MW00577017

LUKE

The Hodder Bible Commentary

Edited by Lee Gatiss

LUKE

DAVID G. PETERSON

HODDER &
STOUGHTON

The Hodder Bible Commentary
Series Editor: Lee Gatiss
First published in Great Britain in 2024 by Hodder & Stoughton
An Hachette UK company

I

Contents

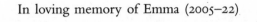

In loving memory of Emma (2005–22)

Series Preface

The unfolding of your words gives light
(Psalm 119:130)

The Hodder Bible Commentary aims to proclaim afresh in our generation the unchanging and unerring word of God, for the glory of God and the good of his people. This fifty-volume commentary on the whole Bible seeks to provide the contemporary church with fresh and readable expositions of Scripture which are doctrinally sensitive and globally aware, accessible for all adult readers but particularly useful to those who preach, teach and lead Bible studies in churches and small groups.

Building on the success of Hodder's NIV Proclamation Bible, we have assembled as contributors a remarkable team of men and women from around the world. Alongside a diverse panel of trusted Consultant Editors, they have a tremendous variety of denominational backgrounds and ministries. Each has great experience in unfolding the gospel of Jesus Christ and all are united in our aim of faithfully expounding the Bible in a way that takes account of the original text, biblical theology, the history of interpretation and the needs of the contemporary global church.

These volumes are serious expositions – not overly technical, scholarly works of reference but not simply sermons either. As well as carefully unpacking what the Bible says, they are sensitive to how it has been used in doctrinal discussions over the centuries and in our own day, though not dominated by such concerns at the expense of the text's own agenda. They also try to speak not only into a white, middle-class, Western context (for example), as some might, but to be aware of ways in which other cultures hear and need to hear what the Spirit is saying to the churches.

As you tuck into his word, with the help of this book, may the glorious Father 'give you the Spirit of wisdom and revelation, so that you may know him better' (Ephesians 1:17).

Lee Gatiss, Series Editor

Consultant Editors

The Series Editor would like to thank the following Consultant Editors for their contributions to the Hodder Bible Commentary:

Shady Anis (*Egypt*)
Kirsten Birkett (*UK*)
Felipe Chamy (*Chile*)
Ben Cooper (*UK*)
Mervyn Eloff (*South Africa*)
Keri Folmar (*Dubai*)
Kerry Gatiss (*UK*)
Kara Hartley (*Australia*)
Julian Hardyman (*Madagascar*)
Stephen Fagbemi (*Nigeria*)
Rosanne Jones (*Japan*)
Henry Jansma (*USA*)
Samuel Lago (*USA*)
Andis Miezitis (*Latvia*)
Adrian Reynolds (*UK*)
Peter Ryan (*Australia*)
Sookgoo Shin (*South Korea*)
Myrto Theocharous (*Greece*)

Author's Preface

For many years I had the privilege of teaching Luke's Gospel to theological students at Moore College in Sydney, Australia, while being asked to preach sermons on the same Gospel. Attempting both tasks at the same time made me aware of the problem that students and pastors experience as they seek to translate what they are taught in academic institutions into authentic and relevant expositions for congregational contexts. At that time, few commentaries moved beyond technical and historical analysis of the text to theological reflection and application. In recent decades, however, more have sought to overcome this problem, and my reliance on their work will be obvious. But even these publications are often occupied with critical matters such as historicity, sources, linguistic and redactional issues. These are important, but not pressing issues for those who gather week by week to hear the Bible expounded. Discerning Christians want to know the theological and practical implications of a passage. Busy preachers find that they must search through many pages of argument in commentaries to find the jewels that they are looking for.

I am grateful, therefore, for the opportunity to write a one-volume, expositional commentary in a series for preachers seeking the best insights from scholarly work on the biblical text and guidelines for conveying them to a contemporary audience. Even so, this commentary does not provide sermon outlines or illustrations that might be found in an application series. Effective biblical preaching is a prophetic ministry, in which the preacher must be captivated by the text and discern its significance for a given audience. The commentator's task is to expose the meaning and significance of passages as much as space will allow, leaving the final task of 'getting it across' to pastors who know the needs of their congregations. I have enjoyed delving into the *Africa Bible Commentary* (2006) and the *South Asia Bible Commentary* (2015) to see how Luke's Gospel is viewed and applied in those two cultures.

Commentaries on the Synoptic Gospels are bound to consider the similarities and differences between these works. This is particularly so where seemingly parallel passages occur in different contexts or are developed differently. Various critical methods have provided insights for interpreters looking at the Gospels in a synchronic way. However, these often raise questions about the authority and reliability of the authors, leading to extensive debates about what Jesus might actually have said or done. Systematic exposition of a Gospel requires a more diachronic approach, considering how a particular evangelist has assembled, arranged and presented his sources, and for what purpose. As with my commentary on the Acts of the Apostles,[1] I have taken a narrative approach to exposition from a biblical–theological perspective. As much as possible, technical details are confined to brackets or footnotes. I have also included a series of reflections at the end of large sections of exposition, drawing together the threads, summarising theological emphases and suggesting practical implications. These should be a guide for preachers about themes to develop and when to introduce such topics in an expository series.

One of the problems facing an interpreter of the Gospels is to discern what structure there may be in the narrative. Sometimes the arrangement of events or teaching segments seems to be thematically determined, but not always. Preachers will rightly be concerned to discover the priorities of a particular Gospel and to present the material in manageable amounts to their congregations. My attention to structure in this commentary has been driven by a concern to discover what seems obvious from the biblical text, but also what would be a helpful way to divide and explain the sequence of the text for preaching.

David G. Peterson

---

[1] David G. Peterson, *The Acts of the Apostles* (Grand Rapids: Eerdmans; Nottingham: Apollos, 2009).

Abbreviations

1QapGen	*Genesis Apocryphon*, DSS
1QH	*Hodayot* (Thanksgiving Hymns), DSS
1QM	*War Scroll*, DSS
1QS	*Rule of the Congregation, Manual of Discipline*, DSS
1QSa	Appendix A (*Rule of the Congregation*) to 1 QS, DSS
BDAG	*A Greek-English Lexicon of the New Testament and Other Early Christian Literature*, edited by Walter Bauer, Frederick W. Danker, William F. Arndt, and F. Wilbur Gingrich (3rd edition; Chicago: University of Chicago, 2000)
CBQ	*Catholic Biblical Quarterly*
CSB	Christian Standard Bible (2016)
DJG	*Dictionary of Jesus and the Gospels*, edited by Joel B. Green (2nd edition; Downers Grove: InterVarsity Press, 2013). Page references are to the print edition.
DNTB	*Dictionary of New Testament Background*, edited by Craig A. Evans and Stanley E. Porter (Downers Grove: InterVarsity/ Leicester: InterVarsity Press, 2000)
DSS	Dead Sea Scrolls
ESV	English Standard Version (2001)
EV	English Versions
JBL	*Journal of Biblical Literature*
KJV	King James Version (1611)
Louw and Nida	*Greek-English Lexicon of the New Testament: Based on Semantic Domains,* (ed.) Johanne P. Louw and Eugene A. Nida (New York: United Bible Societies, 1996)
LXX	Septuagint (Greek) Text of the Old Testament
MT	Masoretic (Hebrew) Text of the Old Testament
NDBT	*New Dictionary of Biblical Theology*, edited by T. Desmond Alexander and Brian S. Rosner (Leicester: InterVarsity Press/Downers Grove: InterVarsity, 2000)

NIDOTTE	*New International Dictionary of Old Testament Theology and Exegesis*, 5 volumes, edited by Willem A. VanGemeren (Carlisle: Paternoster, 1997)
NIV	New International Version (Anglicised) (2011)
NRSVA	New Revised Standard Version with Apocrypha (1995)
TDNT	*Theological Dictionary of the New Testament*, 10 volumes, edited by Gerhard Kittel and Gerhard Friedrich; translated by Geoffrey W. Bromiley (Grand Rapids: Eerdmans, 1964–76)

Introduction

1. Authorship and date

The author of this work introduces himself without disclosing his name (Luke 1:1–4). In his second volume, however, there are several first-person plural indications that he was a companion of the apostle Paul in the later stages of his missionary activity (Acts 16:8–17; 20:5–15; 21:1–18; 27:1–28:16). The earliest extant manuscript of the Gospel (papyrus 75), which is dated between AD 175 and 225, has at its end the ascription 'Gospel according to Luke'. Around AD 180, Irenaeus, Bishop of Lyon, also testified to the belief that 'Luke, the follower of Paul, recorded in a book the gospel as it was preached by him'.[1] Francis Watson observes, 'For Irenaeus, Matthew, Mark, Luke, and John possessed equal status. In writing the gospel they were engaged in a single collective enterprise.'[2]

The Muratorian Canon, which lists the books recognised as Scripture in the Roman church in about AD 170–80, describes the author of the Gospel and Acts as 'Luke the physician' and companion of Paul, who 'wrote in his own name but in accordance with [Paul's] opinion'.[3] This is echoed by the so-called Anti-Marcionite Prologue to the Third Gospel, which possibly belongs to the end of the second century and describes Luke as 'an Antiochene of Syria, a physician by profession. He was a disciple of the apostles and later accompanied Paul until the latter's martyrdom.'[4]

---

[1] Irenaeus, *Against Heresies* 3.1.1, trans. Edward Rochie Hardy, *The Library of Christian Classics Volume I, Early Christian Fathers*, ed. Cyril C. Richardson (London: SCM, 1953), 370.

[2] Francis Watson, *The Fourfold Gospel. A Theological Reading of the New Testament Portraits of Jesus* (Grand Rapids: Baker Academic, 2016), 17.

[3] Translation of Frederick F. Bruce, *The Acts of the Apostles: The Greek Text with Introduction and Commentary* (3rd edition; Grand Rapids: Eerdmans; Leicester: Apollos, 1990), 1.

[4] Translation of Bruce, *Acts*, 8. Compare Colossians 4:14; 2 Timothy 4:11; Philemon

Many scholars contend that the Gospel of Mark was written first, in the period AD 65–70, and that this was a major source for Luke's first volume. Seeking to pinpoint the time when the third Gospel was composed, some would argue that a retrospective awareness of the fall of Jerusalem in AD 70 is reflected in 19:43–4; 21:20–24. Even if this is so – and I dispute the evidence when dealing with those passages – it is not difficult to imagine that Luke published his two-volume work in the early to mid 70s. He could well have been consulting witnesses, assembling his sources and writing them up when he began to make use of Mark's Gospel. If Luke used Matthew as another source, as some have argued, a later date for Luke–Acts should be considered.[5] However, the majority view is that the common material in Matthew and Luke derived from a source, or collection of sources, designated Q for Quelle (German 'source'), and that this pre-dated or was roughly contemporary with Mark.[6]

Certain features of Acts also suggest the possibility of its publication before AD 70, notably its portrayal of Jerusalem and the Temple as still operating at the climax of the story (Acts 21–2), its omission of any reference to the Neronian persecution of Christians and its failure to say anything about the outcome of Paul's imprisonment in Rome.[7]

2. Literary character and purpose

Although Luke associated his work with the 'narrative' approach of his predecessors (1:1), the 'Gospel' character of his first volume was soon identified by early Christian writers such as Irenaeus. The Synoptic Gospels were a unique creation of early Christian writers, determined partly by the life and message of Jesus and partly by the demands of Christian mission. They belong to the broad and flexible genre of Graeco–Roman biography, concentrating on the words and works of Jesus in his three-year public ministry and with special attention to the narrative of his

---

24. See the broader discussion of Luke's identity by James R. Edwards, *The Gospel According to Luke* (Grand Rapids; Cambridge, UK: Eerdmans, 2015), 5–11.
[5] See, for example, Eric Eve, *Solving the Synoptic Puzzle. Introducing the Case for the Farrer Hypothesis* (Eugene: Cascade, 2021).
[6] See the literature cited by J. A. Lloyd, *Archaeology and the Itinerant Jesus* (Tübingen: Mohr Siebeck, 2022), 5, note 34.
[7] David Seccombe, 'Dating Luke–Acts: Further Arguments for an Early Date', *Tyndale Bulletin*, Volume 71, Issue 2, 2020, 207–27, argues for the early 60s.

death and resurrection.[8] Their structure is broadly the same and there is much overlap in content, but Matthew and Luke contain more of Jesus's teaching than Mark does. John's Gospel is another variation of this genre. The four Gospels were written initially to convince Christians about the significance of Jesus and his message, and also to equip them to live as faithful disciples, modelling and propagating his teaching to unbelievers.

Luke's two volumes are linked in terms of subject matter and purpose by their prologues (Luke 1:1–4; Acts 1:1) and by the overlap between Luke 24:36–52 and Acts 1:1–14, both containing predictions that are fulfilled in the rest of Acts. However, Acts has a different literary form and style. Darryl Palmer argues that its length, scope, focus and formal features fit the pattern of 'a short historical monograph'.[9] Acts covers a period of thirty or more years after Jesus's resurrection–ascension and features several journeys with significant speeches by several key leaders. It is a highly selective and theologically reflective history, showing how the message about Jesus was proclaimed in different cultures and how churches were planted there, with special attention to the ministry of the apostle Paul. Despite the differences between these two genres, I conclude that 'Acts is the intended sequel to the Gospel and there is a coherence between the two volumes at the level of story, themes, and theology'.[10]

Luke's acknowledgement that 'many have undertaken to draw up an account of the things that have been fulfilled among us' (1:1–4) need not imply any criticism of his predecessors. He and they were similarly reliant on 'those who from the first were eye witnesses and servants of the word'. Luke claims to have had access to a succession of oral and written sources going back to the time of John the Baptist and Jesus. Nevertheless, having 'carefully investigated everything from the beginning', he intended to write 'an orderly account', suggesting a new and different kind of approach. This could refer to chronological, geographical, logical, but more obviously thematic ordering.[11]

---

[8] Genre can be defined in terms of the content, form and function of a particular text. See Richard A. Burridge, *What are the Gospels? A Comparison with Graeco–Roman Biography* (2nd edition; Grand Rapids: Eerdmans, 2004); R. A. Burridge, 'Gospel: Genre', *DJG*, 335–42.

[9] 'Acts and the Ancient Historical Monograph', in *The Book of Acts in its First Century Setting. Volume 1 Ancient Literary Setting*, eds. Bruce W. Winter and Andrew D. Clarke (Grand Rapids: Eerdmans; Carlisle: Paternoster, 1993), 18.

[10] Peterson, *Acts*, 53.

[11] Joel B. Green, *The Gospel of Luke* (Grand Rapids; Cambridge, UK: Eerdmans, 1997), 1–6, considers more fully what kind of narrative Luke has produced.

Luke's stated aim in writing his two-volume work is that Theophilus and those he represents may know the certainty of the things they have been taught. In other words, his narrative is constructed for the benefit of those who knew something about the matters he records, but who needed to be convinced about their truthfulness, meaning and significance. The contents of Luke's two volumes suggest that he was addressing predominantly Gentile converts, who had some knowledge of the Jewish Scriptures gained from past association with Jewish synagogues.[12] Certainty was needed about the identity, character, teaching and authority of Jesus, God's plan of salvation and how it was fulfilled by Jesus for Jews and Gentiles, how and why Christianity had spread so widely and so quickly in their world, and why there was nevertheless much opposition.

The issue of Luke's historical reliability has been widely discussed, but it will only occasionally be addressed in this commentary.[13] Here I simply want to note the extent to which the Greek translation of the Old Testament (the LXX or Septuagint) influenced the language, form, content and presuppositions of Luke–Acts. Following the argument of Brian Rosner, I conclude, 'Luke was concerned to reflect upon sacred history for the benefit of the believing community, drawing a link between the time of Israel, the time of Jesus, and the time of the early church.'[14] In other words, he wrote a narrative that was driven in various ways by the idea of fulfilment.

3. Major theological themes

In the introduction to my commentary on Acts, I discuss ten theological themes, largely focusing on their development and expression in Luke's second volume.[15] The approach here is to explore a more limited range of topics as they emerge in the setting of Luke's Gospel and occasionally to note how they are developed in Acts.

---

[12] Kevin L. Anderson, 'But God Raised Him from the Dead': The Theology of Jesus' Resurrection in Luke–Acts (Bletchley: Paternoster, 2006), 20, argues more specifically for 'an audience who has an acquaintance with the Jewish hope of resurrection'.
[13] See Peterson, Acts, 8–25 and the literature cited there; Craig Blomberg, The Historical Reliability of the Gospels (2nd edition; Downers Grove: InterVarsity, 2007); Peter J. Williams, Can We Trust the Gospels? (Wheaton: Crossway, 2018).
[14] Peterson, Acts, 14. See Brian S. Rosner, 'Acts and Biblical History', in Winter and Clarke (eds.), The Book of Acts in Its First Century Setting, Volume 1: Ancient Literary Setting, 65–82.
[15] Peterson, Acts, 53–97.

Scripture and the plan of God

Luke follows the lead of his predecessors in drawing up 'an account of the things that have been fulfilled among us' (1:1). His interest in fulfilment is first illustrated with respect to the birth of John the Baptist and the angelic prediction concerning his ministry (1:11–17). This narrative recalls the way other key figures in Scripture are introduced (Genesis 18:1–15; Judges 13; 1 Samuel 1–2) and draws specific attention to the fulfilment of Malachi 3:1; 4:5–6. John's prophetic calling is subsequently emphasised by saying 'the word of God came to John son of Zechariah in the wilderness' (3:2). A quotation from Isaiah 40:3–5 is then formally introduced with the words, 'As it is written in the book of the words of Isaiah the prophet' (Luke 3:3–6). This reinforces the idea announced in 1:16–17, that John was to prepare the Lord's way 'by preparing a repentant people', as Robert Tannehill says, 'whose hearts have turned and who are ready to receive their Lord'.[16]

The notion of God's coming into history to rescue his people from judgment, spiritual alienation and death is then announced in the angelic prediction to Mary concerning the miraculous birth of her son and his future kingdom (1:26–38). The wording of Isaiah 7:14 is recalled, together with the foundational messianic promise in 2 Samuel 7:12–16. Mary's celebratory response picks up several Old Testament themes and applies them first to her own situation (1:46–50) and then to that of her people (1:51–55). The way that God has dealt with Mary in her humble state is consistent with the way he has previously 'lifted up the humble' and brought down the powerful (see 1 Samuel 2:1–10). Her song ends with the claim that God has remembered to be 'merciful to Abraham and his descendants for ever'. This is related to the fulfilment of a broad range of promises and warnings, which will be articulated in subsequent prophecies (1:68–79; 2:29–32) and in Jesus's own teaching (4:18–21; 13:28–30). Tannehill concludes, 'Mary's hymn suggests a set of expectations about God's character and purpose which guide the reader in understanding what is most important in the subsequent story.'[17]

Like Mary's song, Zechariah's prophecy (1:67–79) functions as a narrative pause 'to promote reflection on the events just described', as Green suggests.[18] It answers the question, 'What then is this child going to be?'

[16] Robert C. Tannehill, *The Narrative Unity of Luke–Acts. A Literary Interpretation. Volume 1: The Gospel according to Luke* (Philadelphia: Fortress, 1986), 24.
[17] Tannehill, *Narrative Unity 1*, 29–30.
[18] Green, *Luke*, 112.

(1:66), and clarifies the relationship between John and Jesus.[19] Zechariah begins with praise for God's redemptive visitation of his people in the promised Son of David (1:68–75) and concludes with a message to his son John about his role in God's plan (1:76–9). The messianic redemption involves a release from sin and all its consequences. 'Salvation from our enemies and from the hand of all who hate us' is necessary so that God's people can 'serve him without fear in holiness and righteousness before him all our days'. But who are these enemies?

Old Testament categories are used to describe the messianic salvation. Just as Israel needed to be set free from captivity in Egypt to serve God as a holy nation in the Promised Land (Exodus 7:16; 19:1–8; Psalm 106:10), the Messiah must deliver his people from their enemies – temporal and spiritual – to enable them to serve God faithfully and enter their eternal inheritance. This will happen because of God's original commitment 'to show mercy to our ancestors and to remember his holy covenant, the oath he swore to our father Abraham'. Echoes of Isaiah 9:1–7 in Luke 1:79 suggest that release from sin's dominion and 'the hand of all who hate us' will usher in the promised messianic peace, meaning a right relationship with God and associated blessings (2:14; 7:50; 8:48; 10:5–6; 19:38, 42; 24:36). In due course, this will be offered to people from every nation (Acts 10:36).

Simeon's prophetic response to Jesus in the Temple at Jerusalem (2:28–32) picks up the themes of peace and salvation previously announced. What God has prepared 'in the sight of all nations' (Psalm 98:1–3; Isaiah 40:5; 52:10) has come to Israel in the person of this child. But the promise that Gentiles will be the ultimate beneficiaries is emphasised by allusion to passages such as Isaiah 42:6; 49:5–6: Jesus will be 'a light for revelation to the Gentiles, and the glory of your people Israel'. This focus on the nations recalls again the promise to Abraham (Genesis 12:3; 17:4–6; 22:18), and it anticipates the prediction of Jesus in 13:28–30 and his commission to his disciples in 24:45–7 (see Acts 1:8).

Luke's account of Jesus's preaching in the synagogue at Nazareth (4:16–30) begins with the claim that the prophecy of Isaiah 61:1–2 is being fulfilled. This is met with amazement, but then fury, because Jesus suggests that they might reject him, and that the salvation promised to Israel might be taken to the Gentiles. Words from Isaiah 58:6 are added ('to set the oppressed free') to emphasise the note of liberation in the

---

[19] A helpful summary of the similarities and significant differences between John and Jesus is provided by Takatemjen, 'Luke', in *South Asia Bible Commentary*, ed. Brian Wintle (Grand Rapids: Zondervan, 2015), 1338.

primary text. When Jesus applies Isaiah 61:1–2 to himself, he claims to be the Spirit-anointed proclaimer of God's end-time salvation, implicitly offering this to everyone in the synagogue. In the narratives that follow, Luke progressively shows how Jesus fulfils Isaiah's prophecy, culminating in his answer to the question of John the Baptist (7:18–23), where an echo of this text is linked with allusions to Isaiah 35:5–6. But Jesus's narrow escape from antagonism and death in Nazareth also casts an ominous shadow over his ministry to come (recalling Simeon's prediction in 2:34–5). Further reflection on the significance of Jesus's preaching to 'the poor' can be found on page 17.

There are many biblical allusions in Luke's narrative,[20] but the next text to be formally cited is Malachi 3:1, which is related to John the Baptist by saying, 'This is the one about whom it is written' (7:27). Slightly influenced by the wording of Exodus 23:20, this quotation indicates that John is the messenger whom God sends ahead of him to prepare his way. John is the forerunner of God himself, who comes to save his people in the person of the Messiah. Luke comments that 'all the people, even the tax collectors, when they heard Jesus's words, acknowledged that God's way was right, because they had been baptised by John. But the Pharisees and the experts in the law rejected the plan of God for themselves, because they had not been baptised by John' (7:29–30, my translation).[21]

Jesus paraphrases a portion of Isaiah 6:9 in his explanation to the disciples of why he speaks to the crowds in parables (8:10). Isaiah used both plain and parabolic speech to excite repentance and faith in his day, but he was warned by God from the beginning that his ministry would further harden the hearts of many who heard him. The parables of Jesus were similarly not designed to obscure the truth, but to express his teaching in a way that provoked further inquiry. However, Jesus predicted the range of responses to his message, as illustrated in his parable of the soils (8:4–8, 11–15), and warned his hearers to listen carefully.

Speaking from God's perspective, Jesus reviews the sad history of his dealings with Israel over many centuries (13:34–5). The climax would be his final visit to Jerusalem, which is closely linked with judgment on the

---

[20] See the detailed examination of Luke's use of Scripture by David W. Pao and Eckhard J. Schnabel, 'Luke', in *Commentary on the New Testament Use of the Old Testament*, eds. G. K. Beale and D. A. Carson (Grand Rapids: Baker; Nottingham: Apollos, 2007), 251–414.
[21] The NIV translation ('God's purpose for themselves') obscures the broader significance of the term 'the plan of God' (*hē boulē tou theou*) in Acts 2:23; 4:28; 5:38–9; 13:36; 20:27.

Temple, the city and its people ('Look your house is left to you desolate'). Jesus's visit would bring about his own death (13:33), but he would return as the glorified Messiah ('I tell you, you will not see me again until you say, "Blessed is he who comes in the name of the Lord"'). The words of Psalm 118:26 would soon be uttered by his disciples when they entered Jerusalem, but he speaks here of that greeting being ultimately used by all who would witness his triumphant return.

This psalm text is modified in 19:38 to be more explicitly messianic ('Blessed is the *king* who comes in the name of the Lord'). A further acclamation reminiscent of the angelic revelation at the birth of Jesus declares, 'Peace in heaven and glory in the highest!' Heaven is the divine realm where God the Father is (2:14; 11:13; 20:4), and a place of peace and glory. Jesus's coming into Jerusalem signifies that these blessings are now available for God's people to experience on earth.[22]

When Jesus enters the Temple and begins to drive out those selling there, he says to his disciples, 'It is written . . . "My house will be a house of prayer"; but you have made it "a den of robbers"' (19:46). Isaiah 56:7 is abbreviated to emphasise that the Temple's chief function as a place of prayer had been obscured by commerce. With words from Jeremiah 7:11, Jesus identifies his action with the prophet's protest about the misuse of the Temple in his day. Jesus's prophetic action cleared the way for him to teach in the temple courts and enabled God's people to pray there more easily.[23]

The parable of the tenants is told to the people in the Temple, who react with horror at the outcome (20:9–16). Jesus looks directly at them and asks, 'Then what is the meaning of that which is written: "The stone the builders rejected has become the cornerstone"?' A proverbial saying in Psalm 118:22 is applied to his rejection, death and heavenly exaltation. Joseph Fitzmyer argues that Jesus uses this text to imply that he will become 'the key figure in God's new building, the reconstituted Israel'.[24] In 20:18, imagery from Isaiah 8:14–15, and possibly also Daniel 2:34–5, 44–5, is used to warn those who fail to recognise the significance of his self-identification as the rejected, but soon-to-be restored cornerstone of God's saving plan.

---

[22] See Steve Walton, '"The Heavens Opened": Cosmological and Theological Transformation in Luke–Acts', in *Cosmology and New Testament Theology*, eds. Jonathan T. Pennington and Sean M. McDonough (London; New York: T&T Clark, 2008), 61–3.
[23] An echo of Malachi 3:1–4 may be heard in the words and actions of Jesus here.
[24] Joseph A. Fitzmyer, *The Gospel According to Luke X–XXIV* (Garden City: Doubleday, 1985), 1282.

Jesus raises an important question with the teachers of the law in the Temple about why the Messiah is called the Son of David (20:41–4). The text cited is Psalm 110:1 ('The Lord said to my Lord: "Sit at my right hand until I make your enemies a footstool for your feet"'). Jesus apparently understood that David was reflecting on the promises made to him concerning the eternal reign of his son in a special and exclusive relationship with God (2 Samuel 7:12–16). Jesus repeats his first question in a different way, reflecting on the text of the psalm ('David calls him "Lord." How then can he be his son?'). This was a veiled way of suggesting that Davidic sonship was more than a matter of physical descent and that his kingdom was 'not of this world' (John 18:36). On trial before the Sanhedrin, Jesus again alludes to Psalm 110:1 in a prediction about his heavenly enthronement as Son of Man (22:69).

As Jesus prepares his disciples for his arrest, trials and death (22:31–8), he cites a portion of Isaiah 53:12 ('It is written: "And he was numbered with the transgressors"'). This is accompanied by an emphatic promise of fulfilment ('and I tell you that this must be fulfilled in me. Yes, what is written about me is reaching its fulfilment'). Only here in Luke's Gospel does Jesus clearly align himself with that prophecy, though intimations that he will fulfil the role of God's Servant in Isaiah 52:13–53:12 have previously been given (3:21–2; 9:22, 44; 12:50; 17:25; 18:31–3; 20:13–15) and continue in the narrative that follows.

The risen Lord rebukes his disciples for being 'slow to believe all that the prophets have spoken' and focuses on the need for the Messiah to suffer and then enter his glory (24:25–7).[25] However, 'beginning with Moses and all the Prophets', Jesus explains to them 'what was said in *all* the Scriptures concerning himself' (my emphasis). With this self-identification, his overall concern was to provide them with an open, comprehensive and detailed exposition of God's plan for the Messiah and his people.

Jesus takes this approach again in 24:44–9 with a wider group of disciples, although the scope of fulfilment here includes the need for 'repentance for the forgiveness of sins [to] be preached in his name to all nations, beginning at Jerusalem'. Such teaching, together with the empowerment of the promised Holy Spirit, would enable the first disciples to be effective witnesses of what they had seen and heard 'to the ends of

---

[25] Divine necessity or the plan of God is implied by the use of *dei* ('must') throughout this Gospel, especially in relation to what the Scriptures say about the need for the Messiah to suffer and enter his glory (2:49; 4:43; 9:22; 13:33; 17:25; 22:37; 24:7, 26, 44).

the earth' (Acts 1:8). It also would make possible the spiritual and moral transformation that Jesus had called for throughout his ministry.

With this Christocentric method of interpreting the Scriptures of Israel as part of his narrative, Luke aimed to draw his readers into the same pattern of understanding, belief and experience of the risen Lord that those first witnesses had.[26] His use of what we call the Old Testament pointed to its divine inspiration and continuing authority for Christians. Understood in the light of its fulfilment, it can make us 'wise for salvation through faith in Christ Jesus' (2 Timothy 3:15). At the same time, with his focus on Jesus as the authoritative, end-time interpreter of Scripture and source of new revelation, Luke wrote a Gospel that was foundational for the formation of a New Testament canon of Scripture.

Christology and salvation

These two themes are closely linked in Luke's narrative. 'Son of David' is a title applied to Jesus in Luke 18:38–9 and used by him with reference to the Messiah in 20:41, 44, but the term 'Christ' or 'Messiah' is more extensively employed in this Gospel (2:11, 26; 3:15; 4:41; 9:20; 20:41; 22:67; 23:2, 35, 39; 24:26). Jesus's messianic status and role are first revealed in the angelic prediction to Mary in 1:32–3, which is based on the promise in 2 Samuel 7:12–16. The prophecy of Zechariah in 1:67–79 gives further details about the Messiah and his kingdom (see pages 5–6).[27] John would prepare people to meet their Lord by giving them 'the *knowledge* of salvation through the forgiveness of their sins' (my emphasis). This would enable them to experience in advance the benefits of the salvation that Jesus came to bring (see 7:50; 19:9–10). God's people would know the possibility of being definitively forgiven as beneficiaries of his new covenant (Jeremiah 31:34; Ezekiel 36:25). John would proclaim this in advance of Jesus's coming by 'preaching a baptism of repentance for the forgiveness of their sins' (3:3). But it is actually Jesus who makes available the promised forgiveness to people of every nation through his death and resurrection (22:20; 24:46–7; Acts 2:38; 5:31; 10:43; 13:38; 26:18).

Although messiahship is an important theme in Luke's Gospel, the nature

---

[26] Compare the summary of Luke's approach by Benjamin L. Gladd, *From the Manger to the Throne: A Theology of Luke* (Wheaton: Crossway, 2011), 19–59.
[27] By implication, Jesus is the 'horn of salvation' that God has raised up 'in the house of his servant David' (1:69).

of Jesus's conception points more fundamentally to his divine character and origin (1:34–5). Mary is told by the angel, 'The Holy Spirit will come on you,' reflecting the language of Isaiah 32:15, where the Spirit is expected to renew God's people and restore the created order in a time to come (see Isaiah 44:3–4; Ezekiel 37:1–14). A further expression, 'and the power of the Most High will overshadow you', recalls the overshadowing cloud and the glory of the Lord filling the tabernacle in Exodus 40:34–5. God's presence with his people at the time of their exodus from Egypt expressed his covenant commitment to bless them and bring them into the inheritance he had promised them (Exodus 29:44–6; 33:12–23). His saving presence would now be experienced in and through the person of his Son, making possible the fulfilment of his end-time purpose for his people. The child conceived by the Holy Spirit would be fully human, but holy in the sense of being uniquely related to God as 'the Son' and truly reflecting his character as 'the holy one'. He would be the divine Messiah (2:11) who would enable God's people to share with him eternally in the blessings of his heavenly rule (2:14; 18:29–30; 20:41–4).

The implications of Jesus's divine sonship are further revealed as Luke's narrative proceeds. Eschatological salvation dawns when the transforming light of God shines on 'those living in darkness and in the shadow of death' and guides them 'into the path of peace' (1:78–9). As the unique Son of God, Jesus brings that light and achieves the promised salvation. At his baptism, he is addressed by the heavenly voice as 'my Son' (3:22), reflecting Psalm 2:7 and recalling the angelic prediction that he would be the messianic 'Son of the Most High' (1:32–3). Fitzmyer argues that the term 'whom I love' (*ho agapētos*, 'the beloved') 'adds a specification about the sonship that is not present in Ps. 2:7, expressive of a special love-relationship between the heavenly Father and the Son, Jesus'.[28]

Jesus's anointing at his baptism with the Holy Spirit recalls Isaiah 11:1–2; 61:1–2 and reinforces the messianic implications of this event (see also Acts 4:25–6; 10:37–8). The words 'with you I am well pleased' also echo Isaiah 42:1. As the messianic Son whom God loves and with whom he is well pleased, Jesus must fulfil the role of the Servant of the Lord, culminating in the suffering that brings end-time salvation to Israel and the nations (Luke 9:22; 18:31–3; 22:15, 19–20, 37 (citing Isaiah 53:12), 42; 23:34, 46).

God's personal address to Jesus as 'my Son, whom I love' becomes a title when his calling and identity are challenged by the devil (4:3, 9, 'the

---

[28] Joseph A. Fitzmyer, *The Gospel According to Luke I–IX* (Garden City: Doubleday, 1981), 485–6.

Son of God'). The temptations he faced were distinctly related to his identity and calling as God's Son, though his forty days of testing in the wilderness, together with his quotation of three texts from Deuteronomy concerning Israel's experience (8:3 in 4:4; 6:13 in 4:8; 6:16 in 4:12), suggest that it was God's will for him to be tested representatively as Israel was and to prove faithful. John Nolland concludes that, with respect to both Adam and Israel, Jesus 'marks a new beginning to sonship and sets it on an entirely new footing'.[29] Zechariah's prediction that the Messiah would rescue his people from the hand of their enemies (1:68–75) began to be fulfilled in a cosmic and spiritual way.

Only the demonically possessed acknowledged Jesus as the Son of God in the early stages of his ministry (4:41; 8:28). When his accusers in Jerusalem finally say, 'Are you then the Son of God?' (22:70), they may be asking in another way whether he claims to be the Messiah (22:67). However, the teachers of the law and the chief priests have already posed that question and been rebuffed (22:66–8). They heard him speak about the owner of the vineyard's beloved son in the parable he told against them (20:9–19), and the issue of the Messiah's divine sonship was raised by Jesus in 20:41–4, when he publicly asked how they understood Psalm 110:1. Moreover, when Jesus implied that he would soon sit at God's right hand and rule from there as the Son of Man (22:69), he appeared to be profaning the uniqueness and holiness of God.[30] His answer to their second question ('You say that I am') is a qualified admission to divine sonship.

Jesus's use of the Father–Son language in 10:21–2, together with the heavenly declaration and instruction to the disciples when he is transfigured in their presence (9:35, 'listen to him'), imply that he is able to give a true revelation of the Father and his will. An echo of Deuteronomy 18:15 in 9:35 also implies that Jesus is the eschatological prophet like Moses, who fulfils that prophecy (see also Acts 3:22–3). Although the divine character and authority of Jesus are highlighted in various ways, Luke also presents him as a prophet who proclaims the imminence of the kingdom of God, brings healing and release from demonic powers

---

[29] John Nolland, *Word Biblical Commentary, Volume 35A, Luke 1–9:20* (Dallas: Word, 1989), 173. The implied contrast with Adam as God's 'son' (3:38) and Israel as God's 'son' (Exodus 4:22–3) suggests that in his obedient service as a man Jesus did what they could not do and achieved a transformative salvation for Israel and the nations. See more fully Gladd, *From the Manger to the Throne*, 123–43.
[30] Darrell L. Bock, *Luke Volume 2: 9:51–24:53* (Grand Rapids: Baker, 1996), 1799.

and offers salvation in terms of the forgiveness of sins, reconciliation with God and the possibility of eternal life.[31]

Jesus's preferred self-designation as 'the Son of Man' fills out the cosmic and universal implications of being the messianic Son of God. Eight times he uses the title with reference to his public ministry (Luke 5:24; 6:5; 7:34; 9:58; 11:30; 12:10; 19:10; 22:48), five times with reference to his suffering and resurrection (9:22, 44; 18:31; 22:22; 24:7), but mostly to speak of his return in power and glory to judge (9:26; 12:40; 17:22, 24, 26, 30; 18:8; 21:27, 36; 22:69). This last usage provides the key to understanding the other two. In Daniel 7:13–14, a man-like figure ('one like a son of man') comes 'with the clouds of heaven' into the presence of 'the Ancient of Days' to receive authority, glory and sovereign power over all nations. This recalls the promises made by God to the exalted Son of David in Psalms 2 and 110. Paradoxically, however, Jesus teaches that he must suffer and be rejected as the Son of Man, before being raised to life and exalted to reign at God's right hand.

Although the death of Jesus clearly has salvific significance for Luke, Kevin Anderson observes three ways in which his *resurrection* is also critical to the message of salvation:

> *Theologically,* the resurrection of Jesus is part of God's purpose for Israel and the world. *Christologically,* it confirms his position as the definitive leader of the people of God and the agent of God's coven- ant blessings of salvation. *Ecclesiologically,* it is the inaugural action of God in his promised restoration of Israel. The resurrection of Jesus, in initiating the restoration of Israel, effects both a division within Israel and an expansion of the people of God among the nations.[32]

As Messiah, Son of God, Servant of the Lord, end-time prophet and Son of Man, Jesus fulfilled every aspect of the salvation promised to Israel in different strands of the Old Testament. However, Luke–Acts also stresses that those from any nation, race or culture who seek the blessings of salvation through faith in Christ are united with believing Israelites in the ever-expanding community of his disciples.

---

[31] Jesus fulfilled different prophetic roles in his earthly ministry (see my comments on 4:16–27; 7:11–17; 13:32–5; 24:19–21). His works of healing and restoration had immediate social and spiritual benefits, but they also pointed forward to the promised perfection of a new creation (Isaiah 11:6–9; 35; 65:17–25).
[32] Anderson, *Jesus' Resurrection in Luke–Acts,* 47. Compare Gladd, *From the Manger to the Throne,* 61–97.

It is understandable that Christians in some cultures want to argue that 'salvation includes the restoration of the marginalised' or that salvation in Luke is 'essentially healing'.[33] The gospel has many personal and social implications, but these are not the heart of the message. Commenting on Luke 11:20, Takatemjen rightly argues that Jesus's ministry of healing and exorcism 'signifies a massive shift in the power that controls human life and destiny. A power mightier than Satan is at work, and God's kingdom is being established.'[34] But greater than these victories is the resurrection of Jesus to glory and the pouring out of God's Spirit to empower the proclamation of the gospel in every land and bring many under God's rule for eternity.

Discipleship and the way of Jesus

Luke emphasises that, although many were amazed at Jesus's teaching and mighty works in the early stages of his ministry (4:31–44), Peter and his fishing companions were the first to be called into a special relationship with him (5:1–11). As 'the Holy One of God' (4:34), he facilitated an amazing catch of fish, causing Peter to fall at his knees and say, 'Go away from me, Lord; I am a sinful man!' This echo of Isaiah 6 suggests an identification of Jesus with the God of Israel and a commissioning of Peter and his fishing companions to a prophetic role in declaring his message (5:10, 'you will fish for people'). The implications are drawn out more fully for them in 6:12–16; 9:1–6, 21–62; 22:28–30; 24:36–49, but the pattern of discipleship revealed throughout this Gospel goes beyond the specific calling and empowerment of the twelve apostles for mission. When they leave everything and follow him, they show that their priorities and values have been radically changed because of their encounter with Jesus.[35]

The call of Levi the tax collector is presented in more simple terms (5:27–8, 'Follow me'), but Jesus's invitation excites a response like that of the first disciples: 'Levi got up, left everything and followed him' (see 5:11; 14:33; 18:28). The implication is that he abandoned his occupation and source of income to join Jesus in his itinerant, life-changing work

[33] Takatemjen, 'Luke', 1328. He qualifies this by saying that salvation 'can include physical healing, but it must include the deeper and more pervasive healing that is forgiveness of sins'.

[34] Takatemjen, 'Luke', 1329.

[35] See Fitzmyer, *Luke I–IX*, 236–57; Tokunboh Adeyemo, 'Discipleship', in *Africa Bible Commentary*, ed. Tokunboh Adeyemo (Grand Rapids: Zondervan, 2006), 1249.

(see 9:23, 49, 57, 59, 61; 18:22, 28, 43; 22:39, 54).[36] The call of Jesus –
explicitly or implicitly – involves repentance (5:32), arising from his offer
of forgiveness, the restitution of a right relationship with God and the
promise of eternal salvation (5:20–24; compare 7:44–50; 19:1–10). Jesus
goes on to proclaim that everyone should repent in the face of God's
imminent judgment (13:1–5) and commissions his disciples to preach
repentance for the forgiveness of sins in his name to all nations (24:47).

A growing number of followers learn more about their call and its
significance as they listen to Jesus engage with his opponents (5:29–6:11)
and speak about the ethical implications of belonging to the kingdom he
proclaims (6:17–49). Many of the challenges presented in the so-called
Sermon on the Plain are developed and explained more fully in the
teaching on discipleship given by Jesus in Luke's extensive travel narrative. The Twelve have a distinctive role, which is not revealed until 22:30,
where 'judging the twelve tribes of Israel' means sharing in the Messiah's
rule over a restored or renewed Israel (see Matthew 19:28). When Jesus
names them 'apostles' (6:12–16), he makes them his personal representatives
and envoys, first in his ministry to Israel (9:1–6), and then as witnesses
to the nations (24:45–9; Acts 1:6–8, 21–6).[37] But seventy-two others soon
share in Jesus's outreach to Israel with the message of peace that signals
Satan's downfall (10:1–20).

Jesus's care for women and his desire for them to understand his
teaching is prominent in Luke's account (4:38–9; 7:36–50; 8:40–56; 10:38–
42; 13:10–17). Moreover, his willingness to have them join the inner core
of his disciples was novel, 'involving a sharp break with social expectations
and normal responsibilities'.[38] Their role in 8:2–3 is to help support Jesus

---

[36] See M. J. Wilkins, 'Disciples and Discipleship', *DJG*, 202–12. The verb 'follow' is
also used more broadly by Luke with reference to the crowds, whose association
with Jesus may only have been temporary or occasional (7:9; 9:11; 23:27). 'Come
after me' is another way of expressing the call to personal commitment (14:27,
NIV 'follow me').
[37] Luke mentions the apostles again in 9:10; 17:5; 22:14; 24:10 and many times in
Acts. The related verb (*apostellein*, 'send') is applied differently to various representatives (9:2, 52; 10:1; 22:25; see 11:49).
[38] Tannehill, *Narrative Unity* 1, 138. Jesus's treatment of women and willingness
to have them join the company of his disciples is presented as a challenge to
contemporary African culture by Paul John Isaak, 'Luke', *Africa Bible Commentary*,
1232–4, 1244, and to South Asian culture by Takatemjen, 'Luke', 1328–9. Rebecca
McLaughlin, *Jesus through the Eyes of Women* (Austin: The Gospel Coalition, 2022)
considers some of the implications for women worldwide.

and the Twelve 'out of their own means', presumably with food and money (see also 10:38–42). However, in different ways, they later feature as foundational witnesses to the death, burial and resurrection of Jesus (23:48–24:10; Acts 1:14).

Luke shows that faithful, persevering discipleship depends on a growing apprehension of who Jesus is and what he came to achieve. The Galilean ministry is the context for his self-presentation as God's Messiah, manifesting his divine character in authoritative teaching and in the exercise of supernatural power over the forces of evil, sickness, sin and death. But the time comes for his disciples to acknowledge his identity openly, as Peter does on their behalf (9:18–20). Jesus later indicates that the Father has made this knowledge of the Son possible (10:21–4; compare Matthew 11:25–7; 16:17). Fitzmyer rightly argues that discipleship involves both acceptance of the master's teaching and 'identification of oneself with the master's way of life and destiny in an intimate, personal following of him'.[39]

In each of the Synoptic Gospels, Peter's confession is the moment when Jesus reveals for the first time that he must 'suffer many things and be rejected by the elders, the chief priests and the teachers of the law, and he must be killed and on the third day be raised to life' (9:22). Immediately after this, he begins to teach that would-be disciples must 'deny themselves and take up their cross daily' (9:23). They should not be ashamed of Jesus and his words, since he warns that the Son of Man will be ashamed of those who are ashamed of him 'when he comes in his glory and in the glory of the Father and of the holy angels' (9:26). The related themes of being willing to suffer and give bold testimony to Jesus are developed in subsequent contexts (12:4–12; 51–3; 14:25–35; 18:28–30; 21:12–19; 24:45–9).

The expectation of Jesus's return in judgment as the glorified Son of Man also features at many points in his teaching after this (12:40; 17:22, 24, 26, 30; 18:8; 21:27, 36), climaxing with the declaration before the Sanhedrin in Jerusalem (22:69). The transfiguration of Jesus in the presence of three disciples takes place eight days after Jesus brings this new revelation to them (9:28–36). This provides an assurance that what he has predicted can be believed and gives a hint of the glory that is to come when his suffering is over. But the disciples fail to understand and grasp the significance of what he is saying (9:44–5; 18:31–4), until he is resurrected and opens the Scriptures to them (24:13–49).

Jesus is pictured at prayer more frequently in Luke's Gospel than in

[39] Fitzmyer, *Luke I–IX*, 241.

any of the others, mostly in conjunction with key events in his life (3:21; 5:16; 6:12; 9:18, 28–9; 10:21–2; 11:1; 22:32, 39–46; 23:34, 46). He teaches about prayer and offers a pattern of prayer in response to a request from his disciples (11:1–13). He tells a parable about the need for persistence in prayer (18:1–8) and another about seeking God's mercy in prayer (18:9–14). Implicitly, he calls for prayer in conjunction with his exhortations about worry and watchfulness (12:22–48).[40]

Luke also records more of Jesus's teaching about the disciples' use of material possessions, wealth and money than the other Gospel writers. Related to this, he illustrates what it means from birth to death for the Son of Man to have 'nowhere to lay his head' (9:58).[41] Jesus's teaching about worry, trust, wisdom, generosity and social justice is clearly related to his preaching about end-time salvation and judgment (6:29–30; 12:13–34; 16:1–15, 19–31; 18:1–8, 18–30). However, lifestyle issues flow from his call to repent and believe, rather than being the heart of his gospel message.[42]

'The rich' are mentioned first in Mary's Song with reference to the way God will overturn human values and expectations in fulfilling his promises to Abraham and his descendants (1:46–55). In Jesus's sermon at Nazareth (4:16–21), he quotes from Isaiah 61:1–2, which uses 'poor' as a metaphor for captive Israel, waiting for God's redemption (see 7:18–23). However, in his Beatitudes (6:20–26), Jesus uses similar terms to contrast disciples who are literally poor, weeping, hated and excluded now – because of their commitment to him and God's kingdom – with those who are materially rich, comforted, well fed, happy and highly regarded by others. In his public ministry he reaches out to those who are economically and socially poor, sick or demonically possessed, marginalised and neglected by religious and secular authorities. Although he offers salvation to all, only a few of the rich and powerful respond positively. As Jesus preaches the gospel, he instructs his disciples about the values and behaviour appropriate to those under the rule of God and calls upon them to manifest the imminence of his kingdom in their treatment of one another and care for those in need.[43]

---

[40] Fitzmyer, *Luke I–IX*, 244–47, shows how this teaching is reflected in the prayers of disciples in Acts.
[41] See especially the birth narrative (2:1–20), the extensive travel narrative (9:51–19:10) and 21:37–8.
[42] John the Baptist established a precedent for this (3:3–14). In 3:18 Luke distinguishes John's ministry of exhortation from his proclaiming good news to the people. The latter refers to his preaching about the coming of the Messiah and his baptising 'with the Holy Spirit and fire' (3:15–17).
[43] Fitzmyer, *Luke I–IX*, 247–51, distinguishes two different emphases in Luke–Acts:

Eschatology

The end-time teaching of Luke–Acts has been much discussed, with scholars proposing radically different lines of interpretation. Various emphases emerge as Luke's narrative unfolds, but a cohesive pattern can be discerned.[44] Luke begins as the other Synoptic Gospels do, with claims about the imminent fulfilment of biblical prophecies. These relate to John the Baptist as forerunner of the coming of God himself to judge and to save (1:11–17; 3:1–14) and to the Messiah as God's agent in fulfilling his end-time purpose for Israel and the nations (1:26–33, 46–55, 67–79; 2:10–14, 28–32; 3:15–17).

In his public ministry, Jesus proclaims that 'the kingdom of God' has 'come' or 'drawn near' in an initial but 'not consummative form' (see especially 10:9, 11; 11:20; 17:20–21), as Bock puts it.[45] The signs are both physical and spiritual: healings and exorcisms accompany proclamations of the approaching rule of God (4:40–44; 8:1–2; 9:1–2). Those who respond with faith recognise the power of God already operating through him in these events. However, biblical expectations concerning the ultimate defeat of sin, death and Satanic rule mean that there is more to come.

Jesus constantly warns the crowds about approaching judgment (10:13–15; 11:31–2, 50–51; 12:4–10). In private, however, he tells his followers that he must first suffer many things, be rejected and killed, and on the third day be raised to life (9:22; compare 9:44; 17:25, 31–3). The pattern of their discipleship is determined by this prediction and by the warning about accountability to the Son of Man 'when he comes in his glory and in the glory of the Father and of the holy angels' (9:23–6). Jesus's saying in 9:27 most likely implies that some of his disciples will soon 'see the kingdom of God' and the glory of the Son of Man in anticipation of that great day by witnessing his transfiguration (9:28–36).

The sequence by which end-time events will occur is clarified as Luke's Gospel progresses. Jesus implies that his death in Jerusalem will put in train God's judgment on everything that Jerusalem stood for (13:31–5; compare 19:41–4; 23:27–31), but not immediately. The parable in 19:11–27, which is only found in this Gospel, is told 'because he was near Jerusalem

---

'a prudent use of possessions' by disciples and 'a radical attitude, which recommends the renunciation of all wealth or possessions'.

[44] This is best described as 'Inaugurated Eschatology'. See R. S. Schellenberg, 'Eschatology', *DJG*, 232–9 (especially 234–5).

[45] Bock, *Luke 9:51–24:53*, 1080. See J. B. Green, 'Kingdom of God/Heaven', *DJG*, 468–81.

and the people thought that the kingdom of God was going to appear at once'. The key figure in the parable goes 'to a distant country to have himself appointed king and then to return'. Jesus's death initiates a period requiring watchful waiting and faithful discipleship (21:8–19, 34–6).

Luke's account of Jesus's teaching in 21:20–33 highlights the significance of the city's destruction in fulfilment of earlier predictions and loosely connects this with the return of the Son of Man and the judgment of the nations. But the expression 'the times of the Gentiles' (21:24) marks an unspecified period from the fall of Jerusalem to the consummation of God's plan.[46] The Son of Man's heavenly rule is inaugurated by his death, resurrection and heavenly exaltation (22:69; compare 24:26; Acts 2:32–36), but his triumph will not be apparent to all until his return in glory (12:40; 17:24, 30; 21:27, 36).

Jesus stresses the narrowness of the way into God's kingdom and the limited time before the door is shut (13:22–30), highlighting the sovereign initiative of God in making himself known to those who would experience the eschatological banquet with him (see Isaiah 25:6–9). The interval between his heavenly exaltation and his glorious return will be a period of longing for disciples and alienation from a world where people are preoccupied with everyday life, having no time for God and no fear of imminent judgment (17:22–9). Luke's concern with the delay of the Son of Man's return does not signify a waning interest in eschatology, but as Schellenberg observes, it attests to his effort 'to preserve the credibility of imminent expectation in a new historical situation'.[47] Luke was writing for believers perhaps forty years after Jesus's resurrection–ascension, keen to help them persevere faithfully, while anticipating his return.

Final judgment is represented by Jesus as going down to 'Hades' in Luke 10:15, echoing Isaiah 14:13–15. This Greek term referred to the grave or the shadowy realm of the dead, regularly translating the Hebrew *šᵉʾôl* ('Sheol') in the LXX (see Acts 2:24–32, reflecting on Psalm 16 [15 LXX]:8–11). When convictions about bodily resurrection and retribution after death developed in later Jewish literature, Hades/Sheol came to be regarded as 'a place divided into separate locales', as Fitzmyer puts it.[48] In line with Daniel 12:2–3, however, Jesus envisions only two outcomes:

---

[46] Green, *Luke*, 731, argues that Luke interprets the fall of Jerusalem 'as an eschatological event, but not in immediate relation to the coming of the eschaton'.

[47] Schellenberg, 'Eschatology,' 237, following J. T. Carroll, *Response to the End of History: Eschatology and Situation in Luke–Acts* (Atlanta: Scholars Press, 1988).

[48] Fitzmyer, *Luke X–XXIV*, 855 (e.g., 1 Enoch 22:3–13; 63:10; 99:11). Compare J. B. Green, 'Heaven and Hell', *DJG*, 370–76.

some will be resurrected 'to everlasting life, others to shame and ever-lasting contempt'. Hades is used to represent both death and subsequent punishment for those who are unrepentant in this life (see Matthew 11:23; 16:18; Luke 16:23).[49]

'Hell' is an equivalent term in 12:5 (see Matthew 5:22, 29, 30; 10:28; 18:9; 23:15, 33; Mark 9:43, 45, 47). The Greek *geenna* (often represented as 'Gehenna') derives from the Hebrew *gê-Hinnōm* ('valley of (the son[s] of) Hinnom'), which is variously translated in the LXX. This was where apostate Israelites had once built 'the high places of Baal to burn their children in the fire as offerings to Baal' (Jeremiah 19:4–5; see also 7:31). Jeremiah predicted that this would become 'the Valley of Slaughter' when God acted to punish his people (7:32–4; 19:6–9). Fitzmyer argues that, by the time of Jesus, this smouldering rubbish dump had come to represent 'the place for torment of sinners after judgment, or at least after death'.[50]

Jesus's parable of the rich man and Lazarus (16:19–31) uses images common in mainstream Jewish thought to warn people about listening carefully to Moses and the prophets and repenting before it is too late. The parable was not specifically told to reveal details about the after-life, but it vividly portrays the finality of the situation into which both characters pass. The angels carry Lazarus to 'Abraham's side', while the rich man is in Hades. Being at Abraham's side recalls the image of sitting down with the patriarchs of Israel and all the faithful at the banquet in the kingdom of God (13:28–9). Hades involves separation from God and his saved people, and physical torment. Between these different realms of continuing existence 'a great chasm has been set in place', so that those who would cross from one to the other cannot. From an earthly perspective, these characters have arrived at their ultimate destination, but the general resurrection has not yet taken place in history and the brothers on earth need to hear the message of warning. Some would argue that the rich man and Lazarus are in an intermediate state that anticipates their ultimate destiny, but there is debate about the best way to evaluate the evidence.[51]

Jesus says more about the final destiny of believers in response to the

---

[49] See Paul R. Williamson, *Death and the Afterlife: Biblical Perspectives on Ultimate Questions* (London: Apollos; Downers Grove: InterVarsity, 2017), 38–54.

[50] Fitzmyer, *X–XXIV*, 960. God's judgment had long been associated with fire (Deuteronomy 32:22; Isaiah 31:9; 66:24; Judith 16:17; Jubilees 9:15) and was linked with this valley when its high place was destroyed in the time of Josiah (2 Kings 23:10).

[51] Compare Williamson, *Death and the Afterlife*, 52–4, 61–2, and Murray J. Harris,

Sadducees, 'who say there is no resurrection' (20:27; Acts 23:8). When they come to test him with a question about a woman who married seven times and then died, Jesus replies, 'The people of this age marry and are given in marriage. But those who are considered worthy of taking part in the age to come and in the resurrection from the dead will neither marry nor be given in marriage' (20:34–5). Life in the age to come is clearly related to the general resurrection of the dead. The claim that 'they can no longer die; for they are like the angels' means that, when death has been abolished, there is no further need for human procreation. However, the faithful departed are not merely spiritual beings like angels, since bodily transformation is implied by the expression 'children of the resurrection' (20:36). Moreover, when Jesus argues from Exodus 3:6 that the God of Israel's forefathers is 'not the God of the dead, but of the living' (20:37–8), his conclusion applies to all who have enjoyed a genuine relationship with God in this life. Even though they die, they 'all live to him' (ESV). The verb *zōsin* in the present tense ('they live') suggests that the patriarchs already enjoy resurrection life in anticipation of the end of this age.[52]

Finally, when the man next to Jesus on the cross says, 'Jesus, remember me when you come into your kingdom,' he replies, 'Truly I tell you, today you will be with me in paradise' (23:42–3). The Greek word *paradeisos* was applied to the Garden of Eden in the LXX (Genesis 2:8; 13:10; Ezekiel 31:8) and to God's work of restoring his people and their land after the Babylonian Exile (Isaiah 51:3). In some later Jewish literature, paradise came to mean a pleasant resting place for the righteous prior to the great day of resurrection.[53] However, in view of the biblical promises concerning a new creation or restoration of Edenic life that were broadly linked with the establishment of the Messiah's rule (e.g., Isaiah 11:1–9; 35; 65:17–25; Ezekiel 34:20–31), it is likely that 'paradise' on the lips of Jesus refers to everything promised in Scripture concerning his victory over death and God's new creation. Jesus promises this man an immediate experience of resurrection life with him upon death. The glorification

---

From Grave to Glory: Resurrection in the New Testament (Grand Rapids: Acadamie, 1990), 205–14.

[52] Anderson, *Jesus' Resurrection in Luke–Acts*, 139. Less likely is the view that the verb simply refers to resurrection at the end of the age and that the patriarchs are in an intermediate state. Compare Harris, *From Grave to Glory*, 395–7.

[53] John Nolland, *Word Biblical Commentary Volume 35C Luke 18:35–24:53*, 1152, notes the way an end-time reversal of the expulsion of humanity from the Garden of Eden is expected in *Testament of Levi* 18:10–11; Revelation 2:7, 22.

of the saviour through resurrection and ascension makes it possible for individual believers to experience what is promised to the living and the dead when he returns and brings this age to an end.[54]

4. Cosmological perspectives

Many today find the supernatural aspects of the Gospels a barrier to accepting their veracity. In their understanding of the universe (cosmology), God is unknowable – if he exists at all – and there is no possibility that miracles can occur, or angels appear. But the fundamental message of these ancient documents is that the Creator of all things has acted in a decisive, unprecedented and discernible fashion in the life, death and resurrection–ascension of Jesus of Nazareth. The God of the Bible is not a remote and impersonal force, but a knowable, personal being. Supernatural revelations and events point to the reality of God's presence and self-manifestation in Jesus of Nazareth. They also point to the cosmic significance of his victory over sickness, sin, demonic forces and death for others. Charles Anderson puts it this way:

> Luke may not present a frontal, orderly account of the order of the universe, but his writings are suffused with cosmological claims. God is acclaimed as creator of everything, heaven frequently advances the story, angels and demons show up regularly, and the action spans to the ends of the earth. Most notably, the ascension is a cosmological event. Jesus moves from earth to heaven, with the promise of a future move from heaven to earth. Luke–Acts is not a cosmology, but it does do cosmology from the side.[55]

---

[54] Alexey Somov, *Representations of the Afterlife in Luke–Acts* (London; New York: Bloomsbury, 2017), 229, argues that Luke's understanding of repentance and salvation is 'the main reason why he apparently transfers eschatological issues to the present and emphasizes the importance of individual eschatology'.

[55] Charles Anderson, 'Lukan Cosmology and the Ascension', in *Ascent into Heaven in Luke–Acts. New Explorations of Luke's Narrative Hinge*, eds. David K. Bryan and David Pao (Minneapolis: Fortress, 2016), 177. The intent of ancient cosmology was to give an orderly account of the universe 'to address the ethical–social order of the person and the community' (178).

Angels and the saving intervention of God

Angels appear three times in the opening chapters of Luke (1:11–20, 26–38; 2:9–15) and twice at the end (22:43; 24:4–7 (identified as such in 24:23)), though they are mentioned in several other contexts.[56] An angel of the Lord announces to the parents of John the Baptist that they will conceive a son in their old age. As a prophet of God filled with the Holy Spirit, John will fulfil various biblical predictions and 'bring back many of the people of Israel to the Lord their God' (1:16). The angel introduces himself as Gabriel, who comes from the presence of God to tell them this good news. Gabriel appears a second time to tell Mary that she will conceive and give birth to the long-awaited messianic Son, alluding again to significant biblical promises. The angel explains that her virginal conception will be made possible by the Holy Spirit coming on her and the power of the Most High overshadowing her. Gabriel's role in both contexts is to encourage faith in God's promises and to give understanding of how they will be supernaturally fulfilled.

An angel of the Lord appears next to shepherds in the fields near Bethlehem, announcing 'good news that will cause great joy for all the people. Today in the town of David a Saviour has been born to you; he is the Messiah, the Lord' (2:10–11). The cosmic implications of this are revealed when 'a great company of the heavenly host' appears with the angel, praising God and saying, 'Glory to God in the highest heaven, and on earth peace to those on whom his favour rests.' Reconciliation between heaven and earth through the birth of Jesus and its consequences is indicated.[57] This leads the shepherds to seek for the baby and then spread the word concerning what they have been told about him. In the broader context of Luke 1–2, the significance of John and Jesus is further revealed through prophetic utterances inspired by the Holy Spirit, reflecting on various biblical promises (1:46–55, 67–79; 2:28–35).

Angels appear again at the end of Luke's Gospel to women at the tomb of Jesus in the form of 'two men in clothes that gleamed like lightning'

---

[56] See Luke 2:21; 4:10; 9:26; 12:8, 9; 15:10; 16:22. Human messengers are described as *angeloi* in 7:24, 27; 9:52. See also Acts 5:19; 6:15; 7:30, 35, 38, 53; 8:26; 10:3, 7, 22; 11:13; 12:7–11, 15, 23; 23:8, 9; 27:23–4.

[57] Heaven in this context is the uncreated realm where God dwells (see also Luke 3:21–2; Acts 3:21; 7:55–6). In other contexts, heaven can refer to the visible skies above (e.g., Luke 4:25; 12:56; 17:29; Acts 2:5; 14:17) or both together (e.g., Luke 9:16; 18:13; 24:51; Acts 1:9, 11).

(24:4; compare 24:23).[58] They proclaim his resurrection and remind the women of his prediction that, 'The Son of Man must be delivered over to the hands of sinners, be crucified and on the third day be raised again.' They inform and inspire the women to tell others what has happened, just as they did when appearing to the shepherds (2:9–18). The story of Jesus could have been told without reference to angels, but they function to draw attention to and explain the cosmic significance of key events.

Satan's rule and the establishment of God's dominion

Luke portrays a dark world disordered. Human sin is an obvious factor (3:1–20), but Charles Anderson observes that the problem can also be diagnosed as 'spiritual, demonic darkness. Satan has a kingdom (Luke 11:18). Indeed, he claims authority over all the kingdoms of the world (Luke 4:5–7).'[59] Satan oppresses individuals in different ways (Luke 4:40–41; 8:2; 10:17–20; 13:16, 32; Acts 8:7; 13:6–12; 16:16–18; 19:12), and those who live in darkness and in the shadow of death need to be guided into 'the path of peace' (1:79). Put differently, they need to be turned 'from darkness to light and from the power of Satan to God' (Acts 26:18).

Full of the Holy Spirit, Jesus is led into a direct confrontation with the devil in which his sonship is tested and proven (4:1–13). The implied contrast with Adam and Israel as God's 'son' (Genesis 3:1–7; Exodus 4:22–3) suggests that Jesus is obedient in ways that they were not. When Jesus later cites Isaiah 61:1–2 in the synagogue at Nazareth, he implies that he is the Spirit-anointed prophet sent by God to provide liberation for his people. Without reference to 'the day of vengeance', the quotation indicates that his primary task is to proclaim the Lord's favour, offering his people salvation and not immediately ushering in the day of judgment. His healing miracles and exorcisms are signs of that salvation, though his proclamation of the kingdom of God also signifies imminent judgment in the establishment of God's rule over everything opposing his rule (4:31–44; compare 6:20–26; 10:9–11; 11:20; 13:28–9).

Jesus regularly encounters Satan's personal opposition in those who are demonically possessed (4:33–6, 41; 8:26–39; 11:14–22; 13:10–17). He warns

---

[58] An angel from heaven also appears to Jesus as he prays on the Mount of Olives and strengthens him to face the ordeal ahead of him (22:39–44). Although many Greek manuscripts and ancient versions omit these verses, a sufficient number include them (with variations), and they are cited by early Christian writers.

[59] Anderson, 'Lukan Cosmology', 180.

INTRODUCTION

his disciples about the devil's attempts to discourage belief (8:12; 22:31–2) and sees evidence of Satan's ultimate defeat in the ministry he shares with them (10:17–20). Satan's final attack on Jesus takes place through the betrayal of Judas to the authorities in Jerusalem (22:1–6). Moreover, as Anderson says, 'spiritual darkness and inversion of the world's right order' come into focus with Jesus's prediction of the Temple's destruction and his crucifixion.[60]

God's anticipated judgment on Jerusalem and the Temple is set within the framework of 'fearful events and great signs from heaven' (21:11). Cosmic breakdown is predicted by Jesus in terms familiar from the Old Testament (21:25–6), but this disorder will be reversed by another cosmological event: the coming of the Son of Man 'in a cloud with power and great glory' to bring final redemption (21:27–8). When Jesus is arrested by the Jewish authorities, he describes this as 'your hour – when darkness reigns' (22:53). A link with the coming judgment is made by Jesus in his prediction to those who weep for him (23:27–31). Luke then describes the crucifixion scene in terms of unnatural darkness and the curtain of the Temple being torn in two (23:44–5). At a natural level, however, the centurion rightly discerns a miscarriage of justice in the death of an innocent man (23:47; compare Acts 3:13–15, 17; 7:52–3; 13:28). Both levels of explanation are true and related, since Satan works through human agencies.

Jesus's journey to heaven and back

When Jesus reveals for the first time God's will for him to be rejected and killed and on the third day be raised to life (9:22), he follows this with the prediction that the Son of Man will come back in glory (9:26), which is confirmed by his transfiguration (9:28–36). The time for Jesus to be 'taken up to heaven' begins when he resolutely sets out for Jerusalem (9:51). Luke's actual wording ('the filling up of the days of his being taken up') points to the period leading up to his 'ascension' (*analēmpsis*).[61] This sequence was previously described by Luke as his 'departure' (*exodos*), 'which he was about to bring to fulfilment at Jerusalem' (9:31).

---

[60] Anderson, 'Lukan Cosmology', 181–2.
[61] The related verb is employed in Acts 1:2, 11, 22, and parallel terms are used in Luke 24:51 ('carried up') and Acts 1:9 ('lifted up') to describe how the crucified and resurrected Jesus was exalted to reign at God's right hand as Lord and Messiah (Acts 2:33–6).

Typologically, Jesus's journey to the cross and then his resurrection and ascension complete the journey by which he saves his people and brings them into their eternal inheritance (13:29; 18:28–30; 23:42–3). But final judgment and the renewal of the whole created order cannot happen until the Son of Man returns with power and great glory (21:27–8; Acts 3:21–6).

When Jesus ascends to the Father's 'right hand', he makes the promised Holy Spirit available to 'all people' (Acts 2:16–21, 33), enabling believers in every nation to experience the benefits of his saving work (Acts 10:34–48; 11:15–17). Even more comprehensively, as Anderson argues, the ascension of Jesus 'displays the union of heaven and earth, the unseen and seen, and it paradigmatically expresses the process of the restoration of right order by means of the reversal of the current order'.[62] God definitively reverses the unjust rejection and crucifixion of Jesus by raising him from the dead and glorifying him as a resurrected human being in his presence (20:17–18; 24:26; Acts 2:36; 3:13–15; 4:10–11). Steve Walton concludes:

> The cosmological change of Jesus' presence in heaven at God's right hand produces a theological change in how God is to be seen, understood and known – it is now through and by the Spirit that he is to be known, and that by the Gentiles as well as the Jews (Acts 1:8).[63]

Readers who approach Luke's Gospel with scepticism about any or all of the supernatural manifestations he records should consider the significance given to them on each occasion. The way in which they interconnect in the narrative and relate to what Jesus says about himself should be particularly noticed. Together, they support the fundamental testimony of Luke that, in this extraordinary period of human history, God came to his people and definitively redeemed them (1:68).

---

[62] Anderson, 'Lukan Cosmology', 207. This is so because 'The visible, embodied Jesus has gone to the non-visible divine realm at the right hand of God.'

[63] Walton, 'The Heavens Opened', 71. I would add that Acts envisages the word of Jesus, together with the Spirit, as the means by which he makes himself known in the post-ascension era. See more fully Alan J. Thompson, *The Acts of the Risen Lord Jesus: Luke's Account of God's Unfolding Plan* (Downers Grove: InterVarsity; Nottingham: Apollos, 2011).

I

Preface

LUKE 1:1–4

A brief opening statement in the style of some ancient Greek literary prologues begins this work and is briefly recalled in Acts 1:1–2. Although the author's name is not revealed, several early Christian witnesses testify that Luke the physician and companion of the apostle Paul was responsible for both volumes (see my Introduction, pages 1–2). With this sort of preface, John Nolland contends that Luke is 'evidently claiming some relationship between his own work and published literary, and especially, historical works of his day'.[1] However, several expressions point to the distinctly Christian nature of his subject matter. Many of the claims made in this prologue could apply to Acts as well, although some have a more direct reference to the Gospel.

Introduction

1 Many have undertaken to draw up an account of the things that have been fulfilled[a] among us, ²just as they were handed down to us by those who from the first were eye witnesses and servants of the word. ³With this in mind, since I myself have carefully investigated everything from the beginning, I too decided to write an orderly account for you, most excellent Theophilus, ⁴so that you may know the certainty of the things you have been taught.

_____

a 1 Or *been surely believed*

1. Luke first mentions the achievement of his many predecessors, who 'have undertaken to draw up an account of the things that have been fulfilled among us'. The term *diēgēsis* ('account') suggests that they wrote narratives to explain the significance of events, rather than a loose collection of sayings or stories. Mark's Gospel is likely to have been one of Luke's sources, although he regularly incorporates material from elsewhere. Broadly speaking, his predecessors were concerned with 'the things that

_____

[1] Nolland, *Luke 1–9:20*, 5. See also Peterson, *Acts*, 101–2. Nolland provides a helpful guide to the scholarly literature and the issues involved in this debate.

have been fulfilled among us'. Parallel terms show a significant interest in this theme in Luke–Acts.[2] 'Among us' refers to the community of believers formed by God's extraordinary actions in the life and ministry of Jesus and the subsequent proclamation of the message about him. Luke himself was present for some of the events recorded in his second volume and could have consulted many of the earliest disciples about these matters in his travels with Paul (note the 'we sections' in Acts 16:10–17; 20:4–5; 21:15–19; 27:1–28:16).

2. Both Luke and his literary predecessors were dependent on 'those who from the first were eye witnesses and servants of the word'.[3] The Greek syntax indicates that one group is being identified here, rather than two. It is unlikely that 'the word' should be taken as a reference to the person of Jesus (as in John 1:14), since the gospel of Jesus is regularly described in Luke–Acts as 'the word'.[4] So the expression combines two aspects of their role: those who were eyewitnesses of Jesus and his ministry 'from the first' – that is, from the time of his baptism by John (3:21–3; Acts 1:21–2; 10:37) – soon became devoted agents of the message Jesus preached (Luke 6:12–16; 9:1–6; 24:25–49). Their task was to explain and proclaim the significance of the things they had seen and heard. Such people 'handed down' or delivered their testimony to the Christian community in both oral and written forms (see 1 Corinthians 15:1–8; Hebrews 2:1–4; 1 John 1:1–4; Jude 3).

3. Luke links his own activity with that of his immediate predecessors (ESV, 'it seemed good to me also') and implies no criticism of their work when he claims to have 'carefully investigated everything from the beginning'. This could refer both to his personal engagement with the witnesses and his close examination of the various sources that were

---

[2] The NIV alternative translation ('been surely believed') is less appropriate here. The passive verb *peplērophorēmenōn* suggests God's actions to completely 'fulfil' his purpose (BDAG). More commonly, Luke uses *plēroō* and related terms in relation to the fulfilment of divine revelation (Luke 1:20; 4:21; 24:44; Acts 1:16; 3:18: 13:27, 33). The verb *teleō* ('accomplish, perform, fulfil') and related terms are similarly used in Luke 1:45; 18:31; 22:37; Acts 13:29. See also *pimplēmi* ('fill, fulfil') in Luke 21:22.
[3] This is the only use of the word *autoptēs* ('seeing with one's own eyes') in the Greek Bible, though it was common in secular histories. Luke's preferred term is *martys* ('witness'), as in Luke 24:48; Acts 1:8, 22; 2:32; 3:15; 5:32; 10:39, 41; 13:31; 22:15, 20; 26:16.
[4] See Luke 5:1; 8:11, 12, 13, 15, 21; 11:28; Acts 4:31; 6:2, 7; 8:14, 25; 11:1; 12:24; 13:5, 7, 26, 44, 46, 48, 49; 14:3; 15:35, 36; 16:32; 17:13; 18:11; 19:10, 20.

available to him.[5] Luke asserts his trustworthiness as a historian who has investigated the evidence extensively ('from the beginning'), comprehensively ('everything') and according to the expected standards of his era ('carefully'). 'From the beginning' (*anōthen*) most likely means from the beginning of the gospel story (as in verse 2, *ap' archēs*). When he talks about writing 'an orderly account' (*kathexēs*, 'in order'), he could mean chronological, geographical, logical or thematic order. The same term is used in Acts 11:4, where Peter describes his encounter with Cornelius from his own perspective (NIV 'the whole story'; ESV, 'in order').[6] Both the Gospel and Acts are concerned with chronological and geographical order, but Luke also arranges his material thematically. He includes editorial comments and material from different sources to give his narrative its own distinctive character.

Luke's personal address to Theophilus without mentioning a wider audience is unusual. Most likely, he hoped that Theophilus would recommend his work to others and help to publish it.[7] He may have been a God-fearing Gentile who had embraced Judaism and then Christianity. Although 'most excellent' is an honorific title for Roman officials in Acts 23:26; 24:3; 26:25,[8] applied to Theophilus it may simply mean that he was a socially respected individual.

4. Luke's goal was that Theophilus and those he represented might know 'the certainty' (*asphaleia*, 'security, truth' (BDAG)) of the things they had been taught. The verb *katechō* ('inform, teach, instruct') could imply that Theophilus was an outsider who had merely received reports about Christians and their beliefs and needed assurance about their truthfulness (see Acts 21:21, 24). However, it is more likely that he was an insider who had been formally instructed in the Christian faith (see the use of this verb in Acts 18:25; 1 Corinthians 14:19; Galatians 6:6) and needed assurance about certain issues.[9] The contents of Luke and Acts, their

---

[5] The verb *parakoloutheō* can mean 'follow, accompany, attend' or 'pay careful attention to' (BDAG). See Fitzmyer, *Luke I–IX*, 296–97.

[6] The same Greek word is used for chronological order in Acts 3:24 and geographical order in 18:23. See Darrell L. Bock, *Luke Volume 1: 1:1–9:51* (Grand Rapids: Baker, 1994), 62–3.

[7] Fitzmyer, *Luke I–IX*, 299–300, disputes this, but argues that the dedication means that 'Theophilus stands for the Christian readers of Luke's day and thereafter'.

[8] Compare Josephus, *Antiquities* 18.273; 20.12; *Life* 430.

[9] Patrick Schreiner, *The Mission of the Triune God: A Theology of Acts* (Wheaton: Crossway, 2022), 23, argues that the uncertainty of Luke's first readers 'seems to have stemmed from ethnic, gender, supernatural, social, economic, and political realities'.

emphases and their style of argument suggest that the documents were written for those already reasonably well informed about Christianity, who would be interested in all the details and be able to comprehend the use of Scripture to explain the events. Luke's unique contribution is to provide his readers with a fresh presentation of the gospel story in a salvation–historical framework, from the announcement of John the Baptist's birth to the establishment of Christianity in Rome.

Luke's pastoral aim

As readers of Luke's Gospel, we are challenged to take seriously the author's claim to have researched thoroughly and written thoughtfully about his subject. His reference to 'the things that have been fulfilled among us' expresses his intention to focus particularly on the actions of God to accomplish his plan of salvation for Israel and the nations. To this end, he regularly points to the fulfilment of Scripture and prophecies given within the context of his narrative. In Robert Tannehill's words, Luke establishes an order in his narrative that 'nourishes faith because it discloses a saving purpose behind events'.[10] Luke is interested in people, not just events. He addresses his work to Theophilus and others like him, who have some belief in Jesus but still have questions and doubts about important issues. Set within the context of first-century Judaism and the wider world of the Greco–Roman Empire, Luke's narrative indicates the historical, theological and practical importance of the unique events and teaching he records. At the same time, it introduces us to many characters who bear witness to the impact that Jesus and the gospel had on their lives. Paul John Isaak argues that Luke's Gospel is 'simultaneously the most universal of the four gospels and the most personal', enabling the author to 'embrace diverse groups – the rich, the poor, children, women, men, the powerful and the powerless, the elite and the marginalized'.[11] Luke–Acts as a whole is designed to motivate and equip believers to persevere in the face of doubts and opposition, and to give them resources to communicate and live out their faith in an unbelieving world.[12]

---

[10] Tannehill, *Narrative Unity* I, 12.
[11] Isaak, 'Luke', 1232.
[12] Green, *Luke*, 21–2.

2

Two Significant Births

LUKE 1:5–2:52

After a preface written somewhat in the style of Greek secular histories, Luke adopts a narrative approach reminiscent of the Greek Old Testament, or Septuagint (LXX), and plunges his readers into the world of first-century Palestinian Judaism. God's actions to fulfil his purpose for humanity are set in the broader course of human history, but their significance is revealed in supernatural ways that excite amazement, wonder and praise. This section transitions from the story of Israel to the story of Jesus and provides, in Raymond Brown's words, 'a true introduction to some of the main themes of the Gospel proper'.[1] It begins and ends in the Jerusalem Temple (1:5–25; 2:41–50), as does Luke's Gospel (24:53).

1. God's intentions revealed and acknowledged (Luke 1:5–56)

Luke establishes a close link between John the Baptist and Jesus in the plan of God, echoing biblical scenes where angelic revelations disclose in advance the significance of the birth of a key figure in the history of God's people (e.g., Genesis 18:1–15; Judges 13; 1 Samuel 1–2). This similarity suggests to Tannehill that 'John and Jesus are part of a single divine purpose, which is developing according to the same biblical pattern'.[2] Despite these parallels, however, distinctive differences between John and Jesus are revealed by angelic disclosures and biblical allusions, and by the way each one is described in relation to God's Spirit.[3] The announcement of John's conception (1:5–23) comes first, followed by Elizabeth's pregnancy and praise of God (1:24–5). The announcement of Jesus's conception comes

---

[1] Raymond E. Brown, *The Birth of the Messiah* (London: Chapman, 1977; New York: Image/Doubleday, 1979), 242. Brown compares the way Acts 1–2 transitions from the story of Jesus to the story of the Church.

[2] Tannehill, *Narrative Unity* I, 16. See also Green, *Luke*, 50–51.

[3] See Nolland, *Luke 1–9:20*, 40–41; Fitzmyer, *Luke I–IX*, 313–14.

next (1:26–38), followed by Mary's visit to Elizabeth and her praise of God (1:39–56). Isaak identifies these as the first of a series of 'women's stories' in this Gospel, providing 'female readers with female characters as role models in a world of mainly patriarchal characters'.[4]

The announcement of John's conception (1:5–25)

The birth of John the Baptist foretold

5 In the time of Herod king of Judea there was a priest named Zechariah, who belonged to the priestly division of Abijah; his wife Elizabeth was also a descendant of Aaron. **6** Both of them were righteous in the sight of God, observing all the Lord's commands and decrees blamelessly. **7** But they were childless because Elizabeth was not able to conceive, and they were both very old.

8 Once when Zechariah's division was on duty and he was serving as priest before God, **9** he was chosen by lot, according to the custom of the priesthood, to go into the temple of the Lord and burn incense. **10** And when the time for the burning of incense came, all the assembled worshippers were praying outside.

11 Then an angel of the Lord appeared to him, standing at the right side of the altar of incense. **12** When Zechariah saw him, he was startled and was gripped with fear. **13** But the angel said to him: 'Do not be afraid, Zechariah; your prayer has been heard. Your wife Elizabeth will bear you a son, and you are to call him John. **14** He will be a joy and delight to you, and many will rejoice because of his birth, **15** for he will be great in the sight of the Lord. He is never to take wine or other fermented drink, and he will be filled with the Holy Spirit even before he is born. **16** He will bring back many of the people of Israel to the Lord their God. **17** And he will go on before the Lord, in the spirit and power of Elijah, to turn the hearts of the parents to their children and the disobedient to the wisdom of the righteous – to make ready a people prepared for the Lord.'

18 Zechariah asked the angel, 'How can I be sure of this? I am an old man and my wife is well on in years.'

19 The angel said to him, 'I am Gabriel. I stand in the presence of God, and I have been sent to speak to you and to tell you this good news. **20** And now you will be silent and not able to speak until the day this happens, because you did not believe my words, which will come true at their appointed time.'

21 Meanwhile, the people were waiting for Zechariah and wondering

---

[4] Isaak, 'Luke', 1232. Mary's role is amplified in 2:1–52, where Anna the prophetess is also introduced. Women feature at several other key points in the narrative (7:36–8:3; 8:40–56; 10:38–42; 13:10–17; 15:8–10; 18:1–8; 21:1–4; 23:55–24:12).

why he stayed so long in the temple. **22**When he came out, he could not speak to them. They realised he had seen a vision in the temple, for he kept making signs to them but remained unable to speak. **23**When his time of service was completed, he returned home. **24**After this his wife Elizabeth became pregnant and for five months remained in seclusion. **25**'The Lord has done this for me,' she said. 'In these days he has shown his favour and taken away my disgrace among the people.'

5. John the Baptist's parents lived in the tumultuous era of Herod the Great (73–4 BC), who was appointed 'king of Judea' by the Roman Senate in 40 BC and ruled from 37 to 4 BC. Herod's domain encompassed Galilee, Judea, Samaria, Western Idumea and portions of Perea and Coele–Syria. Edwards describes him as an Idumean by birth but a Jew by religion, 'endowed with strength, stamina, and shrewdness, with a gift for taking strategic risks and landing on his feet, a passionate builder, artistically sensitive and sensuous, but barbarically cruel to his enemies, real or imagined'.[5] Most importantly, he enlarged and magnificently refurbished the Temple that had been built in Jerusalem after the Babylonian Exile. Zechariah is introduced as belonging to 'the priestly division of Abijah' and ministering in that temple.[6] His wife Elizabeth was also from a priestly family ('a descendant of Aaron').

6–7. The righteousness of Zechariah and Elizabeth 'in the sight of God' was expressed in their daily lifestyle ('observing all the Lord's commands and decrees blamelessly').[7] Brown observes, 'Combining priestly origins and blameless observance of the Law, Zechariah and Elizabeth were for Luke the representatives of the best in the religion of Israel; and as a remnant which received the "good news" (1:19), they personified the continuity in salvation history.'[8] Despite their godliness, however, they had no child, 'because Elizabeth was not able to conceive, and they were both very old'. This recalls the situation of Abraham and Sarah (Genesis

---

[5] Edwards, *Luke*, 32. See also H. Bond, 'Herodian Dynasty', *DJG*, 379–82. Judea here means 'the land of the Jews' (see 4:44; 6:17; 7:17; 23:5). Elsewhere, it refers more specifically to the southern area of Palestine.
[6] The word rendered 'priestly division' (*ephēmeria*) is used in 1 Chronicles 23:6; 28:13 LXX with reference to the twenty-four divisions of priests who would do daily service in the Temple for one week, twice in each year, and at the annual festivals. The division of Abijah was the eighth (1 Chronicles 24:10). See C. Fletcher-Louis, 'Priests and Priesthood', *DJG*, 696–702.
[7] See my note on 'the righteous' in verse 17.
[8] Brown, *Birth of the Messiah*, 268.

18:11), and also Samson's mother (Judges 13:2) and Samuel's mother (1 Samuel 1:1–8) who were childless and unable to give birth. The birth of John is thus presented as an extraordinary gift of God 'in continuity with the births of famous figures in the salvific history of Israel'.[9]

8–10. It was 'when Zechariah's division was on duty and he was serving as a priest before God, [that] he was chosen by lot, according to the custom of the priesthood, to go into the temple of the Lord and burn incense'. In association with the daily burnt offerings, incense was offered morning and evening on the altar that stood in the Holy Place before the curtain leading to the Most Holy Place (Exodus 30:1–8). Given the large number of priests available, Nolland considers that 'the privilege of offering incense before the Lord would normally be expected only once or twice in a lifetime'.[10] So it was a special occasion for Zechariah in more ways than one. The statement, 'when the time for the burning of incense came, all the assembled worshippers were praying outside', prepares for the moment when Zechariah comes out of the Temple and the people realise that he has seen a vision (verses 21–2).

11–13. The extraordinary appearance of a divine messenger in the outer sanctuary of the Temple is simply announced: 'Then an angel of the Lord appeared to him, standing at the right side of the altar of incense.' Angelic visitations are actually rare in Scripture, providing special, immediate indications of God's presence and care for his people.[11] The manner in which this 'messenger of the Lord' (called Gabriel in verse 19) announced imminent events is reminiscent of Daniel 8–10. Angels appear three times in Luke's birth narratives (1:11–19, 26–38; 2:9–14), not as bearers of new revelation, but proclaiming the fulfilment of Old Testament prophecies and applying them to either John or Jesus.

Like many recipients of an angelic visitation in the Bible, 'when Zechariah saw him, he was startled and was gripped with fear' (compare Exodus 3:1–6; Judges 6:22–23; Daniel 8:15–17). But the angel insisted that there was nothing for Zechariah to fear, because 'your prayer has been heard'. Since prayer has not been mentioned so far, the following clause, 'your wife Elizabeth will bear you a son', might indicate that he had been praying for this. More likely, Zechariah was praying with others for

---

[9] Brown, *Birth of the Messiah*, 269. Luke 1–2 hints at further specific parallels with the story of Abraham (Green, *Luke*, 53–8).

[10] Nolland, *Luke 1–9:20*, 27. See also Edwards, *Luke*, 34–5.

[11] See C. Fletcher-Louis, 'Angels', *DJG*, 11–17; Green, *Luke*, 72; and my Introduction, pages 23–4.

the coming of the Messiah and the era of salvation (see 2:25, 38; 24:21). The promise of this child was God's surprising answer. Since God-given names generally have significance in Scripture, the instruction to name him John (Hebrew *Yohanan*, 'Yahweh has been gracious') was an important message to both parents and people. God was about to answer their prayers for redemption. Names in many cultures today similarly reflect family heritage, present circumstances or best intentions for a child.

14–15. The angel predicted the impact that John's birth would have on Zechariah and Elizabeth ('he will be a joy and delight to you') and then on his generation ('many will rejoice because of his birth'). These predictions were soon fulfilled (1:58, 64, 68–79). Three Greek words for joy are used here and elsewhere in Luke (*chara* ('joy'); *agalliasis* ('delight'); *chairō* ('rejoice')).[12] The reason for such rejoicing is explained in terms of John being 'great in the sight of the Lord' (see 7:28; 1 Samuel 2:21). This is then related by the angel to Numbers 6:3 ('he is never to take wine or other fermented drink') and the promise that he 'will be filled with the Holy Spirit even before he is born'.[13] John was to be dedicated to the Lord's service from birth, like a Nazirite (compare Samson and Samuel) and filled with the Holy Spirit in his mother's womb (*eti ek koilias*, 'while still in the womb'),[14] so that in due course he could powerfully and effectively proclaim 'the word of God' as a prophet (1:76; 3:2; 7:26–7).

16–17. Alluding to Isaiah 49:6, the angel declared that the Baptist would inaugurate the Servant of the Lord's ministry of bringing back (*epistrepsei*) 'many of the people of Israel to the Lord their God'. The manner of his ministry would be to 'go on before the Lord, in the spirit and power of Elijah'. The first part of this sentence ('go on before the Lord') could refer to his obedient and faithful lifestyle, while the qualifying phrase ('in the spirit and power of Elijah') could refer to his prophetic calling. However, an allusion to Malachi 3:1; 4:5–6 here more likely indicates that he will precede the coming of the Lord God to save and to judge 'with the same spiritual power as Elijah', as Howard Marshall suggests.[15]

---

[12] See J. B. Green 'Joy', *DJG*, 448–50. Joy is a dominant feature of the birth narratives (see 1:28, 44, 46, 58; 2:10).

[13] The term translated 'fermented drink' (*sikera*) is normally used for 'alcoholic drinks not made from grapes, and especially for beer' (Nolland, *Luke 1–9:20*, 30).

[14] This expression points to his prenatal life, suggesting that God relates to foetuses as human persons and may cause them to know him from their earliest days. Even from the womb, John gives a prophetic sign to his mother about the significance of Mary's pregnancy (1:41–4). See Fitzmyer, *Luke I–IX*, 326.

[15] I. Howard Marshall, *The Gospel of Luke: A Commentary on the Greek Text* (Exeter:

More specifically, John's calling is 'to turn the hearts of the parents to their children and the disobedient to the wisdom of the righteous'. These words echo a portion of Malachi 3:23 LXX (4:6 NIV), where the preceding verse contains the divine promise to send Elijah 'before that great and dreadful day of the Lord comes'. As a returning Elijah-figure, John's preaching of repentance would bring about reconciliation at the level of broken human relationships (parents and children), as well as between disobedient Israelites and their God. The phrase 'and the disobedient to the wisdom of the righteous' broadens the implications of the extra phrase in Malachi's prediction ('and the hearts of the children to their parents'). Many will adopt a way of thinking and behaving that reflects a genuine relationship with God (see 7:35).[16] As illustrated in 3:7–14, John called people from every level of Jewish society to 'produce fruit in keeping with repentance'.

The ultimate purpose of the Baptist's ministry will be 'to make ready a people prepared for the Lord'. The task of preparing a people and preparing a way for the Lord (1:76; 3:4; 7:27) are closely related. As Tannehill concludes, John prepares the Lord's way 'by preparing a repentant people, whose hearts have turned and who are ready to receive their Lord'.[17] At this stage, there is no specific indication that John prepares for the Messiah's coming, but rather the focus is on the coming of the Lord God himself, as in Malachi 3–4. These two ideas come together in Luke 1:68–79; 3:1–22.

18–20. Zechariah asks for confirmation of this extraordinary promise, since he knows full well that he and his wife are beyond the age of conceiving a child. The angel answers by identifying himself as God's personal representative (Gabriel means 'God is my hero/warrior'), who stands close to God ('in the presence of God'), ready to bring such news to his people ('and I have been sent to speak to you and to tell you this good news').[18] A judgment is announced ('and now you will be silent and not able to speak until the day this happens'), because Zechariah has doubted the word of God. Daniel was momentarily mute in response

---

Paternoster, 1978), 59. See S. A. Cummins, 'John the Baptist', *DJG*, 436–44.

[16] The term *dikaios* ('righteous') is used positively in 1:6, 17; 2:25; 5:32; 14:14; 23:47, 50 for those who demonstrate a right relationship with God by their behaviour. It is used ironically in 15:7; 18:9; 20:20 for those whose righteousness is questionable. See J. K. Brown, 'Justice, Righteousness', *DJG*, 463–7.

[17] Tannehill, *Narrative Unity* 1, 24.

[18] The verb *euangelizomai* ('bring good news') is used here for the first time in Luke (see also 2:10; 3:18; 4:18, 43; 7:22; 8:1; 9:6; 16:16; 20:1).

to a divine revelation (Daniel 10:15–16), but Zechariah's punishment for not believing the angel's words would last until they 'come true at their appointed time'. Marshall observes that this enforced silence confirms the truth of the angel's promise, while concealing from others 'the wonder of what was to happen until the due time'.[19]

21–2. The people outside 'were waiting for Zechariah and wondering why he stayed so long in the temple'. Normally, the priest on duty would remain in the sanctuary for a short while and reappear to give the Aaronic blessing (Numbers 6:24–6; Sirach 50:19–21). When Zechariah came out, however, 'they realised he had seen a vision in the temple, for he kept making signs to them but remained unable to speak'.

23–5. When Zechariah's time of service was completed, he returned home to a town in the hill country of Judea (verse 39), after which his wife Elizabeth became pregnant and for five months remained in seclusion. The timing is precise here and in verses 26, 36, 56, because Luke wishes to demonstrate how the stories of Elizabeth and Mary interlock. In those five months, Elizabeth gave glory to God, saying, 'The Lord has done this for me,' and thanking him that the reproach of barrenness had been taken away from her ('in these days he has shown his favour and taken away my disgrace among the people'). The affliction of childlessness is mentioned in several biblical contexts, where a woman's shame is often exacerbated by the attitude of others (e.g., Genesis 16:5; 29:32; 30:1, 23; 1 Samuel 1:6–7, 11). But God can make the childless woman 'a happy mother' (Psalm 113:9). Barrenness is not portrayed as a punishment for individual sin, but as 'a difficult human experience through which God can act'.[20]

THE FIRST STIRRINGS OF HOPE

Luke alone among the Gospel writers begins his narrative in the sacred precincts of the Jerusalem Temple, where the significance of John the Baptist in the plan of God is first revealed. The miraculous nature of John's conception links him with key figures in Israel's history and the name he is given expresses God's continuing graciousness to his people. The angel's prediction about his ministry confirms that every biblical prediction concerning end-time salvation will be fulfilled: God is about

---

[19] Marshall, *Luke*, 60.

[20] K. T. Magnuson, 'Childlessness', *NDBT*, 406. The shame of barrenness reflects an exaggerated emphasis on the significance of childbirth for a woman's worth in society. Isaak, 'Luke', 1232–3 discusses the impact of this on African cultures today.

to 'visit' his people (1:68; 7:16). John's godly parents were part of a faithful remnant, waiting for 'the consolation of Israel' (2:25) and 'the redemption of Jerusalem' (2:38; see also 23:51; 24:21). John's task was to prepare many more to meet with their God. His significance is further indicated in Luke 1:68–80; 3:1–18; 7:24–35; 9:7–9, 19; 11:1; 16:16; 20:3–6, and his ministry is regarded as the beginning of the gospel story in Acts 10:37; 13:24–5. Some readers may baulk at the mention of angels, regarding this as an unnecessary and embarrassing feature of the narrative. But Luke is claiming that God intervened in human history in a decisive and unprecedented fashion in the period he records. This involved angelic and prophetic proclamations, miracles and other supernatural events, showing God's unique relationship with Jesus and God's purpose for him. Angels function in this remarkable story to announce the fulfilment of ancient prophecies and prepare the participants for the coming of God into their midst. See my Introduction, pages 22–4.

The announcement of Jesus's conception (1:26–38)

The birth of Jesus foretold

26 In the sixth month of Elizabeth's pregnancy, God sent the angel Gabriel to Nazareth, a town in Galilee, 27 to a virgin pledged to be married to a man named Joseph, a descendant of David. The virgin's name was Mary. 28 The angel went to her and said, 'Greetings, you who are highly favoured! The Lord is with you.'

29 Mary was greatly troubled at his words and wondered what kind of greeting this might be. 30 But the angel said to her, 'Do not be afraid, Mary, you have found favour with God. 31 You will conceive and give birth to a son, and you are to call him Jesus. 32 He will be great and will be called the Son of the Most High. The Lord God will give him the throne of his father David, 33 and he will reign over Jacob's descendants

for ever; his kingdom will never end.'

34 'How will this be,' Mary asked the angel, 'since I am a virgin?'

35 The angel answered, 'The Holy Spirit will come on you, and the power of the Most High will overshadow you. So the holy one to be born will be called[b] the Son of God. 36 Even Elizabeth your relative is going to have a child in her old age, and she who was said to be unable to conceive is in her sixth month. 37 For no word from God will ever fail.'

38 'I am the Lord's servant,' Mary answered. 'May your word to me be fulfilled.' Then the angel left her.

---

b 35 Or *So the child to be born will be called holy,*

26–8. A temporal link with Elizabeth's pregnancy ('in the sixth month') prefaces the record of an angelic visitation to her younger relative ('God sent the angel Gabriel to Nazareth, a town in Galilee').[21] The focus turns from the Temple in Jerusalem to a humble home in an obscure northern town. Mary is 'a virgin pledged to be married to a man named Joseph, a descendant of David'. Joseph's role is stressed in Matthew 1:18–25, including the fact that he must ultimately name the child, but Mary (Hebrew, *Miryam* (see Exodus 15:20)) is the focus in Luke's narrative.[22] 'Virgin' is an appropriate translation of the Greek (*parthenos*) with reference to 'a young, unmarried girl' (BDAG), who was 'pledged to be married' (*emnēsteumenēn*; see Matthew 1:18–19). A betrothal at that time was considered to be as binding as marriage, but sexual intercourse could not take place until the girl went to live in the bridegroom's home. The usual age for a girl's betrothal was between twelve and twelve and a half, but Mary could have been betrothed for some years before this angelic visitation.[23] The angel's greeting indicates that God's grace had been shown to her in a personal way: 'Greetings, you who are highly favoured!'[24] The claim that 'the Lord is with you' suggests the powerful presence of God to fulfil his purpose for Mary (see verse 35). As Joel Green puts it, 'God has given his favor to one who had no claim to worthy status, raised her up from a position of lowliness, and has chosen her to have a central role in salvation history.'[25]

29–33. Despite the angel's encouraging declaration, Mary was 'greatly troubled at his words and wondered what kind of greeting this might be'. Gabriel acknowledged her fear ('Do not be afraid, Mary') and repeated his affirmation in a different form: 'you have found favour with God' (*charin para tō theō*).[26] A cumulative explanation of what this means is

---

[21] Green, *Luke*, 83–4, lists the parallels between the angel's encounter with Zechariah in 1:11–20 and Mary in 1:28–38, but then highlights the differences.
[22] Fitzmyer, *Luke I–IX*, 307 lists twelve parallels between the infancy narratives in Matthew and Luke. The angelic visitation in Matthew comes after Mary's conception and directs Joseph's response to the situation.
[23] Joachim Jeremias, *Jerusalem in the Time of Jesus* (Philadelphia: Fortress; London: SCM, 1978), 364–5; Nolland, *Luke 1–9:20*, 49.
[24] The perfect participles *emnēsteumenēn* (verse 27, 'pledged to be married') and *kecharitōmenē* (verse 28, 'you who are highly favoured') emphasise her current state. See Constantine R. Campbell, *Verbal Aspect and Non-Indicative Verbs: Further Soundings in the Greek of the New Testament* (New York: Peter Lang, 2008), 24–6.
[25] Green, *Luke*, 87 (emphasis removed).
[26] See Genesis 6:8; Judges 6:17; 1 Samuel 1:18; 2 Samuel 15:25. The word *charis*

then given. First, Mary is told that she will 'conceive and give birth to a son', echoing the language of angelic announcements in Genesis 16:11 and Judges 13:5, and more importantly the wording of Isaiah 7:14 (see Matthew 1:22–23). Second, the instruction 'to call him Jesus' (Hebrew *yᵉhôšua*, 'Yahweh saves' or 'Yahweh is salvation') points to his significance as the agent of God's salvation (explicit in Matthew 1:21). Third, the claim is made that 'he will be great and will be called the Son of the Most High'. Zechariah was told that his son would be 'great in the sight of the Lord' (verse 15) as the prophet who would prepare God's people to meet him (verses 16–17), but Jesus is greater as God's Son.

The title 'Son of the Most High' is first explained in messianic terms, with deeper implications revealed in verse 35. Echoing the language of 2 Samuel 7:12–16, the angel promises that 'the Lord God will give him the throne of his father David, and he will reign over Jacob's descendants for ever; his kingdom will never end'. This recalls the special relationship God promised to have with David's son in 2 Samuel 7:14 ('I will be his father, and he shall be my son'). Initially, God's covenant with David was fulfilled in the succession of Davidic kings before the Babylonian Exile. When that rule ceased, God's promises reappeared in prophecies concerning an end-time deliverer of his people (e.g., Isaiah 9:6–7; 11:1–5; Jeremiah 23:5–6; 33:14–22; Ezekiel 34:22–4; Amos 9:11; Zechariah 6:12–13; 9:9). God would establish his eternal rule over Israel and the nations through the Son of David he would raise up (see Psalms 2, 89, 110). Similar expectations appear in Jewish intertestamental literature.[27] 'Son of David' is a title applied to Jesus in Luke 18:38–9 and used by him with reference to the Messiah in 20:41, 44, but the term 'Christ' or 'the Messiah' is more extensively employed in this Gospel (2:11, 26; 3:15; 4:41; 9:20; 20:41; 22:67; 23:2, 35, 39; 24:26).[28]

34–5. Mary asks, 'How will this be . . . since I am a virgin?' (*epei andra ou ginōskō*, 'since I do not know a man'), meaning that she has not had sexual relations. She does not express unbelief but requests clarification: pregnancy before marriage would have been more shameful than

---

('grace, favour') is found again in Luke 2:40, 52; 4:22; 6:32–4; 17:9.

[27] For example, Edwards, *Luke*, 43, notes how the Qumran document 4Q246 predicts the coming of a messianic ruler, who will be 'Son of the Most High' and 'Son of God', and uses a number of phrases reminiscent of 2 Samuel 7:12–14; Isaiah 9:6–7. Document 4Q174:10–11 combines elements of 2 Samuel 7:12–14 with Amos 9:11. See Geza Vermes, *The Complete Dead Sea Scrolls in English* (7th edition; Penguin Classics, 2012).

[28] See Y. Miura, 'Son of David', *DJG*, 881–6; A. Winn, 'Son of God', *DJG*, 886–94.

childlessness. The answer reveals more clearly what it means for Jesus to be the Son of the Most High (verse 32): the nature of his conception points to his divine character and origin. Mary is told by the angel, 'The Holy Spirit will come on you,' reflecting the language of Isaiah 32:15 LXX, where the Spirit is expected to renew God's people and restore the created order in a time to come (Isaiah 44:3–4; Ezekiel 37:1–14). God's transforming Spirit would bring about a miraculous conception in the virgin's womb to fulfil his saving plan (see Matthew 1:18–25).[29] A further expression, 'and the power of the Most High will overshadow you', recalls the overshadowing cloud and the glory of the Lord filling the tabernacle in Exodus 40:34–5 (see Luke 9:34). God's presence in the midst of his people expressed his covenant commitment to bless them and bring them into the inheritance he had promised them (Exodus 29:44–6; 33:12–23). Salvation would now be experienced in and through the person of his Son, making possible the fulfilment of his end-time purpose for his people (see Isaiah 7:14, 'Immanuel' ('God with us')).[30]

The conclusion to this revelation (*dio*, 'therefore, so') is that 'the holy one to be born will be called the Son of God'. The child conceived by the Holy Spirit will be fully human, but holy in the sense of being uniquely related to God as his Son and truly reflecting his character as the Holy One. The implications of Jesus's divine sonship are further revealed as Luke's narrative proceeds (see especially 3:22; 4:3, 9, 41; 8:28; 9:35; 10:21–2; 22:42, 70). In the present context, the focus is on his conception, calling and unique ability to fulfil God's kingdom plan. The messianic emphasis in 1:32–4 indicates that the supernatural conception of Jesus brings God's presence and rule into human history, as envisaged by the prophets of Israel.[31]

36–8. As a confirmation that this extraordinary promise will be fulfilled, the angel says, 'Even Elizabeth your relative is going to have a child in her old age, and she who was said to be unable to conceive is in her sixth month.' The word 'relative' (*syngenis*) has a broad meaning and does not specify the nature of their kinship. Although their life situations were different, Elizabeth's advanced pregnancy was a proof that 'no word from God will ever fail' (ESV, 'For nothing will be impossible with God'; see

---

[29] See also M. Wenk, 'Holy Spirit', *DJG*, 387–94.

[30] John 1:14 uses related terminology to express the same idea: 'the Word became flesh and made his dwelling among us' (*eskēnōsen*, 'tabernacled').

[31] Bock, *Luke 1:1–9:50*, 123–25, argues that the title 'Son of God' *may* have ontological implications, but Luke only uses it in an enhanced messianic sense. This seems to play down the contextual emphasis on the coming of God into history in the person of Jesus. See G. L. Parsenios, 'Incarnation', *DJG*, 399–403; Green, *Luke*, 91.

Genesis 18:14; Job 42:2; Jeremiah 32:27; Zechariah 8:6; Mark 10:27; Luke 18:27). Mary's willingness to believe and submit to God's will in an even more difficult situation is simply expressed, 'I am the Lord's servant . . . May your word to me be fulfilled' (contrast Zechariah in verse 18). As Edwards observes, 'Mary demands no outside proofs or signs that the impossible shall be made possible. She receives God's word in abandonment and trust.'[32] Although this meant living with the potential scandal that she had conceived a child before her marriage to Joseph, she acknowledges that she belongs to God as a slave to her master (*doulē*, 'female slave, bondwoman' (BDAG); see verse 48 and 1 Samuel 1:11). When Mary has expressed her desire for God's word to be fulfilled, the angel leaves her.

THE VIRGIN BIRTH AND GOD'S SAVING PLAN

The links between John and Jesus developed by Luke emphasise the unity of their task, but they also point to the uniqueness of Jesus and his calling. John will be 'great' as 'a prophet of the Most High' who precedes the coming of the Lord God himself, but Jesus as 'the Son of the Most High' who will reign as Son of David over Jacob's descendants forever. John's birth to a childless and aged couple is a miracle with biblical precedents and John is filled with the Spirit from the womb, but Jesus's virginal conception by the power of the Holy Spirit is 'an unheard-of wonder'.[33] Luke does not explicitly assert the pre-existence of the Son of God as the Fourth Gospel does (John 1:1–3, 9–14, 18), though this could be inferred from the angel's prediction in verse 35. Luke certainly proclaims the coming of God himself in the person of Jesus. As the ancient carol puts it, 'True God of true God, Light of Light eternal, lo, he abhors not the virgin's womb.'[34] There is no hint in Luke's record that Mary herself needed to have an 'immaculate conception' for this to take place: the focus is on God's radically new initiative in the birth of Jesus. Although many find the idea of a virgin birth hard to believe and reject the notion of a divine incarnation (often confusing this with 'immaculate conception'), Luke explains how this was made possible by God's creative power. Such a birth was

---

[32] Edwards, *Luke*, 50.

[33] Nolland, *Luke 1–9:20*, 41. Nolland (43–6) discusses possible parallels to the virgin birth of Jesus in ancient pagan sources and concludes that Luke's narrative is much more obviously influenced by Old Testament motifs and themes. Compare Edwards, *Luke*, 41–2.

[34] *Adeste Fideles* ('O come all ye faithful'), translated by Frederick Oakeley (1802–80), William Mercer (1811–73), and others.

also necessary to fulfil prophetic expectations about the Messiah as the Son of God, whose kingdom will never end (especially 2 Samuel 7:16; Isaiah 9:6–7). Mary's child had to be both human and divine to fulfil God's covenant promises and accomplish his plan of redemption. God was present with human beings in a new and intimate way through Jesus, to save and to bless them in fulfilment of his ancient promises. This narrative reveals profound truths that will only gradually become known to participants in Luke's larger story.

Mary's visit to Elizabeth and her praise to God (1:39–56)

Mary visits Elizabeth

39At that time Mary got ready and hurried to a town in the hill country of Judea, **40**where she entered Zechariah's home and greeted Elizabeth. **41**When Elizabeth heard Mary's greeting, the baby leaped in her womb, and Elizabeth was filled with the Holy Spirit. **42**In a loud voice she exclaimed: 'Blessed are you among women, and blessed is the child you will bear! **43**But why am I so favoured, that the mother of my Lord should come to me? **44**As soon as the sound of your greeting reached my ears, the baby in my womb leaped for joy. **45**Blessed is she who has believed that the Lord would fulfil his promises to her!'

Mary's song

46And Mary said:

'My soul glorifies the Lord
47   and my spirit rejoices in God my
        Saviour,
48for he has been mindful
        of the humble state of his
            servant.

From now on all generations will
        call me blessed,
49 for the Mighty One has done
        great things for me –
    holy is his name.
50His mercy extends to those who
        fear him,
    from generation to generation.
51He has performed mighty deeds
        with his arm;
    he has scattered those who
        are proud in their inmost
            thoughts.
52He has brought down rulers from
        their thrones
    but has lifted up the humble.
53He has filled the hungry with good
        things
    but has sent the rich away
        empty.
54He has helped his servant Israel,
        remembering to be merciful
55to Abraham and his descendants
        for ever,
    just as he promised our
        ancestors.'

56Mary stayed with Elizabeth for about three months and then returned home.

39–45. 'Mary got ready and hurried to a town in the hill country of Judea,' which was a two- or three-day journey from Nazareth. Particular attention is paid to the impact that Mary's greeting had on Elizabeth and her baby: 'the baby leaped in her womb, and Elizabeth was filled with the Holy Spirit'. Presumably, Mary told Elizabeth what the angel had revealed to her and how she had responded. Mary's greeting and the baby's foetal leap are mentioned together again for emphasis in verse 44. John, who is 'filled with the Holy Spirit even before he is born' (verse 15), acknowledges in some inarticulate way the significance of Mary's greeting (see Genesis 25:22–3). His mother's Spirit-led response, however, is 'in a loud voice'. She offers three blessings and asks a rhetorical question, demonstrating prophetic insight into the significance of what Mary has told her.[35]

The first two blessings are joined together: 'Blessed are you among women, and blessed is the child you will bear' (*ho karpos tēs koilias sou*, 'the fruit of your womb'). Elizabeth's own sense of being blessed by God is expressed in her question, 'But why am I so favoured, that the mother of my Lord should come to me?' Describing Mary's child as her Lord, she acknowledges the deepest implication of the angelic revelation to Mary (1:31–3, 35; see 2:11).[36] The third blessing commends Mary for her trust in God's promise: 'Blessed is she who has believed that the Lord would fulfil his promises to her' (contrast verses 18, 20). Both Elizabeth and Mary are identified as exemplary believers and godly members of the covenant community (see 8:15, 19–21).

46–9. Mary responds to Elizabeth's blessings with a personal expression of praise to God. Mary's song is marked by a several Old Testament allusions and themes that are applied first to her own situation (verses 46–50) and then to that of her people (verses 51–5). Commentators often question whether this song could have been composed by Mary, sometimes arguing that it must have originated in the context of early Jewish Christian worship.[37] However, even if Mary's testimony was preserved in this way, there is no intrinsic reason why she could not have been the original source of such praise. The use of LXX language in the final form of this

---

[35] A blessing acknowledges an existing state of divine favour and rejoices in it. A verbal form is used here (*eulogēmenē*) and in 1:48 (*makariousin*). An adjectival form (*makarios*, 'fortunate') occurs in 1:45; 6:20–22; 11:27–8. Such terms implicitly praise God for the blessings.

[36] See B. Witherington III and K. Yamazaki-Ransom, 'Lord', *DJG*, 526–35.

[37] See Brown, *Birth of the Messiah*, 346–52; Bock, *Luke 1:1–9:50*, 142–5; R. B. Vinson, 'Songs and Hymns', *DJG*, 900–03.

hymn does not preclude the possibility that it was originally uttered in Hebrew or Aramaic. Hannah's song (1 Samuel 2:1–10) could easily have come into Mary's mind and influenced her praise.[38] Contextually, Luke's emphasis is on the Spirit's enabling of prophetic declarations (verses 41–5, 67). As a divinely inspired utterance, Mary's song could have surpassed her natural ability as a speaker.[39]

The song opens with Mary's desire to magnify or glorify God for the joy she experienced in her inner being: 'My soul glorifies the Lord and my spirit rejoices in God my Saviour.' No distinction should be made between soul and spirit in this poetic parallelism: Mary delights in God wholeheartedly.[40] Her address to God as 'my Saviour' affirms that she will personally benefit from the messianic salvation promised in Scripture (verses 31–3). Mary is a sinner in need of God's forgiveness, like everyone else (verses 68–79). She is especially grateful that God has favoured such a lowly person with the honour of giving birth to his Son: 'for he has been mindful of the humble state of his servant'.[41] Mary perceives that the blessings pronounced by Elizabeth mark the beginning of a new stage in human history ('From now on all generations will call me blessed'), because of the miraculous conception that has taken place in her womb ('for the Mighty One has done great things for me'). In this exercise of his power, God has shown himself to be 'holy' (see Exodus 15:11; 1 Samuel 2:2), acting distinctively as Creator and Redeemer to fulfil his promises and bring about the incarnation of his Son!

50–55. The second part of Mary's song sets her experience within the context of God's historic dealings with his people. The 'mercy' shown to her 'extends to those who fear him, from generation to generation' (see

---

[38] Edwards, *Luke*, 54, suggests that it is not difficult to imagine that 'a marginalised young peasant woman steeped in the psalms of Israel could have composed what we know as the Magnificat'. Contrast Brown, *Birth of the Messiah*, 340; Fitzmyer, *Luke I–IX*, 359–62.

[39] The textual evidence for reading Mary as the author of this song, rather than Elizabeth, is evaluated by Bruce M. Metzger, *A Textual Commentary on the Greek New Testament* (2nd edition; Stuttgart: German Bible Society; New York: American Bible Society, 1994), 109; Green, *Luke*, 97, note 13.

[40] Bock, *Luke 1:1–9:50*, 149–50, understands the aorist verb *ēgalliasen* ingressively ('has begun to delight'), but it is more likely a timeless use following the present tense (*megalynei*, 'magnifies').

[41] The word *tapeinōsis* ('humble state') often relates to social and economic deprivation. See W. Grundmann, 'ταπεινός, κτλ.', *TDNT* 8:10–11, 20–21.

verse 54; Psalm 103:17). This is explained in terms of having 'performed mighty deeds with his arm,' meaning that God has acted powerfully to save them (see Exodus 6:1, 6; 15:16; Isaiah 51:9–10). At the same time, the Divine Warrior 'has scattered those who are proud in their inmost thoughts', referring to those who do not fear him (verse 50; see Psalms 18:27; 119:21, 78) and who oppose his people (see Numbers 10:35; Psalm 68:1). More specifically, 'he has brought down the rulers from their thrones but has lifted up the humble'. The way that God has dealt with Mary in her humble state (verse 48) is consistent with the way he has previously 'lifted up the humble' and brought down the powerful more generally.[42] Mary rejoices, as Hannah did in 1 Samuel 2:1–10 anticipating that the birth of her baby (Samuel) would lead to the defeat of Israel's enemies and the eventual establishment of God's rule through his anointed king (David).

Socio-economic terms are used in verse 53 (hungry–rich) in a way that inversely parallels the use of political terms in verse 52 (rulers–humble). But the context shows that both sets of terms are primarily ways of referring to Israel in relation to her enemies (see verses 50–51 and 54–5). The proud are identified with the rulers who oppose God's people and with the rich who oppress the poor; the humble are identified with the hungry and with God's needy servant Israel (verse 54, 'he has helped his servant Israel'; see Isaiah 41:8–9). As David Seccombe suggests, 'It is the oppressors of God's people, the heathen overlords, who are to be driven away. They are characterized as rich because, from the point of view of the exploited nation, they are, and at Israel's expense.'[43] The tense of the verbs in these verses may be understood in relation to both past and future events (see also my comment on verses 67–8). What God has done in the past is the model of what will happen again with the coming of Jesus, only this time the benefits will be eternal.[44]

Just as this part of Mary's song began with a reference to God's mercy (verse 50), so it ends with the claim that God has remembered to 'be merciful to Abraham and his descendants for ever' (verses 54–5; see Exodus 2:24; 32:13; Deuteronomy 9:27). This is related to the fulfilment

---

[42] The word translated *rulers* (*dynastas*) means 'powerful' and should be compared with the description of God as 'the Mighty One' (*ho dynatos*) in verse 49. Clearly, God's power is greater than theirs and is used to release the oppressed and raise them up.
[43] David P. Seccombe, *The Poor and Their Possessions. Possessions and the Poor in Luke–Acts* (Eugene: Wipf and Stock, 2022), 86. Compare Tannehill, *Narrative Unity* 1, 29–30.
[44] Bock, *Luke 1:1–9:50*, 155, plays down the historical or retrospective dimension to Mary's praise.

of a broad range of promises ('just as he promised our ancestors'), which will be articulated in subsequent prophecies (1:68–79; 2:29–32) and in Jesus's own teaching (4:18–21; 13:28–9). The birth of Mary's child will bring about the consummation of God's *eternal* purpose for his people ('for ever'). From a narrative perspective, Tannehill argues that 'Mary's hymn suggests a set of expectations about God's character and purpose which guide the reader in understanding what is most important in the subsequent story'.[45]

56. 'Mary stayed with Elizabeth for about three months,' suggesting that she waited until John was born (see verse 26). If she was not yet married, returning home would have meant returning to live with her parents.

SINGING MARY'S SONG

Mary's song begins as a personal expression of praise to God for acting so powerfully to conceive a child in her womb. However, following the pattern of Hannah's song (1 Samuel 2:1–10), her praise soon becomes a celebration of God's long-standing pattern of dealing with his people. Salvation is pictured in traditional terms, with the language of reversal having both national and personal dimensions: rulers dethroned, but the humble exalted; the hungry fed, but the rich sent empty away. The way in which God showed mercy to those who feared him in the past sets the pattern for his end-time salvation. As Green says, Mary's song is not 'a revolutionary call to human action but a celebration of God's action. Indeed, God's dramatic work is *against* those who would take power into their own hands.'[46] Nevertheless, this prophetic word invites reflection on how God's saving action should influence those who believe and live by the gospel. Christians can share Mary's praise by acknowledging the impact her child has had on their own lives and on human history ever since. They can celebrate the way God's promises to Israel have been fulfilled and the blessings that have come to those in every nation who believe the gospel. They can identify with those who fear God, rather than with those who oppose him and are 'proud in their inmost thoughts'. They

---

[45] *Narrative Unity* 1, 29–30.

[46] Green, *Luke*, 100. In his passion to address issues in African culture that shame women and deny them honour, Isaak, 'Luke', 1234, describes Mary's song as 'a revolutionary document of intense conflict and victory, produced by a woman who proclaims the virtues and values of peace, justice, humanness, compassion and the equality of humankind'. However, he fails to consider the salvation–historical significance of Mary's song and how this could provide a foundation for Christian social ethics, politics and economics.

can stand with the marginalised and demonstrate God's mercy to them in practical ways, as Jesus did in his ministry. Mary's son has inaugurated the ultimate rule of God, which will involve the complete reversal of values and outcomes anticipated in her song. Meanwhile, Christians continually struggle to make their voice heard in a world that resists the actions and intentions of God revealed in the gospel.

2. God's promises fulfilled (Luke 1:57–2:52)

The prophecies and narratives in this section reveal more links between John the Baptist and Jesus. There are parallel sequences of birth, circumcision and naming for each child, and the things that are said about them in prophetic utterances (1:67–79; 2:29–35, 38) and angelic revelations (2:10–14) describe their interconnected but different destinies. Although these sequences appear to end in the same way (1:80; 2:40), the extra narrative concerning the boyhood visit of Jesus to the Temple in Jerusalem affords further insight into his distinct identity and calling (2:41–52).

The birth of John the Baptist and its significance proclaimed (1:57–80)

The birth of John the Baptist

57 When it was time for Elizabeth to have her baby, she gave birth to a son. **58** Her neighbours and relatives heard that the Lord had shown her great mercy, and they shared her joy.

59 On the eighth day they came to circumcise the child, and they were going to name him after his father Zechariah, **60** but his mother spoke up and said, 'No! He is to be called John.'

61 They said to her, 'There is no one among your relatives who has that name.'

62 Then they made signs to his father, to find out what he would like to name the child. **63** He asked for a writing tablet, and to everyone's astonishment he wrote, 'His name is John.' **64** Immediately his mouth was opened and his tongue set free, and he began to speak, praising God. **65** All the neighbours were filled with awe, and throughout the hill country of Judea people were talking about all these things. **66** Everyone who heard this wondered about it, asking, 'What then is this child going to be?' For the Lord's hand was with him.

Zechariah's song

67 His father Zechariah was filled with the Holy Spirit and prophesied:

68 'Praise be to the Lord, the God of Israel,

because he has come to his
people and redeemed them.
69 He has raised up a horn[c] of salvation for us
in the house of his servant David
70 (as he said through his holy
prophets of long ago),
71 salvation from our enemies
and from the hand of all who
hate us –
72 to show mercy to our ancestors
and to remember his holy
covenant,
73   the oath he swore to our father
Abraham:
74 to rescue us from the hand of our
enemies,
and to enable us to serve him
without fear
75   in holiness and righteousness
before him all our days.

76 And you, my child, will be called a
prophet of the Most High;

for you will go on before the
Lord to prepare the way for
him,
77 to give his people the knowledge
of salvation
through the forgiveness of their
sins,
78 because of the tender mercy of our
God,
by which the rising sun will
come to us from heaven
79 to shine on those living in
darkness
and in the shadow of death,
to guide our feet into the path of
peace.'

80 And the child grew and became
strong in spirit[d]; and he lived in the
wilderness until he appeared publicly
to Israel.

---

c 69 *Horn* here symbolises a strong king.
d 80 Or *in the Spirit*

57–8. John's arrival is simply recorded: 'When it was time for Elizabeth to have her baby, she gave birth to a son.' The reaction of her 'neighbours and relatives' is described in terms recalling the announcement of John's conception (verse 14) and Elizabeth's first response (verse 25). They perceived that 'the Lord had shown her great mercy' (more literally, 'magnified his mercy with her' (see verses 46–50)) 'and they shared her joy.'

59–60. The circumcision of the child took place 'on the eighth day', when his membership of the covenant community was celebrated (Genesis 17:11–12; Leviticus 12:3; Joshua 5:2–9). A child's name was normally given at birth by the parents (Genesis 21:1–3; 25:24–6), but the statement that 'they were going to name him after his father Zechariah' suggests that others had begun to call him Zechariah (*ekaloun*, 'they were calling').[47] His

---

[47] Nolland, *Luke 1–9:20*, 79, notes the precedent of naming a son after his father in

49

circumcision became a public opportunity for his mother to clarify that his name would be John. This is the first historical record of circumcision and naming taking place together, though in later Judaism it became common.[48]

61–4. When people said to Elizabeth, 'There is no one among your relatives who has that name,' they made signs to his father to find out what he would like to call him. Apparently, Zechariah was deaf as well as mute (*kōphos* in 1:22 can have both meanings, as in 7:22 (BDAG)). He then asked for a writing tablet, and to the astonishment of all present, he wrote, 'His name is John.' Neighbours and friends were not aware of the angel's prediction and so they were amazed at this confirmation of Elizabeth's unexpected name-choice. The angel's prediction about Zechariah was then fulfilled (verse 13): 'Immediately his mouth was opened and his tongue set free, and he began to speak, praising God.' Zechariah could now join with Elizabeth in blessing God for John's birth and what it represented for his people.

65–6. 'All the neighbours were filled with awe' (see 5:26; 7:16; 8:37; Acts 2:43; 5:5, 11), recognising that an extraordinary act of God had taken place in their midst. Zechariah had been prevented from speaking for nine months and now he was praising God! A child had been born to this aged couple and they had agreed to give him the unusual name of John. 'Throughout the hill country of Judea people were talking about all these things,' but their focus was not simply on the immediate events. 'Everyone who heard this wondered about it' (ESV, 'all who heard them laid them up in their hearts'),[49] and they questioned what this might mean for John's future, saying, 'What then is this child going to be?' God's powerful presence in John's life is asserted when Luke says, 'For the Lord's hand was with him' (see Exodus 14:31; Isaiah 31:3; 41:20; 66:14; Acts 11:21).

67–75. Like Mary's song (verses 46–55), Green notes that Zechariah's prophecy functions as a narrative pause 'to promote reflection on the events just described'.[50] It answers the question, 'What then is this child going to be?' (verse 66). Despite the claims of some that these words could not have originated with Zechariah, there are no real reasons why

---

Josephus, *Antiquities* 14.10, but says naming after the grandfather is better attested (1 Maccabees 2:1–2; Jubilees 11:15; Josephus, *Life* 1.5).

[48] See Edwards, *Luke*, 58. The Jewish Talmud records the practice of circumcising and naming together, but the first known examples of this are in Luke 1:59; 2:21.

[49] Literally, 'they set (these things) in their heart' (*ethento . . . en tē kardia autōn*), meaning that that the events were registered 'in the core of their being' (Edwards, *Luke*, 60). See 2:19, 51; 3:15; 5:22.

[50] Green, *Luke*, 112.

an elderly Jewish priest with a lifetime of reflecting on the Scriptures could not have uttered them. As with Mary's song, the final form of this prophecy in Greek should not prejudice the debate about whether it was originally composed in Hebrew or Aramaic. Elizabeth is said to have been 'filled with the Holy Spirit' (1:41) when she began to praise God with spiritual insight, but Zechariah is the first person in Luke–Acts who is actually said to be 'filled with the Holy Spirit and prophesied' (see Acts 2:4, 16–21; 4:8, 31; 9:17; 13:9, 52).

There are similarities with Mary's song in vocabulary and ways of alluding to the Old Testament, though Mary largely draws her inspiration from Psalms and Zechariah from prophetic oracles. However, while Mary begins with praise for God's intervention in her life in a very personal way and moves to consider the broader implications for her people, Zechariah begins with praise for God's redemptive visitation of his people in the promised Son of David (verses 68–75) and concludes with a personal word to his son John about his role in God's plan (verses 76–9). The first section speaks in the past tense and the third person as if these things have already happened, while the second section is in the future tense and second person.

Zechariah's song celebrates God's saving activity and invites others to praise him for it (see 1 Samuel 25:32; 1 Kings 1:48; 8:15–21; Psalm 41:13 [40:14 LXX]; Ephesians 1:3–14; 1 Peter 1:3–9).[51] Using familiar biblical terms, Zechariah speaks about the Lord God of Israel having 'come to his people and redeemed them'.[52] God has 'made a release' (epoiēsen lytrōsis) or liberated his people from an oppressive situation, initially described in political terms as rescue from enemies (verses 71, 74; compare 2:38, 'the redemption of Jerusalem'). The tense of the aorist verb epoiēsen expresses the certainty of this, as if the release has already taken place. As the prophecy continues, it becomes clear that redemption will involve a release from sin and all its consequences (verses 77–9).[53] This activity

---

[51] The adjective eulogētos ('blessed') is related to the verb eulogeō, which is rendered 'speak well of, praise, give thanks' in 1:64; 2:28; 9:16; 13:35; 19:38; 24:30, 53; 'ask for the bestowal of a special favour (from God)' in 2:34; 24:50, 51; and 'bestow a favour, provide with benefits' in 1:42; 6:28.

[52] The NIV ('come to') renders Greek episkeptomai (ESV, 'visited'). This verb is used in the LXX when God brings deliverance or help in various situations (e.g., Genesis 21:1; Exodus 4:31; Ruth 1:6; Psalm 106:4; Jeremiah 15:15).

[53] See my comment on freedom (aphesis) in 4:18. Redemption in 21:28 (apolytrōsis, as in 2:38) is finally shown to mean deliverance from a world under judgment to enjoy the eternal benefits of Christ's kingdom (21:31).

is related to the coming of the Messiah, which is once again described with certainty, because Zechariah has heard about the promises made to Mary concerning the child in her womb (verses 39–45). God has already 'raised up a horn of salvation for us in the house of his servant David' (verse 69; see 1:32–3). In the Old Testament, God himself is portrayed as a 'horn of salvation' (Psalm 18:2), meaning a powerful provider of salvation, who specifically promises to 'make a horn grow for David' (Psalm 132:17), signifying a strong successor for David (see 2 Samuel 7:26, 'the house of your servant David'). Before Zechariah teases out the nature of this salvation, he states his authority for making such a claim ('as he said through his holy prophets of long ago'; see Acts 3:21).

'Salvation from our enemies and from the hand of all who hate us' (verse 71) involves liberating God's people 'to serve him without fear in holiness and righteousness before him all our days' (verses 74–5; compare Joshua 24:14; Jeremiah 32:39). Israel in Egypt needed to be set free from physical captivity to serve God as a holy nation in the Promised Land (Exodus 7:16; 19:1–8; Psalm 106:10). As Luke's narrative will show, the Messiah must deal with different enemies – temporal and spiritual – to enable the sort of covenant faithfulness that God requires and bring his people into their eternal inheritance. This will happen because of God's original commitment 'to show mercy to our ancestors and to remember his holy covenant, the oath he swore to our father Abraham' (verses 72–3; see Genesis 22:16–17; Exodus 2:24; Leviticus 26:42; Micah 7:20). But the focus on forgiveness of sins and deliverance from the shadow of death to walk in the path of peace (verses 77, 79) highlights the moral and spiritual dimensions to the messianic redemption.

76–9. Zechariah's word to his son reflects the message of the angel in verses 16–17 and the biblical prophecies to which it alludes. John himself will be 'a prophet of the Most High' with a special calling: 'for you will go on before the Lord to prepare the way for him'. The precise way in which John will prepare Israel to meet her Lord is 'to give his people the knowledge of salvation through the forgiveness of their sins'. Knowledge of salvation here means experiencing in advance the benefits of the salvation that Jesus will make available (see 7:50; 19:9–10).[54] God's people will know the possibility of being definitively forgiven (Jeremiah 31:34; Ezekiel 36:25). This will go hand in hand with repentance (Isaiah 55:7; 59:20), which John will proclaim, while offering 'a baptism of repentance

---

[54] The forgiveness of sins comes 'not through John, but through the salvation he makes known' (Edwards, *Luke*, 63).

for the forgiveness of their sins' (3:3). But it will be Jesus who actually makes possible the promised forgiveness (24:46–7; Acts 2:38; 5:31; 10:43; 13:38; 26:18). John will offer a preliminary experience of this extraordinary mercy of God ('because of the tender mercy of our God').[55]

The linkage of this mercy with the coming of the Messiah is clarified by the second half of verse 78 ('by which the rising sun will come to us from heaven'). The subject of the verb 'will come' is most naturally God himself (the same verb is translated 'has come' in verse 68). The next phrase means 'as a rising from on high' or 'as a sunrise from heaven' (*anatolē ex hypsous*), which recalls Isaiah 60:2 ('The Lord rises upon you'; see 2 Samuel 23:4; Malachi 4:2).[56] But the coming of God and the coming of the Messiah have already been closely linked (verses 68–9). Moreover, Isaiah 9:1–7 calls the Messiah 'Wonderful Counsellor, Mighty God, Everlasting Father, Prince of Peace' and describes the benefits of his rule in terms of light, joy, justice, righteousness and peace.

Zechariah's prophecy reflects such prophetic predictions by claiming that the one who comes from heaven will 'shine on those living in darkness and in the shadow of death', and he will also 'guide our feet into the path of peace'. The peace proclaimed here and in Luke 2:14, 29 fundamentally concerns a right relationship with God (see 7:50; 8:48; 10:5–6; 19:38, 42; 24:36; Acts 10:36). But the light that shines in Israel will ultimately bring spiritual renewal and moral transformation to people from every nation (see 2:29–32). Zechariah knows that the issue is not simply deliverance from earthly oppressors.

80. Luke concludes his narrative of John's infancy with two observations. The first is that 'the child grew and became strong in spirit' (see 2:40, 52, recalling 1 Samuel 2:26; 3:19–20; Judges 13:24–5). 'Strong in spirit' describes his spiritual maturation which, by implication, was due to the work of God's Spirit in his life (see 1:15). The second observation is related to the first: 'he lived in the wilderness until he appeared publicly to Israel'. John's devotion to God and preparation for his ministry was nurtured in a desert place.[57]

---

[55] More literally, this salvation is achieved 'through the deep affection (*splagchna*, "bowels") of the mercy of our God'.

[56] In 24:49 *ex hypsous* is similarly translated 'from on high'. Edwards, *Luke*, 63, follows Fitzmyer, *Luke I–IX*, 387, in taking the image of 'the rising one' to be a metaphor for the Messiah (Jeremiah 23:5; Zechariah 3:8; 6:12; *Testament of Levi* 4:4) and reads it as the subject of the verb 'will come'. Contrast Nolland, *Luke 1–9:20*, 90.

[57] Fitzmyer, *Luke I–IX*, 389, considers the possibility that John may have spent some of this time with the Essenes of Qumran in the Judean desert.

THE MESSIANIC SALVATION ANTICIPATED

Luke draws attention to the impact that John's birth had on people living in the Judean hill country. There was joy, astonishment, awe and wonder, as foretold by the angel. The miracle of John's birth to such aged parents was followed by his unexpected naming and the restoration of his father's ability to speak. This raised questions about what the child might become, which Zechariah began to answer in his Spirit-directed prophecy. Old Testament expectations concerning Israel's salvation would be fulfilled by the coming Messiah and anticipated in the ministry of his predecessor John. In effect, John would offer in advance the benefits of the new covenant promised in Jeremiah 31:33–4. 'Knowledge of salvation through the forgiveness of their sins' would enable God's people 'to serve him without fear in holiness and righteousness before him all our days'. In addition to these new covenant benefits, Zechariah points to the specifically messianic nature of this salvation, alluding to the foundational promise in 2 Samuel 7:12–16 and the particular portrayal of its fulfilment in Isaiah 9:1–7. Salvation will come when the transforming light of God shines on 'those living in darkness and in the shadow of death' and guides them 'into the path of peace'. Luke's narrative illustrates this by using these terms in significant contexts: *forgiveness* (3:3; (4:18, 'freedom'); 24:47; Acts 2:38; 5:31; 10:43; 13:38; 26:18); *peace* (2:14, 29; 7:50; 8:48; 10:5, 6; 12:51; 14:32; 19:38, 42; 24:36; Acts 9:31; 10:36; 15:33); and *light* (2:32; 8:16; 11:33, 35; 12:3; 16:8; Acts 9:3; 12:7; 13:47; 22:6, 9, 11; 26:13, 18, 23).[58] Christians can rejoice with Zechariah as they reflect on the way his prophecy and the biblical expectations it conveys have already been fulfilled. All these amazing benefits can now be experienced by people in every nation who turn to Jesus in repentance and faith and experience the blessing of reconciliation with God (Acts 10:36). Divine forgiveness, peace with God and spiritual enlightenment continue to be sought through many religious practices in our world, but they can only be found in a relationship with God through his Son, the promised Messiah. The consummation of these blessings will be experienced when he returns to usher in a renewed creation (21:28; Acts 3:19–21).

---

[58] The verb 'forgive' is used in Luke 5:20, 21, 23, 24; 7:47, 48, 49; 11:4; 12:10; 17:3, 4; 23:34; Acts 8:22. See Gladd, *From the Manger to the Throne*, chapter 3.

The birth of Jesus and its significance proclaimed (2:1–52)

With brief locational references (verses 1–3), Luke explains how Mary and Joseph came to be in Bethlehem when their son was born (verses 4–7). Angelic announcements of his birth to shepherds in the fields (verses 8–20) pick up some of the wording of the promise to Mary in 1:32–3, proclaiming 'good news that will cause great joy for all the people' and 'peace on earth to those on whom [God's] favour rests' (see 1:79). A simple report of the circumcision and naming of Jesus follows (verse 21). The more public occasion of Mary's purification in Jerusalem provides the opportunity for Jesus to be presented to the Lord and for Simeon and Anna to reveal more of his significance in Spirit-directed utterances (verses 22–38). After the return of Joseph and Mary to Nazareth, their son's maturation is described in terms that recall what was said about John (verses 39–40; compare 1:80). However, Jesus's later experience in the Temple points to his unique relationship with God as Father and his surprising ability to engage with the teachers of Israel (verses 41–52).

The birth of Jesus

2 In those days Caesar Augustus issued a decree that a census should be taken of the entire Roman world. 2 (This was the first census that took place while[a] Quirinius was governor of Syria.) 3 And everyone went to their own town to register.

4 So Joseph also went up from the town of Nazareth in Galilee to Judea, to Bethlehem the town of David, because he belonged to the house and line of David. 5 He went there to register with Mary, who was pledged to be married to him and was expecting a child. 6 While they were there, the time came for the baby to be born, 7 and she gave birth to her firstborn, a son. She wrapped him in cloths and placed him in a manger, because there was no guest room available for them.

8 And there were shepherds living out in the fields near by, keeping watch over their flocks at night. 9 An angel of the Lord appeared to them, and the glory of the Lord shone around them, and they were terrified. 10 But the angel said to them, 'Do not be afraid. I bring you good news that will cause great joy for all the people. 11 Today in the town of David a Saviour has been born to you; he is the Messiah, the Lord. 12 This will be a sign to you: you will find a baby wrapped in cloths and lying in a manger.'

13 Suddenly a great company of the heavenly host appeared with the angel, praising God and saying,

14 'Glory to God in the highest
>heaven,
>and on earth peace to those on
>whom his favour rests.'

15 When the angels had left them and gone into heaven, the shepherds said to one another, 'Let's go to Bethlehem and see this thing that has happened, which the Lord has told us about.' 16 So they hurried off and found Mary and Joseph, and the baby, who was lying in the manger. 17 When they had seen him, they spread the word concerning what had been told them about this child, 18 and all who heard it were amazed at what the shepherds said to them. 19 But Mary treasured up all these things and pondered them in her heart. 20 The shepherds returned, glorifying and praising God for all the things they had heard and seen, which were just as they had been told.

21 On the eighth day, when it was time to circumcise the child, he was named Jesus, the name the angel had given him before he was conceived.

Jesus presented in the temple

22 When the time came for the purification rites required by the Law of Moses, Joseph and Mary took him to Jerusalem to present him to the Lord 23 (as it is written in the Law of the Lord, 'Every firstborn male is to be consecrated to the Lord'b), 24 and to offer a sacrifice in keeping with what is said in the Law of the Lord: 'a pair of doves or two young pigeons.'c

25 Now there was a man in Jerusalem called Simeon, who was righteous and devout. He was waiting for the consolation of Israel, and the Holy Spirit was on him. 26 It had been revealed to him by the Holy Spirit that he would not die before he had seen the Lord's Messiah. 27 Moved by the Spirit, he went into the temple courts. When the parents brought in the child Jesus to do for him what the custom of the Law required, 28 Simeon took him in his arms and praised God, saying:

29 'Sovereign Lord, as you have
>promised,
>you may now dismissd your
>servant in peace.
30 For my eyes have seen your
>salvation,
31 which you have prepared in the
>sight of all nations:
32 a light for revelation to the
>Gentiles,
>and the glory of your people
>Israel.'

33 The child's father and mother marvelled at what was said about him. 34 Then Simeon blessed them and said to Mary, his mother: 'This child is destined to cause the falling and rising of many in Israel, and to be a sign that will be spoken against, 35 so that the thoughts of many hearts will be revealed. And a sword will pierce your own soul too.'

36 There was also a prophet, Anna, the daughter of Penuel, of the tribe of Asher. She was very old; she had

lived with her husband seven years after her marriage, **37** and then was a widow until she was eighty-four.^e She never left the temple but worshipped night and day, fasting and praying. **38** Coming up to them at that very moment, she gave thanks to God and spoke about the child to all who were

looking forward to the redemption of Jerusalem.

_____

a 2 Or *This census took place before*
b 23 Exodus 13:2,12
c 24 Lev. 12:8
d 29 Or *promised, / now dismiss*
e 37 Or *then had been a widow for eighty-four years.*

1. The birth of Jesus is broadly located 'in those days' when 'Caesar Augustus issued a decree that a census should be taken of the entire Roman world'. This should be compared with 1:5, where we are told that the births of John and Jesus took place when Herod the Great was king of Judea (34 to 4 BC).[59] The narrative of John's public ministry is also introduced with historical cross-referencing in 3:1–2. Caesar Augustus was born in 63 BC and named Octavian. As the sole ruler of the Roman Empire from 31 BC to AD 14, he was granted the Latin title *Augustus* by the Senate in 27 BC (Greek *Sebastos*, 'worthy of reverence, revered' (BDAG)).[60] Augustus achieved a peace and solidity in the Empire that lasted for centuries, and he was soon divinised as saviour of the whole world. But in Luke's narrative, these qualities are about to be attributed to Jesus!

There is no extant record of an empire-wide census being initiated by Augustus, although several localised censuses did take place in his reign.[61] The infinitive *apographesthai* can be translated as passive 'to be registered (for taxation)' or middle voice 'to register oneself' (BDAG). 'The entire Roman world' refers to the Roman Empire here (as in Acts 11:28): elsewhere the term *oikoumenē* is used for 'the inhabited earth, the world' (4:5; 21:26; Acts 17:31 (BDAG)). As Fitzmyer observes, Luke depicts Augustus as an unwitting 'agent of God, who by his edict of registration brings it about that Jesus is born in the town of David'.[62]

_____

[59] According to Stanley Porter, 'Chronology, New Testament', *DNTB*, 201–3, the available evidence suggests that Jesus was born shortly before the death of Herod in 4 BC (see Matthew 2:15, 19–20). In the sixth century AD a mistake was made in calculating dates, so the reckoning of Jesus's birth in our calendar as year 0 is incorrect.
[60] See Acts 25:21, 25. Sebastos was also used as a proper name, as was Caesar. See P. Oakes, 'Rome', *DJG*, 810–19.
[61] See Fitzmyer, *Luke I–IX*, 400; Porter, 'Chronology', 202.
[62] Fitzmyer, *Luke I–IX*, 393.

2. A chronological problem is raised by the apparent linkage of Caesar's decree with 'the first census that took place while Quirinius was governor of Syria'. Judea was annexed to the Roman province of Syria when Quirinius was governor (AD 6–9). Acts 5:37 speaks about this registration, which led to Jewish revolts.[63] But these events took place some ten years after the death of Herod the Great. Furthermore, we know of only one census in the brief period when Quirinius was governor. This problem has stimulated much scholarly debate and given rise to different possible solutions.[64] Some argue that Quirinius began the process of registration during a previous period of leadership in Syria, but convincing evidence is lacking for this. Others have translated *hautē apographē prōtē egeneto* 'this registration took place before' (NIV margin), allowing for a registration by Herod under Roman direction before the infamous one associated with Quirinius in AD 6. Although there is no external support for this historical reconstruction, the adjective *prōtos* can be understood in a comparative way (as in John 1:15, 30; 15:18 ['before'], where a genitive of comparison follows). The Greek of Luke's sentence is awkward either way but, in Nolland's estimation, such a reading is 'better than forcing an earlier governorship on Quirinius and more likely than the contradiction in the Lukan infancy narratives created by an identification of the census here as that of AD 6'.[65] Luke states his care in investigating such matters in 1:1–4 and demonstrates his reliability in other dating references.

3–5. Luke implies that it was Caesar's will for everyone in the region to go 'to their own town to register'. 'So, Joseph also went up from the town of Nazareth in Galilee to Judea, to Bethlehem the town of David' (see 1 Samuel 16:1, 18; 17:12, 58; 20:6). Bethlehem was the town from which the Messiah was predicted to come (Micah 5:2; Matthew 2:3–8). Joseph went there 'because he belonged to the house and line of David' (see 1:27, 'a descendant of David'). The Romans customarily based taxation on residency rather than ancestry, and so it may be that Joseph or his family had property in Bethlehem.[66] Whatever the human reason, as Marshall concludes, Luke is demonstrating how 'the fiat of an earthly ruler

---

[63] See Josephus, *Antiquities* 17.35; 18.1–2, 26.
[64] See Marshall, *Luke*, 98–104; Nolland, *Luke 1–9:20*, 99–104; Bock, *Luke 1:1–9:50*, 903–9; Porter, 'Chronology', 202–3.
[65] Nolland, *Luke 1–9:20*, 102. See also H. W. Hoehner and J. K. Brown, 'Chronology', *DJG*, 134–8.
[66] Marshall, *Luke*, 101. See Fitzmyer, *Luke I–IX*, 405. Brown, *Birth of the Messiah*, 549, allows for the possibility that the Romans allowed a census to be taken according to local custom.

can be utilized in the will of God to bring his more important purposes to fruition'.[67] Mary went with Joseph to register, though normally only the heads of families were required to appear. Mary is described in a way that confirms her virginal conception: she was 'pledged to be married to him' (as in 1:27) and 'was expecting a child' (1:31–7; compare Matthew 1:24–25). Despite the difficulty of the journey, Mary needed to be with Joseph during her pregnancy and delivery.

6–7. While they were in Bethlehem, 'the time came for the baby to be born' (compare 1:57; Genesis 25:24) and 'she gave birth to her firstborn, a son'. The term 'firstborn' (*prōtotokos*) prepares for the account of Jesus's dedication to the Lord in verses 22–4, though it also allows for the possibility that he had younger siblings (see Mark 6:3). Mary 'wrapped him in cloths' (ESV, 'swaddling cloths'), which Marshall describes as 'strips of cloth like bandages, wrapped around young infants to keep their limbs straight (Ezekiel 16:4; Wisdom 7:4)'.[68] She placed him 'in a manger', most likely meaning a feeding trough for animals here (though *phatnē* is rendered 'stall' in 13:15). This could have been downstairs in the main living area of the house, where cattle, sheep and goats were kept in close proximity to the family, rather than outside 'in a lowly cattle shed'.[69] Luke provides a practical explanation for this: 'because there was no guest room available for them'. The word *katalyma* means 'lodging place' (BDAG) and could refer to the guest room in the house of a relative or friend, which was normally upstairs (22:11). The traditional interpretation of this as an 'inn' (KJV, ESV) is unlikely (another word is used in 10:34 for 'inn'). Luke's expression (*ouk ēn autois topos en tō katalymati*) could mean that there was no place for the child in the guest room provided for the parents and so they put him in a manger.[70] Whatever the exact circumstances, Mary was deprived of appropriate comfort and privacy when she gave birth. When 'lying in a manger' is repeated in verses 12 and 16 its significance is amplified. It is a strangely incongruent sign of the coming of 'the Messiah, the Lord' (2:11; compare 9:58).

8–9. The first to learn about the significance of this birth were 'shepherds living out in the fields near by, keeping watch over their flocks at

---

[67] Marshall, *Luke*, 98. Contrast Edwards, *Luke*, 72.

[68] Marshall, *Luke*, 106.

[69] Cecil Alexander, 'Once in Royal David's City' (1848). Martin Hengel, 'φάτνη', *TDNT* 9:52, details the evidence for concluding that feeding-troughs would be either at the approach to the platform where the family lived 'or by the wall often in the form of niches'.

[70] Nolland, *Luke 1–9:20*, 105–6.

night'. Shepherding was a lowly, but honourable task in ancient Israel.[71] The shepherd image is applied to God in Psalm 23 and to the Messiah in prophecies such as Ezekiel 34:23–4; Micah 5:4 (see also 2 Samuel 5:2; Psalm 78:70–72). These humble Israelites encountered 'an angel of the Lord' as Zechariah (1:11–20) and Mary (1:26–38) did. However, what they experienced was even more awesome: 'the glory of the Lord shone around them, and they were terrified'. 'Glory' refers to the splendour of God's self-manifestation, which appears in different ways throughout Scripture (e.g., Exodus 16:7, 10; 24:17; 33:21–3; Psalm 63:3; Isaiah 60:1–3; Luke 9:26, 29–32; 21:7). What the shepherds saw was the first sign of the dawning light that Zechariah spoke about (1:78–9) and their fear was extreme (*ephobēthēsan phobon megan*, 'they feared with great fear').

10–11. The angel comforted the shepherds by saying, 'Do not be afraid. I bring you good news that will cause great joy for all the people.' This was an occasion for joy, not fear, because of the 'good news' that could now be proclaimed. As in 1:19, the verb *euangelizomai* ('bring good news') is employed, but it is now given explicit content concerning Jesus.[72] His birth is predicted to bring 'great joy for all the people', meaning Israel in the first instance (see 3:21; 7:29; 8:47; 9:13; 18:43; 19:48; 20:6, 45; 21:38; 24:19). Echoing the promise to Mary in 1:32–3, the angel reveals, 'Today in the town of David a Saviour has been born to you: he is the Messiah, the Lord.' 'Today' signifies an important moment in the coming of the messianic salvation (see 4:21; 5:26; 12:28; 13:32, 33; 19:5, 9; 22:34, 61; 23:43). God was identified as 'Saviour' in 1:47, but now it is made clear that he will save his people specifically through one who is identified as 'the Messiah, the Lord' (see Acts 5:31; 13:23).[73]

'Messiah' (*Christos*) is used here for the first time in Luke. The combination *Christos kyrios* occurs nowhere else in the New Testament and means 'the Messiah (and) the Lord'.[74] As the Messiah born in David's town, he is 'the Son of the Most High' (1:32, 35) and David's Lord, who will reign

---

[71] Edwards, *Luke*, 74, cites later Jewish texts that have a low view of shepherds, but there is no hint of such negativity in Luke's record. Compare Green, *Luke*, 130–31.

[72] Compare the use of this verb in Isaiah 40:9; 52:7; 61:1 LXX; Luke 1:19; 2:10; 3:18; 4:18, 43; 7:22; 8:1; 9:6; 16:16; 20:1; Acts 5:42; 8:4, 12, 25, 35, 40; 10:36; 11:20; 13:32; 14:7, 15, 21; 15:35; 16:10; 17:18.

[73] The language of salvation is extensively used throughout Luke–Acts in relation to Jesus and his work. See J. G. van der Watt and D. S. du Toit, 'Salvation', *DJG*, 826–32.

[74] See Marshall, *Luke*, 110. Contrast *ton Christon kyriou* (verse 26, 'the Lord's Messiah'), which is apparently the reading understood by some ancient versions of verse 11 (Metzger, *Textual Commentary*, 110).

at God's right hand (20:41–4). The title 'Lord' is crucial for understanding who Jesus is in Luke–Acts, though its true significance is not perceived until after his resurrection.[75] This lordship of Jesus is a central claim of the gospel that the apostles preached to Jewish audiences (Acts 2:29–36; 5:30–32) and in due course to Gentiles as well (Acts 10:36–43). The good news of peace with God through the Messiah Jesus, 'who is Lord of all' (Acts 10:36), should be the source of great joy for everyone who hears it. Although the narrative here is thoroughly Jewish, Nolland observes that 'a first-century Hellenistic reader would find in the configuration created by good news (v. 10) concerning the birth of one who is to be a savior and bringer of peace (v. 14) an echo of the language in which Augustus had been honoured'.[76] The superiority of the Messiah and his rule to the greatest political authority of that day or any era since is thus implied.

12. The sign that is given to the shepherds ('you will find a baby wrapped in cloths and lying in a manger') is designed, in Marshall's words, 'not only to identify the child by indicating where he is to be found (see Matt. 2:9) but also in this way to authenticate the messianic proclamation'.[77] When they find a baby in this strange and humble context, the shepherds will know for sure that he is the promised Saviour!

13–14. A further, unannounced, confirmation is then given to the shepherds: 'Suddenly a great company of the heavenly host appeared with the angel'. This vision of a huge army of angels (compare 1 Kings 22:19; Isaiah 6:1–4) reveals them to be 'praising God' (see Hebrews 12:22; Revelation 5:11–12). They attribute 'glory to God in the highest heaven', meaning that angels acknowledge the unique character of God in the realm where they exist with him.[78] As Scripture shows in many places, God is holy and gracious, perfectly righteous, faithful, and loving. This glory is being revealed 'on earth' (see verse 9) in the birth of the Messiah and the benefits that will flow from his coming, specifically 'peace to those on whom his favour rests'. This does not fundamentally refer to

---

[75] See B. Witherington III and K. Yamazaki-Ransom, 'Lord', *DJG*, 526–35. Luke as narrator regularly speaks about Jesus as 'the Lord', reflecting the full post-resurrection meaning of this term, but he is careful not to place this in the mouth of human characters before 24:34. See, however, Elizabeth's prophetic insight in 1:43.

[76] Nolland, *Luke 1–9:20*, 107.

[77] Marshall, *Luke*, 110.

[78] When God is 'glorified' or 'honoured' in Scripture (*doxazō*), his people indicate why glory (*doxa*), honour and praise are due to him (e.g., Psalms 50:15 [49:15 LXX]; 86:9, 12 [85:9 LXX, 12]). See G. Kittel and G. von Rad, 'δόξα, δοξάζω, κτλ.', *TDNT* 2: 233–54.

peace between nations or warring individuals, though peace with God can bring reconciliation of that sort (see Isaiah 9:1–7). God achieves peace with 'those living in darkness and the shadow of death' by guiding their feet 'into the path of peace' (Luke 1:79). This messianic peace is linked to the forgiveness of sins, which is made possible 'because of the tender mercy of our God' (1:77–8). Peace with God and its consequences is another way of speaking about the salvation brought by the Messiah (see Romans 5:1; Ephesians 2:11–18).[79]

The messianic salvation is declared to be for 'those on whom his favour rests' (*en anthrōpois eudokias*, 'among people of [his] favour'). The KJV rendering ('good will toward men'), which has found its way into common parlance, is often taken to mean that human beings should show good will to one another, especially at Christmas! It follows a later variant that is not now regarded as the original text (*en anthrōpois eudokia*).[80] But peace with God in the angelic proclamation is an expression of God's 'favour' (*eudokia*, as in 10:21; Ephesians 1:5, 9, 'pleasure') towards a particular group of people. The better-attested expression 'those on whom his favour rests' is Semitic in form, as Nolland points out, 'having overtones of election and of God's active initiative in extending his favour'.[81] Luke will go on to show how this favour extends through Jesus to believers from every nation (2:32; 7:1–10; 17:11–19; 24:45–7; Acts 13:48), but his wording excludes the idea that *all* will be saved, whether they trust in Jesus or not.

15–17. 'When the angels had left them and gone back into heaven, the shepherds said to one another, "Let's go to Bethlehem and see this thing that has happened, which the Lord has told us about."' Like Mary (1:38–9) and Elizabeth (1:41–5), the shepherds instantly believed and obeyed the angelic word. In fact, 'they hurried off and found Mary and Joseph, and the baby, who was lying in the manger'. When they had seen the incongruous sign of the baby 'wrapped in cloths and lying in a manger' (see comments on verses 7, 12), 'they spread the word concerning what had been told them about this child'. Luke portrays them as faithful Israelites, faced with a divine encounter, a clear word about the fulfilment of ancient

---

[79] See R. S. Schellenberg, 'Peace', *DJG*, 666–9.

[80] Metzger, *Textual Commentary*, 111, observes that the genitive case (*eudokias*), which is a more difficult reading than the nominative (*eudokia*), is supported by the oldest representatives of the Alexandrian and the Western groups of witnesses.

[81] Nolland, *Luke 1–9:20*, 109, cites the use of Hebrew and Aramaic expressions like this in the DSS. John M. G. Barclay, *Paul and the Gift* (Grand Rapids: Eerdmans, 2015), 244, observes that the DSS are selective, rather than national or ancestral, in using such expressions.

prophecies, and a fulfilled sign. Consequently, they were keen to spread the message about the significance of this birth (see also verses 20, 25–38).

18–20. Three different responses to the message are recorded. First, those who heard what the shepherds reported were amazed. This probably refers to a wider group than those gathered at the manger. Luke regularly uses the verb 'amaze' to describe initial responses to unusual events (1:21, 63; 2:18, 33; 4:22; 8:25; 9:43; 11:14; 24:12, 41), but amazement does not always lead to a deeper understanding and increased faith. Second, Mary 'treasured up all these things and pondered them in her heart'. There is an echo of Genesis 37:11 here, where Jacob is said to have 'kept the matter in mind', and Daniel 7:28 LXX, where Daniel says, 'I kept the matter to myself' (*en kardia mou*, 'in my heart'). Mary continued to reflect on all the things that had happened and the angelic messages interpreting these events (see verse 51).[82] Third, Luke continues to highlight the exemplary response of the shepherds, who 'returned glorifying and praising God for all the things they had heard and seen, which were just as they had been told'. They spontaneously followed the example of the angels in 'glorifying and praising God'. There is a time for pondering and a time for proclaiming what God has revealed about his Son the Messiah.

21. The circumcision of this baby boy 'on the eighth day' followed the direction of Scripture (Genesis 17:11–12; Leviticus 12:3), affirming his membership of the covenant community. This presumably took place when they returned to Nazareth. As with John, the circumcision of Jesus was unusually accompanied by his naming (see comment on 1:59). A child's name was normally given at birth (e.g., Genesis 21:1–3; 25:24–6), but there was a special reason for making known on this occasion the name that God had given him. Jesus (Hebrew, *yᵉhôšuaʿ*, 'Yahweh saves') was 'the name the angel had given him before he was conceived' (1:31).

WELCOMING THE DIVINE SAVIOUR
Luke links the birth of Jesus with important historical events in the Roman Empire. The temporary relocation of his parents to Bethlehem took place because of an imperial decree, forcing them to accept less-than-ideal accommodation in David's town for his birth. An angel of the

---

[82] With these words Luke may have been drawing attention to Mary as the source for his knowledge of these events and the revelations about their significance. John W. Kleinig, *Grace upon Grace: Spirituality for Today* (St. Louis: Concordia, 2008), 116–18, also observes how Mary functions as a model for Christian meditation or reflection in this Gospel.

Lord announced to shepherds in the fields nearby that Mary's child was in fact the promised Saviour, Israel's Messiah and Lord. The full significance of this began to be revealed when 'the glory of the Lord shone around them' and a great company of angels appeared, praising God and proclaiming peace on earth to those on whom God's favour rests. Angels rarely appear in biblical narratives, so that their manifestation in this way signalled the coming of God into human history and the fulfilment of prophetic predictions (see especially Isaiah 9:6–7; 25:9; 40:9–11).[83] Caesar Augustus was not the Saviour of the world and bringer of ultimate peace, as was commonly thought, but Jesus was! The first people to be favoured with this news were lowly shepherds in a distant corner of the Empire, illustrating the reversal of human values and expectations proclaimed in Mary's Song (1:52–5). The angels restated in different words the promise to Mary (1:31–3, 35) and the claims of Zechariah (1:68–75). The shepherds obeyed the call to visit the baby and began to spread the message concerning what had been told them about this child, 'glorifying and praising God for all the things they had heard and seen'. Luke's narrative focuses on the way the wonderful news about Jesus was first proclaimed and then passed on joyfully to others. His extensive use of the verb euangelizomai ('bring good news'), which begins with the angelic announcements in 1:19; 2:10, highlights a central feature of the ministry of Jesus and his followers in the apostolic period and beyond.[84] Whatever options there seem to be for peace and salvation in our world today, the God-given gospel of Jesus reveals the only adequate and truly satisfying solution. Human beings need to be reconciled to God before they can be comprehensively reconciled to one another. Those who are certain about this and have tasted the blessings themselves are encouraged by Luke's narrative to find ways of sharing this news with others.

Mary's purification and the consecration of her son to the Lord (2:22–38)

22–4. The next event is introduced with the same Greek expression that was used in verse 21, here translated, 'When the time came' (see also verse 6). This signals a new event with an emphasis on the appropriate timing and ordering of the occasion according to Scripture. When a son

---

[83] See also my Introduction, pages 23–4.
[84] See also Luke 3:18; 4:18, 43; 7:22; 8:1; 9:6; 16:16; 20:1; Acts 5:42; 8:4, 12, 25, 35, 40; 10:36; 11:20; 13:32; 14:7, 15, 21; 15:36; 16:10; 17:18.

was born, a Jewish mother was required to engage in a purification rite at the Temple thirty-three days after his circumcision (Leviticus 12:6). Childbirth involved the issue of blood and necessitated the cleansing ritual prescribed in the Law of Moses. The reference to 'their purification' (*tou katharismou autōn*) is obscured by NIV (compare ESV). This probably signified that for Joseph and Mary it was a family matter.[85] All the purification requirements of the law were soon to be fulfilled in the sacrificial death of Jesus (Acts 10:28; 15:8–9; Hebrews 1:3; 9:13–14).

Mary's ritual purification is linked to the presentation of her baby to the Lord, 'as it is written in the Law of the Lord, "Every firstborn male is to be consecrated to the Lord"' (*hagion tō kyriō*, 'holy to the Lord', ESV). This requirement was initially associated with the Passover (Exodus 13:2, 12, 15) and was linked to the demand for the firstborn of animals to be sacrificed to the Lord (Exodus 34:19–20). But God chose the tribe of Levi to serve him in place of the first male offspring of every Israelite woman, telling Moses, 'The Levites are mine, for all the firstborn are mine. When I struck down all the firstborn in Egypt, I set apart for myself every firstborn in Israel, whether human or animal' (Numbers 3:12–13). Firstborn sons could be ritually 'redeemed' or released from priestly service at the price of five shekels of silver (Numbers 18:15–16; see 8:15–19). Since no ransom price is mentioned by Luke, the emphasis is on Jesus being 'consecrated to the Lord,' rather than 'redeemed'.[86] The scene is reminiscent of 1 Samuel 1:11, 22, 28, where Samuel is offered to God by his mother for a lifetime of service. Believers are now consecrated to God through 'the sacrifice of the body of Jesus Christ once for all' (Hebrews 10:10). This benefit is received through faith in the crucified and resurrected Lord (Acts 20:32; 26:18; 1 Corinthians 1:2; 6:11).

Luke returns to the subject of Mary's purification, which includes the requirement 'to offer a sacrifice in keeping with what is said in the Law of the Lord: "a pair of doves or two young pigeons"' (Leviticus 5:11; 12:8). This was the provision for a poor mother who could not afford to bring a lamb for a burnt offering, and it confirms that Mary's previous reference to her 'humble estate' (1:48) included economic poverty.

---

[85] Nolland, *Luke 1–9:20*, 117, rightly opposes the view that Luke was uninformed about the requirement for the mother alone to be purified. Marshall, *Luke*, 116, discusses variant readings. See M. C. Mulder, 'The "Presentation" of the Infant Jesus in Luke 2:22–24', *Unio cum Christo* 2.2 (2016), 83–96.

[86] See Marshall, *Luke*, 117. Whether or not any redemption money was paid, Luke views the event as an opportunity for Jesus to be consecrated to the Lord's service in a traditional way. See also my comments on his baptism in 3:21–2.

25–7. When Mary and Joseph brought Jesus to the Temple 'to do what the custom of the Law required' (verse 27), they encountered two significant people. The sequence in verses 25–38 begins and ends with similar expressions, linking Simeon and Anna together. Simeon is first described as 'righteous and devout' and 'waiting for the consolation of Israel' (verse 25), while Anna is numbered among 'all who were looking forward to the redemption of Jerusalem' (verse 38, *lytrōsis*).[87] Elizabeth and Zechariah, Mary and Joseph were previously identified as belonging to this faithful and expectant group (see also 23:50–51; 24:21). The 'consolation' (*paraklēsis*) of Israel recalls Isaiah's emphasis on the comfort that God would bring to his people in desperate need of his salvation (Isaiah 40:1; 49:13; 51:3; 52:9; 57:18; 66:10–11). The redemption of Jerusalem is a parallel notion, recalling prophetic predictions about the liberation of its people from the consequences of their sin.

Luke mentions the pre-Pentecost operation of the Spirit of God three times in relation to Simeon. The Holy Spirit was 'on him', and it had been 'revealed to him by the Holy Spirit that he would not die before he had seen the Lord's Messiah', and, 'Moved by the Spirit, he went into the temple courts.' The Spirit's guidance enabled him to meet the baby with his parents in the Temple, to recognise him as the promised Messiah, and then (by implication) to prophesy about him. The prophetic characters in Luke 1–2 function like Old Testament prophets in a revelatory way, anticipating the more derivative form of prophesying by believers in the post-Pentecost situation (Acts 2:1–4, 14–21).[88] The songs of Mary, Zechariah and Simeon offer divinely given patterns of praise and thanksgiving for Christians in every generation to share in corporate worship and deepen their understanding of the gospel and its implications. This is particularly so when they celebrate ways in which Scripture has been fulfilled.

28–32. Simeon's reception of the child 'in his arms' is the preliminary to blessing God for him (*eulogēsen*).[89] The presentation of the baby (verse 22), followed by Simeon's reception of him, could imply that he was a priest, who blessed God for the child (verses 28–32) and then blessed his parents (verse 34).[90] However, the form that follows is not strictly a

---

[87] See 1:68. The verb *prosdechomai* ('wait for, welcome') is used in both contexts and in 12:36; 15:2; 23:51; Acts 23:21; 24:15.

[88] See Peterson, *Acts*, 60–65, 129–44.

[89] See my notes on 1:39–45, 67–75, regarding the terminology of blessing.

[90] See Nolland, *Luke 1–9:20*, 119. Edwards, *Luke*, 83, notes later apocryphal accounts of Simeon as a priest and great teacher, but he considers them of doubtful historical value.

blessing (see 1:68), but a prayer that issues in praise for allowing him to see with his own eyes the salvation associated in Scripture with the coming of 'the Lord's Messiah' (verse 26, *ton christon kyriou*). King Saul was the first to be called 'the Lord's Anointed' (1 Samuel 2:10; 24:6, 10), but here the title points to the ruler and deliverer of God's people predicted by the prophets (Isaiah 9:6–7; 11:1–5; Jeremiah 23:5–6). See also Luke 9:20; 23:35; Acts 3:18; 4:26 (Psalm 2:2); Revelation 11:15; 12:10.

Simeon addresses God as 'Sovereign Lord' (*Despota*) and describes himself as 'your servant' (see 1:38). Encountering the baby Jesus was a dramatic moment for him. God's promise to him that he would 'not die before he had seen the Lord's Messiah' (verse 26) was fulfilled. When he says, 'you may now dismiss your servant in peace', he may mean that he is ready to die and be released from his service to God (*apolyō*, 'set free, dismiss'), suggesting a lifetime of dedication now brought to its climax. Simeon could say this because he believed that the messianic peace was in the process of being established (1:76–9).[91] He immediately links seeing the Messiah with seeing the salvation (*sōtērion*, as in Acts 28:28) that God had 'prepared in the sight of the nations' (Psalm 98:1–3; Isaiah 40:5; 52:10). The prophetic hope of God's salvation being for 'all nations' is emphasised by reversing the order implied in passages like Isaiah 42:6; 49:5–6 and putting the Gentiles before Israel: 'a light for revelation to the Gentiles, and the glory of your people Israel'.[92] 'Light' and 'glory' should probably be read as parallel terms here: the light that goes to the Gentiles is the glory of the Lord manifested to Israel by the Messiah (see Isaiah 60:1–3). The risen Lord restates the familiar order of events when he commands that the gospel be preached 'to all nations, beginning at Jerusalem' (Luke 24:47; see Acts 1:8). Simeon proclaims in his own way the universal blessing that will result from the coming of the Messiah to Israel, significantly broadening the picture given in 1:32–3, 46–55, 68–79; 2:10–11.

33–4. When Luke says, 'The child's father and mother marvelled about what was said about him,' the context suggests an emerging

---

[91] Although the passive form of *apolyō* can be used with reference to death (e.g., Numbers 20:29; Tobit 3:6, 13; 2 Maccabees 7:9), the active form of the present tense here (*apolyeis*, 'you are releasing') in conjunction with *nyn* ('now') more likely means mean that this patient 'servant' (*doulos*) is being released by his 'master' (*Despota*) from duty as a 'watchman' (verse 25), 'because the goal of his watching is now accomplished' (Nolland, *Luke 1–9:20*, 119).

[92] Green, *Luke*, 148, rightly observes that 'a light for revelation to the Gentiles' implies the offer of salvation to them.

apprehension of the implications of Jesus's birth.[93] Then Simeon blessed
them (*eulogēsen*), perhaps meaning that he prayed for God to meet their
needs (as in Numbers 6:23–7; 1 Samuel 2:20). But he also said to Mary,
'This child is destined to cause the falling and rising of many in Israel,
and to be a sign that will be spoken against.' This ominous prediction
recalls biblical warnings about the Lord God being 'a stone that causes
people to stumble and a rock that makes them fall' (Isaiah 8:14; see 28:16;
Psalm 118:22). Various combinations of these 'stone' passages are applied
to Jesus in other New Testament contexts (e.g., Luke 20:17–18; Romans
9:32–3; 1 Peter 2:6–8). Simeon's addition of the word 'rising' offers the
hope that not all will reject the Lord's Messiah (or perhaps many will
fall and then rise). Jesus will be 'a sign' of the presence of God and his
salvation, but for those who stumble and fall he will be 'a sign that
will be spoken against'. There may be an echo of Isaiah 8:16–18 in this
saying, where the prophet speaks of himself and his disciples as 'signs and
symbols in Israel from the Lord Almighty'. A sign that is 'spoken against'
is contradicted or contested, even though it is God-given.

35. Simeon's prophecy about the future of Mary's child continues
with the words 'so that the thoughts of many hearts will be revealed'.
As people 'rise' or 'fall' in response to Jesus and his ministry, what they
secretly think and feel about him will be exposed. A further clause
describes Mary's fate in relation to that of her son and should perhaps
be put in brackets ('And a sword will pierce your own soul too').
The same image is used in Psalm 37:15 (36:15 LXX) with a different
meaning (the swords of the wicked 'will pierce their own hearts'). The
emphatic term 'too' suggests that the image of a sword piercing the
Messiah is the prior allusion.[94] This could be based on a combination
of biblical texts (Psalm 22:20; Zechariah 12:10; 13:7). Simeon implies
that the opposition to Jesus will reach its climax in his death, but the
main emphasis in this prediction is on what will happen to Mary. Her
'own soul' will *also* be metaphorically pierced as her son is opposed
and finally killed.[95] This subtle rhetoric only hints at what is to come
in Luke's narrative.

---

[93] Some manuscripts replace 'his father' with 'Joseph', presumably to safeguard
the doctrine of the virgin birth, but this is a later and unnecessary change. See
Metzger, *Textual Commentary*, 111–12.

[94] The combination *kai sou de* ('and of you also') is read by certain key manuscripts
and is likely to be original. But *de* is omitted by others, possibly because it adds
to the awkwardness of the phrase.

[95] Brown, *Birth of the Messiah*, 262–3, 463–6, discusses a range of possible

36–8. Anna is introduced in an elaborate way. Like Simeon, she is an important witness to the presence of the Messiah in the Temple. She is first called 'a prophet' (*prophētis*, as in Exodus 15:20; Judges 4:4 LXX), though her words are not actually recorded. She is further described as 'the daughter of Penuel, of the tribe of Asher', meaning that she belonged to one of the ten northern tribes that were deported to Assyria in the eighth century BC (2 Kings 17). Great stress is laid on her age and piety: 'she was very old; she had lived with her husband seven years after her marriage, and then was a widow until she was eighty–four' (see Judith 8:4–8; 16:22–23). The implication is that she never remarried because of her devotion to God: 'She never left the temple but worshipped night and day, fasting and praying' (see Judith 11:17; Luke 24:53; Acts 26:7).

Like Simeon (verse 27), and at the 'very moment' when he was prophesying, she was led by the Spirit to meet the family and discern that Jesus was the promised Messiah. Her prophetic ministry involved giving thanks to God and speaking about the child 'to all who were looking forward to the redemption of Jerusalem'. This more obviously anticipates the perspective of Acts, where prophesying by men and women includes both praise (2:11, 47) and gospel proclamation (2:14–36; see 4:31), rather than imparting new revelation. As noted previously, the 'redemption of Jerusalem' parallels 'the consolation of Israel' (verse 25). The notion of redemption from enemy oppression (*lytrōsis*) was linked by Zechariah to the forgiveness of sins and the restoration of Israel's relationship with God (1:68–79; see Psalms 111:9 [110:9 LXX]: 130:7 [129:7 LXX]). This is consistent with the portrayal of God as the Redeemer of Israel in many predictions arising out of the Babylonian Exile (e.g., Isaiah 41:14; 43:1, 14; 44:22–3; 48:17; 52:3; 62:12). Anna kept speaking (*elalei*, imperfect tense) about the birth of the Messiah to those who were waiting expectantly for God to bring the end-time fulfilment of these promises.[96]

HINTS OF DIVISION AND SUFFERING

The circumcision and naming of Jesus eight days after his birth in Bethlehem was followed by his first visit to the Temple in Jerusalem for the purification of his mother and his consecration to the Lord as her

---

interpretations of this expression. See also Fitzmyer, *Luke I–IX*, 430; Bock, *Luke 1:1–9:50*, 249–50.

[96] The present participle that defines them (*prosdechomenois*) shows that this was the ongoing hope of their lives. Fitzmyer, *Luke I–IX*, 432, draws attention to Jewish sources that reflect such aspirations of Palestinian Jews at that time.

firstborn son. There the family met Simeon and Anna, who belonged to that faithful group of Israelites who were waiting expectantly for God to bring the promised 'consolation of Israel' and 'redemption of Jerusalem'. Simeon spoke prophetically about the imminent fulfilment of these expectations for Israel and the nations. But he also revealed to Mary that her son would cause division and opposition in Israel, leading to his death. This tragic outcome would inevitably pierce her own soul. On the one hand, Luke emphasises again that the glorious news about the Saviour's birth should be received with joy and indicates that it will ultimately bring blessing to people of every nation. On the other hand, Simeon's sombre prediction warns about the opposition Jesus will experience and the difficulties this will bring for those who identify with him (see 9:49–53; 12:49–53; Acts 4–7; 9:15–16; 14:21–2). Simeon highlights both the positive and negative implications of being linked to Israel's Messiah, then and now.

Jesus with the teachers in the Temple (2:39–52)

39 When Joseph and Mary had done everything required by the Law of the Lord, they returned to Galilee to their own town of Nazareth. **40** And the child grew and became strong; he was filled with wisdom, and the grace of God was on him.

The boy Jesus at the temple

41 Every year Jesus' parents went to Jerusalem for the Festival of the Passover. **42** When he was twelve years old, they went up to the festival, according to the custom. **43** After the festival was over, while his parents were returning home, the boy Jesus stayed behind in Jerusalem, but they were unaware of it. **44** Thinking he was in their company, they travelled on for a day. Then they began looking for him among their relatives and friends. **45** When they did not find him, they went back to Jerusalem to look for him. **46** After three days they found him in the temple courts, sitting among the teachers, listening to them and asking them questions. **47** Everyone who heard him was amazed at his understanding and his answers. **48** When his parents saw him, they were astonished. His mother said to him, 'Son, why have you treated us like this? Your father and I have been anxiously searching for you.'

49 'Why were you searching for me?' he asked. 'Didn't you know I had to be in my Father's house?'**f 50** But they did not understand what he was saying to them.

51 Then he went down to Nazareth with them and was obedient to them. But his mother treasured all these things in her heart. **52** And Jesus grew in wisdom and stature, and in favour with God and man.

_____
f 49 Or *be about my Father's business*

39–40. As faithful, law-abiding Jews, Jesus's parents returned from Jerusalem to Galilee 'to their own town of Nazareth', when they had done 'everything required by the Law of the Lord'. A brief summary of Jesus's early life follows: 'And the child grew and became strong; he was filled with wisdom, and the grace of God was on him.' This echoes what was said about John the Baptist in 1:80, though more detail is given concerning the development of Jesus (note also parallels with 1 Samuel 2:21, 26). In particular, the claim that he was 'filled with wisdom' prepares for the next incident. Jesus was nurtured in the context of a pious Galilean family and grew as any normal child would, but the favour of God was especially manifested in the wisdom he was given (see also verse 52). Luke highlights the true humanity of Jesus by describing his maturation in this way, and then discloses his early awareness of a unique relationship with God as Father. John 1:14–18 exposes more clearly the significance of what is claimed here: 'the one and only Son, who is himself God and is in the closest relationship with the Father', at a particular moment in human history 'became flesh and made his dwelling among us.'

41–3. Luke has progressively demonstrated the similarities and differences between John the Baptist and Jesus. But the account of Jesus's visit to the Temple at age twelve stands alone in the structure of the narrative and adds significantly to the portrayal of Jesus's identity. This is the only record in the Gospels of the whole period between his return to Nazareth as a baby and his baptism by John in the Jordan River (3:21–2) at about thirty years of age (3:23). It illustrates the meaning of verse 40 and anticipates the critical confession in 10:21–4. Apocryphal Gospels dating from the second century and later provide specious accounts of the 'lost years' of Jesus's youth, focusing on the marvellous and miraculous in ways that are out of character with the evidence of the canonical Gospels.[97]

The piety of Mary and Joseph is once again highlighted by the introduction to the story: 'Every year Jesus' parents went to Jerusalem for the Festival of the Passover' (verse 41). Jewish males were obligated to 'appear before the Lord' to celebrate the Festivals of Passover (technically 'the feast of Unleavened Bread'), Pentecost and Tabernacles (differently named in Exodus 23:14–17; Deuteronomy 16:1–16).[98] There was no requirement for women or children to participate in this pilgrimage, but when Jesus

---

[97] See Edwards, *Luke*, 90–91; B. Ehrman and Z. Pleše, *The Apocryphal Gospels: Texts and Translations* (Oxford: Oxford University Press, 2011); T. P. Henderson, 'Gospels: Apocryphal', *DJG*, 346–52.

[98] See G. H. Twelftree, 'Feasts', *DJG*, 270–78.

was twelve years old, his parents took him with them to the Festival. This may have been Jesus's first visit to the city since his presentation to the Lord as a baby in the Temple (verses 22–4). It was an important moment in his life as a Jewish boy, since he would be obligated to keep every aspect of the Law from the age of thirteen.[99] When the Festival was over, while his parents were returning home with the crowd from Galilee, the boy Jesus stayed behind in Jerusalem, but they were unaware of this. His parents' later reprimand (verse 48, 'Son, why have you treated us like this?') reinforces the idea that it was his choice to stay.

44–5. Mary and Joseph wrongly thought that Jesus was in the safety of their 'company' (*synodia*, 'a group of travelers, caravan', BDAG), which after a day could have been some twenty to twenty-five miles (30 to 40km) along the road to Nazareth. They began looking for him 'among their relatives and friends', perhaps not even beginning the search until they struck camp in the evening. When they could not find him, they went back to Jerusalem to look for him there.

46–8. 'After three days they found him in the temple courts, sitting among the teachers, listening to them and asking them questions.' The 'three days' probably included the time taken to search for him among the travellers, return to Jerusalem and then look for him in the city. The 'temple courts' (*to hieron*) refers to the whole Temple complex. Jesus was found in a space where instruction could take place, listening to the scribes and lawyers and asking them questions. Remarkably, however, 'everyone who heard him was amazed at his understanding and his answers'. Jesus was not only seeking wisdom, but already manifesting a mature understanding in his answers to questions (see Isaiah 11:2). Finding Jesus in this context, his parents 'were astonished' (*exeplagēsan*, 'amazed to the point of being overwhelmed', BDAG).[100] Mary's challenge combines affectionate concern with a rebuke about the pain he has caused them: 'Son, why have you treated us like this? Your father and I have been anxiously searching for you.' The Greek emphasises that they were searching for him 'in great distress' (*odynōmenoi* [see 16:24–5; Acts 20:38]).

49–50. The first words Jesus utters in Luke's Gospel are, 'Why were you searching for me? . . . Didn't you know I had to be in my Father's

---

[99] Edwards, *Luke*, 92, notes the later rabbinic tradition that a father should begin teaching his son Torah no later than puberty. This included the observance of the Passover 'one or two years before (they are of age)'.

[100] The verb here is even more emphatic than *existanto* ('confused, amazed, astounded', BDAG) in the previous verse. See 4:32; 9:43; Acts 13:12.

house?' He responds to his mother's reproach with surprise, suggesting that his parents should have known that he would be found in that context. More profoundly, as Fitzmyer states, he reveals himself to be 'an obedient son of his heavenly Father'.[101] The expression *en tois tou patros mou* could mean 'be about my Father's business' (NIV note f), 'among those people belonging to my Father', or 'in my Father's house'. The first two alternatives are possible readings of the Greek, though there are grammatical difficulties associated with them. Parallels to the third reading have been found in biblical and extrabiblical texts, where the meaning is 'in the house/household of X'.[102] Properly understood, the third reading embraces the sense of the other two. The expression is deliberately enigmatic, anticipating Jesus's entire mission.[103] If Jesus saw the need to be in the Temple, engaging with the teachers about the revelation God had given to his people in the Scriptures, it was because he saw this as an essential preparation for the ministry he had been given by his heavenly Father.

The phrase 'had to be' points to a divine necessity (the impersonal verb *dei* is used with that sense in 2:49; 4:43; 9:22; 13:33; 17:25; 22:37; 24:7, 26, 44). Jesus's awareness of his unique relationship to God produced in him a profound sense of obligation to do the will of his heavenly Father (see John 4:34). But his parents 'did not understand what he was saying to them'. Despite the angelic revelations and prophecies that they had heard about him, there was still much for them to comprehend about their son's identity and mission. They were like his later disciples, who failed to understand what he was saying to them at various key points in his ministry (9:44–5; 18:31–4; 24:25–6).

51–2. When Jesus returned to Nazareth with his parents, he continued to be 'obedient to them' (*ēn hypotassomenos*, 'was submissive', ESV). His commitment to do the will of his heavenly Father (verse 49) enabled him to keep submitting to his earthly mother and father. They did not understand the significance of what he had said to them, but 'his mother treasured all these things in her heart' (see verse 19), meaning that she continued to reflect on them and ponder the implications. Meanwhile, 'Jesus continued to grow in wisdom and stature, and in favour with God and man.' This summary–conclusion is similar to the previous one: 'stature' (*hēlikia*) most likely refers to size (19:3), rather than age (12:25),

---

[101] Fitzmyer, *Luke I–IX*, 436.
[102] See Fitzmyer, *Luke I–IX*, 443–4. The Temple in Jerusalem is indirectly referred to as God's 'house' (*oikos*) in Luke 19:46. See also Nolland, *Luke 1–9:20*, 131–2.
[103] Tannehill, *Narrative Unity* I, 54.

corresponding with 'became strong' in verse 40. But it was his growing wisdom that especially pleased God and those who came to know him (see 1 Samuel 2:26). This was a wisdom that developed because 'the fear of the Lord' was foundational to his human life (see Proverbs 1:7). It was a sign that the messianic prophecy of Isaiah 11:1–3a was being fulfilled, but also that the mystery of his divine sonship was being unfolded (Luke 1:31–5).

THE OBEDIENT SON

Jesus's visit to the Temple at age twelve reveals his consciousness of a unique relationship with God as Father and an early sense of devotion to him. This passage highlights the humanity of Jesus as he seeks to learn more about the will of God from the teachers in the Temple, and yet he calls God 'my Father', anticipating significant moments later in the Gospel (10:21–2; 22:29, 42; 23:34, 46; 24:49). More is revealed about the divine sonship of Jesus in important incidents that Luke records (3:22; 4:1–12; 9:26, 35; 22:29–30, 41–2; 23:34, 46; 24:49). When Jesus invites his disciples to relate to God as Father (6:36; 11:2, 13; 12:30, 32), he demonstrates his unique ability to reveal the Father and bring others to know him (10:21–4). Despite the revelations they had received at the time of his birth, Mary and Joseph did not understand the importance of Jesus's claim. Nevertheless, he returned to Nazareth to live in obedience to them and in this way please his heavenly Father and experience the approval of others. From a narrative perspective, Luke shows that Jesus's self-awareness as the Son of God is a key to understanding his mission and responding to him appropriately. Although the Christmas carol is correct in saying, 'For he is our childhood's pattern. Day by day like us he grew,'[104] Luke's emphasis is on the uniqueness of this child and the way he developed and expressed himself in relation to God as his Father. The apostle Paul put it this way: 'When the set time had fully come, God sent his Son, born of a woman, born under the law, to redeem those under the law, that we might receive adoption to sonship' (Galatians 4:4–5).

THE AUTHENTICITY AND FUNCTION
OF THE INFANCY NARRATIVES

Some scholars deny an organic relationship between the infancy narratives and the rest of Luke's work, although there are significant verbal and

---

[104] Cecil Francis Alexander, 'Once in Royal David's City'.

thematic links that cannot be fairly dismissed.[105] They argue that these narratives developed at a later stage than the main Gospel traditions and reflect post-resurrection confessions about Jesus in the form of myths or legends.[106] But are such approaches necessary and warranted? Matthew and Luke's accounts differ in content and style, but theological complementarity can be discerned even when the details differ. So Francis Watson contends, 'Luke's and Matthew's infancy narratives are not two separate stories, but the same story told from different perspectives.'[107] The testimony of Luke 1–2 is that the revelations recorded here were made to a limited few. They were brief and sometimes enigmatic in content, and they were only partially understood at the time. They describe in broad outline the salvation Jesus came to bring and hint at the significance of his person and work. However, as Joel Green observes, 'Luke 1–2 is incomplete in itself and utterly dependent on the narrative that follows.'[108] These chapters lead readers to assume that the expectations they convey will be fulfilled in what follows. What is said about Mary remembering the things that were said and done and pondering them in her heart (2:19, 51) suggests that she was a reliable source for the development of Luke's story. Moreover, as Nolland observes, 'Mary alone bridges in her person the infancy gospel, the ministry of Jesus (8:19–21), and the early life of the post-resurrection church (Acts 1:14).'[109] In other words, she represents the sort of journey to understanding the full significance of Jesus that Luke invites his readers to take. When the story of Jesus reaches its climax in his death and resurrection, he teaches his disciples to understand from the Scriptures the full implications of what was only partially revealed in the earliest traditions about him (24:13–49; Acts 1:1–8). Luke gives assurance to Theophilus about the things he has been taught (1:4) by showing how these early revelations were given, received and cohere with what was later understood and proclaimed to him.

---

[105] Discussed by Edwards, *Luke*, 97–100.

[106] See Fitzmyer, *Luke I–IX*, 304–9. Fitzmyer argues that these chapters were 'in large part freely composed by Luke on the basis of information obtained from earlier models and in imitation of some OT motifs' (309).

[107] Watson, *Fourfold Gospel*, 76

[108] Green, *Luke*, 49.

[109] Nolland, *Luke 1–9:20*, 133.

3

Preparation for the Ministry of Jesus

LUKE 3:1–4:13

Luke provides a detailed summary of the public ministry of John the Baptist, somewhat paralleling Matthew 3:1–12 and Mark 1:1–8 (see also John 1:15–28), but with his own distinctive additions (3:1–20).The baptism of Jesus is briefly recorded, and a genealogy follows, linking Jesus back to Adam 'the son of God' (3:21–38; compare Matthew 1:1–17; 3:13–17; Mark 1:9–11; John 1:29–34). Luke then provides an account of the testing of Jesus in the wilderness (4:1–13; compare Matthew 4:1–11; Mark 1:12–13), before beginning his lengthier narrative of Jesus's Galilean ministry (4:14–9:50). Many flashbacks to the intertwined accounts of the birth of John and Jesus in 1:5–2:52 are provided, and God remains the primary actor in the narrative.[1]

1. John the Baptist prepares the way (3:1–20)

Luke first establishes the context of the Baptist's ministry with respect to what was happening in the wider world and in Judea (verses 1–2). Then he provides a more detailed description of John's calling and ministry than either Matthew or Mark and cites more of the biblical text that is used by each of the evangelists to explain John's significance (verses 3–6). Luke omits any reference to John's clothing and diet and moves straight to an expanded version of his preaching to those who came for baptism (verses 7–14). John's prediction about the one coming after him climaxes each of the Gospel accounts, but Luke sets this in the context of a question about whether John might be the Messiah and follows it with the claim that John exhorted the people and proclaimed the good news to them with many other words (verses 15–19). Luke alone gives a brief report about the arrest of the Baptist at this point in his narrative (verses 19–20).

---

[1] Green, *Luke*, 159–61.

The context of John's ministry (3:1–6)

John the Baptist prepares the way

3 In the fifteenth year of the reign of Tiberius Caesar – when Pontius Pilate was governor of Judea, Herod tetrarch of Galilee, his brother Philip tetrarch of Iturea and Traconitis, and Lysanias tetrarch of Abilene – **2** during the high-priesthood of Annas and Caiaphas, the word of God came to John son of Zechariah in the wilderness. **3** He went into all the country around the Jordan, preaching a baptism of repentance for the forgiveness of sins. **4** As it is written in the book of the words of Isaiah the prophet:

'A voice of one calling in the wilderness,
"Prepare the way for the Lord,
    make straight paths for him.
5 Every valley shall be filled in,
    every mountain and hill made low.
The crooked roads shall become straight,
    the rough ways smooth.
6 And all people will see God's salvation." '**a**

———

a 6 Isaiah 40:3-5

1. For the third time in his narrative so far, Luke provides a setting in world history for the events he records (see 1:5; 2:1–2), suggesting their international significance (verse 6). He begins by noting that John began his public ministry 'in the fifteenth year of the reign of Tiberius Caesar', which was AD 28–29.[2] Tiberius became emperor upon the death of his stepfather Augustus, at which time some imperial provinces came directly under the emperor's care and others operated under the care of legates or prefects appointed by the Senate. Pontius Pilate as 'governor of Judea' was a prefect, serving in that capacity from AD 26 to 36.[3] Herod the Great's extensive kingdom was split among his sons upon his death in 4 BC. Archelaus the oldest son received Judea and Samaria until his banishment in AD 6; Herod Antipas received Galilee and Perea, ruling as 'tetrarch' until AD 39; and his half-brother Philip was 'tetrarch of Iturea and Traconitis' in the Transjordan region until AD 34. A tetrarch was the ruler of one of four regions in a country or province of the Empire. The

———

[2] Dating the fifteenth year of the reign of Tiberias as AD 28 or 29 depends on which calendar Luke used and how he reckoned the accession year of Tiberias. See Marshall, *Luke*, 133; Fitzmyer, *Luke I–IX*, 455.

[3] Pilate was literally 'leading' Judea (*hēgemoneuontos*) at this time (20:20, *hēgemonos*, 'the leader, governor'). A Latin inscription discovered at Caesarea describes him as *praefectus* ('prefect'). The title 'procurator' was only applied to the governor of Judea at a later date. See Bock, *Luke 1:1–9:50*, 60–61, 283; Edwards, *Luke*, 663–6.

evidence concerning the beginning of the tetrarchy of Lysanias in Abilene is uncertain, although it is likely to have ended in AD 40.[4]

2. The high priesthood of Annas and Caiaphas was the most immediate setting for John the Baptist's ministry. A singular term is used to describe the high priesthood of two men who held the office at different periods: Annas was high priest from AD 6 to 15 and his son-in-law Caiaphas from AD 18 to 37. Luke recognises that there was one high priest in office at the time but, as Marshall suggests, he 'shows his consciousness of the powerful position of the retired high priest'.[5] The ancient kingdom of Israel was divided into different regions and ruled by secular authorities, with varying degrees of sympathy towards Judaism. In Jerusalem, however, the high priest continued to have both political and religious influence. Jeremias observes that, 'as president of the Sanhedrin and principal agent of the people at a time when there was no king, he represented the Jewish people in all dealings with Rome'.[6] Herod Antipas and his household, Pontius Pilate, Annas and Caiaphas all reappear in Luke's narrative as it develops (3:19; 8:3; 9:7–9; 13:1, 31; 23:1–25, 52; Acts 3:13; 4:6–7, 27; 13:1, 28). However, as Isaak discerns, 'While the politicians and religious leaders possessed the highest authority in the political and religious arena, John came with a higher authority.'[7]

John's prophetic calling is emphasised by Luke saying that 'the word of God came to John son of Zechariah in the wilderness'. Luke gives no details about his manner of life (compare Matthew 3:4; Mark 1:6), but simply focuses on him as 'a voice of one calling in the wilderness' (verse 4). The testimony to John's prophetic ministry by the Jewish historian Josephus pays special attention to the political fears he aroused in Herod.[8] God's revelation to his prophets in the Old Testament was often expressed in terms of his 'word' or message coming to them (Isaiah 38:4; Jeremiah 1:2, 4, 11, 13; Hosea 1:1). 'Son of Zechariah' recalls Luke's account of

---

[4] Josephus, *Antiquities* 19.5.1; 20.7.1 says that the tetrarchy of Lysanias was given by the Emperor Claudius to Herod Agrippa 1, who ruled Galilee and Perea from AD 40 to 44 in succession to his uncle Herod Antipas. Edwards, *Luke*, 666–8, reviews the life and character of Herod Antipas.

[5] Marshall, *Luke*, 134. John 18:13–27 and Acts 4:5–6 indicate that Annas continued to exercise power behind the scenes when Caiaphas was the ruling high priest. See Jeremias, *Jerusalem*, 157–8.

[6] Jeremias, *Jerusalem*, 159.

[7] Isaak, 'Luke', 1236.

[8] Josephus, *Antiquities* 18.5.2. See Frederick F. Bruce, *Jesus and Christian Origins Outside the New Testament* (Grand Rapids: Eerdmans, 1974), 34–5; Fitzmyer, *Luke I–IX*, 451.

John's origin (1:5–25, 57–79) and follows the occasional biblical custom of giving a father's name when introducing a prophet (Hosea 1:1; Joel 1:1; Zechariah 1:1). The reference to John's being 'in the wilderness' takes us back to where he was last located (1:80; compare 7:24). The flow of the narrative suggests that Isaiah 40:3–5 was the particular word that came to him, clarifying the nature of his calling (verses 4–6) and identifying the means by which the angelic and prophetic revelations given at the time of his birth would be fulfilled (1:16–17; 67–79).

3. John's entrance 'into all the country around the Jordan, preaching a baptism of repentance for the forgiveness of sins', recalls Israel's first entrance into the Promised Land, when they crossed the Jordan river (Joshua 3–4). There, John offered his contemporaries the chance to return to the God of the covenant and serve him in a new way (compare Hosea 2:14–15).[9] Repentance in biblical thought involves a change of behaviour and orientation of life, rather than simply a change of mind (Jeremiah 3:7; 4:1; Hosea 6:1; 7:10). Repentance (*metanoia*) is mentioned again in Luke 3:8; 5:32; 15:7; 24:47; Acts 5:31; 11:18; 13:24; 19:4; 20:21; 26:20. The related verb is used in 10:13; 11:32; 13:3, 5; 15:7, 10; 16:30; 17:3, 4; Acts 2:38; 3:19; 8:22; 17:30; 26:20.[10] Repentance is a gift or offer from God (Acts 5:31; 11:18) that must be exercised or expressed in obedience to his call. The promise of forgiveness is regularly the motivation for repentance in Luke–Acts. Forgiveness was offered by John verbally in his preaching and symbolically in the washing of baptism.

Ritual washing to provide cleansing from sin was required for membership of the Qumran community. This group of pious Jews had established a monastic way of life in the Judean wilderness, where they sought to live perfectly before God by obeying his laws.[11] A complex system of penance and discipline was ordered to maintain their purity (1QS 6:24–7:24). But John's strategy was different: he challenged fellow Jews to come to the Jordan and be baptised, to express definitive repentance, receive God's

---

[9] Nolland, *Luke 1–9:20*, 140, notes that John did not strictly leave the wilderness, but he moved to a place where there was water for baptism in the Jordan region.

[10] The verb *metanoeō* ('repent') is used in conjunction with *epistrephō* ('turn') in Luke 17:4; Acts 3:19; 26:20, reflecting the emphasis of the prophets, who called upon the people to 'turn back' to God (Hebrew *shuv*). This second verb identifies the foundation of a right relationship with God in Luke 1:16; Acts 9:35; 11:21; 14:15; 15:19; 26:18, 20. See F. Mendez-Moratalla, 'Repentance', *DJG*, 771–4.

[11] 1QS 3:3–12. Geza Vermes, *The Dead Sea Scrolls: Qumran in Perspective* (London: Collins, 1977), 147, dates the existence of this community between 150–140 BC and AD 68.

PREPARATION FOR THE MINISTRY OF JESUS

forgiveness and then return to everyday life to 'produce fruit in keeping with repentance' (verse 8).[12]

Little is said about John's act of baptising, except that it was the context for his preaching (verses 7, 16). John presented baptism as a public opportunity to return to God and receive forgiveness apart from the sacrificial ritual of the Temple ('confessing their sins' is added in Matthew 3:6; Mark 1:5). Although Luke goes on to reveal that definitive forgiveness is ultimately made possible by the Messiah's death and resurrection (24:46–7; Acts 2:36–9; 13:38–9), John was offering his contemporaries the 'knowledge' or experience of that forgiveness in advance of its accomplishment (1:77). Christian baptism supersedes John's baptism because it proclaims the achievement of that forgiveness, provides an opportunity to call upon Jesus as Lord and Saviour with repentance and faith and offers those who do so the associated new covenant gift of the Spirit (Acts 2:38–9; 19:1–6; compare Ezekiel 36:25–7).[13] If conversion and the Holy Spirit come before baptism, the ceremony essentially confirms the covenantal relationship with God which the new believer shares with others (Acts 10:44–8).

4–5. Luke introduces the quotation from Isaiah with a formula that indicates its importance (see 2 Chronicles 35:12; Acts 13:33): 'As it is written in the book of the words of Isaiah the prophet' (compare Matthew 3:2; Mark 1:2). Significantly also, Luke cites most of Isaiah 40:3–5, whereas Matthew and Mark only record 40:3 (prefaced by words from Malachi 3:1 in Mark 1:2). The phrase 'in the wilderness' echoes what is said about John in Luke 1:80; 3:2, suggesting that he was in the right place to receive this calling and obey its challenge. Each of the Synoptic Gospels follows the LXX version ('A voice of one calling in the wilderness, "Prepare the way for the Lord"'), rather than the Hebrew ('A voice of one calling: "In the wilderness prepare the way for the Lord"'). Applied to John, the LXX version means that he is the one calling from the wilderness for others to prepare for the Lord's coming. The Hebrew version could simply mean that God called John to prepare the way for the Lord in the wilderness. Both readings are relevant, but the former was probably intended because the tradition about John's ministry emphasised the way he challenged others to prepare for God's coming. As indicated in

---

[12] Bock, *Luke 1:1–9:50*, 288–9, discusses the difference between John's baptism and the ritual washings at Qumran. He also contrasts it with the practice of Jewish proselyte baptism. Edwards, *Luke*, 107–8, thinks John's baptism more likely reflects the ritual washing of Israel before entering into the covenant with God at Sinai (Exodus 19:10). See also E. Ferguson, 'Baptism', *DJG*, 143–8.

[13] Peterson, *Acts*, 153–6; 527–33.

connection with 1:17, the task of preparing a people and preparing a way for the Lord (1:76; 3:4; 7:27) are closely related. In Tannehill's words, John was to prepare the Lord's way 'by preparing a repentant people, whose hearts have turned and who are ready to receive their Lord'.[14]

Isaiah uses the image of a smooth road being made for a king to enter his domain ('make straight paths for him') to explain how to 'prepare the way for the Lord'. This is expanded in grandiose terms appropriate to the visitation of God as Creator and Redeemer:

> Every valley shall be filled in,
>   every mountain and hill made low.
> The crooked roads shall become straight,
>   the rough ways smooth.

If John became convinced that Isaiah 40:3–5 was setting forth the pattern for his ministry, he must have considered the spiritual and moral dimensions of this road-building challenge (as, for example, in Isaiah 52:1–6; 55; 57:14–21; 59:20–21). In that broader context, he would have reflected on the need for Israel to return to God with repentance and faith, seeking cleansing from sin and the renewing work of his Spirit.

6. Luke has shortened the LXX version of Isaiah 40:5 to read, 'And all people will see God's salvation.'[15] This text was obviously included to highlight the universal implications of God's coming to save his people in the way that Isaiah outlines (e.g., Isaiah 45:22–5; 49:5–6; 52:7–10; 60:1–3). Simeon used similar language with reference to Jesus, seeing in him the promised salvation which God had 'prepared in the sight of all nations' (Luke 2:30–32). John went on to predict that the process of end-time judgment and salvation would begin in the ministry of the Messiah (3:16–17). Jesus similarly preached repentance for the forgiveness of sins (5:17–32) and sent out messengers 'before his face' (9:52; 10:1) to preach the same message, ultimately linking this to his saving death and resurrection and calling for it to be preached to all nations (24:46–7). Green rightly concludes, 'John's ministry may be more narrowly directed to Israel (see 1:16; 3:3), but it is part of God's larger project of bringing redemption to all humanity.'[16]

---

[14] Tannehill, *Narrative Unity* 1, 24.
[15] The Hebrew says that 'all flesh will see it together', referring to the glory of the Lord.
[16] Green, *Luke*, 172.

John's preaching of repentance (3:7–14)

7 John said to the crowds coming out to be baptised by him, 'You brood of vipers! Who warned you to flee from the coming wrath? **8** Produce fruit in keeping with repentance. And do not begin to say to yourselves, "We have Abraham as our father." For I tell you that out of these stones God can raise up children for Abraham. **9** The axe has been laid to the root of the trees, and every tree that does not produce good fruit will be cut down and thrown into the fire.'

10 'What should we do then?' the crowd asked.

11 John answered, 'Anyone who has two shirts should share with the one who has none, and anyone who has food should do the same.'

12 Even tax collectors came to be baptised. 'Teacher,' they asked, 'what should we do?'

13 'Don't collect any more than you are required to,' he told them.

14 Then some soldiers asked him, 'And what should we do?'

He replied, 'Don't extort money and don't accuse people falsely – be content with your pay.'

7. Whereas Matthew identifies 'many of the Pharisees and Sadducees' as the particular focus of John's challenge (3:7), Luke has him more generally addressing 'the crowds coming out to be baptised by him'. These people 'went out to him from Jerusalem and all Judea and the whole region of the Jordan' (Matthew 3:5; see Mark 1:5; Luke 7:29–30, 'all the people'). John likens them to 'a brood of vipers' (see Matthew 3:7; 12:34; 23:33). As Isaak suggests, 'They are behaving like snakes fleeing before a grass fire; trying to escape the flames without any intention of having their evil nature changed.'[17] With prophetic irony John asks, 'Who warned you to flee from the coming wrath?' (see Isaiah 13:9; Ezekiel 7:19; Zephaniah 1:14–16; 2:2). John implies that they were dangerously misled if they thought that the act of baptism and token repentance would be sufficient to rescue them from God's condemnation.

8. John's positive message to those coming to be baptised is to 'produce fruit in keeping with repentance'. Fitzmyer takes this to mean, 'Show by your actions and conduct that an inner revitalization has taken place.'[18] Put differently, this is a challenge to demonstrate your repentance by the way you now live (see 6:43–5). Negatively, John warns, 'And do not begin to say to yourselves, "We have Abraham as our father."' This presumes an arrogance about covenant membership by some and the belief that

---

[17] Isaak, 'Luke', 1236.
[18] Fitzmyer, *Luke I–IX*, 468.

physical descent from Abraham could protect them from the coming wrath of God (see 16:19–31; John 8:39–40). The claim that 'out of these stones God can raise up children for Abraham' suggests that God can fulfil his promises to the patriarchs by raising up a new or reconstituted Israel without them (see Exodus 32:25–33:3; Luke 19:8–10), possibly echoing Isaiah 51:1b–2. As Isaak concludes, 'The criterion for salvation is not birth, national identity, religion, class or status.'[19]

9. The nearness of God's judgment is conveyed with another powerful image: 'The axe has been laid to the root of the trees.' In other words, the process of lopping off boughs and felling trees has begun and the Day of the Lord is at hand (see Isaiah 10:33–4). The outcome will be that 'every tree that does not produce good fruit will be cut down and thrown into the fire'. Judgment will be based on moral and spiritual fruit, revealing the genuineness of a person's repentance and faith (see 6:43–9; 13:6–9). The judgment of God is described in terms of 'unquenchable fire' in verse 17 (see my comment on hell in 12:5 and Hades in 16:23–4).

10–14. The same question, 'What shall we do then?', is successively put by three groups of people, asking what John means by 'fruit in keeping with repentance'. The ethical teaching of the Baptist is first illustrated with respect to 'the crowd': 'Anyone who has two shirts should share with the one who has none, and anyone who has food should do the same.' This is a call for genuine acts of love and mercy to be shown towards neighbours, reflecting the teaching of various biblical passages and anticipating the radical challenge of Jesus (6:27–38; 10:25–37; 12:33; 14:12–14; 18:22). Clothing and food represent the essentials of daily life.

Luke then marvels that 'even tax collectors came to be baptised', addressing John as 'Teacher' and asking, 'What should we do?' John replies, 'Don't collect more than you are required to.' Jewish 'toll collectors' (*telōnai*) worked for the Romans, collecting various indirect taxes. They figure prominently in later narratives, because the Pharisees and teachers of the law treated them as outcasts from their society (see 5:27, 29–30; 7:34; 15:1 18:10–13; 19:2). The Roman taxation system was open to abuse and dishonesty, because expenses and profits could be added by collectors to the authorised amount.[20] John does not tell them to get a new job

---

[19] Isaak, 'Luke', 1236. Isaak reflects on the communal aspects of repentance appropriate to African culture.
[20] Fitzmyer, *Luke I–IX*, 469–70, and Edwards, *Luke*, 111–12, detail how the system operated, encouraging graft and greed. See also D. Downs, 'Economics', *DJG*, 381–7.

but, as Green says, 'to work out the substance of repentance within the day-to-day activities of their duties as toll collectors'.[21]

'Soldiers' were the third group that John encountered. These would have been 'Jewish men enlisted in the service of Herod Antipas, of whose troops Josephus gives testimony'.[22] The warning to them was, 'Don't extort money and don't accuse people falsely – be content with your pay.' The first temptation was to 'take money from anyone by force' (Louw and Nida, *diaseiō*). The second temptation was to 'bring charges against an individual and receive a part of the fine or indemnity paid to the court' (Louw and Nida, *sykophanteō*). In both cases, a soldier could misuse the authority and privilege of his office for personal gain. The positive alternative is 'be content with your pay' (*opsōnion*, 'ration money'). John did not directly call for social structures to be radically changed, but for people to participate in society with generosity, justice, love and contentment, themes that Jesus goes on to emphasise in his teaching also (e.g., 12:13–34; 16:1–31; 19:1–10).

John's preaching about the Messiah (3:15–18)

15 The people were waiting expectantly and were all wondering in their hearts if John might possibly be the Messiah. 16 John answered them all, 'I baptise you with[b] water. But one who is more powerful than I will come, the straps of whose sandals I am not worthy to untie. He will baptise you with[b] the Holy Spirit and fire. 17 His winnowing fork is in his hand to clear his threshing-floor and to gather the wheat into his barn, but he will burn up the chaff with unquenchable fire.' 18 And with many other words John exhorted the people and proclaimed the good news to them.

b 16 Or *in*

15. Despite the continuity between the ministries of John and Jesus, the distinction between them is clearly stated now. John's message about imminent judgment and the need to prepare for the Lord's coming arouses a godly anticipation in many: 'The people were waiting expectantly and were all wondering in their hearts if John might be the Messiah.' The reference to 'their hearts' indicates that deep reflection is taking place, as

---

[21] Green, *Luke*, 179.

[22] Fitzmyer, *Luke I–IX*, 470, citing Josephus, *Antiquities* 18.5. Fitzmyer observes, 'Palestinian Jews were exempt from service in Roman armies since the time of Julius Caesar . . . some of them, however, did serve as mercenaries.'

questions about the significance of John's ministry and his relation to the Messiah are asked (see 7:18–35; John 1:19–28). The Greek expression Luke uses (*mēpote autos eiē*, 'whether he might be', ESV) expresses uncertainty about identifying John with the Messiah.[23]

16–17. In response to questions about himself and the Messiah, John makes three related claims: the coming one will be 'more powerful' than he is; he will baptise 'with the Holy Spirit and fire'; and he will inaugurate the end-time judgment of God. Matthew 3:11–12 provides a close parallel. Mark 1:7–8 is briefer and puts the claim about the Messiah being more powerful first, while John 1:26–7 is briefer still. Bock observes that 'the figure of the Strong One for Luke is tied to an anointing with power, a picture that looks not so much at divinity as it does at Jesus' regal office'.[24] The Baptist presents himself as a slave in relation to the coming King, who will be more powerful than he is ('the straps of whose sandals I am not worthy to untie'). As well as this personal comparison, John highlights the difference in their roles ('I baptise you with water . . . He will baptise you with the Holy Spirit and fire').[25] John's prediction first relates to the impact that the Spirit-empowered Messiah will have on his contemporaries. Jesus is anointed by the Spirit at his baptism (verse 22; see Isaiah 11:1–2) and equipped to be the faithful Son of God (4:1–13) and agent of final salvation (4:14–44; see Acts 10:38). His teaching and his mighty works test and divide people (5:27–32; 6:6–11; 7:29–35; 8:34–9), bringing 'fire on the earth' and making it necessary for Jesus himself to undergo a baptism of fire (12:49–53). As the Messiah anointed by the Spirit, he fills his disciples with the Holy Spirit after he has accomplished their salvation, enabling them to continue his prophetic work in all the world (Acts 1:8; 2:1–21). John's baptism with water prepares people to benefit from the full scope of the Messiah's baptism 'with the Holy Spirit and fire'.

Much debate has taken place about the relationship between 'Spirit' and 'fire' in the ministry of Jesus. 'Tongues of fire' in Acts 2:3 signify the later distribution of the Spirit to all present, but baptism with the Holy Spirit is mentioned without reference to fire in Mark 1:8; Acts 1:5;

---

[23] Messiah as a title ('the Anointed One') is only used in the Old Testament of a future figure in Daniel 9:25. However, some DSS (1QS 9:11; 1QSa 2:14, 20) and the intertestamental *Psalms of Solomon* 17:23, 36; 18:6, 8 reveal 'a clear Jewish expectation of the coming of a messiah (or messiahs) in the period prior to the emergence of Christianity', Fitzmyer, *Luke I–IX*, 471–2.

[24] Bock, *Luke 1:1–9:50*, 320.

[25] See M. Wenk, 'Holy Spirit', *DJG*, 637–9; Bock, *Luke 1:1–9:50*, 322–4.

11:16. In Luke 3:17 and Matthew 3:12, fire is associated with separation and judgment. A winnowing fork was used to lift harvested wheat so that the wind could blow away the chaff and the grain could fall on the threshing-floor and be collected ('His winnowing fork is in his hand to clear his threshing-floor'; see Jeremiah 15:7). In the ministry of Jesus, some will be saved (he will 'gather the wheat into his barn') and some will be lost ('he will burn up the chaff with unquenchable fire'; see Isaiah 66:24; Mark 9:43, 48). In Isaiah 4:4, 'spirit' and 'fire' are brought together in a promise about the purging and renewing of God's people. Similarly, the Qumran document 1QS 4:20–21 speaks of God cleansing people 'with a holy Spirit' from all their wicked practices and sprinkling them 'with a spirit of truth like purifying water'. *Spirit and fire together describe the effect of the Messiah's coming,* 'experienced by the penitent as purification in the refiner's fire and by the godless as destruction by wind and fire'.[26]

18. John spoke 'with many other words' than Luke has recorded, but the pattern was the same: he 'exhorted' the people (*parakalōn*) to express genuine repentance (verses 7–14) and 'proclaimed the good news' to them (*euēggelizeto*, verses 15–17). The second verb recalls the emphasis on proclaiming Israel's restoration in Isaiah 40:9; 52:7; 60:6; 61:6 LXX and anticipates the use of this term with respect to the ministry of Jesus (4:43; 7:22; 8:1; 16:16; 20:1) and his followers (9:6; Acts 5:42; 8:4, 12, 25, 35, 40; 10:36; 11:20; 13:32; 14:7, 15, 21; 15:35; 16:10; 17:18). Authentic gospel proclamation offers salvation in the face of approaching judgment to all who will respond with repentance and faith.

John's imprisonment (3:19–20)

19 But when John rebuked Herod the tetrarch because of his marriage to Herodias, his brother's wife, and all the other evil things he had done, **20** Herod added this to them all: he locked John up in prison.

John's prophetic ministry led him to rebuke Herod Antipas the tetrarch of Galilee, 'because of his marriage to Herodias, his brother's wife, and all the other evil things he had done' (compare Matthew 14:3–4; Mark

---

[26] Nolland, *Luke 1–9:20*, 153. Nolland contends that 'the double possibility for the fire is present in the imagery of the refiner's fire which destroys the dross, but purifies the precious metals' (see Isaiah 1:25; Zechariah 13:9; Malachi 3:2–3). Jeremiah 4:11–12 speaks of a scorching wind that can destroy, rather than simply winnow and cleanse.

LUKE

6:17–18). Luke wants to focus on Jesus from now on and concludes his record of John's life and ministry briefly. Both Herod and Herodias left previous marriages to enter into this new relationship. In so doing, Herod married the wife of his half-brother Philip and violated the prohibition of Leviticus 18:16. When Luke says that Herod added to all the evil he committed by imprisoning John, he means that this was the crowning example of his wickedness. Rather than responding to the prophet's challenge, he sought to silence him! The rich and powerful don't like to be challenged about their sexual sins, especially if they are ignored by the wider society, and it requires much courage to call them out. John was eventually beheaded by Herod, because Herodias continued to nurse a grudge against him (Matthew 14:6–12; Mark 6:19–29; Luke 9:9).[27] Observing that 'this prophet from the desert did not remove himself from the political arena', Isaak points to the need for Christians today to consider carefully the relationship between church and state in their own context, 'because there is a high price to pay if the church becomes too politicized or our faith too privatized'.[28]

PREPARING THE WAY FOR JESUS

John's prophetic call is set within the political and religious context of his day and related to Isaiah's prediction that 'all people' would see the salvation of God. John set in motion a pattern of exhortation and preaching that eventually brought the promised salvation 'to the ends of the earth' (Acts 1:8). His specific task was to 'prepare the way for the Lord' by preaching 'a baptism of repentance for the forgiveness of sins'. This involved challenging fellow Jews to flee from the coming wrath and to be ready for the Messiah, who would bring judgment for some and salvation for others. The ethical dimension of John's preaching was the call to 'produce fruit in keeping with repentance', which he illustrated with examples applicable to different groups in his community. John's reference to the Messiah's baptising 'with the Holy Spirit and fire' was a global way of describing the effect that Jesus's ministry would have on those he encountered. Both John and Jesus called for a radical reorientation of people's lives towards God and his purpose for them, but in Jesus's

---

[27] Josephus, *Antiquities* 18.5, 2, emphasises the political motivation for John's arrest and records that he was imprisoned in the fortress of Machaerus on the east side of the Dead Sea.
[28] Isaak, 'Luke', 1237. He argues for 'institutional separation *and* functional interaction'.

88

public ministry the immanence of the kingdom of God was more obvious and its blessings more immediately accessible (see 4:14–44; 7:18–28). As Luke's Gospel progresses, Jesus presents himself as the Son of Man who must suffer many things, be rejected and killed, and on the third day be raised to life (9:22). Moreover, he predicts his return as the Son of Man 'in his glory and in the glory of the Father and of the holy angels' (9:26). Much of his teaching about discipleship concerns watchfulness, faithful stewardship and enabling others to be prepared for these great events. Christian preaching takes place between his finished work and promised return with all its consequences (Acts 1:11; 3:19–23).

2. The baptism of Jesus and his genealogy (3:21–38)

Luke's account of the baptism of Jesus is briefer than the parallels (Matthew 3:13–17; Mark 1:9–11), but he adds that Jesus was praying when the Holy Spirit descended on him and that the Spirit's coming was 'in bodily form', in the manner of a dove (verse 22). The climactic moment in each of these narratives is the address to Jesus from heaven, identifying him as the Son whom God loves and with whom he is 'well pleased' (verse 22). Luke's record that Jesus began his ministry when he was 'about thirty years old' introduces a genealogy stretching back to Adam, who in another sense is 'the son of God' (verses 23–38). With this literary device the story of Jesus is related to human history from the beginning. Jesus is human like Adam, but he is the true and faithful Son of God (4:1–13), who restores human beings to the sort of relationship with God for which they were created.

The baptism and genealogy of Jesus

21 When all the people were being baptised, Jesus was baptised too. And as he was praying, heaven was opened **22** and the Holy Spirit descended on him in bodily form like a dove. And a voice came from heaven: 'You are my Son, whom I love; with you I am well pleased.'

23 Now Jesus himself was about thirty years old when he began his ministry.

He was the son, so it was thought, of Joseph,

the son of Heli, **24** the son of Matthat,
the son of Levi, the son of Melki,
the son of Jannai, the son of Joseph,
25 the son of Mattathias, the son of Amos,
the son of Nahum, the son of Esli,
the son of Naggai, **26** the son of

Maath,
the son of Mattathias, the son of
Semein,
the son of Josek, the son of Joda,
27 the son of Joanan, the son of
Rhesa,
the son of Zerubbabel, the son of
Shealtiel,
the son of Neri, 28 the son of Melki,
the son of Addi, the son of Cosam,
the son of Elmadam, the son of Er,
29 the son of Joshua, the son of
Eliezer,
the son of Jorim, the son of
Matthat,
the son of Levi, 30 the son of
Simeon,
the son of Judah, the son of
Joseph,
the son of Jonam, the son of
Eliakim,
31 the son of Melea, the son of
Menna,
the son of Mattatha, the son of
Nathan,
the son of David, 32 the son of
Jesse,
the son of Obed, the son of Boaz,
the son of Salmon,c the son of
Nahshon,

33 the son of Amminadab, the son of
Ram,d
the son of Hezron, the son of
Perez,
the son of Judah, 34 the son of
Jacob,
the son of Isaac, the son of
Abraham,
the son of Terah, the son of Nahor,
35 the son of Serug, the son of Reu,
the son of Peleg, the son of Eber,
the son of Shelah, 36 the son of
Cainan,
the son of Arphaxad, the son of
Shem,
the son of Noah, the son of
Lamech,
37 the son of Methuselah, the son of
Enoch,
the son of Jared, the son of
Mahalalel,
the son of Kenan, 38 the son of
Enosh,
the son of Seth, the son of Adam,
the son of God.

c 32 Some early manuscripts *Sala*
d 33 Some manuscripts *Amminadab, the son of Admin, the son of Arni*; other manuscripts vary widely.

21–2. John is not mentioned in this brief account, though his presence is implied by the introductory words, 'When all the people were being baptised, Jesus was baptised too.' Jesus was introduced by Luke as the Son of God, who was conceived by the Holy Spirit and born of the virgin Mary (1:31–5). So why did he need to submit to John's 'baptism of repentance for the forgiveness of sins' (3:3) and have the Spirit descend on him? At one level, baptism was a way of endorsing John's ministry, acknowledging that it was authorised by God (see 20:4–7; Matthew 3:14–15). At the same time, Jesus identified with those who responded positively to John's ministry, indicating that this was the way of renewal and transformation for Israel. Luke's focus on Jesus 'praying' suggests that Jesus saw baptism as a way of personally dedicating himself to do his Father's will (see 2:49; 9:28; 22:39–42). The answer to his prayer was that 'heaven opened and the Holy Spirit descended on him in bodily form like a dove'. The opening of heaven signified the supernatural intervention of God (see Exodus 19:9–22; Isaiah 64:1–3) to speak and equip his Son for service with the anointing of his Spirit (see Ezekiel 1:1; 2:1–8). Nolland rightly observes that 'the historicity of the voice from heaven is finally beyond the scope of critical inquiry', but something set Jesus apart from others who came to be baptised, and each of the Synoptic Gospels bears witness to the same sequence of events.[29]

The address to Jesus as 'my Son' (*ho hyios mou*) reflects Psalm 2:7 and recalls the angelic prediction that he would be the messianic 'Son of the Most High' (Luke 1:32–3).[30] The Father confirms the uniqueness of this relationship and expresses delight in his Son, even before he begins his public ministry. Fitzmyer suggests that the term 'whom I love' (*ho agapētos*, 'the beloved') 'adds a specification about the sonship that is not present in Ps. 2:7, expressive of a special love-relationship between the heavenly Father and the Son, Jesus'.[31] His anointing with the Spirit recalls Isaiah 11:1–2; 61:1–2 (see also the intertestamental *Psalms of Solomon* 17:37, 42) and reinforces the messianic implications of this event (see Acts 4:25–6; 10:37–8). The words 'with you I am well pleased' also echo Isaiah 42:1:

> Here is my servant, whom I uphold,
>   my chosen one in whom I delight:
> I will put my Spirit on him,
>   and he will bring justice to the nations.[32]

As the messianic Son whom God loves and with whom he is well pleased, Jesus must fulfil the role of the Servant of the Lord, culminating in the

---

[29] Nolland, *Luke 1–9:20*, 159.

[30] Some later manuscripts include words from Psalm 2:7 ('today I have begotten you'), but this is clearly a secondary reading. See Metzger, *Textual Commentary*, 112–13.

[31] Fitzmyer, *Luke I–IX*, 485–6. Bock, *Luke 1:1–9:50*, 342–3, considers whether *ho agapētos* echoes Genesis 22:2, 12 LXX ('only') or Isaiah 41:8 (*hon ēgapēsa*, 'whom I loved'). See Luke 20:13 (*ton huion mou ton agapēton*, 'my only son'). See also Green, *Luke*, 187.

[32] The address to Jesus in Luke 3:22 is closer to the individual sense of Isaiah 42:1 in Hebrew. See H. Beers, 'Servant of Yahweh', *DJG*, 1348–55.

suffering that brings salvation to others (see Luke 22:19–20, 37). Jesus did not need to seek forgiveness for his own sins in baptism but dedicated himself to be numbered with the transgressors, to bear the sin of many and to make intercession for the transgressors (Isaiah 53:12). The heavenly voice at Jesus's baptism draws together various strands of biblical expectation and points to their fulfilment in his person and work.[33]

Mark 1:10 presents this as a moment of revelation for Jesus alone ('he saw heaven being torn open and the Spirit descending on him like a dove'), but Luke is less specific. Although the descent of the Spirit and the divine words of affirmation were for Jesus's benefit, according to John 1:32–3, the Baptist was a witness of what happened.[34] The phrase 'in bodily form like a dove' expresses approximation, not identification. Jesus experienced something tangible when the Spirit descended on him, but it was more like the gentleness of a dove alighting on him than a violent rushing wind (contrast Acts 2:1–4).[35] The coming of the Spirit in some manifest way affirmed his messianic calling and empowered him to fulfil it (compare 4:36; 5:17; 6:19; 8:46; 9:1; 10:19; 21:27; Acts 2:22; 10:38). Note the simultaneous appearance of all three persons of the Trinity at once here, as Jesus sets out to do the will of his heavenly Father.

Baptism 'in the name of Jesus Christ' (Acts 2:38–9) maintains a continuity with the baptism of John in expressing 'repentance for the forgiveness of sins' (Luke 3:3). But it also acknowledges the fulfilment of John's prediction that the Messiah would 'baptise you with the Holy Spirit and fire' (3:16). Christian baptism affirms the saving death and resurrection of Jesus, his exaltation to God's right hand and his pouring out of the promised Holy Spirit (Acts 2:32–41). It provides an opportunity for those who believe the gospel to appropriate by faith the benefits of Jesus's saving work.[36]

23–38. Luke's genealogy of Jesus is introduced with a reference to the beginning of his public ministry ('Now Jesus himself was about thirty years old when he began his ministry') and it concludes with an oblique reference to 'Adam, the son of God' (*Adam tou theou*). Adam is identified

[33] Bock, *Luke 1:1–9:50*, 336–7, outlines different explanations for the baptism of Jesus that have been given throughout Christian history.
[34] Matthew 3:16–17 reflects Mark's focus on Jesus's perception of the Spirit of God 'descending like a dove and alighting on him', but the voice from heaven is presented as addressing a wider audience. Compare Luke 9:35.
[35] Bock, *Luke 1:1–9:50*, 338–9, rightly dismisses all attempts to make a theological symbol out of the dove, pointing out that *hōs* ('like') is an adverb of manner.
[36] See also my comments on baptism in relation to 3:3.

in this way as the first human being, created in the image and likeness of God (Genesis 1:26–27; 5:1–3). The distinctive address by God to Jesus as 'my Son, whom I love' at his baptism (verse 22, *ho hyios mou ho agapētos*) becomes a title ('the Son of God') when his calling and identity are later challenged by the devil (4:3, 9, *ho hyios tou theou*). In between these claims, Jesus is identified as a descendant of Adam, truly human, but not a fallen and disobedient son of God as Adam was.

Matthew's genealogy begins with Abraham, highlights the significance of David and the exile to Babylon in biblical history, and ends with 'Jesus who is called the Messiah' (1:1–16). Matthew wants to show that Jesus is 'the son of David, the son of Abraham' – the one who fulfils the promises made to these key figures in biblical history. Luke's genealogy is not so carefully structured or elaborate. It proceeds in reverse order, beginning with Jesus 'the son, so it was thought, of Joseph'. The qualification 'so it was thought' affirms the record of Jesus's virginal conception (1:34–5) and implies that Joseph can only have been the adoptive father of Jesus (see Matthew 1:18–21).[37] Luke traces his earthly family back through David (verse 31) and Abraham (verse 34) to Adam (verse 38), identifying him more broadly as part of the human race and destined to have an impact on people from every nation (see 2:29–32; 3:6). Luke alone includes the list of names between Abraham and Adam, which were likely gleaned from genealogies in the Pentateuch. Luke shares with Matthew the list from Abraham to David, though textual variation exists with reference to some names in verse 33.[38] Luke diverges from Matthew in the section of the genealogy from David to Joseph, though both lists mention Zerubbabel and Shealtiel. The Davidic descent of Jesus is traced through Solomon in Matthew and through Nathan in Luke. Although it is speculative, the most attractive harmonising solution is that 'Matthew gives Joseph's ancestry by birth, Luke that by adoption'.[39]

---

[37] Fitzmyer, *Luke I–IX*, 489–90, considers the variety of ways in which genealogies were constructed and used in biblical times. See also Nolland, *Luke 1–9:20*, 168–9; D. R. Bauer, 'Genealogy', *DJG*, 497–503.

[38] NIV presents the same succession in Luke 3:33 as in Matthew 1:4 (Ram–Amminadab–Nashon), but the marginal note acknowledges that some manuscripts have 'Amminadab, the son of Admin, the son of Arni'. These last two names are unknown in the Old Testament.

[39] Nolland, *Luke 1–9:20*, 170. Nolland argues that Joseph was adopted by Mary's father Eli as son and heir when he married Mary. Fitzmyer, *Luke I–IX*, 496–7, and Edwards, *Luke*, 123–4, consider other possible reasons for differences in the lists.

3. The testing of Jesus (4:1–13)

This narrative broadly parallels Matthew 4:1–11, though the temptations are in a different order, coinciding with Luke's focus on Jerusalem and the Temple as the place of Jesus's ultimate challenge (9:22, 44, 51; 13:31–5; 18:31–3; 19:28–24:53). Most likely, the details came from Jesus himself, who warned his disciples about the way Satan would test them (22:31–2, 46). Edwards argues that 'the fact that no known prototype of the temptation of Jesus exists makes it unlikely that the temptation narrative was a later Christian invention'.[40] Zechariah's prediction that the Messiah would rescue his people from the hand of their enemies (1:68–75) was manifested in a cosmic and spiritual way with this encounter. Jesus used Scripture to resist the devil's enticements to sin, affirming its truth and submitting himself to obey it. The temptations he faced were distinctly related to his identity and calling as God's Son, though his pattern of resistance in some respects is also a model for believers to follow. Challenges that he would face in the course of his ministry were presented to him to prepare him in advance for a life of obedient service to his heavenly Father.

Jesus is tested in the wilderness

4 Jesus, full of the Holy Spirit, left the Jordan and was led by the Spirit into the wilderness, ²where for forty days he was tempted[a] by the devil. He ate nothing during those days, and at the end of them he was hungry.

³The devil said to him, 'If you are the Son of God, tell this stone to become bread.'

⁴Jesus answered, 'It is written: "Man shall not live on bread alone."[b]'

⁵The devil led him up to a high place and showed him in an instant all the kingdoms of the world. ⁶And he said to him, 'I will give you all their authority and splendour; it has been given to me, and I can give it to anyone I want to. ⁷If you worship me, it will all be yours.'

⁸Jesus answered, 'It is written: "Worship the Lord your God and serve him only."[c]'

⁹The devil led him to Jerusalem and had him stand on the highest point of the temple. 'If you are the Son of God,' he said, 'throw yourself down from here. ¹⁰For it is written:

' "He will command his angels
  concerning you
  to guard you carefully;
¹¹ they will lift you up in their hands,
  so that you will not strike your
  foot against a stone."[d]'

---

[40] Edwards, *Luke*, 131. See Bock, *Luke 1:1–9:50*, 60–61, 364–6; M. J. Wilkins, 'Temptation of Jesus', *DJG*, 1498–1509.

12 Jesus answered, 'It is said: "Do not put the Lord your God to the test."ᵉ'
13 When the devil had finished all this tempting, he left him until an opportune time.

a 2 The Greek for *tempted* can also mean *tested.*
b 4 Deut. 8:3
c 8 Deut. 6:13
d 11 Psalm 91:11,12
e 12 Deut. 6:16

1–2. A link with Jesus's baptism is made with the declaration that he was 'full of the Holy Spirit' when he 'left the Jordan and was led by the Spirit into the wilderness'.[41] Israel was led by God for forty years in the wilderness (Deuteronomy 8:2) and tested to learn what was in their heart. Jesus's forty days of testing, together with his quotation of three texts from Deuteronomy concerning Israel's experience (8:3 in verse 4; 6:13 in verse 8; 6:16 in verse 12), suggest that it was God's will for him to be similarly tried. In view of the way the genealogy concludes (3:38), an echo of Adam's temptation may also be heard in this context (Genesis 2:16–17; 3:1–7). God allowed 'the devil' to be his agent in presenting these challenges, though his designs were evil (4:2, 3, 6, 13; see also Job 1:6–12; 2:1–6). Jesus experienced temptation from an external, personal, spiritual adversary, whose influence he knew he must resist.[42] He succeeded where both Adam and Israel failed. The verb *peirazō* can be rendered 'tempted' or 'tested', depending on the context. From Satan's perspective, it was an opportunity to turn Jesus away from serving his heavenly Father. From God's perspective, it was a way of proving the sonship of Jesus and preparing him for what lay ahead. When Luke says, 'He ate nothing during those days, and at the end of them he was hungry,' the likely meaning is that Jesus was fasting and ate nothing substantial (see Matthew 4:2).

3–4. The devil's first challenge ('If you are the Son of God') does not express doubt about Jesus's identity but invites him to use his power to satisfy his own needs ('tell this stone to become bread'), rather than being 'nourished in filial dependence on God', as Nolland puts it.[43] Jesus

---

[41] Luke's Greek means 'in the Spirit' (*en tō pneumati*), as in verse 14 (*en tē dynamei tou pneumatos*, 'in the power of the Spirit'). Matthew 4:1 emphasises the personal agency of the Spirit (*hypo tou pneumatos*, 'by the Spirit') and Mark 1:12 reads 'the Spirit sent him out'.

[42] Luke identifies 'Satan' (Hebrew, 'adversary, accuser'; 10:18; 11:18; 13:16; 22:3, 21; Acts 5:3; 26:18) with 'the devil' (Hebrew, 'the slanderer'; 8:12; 22:3, 31; Acts 5:5; 13:10; 26:18). See Bock, *Luke 1:1–9:50*, 60–61, 370–71; R. H. Bell, 'Demon, Devil, Satan', *DJG*, 336–40.

[43] Nolland, *Luke 1–9:20*, 179. Bock, *Luke 1:1–9:50*, 372–4 discusses alternative

does not debate the issue but responds immediately with a quotation from Deuteronomy 8:3. This is introduced with a formula emphasising its authority as Scripture, 'It is written: "Man shall not live on bread alone."' The Israelites in the wilderness had to rely on God to meet their daily needs. Moses explained this in terms of depending 'on every word that comes from the mouth of God' (cited in Matthew 4:4). Jesus could have acquired food for himself miraculously (Luke 9:10–17) but, as Wilkins says, this would have led him 'outside the will of the Father for the Son's incarnational experience'.[44]

5–8. The devil's second challenge takes place after he has led Jesus 'up to a high place and showed him in an instant all the kingdoms of the world'. There is no need to insist on a literal transfer of Jesus from the wilderness to a high mountain and then to Jerusalem (verse 9). The language is visionary, because there is no mountain where one can see 'in an instant all the kingdoms of the world'. Satan appeals to Jesus's imagination, alluding to God's promise concerning the Messiah's inheritance of the nations (Psalm 2:8) and putting himself in the place of God: 'I will give you all their authority and splendour'. He arrogantly assumes that he has absolute power over the nations ('it has been given to me, and I can give it to anyone I want to'), but his power is limited (John 12:31; 14:30–31; 16:11). To share the devil's power, Jesus would have to treat him as God ('If you worship me, it will all be yours'). An act of homage is implied here, expressing submission to the devil's rule and control.[45] This would mean abandoning his trust in God to fulfil his promises. Jesus responds with a reference to Deuteronomy 6:13: 'It is written: "Worship the Lord your God and serve him only."' This reflects the LXX A text, which begins with the same verb used in the devil's challenge.[46] The verb 'serve' clarifies that true homage to God will lead to a life of obedience to him. Obedience will involve suffering for Jesus, before he is glorified and his rule over the nations is fully established (9:26; 24:26), and it will also involve suffering for those who follow him (9:23–6; 12:4–7; 21:12–19).

---

interpretations.

[44] Wilkins, 'Temptation of Jesus', *DJG*, 1505.

[45] The verb *proskyneō* ('worship') can indicate a physical or spiritual submission. Luke's use of *enōpion emou* ('before me') emphasises the need for an outward expression of homage (see Matthew 4:9).

[46] Deuteronomy 6:13 (LXX B) follows the Hebrew, 'Fear the Lord your God, serve him only.' This expresses the parallel notion that true reverence or respect for God should lead to a life of serving him.

9–12. The devil's third challenge takes place when he has led Jesus to Jerusalem and 'had him stand on the highest point of the temple'. As with the previous temptation, this is likely to have been a visionary experience or appeal to Jesus's imagination. Edwards notes that 'the highest point of the temple' cannot be confidently identified, though it must have been a place where Jesus could contemplate putting his life at risk in a spectacular way.[47] The form of the challenge is the same as verse 3, with an assumption that he is 'the Son of God' and an encouragement to prove it ('throw yourself down from here'). The devil suggests an alternative to the way of the cross, supported by the misuse of Psalm 91:11–12. This text promises angelic protection to those who make God their refuge and put their trust in him for rescue:

> He will command his angels concerning you
>> to guard you carefully;
> they will lift you up in their hands,
>> so that you will not strike your foot against a stone.

The devil tempts Jesus to take God at his word and force his hand! But Jesus answers with another Scripture by way of rebuke: 'It is said: "Do not put the Lord your God to the test."' Deuteronomy 6:16 refers to the testing of God at Massah (Exodus 17:7), when the people said, 'Is the Lord among us or not?' Despite his many provisions for them, the Israelites doubted God's love for them and sought to provoke him into action, but Jesus refuses to dictate to his Father how he must fulfil his promises. Satan still uses the misinterpretation of Scripture to lead people astray!

13. When Luke records that the devil had 'finished all this tempting' (*syntelesas panta peirasmon*; ESV, 'ended every temptation'), he implies that Jesus had withstood a comprehensive attack on his mission (see my comment on 11:22). The devil then left him 'until an opportune time' (*achri kairou*), ultimately referring to his betrayal and death (22:1–6), though Jesus's public ministry was not 'Satan-free', since he encountered the devil in several ways in Luke's ongoing narrative.[48] According to Matthew 4:11 and Mark 1:13, angels came to serve him as the testing in the wilderness ended and he set out to fulfil God's kingdom plan.

---

[47] Edwards, *Luke*, 129–30. The *pterygion* (BDAG, 'tip or extremity') could refer to the southeast corner of the Temple, which stood 150 feet (45m) above the Kidron Valley.
[48] See Fitzmyer, *Luke I–IX*, 186–7.

THE PROVING OF GOD'S SON

When Jesus prayerfully submitted to John's baptism and was anointed with God's Spirit, he was confirmed as the unique Son, with whom the Father is well pleased (see 2:49, 52). Biblical echoes in the divine address to Jesus identify him as the Son who is also the promised Messiah and Servant of the Lord. Full of the Holy Spirit, he was led into a direct confrontation with the devil in which his sonship was tested and proven. The implied contrast with Adam and Israel as God's 'son' (Genesis 3:1–7; Exodus 4:22–3) suggests that in his obedient service as a man he did what they could not do. Nolland observes that Jesus 'marks a new beginning to sonship and sets it on an entirely new footing'.[49] More than a model to believers of how to resist temptation, he is the Son who uniquely defeats the devil and releases people from his power (see 11:21–2; 13:16; Colossians 1:13–14; Hebrews 2:14–15; 1 John 3:8). In his public ministry, Jesus regularly encountered Satan's personal opposition in those who were demonically possessed (4:33–6, 41; 8:26–39; 11:14–22; 13:10–17) and viewed every victory as a sign of Satan's final defeat (10:17–20). His trials were many (22:28), culminating in Satan's attack through the betrayal of Judas (22:1–6), his prayer for the Father's will to be done (22:42) and his struggle on the cross to be faithful to the end (23:35–46). Martin Luther rightly insisted, 'The chief article and foundation of the gospel is that before you take Christ as an example, you accept and recognize him as a gift, as a present that God has given you and that is your own.'[50] Christians caught up in the same spiritual battle should look to Jesus for deliverance. His life of resistance to sin and obedience to the Father's will, even to death, make him the helper we need in times of testing (Hebrews 2:17; 4:14–16; 5:7–10; 7:25; 9:14).

---

[49] Nolland, *Luke 1–9:20*, 173. Nolland concludes that 'the narrative presents both moral challenge as well as Christological affirmation' (182). See more fully Gladd, *From the Manger to the Throne*, 123–43.

[50] *Luther's Works*, edited by J. Pelikan and H. L. Lehmann (St. Louis: Concordia; Philadelphia: Fortress Press, 1955–86), volume 35, 119.

4

The Galilean Ministry of Jesus

LUKE 4:14–9:50

Luke broadly follows Mark here, mostly abbreviating his material. However, whereas just over half of Mark's Gospel is devoted to this period (1:14–9:41 (350 verses)), the comparable section in Luke (274 verses) is barely a quarter of the book. Three passages paralleling Matthew are inserted into this (Luke 6:27–49; 7:1–10; 7:18–35), together with material from other sources (4:16–30; 5:1–11; 6:17–26; 7:11–17, 36–50). The overall effect is to highlight the impact that the words and deeds of Jesus had on his contemporaries in Galilee.[1] Many were amazed and spoke well of him (4:15, 22, 32, 36–7; 5:15, 26; 7:16–17), gathering to hear him teach and be healed of their diseases (4:40; 5:15; 6:17–19; 8:40; 9:11). Some turned against him (4:28–9; 5:21; 6:1–11), while others became disciples (5:1–11, 27–8; 6:12–15; 7:36–50). The latter progressively came to understand more of the significance of his person and mission (6:20–49; 8:1–18, 22–56; 9:18–50).

1. Proclamation and rejection at Nazareth (Luke 4:14–30)

A brief introduction to this section reports Jesus's teaching in the synagogues of Galilee and the positive response it aroused (verses 14–15; compare Mark 1:14–15). Luke then recounts a meeting in the synagogue at Nazareth, paralleled in Matthew 13:53–8; Mark 6:1–6a at a later stage in the ministry of Jesus. Luke orders his narrative in this way to highlight from the beginning the paradox of Jesus's gracious, saving message and the opposition it provoked. His claim to be fulfilling the prophecy of Isaiah 61:1–2 met with amazement (verses 16–22), but then fury. People in the

---

[1] Josephus, *War* 3.35–8 identifies first-century Galilee as the northern region of *Jewish* settlement, surrounded by Phoenicia in the west and north, the Decapolis in the east and Samaria in the south. Lloyd, *Itinerant Jesus*, 65–206, discusses archaeological evidence for Jewish ethnicity in Galilee, settlements, population density and travel options.

LUKE

synagogue were angry when he suggested that they might reject him and
that the salvation promised to Israel might be taken to the Gentiles (verses
23–8). Jesus's narrow escape from antagonism and death in Nazareth (verses
29–30) casts an ominous shadow over his ministry to come (see 2:34–5),
but he continues on the way established for him by God in Scripture.

Jesus rejected at Nazareth

14 Jesus returned to Galilee in the power of the Spirit, and news about him spread through the whole countryside. **15** He was teaching in their synagogues, and everyone praised him.

16 He went to Nazareth, where he had been brought up, and on the Sabbath day he went into the synagogue, as was his custom. He stood up to read, **17** and the scroll of the prophet Isaiah was handed to him. Unrolling it, he found the place where it is written:

18 'The Spirit of the Lord is on me,
      because he has anointed me
   to proclaim good news to the
      poor.
   He has sent me to proclaim
      freedom for the prisoners
   and recovery of sight for the
      blind,
   to set the oppressed free,
19 to proclaim the year of the
      Lord's favour.'[f]

20 Then he rolled up the scroll, gave it back to the attendant and sat down. The eyes of everyone in the synagogue were fastened on him. **21** He began by saying to them, 'Today this scripture is fulfilled in your hearing.'

22 All spoke well of him and were amazed at the gracious words that came from his lips. 'Isn't this Joseph's son?' they asked.

23 Jesus said to them, 'Surely you will quote this proverb to me: "Physician, heal yourself!" And you will tell me, "Do here in your home town what we have heard that you did in Capernaum."'

24 'Truly I tell you,' he continued, 'no prophet is accepted in his home town. **25** I assure you that there were many widows in Israel in Elijah's time, when the sky was shut for three and a half years and there was a severe famine throughout the land. **26** Yet Elijah was not sent to any of them, but to a widow in Zarephath in the region of Sidon. **27** And there were many in Israel with leprosy[g] in the time of Elisha the prophet, yet not one of them was cleansed – only Naaman the Syrian.'

28 All the people in the synagogue were furious when they heard this. **29** They got up, drove him out of the town, and took him to the brow of the hill on which the town was built, in order to throw him off the cliff. **30** But he walked right through the crowd and went on his way.

------

[f] 19 Isaiah 61:1,2 (see Septuagint); Isaiah 58:6
[g] 27 The Greek word traditionally translated *leprosy* was used for various diseases affecting the skin.

14–15. Luke's summary introduction to this section begins with a geographical and theological link to what has gone before (compare Matthew 4:12–17; Mark 1:14–15). Jesus returned to Galilee from his baptism in the Jordan and his testing in the Judean wilderness 'in the power of the Spirit'. The Spirit who anointed him at his baptism (3:22) and led him into direct confrontation with the devil (4:1) empowered him to begin a ministry of 'teaching in their synagogues'.[2] In 4:43 are we specifically told that he proclaimed 'the good news of the kingdom of God'. The initial result of this ministry was that 'news about him spread through the whole countryside' and 'everyone praised him.'

16–17. Luke now focuses on Jesus's ministry in the synagogue at Nazareth, 'where he had been brought up' (1:26; 2:4, 39, 51–2). The narrative is positioned here with more detail than in the parallel accounts for thematic reasons.[3] The pattern of first-century synagogue services is much disputed, but Acts 13:15 testifies to the centrality of readings from the Law and the Prophets, followed by an exposition or 'word of exhortation', and Matthew 6:5 mentions prayer. When Jesus stood up to read, 'the scroll of the prophet Isaiah was handed to him'. Unrolling it, he found the place he was looking for, perhaps the passage set for the day or one he chose for himself. It is likely that a longer section of Isaiah 61 was read but that Jesus only drew attention to the significance of the first two verses.

18–19. The quotation from Isaiah 61:1–2a follows the Greek version (LXX), but it leaves out 'to bind up the broken hearted', which is covered by parallel expressions: 'to proclaim good news to the poor, . . . to proclaim freedom for the prisoners and recovery of sight to the blind'. Words from Isaiah 58:6d are added ('to set the oppressed free') to emphasise the note of liberation. Without reference to 'the day of vengeance', the quotation suggests that Jesus's primary task was to proclaim the Lord's 'favour' (*dektos*, 'approval'), offering his people salvation in the face of imminent judgment, as John predicted (3:17). Judgment becomes a more prominent theme in Luke 10:8–15; 11:29–32 and subsequent passages. The prophet reveals

---

[2] The word *synagōgē* can describe either 'a place of assembly' or those who gather together (BDAG). Fitzmyer, *Luke I–IX*, 523–4, gives a brief description of the development and purpose of this Jewish institution. See also A. Runesson, 'Synagogue', *DJG*, 903–11.

[3] Luke could have used another source that paralleled Mark 6:1–6a; Matthew 13:53–58 and contained greater detail of the same event (see Marshall, *Luke*, 179–80; Bock, *Luke 1–9:50*, 397). Luke's narrative begins without a time reference and is presented as an example of Jesus's synagogue preaching with an unexpectedly hostile response.

that the Spirit of the Lord had anointed him 'to proclaim good news to the poor' (*euaggelisasthai ptōchois*). His task was to announce salvation to Israel at the time of the Babylonian Exile, 'suffering and in great need', as David Seccombe puts it.[4] The parallel charge 'to proclaim freedom for the prisoners' pointed even more clearly to 'release' (*aphesis*) from this captivity. 'Recovery of sight for the blind' was another parallel, since prisoners regularly lived in darkness (the Hebrew version says 'release from darkness for the prisoners'). The call to 'set the oppressed free' repeats the emphasis on liberation, alluding to the Jubilee provision in Leviticus 25:8–13; Deuteronomy 15:1–2. Seccombe argues that the Lord's salvation is presented in terms of '*his* Jubilee, a period in which he intervenes to bring freedom to his people'.[5] Isaiah's prophecy was not a challenge for God's people in exile to implement a Jubilee, but a way of portraying God's intention to release *them* from captivity. This began in the sixth century BC, when many Jews returned to their homeland, but the renewal predicted by the prophet was only partially experienced. At the time of Jesus, many were still looking for the messianic 'consolation of Israel' (2:25) and the 'redemption of Jerusalem' (2:38). Since Jesus did not set out to liberate his people in any political sense, we are bound to search carefully in Luke's narrative to discover the true nature of the freedom he proclaimed.

20–21. When Jesus 'rolled up the scroll, gave it back to the attendant and sat down', the 'eyes of everyone in the synagogue were fastened on him'. The thrust of his sermon was, 'Today this scripture is fulfilled in your hearing,' implying that he would bring to his people the liberation they needed. The words spoken to him at his baptism suggested that he was anointed with the Holy Spirit as Messiah (see Isaiah 11:2; Acts 4:26–7) and Servant of the Lord (see Isaiah 42:1), but the focus in this text is on his anointing as the prophetic liberator of his people (see 4:24–7; 7:16, 39; 9:8, 19; 13:33; 24:19).[6] These roles overlap in Luke's portrayal of Jesus. The word 'Today' (*sēmeron*),

---

[4] Seccombe, *The Poor*, 41. The poor in Isaiah 61:1 are 'the dispirited nation of the restoration': 'those who mourn in Zion' (61:3) are not a group among the people, but the people itself. Their situation was 'in many ways analogous to the state of affairs at the time of Jesus' (40).

[5] Seccombe, *The Poor*, 53 (my emphasis). The blending of Isaiah 58:6d ('to set the oppressed free') with Isaiah 61:2a ('to proclaim the year of the Lord's favour) emphasises this. The DSS document 11QMelchizedek 9 also links the idea of a Jubilee release of debts with eschatological salvation. See J. B. Green and N. Perrin, 'Jubilee', *DJG*, 450–52.

[6] Luke 9:30–35 and Acts 3:22–3 point to Jesus as the anticipated prophet like Moses (Deuteronomy 18:15, 19). See Nolland, *Luke 1–9:20*, 196; Tannehill, *Narrative Unity* 1, 96–9.

together with the tense of the verb 'fulfilled' (*peplērōtai*), stress the immediate availability of the salvation Jesus proclaimed. The promised redemption was offered to everyone present ('in your hearing'), though they needed to believe what they heard if the benefits were to be experienced.

In the narratives that follow, Luke progressively shows how Jesus fulfilled Isaiah's prophecy. Proclaiming good news to the poor was closely associated with the release of people from demonic powers (4:33–5, 41) and from the consequences of sin through healing, resurrection from death and forgiveness (4:38–40; 5:12–26; 7:11–17, 36–50). Jesus's allusion to Isaiah 61:1 in a later review of his ministry (7:20–23) clarifies the link between his preaching and his mighty works. He both proclaimed and demonstrated the availability of this liberation for those who believed in him.

22–3. Initially, 'all spoke well of him' (*emartyroun autō*, 'were testifying to him') and 'were amazed at the gracious words that came from his lips'. 'Gracious words' (*tois logois tēs charitos*, 'words of grace') most likely refers to the gracious content of his teaching, rather than his manner (see Acts 14:3; 20:32). But the questioning of the crowd ('Isn't this Joseph's son?') exposed an element of doubt, even contempt, which caused them to be offended by him (Matthew 13:56–7a; Mark 6:3). They could not accept that one of their own might be the promised deliverer. Jesus spoke with prophetic insight about what they were thinking ('Surely you will quote this proverb to me: "Physician, heal yourself!"').[7] This implied that he should attend to faults in his own life before presuming to preach to them! Jesus further anticipated that they would say, 'Do here in your home town (*patris*) what we have heard that you did in Capernaum' (see 4:31–41). He knew that people would demand miracles to dispel their unbelief and he refused to oblige (Matthew 13:58; Mark 6:4–6; compare Luke 11:16; 22:64; 23:8).

24–7. A solemn warning is introduced with the declaration, 'Truly I tell you' (*amēn legō hymin*, as in 12:37; 18:17, 29; 21:32; 23:43): 'no prophet is accepted in his home town'.[8] A longer form of this saying can be found in Mark 6:4; Matthew 13:57, without the opening assertion (see John 4:44). Jesus implies that he is a prophet like Elijah and Elisha, highlighting the way they became a source of blessing to those outside their homeland (*patris*). Elijah predicted a great drought as the judgment

---

[7] Different forms of this 'proverb' (*parabolē*) or wise saying can be found in Greek and rabbinic literature of the time (see Bock, *Luke 1:1–9:50*, 416).

[8] Jesus's use of *amēn* implies 'a finality and authority in the words that follow which is quite unparalleled and transcends that of any religious leaders of his day' (Robert H. Stein, *The Method and Message of Jesus' Teachings* (Philadelphia: Westminster, 1978), 117).

of God on his rebellious people, and a severe famine followed (1 Kings 17:1–6).[9] There were many widows in Israel in Elijah's time, yet he was not sent to bring relief to any of them, 'but to a widow in Zarephath in the region of Sidon' (1 Kings 17:7–24). Ministry to a Gentile, rather than to a Jew, is further illustrated in the example of Elisha. There were many in Israel with leprosy in his time, 'yet not one of them was cleansed – only Naaman the Syrian' (2 Kings 5). The power and grace of God was experienced by those who sought it, but not by those in Israel who rejected the prophets and disdained them.

28–30. 'All the people in the synagogue were furious when they heard this.' The suggestion that they might be like their ancestors who had rejected the prophets immediately proved true: 'They got up, drove him out of the town, and took him to the brow of the hill on which the town was built, in order to throw him off the cliff.' Nazareth is built on a slope and surrounded by hills. Nolland observes that if the intention was to treat him as a false prophet (Deuteronomy 13:5), 'the cliff' need only to have been high enough for a stoning.[10] Jesus's escape ('he walked right through the crowd and went on his way') illustrated his determination to continue his mission in the face of such unbelief (see 9:51; 13:31–3).

THE DELIVERANCE PROCLAIMED BY JESUS

When Jesus applied Isaiah 61:1–2 to himself, he was claiming to be the Spirit-anointed fulfiller of the end-time salvation anticipated by the prophet. Even as he spoke, he implicitly offered this to everyone in the synagogue. Salvation was expressed in terms of a Jubilee-type release from the bondage in which his contemporaries found themselves. Jesus fulfilled this prophecy by addressing both the physical and spiritual needs of those he encountered, providing forgiveness of sins and release from every power that hindered peace with God, a life of godly service and eternal life. His works of healing and restoration had immediate social and spiritual benefits for those involved, but they also pointed forward to the promised perfection of a new creation (Isaiah 11:6–9; 35; 65:17–25). Those who saw their need for what he offered came to him in faith and were taught this 'now and not yet' perspective (6:20–26). At the same time,

---

[9] Elijah was told to present himself to the king in the third year of the drought and rain would come (18:1). Jesus's reference to the sky being closed for three and a half years allows for the outworking of events in 1 Kings 18:2–46. See Bock, *Luke 1:1–9:50*, 421.

[10] Nolland, *Luke 1–9:20*, 193–4, 201.

Jesus boldly exposed the unbelieving attitudes of those he had grown up with and warned them about the danger of rejecting him. Murderous rage was aroused when he suggested that they might treat him as their ancestors treated the prophets, miss out on the promised salvation and witness it being offered to the nations (4:23–9).

This narrative anticipates the rejection that Jesus experienced throughout his ministry, culminating in his betrayal and death. It also anticipates the rejection of his followers and their message at various stages throughout the narrative of Acts and beyond. Some interpreters have understood this passage to be essentially a call to liberate the socially and politically oppressed, but that was not the message of Jesus in Luke or of his apostles in Acts. The challenge for Christians in every generation is to proclaim the kingdom of God as they did, with all its 'now and not yet' implications. Nevertheless, God's saving activity in Jesus must influence the way we live and testify to the gospel in the social and political context in which we find ourselves. Speaking from his African experience, Paul John Isaak argues:

> God's creation is social and cultural as well as natural and physical. As a consequence, we have to take the secular world and the civil community seriously. The church's social ministry should not be limited to charitable activities that merely bind up the wound of society's victims. We should be actively engaged in shaping society to prevent such wounds.[11]

2. Authority in word and deed (Luke 4:31–44)

The call of Jesus's first disciples is not reported until 5:1–11 (compare Mark 1:16–20; Matthew 4:18–22). Luke first narrates the events of a single Sabbath day in Capernaum and its sequel, mostly following Mark 1:21–39 (see also Matthew 4:23–5; 7:28–9; 8:14–17). The effect of this is to fill out the summary report in verses 14–15 by illustrating the *positive* impact of Jesus's synagogue teaching and the way 'the power of the Spirit' was shown in exorcisms and healings (verses 31–41). These extraordinary events begin to illustrate what Jesus meant when he applied the prophecy of Isaiah 61:1–2 to himself (verses 16–21). The summary in verses 42–4 forms an inclusion

---

[11] Isaak, 'Luke', 1237. The ability to shape society will vary from culture to culture, but the challenge is to express God's justice and grace in whatever circumstance we live.

with verses 14–15 and also with verse 18, clarifying that preaching was his priority and that proclaiming the good news of the kingdom of God was another way of speaking about proclaiming good news to the poor.

Jesus drives out an impure spirit

31 Then he went down to Capernaum, a town in Galilee, and on the Sabbath he taught the people. **32** They were amazed at his teaching, because his words had authority.

33 In the synagogue there was a man possessed by a demon, an impure spirit. He cried out at the top of his voice, **34** 'Go away! What do you want with us, Jesus of Nazareth? Have you come to destroy us? I know who you are – the Holy One of God!'

35 'Be quiet!' Jesus said sternly. 'Come out of him!' Then the demon threw the man down before them all and came out without injuring him.

36 All the people were amazed and said to each other, 'What words these are! With authority and power he gives orders to impure spirits and they come out!' **37** And the news about him spread throughout the surrounding area.

Jesus heals many

38 Jesus left the synagogue and went to the home of Simon. Now Simon's mother-in-law was suffering from a high fever, and they asked Jesus to help her. **39** So he bent over her and rebuked the fever, and it left her. She got up at once and began to wait on them.

40 At sunset, the people brought to Jesus all who had various kinds of illness, and laying his hands on each one, he healed them. **41** Moreover, demons came out of many people, shouting, 'You are the Son of God!' But he rebuked them and would not allow them to speak, because they knew he was the Messiah.

42 At daybreak, Jesus went out to a solitary place. The people were looking for him and when they came to where he was, they tried to keep him from leaving them. **43** But he said, 'I must proclaim the good news of the kingdom of God to the other towns also, because that is why I was sent.' **44** And he kept on preaching in the synagogues of Judea.

31–2. Luke presents this as a return visit to Capernaum (see verse 23), whereas Mark 1:21–8 records it as the first example of Jesus's teaching in a Galilean synagogue.[12] Both Gospels emphasise that the people 'were amazed at his teaching, because his words had authority'. There was a prophetic

---

[12] Capernaum is mentioned again in 7:1; 10:15. It was on the northwest shore of Lake Gennesaret (also called the Sea of Galilee or Sea of Tiberias). See R. Riesner, 'Galilee', *DJG*, 297–9. Lloyd, *Itinerant Jesus*, 148–53 reviews evidence for a first-century synagogue there and estimates a population of 1,200 to 2,500 at that time.

character to his message, as illustrated in verses 21–8 (see Mark 1:22). This reflected the commission and empowerment he had received at his baptism (3:21). A similar response occurs at the end of the account (verse 36), where a different Greek term is used to express the amazement of the congregation at his authority and power to exorcise demons (see 9:43).

33–4. 'In the synagogue there was a man possessed by a demon, an impure spirit' (ESV, 'who had the spirit of an unclean demon'). The presence of an 'unclean demon' in a synagogue is remarkable. The adjective *akathartos* ('unclean, impure') describes the moral and spiritual influence that such a 'spirit' might have on an individual and a congregation. God promised to remove such influences on the 'day' when he acted to cleanse his people from sin and impurity (Zechariah 13:1–2). Luke regularly uses the expression 'impure spirit' (4:33, 36; 6:18; 8:29; 9:42; 11:24–6; 13:11), and sometimes 'evil spirit' (7:21; 8:2).[13] Greek *pneuma* can refer to the human spirit (1:17, 47, 80; 8:55; 23:46), which may be controlled and directed by the Spirit of God (1:41, 67; 2:25, 26, 27; 4:1, 14, 18; 10:21; 12:12) or by Satan and his minions. More than the other evangelists, Luke uses the term *daimonion* ('demon') to refer to an evil, supernatural force controlling a person's spirit (4:33, 41; 7:33; 8:2, 27, 29, 30, 33, 35, 38; 9:1, 42, 49; 10:17). Sometimes the presence of a demon is linked to sickness or a physical impediment (9:38–42; 11:14; 13:11), so that the driving out of the demon brings both spiritual and physical healing. In other contexts, the casting out of demons and physical healing are associated but distinct activities (4:40–41; 6:18; 7:21; 8:2; 9:1; 13:32). When Jesus is accused of casting out demons in the name of 'Beelzebul, the prince of demons', he makes it clear that demons are under the control of Satan, so that they can only be driven out by the power of God (11:15–20; compare 13:16; Acts 10:38).

At Capernaum, the demon's presence was recognised when the man 'cried out at the top of his voice' (see 9:39). He first expressed hostility to Jesus and his authoritative teaching ('Go away!'). The next cry denied any common interest ('What do you want with us, Jesus of Nazareth?' (ESV, 'What have you to do with us?')).[14] The plural 'us' could refer to the man and the demon, but it more likely suggests that the whole realm

---

[13] Fitzmyer, *Luke I–IX*, 544–5, notes Aramaic counterparts in the DSS. W. Foerster, 'δαίμων, δαιμόνιον', *TDNT* 2: 10–16, outlines the development of demonology in Judaism and explores the link with angelology. See also R. Kotansky, 'Demonology', *DNTB*, 269–73.

[14] NIV ('Go away') is a contextually justifiable rendering of the Greek *Ha* (CSB, 'Leave us alone'). The second cry recalls the words spoken by the widow to Elijah in 1 Kings 17:18 LXX, expressing a sense of alienation.

of the demonic is under threat since Jesus has come. This fear is based on a supernatural recognition of his identity and intention ('Have you come to destroy us? I know who you are – the Holy One of God!'). The first expression could be a statement ('you have come to destroy us'), rather than a question: they acknowledge that a battle has begun, which they cannot win. 'The Holy One of God' is an unusually perceptive way of addressing Jesus (see Mark 1:24; John 6:69; Acts 4:27). It recalls the angel's words in 1:35 and prepares the reader for the response of Peter in 5:8. As Nolland suggests, 'the demon is aware that the holy and the unclean are implacably opposed'.[15]

35. Jesus responded with a stern command: 'Be quiet! . . . Come out of him!' The verb *epetimēsen* ('rebuke, reproach') normally expresses strong disapproval or censure (BDAG; 9:55; 17:3; 18:15), but its use in exorcism (4:35, 41; 9:42) suggests to Fitzmyer 'the pronouncement of a commanding word whereby God or his spokesman brings evil powers into submission'.[16] Jesus commanded silence because he did not wish his identity and calling to be revealed by an evil spirit ('Be quiet!'). He then released the man from its control with a simple imperative ('Come out of him!'). This illustrates one aspect of the freedom from oppression Jesus had promised in fulfilling Isaiah 61:1–2 (see verses 18–21). The demon's last act of defiance was to throw the man down 'before them all', and Jesus's superior authority was shown by the fact that the demon 'came out without injuring him'.

36–7. 'All the people were amazed and said to each other, 'What words these are!' The Greek might be better rendered, 'What kind of command is this?' Jesus does not use magic potions, incantations or rituals to exorcise demonic forces, as was common in his day.[17] He simply utters a commanding word: 'With authority and power he gives orders to impure spirits and they come out.' Todd Klutz argues that 'authority' (*exousia*) relates to Jesus's 'prerogative to issue commands to the unclean spirits', while his 'power' (*dynamis*) is evident 'in the spirits' obedience to these commands'.[18] As a result, 'the news [*ēchos*, 'report'] about him spread throughout the surrounding area'. The focus on Jesus's authoritative word continues in verses 38–44.

---

[15] Nolland, *Luke 1–9:20*, 209.

[16] Fitzmyer, *Luke I–IX*, 546. Different command words are used for exorcism in 4:36; 8:29.

[17] See Nolland, *Luke 1–9:20*, 204; Bock, *Luke 1:1–9:50*, 427, 434, note 19; Todd Klutz, *The Exorcism Stories in Luke–Acts: A Sociostylistic Reading* (Cambridge: Cambridge University Press, 2004), 61–78.

[18] Klutz, *Exorcism Stories*, 48–9.

38–9. 'Jesus left the synagogue and went to the home of Simon.' Luke follows Mark 1:29 in recording this encounter with Simon, although he omits any reference to James, John and Andrew here. The seriousness of the situation is highlighted ('Simon's mother-in-law was suffering from a high fever'), together with the faith of those who 'asked Jesus to help her'. She was probably a widow, living with Peter because she had no sons of her own to care for her. The description of her healing is unusual: 'he bent over her and rebuked the fever'. Luke uses the verb 'rebuked' (*epetimēsen*, as in verse 35) to refer to the sovereign command of Jesus. The repetition of this term could imply a demonic causation (see verse 41; 13:16; Acts 10:38), though the process is otherwise different from an exorcism. More broadly, use of this term in relation to sickness, demonic possession and even 'the wind and the raging waters' (8:24) suggests that Jesus opposes everything that hinders human flourishing. The immediacy and completeness of the cure is stressed by saying, 'it left her' and that she 'got up at once and began to wait on them'.

40–41. Luke's summary of that evening of ministry in Capernaum makes a clear distinction between Jesus's healing activity and his exorcisms (see Mark 1:32–4). 'At sunset, the people brought to Jesus all who had various kinds of illness.' Healing is associated with 'laying his hands on each one'.[19] This gesture could express both compassion and hope, though it might also represent his power to heal. 'Moreover' (*de kai*, 'and also'), 'demons came out of many people, shouting "You are the Son of God!"' This echoes the cry of recognition in verse 34 ('the Holy One of God'), though the messianic implications are clearer here. Jesus 'rebuked them and would not allow them to speak, because they knew he was the Messiah'. He did not want them to be the agents of his self-disclosure! Luke's presentation of Jesus's divine sonship began with the angelic promise in 1:31–3, amplified by the promise in 1:35 that 'the holy one to be born will be called the Son of God'. Properly understood, the messiahship of Jesus relates to his divine origin and achievement of a kingdom that will never end. 'Son of God' in Luke must be understood in this comprehensive sense.

42–3. This account of Jesus's departure from Capernaum appears to be based on Mark 1:35–9. 'At daybreak, Jesus went out to a solitary place,' though Luke does not mention his intention to pray at this point. There

---

[19] Fitzmyer, *Luke I–IX*, 553, observes that 'the imposition of hands as a gesture of healing is unknown in the OT and in rabbinic literature, but it has turned up in 1QapGen 20:28–29'.

is no mention of Simon and his companions searching for him either, but Luke simply says, 'The people were looking for him and when they came to where he was, they tried to keep him from leaving them.' Jesus's response reveals the priority of his mission: 'But he said, "I must proclaim the good news of the kingdom of God to the other towns also, because that is why I was sent."' People were apparently seeking more healings and exorcisms, but Jesus asserted the vital importance of preaching the kingdom of God as extensively as possible. Two verbal expressions indicate his calling to do this: 'I must' (*dei*, as in 2:49) and 'I was sent' (*apestalēn*, as in 4:18). Luke uses the term 'proclaim good news' (*euaggelisasthai*) to describe the essential task (see also 1:19; 2:10; 3:18; 4:18; 7:22; 8:1; 9:6; 16:16; 20:1).

The term 'the kingdom of God' does not occur in the Old Testament, but it picks up the biblical notion that God is lord of heaven and earth and that he blesses those who live under his rule. Human beings reject him and seek to go their own way, bringing judgment upon themselves and alienation from God. Speaking though the prophets, however, God promised to come and restore his rule over rebellious Israel and the rest of the nations for their good (Isaiah 40:1–11; 52:7–10). He would do this through a son, who would bring justice and righteousness to the whole world and reign for ever over God's people (Isaiah 9:6–7; 11:1–5). Both judgment and salvation would be involved in this end-time visitation. Every form of evil would be cast out to enable his people to live in a renewed creation (Isaiah 11:6–9; 65:17–25). Luke has already clarified that the kingdom refers to the eternal rule promised to Jesus as the anticipated Son of David or Messiah (1:31–3, citing 2 Samuel 7:13–14a). At his baptism, Jesus was anointed with the Spirit for this role and function (3:21–2).[20]

44. Luke's conclusion that Jesus 'kept on preaching in the synagogues of Judea' is unexpected. People came to Jesus from the region of Judea and Jerusalem at different stages in his Galilean ministry (5:17; 6:17;) and news about him spread 'throughout Judea and the surrounding country' (7:17). When Luke refers to a proactive synagogue ministry in 'Judea' here, he probably uses the term to refer to 'the whole of Palestine' (see 1:5; 23:5; Acts 10:37).[21]

---

[20] 'The kingdom of God' is mentioned again in 6:20; 7:28; 8:1, 10; 9:2, 11, 27, 60, 62; 10:9, 11; 11:20; 13: 18, 20, 28, 29; 14:15; 16:16; 17:20 (twice), 21; 18:16, 17, 24, 25, 29; 19:11; 21:31; 22:16, 18; 23:51. 'The kingdom' is mentioned in 11:2; 12:31, 32; 22:29, 30; 23:42. See J. B. Green, 'Kingdom of God/Heaven', *DJG*, 468–81.
[21] Nolland, *Luke 1–9:20*, 216. Some manuscripts read 'of Galilee', following the

EXORCISMS, HEALINGS AND THE KINGDOM OF GOD

Demonic forces are real to people in other cultures, but, as Darrell Bock observes, in the contemporary Western world, 'demonic forces are explained away, rationalized as vestiges of an ancient worldview, or placed in modern categories of mental illness'.[22] But such explanations do not engage seriously enough with the evidence of the Gospels. Jesus believed in the demonic world and had important things to say about its defeat (10:17–20; 11:14–26; 13:10–17; John 12:31–3). Luke normally distinguishes between demonic possession, sickness and disability in three ways. First, the demon-possessed address Jesus as 'the Holy One of God' (verse 34) or 'the Son of God' (verse 41; see 8:28), acknowledging his divine origin and messiahship. Those who are sick call him 'Lord', meaning 'Sir' or 'Master' (5:12; 17:13), and 'Son of David' (18:38), not perceiving the full significance of what they are saying. Second, the sick eagerly seek Jesus's help, but the demon-possessed express hostility, alienation and the desire for him to leave them alone. Third, although the physical and psychological effects of demon possession vary from person to person, the common factor is an attempt to resist and control Jesus by speaking his name. His proclamation of the kingdom of God signalled the ultimate defeat of every form of spiritual oppression, while his healings and exorcisms demonstrated his authority to bring the transforming rule of God to bear on every aspect of human life. Healing and exorcism in the name of Jesus continued in the apostolic era, although preaching the gospel was the dominant way of releasing people from Satan's dominion and its effects (Acts 3; 5:12–16; 8:4–8; 14:8–18; 19:8–12). If Satan is 'the spirit who is now at work in those who are disobedient' (Ephesians 2:2), demon possession may be evident today in different cultural, social and personal manifestations. Christians should be alert to 'the devil's schemes' and play their part in opposing his evil influence wherever they see it, clothed with the armour of the gospel (Ephesians 6:10–20).[23]

---

parallels in Matthew 4:23; Mark 1:39, but the harder reading ('of Judea') is found in a range of better attested manuscripts. See Metzger, *Textual Commentary*, 114–15.
[22] Bock, *Luke 1:1–9:50*, 426. Compare R. H. Bell, 'Demon, Devil, Satan', *DJG*, 193–202.
[23] Isaak, 'Luke', 1240, offers an interesting reflection on the way health and healing in the African world is perceived to be more than physical. True health is seen to involve 'spiritual, mental, physical, social and environmental harmony'.

3. Peter and his companions drawn into the mission of Jesus (Luke 5:1–11)

This narrative somewhat parallels Mark 1:16–20 and Matthew 4:18–22, but it has extra features.[24] According to Mark, the first thing Jesus did when he came into Galilee proclaiming the good news of God's kingdom was to call Simon, Andrew, James and John to follow him and be sent to out to 'fish for people'. However, as Fitzmyer observes, Luke focuses specifically on how Simon as the future leader of the Twelve (6:12–16; 9:18–20; 22:31–2) is 'brought personally into the sphere of Jesus's mighty power, and that experience becomes the basis of a promise that is made to him'.[25] Simon's previous association with Jesus is mentioned in 4:38–9 and assumed in 5:1–5. Luke's narrative explains why Simon and his fishing partners were attracted to Jesus and immediately willing to leave everything and follow him.

Jesus calls his first disciples

5 One day as Jesus was standing by the Lake of Gennesaret,[a] the people were crowding round him and listening to the word of God. **2** He saw at the water's edge two boats, left there by the fishermen, who were washing their nets. **3** He got into one of the boats, the one belonging to Simon, and asked him to put out a little from the shore. Then he sat down and taught the people from the boat.

4 When he had finished speaking, he said to Simon, 'Put out into deep water, and let down the nets for a catch.'

5 Simon answered, 'Master, we've worked hard all night and haven't caught anything. But because you say so, I will let down the nets.'

6 When they had done so, they caught such a large number of fish that their nets began to break. **7** So they signalled to their partners in the other boat to come and help them, and they came and filled both boats so full that they began to sink.

8 When Simon Peter saw this, he fell at Jesus' knees and said, 'Go away from me, Lord; I am a sinful man!' **9** For he and all his companions were

---

[24] Bock, *Luke 1:1–9:50*, 450–51, considers the possibility that there was an initial calling of these disciples and then the miraculous catch of fish to assure them of success in the task Jesus had given them. Luke may have incorporated the miracle story in a framework based on Mark 1:16–20 (see Marshall, *Luke*, 201).

[25] Fitzmyer, *Luke I–IX*, 562. He concludes that the same piece of gospel tradition has been developed independently in John 21:1–11. But it seems equally plausible to argue that there were two similar events, one in relation to the call of Simon (Luke) and the other to reinstate him after his betrayal (John), with deliberate echoes of the first.

astonished at the catch of fish they had taken, **10** and so were James and John, the sons of Zebedee, Simon's partners.

Then Jesus said to Simon, 'Don't be afraid; from now on you will fish for people.' **11** So they pulled their boats up on shore, left everything and followed him.

_____

a 1 That is, Sea of Galilee

1. The time reference is vague ('One day'), but the thematic and geographical links with 4:42–3 are clear. Luke uses the same introductory expression to bind together the passages that follow in a loose fashion (5:12, 17; 6:1, 6, 12). Jesus is in Galilee, 'standing by the Lake of Gennesaret', not far from Capernaum.[26] Only here in this Gospel are the people by the lakeside, 'crowding around him and listening to the word of God'. Luke introduces the term 'the word of God' to describe the message preached by Jesus (see 8:11, 21; 11:28) and the earliest believers (Acts 4:31; 6:2, 7; 8:14; 11:1; 12:24; 13:5, 7, 44, 46, 48; 16:32; 17:13; 18:11).[27] Contextually, 'the word of God' means 'the good news of the kingdom of God' (4:43). Although the Greek term (_ho logos tou theou_) could mean 'the message about God', it more likely means 'the message from God', expressing its divine origin and authority (see the 'word of God' that came to John the Baptist (3:2)). Use of the term here is significant because Jesus is about to invite others to share in his ministry of the word. Those whom he calls to this task first need to be impacted by his message themselves.

2–3. Two boats at the water's edge are mentioned in preparation for verse 7. The fact that the fishermen were washing their nets indicates that it was morning; they were no longer trying to catch fish and their boats were lying idle. When Jesus got into one of the boats, specifically 'the one belonging to Simon, and asked him to put out a little from the shore', he was intent on engaging with Simon personally once more (see 4:38–9). But his broader aim was to sit and teach the people from Simon's boat (see Mark 4:1). His voice would have been amplified over the water and he could have been seen by a large crowd.[28]

_____

[26] '_Gennesaret_ is the Greek name of a small, fertile, and heavily populated district west of the lake that some writers refer to as the Sea of Galilee. From the district the name was extended to the lake' (Fitzmyer, _Luke I–IX_, 565). Compare Lloyd, _Itinerant Jesus_, 176–7.

[27] See Peterson, _Acts_, 70–75; Edwards, _Luke_, 152. In Matthew 15:6; Mark 7:13; John 10:35, 'the word of God' more broadly refers to Old Testament Scripture.

[28] Edwards, _Luke_, 153, notes the existence of a natural amphitheatre near Capernaum, where the land slopes gently down to a natural bay, which can 'transmit a human

4–5. Jesus's control of the situation is stressed: 'When he had finished speaking, he said to Simon, "Put out into deep water, and let down the nets for a catch."' This command is followed by the professional fisherman's cautious reply: 'Master, we've worked hard all night and haven't caught anything.' Jesus is called 'Master' (*epistata*) here and in 8:24, 45; 9:33, 49, 17:13 (parallels in other Gospels are 'Teacher' or 'Rabbi'), expressing confidence in his spiritual authority. Peter obeys in spite of his reticence ('But because you say so, I will let down the nets'), presumably encouraged by his previous experience of Jesus's healing power (4:31–42). What happens next may be more of 'a miracle of knowledge' than a sign of his control over nature (see 8:22–5), as Bock suggests.[29] Jesus knows where the fish are!

6–7. The enormity of the catch is indicated in two ways. First, when they put out into deep water and put down their nets, 'they caught such a large number of fish that their nets began to break'. The plurals here ('they . . . their') suggest the presence of Simon's brother Andrew with him in the boat (see verses 9–10; Matthew 4:18; Mark 1:16; Luke 6:14). Second, 'they signalled to their partners in the other boat to come and help them, and they came and filled both boats so full that they began to sink'. These fishing 'partners' (*metochoi*) are identified as James and John, the sons of Zebedee, in verse 10. As Nolland notes, the miracle of this catch is 'only fully known when the fish have been drawn from the water'.[30]

8. The double name Simon Peter is used in anticipation of 6:14 (see also Acts 10:5, 18, 32; 11:13). Simon's significance in the story of Jesus and the early church is determined by his response on this occasion. When he saw the amazing catch, he fell at Jesus's knees in the boat and said, 'Go away from me, Lord; I am a sinful man!' This is Luke's first use of the term 'sinner' (*hamartōlos*), a notion that clearly interests him (5:30, 32; 6:32, 33, 34; 7:34, 37, 39; 13:2; 15:1, 2, 7, 10; 18:13; 19:7; 24:7). The expression 'Go away from me' recalls the demon-possessed man's supernatural perception of Jesus's identity and sense of belonging to a different spiritual realm (4:34). But Peter's reaction is more like that of Isaiah, when he was confronted with a vision of the holiness of God and his own unworthiness to be in the presence of God (Isaiah 6:5; compare Revelation 1:17). Peter was suddenly aware of a great distance between himself and Jesus. As Tannehill observes, 'a sinful man cannot associate

---

voice effortlessly to several thousand people'. Edwards also gives details about the nets used at this time.

[29] Bock, *Luke 1:1–9:50*, 457. See, however, my comment on 7:10.

[30] Nolland, *Luke 1–9:20*, 222.

with one who wields divine power'.[31] Peter had previously seen Jesus do amazing things, but this time, as Kent Hughes discerns, 'Jesus ministered in Peter's personal universe – his sea, his boat, his nets – and so the significance came to him as never before.'[32] When he called Jesus 'Lord' (*Kyrie*, see 5:12; 7:6; 9:54, 59, 61), the meaning may be no more than 'Master' (see verse 5). But Peter had edged closer to understanding the significance of who Jesus was, even if he had a way to go in perceiving the full meaning of 'Lord' as a title (see 8:25).

9–10. Simon and 'all his companions were astonished at the catch of fish they had taken'. The latter appear to be those in Simon's boat, because James and John the sons of Zebedee are then mentioned as Simon's fishing 'partners' (*koinōnoi*) in the other boat. They too would soon be designated as apostles (6:14) and would appear again at later stages in the Gospel (8:51; 9:28, 54) and Acts (1:13; 12:2). Even though Simon is the central character, the others are drawn to follow Jesus with him. The first words to Simon ('Don't be afraid') suggest that he has found favour with God and is about to discover God's will for his life (see 1:13, 30; 2:10). The phrase 'from now on' indicates a new beginning for Peter and his companions, replacing, 'Come, follow me' in Mark 1:17; Matthew 4:19. The simple promise, 'you will fish for people', implies a new status and a calling. The fishing metaphor obviously relates to their previous vocation, signifying now a lifetime of catching *people* for the kingdom of God. Luke employs the present participle *zōgrōn* ('taking alive') to express the idea of fishing for people, whereas the other Gospels have the noun *halieis* ('fishers').[33] The implications of their calling are not clarified until they are sent out to preach his message and demonstrate his power and authority in exorcism and healing (9:1–6). They must learn to be disciples before fishing for others.

11. When they pulled their boats up on the shore, they 'left everything and followed him' (see 5:28; 18:28). Their priorities in life had been radically changed because of this experience. Simon and his companions showed that they understood the promise of Jesus to be first and foremost a call to discipleship. The verb 'follow' is regularly used throughout Luke's

---

[31] Tannehill, *Narrative Unity* 1, 204.

[32] R. Kent Hughes, *Luke: That You May Know the Truth* (Wheaton: Crossway, 2015), 167.

[33] The fishing metaphor recalls Jeremiah 16:16, where God promises to bring his people into judgment (compare Amos 4:2–3), though Jesus's application of the metaphor more likely means rescuing individuals *from* judgment through preaching his message.

Gospel in contexts where it is demonstrated that it involves accepting the teaching of Jesus, believing in him, walking in his footsteps and, in Fitzmyer's words, having 'an internal attachment and commitment to Jesus and the cause that he preaches'.[34]

ENGAGING WITH THE HOLY ONE

Luke's narrative focuses on the character and authority of Jesus: his supernatural knowledge of what will happen, his apparent closeness to God and the compelling attractiveness of his person and his promises. As people came to meet Jesus, they experienced his authority, grace and calling in different ways. Simon and his fishing partners had a remarkable encounter in the context of their everyday work, when they heard his teaching, witnessed an unprecedented catch of fish and received words of assurance effectively calling them to leave everything and follow him. In this way, they moved from having a simple trust in Jesus (verse 5) to being his committed followers (verse 11). Moreover, as Robert Tannehill asserts, 'the great catch of fish becomes a symbolic narrative of the amazingly successful mission which Simon and others will have'.[35] Simon Peter is at the centre of this calling and Jesus is the one who calls. As 'the Holy One of God' (4:34), he acts in a way that causes Peter to fall at his knees and say, 'Go away from me, Lord; I am a sinful man!' This echo of Isaiah 6 identifies Jesus with the God of Israel and suggests a commissioning of these fishermen to a prophetic role in declaring his word. The implications are drawn out more fully for them in 6:12–16; 9:1–6; 22:28–30; 24:36–49, but the pattern of discipleship revealed throughout this Gospel goes beyond the specific calling and empowerment of the twelve apostles. The living Lord Jesus continues to draw people to himself through the preaching of his word, and he invites believers to join with the earliest witnesses in spreading his message to the nations.

4. Jesus heals and forgives (Luke 5:12–26)

Luke returns to the sequence of Mark 1:40–2:12, using many words and phrases from this source, but adding new details as well. The first episode concentrates on the healing of a man with leprosy, who begged

---

[34] Fitzmyer, Luke I–IX, 569. Compare M. J. Wilkins, 'Disciples and Discipleship', DJG, 202–12.
[35] Tannehill, Narrative Unity 1, 203.

Jesus to help him (5:12–16; see also Matthew 8:1–4). Jesus charged him not to tell anyone, but to go and fulfil the cleansing process that Moses commanded. Nevertheless, this did not stop the news from spreading. Crowds of people came to hear him and be healed, so that Jesus regularly withdrew to lonely places to pray. The linked narrative about the healing of a paralysed man (5:17–26) abbreviates Mark 2:1–12 and adds a different introduction and conclusion (compare Matthew 9:1–8). Luke mentions the Pharisees and teachers of the law for the first time, preparing for the conflict Jesus has with them in 5:21–4, 30–32. Jesus implies that he is the Son of Man who has authority on earth to forgive sins, before healing the man with a simple command and amazing all present.

Jesus heals a man with leprosy

12 While Jesus was in one of the towns, a man came along who was covered with leprosy.[b] When he saw Jesus, he fell with his face to the ground and begged him, 'Lord, if you are willing, you can make me clean.'

13 Jesus reached out his hand and touched the man. 'I am willing,' he said. 'Be clean!' And immediately the leprosy left him.

14 Then Jesus ordered him, 'Don't tell anyone, but go, show yourself to the priest and offer the sacrifices that Moses commanded for your cleansing, as a testimony to them.'

15 Yet the news about him spread all the more, so that crowds of people came to hear him and to be healed of their illnesses. **16** But Jesus often withdrew to lonely places and prayed.

Jesus forgives and heals a paralysed man

17 One day Jesus was teaching, and Pharisees and teachers of the law were sitting there. They had come from every village of Galilee and from Judea and Jerusalem. And the power of the Lord was with Jesus to heal those who were ill. **18** Some men came carrying a paralysed man on a mat and tried to take him into the house to lay him before Jesus. **19** When they could not find a way to do this because of the crowd, they went up on the roof and lowered him on his mat through the tiles into the middle of the crowd, right in front of Jesus.

20 When Jesus saw their faith, he said, 'Friend, your sins are forgiven.'

21 The Pharisees and the teachers of the law began thinking to themselves, 'Who is this fellow who speaks blasphemy? Who can forgive sins but God alone?'

22 Jesus knew what they were thinking and asked, 'Why are you thinking these things in your hearts? **23** Which is easier: to say, "Your sins are forgiven," or to say, "Get up and walk"? **24** But I want you to know that the Son of Man has authority on earth to forgive sins.' So he said to the paralysed man, 'I tell you, get up, take your mat and go home.' **25** Immediately he stood up in front of them, took what he had been lying on and went home praising God. **26** Everyone was amazed and gave praise to God. They were filled with awe and said, 'We have seen

remarkable things today.'

b 12 The Greek word traditionally translated *leprosy* was used for various diseases affecting the skin.

12. 'While Jesus was present in one of the towns' – most likely in Galilee (verse 1) – a man was there who was 'covered with leprosy' (ESV, 'full of leprosy'). In the LXX, the word *lepra* translates the Hebrew ṣāra'at, which refers to a variety of inflammatory or scaly skin diseases (Leviticus 13:1–46), mould on clothes (13:47–59), and mould in houses (14:34–53). It is unlikely that the malignant form of leprosy known to modern medicine as Hansen's disease can be identified here.[36] Leviticus 13 contains regulations about the detection of such defilements, enabling priests to declare individuals clean or unclean. Those who were unclean had to live outside human settlement, separated from family and sanctuary (Numbers 5:1–4; 2 Kings 7:3–8). This may have been necessary to stop the spread of infection, but the main reason was spiritual. Gordon Wenham argues that 'holiness in Leviticus is symbolized by wholeness . . . God's abiding presence with his people depended on uncleanness being excluded from their midst (see Isaiah 6:3–5).'[37]

This man ignored the restrictions of the law by coming into town to seek for help. 'When he saw Jesus, he fell with his face to the ground and begged him, "Lord, if you are willing, you can make me clean."' The verb *katharizein* ('make clean') is specifically employed in relation to skin diseases. The man's appeal (Mark 1:40, 'begged him on his knees') was for Jesus to heal him in a way that would restore him to the life of his family and community. His address to Jesus as 'Lord' (*Kyrie*, as in verse 8) was respectful, but unlikely to be a confession of Jesus's divinity at this stage in the Gospel.

13. Both Luke and Matthew omit any reference to Jesus's emotion at this point (compare Mark 1:41), focusing on his action ('Jesus reached out his hand and touched the man') and his words ('I am willing . . . Be clean!'). Luke continues to emphasise his power to heal with a single

[36] Gordon J. Wenham, *The Book of Leviticus* (Grand Rapids: Eerdmans, 1979), 194–7, cites medical opinion that Hansen's disease is not being described in Leviticus. T. Omiya, 'Leprosy', *DJG*, 517, also concludes that Hebrew ṣāra'at is 'a ritual term, not a medical one'.

[37] Wenham, *Leviticus*, 203. Wenham (200) observes that 'outside the camp' of Israel is 'the place farthest removed from God, the place to which the sinner and the impure were banished'.

word of command (see 4:35, 36, 39, 41; 5:24–5). The instantaneous effect is then clarified ('immediately the leprosy left him').[38] Jesus does not violate the regulations in Leviticus with this touch, but he signifies that the man is healed and restored to fellowship with God and his people.

14. The need for secrecy is not expressed as strongly as in Mark's account.[39] Nevertheless, Jesus 'ordered him, "Don't tell anyone."' Previously overwhelmed by the number of people seeking help (4:40, 42), Jesus knew that news of this remarkable healing could spread quickly and limit his itinerant preaching ministry (4:43). More immediately, however, he was concerned that the man should fulfil the requirements of the law and avoid contact with others (compare 17:14): 'go, show yourself to the priest and offer the sacrifices that Moses commanded for your cleansing, as a testimony to them' (see Leviticus 14:1–32). The expression 'as a testimony to them' suggests providing proof of healing to the community through the priestly ritual. Of course, this would inevitably disclose that Jesus was responsible for the healing, meaning that his desire for silence could not have been absolute.

15–16. Luke does not mention that the man 'went out and began to talk freely, spreading the news' (Mark 1:45), but more indirectly writes, 'Yet the news about him spread all the more.' The inevitable consequence was that 'crowds of people came to hear him and to be healed of their illnesses' (see 4:42–3; 7:17). Mark records that 'Jesus could no longer enter a town openly but stayed outside in lonely places,' while Luke generalises that 'Jesus often withdrew to lonely places and prayed.' Jesus deliberately detached himself from teaching and healing so that he could commune with his heavenly Father. More than the other evangelists, Luke shows how prayer was an essential feature of his life and ministry (3:21; 6:12; 9:18, 28–9; 11:1; 22:39–46; 23:34, 46).

17. 'One day' loosely links this narrative to the preceding one.[40] Luke immediately highlights the presence of 'Pharisees and teachers of the law'. These religious leaders 'had come from every village of Galilee and from Judea and Jerusalem' in what seemed like an official delegation to examine Jesus's teaching and investigate what he was doing. The extraordinary miracle to come is anticipated when Luke adds that 'the power of the Lord was with Jesus to heal those who were ill' (see 6:19; 8:44; 24:19). Pharisees were one of the three main 'sects' in Palestinian Judaism at that

---

[38] The word *eutheōs* ('immediately') parallels the term used in 4:39; 5:25. See C. Wahlen, 'Healing', *DJG*, 362–70.

[39] Mark 1:43 (*embrimēsamenos*, 'sternly charged') indicates a strong warning.

[40] Mark 2:1 locates the event more precisely in Capernaum.

time, the others being the Sadducees and the Essenes (Acts 15:5; 23:6–8).[41] The Greek name *Pharisaioi* is probably a transcription of the Aramaic term for 'separated ones'. Their strictness in interpreting and obeying the law of Moses is noted in Acts 26:5. But they were also devoted to keeping the oral law (Mark 7:8, 'human traditions'), which Fitzmyer says, had developed in postexilic times to be 'a "fence for the law," guarding it against violation'.[42] Luke uses the unusual term *nomodidaskaloi* ('teachers of the law') to introduce those who are more regularly identified as *grammateis* (verse 21, 'scribes', ESV), some of whom belonged to the party of the Pharisees (5:30).[43] Some teachers of the law were members of the ruling council in Jerusalem (22:66), having both teaching authority and a role in the administration of justice.

18–19. 'Some men came carrying a paralysed man on a mat.'[44] They tried to take him into the house where Jesus was teaching, 'to lay him before Jesus'. Finding no way to do this because of the crowd, 'they went up on the roof and lowered him on his mat through the tiles into the middle of the crowd, right in front of Jesus'. The word translated 'mat' is first *klinē* ('pallet, stretcher', BDAG), and then the diminutive form *klinidion*, which is probably used for stylistic variation. Ropes could have been used to lower this to the feet of Jesus. Fitzmyer notes that 'the roof of the common Palestinian house was made of wooden beams placed across stone or mudbrick walls; the beams were covered with reeds, matted layers of thorns and several inches of clay'.[45] Mark 2:4 speaks of the men digging through the roof, but Luke mentions that they lowered the man 'through the tiles', perhaps using this expression for the benefit of readers in contexts where tiled roofs were more common.[46]

20. 'When Jesus saw their faith, he said, "Friend, your sins are forgiven."' Faith is mentioned for the first time here by Luke, although it was implicit in previous references to people seeking help from Jesus (4:38;

---

[41] See also Josephus, *Antiquities* 13.5, 9; 18.1–5.
[42] Fitzmyer, *Luke I–IX*, 581. See Edwards, *Luke*, 162–3; L. Cohick, 'Pharisees', *DJG*, 673–9.
[43] NIV translates *grammateis* 'teachers of the law' in 5:21, 30; 6:7; 9:22; 11:53; 15:2; 19:47; 20:1, 19, 39, 46; 22:2, 66; 23:10. The parallel *nomikos* is translated 'an expert in the law' in 7:30; 10:25; 11:45, 46, 52; 14:3. See G. Thelmann, 'Scribes', *DJG*, 840–42.
[44] ESV, 'a man who was paralysed' (*anthrōpon hos ēn paralelymenos*). Compare Mark 2:3 (*paralytikos*, 'a paralysed man').
[45] Fitzmyer, *Luke I–IX*, 582.
[46] Bock, *Luke 1:1–9:50*, 480–81, thinks Luke may be describing 'the removed lumps of clay with a word that also indicated their function (as tiles)'.

5:12; see 7:9, 50; 8:25, 48; 17:5, 6, 19; 18:8, 42; 22:32). The related verb 'believe' was used in 1:20, 45. 'Their faith' must surely include the faith of the paralysed man, though the story so far has been about the determination and ingenuity of those who brought him to Jesus. The claim that 'your sins are forgiven' includes the singular pronoun *soi* ('to you'), which emphasises the personal nature of the promise to the paralysed man. The passive verb would normally imply that his sins are forgiven by God,[47] but Jesus's opponents rightly understood him to be claiming that prerogative for himself. The forgiveness of sins is a critical aspect of the freedom or release (*aphesis*) that Jesus was sent to proclaim (4:18, citing Isaiah 61:1). When Jesus saw their faith, he offered the man what he most needed, namely the forgiveness that would enable him to share in all the blessings of the kingdom of God.

21. 'The Pharisees and the teachers of the law' come into the foreground now (see my comment on verse 17). What they 'began thinking to themselves' is exposed in Jesus's perceptive questioning of them (verse 22).[48] As Simeon predicted, 'the thoughts of many hearts' were being revealed by Jesus (2:35). They were pondering, 'Who is this fellow who speaks blasphemy? Who can forgive sins but God alone?' (see 7:48–9). The seriousness of speaking 'blasphemies' can be understood in the light of Leviticus 24:10–11, 14–16, 23, where the command is given to put to death someone who misuses the name of God and dishonours him (see Exodus 20:7). More broadly, ridiculing God or denying his ability in some way is a form of blasphemy (2 Kings 19:4, 6, 22). Jesus appeared to have blasphemed by usurping a role considered to be uniquely his (Exodus 34:7).[49] Human beings can forgive those who sin against *them* (Luke 6:37; 11:4), but only God can forgive those who sin against *him*.

22–3. 'Jesus knew what they were thinking' (see 4:23; 6:8; 7:39–47; 9:47) and so he asked, 'Why are you thinking these things in your hearts?' His further question ('Which is easier to say, "Your sins are forgiven," or to say, "Get up and walk"?') links his offer of forgiveness with the possibility of

---

[47] An unusual form of the perfect passive indicative (*apheōntai*) indicates a present activity ('your sins are being forgiven'). See Constantine R. Campbell, *Verbal Aspect, the Indicative Mood, and Narrative: Soundings in the Greek of the New Testament* (New York: Peter Lang, 2007), 210.

[48] The verb *dialogizesthai* can mean 'discuss, argue' or 'consider, ponder, reason' (BDAG). The latter sense is clarified by 'in your hearts' (verse 22).

[49] See D. L. Bock, 'Blasphemy', *DJG*, 84–7. The charge of blasphemy was made again at the trial of Jesus in Matthew 26:65; Mark 14:64, but not in Luke. See John 5:18; 10:36.

healing. Neither is easier for a mere human being, but Jesus can do both! The plural 'sins' is deliberately general. Sickness and disability are sometimes presented in Scripture as the judgment of God for specific sins (e.g., Numbers 12:9–12; 1 Samuel 16:14–16; 2 Samuel 12:13–17; 2 Chronicles 26:16–21), but mostly they are viewed as an inevitable feature of life in a world needing redemption and transformation by God (Isaiah 35:1–7; 65:17–25; Romans 8:18–25; Revelation 21:1–4). There is no suggestion in this passage that the man's paralysis is directly caused by his sin. Rather, he is being told that his greatest need as a human being is for the forgiveness of his sins and that Jesus can provide this as well as heal him physically.

24–5. Jesus's authority to forgive sins is first declared in relation to the objectors:[50] 'I want you to know that the Son of Man has authority on earth to forgive sins.' The present infinitive (*aphienai*, 'to forgive') suggests repeated action and his authority to do this is exercised as 'the Son of Man . . . on earth'. Then Jesus turns to the paralysed man and says, 'I tell you, get up, take your mat and go home.' The wonder of the miracle is simply stated: 'Immediately he stood up in front of them, took what he had been lying on and went home praising God.' As in verse 13, a divine act of healing took place in response to Jesus's word of command, and this confirmed his authority to forgive sins.

The expression 'the Son of Man' (*ho huios tou anthrōpou*) appears for the first time here. Much debate has taken place about the origin of this term and its use by Jesus. Some scholars claim that it should be understood in the generic sense of 'a human being' or be taken to refer to 'a corporate figure'.[51] But the term regularly functions in the Gospels as an indirect form of self-reference by Jesus. It is not used by others (though see Acts 7:56) and played no part in the confessional and doctrinal statements of the early church. Nevertheless, the Son of Man passages in the Gospels have much to teach us about Jesus's person and work. Luke records twenty-five uses, nine of which correspond with Mark (Luke 5:24; 6:5; 9:22, 26, 44; 18:31; 21:27; 22:22, 69) and eight exclusively with Matthew (Luke 7:34; 9:58; 11:30; 12:10, 40; 17:24, 26, 30), while six are peculiar to Luke (17:22; 18:8; 19:10; 21:36; 22:48; 24:7). Some texts relate primarily to Jesus's public ministry (Luke 5:24; 6:5;

---

[50] The introductory words *hina de eidēte* have been understood imperatively ('know'; see Nolland, *Luke 1–9:20*, 230, 237) or as a purpose clause ('that you may know') prefacing an editorial comment to the reader (Fitzmyer, *Luke I–IX*, 579, 585). But it is also possible to read this as a purpose clause spoken by Jesus to his opponents before he speaks to the man (NIV, ESV). Compare the same pattern in 19:9–10.
[51] Nolland, *Luke 9:21–18:34*, 468–74, provides a helpful summary of the debate.

7:34; 9:58; 11:30; 12:10; 19:10; 22:48), others to his predicted suffering and resurrection (9:22, 44; 18:31; 22:22; 24:7), while the majority speak of his return in power and glory to judge (9:26; 12:40; 17:22, 24, 26, 30; 18:8; 21:27, 36; 22:69). This last usage provides the key to understanding the other two.[52]

There are specific echoes of Daniel 7:13–14 in Luke 9:26; 21:27, 36; 22:69. A man-like figure in Daniel's vision (Aramaic, $k^e\underline{b}ar$ $^{\prime e}n\bar{a}\check{s}$ (or $^{\prime}en\bar{o}\check{s}$), 'one like a son of man') comes 'with the clouds of heaven' into the presence of 'the Ancient of Days' to receive authority, glory and sovereign power over all nations. This recalls the promises made by God to the exalted Son of David in Psalms 2 and 110. God's judging of the nations precedes the handing over of power and authority to this heavenly ruler in Daniel 7:9–10. Daniel is then told that his vision relates to the salvation of 'the holy people of the Most High' through the defeat of their enemies (7:15–18, 26–7).[53]

Jesus uses the cryptic term 'the Son of Man' to refer to himself allusively as Daniel's man-like figure. Paradoxically, he must be rejected and suffer as the Son of Man, before being exalted to reign at God's right hand and return in great power and glory to judge and to save.[54] In Luke 5:24 and parallels, Jesus implies that, as the one destined to be the world ruler and judge of all, he is able to forgive sins on earth in advance of his coming at the end of the age. Jesus uses the title Son of Man deliberately, but enigmatically, to indicate how he fulfils God's plan of salvation. He brings the definitive forgiveness of sins promised by the prophets (Isaiah 43:25; Jeremiah 31:34; Ezekiel 16:63; 36:25), anticipated by

---

[52] Bock, 'Son of Man', *DJG*, 894–900, thinks there is no need to invoke Daniel 7 to make sense of the indirect self-reference in passages such as Luke 5:24; 6:5, but this diminishes the eschatological significance of these sayings. If Jesus made a linguistic link with Daniel 7:13, it is likely that some theological connection should be discerned with every usage of the term (even paradoxical, as in 7:34; 9:22, 44, 58).
[53] The man-like figure represents and rules over God's people, just as the beasts appear to represent both enemy kingdoms and their rulers. The imagery of Daniel 7:13–14 is picked up in Jewish apocalyptic literature (1 Enoch 37–71; 4 Ezra 11–13), portraying an expected judge–deliverer, who has royal and divine qualities. See Bock, *Luke 1:1–9:50*, 924.
[54] Some have related Jesus's passion predictions to the suffering of the people of God at the hands of their enemies in Daniel 7:21, 25. But it is more likely that verses from Psalms and Isaiah 52:13–53:12 inform what is said about the suffering and vindication of the Son of Man in the Gospels. Different strands of biblical expectation are combined in this way.

Zechariah (Luke 1:77) and offered in advance through John the Baptist (3:3), as an essential step in realising that plan.

26. 'Everyone was amazed' (ESV 'amazement seized them all') and they 'gave praise to God'. Perhaps even the scribes and Pharisees shared this initial response, though their questioning of Jesus continued (5:30, 33; 6:2). They soon became more implacably opposed to what he was saying and doing (6:7, 11). Luke elaborates Mark's conclusion (2:12) by adding that people were 'filled with awe' (*phobos*, 'fear'). They acknowledged with reverent fear, as well as praise, that they had seen God at work in their midst (see 1:12, 65; 2:9; 7:16), saying 'We have seen remarkable things today.'

THE SON OF MAN ON EARTH

John Nolland observes that 'the uncleanness of leprosy is a potentially powerful image for human defilement in sin'.[55] In the time of Jesus, infectious diseases associated with the term 'leprosy' afflicted individuals physically, socially and spiritually. They were ritually unclean, isolated and alienated from the worshipping community. Jesus healed those 'covered with leprosy' by the power of his word, while his touch expressed the restoration of relationships with God and his people. But Jesus was also concerned that, until his work of atonement and ultimate cleansing from the effects of sin could be accomplished, the prescriptions of the Mosaic law should be followed. Healing, cleansing and forgiveness were experienced by Israelites who approached Jesus with faith, but his death and resurrection made these benefits potentially available to all (see 22:17–20; 24:46–7; Hebrews 1:3; 2:17; 9:14). The forgiveness and healing of a man who was paralysed demonstrated Jesus's authority as 'the Son of Man . . . on earth' to act in advance of his anticipated role as ruler, judge and deliverer of people from every nation (verses 20–24; see Daniel 7:13–14). His allusive self-description in this way pointed to the end-time significance of his words and works. Forgiveness of sins is now possible for all who seek it through the Son of Man who is 'seated at the right hand of the mighty God' (22:69), but full and permanent healing from disability and disease will not be available 'until the time comes for God to restore everything, as he promised long ago through his holy prophets' (Acts 3:21).

---

[55] Nolland, *Luke 1–9:20*, 227.

5. Jesus eats with outcasts and sinners (Luke 5:27–39)

Luke adapts Mark 2:13–22 to highlight certain issues. The call of Levi and Jesus's subsequent meal with 'tax collectors and sinners' shocks 'the Pharisees and the teachers of the law who belonged to their sect' (verses 27–30). Their questioning about this elicits another programmatic statement from Jesus about his mission. As the divine physician he has come to make forgiveness and repentance possible for sinners (verses 31–2; see 4:17–20; 5:24). A further question from objectors about fasting provokes him to speak in a parabolic way about his coming as 'the bridegroom' of God's people and its implications (verses 33–9).

Jesus calls Levi and eats with sinners

27 After this, Jesus went out and saw a tax collector by the name of Levi sitting at his tax booth. 'Follow me,' Jesus said to him, **28** and Levi got up, left everything and followed him.

29 Then Levi held a great banquet for Jesus at his house, and a large crowd of tax collectors and others were eating with them. **30** But the Pharisees and the teachers of the law who belonged to their sect complained to his disciples, 'Why do you eat and drink with tax collectors and sinners?'

31 Jesus answered them, 'It is not the healthy who need a doctor, but those who are ill. **32** I have not come to call the righteous, but sinners to repentance.'

Jesus questioned about fasting

33 They said to him, 'John's disciples often fast and pray, and so do the disciples of the Pharisees, but yours go on eating and drinking.'

34 Jesus answered, 'Can you make the friends of the bridegroom fast while he is with them? **35** But the time will come when the bridegroom will be taken from them; in those days they will fast.'

36 He told them this parable: 'No one tears a piece out of a new garment to patch an old one. Otherwise, they will have torn the new garment, and the patch from the new will not match the old. **37** And no one pours new wine into old wineskins. Otherwise, the new wine will burst the skins; the wine will run out and the wineskins will be ruined. **38** No, new wine must be poured into new wineskins. **39** And no one after drinking old wine wants the new, for they say, "The old is better."'

27–8. A precise temporal link with the previous episode is indicated ('After this, Jesus went out and saw a tax collector by the name of Levi sitting at his tax booth').[56] In Mark 2:14 this man is called Levi son of Alphaeus, but in Matthew 9:9, he is simply called Matthew. A link between Matthew the apostle and Levi is suggested in Matthew 10:3 ('Matthew the tax collector'). First-century Palestinian Jews often had two names and so it is possible that he was called Levi Matthew or Matthew Levi.[57] Jesus's invitation ('Follow me') was immediately accepted: 'Levi got up, left everything and followed him' (see 5:11; 14:33; 18:28). The verb 'followed' is a key to understanding the nature of discipleship in the Gospels. 'Come after me' is another way of expressing the call to personal commitment (14:27 ESV; NIV 'follow me'). Being a disciple means believing in Jesus and learning from him, but his call to repent (verse 32) implies also a radical change of values, commitments and lifestyle. For Levi, repentance involved leaving his despised occupation and source of income to join Jesus in his itinerant, life-changing mission (see 5:11; 9:23, 49, 57, 59, 61; 18:22, 28, 43; 22:39, 54).[58]

29. As an expression of his repentance, Levi used his financial resources generously and 'held a great banquet for Jesus at his house'. Meals with Jesus are mentioned often in Luke's narrative and have different functions (see 7:36–50; 9:10–17; 10:38–42; 11:37–54; 14:1–24; 19:1–10; 22:7–38; 24:29–32, 41–3).[59] This sumptuous event was an indication of Levi's gratitude for the grace shown to him by Jesus and his desire for 'a large crowd of tax collectors and others' to meet his new master and experience the same grace (Mark 2:15 mentions that many tax collectors and sinners were already following Jesus).

30. The Pharisees and 'the teachers of the law who belonged to their sect' (ESV, 'their scribes' (see verses 17, 21)) became aware of what Jesus was doing. They 'complained' (see 15:2; 19:7 'muttered') to his disciples, 'Why do you [plural] eat and drink with tax collectors and sinners?' In Mark 2:16, the question is more specifically about Jesus, but his disciples are charged with the same improper association here (with the obvious implication that Jesus is responsible for it). Luke heightens the note of

---

[56] See my comment on 3:12 about 'toll collectors' (telōnai) who worked for the Romans, collecting various indirect taxes.

[57] Fitzmyer, Luke I–IX, 590; Bock, Luke 1:1–9:50, 493–4.

[58] See M. J. Wilkins, 'Disciples and Discipleship', DJG, 202–12. The verb 'follow' is also used in a more limited way by Luke with reference to crowds, whose association with Jesus may only have been temporary or occasional (7:9; 9:11; 23:27).

[59] See Craig L. Blomberg, Contagious Holiness: Jesus' Meals with Sinners (Leicester: Apollos; Downers Grove: IVP Academic, 2005), 32–163; M. A. Powell, 'Table Fellowship', DJG, 925–31.

celebration by adding that they *drank* with tax collectors and sinners (see 7:34). The Pharisees linked tax collectors with sinners because of their immoral lifestyle (see 18:11). As well as mixing with Gentiles and collaborating with the Roman authorities, they used their position to accumulate personal wealth.[60] 'Sinners' in the Gospels and in Jewish literature at that time fall into two categories: those who oppose God and his will in any sense (e.g., Luke 7:37, 39; 13:2; 18:13; 19:7) and those who fall short of the demands of particular Jewish factions (e.g., John 9:16, 24).[61] The Pharisees and their scribes in this context seem to be using the term in the first sense.

31–2. Jesus replied to them, 'It is not the healthy who need a doctor, but those who are ill' (see Jeremiah 8:22; Sirach 38:1–15). Sin is a sickness that only God can cure. Forgiveness that brings repentance is the solution (5:20–24). Jesus's wisdom saying prepares for the declaration that follows: 'I have not come to call the righteous, but sinners to repentance' (see 15:7). Further statements about why he 'came' appear in 7:34; 12:49, 51; 19:10 (see also Mark 1:38; 10:45; Matthew 20:28), but here the pattern is different. He makes a negative claim first (as in Matthew 5:17) to highlight the positive claim that follows. Luke frequently uses the adjective 'righteous' (*dikaios*) to express, in Brown's words, 'loyalty to God's ways and commandments in concert with OT covenantal understandings'.[62] Those who are truly righteous are spiritually healthy and do not need the kind of radical reorientation of their lives towards God that 'sinners' do. Paradoxically, however, righteous Israelites were drawn to Jesus, as they came to recognise his significance as the promised Saviour of his people (e.g., 2:25–38; 23:50–58; 24:13–35). Jesus did not directly challenge the status of his critics here, who doubtless considered themselves to be righteous. But his generous engagement with sinners exposed the exclusivism, lack of compassion and self-righteousness of his opponents. Like a physician with the sick, Nolland says Jesus treated sinners as 'needy and able to be helped, rather than as contaminating and deserving to be spurned'.[63] In this way, they experienced through him the mercy of God (note the addition of Hosea 6:6 in Matthew 9:13).

---

[60] Bock, *Luke 1:1–9:50*, 495 note, considers different ways in which Jesus's action may have offended the separatism of the Pharisees.

[61] See M. F. Bird, 'Sin, Sinner', *DJG*, 863–9; Blomberg, *Contagious Holiness*, 24–6.

[62] J. K. Brown, 'Justice, Righteousness', *DJG*, 465. See Luke 1:6, 17; 2:25; 14:14; 15:7; 23:50.

[63] Nolland, *Luke 1–9:20*, 246. Green, *Luke*, 248, observes that healing is understood in this context as 'restoration to relationship with Yahweh and his people – that is, as forgiveness'.

Jesus's welcoming attitude did not condone sinful behaviour, since he came to call sinners 'to repentance' (*eis metanoian*). Luke alone uses the term here (compare Matthew 9:13; Mark 2:17), showing that there is another side to Jesus's role as the forgiver of sins (verse 24). As noted in connection with the preaching of John the Baptist, repentance involves a change of behaviour and orientation of life, rather than simply a change of mind (3:3, 8; 5:32; 15:7; 24:47). The related verb *metanoeō* ('repent', in 10:13; 11:32; 13:3, 5; 15:7, 10; 16:30; 17:3, 4), together with *epistrephō* ('turn', in Luke 17:4; Acts 3:19; 26:20), reflects the emphasis of the prophets, who often called upon God's people to return to him (Hebrew, *shuv*).[64] Tannehill argues that, in Luke–Acts, 'repentance and forgiveness together refer to the transformation in human lives that results from God's saving action in fulfilling the promises of salvation through Israel's Messiah, Jesus'.[65] Jesus is both the agent and the focus of genuine repentance.

33. Unnamed characters now question Jesus about a related issue (compare Matthew 9:14–17; Mark 2:18–22). They say, 'John's disciples often fast and pray, and so do the disciples of the Pharisees, but yours go on eating and drinking.' Luke adds the words 'and pray', indicating that such fasting was in the context of prayer. The adverb 'often' reveals that this was their regular practice (the Pharisee in 18:12 claims to fast 'twice a week'). Such piety seemed to be in stark contrast with the lifestyle of Jesus's disciples, who were continually 'eating and drinking'. Moreover, none of the customary signs of repentance could be seen in their converts, identified by Tannehill as 'weeping and mourning, fasting, donning sackcloth and ashes'.[66]

34–5. Jesus did not reject the practice of fasting, but he focused on the joy and celebration that is appropriate when a sinner returns to God and experiences his forgiveness (see Luke 15). His answer to the question about fasting makes a distinction between the time when he was with his disciples and a time to come, when he would be taken away from them. He used the expression 'the friends of the bridegroom' (*tous huious tou nymphōnos*, 'sons of the wedding hall/bridal chamber'), which referred

---

[64] The verb *epistrephō* ('turn back') occurs on its own in Luke 1:16; Acts 9:35; 11:21; 14:15; 15:19; 26:18, 20. See F. Mendez-Moratalla, 'Repentance', *DJG*, 771–4.
[65] Robert C. Tannehill, *The Shape of Luke's Story: Essays on Luke–Acts* (Eugene: Cascade, 2005), 88.
[66] Tannehill, *Shape*, 94. Fitzmyer, *Luke I–IX*, 596, notes the practice of fasting on the Day of Atonement (Leviticus 16:29–31), and on other occasions for penitence (1 Kings 21:27; Isaiah 58:19; Joel 1:14; 2:15–27), as well as for mourning (Esther 4:3). See also Esther 9:31; Zechariah 8:19.

to the attendants of a bridegroom.[67] First, Jesus asked, 'Can you make the friends of the bridegroom fast while he is still with them?' Images of marriage and feasting point to the consummation of God's saving plan for his people (Isaiah 25:6–9; Revelation 19:7–9). As 'the bridegroom'(*ho nymphios*) in that context, Jesus assumes the role of God, who is sometimes described by the prophets as Israel's husband and lover (Isaiah 5:1; 54:5–6; 62:4–5; Hosea 2:19).[68] Second, Jesus predicts that 'the time will come when the bridegroom will be taken from them; in those days they will fast'. The picture of the bridegroom being removed from his own marriage celebration is dramatic. Jesus implies that his death may come suddenly and be the time for disciples to mourn their loss (see 4:28–9; 9:21–2; 13:32–3). When this prediction is fulfilled, however, the period of mourning will be short, and joy will return because of Jesus's resurrection (24:41, 52–3; Acts 2:46–7). Fasting in the post-resurrection era takes place at significant moments of prayer (Acts 13:2–3; 14:23) and ministry (2 Corinthians 6:5; 11:27), but voluntarily, not as an imposed form of self-discipline.

36. Although Jesus had spoken parabolically in verses 34–5, Luke specifically identifies what follows as a 'parable' that he told to high-light the difference between the past and the present, the old and the new.[69] 'No one tears a piece out of a new garment to patch an old one. Otherwise, they will have torn the new garment, and the patch from the new will not match the old.' Luke specifies 'a piece out of a new garment' instead of 'a piece of unshrunk cloth' (Mark 2:21). When an old garment is washed, a new patch shrinks and tears away, no longer functioning as a patch. Nolland takes this to mean that the new situation brought about by the coming of Jesus 'is not to be reduced to a patch on the old; nor is it right to attempt to contain the new within the constraints of the old'.[70]

37–8. A second parable or metaphor is offered without introduction. 'And no one pours new wine into old wineskins. Otherwise, the new wine will burst the skins; the wine will run out and the wineskins will be ruined. No, new wine must be poured into new wineskins.' Newly

---

[67] Nolland, *Luke 1–9:20*, 247–8.
[68] See Edwards, *Luke*, 174; J. McWhirter, 'Bride, Bridegroom', *DJG*, 95–7.
[69] The term *parabolē* is used here to refer to a simple metaphor or similitude (compare 4:23; 6:39; 12:16, 41; 13:6; 14:7; 18:1, 9; 19:11; 20: 9, 19; 21:29). Fitzmyer, *Luke I–IX*, 600, outlines other uses of the term in the Gospels. See also my comment on 8:4.
[70] Nolland, *Luke 1–9:20*, 247. Nolland insists that the issue is 'the need for the new to be allowed to have its own integrity'. But Bock, *Luke 1:1–9:50*, 520, nuances this conclusion by saying that Jesus brings 'discontinuity in the midst of continuity'.

fermented wine is too strong for old wineskins and will rupture them. As in the previous illustration, the new cannot be contained within the old. Both the old and the new are spoiled if they are simply mixed. Fitzmyer interprets this to mean that, 'the new economy of salvation must find for itself forms of piety that suit it'.[71]

39. Luke adds a further parabolic saying that is not present in the parallel accounts: 'And no one after drinking old wine wants the new, for they say, "The old is better."' There are similar proverbs in Jewish literature of that era (e.g., Sirach 9:10). Some have argued that the version here contradicts Jesus's previous sayings because it seems to favour the old order over the new. But Fitzmyer takes this to be 'a wry comment on the effect that clinging to the old has on those who have closed their minds to his message about the new economy of salvation'.[72] As Edwards concludes, the question is whether people will 'forsake business as usual and join the wedding celebration; whether they will become entirely new receptacles for the expanding fermentation of Jesus and the gospel in their lives'.[73]

FORGIVENESS, REPENTANCE AND CELEBRATION

The call of Levi and Jesus's subsequent feasting with his disciples and the social and religious outcasts of his day sent shockwaves into the region (see also 7:36–50; 15:1–32; 19:1–10). Jesus's call to repent meant more than mourning over sin and guilt: it involved turning back to God by following *him* and joyfully discovering that 'one is included in God's salvation, making possible a transformed life', as Tannehill suggests.[74] Responding to the criticism of the Pharisees and scribes, Jesus adopted their terminology, contrasting the righteous with sinners. The righteous are those who live to please God and sinners are those who turn their backs on him to live disobediently. But Jesus's willingness to receive sinners and eat with them called into question the righteousness of those who sat in judgment on him and his disciples. They had no heart for the lost and saw no need for the forgiveness he offered.

---

[71] Fitzmyer, *Luke I–IX*, 601. Bock, *Luke 1:1–9:50*, 521, relates this to the problem of trying to 'Judaize' Christianity, as witnessed in Acts 15 and other New Testament passages.

[72] Fitzmyer, *Luke I–IX*, 602. Nolland, *Luke 1–9:20*, 250, observes that 'the inappropriate behavior of vv. 36 and 37–38 in each case has involved a preference for the old'. The verse is well attested, but it is omitted from several Western texts (Metzger, *Textual Commentary*, 115–16), perhaps because of confusion over its meaning.

[73] Edwards, *Luke*, 176.

[74] Tannehill, *Shape*, 94.

Jesus went on to proclaim that everyone should repent in the face of God's imminent judgment (13:1–5). Ultimately, he commissioned his disciples to preach repentance for the forgiveness of sins in his name to all nations (24:47). Jesus likened his eating and drinking with tax collectors and sinners to a joyful wedding feast, in which his presence as the bridegroom made fasting inappropriate. Images of marriage and feasting pointed to the consummation of God's saving plan for his people (Isaiah 25:6–9; Revelation 19:7–9). Jesus used the debate about fasting to highlight the newness of the situation brought about by his coming, but also to hint at the possibility of his sudden removal and the need for his disciples to mourn when that happened. Jesus's parabolic sayings warn about trying to constrain the newness of the gospel in patterns of devotion to God that obscure the blessings of the New Covenant that he came to make possible. This could include rituals such as circumcision and regulations that 'have an appearance of wisdom, with their self-imposed worship, their false humility and their harsh treatment of the body, but they lack any value in restraining sensual indulgence' (Colossians 2:23).

6. Jesus is Lord of the Sabbath (Luke 6:1–11)

Luke follows Mark 2:23–3:6 with minor modifications (see the expansion in Matthew 12:1–14). Two linked narratives reveal Jesus's attitude towards Sabbath observance, which was a defining characteristic of first-century Judaism along with circumcision and the clean–unclean regulations alluded to in 5:12–14, 27–32. The behaviour of Jesus's disciples, who had been casually picking ears of corn, rubbing them in their hands, and eating the grain on the Sabbath (verses 1–2), aroused the opposition of the Pharisees. Jesus responded with an argument from Scripture and made the enigmatic claim to be 'Lord of the Sabbath' (verses 3–5). On another Sabbath, the Pharisees and the teachers of the law were present in a synagogue with Jesus, watching to see if he would heal a man with a shrivelled hand (verses 6–7). Jesus questioned their presuppositions about what is lawful on the Sabbath and openly healed the man (verses 8–10). The furious response of his opponents marks a sinister turning-point in their opposition to him (verse 11).

Jesus is Lord of the Sabbath

6 One Sabbath Jesus was going through the cornfields, and his disciples began to pick some ears of corn, rub them in their hands and eat the grain. **2**Some of the Pharisees asked, 'Why are you doing what is unlawful on the Sabbath?'

3Jesus answered them, 'Have you never read what David did when he and his companions were hungry? **4**He entered the house of God, and taking the consecrated bread, he ate what is lawful only for priests to eat. And he also gave some to his companions.' **5**Then Jesus said to them, 'The Son of Man is Lord of the Sabbath.'

6On another Sabbath he went into the synagogue and was teaching, and a man was there whose right hand was shrivelled. **7**The Pharisees and the teachers of the law were looking for a reason to accuse Jesus, so they watched him closely to see if he would heal on the Sabbath. **8**But Jesus knew what they were thinking and said to the man with the shrivelled hand, 'Get up and stand in front of everyone.' So he got up and stood there.

9Then Jesus said to them, 'I ask you, which is lawful on the Sabbath: to do good or to do evil, to save life or to destroy it?'

10He looked round at them all, and then said to the man, 'Stretch out your hand.' He did so, and his hand was completely restored. **11**But the Pharisees and the teachers of the law were furious and began to discuss with one another what they might do to Jesus.

1–2. The first Sabbath event seems innocent enough: 'Jesus was going through the cornfields, and his disciples began to pick some ears of corn, rub them in their hands and eat the grain.' They were acting legitimately in casually eating someone else's corn (Deuteronomy 23:25), but when some of the Pharisees learned about it, they questioned Jesus about this behaviour ('Why are you [plural] doing what is unlawful on the Sabbath?'). Resting on the Sabbath was commanded in Scripture 'even during the ploughing season and harvest' (Exodus 34:21). Pharisaic tradition defined ploughing and harvesting in many restrictive ways, so that even removing the kernel from the husk came to be treated as work.[75]

3–4. Jesus answered the charge, not by engaging in a discussion about the definition of work on the Sabbath but by citing an example of apparent disobedience to God's Law in Scripture ('Have you never read what

---

[75] Mishnah, *Shabbat* 7:2 lists thirty-nine forms of work prohibited on the Sabbath. See Christopher Rowland, 'A Summary of Sabbath Observance in Judaism at the Beginning of the Christian Era', in *From Sabbath to Lord's Day: A Biblical, Historical, and Theological Investigation*, ed. Donald A. Carson (Grand Rapids: Zondervan, 1982), 42–55; Edwards, *Luke*, 176–8.

David did when he and his companions were hungry?'). According to 1 Samuel 21:1–6, David 'entered the house of God,' which must refer to the tent where the consecrated bread was 'set out before the Lord regularly, Sabbath after Sabbath, on behalf of the Israelites, as a lasting covenant' (Leviticus 24:8).[76] With the permission of Ahimelek the priest, David took and ate 'what is lawful only for priests to eat. And he also gave some to his companions.' This was not an example of Sabbath-breaking by David and his men, nor of David exercising authority over Ahimelek.[77] They were simply allowed to feed on the consecrated bread because of their genuine need. Jesus's point was that this biblical event calls into question the rigid interpretation of the Sabbath law by the Pharisees and suggests the need to exercise mercy and compassion in its application.

5. Luke does not record the saying, 'The Sabbath was made for man, not man for the Sabbath' (Mark 2:27), though this is implied in verses 8–9. Jesus is simply heard to say, 'The Son of Man is Lord of the Sabbath.' Given the use of the title 'the Son of Man' in 5:24, Fitzmyer argues that Jesus's pronouncement in 6:5 should be read as 'part of the Christological buildup of the Gospel as it develops'.[78] If the Son of Man relates to the man-like figure in the vision of Daniel 7:13–14, the saying here identifies another aspect of his authority 'on earth' (5:24), in anticipation of his heavenly exaltation and rule. As 'Lord of the Sabbath,' Jesus has the right to determine how the Sabbath command should be understood and obeyed. Nolland asserts that 'in this new situation the Son of Man is able to open up the full potential of the Sabbath as God's gift to humankind'.[79] More broadly, Luke's ongoing presentation of Jesus's approach to the Mosaic Law shows us how it loses its 'central and mediating position and is replaced by the person and teaching of Jesus'.[80]

---

[76] NIV ('the consecrated bread') is an interpretation of the expression *tous artous tēs protheseōs* ('the loaves of presentation'). This reflects the sense of Leviticus 24:8 LXX that the loaves should be 'set out before the Lord', elsewhere described as 'the bread of the Presence' (Exodus 25:30; 35:13; 39:36; 40:23).

[77] Edwards, *Luke*, 178, reads too much into this when he claims that David is being viewed by Jesus as 'Israel's royal messianic prototype'.

[78] Fitzmyer, *Luke I–IX*, 610.

[79] Nolland, *Luke 1–9:20*, 258. D. A. Carson, 'Jesus and the Sabbath', in *From Sabbath to Lord's Day*, ed. D. A. Carson, 66, describes this as 'a messianic claim of grand proportions'. Contrast Bock, *Luke 1:1–9:50*, 525–7.

[80] Max M. B. Turner, 'The Sabbath, Sunday and the Law in Luke/Acts', in *From Sabbath to Lord's Day*, ed. D. A. Carson, 108. Jesus appears to assert both the law's continuity and, in some respects, its discontinuity, as Turner goes on to argue.

6–7. Luke clarifies that a related incident took place 'on another Sabbath', when Jesus went into an unnamed synagogue and was teaching. A man was present 'whose right hand was shrivelled' (*xēra*, 'withered, shrunken, paralyzed', BDAG; see 23:31). The Pharisees and teachers of the law were deliberately watching Jesus, 'to see whether he would heal on the Sabbath, so that they might find a reason to accuse him' (ESV; see 11:53–4). They had already made up their minds that he was a lawbreaker, and they wanted to bring him to trial for this.

8–9. As in 4:23; 5:22, 'Jesus knew what they were thinking' and was intent on challenging their rigid views. He wanted to heal the man in a public way, and so he said to him, 'Get up and stand in front of everyone.' Given the shame of his disability, this must have been quite a challenge for him. Nevertheless, at the command of Jesus, he got up and stood there. Jesus then questioned his opponents, 'I ask you, which is lawful on the Sabbath: to do good or to do evil, to save life or to destroy it?' These questions reflect the sorts of debates about the Sabbath evidenced in later rabbinic sources.[81] Jesus equated the saving of life with doing good, which was especially appropriate on the day set apart to honour God as Creator and Redeemer (Exodus 20:8–11; Deuteronomy 5:12–15). Salvation in this context meant healing or rescue from physical impediment, rather than restoration to a right relationship with God (as in 7:50; 19:9–10). The Pharisees agreed with saving life in extreme situations, but Nolland notes that 'rabbinic thought set itself to keep to a strict minimum on the Sabbath any help to another that could be in any way construed as work'.[82] Rabbinic teaching even prohibited 'straightening a deformed body or setting a broken limb' on the Sabbath (Mishnah, *Shabbat* 22:6). For Jesus, however, not to heal someone when there was an opportunity to do so was the same as destroying life and was therefore evil. He lifted the discussion from the legal to the moral realm. Love of God and love of neighbour belong together and cannot be legitimately separated. The latter involves positively seeking the best interests of another (see Matthew 12:7, citing Hosea 6:6; Luke 10:25–37).

10–11. When Jesus had asked these questions, 'he looked round at them all' (Mark 3:5 adds 'deeply distressed at their stubborn hearts'). The silence of his opponents showed that they were unwilling to have a serious debate about the issue. Jesus had challenged their whole way of

---

[81] See Rowland, 'Sabbath Observance', 47–51.

[82] Nolland, *Luke 1–9:20*, 261. Rabbinic tradition allowed for medical aid on the Sabbath in case of mortal illness (Mishnah, *Yoma* 8:6) and also midwifery and circumcision (Mishnah, *Shabbat* 18:3; 19:2).

interpreting the law and their moral compass. When he said to the man, 'Stretch out your hand', he obeyed, 'and his hand was completely restored'. Jesus did no 'work', but the man was healed! This action demonstrated his authority to speak as Lord of the Sabbath and further showed him to be the agent of God's end-time redemption (see 5:17–26; Isaiah 35:3–6; 61:1–2; 65:17–25). The Pharisees and teachers of the law were 'furious and began to discuss with one another what they might do to Jesus'. Luke moderates the language of Mark 3:6, but he still indicates that this was a moment when the opposition to Jesus became more intense. When challenged again about his healing on the Sabbath in 13:10–17; 14:1–5, Jesus restated the argument about doing good. Despite the importance of these debates, Sabbath-breaking was surprisingly not mentioned in his trial before the Sanhedrin (22:66–71). By that stage, the central issue was his apparent claim to be the Messiah.

JESUS AND THE LAW OF GOD

Luke contains no exact parallel to Matthew 5:17–48, which exposes what it meant for Jesus to 'fulfil' the law. However, repeated contrasts in that passage between, 'You have heard that it was said . . .' and, 'But I tell you . . .' find an echo in Luke 6:1–11. When the Pharisees accused Jesus and his disciples of 'doing what is unlawful on the Sabbath', they were thinking in terms of their own interpretation of Exodus 34:21. Jesus did not debate the meaning of that text, but he drew attention to a biblical narrative in which the divine requirement in Leviticus 24:9 was set aside by a priest wishing to help David and his men in their time of need. Jesus used this passage to challenge the narrow legalism of the Pharisees and expose deeper issues regarding Sabbath observance. His claim that 'the Son of Man is Lord of the Sabbath' expressed his authority to determine such matters. More broadly, it suggests his role as the interpreter of Scripture for his people (see 6:20–49; 24:44–9), and that he actually brings the Sabbath to its fulfilment in the 'rest' of God's new creation (see Matthew 11:28–30).

Opposition to Jesus intensified when he pointed to the logic of doing good on the Sabbath and healed a man with a shrivelled hand (6:6–11). This further emphasised the need for compassion to be shown in applying God's Law to individual situations. Moreover, his healing of this man pointed to the newness of the situation his ministry introduced, reinforcing the expectation of change expressed in 5:34–9. Jesus says nothing about the observance of the Sabbath by his disciples in the future, but his own resurrection and teaching about the kingdom of God led to new ways of thinking about the Sabbath and eventually moved Christians to take the radical step of meeting to celebrate his resurrection on Sunday, the first day of the week.[83] We are not under the Law as Israel was, but as Robert Banks argues, 'It is in the law's transformation and fulfilment in the teaching of Jesus that its validity continues.'[84]

7. The blessings and challenges of discipleship (Luke 6:12–49)

A new phase in Luke's account of Jesus's public ministry is introduced with the mention that he withdrew to pray, before 'he called his disciples to him and chose twelve of them, whom he also designated apostles' (6:12–16). Although Jesus experienced growing opposition to his ministry from the Pharisees and the teachers of the law (5:17–6:11), Luke affirms once more his popularity with the crowds (6:17–19; compare 4:40–44; 5:17–19), before focusing on his teaching to disciples (6:20–49).[85] This discourse is often called the Sermon on the Plain, because of its setting (6:12, 17) and because of its likeness to Matthew's Sermon on the Mount. In both contexts, a large crowd is present to overhear what Jesus says to his disciples. Promises of blessing for those who follow Jesus are given at the beginning (Matthew 5:3–12; Luke 6:20–22), and the concluding parable challenges all who hear his words to put them into practice (Matthew 7:24–7; Luke 6:46–9). Luke does not record most of the material found in Matthew 5:13–6:34 concerning the Law, devotional practices, possessions and worry, though he includes similar teaching in other contexts. Despite the disparity in size, the two versions agree with respect to the order of the teaching they have in common. It is possible that both sermons derive from a common source, showing the link between the gospel Jesus preached and the demands of discipleship.[86] However, it is also possible that Jesus preached similar material on different occasions.

---

[83] See Turner, 'Sabbath', 124–157; Andrew T. Lincoln, 'Sabbath, Rest, and Eschatology in the New Testament', in *From Sabbath to Lord's Day*, ed. D. A. Carson, 197–220; A. G. Shead, 'Sabbath', *NDBT*, 745–50.

[84] Robert J. Banks, 'Matthew's Understanding of the Law: Authenticity and Interpretation in Matt. 5:17–20', *JBL* 93 (1974), 237. See further what is said about Jesus and the Law in my exposition of Luke 6:20–49.

[85] Mark 3:7–18 has a broadly parallel passage about Jesus's public ministry before the appointment of the apostles. Compare Matthew 4:23–5; 10:1–8.

[86] See Bock, *Luke 1:1–9:50*, 548–60, 931–44. Many scholars argue that where Matthew and Luke overlap, they were working from a written source called Q (for German 'Quelle'), which no longer exists. The possibility that Luke used Matthew

The choosing of the Twelve (6:12–16)

The twelve apostles

12 One of those days Jesus went out to a mountainside to pray, and spent the night praying to God. **13** When morning came, he called his disciples to him and chose twelve of them, whom he also designated apostles:

14 Simon (whom he named Peter), his brother Andrew, James, John, Philip, Bartholomew, **15** Matthew, Thomas, James son of Alphaeus, Simon who was called the Zealot, **16** Judas son of James, and Judas Iscariot, who became a traitor.

12–13. Luke marks a transition in his narrative with a broad link with what has gone before ('One of those days'). The importance of prayer in Jesus's life is highlighted again by saying that he 'went out to a mountainside to pray' (see 3:21; 9:18, 28–9; 11:1; 22:39–46; 23:34, 46). Apparently, he 'spent the night praying to God' because he was seeking his Father's guidance about the choice of the Twelve. When morning came, Jesus called the larger group of his disciples to come to him on the mountain and from that group he 'chose twelve of them, whom he also designated apostles'. Wilkins discerns, 'The distinctions between the general group of disciples and the specific group of the Twelve has to do with function or role, not status or worth.'[87] The significance of the number twelve is not revealed until 22:30, where 'judging the twelve tribes of Israel' means sharing in the Messiah's rule over a restored or renewed Israel (see Matthew 19:28). When Jesus named them 'apostles' (*apostoloi*), he could have used the Hebrew or Aramaic term *šālîaḥ* to convey the idea that they were his personal envoys.[88] Luke mentions the apostles again in 9:10; 17:5; 22:14; 24:10 and many times in Acts. The related verb (*apostellein*, 'send') is applied to various representatives (9:2, 52; 10:1; 22:25; see 11:49), but the Twelve are especially commissioned to share in Jesus's ministry to Israel (9:1–6), and then to be his foundational witnesses to the nations (24:45–9; Acts 1:6–8, 21–26).[89]

---

as a source is examined by Eric Eve, *Solving the Synoptic Puzzle: Introducing the Case for the Farrer Hypothesis* (Eugene: Cascade, 2021).

[87] Wilkins, 'Disciples and Discipleship', *DJG*, 353.

[88] Nolland, *Luke 1–9:20*, 266, observes that the evidence for the use of this noun with this meaning is much later than the New Testament, but the cognate verb is used in the Old Testament for the act of entrusting someone with a task.

[89] See Peterson, *Acts*, 79–83, 103–4, 108–33, 126–9. Note, however, the incidental description of Paul and Barnabas as 'the apostles' in Acts 14:4, 14, and Paul's testimony about his calling to be a 'witness' in Acts 26:16.

14–16. The order of the names here and in Acts 1:13 differs slightly from the lists in Mark 3:16–19 and Matthew 10:2–4, which are virtually synonymous. The first name in all the lists is Simon ('whom he named Peter'). Luke uses the name 'Peter' from this point (though 'Simon Peter' occurs in 5:8) without explanation of its significance (see Matthew 16:18). Simon's brother Andrew was an early follower of Jesus, as were James and John (Mark 1:16–19; Matthew 4:18–22; John 1:35–51), but Andrew is not mentioned in Luke 5:4–11. Luke says nothing about the call of the other eight to be disciples, though Matthew is probably another name for Levi (see my comment on 5:27–8). 'Simon who was called the Zealot' corresponds with 'Simon the Cananaean' in Mark 3:18 and Matthew 10:4, which the NIV translates as 'Simon the Zealot' to indicate that the same person is meant (*Kananaios* represents the Aramaic *qan'ān*, 'zealous one'). The Greek term *zēlōtēs* referred to someone 'earnestly committed to a side or cause' (BDAG). It has that general meaning here, rather than technically identifying Simon as a member of the Zealot party, which was not formed to oppose the Roman occupation of Palestine until AD 67–8.[90] Luke also has 'Judas son of James' instead of Thaddeus. Since several of the apostles have second names, it seems likely that this is the case here.[91] Each of the Gospels has Judas Iscariot at the end of the list with a comment about his future betrayal of Jesus. The best explanation for 'Iscariot' is that it is a Greek transcription of the Hebrew for 'man of Kerioth', making him the only non-Galilean apostle.[92] Like verse 11, the mention of betrayal sounds another warning note in Luke's narrative.

Disciples and the crowds: blessings and woes (6:17–26)

Blessings and woes

17 He went down with them and stood on a level place. A large crowd of his disciples was there and a great number of people from all over Judea, from Jerusalem, and from the coastal region around Tyre and Sidon, 18 who had come to hear him and to be healed of their diseases. Those troubled by impure spirits were cured, 19 and the

---

[90] See W. J. Heard and K. Yamazaki-Ransom, 'Revolutionary Movements', *DJG*, 796. Contrast Bock, *Luke 1:1–9:50*, 545–6.
[91] Nolland, *Luke 1–9:20*, 265; Bock, *Luke 1:1–9:50*, 546.
[92] Fitzmyer, *Luke I–IX*, 620. Kerioth Hezron was a village about twelve miles (19km) south of Hebron in Judea (Joshua 15:25). Bock, *Luke 1:1–9:50*, 546–7, notes alternative proposals for the meaning of 'Iscariot', but he agrees with Fitzmyer. Compare John 6:71; 13:26 ('the son of Simon Iscariot').

people all tried to touch him, because power was coming from him and healing them all.

20 Looking at his disciples, he said:

'Blessed are you who are poor,
for yours is the kingdom of God.
21 Blessed are you who hunger now,
for you will be satisfied.
Blessed are you who weep now,
for you will laugh.
22 Blessed are you when people hate you,
when they exclude you and insult you
and reject your name as evil,
because of the Son of Man.

23 'Rejoice in that day and leap for joy, because great is your reward in heaven. For that is how their ancestors treated the prophets.

24 'But woe to you who are rich,
for you have already received your comfort.
25 Woe to you who are well fed now,
for you will go hungry.
Woe to you who laugh now,
for you will mourn and weep.
26 Woe to you when everyone speaks well of you,
for that is how their ancestors treated the false prophets.

17–19. To resume his public ministry, Jesus 'went down with them and stood on a level place'. This prepares for the discourse to come, as does the mention of 'a large crowd of his disciples' (see verse 20). Luke also emphasises again the growing popularity of Jesus with the masses (see 4:40–44; 5:15, 17–19). 'A great number of people from all over Judea, from Jerusalem, and from the coastal region around Tyre and Sidon' had come 'to hear him and to be healed of their diseases' (as in 5:15). 'All over Judea' means Jewish Palestine (as in 4:44). 'The coastal region around Tyre and Sidon' probably refers to Jews who lived in that area: Gentiles are not yet in view (see 7:1–10).[93] Luke especially notes that 'those troubled by impure spirits were cured'. This took place as people tried to touch him, because they perceived that 'power was coming from him and healing them all' (see 5:17). They may have thought that Jesus had magical power, which could be experienced through touch, but the incident in 8:43–8 shows how he sought to draw such people into a more personal relationship of trust.

20–26. Jesus was specifically looking at his disciples when he pronounced four memorable blessings and encouraged them to rejoice in the social exclusion they might experience because of their attachment to him (verses 20–3). But his pattern of speech implicitly also commended discipleship to

---

[93] Nolland, *Luke 1–9:20*, 276; Lloyd, *Itinerant Jesus*, 299–346.

everyone listening (see verses 27, 47; 7:1; Matthew 5:1–2). The first three blessings affirm biblical expectations about the kingdom of God: 'yours is the kingdom of God . . . you will be satisfied . . . you will laugh' (verses 20–21).[94] The corresponding woes warn about the eternal consequences of rejecting Jesus and his teaching: 'you have already received your comfort . . . you will go hungry . . . you will mourn and weep' (verses 24–5). The fourth blessing narrows the focus to the persecution of disciples 'because of the Son of Man' (verse 22), and the corresponding woe contrasts those about whom 'everyone speaks well' (verse 26).[95]

Jesus's messages to the 'poor' (verse 20) and the 'rich' (verse 24), 'you who hunger now' (verse 21) and 'you who are well fed now' (verse 25) recall Mary's song (1:46–55) and his own use of Isaiah 61:1–2. These passages relate first to Israel in need of national deliverance ('you who weep now' specifically recalls Isaiah 61:2, 3). When Jesus applies Isaiah's predictions to his own ministry (4:16–21), he claims to be the agent of end-time salvation for those who believe. Deliverance from exile in Babylon established a pattern for the end-time rescue of God's people. Against S. A. Yang, the first blessing and woe (6:20, 24) are not simply 'a general proclamation that the kingdom of God belongs to those who suffer from marginalization and oppression, while those who marginalize and oppress others have no place in God's kingdom'.[96] In Luke's narrative, those who are poor, hungry and weep now come to Jesus with specific physical, social and spiritual needs. They experience restoration and renewal through him, but they also find themselves hated, excluded, insulted and rejected 'because of the Son of Man'. The fourth blessing (verse 22), in Seccombe's view, forms 'an interpretative climax and explanation or application of the other three'.[97] This suggests that the salvation which Jesus openly proclaims to all Israel 'will ultimately rest only upon his disciples'.[98] Nolland rightly judges that it is best 'neither to spiritualize

---

[94] See my comment on 4:43 concerning the kingdom of God, which these sayings explicate.

[95] The LXX uses the language of blessing to identify the happiness of those who trust God and walk in his way (e.g., Psalms 1:1; 119:1–2) and the term 'woe' to express the danger facing those who do not (e.g., Isaiah 5:8). Blessings are pronounced in Luke 1:45; 7:23; 10:23; 11:27–8; 12:37, 38, 43; 14:14, 15; 23:29 and woes in 10:13; 11:42–52; 17:1; 21:23; 22:22.

[96] S. A. Yang, 'Sermon on the Mount/Plain', *DJG*, 853. Compare Green, *Luke*, 264–7.

[97] Seccombe, *The Poor*, 96. Bock, *Luke 1:1–9:50*, 578–9, considers the different forms of opposition identified by the language in verse 22.

[98] Seccombe, *The Poor*, 96.

THE GALILEAN MINISTRY OF JESUS

away the reference to actual poverty, nor to make the whole thing a matter of social justice for the proletariat'.[99]

The exhortation to 'rejoice in that day and leap for joy, because great is your reward in heaven' (verse 23) repeats the note of joy from verse 21 and expresses the blessings of the kingdom of God in terms of vindication and a heavenly reward. Paradoxically, however, the phrase 'in that day' encourages rejoicing in the present, when disciples are hated, excluded, insulted and maligned, because of their attachment to 'the Son of Man' (see my comment on this term in 5:24). The expression 'reject your name as evil' is a Semitic idiom for giving someone a bad reputation (Deuteronomy 22:14, 19). Disciples can rejoice when they are treated that way, because they are in good company: 'for that is how their ancestors treated the prophets' (see Jeremiah 15:15; 20:8).

Those who are rich, well fed and laugh now find their satisfaction in the present age and have no longing for salvation (verses 24–5). Nolland draws attention to the way that riches ensnare those who possess them in 'a false set of values and loyalties which involve a foreshortened perspective in which love for the things of this world proves to be greater than the desire for the kingdom of God (18:23). One cannot serve God and mammon (16:13).'[100] As in Israel's past, those who are rich, well fed and seemingly happy with their material existence desire others to speak well of them. They attach themselves to 'false prophets', who reinforce their values and lifestyle rather than criticise them (verse 26; see Isaiah 30:10–11; Jeremiah 6:14; 23:16–17; Micah 2:11). Seccombe describes such people as 'withdrawing themselves from the true suffering Israel and forfeiting their coming consolation'.[101]

The call to love, generosity and a non-judgmental spirit (6:27–42)

Love for enemies

27 'But to you who are listening I say: love your enemies, do good to those who hate you, 28 bless those who curse you, pray for those who ill-treat you. 29 If someone slaps you on one cheek, turn to them the other also. If someone takes your coat, do not withhold your shirt from them. 30 Give to everyone who asks you, and if anyone takes what

---

[99] *Luke 1–9:20*, 288. See also Bock, *Luke 1:1–9:50*, 573–7.
[100] Nolland, *Luke 1–9:20*, 290. The rich are mentioned again in 12:16; 14:12; 16:1, 19, 21, 22; 18:23, 25; 19:2; 21:11.
[101] Seccombe, *The Poor*, 97. The word *paraklēsis* ('consolation' or 'comfort') is used in 2:25 to describe everything the prophets predicted concerning the salvation of Israel.

LUKE

belongs to you, do not demand it back. ³¹Do to others as you would have them do to you.

³²'If you love those who love you, what credit is that to you? Even sinners love those who love them. ³³And if you do good to those who are good to you, what credit is that to you? Even sinners do that. ³⁴And if you lend to those from whom you expect repayment, what credit is that to you? Even sinners lend to sinners, expecting to be repaid in full. ³⁵But love your enemies, do good to them, and lend to them without expecting to get anything back. Then your reward will be great, and you will be children of the Most High, because he is kind to the ungrateful and wicked. ³⁶Be merciful, just as your Father is merciful.

Judging others

³⁷'Do not judge, and you will not be judged. Do not condemn, and you will not be condemned. Forgive, and you will be forgiven. ³⁸Give, and it will be given to you. A good measure, pressed down, shaken together and running over, will be poured into your lap. For with the measure you use, it will be measured to you.'

³⁹He also told them this parable: 'Can the blind lead the blind? Will they not both fall into a pit? ⁴⁰The student is not above the teacher, but everyone who is fully trained will be like their teacher.

⁴¹'Why do you look at the speck of sawdust in your brother's eye and pay no attention to the plank in your own eye? ⁴²How can you say to your brother, "Brother, let me take the speck out of your eye," when you yourself fail to see the plank in your own eye? You hypocrite, first take the plank out of your eye, and then you will see clearly to remove the speck from your brother's eye.

27–8. Jesus continues to speak to his disciples and others who are listening (verse 17–19). First, he deals with love of enemies (verses 27–36) and then with being non-judgmental (verses 37–42). The first section begins with a general statement ('love your enemies'),[102] followed by a detailed description of how to respond to them ('do good to those who hate you, bless those who curse you, pray for those who ill-treat you'). This injunction clearly relates to the threat of persecution mentioned in verses 22–3. Jesus takes love of neighbour (Leviticus 19:18) to include not taking revenge on enemies, but positively seeking their best interests by doing good to them, blessing them and praying for them (see Exodus 23:4–5; Proverbs

---

[102] The verb used here (*agapaō*, as in 6:32, 35; 7:5, 42, 47; 10:27; 11:43; 16:13) has special significance in the New Testament, being used to describe 'God's love and the behavioral expectation of those who belong to God through Jesus Christ' (Edwards, *Luke*, 196). See E. Stauffer, 'ἀγαπάω, ἀγάπη, ἀγαπητός', *TDNT* 1:44–8; E. E. Popkes, 'Love, Love Command', *DJG*, 535–40.

25:21–2). These imperatives are in the present tense, encouraging habitual behaviour. Although some pagan and Jewish thinkers in that era argued for love of enemies in one form or another, Nolland observes that 'Jesus calls for an aggressive pitting of good against evil'.[103] The apostle Paul echoes this teaching in Romans 12:14, 19–21. Jesus modelled such behaviour in dealing with his opponents, even praying for their forgiveness (23:34).

29–30. Jesus offers further examples of how to deal with persecutors (see Matthew 5:38–42), identifying 'various ways believers are maltreated by physical violence, extortion or coercion, being imposed upon, and being robbed', as Edwards puts it.[104] Turning the other cheek and not withholding your shirt from someone who takes your coat means not retaliating and going beyond what is demanded of you. The second-person singular address in these verses highlights the need for individuals to make this choice. Such teaching is not a warrant for societies to let evil go unpunished. Moreover, self-defence cannot be ruled out 'where there is danger to life and limb', as Nolland warns.[105] But the aim in such personal attacks is to reduce aggression and express trust in God (see 1 Peter 4:19). The more general charge to 'give to everyone who asks you' calls for a generosity that reflects the grace and mercy of God (verses 35–6). The related injunction ('if anyone takes what belongs to you, do not demand it back') brings the focus back to the specific context of unwarranted personal attack.

31. Different forms of the 'golden rule' can be found in Jewish and Graeco–Roman sources. This positive version ('Do to others as you would have them do to you') specifically relates to Jesus's teaching about love for enemies, whereas in Matthew 7:12 it is part of a more general statement about the demands of 'the Law and the Prophets'. Nolland takes Jesus to mean that actions towards others should be determined not by the behaviour of the other, 'but only by what one would recognize as the good if one were on the receiving end'.[106] However, even this golden rule does not fully express the radical nature of Jesus's teaching about love, since 'the good' he wants his disciples to demonstrate far exceeds what might naturally be expected of them.

---

[103] Nolland, *Luke 1–9:20*, 302.
[104] Edwards, *Luke*, 198.
[105] Nolland, *Luke 1–9:20*, 297. The retaliation allowed in Exodus 21:24; Leviticus 24:20; Deuteronomy 19:21 was limited and meant to be determined in a legal context, not by personal acts of vengeance.
[106] Nolland, *Luke 1–9:20*, 298. Nolland lists versions of this saying that predate Jesus's usage and argues that they are mostly concerned with 'moral consistency or an ethic of reciprocity'.

32–4. Jesus calls for a love that is self-giving, not reciprocal or expecting a reward. Three hypothetical situations are considered. First, 'If you love those who love you, what credit is that to you?' (Matthew 5:46 has *misthos*, 'reward', instead of *charis*, 'credit'). Jesus answers his own question when he says, 'Even sinners love those who love them' (Matthew 5:46 has 'tax collectors', but Luke uses the more general term 'sinners' three times). Second, 'If you do good to those who do good to you, what credit is that to you?' Once again, the answer is, 'Even sinners do that' (Matthew 5:47 has *ethnikoi* ['foreigners, pagans']). Third, 'If you lend to those from whom you expect repayment, what credit is that to you?' Jesus answers emphatically, 'Even sinners lend to sinners, expecting to be paid in full,'[107] and calls for acts of sheer grace and mercy to opponents (see more broadly 11:41; 14:12–14).

35–6. Jesus repeats and expands his exhortation to 'love your enemies' by returning to the language of verses 33–4 ('do good to them, and lend to them without expecting to get anything back'). The theological foundation for his radical ethic is then revealed: God shows grace to those who act with grace ('your reward will be great'). God's 'reward' (*misthos*) is not a payment that is earned, but his gift to those who show themselves to be truly 'children of the Most High' (see Matthew 5:44). They know from Scripture and their own experience that God is 'kind to the ungrateful and wicked' (e.g., Psalms 34:8 (33:9 LXX); 86:5 (85:5 LXX)), and they seek to reflect this kindness in their own lives.[108] As 'the Son of the Most High' (1:32), Jesus perfectly reflected it and called upon his disciples to 'be merciful, just as your Father is merciful' (*oiktirmōn*, as in Exodus 34:6; Deuteronomy 4:31; Joel 2:13; Jonah 4:2 LXX).[109] Believers become children of God by his gracious initiative and should demonstrate that grace to others. Ultimately, they will experience the reward of God's grace in the eternal fellowship of his heavenly kingdom (see 20:35–6).

37–8. The next section of the sermon begins with the warning, 'Do not judge, and you will not be judged.' Judging is appropriate in properly

---

[107] Edwards, *Luke*, 201 argues that *apolabōsin ta isa* (NIV, 'paid in full') is better rendered 'paid in equal measure'.

[108] The word *chrēstos* ('kind') is often translated 'good' by the NIV. In a passage like Psalm 145:7–9 (144:7–9 LXX), it is used with other terms such as 'gracious', 'merciful' and 'compassionate'. Barclay, *Paul and the Gift*, 316, draws attention to Jewish texts celebrating 'a form of divine grace that rewarded those who were fitting recipients of its free and lavish beneficence'.

[109] The corresponding challenge in Matthew 5:48 ('Be perfect, therefore, as your heavenly Father is perfect') reflects the more general call of Leviticus 19:2 to be holy as God is holy.

constituted legal situations and for the discernment of right and wrong more generally (verses 39–40, 43–5; see 7:43), but what Jesus describes here is what Fitzmyer calls 'the human tendency to criticize and find fault with one's neighbor'.[110] The promise that 'you will not be judged' could refer to the way the other person responds, but more likely the passive verb refers to the judgment of God. The related warning, 'Do not condemn and you will not be condemned', speaks about the further step of pronouncing someone guilty (BDAG, *katadikazō*). In this sequence, 'Forgive, and you will be forgiven' suggests that those who forgive others may hope to be forgiven by God (see 11:4). A further antidote to presumption and contempt for others is expressed with two promises. The first, 'Give, and it will be given to you', recalls what is said about grace in verses 35–6, enhanced with the image of an abundant harvest of grain ('A good measure, pressed down, shaken together and running over, will be poured into your lap'). The giving here involves being generous about the motives and intentions of others. Those who are generous in this way will experience the superabundance of God's generosity.[111] The second promise develops the harvest imagery, 'For with the measure you use, it will be measured to you', and resumes the like-for-like pattern in verse 37.

39–40. A link with the preceding teaching is indicated by the words, 'He also told them this parable' (see my comment on 'parable' in 5:36; 8:4). A simple comparison is introduced with two rhetorical questions: 'Can the blind lead the blind? Will they not both fall into a pit?' A blind leader will resist the call for the sort of behaviour Jesus has been commending. The point of the parable is then stated: 'The student is not above the teacher, but everyone who is fully trained will be like their teacher.' Would-be disciples are warned against choosing teachers who are 'blind' and will lead them 'into a pit' (see Matthew 15:14). They need to discern the negative influence that blind teachers will have on them (see Matthew 10:24–5) and compare the positive influence that Jesus has on those who follow him.

41–2. Jesus returns to the subject of criticising others, using an exaggerated comparison to make his point ('Why do you look at the speck of

---

[110] Fitzmyer, *Luke I–IX*, 641. The verb *krinō* ('judge') can refer to a thoughtful decision (BDAG), but here it means making an unfavourable judgment on someone without sufficient evidence or cause (see Romans 14:10–13).
[111] Fitzmyer, *Luke I–IX*, 641. See 8:18; 19:25–6. Contrast Isaiah 65:7; Jeremiah 32:18; Psalm 79:12.

sawdust in your brother's eye and pay no attention to the plank in your own eye?'). The absurdity of this is reinforced by repetition ('How can you say to your brother, "Brother, let me take the speck out of your eye," when you yourself fail to see the plank in your own eye?'). The fundamental issue is hypocrisy ('You hypocrite'), caused by an unwillingness to deal with one's own more serious faults ('first take the plank out of your eye, and then you will see clearly to remove the speck from your brother's eye').[112]

Putting Jesus's words into practice (6:43–9)

A tree and its fruit
43 'No good tree bears bad fruit, nor does a bad tree bear good fruit. 44 Each tree is recognised by its own fruit. People do not pick figs from thorn-bushes, or grapes from briers. 45 A good man brings good things out of the good stored up in his heart, and an evil man brings evil things out of the evil stored up in his heart. For the mouth speaks what the heart is full of.

The wise and foolish builders
46 'Why do you call me, "Lord, Lord," and do not do what I say? 47 As for everyone who comes to me and hears my words and puts them into practice, I will show you what they are like. 48 They are like a man building a house, who dug down deep and laid the foundation on rock. When the flood came, the torrent struck that house but could not shake it, because it was well built. 49 But the one who hears my words and does not put them into practice is like a man who built a house on the ground without a foundation. The moment the torrent struck that house, it collapsed and its destruction was complete.'

43–5. The final section of this discourse contains various forms of parabolic speech, beginning with, 'No good tree bears bad fruit, nor does a bad tree bear good fruit.'[113] Jesus restates the general principle ('Each tree is recognised by its own fruit') and then refers to a choice that has to be made ('People do not pick figs from thorn-bushes, or grapes from briers'). In view of verses 39–40, this could reinforce the idea that disciples must discern the character of those who would teach and influence them. In Matthew 7:15–20, this imagery is associated with a warning to 'watch out

---

[112] Nolland, *Luke 1–9:20*, 307–8, argues that the 'plank' and the 'speck' express the difference between the great demands of discipleship and 'ethical minutiae'. Hypocrisy is identified again in 12:1, 56; 13:15.
[113] Fruit is often an image for deeds in the Old Testament (e.g., Isaiah 3:10; Jeremiah 17:10; 21:14; Hosea 10:13). See Luke 3:8.

for false prophets'. But Luke's version offers a more general application: 'A good man brings good things out of the good stored up in his heart' (ESV, 'out of the good treasure of his heart'), 'and an evil man brings evil things out of the evil stored up in his heart' (see 11:39–41). This picks up on the need for self-examination and honesty about one's faults (verse 42), while focusing on the way speech particularly reveals character ('For the mouth speaks what the heart is full of'). In Nolland's judgment, Jesus calls for 'a true inner goodness of the heart, of which one's concrete acts of goodness will be the natural fruit'.[114] Teachers and disciples alike need to heed this warning (see Matthew 12:33–7; James 3:1–12).

46–9. An implied rebuke climaxes the sermon ('Why do you call me, "Lord, Lord," and do not do what I say?').[115] Jesus describes a genuine follower as one who comes to him, hears his words and puts them into practice. Such a person is like a man who built his house with a deep foundation on rock, and, 'When the flood came, the torrent struck that house but could not shake it, because it was well built.' Given his teaching in verses 20–26, this is an image of surviving persecution and suffering and experiencing the promised blessings of God's kingdom. The person who hears his words and does not put them into practice is like 'a man who built a house on the ground without a foundation. The moment the torrent struck that house, it collapsed and its destruction was complete.' This is a picture of the ultimate ruin facing those who do not take the challenge of discipleship seriously.

THE ETHICAL DEMANDS OF JESUS

The blessings and woes pronounced by Jesus were a way of proclaiming the gospel of the kingdom of God and its ethical implications. Jesus contrasted two different ways of life, one characterised by poverty, hunger, weeping and social alienation 'because of the Son of Man' (see 9:23–6, 57–62), and the other by contentment with riches, being well fed and happy in the present, enjoying the approval of others and listening to false prophets. The lifestyle consistent with his kingdom message includes a willingness to suffer for it, while looking to a heavenly reward. Those who are satisfied with what this world offers will miss out on the blessings of the world to come. At the heart of his 'sermon' there is a radical demand for love of neighbour, even enemies who mistreat disciples and deprive them of what is rightfully

---

[114] Nolland, *Luke I–IX*, 309. See S. McKnight, 'Ethics of Jesus', *DJG*, 242–51.
[115] *Kyrios* ('Lord') at this stage in Jesus's public ministry will mean 'Sir or 'Master' (see 5:8, 12; 7:6; 9:54, 59, 61).

theirs. The inspiration and motivation for such love is the kindness, generosity and mercy of God, which Jesus demonstrated and proclaimed. His emphasis on not judging others is another way of expressing genuine love. But this warning is balanced by a challenge to discern the true character of would-be teachers and the influence they might have on their followers. Love and truth belong together here. Jesus calls for an inner transformation of the heart that will be identified by the good fruit it produces. His subtle appeal for people to follow him concludes with the demand to treat him as Master by hearing his words and putting them into practice.

8. Further revelations of the authority of Jesus (Luke 7:1–50)

This series of episodes begins by highlighting the reasons for a widespread recognition of Jesus as a great prophet (verses 1–17). However, the question of John's disciples ('Are you the one to come, or should we expect someone else?') leads Jesus to claim a greater significance for himself than any of the prophets who went before him, including John himself (verses 18–35). The issue of his prophetic status is raised again by a Pharisee who invites him to dinner (verses 36–9). Jesus encounters a woman whom the Pharisee dismisses as a sinner, assures her of the forgiveness she is seeking, warns the Pharisee that his lack of love is a sign of being 'forgiven little' and declares that the woman's faith has 'saved' her (verses 40–50).

Healing a Gentile centurion's servant (7:1–10)

The faith of the centurion

7 When Jesus had finished saying all this to the people who were listening, he entered Capernaum. 2There a centurion's servant, whom his master valued highly, was ill and about to die. 3The centurion heard of Jesus and sent some elders of the Jews to him, asking him to come and heal his servant. 4When they came to Jesus, they pleaded earnestly with him, 'This man deserves to have you do this, 5because he loves our nation and has built our synagogue.' 6So Jesus went with them.

He was not far from the house when the centurion sent friends to say to him: 'Lord, don't trouble yourself, for I do not deserve to have you come under my roof. 7That is why I did not even consider myself worthy to come to you. But say the word, and my servant will be healed. 8For I myself am a man under authority, with soldiers under me. I tell this one, "Go", and he goes; and that one, "Come", and he comes. I say to my servant, "Do this", and he does it.'

9When Jesus heard this, he was

amazed at him, and turning to the crowd following him, he said, 'I tell you, I have not found such great faith even in Israel.' **10** Then the men who had been sent returned to the house and found the servant well.

Both Luke and Matthew locate this event soon after Jesus has spoken extensively about discipleship (see Matthew 8:5–13).[116] Jesus commends the centurion's faith, although in Luke's version his engagement with Jesus is more remote. The centurion sends some Jewish elders as intermediaries, asking Jesus to come and heal his servant, who is close to death (verses 3–5). Then he sends unspecified friends with the message that he does not deserve to have Jesus come under this roof, acknowledging that he can heal his servant from a distance with a simple command (verses 6–8). The narrative climaxes with Jesus's pronouncement, 'I have not found such great faith even in Israel,' and an indication that the servant was healed (verses 9–10). The focus is thus on a faith that genuinely acknowledges Jesus's authority and trusts him to bless, even without seeing him.[117]

1–2. The link between this episode and the preceding section is strong ('When Jesus had finished saying all this to the people who were listening, he entered Capernaum'). In that Galilean town, 'a centurion's servant, whom his master valued highly, was ill and about to die' (Matthew 8:6 adds 'paralysed, suffering terribly'). The centurion was an important represent-ative of the occupying power, notionally in charge of a hundred soldiers. Since it is unlikely that there was a Roman garrison in Capernaum at that time, he could have been responsible to Herod Antipas as the leader of mercenary troops or, as Fitzmyer suggests, he may have been in 'police-service or customs-service'.[118] The terms *doulos* ('slave') and *pais* ('servant') are used interchangeably in this narrative. The centurion's concern for his servant was unusual and exemplary, with no hint of impropriety.[119]

3–5. The centurion could have heard of Jesus because of his previous ministry in Capernaum (4:31–7), or from those who had been part of the great gathering mentioned in 6:17–49. Luke alone records that he 'sent some elders of the Jews to him, asking him to come and heal his

---

[116] Nolland, *Luke 1–9:20*, 314, 316, argues for the originality of Luke's version, which has been abbreviated by Matthew (though Matthew 8:11–12 adds sayings found in Luke 13:28–9). See Bock, *Luke 1:1–9:50*, 630–32.

[117] The issue of Jesus's authority and its source is highlighted in 4:32, 36; 5:24; 20:2, 8.

[118] Fitzmyer, *Luke I–IX*, 651. Bock, *Luke 1:1–9:50*, 635, argues that the centurion need not have been a Roman, but the wording of verse 9 suggests that he was certainly not a Jew.

[119] J. A. Harrill, 'Slavery', *DNTB*, 1124–7.

servant'. These elders were probably leaders of the local Jewish community (see 20:1; 22:52; Acts 4:5, 8, 23). As a Gentile, the centurion recognised that he had no claim on Jesus and wanted the elders to intercede on his behalf. When they came to him, they emphasised the centurion's merits: 'This man deserves to have you do this (ESV, 'he is worthy' (*axios*)), because he loves our nation and has built our synagogue'. His love for the Jewish people had been generously expressed, suggesting that he was a wealthy 'Godfearer', like the centurion in Acts 10:2, 22.[120] But this did not make him more worthy of Jesus's help than anyone else! The centurion's humble approach in verse 7 exposes the false values and reasoning of the Jewish elders.

6–8. Jesus responded to the appeal of the elders and went with them, showing no concern about being defiled by contact with a Gentile. He was not far from the house when the centurion sent friends to forestall the visit. Speaking through them, the centurion says, 'Lord, don't trouble yourself, for I do not deserve to have you come under my roof. That is why I did not consider myself worthy to come to you.' These two expressions ('I do not deserve' (*ou gar hikanos eimi*)) and 'I did not consider myself worthy' (*oude emauton ēxiōsa*)) show the centurion's genuine humility and surprising respect for Jesus.[121] More profoundly, the second part of his message expresses some perception of Jesus's divine authority: 'But say the word, and my servant will be healed. For I myself am a man under authority, with soldiers under me. I tell this one, "Go", and he goes; and that one, "Come", and he comes. I say to my servant "Do this", and he does it.' His military experience enabled him to understand how Jesus's command could achieve healing, even at a distance.

9. 'When Jesus heard this, he was amazed at him.' No one in Israel so far had expressed such confidence in the power of his word to achieve such an outcome (4:36 relates the response of those in the synagogue *after* Jesus had exorcised a demon). Turning to the crowd following him, Jesus commended the centurion's faith: 'I tell you, I have not found such great faith in Israel' (see 4:24–7; 23:47). This incident anticipates the record of Luke's second volume, where many Gentiles come to believe in Jesus, while Jews remain unresponsive and even antagonistic to the

---

[120] See Peterson, *Acts*, 323–4, 326–7. Nolland, *Luke 1:1–9:20*, 316, notes inscriptional evidence for the erection of synagogues by Gentiles. See also Edwards, *Luke*, 211.
[121] The centurion would have known that Jews regarded the dwellings of Gentiles as unclean (see Acts 10:28; 11:12) and sought to relieve Jesus of the need to visit him. Compare the healing of Naaman at a distance by Elisha in 2 Kings 5.

gospel (e.g., Acts 13:42–14:7). Matthew 8:11–12 adds a prediction about many Gentiles taking their places with Abraham, Isaac and Jacob in the kingdom of heaven, while 'the subjects of the kingdom' are 'thrown outside'. Luke reserves this warning until 13:28–30, choosing rather to show how positive evaluations of Jesus's ministry continued to spread throughout Judea and the surrounding country (7:11–17).

10. 'Then the men who had been sent returned to the house and found the servant well.' He had been healed while the centurion's friends were talking to Jesus. In fact, no explicit command was given to achieve this. The outcome was even more amazing than the centurion had hoped for: Jesus was in such communion with his heavenly Father that he could simply heal by willing it.

Jesus raises a widow's son from death (7:11–17)

Jesus moves from healing a man who was about to die (verse 2) to raising a young man who was already dead (verses 11–15). Similarities to events in the ministries of Elijah and Elisha (1 Kings 17:17–24; 2 Kings 4:8–37) probably contributed to the widespread conclusion that 'a great prophet has appeared among us' and 'God has come to help his people' (verse 16). The incident has no parallel in the other Gospels, though the raising of Jairus's daughter is recorded in Matthew 9:18–25; Mark 5:22–43; Luke 8:40–56, and John testifies to the raising of Lazarus (John 11:1–44).[122] Luke's narrative continues to focus on Jesus's extraordinary authority over life and death (see 7:7–10).

Jesus raises a widow's son

11 Soon afterwards, Jesus went to a town called Nain, and his disciples and a large crowd went along with him. **12** As he approached the town gate, a dead person was being carried out – the only son of his mother, and she was a widow. And a large crowd from the town was with her. **13** When the Lord saw her, his heart went out to her and he said, 'Don't cry.'

14 Then he went up and touched the bier they were carrying him on, and the bearers stood still. He said, 'Young man, I say to you, get up!' **15** The dead man sat up and began to talk, and Jesus gave him back to his mother.

---

[122] Nolland, *Luke 1–9:20*, 324, rightly observes that 'once a naturalistic perspective has been transcended to allow for the historicity of any of Jesus's healings (understood as more than psychosomatic healings), there seems to be no good reason for stumbling over the resuscitation of the dead'.

16 They were all filled with awe and praised God. 'A great prophet has appeared among us,' they said. 'God has come to help his people.' **17** This news about Jesus spread throughout Judea and the surrounding country.

11–13. A close connection with the previous incident is indicated by the words 'Soon afterwards'. Nain was on the southern border of Galilee, a few kilometres south of Nazareth, 'and his disciples and a large crowd went along with him.' As they approached the town gate, they met another large crowd coming in the other direction, while 'a dead person was being carried out'. The chief mourner was a widow, who had lost her only son. Apart from the emotional impact, this loss exposed her to economic and social deprivation, with no male to look after her and supply her needs. The large crowd of mourners no doubt heightened the sense of grief and loss she felt. From this point in his narrative, Luke begins to call Jesus 'the Lord', expressing his own post-resurrection belief in the divinity of Jesus (see 24:34, 52; Acts 2:36), though the characters in the story do not have that perception. Along with this exalted title, Luke stresses the compassionate humanity of Jesus: 'When the Lord saw her, his heart went out to her (ESV, 'he had compassion on her').' The verb used here (*splagchnidzomai*) and in 10:33; 15:20 describes a deep-seated feeling that propels people into action (the corresponding noun is used in 1:78). Jesus took the initiative and said to the woman, 'Don't cry,' and then he proceeded to help her in a remarkable and unexpected way.

14–15. When Jesus touched 'the bier they were carrying him on' (*sporos* could mean 'coffin' rather than 'bier'), he was silently asking for the procession to stop, and 'the bearers stood still'. There are several echoes of the raising of the widow's son by Elijah (1 Kings 17:19–23) in what follows. However, Jesus's approach was less elaborate, and he had no need to cry out to God in prayer, but simply said, 'Young man, I say to you, get up!' The authority of Jesus's word of command is once more demonstrated (see verses 7–8, 10). 'The dead man sat up and began to talk,' signifying his immediate and complete recovery. The relational significance of this restoration to life is stressed when Luke says that 'Jesus gave him back to his mother' (see 1 Kings 17:23).[123]

---

[123] Green, *Luke*, 289–92, notes the extent to which the raising of this young man would have led to the restoration of his mother within her community. His resuscitation to earthly life anticipated the resurrection to eternal life, though the latter involves a transformation of the body (according to 20:34–8; 24:28–43; 1 Corinthians 15:35–56).

16–17. All who witnessed this mighty work 'were filled with awe' (*elaben de phobos pantas*, 'fear seized all'), which is a common reaction to a divine intervention in Luke (1:12, 65; 2:9; 5:26; 8:25, 37; Acts 2:43; 5:5, 11; 19:17), sometimes linked to praise ('and they praised God'). Echoes of 1 Kings 17:17–24 lead the people to say, 'A great prophet has appeared among us' (*ēgerthē*, 'has been raised up') and 'God has come to help his people' (*epeskepsato*, 'visited'). This is an encouraging response, even though subsequent narratives question the adequacy of simply linking Jesus with Elijah or Elisha. The language of divine visitation recalls Zechariah's prophecy (1:68, 78–9), giving a hint that end-time expectations might be in the process of fulfilment. 'This news about Jesus spread throughout Judea', implying the whole of Jewish Palestine (4:44; 6:17) and even further to 'the surrounding country'.

JESUS AND GOD

Although there is a focus on the prophetic character of Jesus's ministry in Luke 7, the claim that 'God has come to help his people' takes on a deeper meaning when these narratives are viewed in the light of what has been progressively disclosed about Jesus. Earlier claims of a divine visitation to save his people are specifically associated with the messiahship of Jesus (1:67–75; 2:10–11). In 7:1–15, Jesus does God-like things, such as healing the centurion's servant at a distance without a word and raising the widow's son from death with a simple command. These actions confirm the earlier claim that the power of the Lord was with him to heal and restore in remarkable ways (see 5:17). What Jesus says about himself further exposes his divine authority and unique relationship with God (e.g., 5:20–24, 31–2; 6:5). In his 'Sermon on the Plain' he goes beyond anything said by the prophets, asserting that the kingdom of God belongs to those who come to *him* in faith and put *his* words into practice (6:20–49). It is notable, therefore, that at this stage in his narrative Luke begins to call Jesus 'the Lord' and implicitly invites his readers to affirm this too. In both incidents, Jesus shows himself to be the Lord of life and death.

Jesus and John the Baptist (7:18–35)

Three linked passages deal with the relationship between Jesus and John the Baptist, as in Matthew 11:2–19.[124] However, in Luke's account they

---

[124] The similarities and differences between these narratives are discussed by Fitzmyer, *Luke I–IX*, 662–5; Nolland, *Luke 1–9:20*, 326–7.

function particularly in relation to the claims that 'a great prophet has appeared among us' and 'God has come to help his people' (verse 16). Jesus first responds to John's question through his disciples about his identity and calling (verses 18–23). Then he speaks to the crowd about John's role in the purpose of God and the different ways he was received (verses 24–30). Finally, he reflects on the contradictory expectations of the people regarding John and himself (verses 31–5).

Jesus and John the Baptist

18 John's disciples told him about all these things. Calling two of them, **19** he sent them to the Lord to ask, 'Are you the one who is to come, or should we expect someone else?'

20 When the men came to Jesus, they said, 'John the Baptist sent us to you to ask, "Are you the one who is to come, or should we expect someone else?"'

21 At that very time Jesus cured many who had diseases, illnesses and evil spirits, and gave sight to many who were blind. **22** So he replied to the messengers, 'Go back and report to John what you have seen and heard: the blind receive sight, the lame walk, those who have leprosy[a] are cleansed, the deaf hear, the dead are raised, and the good news is proclaimed to the poor. **23** Blessed is anyone who does not stumble on account of me.'

24 After John's messengers left, Jesus began to speak to the crowd about John: 'What did you go out into the wilderness to see? A reed swayed by the wind? **25** If not, what did you go out to see? A man dressed in fine clothes? No, those who wear expensive clothes and indulge in luxury are in palaces. **26** But what did you go out to see? A prophet? Yes, I tell you, and more than a prophet. **27** This is the one about whom it is written:

' "I will send my messenger
    ahead of you,
who will prepare your way
    before you."[b]

28 I tell you, among those born of women there is no one greater than John; yet the one who is least in the kingdom of God is greater than he.'

29 (All the people, even the tax collectors, when they heard Jesus' words, acknowledged that God's way was right, because they had been baptised by John. **30** But the Pharisees and the experts in the law rejected God's purpose for themselves, because they had not been baptised by John.)

31 Jesus went on to say, 'To what, then, can I compare the people of this generation? What are they like? **32** They are like children sitting in the market-place and calling out to each other:

' "We played the pipe for you,
    and you did not dance;
we sang a dirge,
    and you did not cry."

33 For John the Baptist came neither eating bread nor drinking wine, and you say, "He has a demon." 34 The Son of Man came eating and drinking, and you say, "Here is a glutton and a drunkard, a friend of tax collectors and

sinners." 35 But wisdom is proved right by all her children.'

---

a 22 The Greek word traditionally translated *leprosy* was used for various diseases affecting the skin.

b 27 Mal. 3:1

18–19. 'John's disciples told him about all these things', meaning the teaching and mighty works of Jesus and the various responses recorded in 4:31–7:17. John called two of his disciples and 'sent them to the Lord' to ask, 'Are you the one who is to come, or should we expect someone else?' Jesus did not appear to have fulfilled John's expectations (see 3:16–17). 'The one who is to come' is not necessarily a messianic title (Isaiah 40:10; Zechariah 14:5; Malachi 3:1), but John's prediction was specifically in the context of the people 'wondering in their hearts if [he] might possibly be the Messiah' (3:15).[125]

20–22. John's question is repeated by Luke for dramatic effect, as his disciples relay it to Jesus. Luke also adds his own summary of what Jesus had been doing 'at that very time' (ESV, 'in that hour'): 'Jesus cured many who had diseases, illnesses and evil spirits, and gave sight to many who were blind' (see 4:40–41; 5:15; 6:18–19).[126] Jesus then called John's messengers to act as witnesses of what they had 'seen and heard' (see Deuteronomy 19:15): 'the blind receive sight, the lame walk, those who have leprosy are cleansed, the deaf hear, the dead are raised, and the good news is proclaimed to the poor'. Jesus alludes to Isaiah 35:5–6 with its portrayal of physical healing in the context of a renewed creation (see Isaiah 29:18–19). Isaiah 26:19 may also have been in mind, with its promise of bodily resurrection, and Isaiah 61:1–2, with its gospel of release for captive Israel.[127] In his sermon at Nazareth, Jesus identified himself with the Spirit-anointed prophet who would proclaim that release and make the end-time blessings of salvation available (4:18–21). However, Luke's narrative has created specifically messianic expectations, with John as the forerunner (1:31–2, 68–79; 2:11, 26; 3:15). By implication these are indeed 'the deeds of the Messiah' (Matthew 11:2).

---

[125] Fitzmyer, *Luke I–IX*, 666–7, rejects this explanation and argues that the title should be understood of 'the messenger of Yahweh' (Malachi 3:1), who is a Second Elijah. Nolland, *Luke 1–9:20*, 328–9, more helpfully suggests that the title brings together every strand of eschatological expectation.
[126] The healing of a blind person is not recorded until 18:35–43.
[127] There is no specific Old Testament prophecy about lepers being cleansed, and Luke does not record the healing of a deaf person. However, the latter may be implied in 11:14 (*kōphos* can mean 'mute' or 'deaf' (BDAG)).

23. Jesus says nothing here about the coming of God with vengeance and retribution, which is an aspect of prophetic expectation in the passages he alludes to (Isaiah 35:5; 61:2). This theme is emphasised in Luke 10:13–15; 13–14; 21, but Jesus's earlier teaching and actions essentially 'proclaim the year of the Lord's favour' (4:19). His focus on grace, rather than imminent judgment (3:7–9, 16–17), apparently caused John to question the identity and significance of Jesus. John is therefore included in the challenge that Jesus gives: 'Blessed is anyone who does not stumble on account of me' (see 2:34). This blessing is worded in the singular, though it is intended to be a general warning (*hos ean*, 'whoever'). The verb used here (*skandalisthē*) implies that someone might be tripped up and 'fall away' because of unbelief (see Mark 14:27, 29; Luke 17:2; John 16:1). Jesus must be received on his own terms, not as one might like him to be!

24–7. 'After John's messengers left, Jesus began to speak to the crowd about John.' Several rhetorical questions were posed to remind them that, when John was preaching in the wilderness, they went out to see a prophet. They were not looking for 'a reed swayed by the wind' or 'a man dressed in fine clothes'. 'No, those who wear expensive clothes and indulge in luxury are in palaces.' In fact, John was 'more than a prophet'. He was the greatest prophet of the Old Testament era because of his calling: 'the one about whom it is written: "I will send my messenger ahead of you, who will prepare your way before you."' This quotation from Malachi 3:1 is slightly influenced by the wording of Exodus 23:20 LXX (see Mark 1:2) to hint at the prospect of a new exodus. Malachi uses the pronouns 'my' and 'me' to indicate that the messenger prepares for the coming of God himself. Exodus 23:20 uses the pronoun 'you' to refer to Israel ('I am sending an angel ahead of you to guard you along the way and to bring you to the place I have prepared'). John is the messenger (*angelos*) whom God sends ahead of his Son, 'to make ready a people prepared for the Lord' (Luke 1:17; see 1:76–9; 3:4–6). He is the Elijah figure of Malachi 4:5 (ET), who prepares for the coming of God in the person of Jesus to save his people (Luke 7:16) and bring them into their ultimate inheritance.

28. Despite the greatness of John, however, Jesus insists that 'a new state of affairs has been inaugurated now by the in-breaking of the kingdom of God', as Nolland puts it.[128] The first part of this verse affirms in different terms what Jesus has already said: 'I tell you, among those born of women there is no one greater than John.' Jesus apparently excludes himself from the general category of 'those born of women' because of

---

[128] Nolland, *Luke 1–9:20*, 335.

his divine conception and identity (see 1:34–5). As the forerunner of God himself in the person of the Messiah, John surpassed every other human being, but he belonged to the old era and not the new ('the one who is least in the kingdom of God is greater than he'). Since the Greek term *mikroteros* is a comparative adjective, it can be translated 'the one who is less' and has been taken as a humble form of self-reference by Jesus.[129] However, the term is better read as a superlative ('least') and understood as a reference to any one of Jesus's disciples (9:48; Matthew 10:42; 18:10, 14; Mark 9:42) who has witnessed what prophets and kings wished to see and to hear (10:23–4). When John was imprisoned (3:20), he was excluded from being 'in the kingdom of God' in this anticipatory way, though he is certainly among the prophets who will enjoy the consummation of the kingdom with Jesus and his followers (13:28).[130]

29–30. These verses have no parallel in Matthew's account and are likely to be an editorial comment by Luke (rightly placed in brackets by the NIV). John and Jesus are linked together, as similar reactions to their ministries are considered. 'All the people' whom Jesus has just addressed (verse 24), among whom there were even tax collectors, 'acknowledged that God's way was right' (*edikaiōsan ton theon*, 'they declared God just' (ESV)), 'because they had been baptised by John' (see 3:12). Fitzmyer calls their positive response 'a verdict of approval on God's plan of salvation'.[131] 'But the Pharisees and the experts in the law rejected God's purpose for themselves, because they had not been baptised by John.' When they rejected John's call to repent and be baptised, they set aside *for themselves* God's plan (*tēn boulēn tou theou*), which Jesus came to fulfil.[132] Their growing opposition to Jesus and his ministry (5:17–6:11) continued to express this disregard for God's will and purpose.

31–4. Jesus goes on to provide a parable or simile about his generation (verses 31–2), an explanation of this (verses 33–4), and a final wisdom saying (verse 35). This sequence is paralleled in Matthew 11:16–19. Two rhetorical questions identify the issue: 'To what, then, can I compare the people of this generation? What are they like?' The term 'generation' (*genea*)

---

[129] Fitzmyer, *Luke I–IX*, 675, argues for this possibility and notes that it allows for John to be included in the kingdom of God.

[130] Nolland, *Luke 1–9:20*, 337–9. Compare Marshall, *Luke*, 296–7. This interpretation is confirmed by the verses that follow the saying in Matthew 11:12–14. Compare Luke 16:16.

[131] Fitzmyer, *Luke I–IX*, 676; see Green, *Luke*, 301.

[132] Since the 'plan of God' has a broad reference in Acts 2:23; 4:28; 5:38–39; 13:36; 20:27, the NIV translation 'God's purpose for themselves' seems too restricted here.

has a negative sense here (as in 9:41; 11:29–32, 50–51; 17:25; Acts 2:40; compare Jeremiah 2:31; 7:29) and broadly applies to the contemporaries of Jesus and John (verse 35 identifies exceptions to this generalisation). The parable is about:

> . . . children sitting in the market-place and calling out to each
>   other:
> 'We played the pipe for you,
>   and you did not dance;
> we sang a dirge,
>   and you did not cry.'

Many interpretations have been offered to explain this imagery, but certain things seem to be clear from the context. The children represent conflicting attitudes and expectations, some wanting to rejoice (as at a wedding) and others to mourn (as at a funeral). They cannot agree about what is needed. Their expectations are then related to the ministries of John and Jesus. 'John the Baptist came neither eating bread nor drinking wine, and you say, "He has a demon."' Even those who thought it was time for mourning and repentance regarded John's asceticism as unreasonable.[133] 'The Son of Man came eating and drinking, and you say, "Here is a glutton and drunkard, a friend of tax collectors and sinners."' As Nolland observes, 'Jesus seemed to behave as though there was continually something to celebrate (see 5:33–34), and he drew into this celebration tax collectors and sinners – people known to be unsavoury types who lived beyond the edge of respectable society.'[134] John and Jesus were rejected for apparently contradictory behaviours, which were in fact different manifestations of the same plan of God for Israel's salvation.

35. A final saying provides the counterpart to the gloomy picture provided in verses 30–34. 'Wisdom' is personified (as in Proverbs 1:20–33; 8:1–9:6; Wisdom 6:22–9:18) and is said to be 'proved right by all her children' (see Proverbs 8:32; Sirach 4:11; Matthew 11:19, 'by her deeds'). Although it has been suggested that John and Jesus themselves are wisdom's children, the context points to those who acknowledge the wisdom of God in their ministries. The disciples of John and Jesus showed by their lives that God's provision for his people in these complementary

---

[133] Fitzmyer, *Luke I–IX*, 681. Fitzmyer (678–9) discusses various possible lines of interpretation.
[134] Nolland, *Luke 1–9:20*, 348.

ministries was right.[135] Indeed, the wisdom of God in the ministry of Jesus has been demonstrated in subsequent history and the multitudes that have been transformed by him. Christianity has been good for the world, and it brings wonderful outcomes when it is embraced honestly and seriously!

Salvation for a sinful woman (7:36–50)

Fitzmyer suggests:

> This scene is one of the greatest episodes in the Lucan Gospel, for it depicts Jesus not merely defending a sinful woman against the criticism of a Pharisee, but drives home in a special way the relationship between the forgiveness of sins (by God) and the place of human love and the giving of oneself in that whole process.[136]

The Pharisee who invites Jesus to dinner knows that many regard Jesus as a prophet (verse 16), but he cannot reconcile this view with the fact that Jesus allows a notoriously sinful woman to touch him (verses 36–9). Jesus tells a parable about two debtors to explain why the woman has shown such great love (verses 40–47) and then assures her that her sins have been forgiven, that her faith has saved her and that she can 'go in peace' (verses 48–50). This woman perfectly illustrates the claim that 'wisdom is proved right by all her children' (verse 35).

Jesus anointed by a sinful woman

36 When one of the Pharisees invited Jesus to have dinner with him, he went to the Pharisee's house and reclined at the table. **37** A woman in that town who lived a sinful life learned that Jesus was eating at the Pharisee's house, so she came there with an alabaster jar of perfume. **38** As she stood behind him at his feet weeping, she began to wet his feet with her tears. Then she wiped them with her hair, kissed them and poured perfume on them.

39 When the Pharisee who had invited him saw this, he said to himself, 'If this man were a prophet, he would know who is touching him and what kind of woman she is – that she is a sinner.'

---

[135] Marshall, *Luke*, 303–4. The verb used in verse 29 reappears in a timeless passive form here (*edikaiōthē*, 'is justified, proved right').
[136] Fitzmyer, *Luke I–IX*, 687. He goes on to consider the distinctive features of this narrative in relation to the account of the anointing of Jesus in Bethany (Mark 14:3–9; Matthew 26:6–13; John 12:1–8). See also Bock, *Luke 1:1–9:50*, 689–91; Edwards, *Luke*, 225, note 61.

40Jesus answered him, 'Simon, I have something to tell you.'

'Tell me, teacher,' he said.

41'Two people owed money to a certain money-lender. One owed him five hundred denarii,^c and the other fifty. **42**Neither of them had the money to pay him back, so he forgave the debts of both. Now which of them will love him more?'

43Simon replied, 'I suppose the one who had the bigger debt forgiven.'

'You have judged correctly,' Jesus said.

44Then he turned towards the woman and said to Simon, 'Do you see this woman? I came into your house. You did not give me any water for my feet, but she wet my feet with her tears and wiped them with her hair.

45You did not give me a kiss, but this woman, from the time I entered, has not stopped kissing my feet. **46**You did not put oil on my head, but she has poured perfume on my feet. **47**Therefore, I tell you, her many sins have been forgiven – as her great love has shown. But whoever has been forgiven little loves little.'

48Then Jesus said to her, 'Your sins are forgiven.'

49The other guests began to say among themselves, 'Who is this who even forgives sins?'

50Jesus said to the woman, 'Your faith has saved you; go in peace.'

---

c 41 A denarius was the usual daily wage of a day labourer (see Matt. 20:2).

36. The Pharisees as a group had become progressively antagonistic to Jesus and his ministry (5:30, 33; 6:2, 7; 7:30). It comes as a surprise, therefore, that 'one of the Pharisees invited Jesus to have dinner with him' (see also 11:37; 14:1). He seems to have done so because of Jesus's reputation as a prophet (verse 39) and teacher (verse 40). Fitzmyer concludes that the occasion was 'a festive banquet, since reclining at table was practiced only for such occasions in Palestine at that time'.[137] Although he displays an unexpected degree of generosity and openness to Jesus, the Pharisee's hospitality is soon shown to be limited (see verses 44–7).

37–8. The woman who was known in the town as 'a sinner' (*hamar-tōlos*; see 5:8, 30, 32; 6:32, 33, 34; 7:34) was probably a prostitute, especially since the Pharisee was concerned about her touching Jesus (verse 39).[138] Attempts have been made to identify this woman as Mary Magdalene (see 8:2; 24:10) or as Mary of Bethany, the sister of Martha (see 10:39, 42; John

---

[137] Fitzmyer, *Luke I–IX*. 688. Bock, *Luke 1:1–9:50*, 694–5, suggests that such a public meal would have made it easy for the woman to enter and approach Jesus.
[138] The NIV softens the impact of *hamartōlos* in verse 37 by translating 'who lived a sinful life'. See Nolland, *Luke 1–9:20*, 353–4; M. F. Bird, 'Sin, Sinner', *DJG*, 863–9.

11:1–2; 12:3), but there is insufficient evidence for either connection. The Pharisee treated her as a person without hope, but she dared to invade his space, because she had learned that Jesus was eating at his house. She may have heard about the grace that Jesus had shown towards 'tax collectors and sinners' on similar occasions (5:27–32; 7:34) or directly experienced it herself in some way. Bringing 'an alabaster jar of perfume', she stood behind him at his feet, weeping, so that she could attend to his feet, while he reclined at the table. 'She began to wet his feet with her tears. Then she wiped them with her hair, kissed them and poured perfume on them.'[139] This was not a symbolic preparation of his body for burial (contrast the incident closer to the time of his death in Mark 14:3–9; Matthew 26:6–13), but an expression of personal sorrow for sin mixed with gratitude. She came believing that Jesus would receive her and forgive her.

39–40. With prophetic insight, Jesus becomes aware of what the Pharisee is thinking (see 4:23; 5:21–2; 6:8), questioning his reputation and orthodoxy, because he allowed such a woman to touch him ('If this man were a prophet, he would know who is touching him and what kind of woman she is – that she is a sinner'). Jesus answers this unspoken criticism, addressing the Pharisee by name and seeking to challenge his attitude personally ('Simon, I have something to tell you'). Simon's response is courteous and respectful ('Tell me, teacher'; as in 3:12; 8:49; 9:38; 10:25; 11:45; 12:13; 19:39; 20:21, 39).

41–3. Jesus first tells a parable about two people who 'owed money to a certain money-lender. One owed him five hundred denarii, and the other fifty' (see Matthew 18:21–35). A denarius was the usual daily wage for a labourer (Matthew 20:2) and so both debts would have been considerable. The conclusion is dramatic and unexpected: 'Neither of them had the money to pay him back, so he forgave the debts of both.'[140] Simon is asked a question that draws him into the interpretation of this parable ('Now which of them will love him more?'). The verb 'love' (*agapaō*, as in 6:32, 35; 7:5, 47; 10:27; 11:43; 16:13) denotes gratitude and appreciation here (see Psalm 116:1 [114:1 LXX]). Simon replies somewhat cautiously ('I suppose the one who had the bigger debt forgiven'), and his answer is commended by Jesus ('You have judged correctly').

---

[139] Edwards, *Luke*, 227–8, disputes that there are sexual innuendos here, but Green, *Luke*, 310, imagines that her actions may have been viewed that way because of her reputation in the town.

[140] The verb 'forgave' in verses 42, 43 (*echarisato*) means 'to give freely as a favour' and so 'to cancel a sum of money that is owed' (BDAG). Another verb is used for the forgiving of sins in verses 47, 48.

44–6. Jesus turns towards the woman, while still addressing Simon. Drawing attention to the woman's actions, he implies that there is something to learn from her loving welcome:

> You did not give me any water for my feet, but she wet my feet with her tears and wiped them with her hair. You did not give me a kiss, but this woman, from the time I entered, has not stopped kissing my feet. You did not put oil on my head, but she has poured perfume on my feet.

Simon's welcome was correct and formal, but, in Nolland's words, the woman had shown 'the extra thoughtfulness that would mark the hospitality of a host who owed a debt of affectionate gratitude to his guest'.[141] She was far more welcoming and appreciative of Jesus than the Pharisee was!

47. Jesus's two-part conclusion explains the significance of what he has just said. The woman's extravagant actions demonstrated that 'her many sins have been forgiven'. Jesus does not minimise her need for forgiveness, but he refers to her many sins. The passive verb *apheōntai* could imply that God has already forgiven her in response to her prayers of repentance or that Jesus has previously made this clear to her. In this antagonistic context, however, she still needs both the personal and public assurance of forgiveness that Jesus will give her (verse 48). The next expression ('as her great love has shown') cannot mean that her love was the reason for her forgiveness, because that would contradict the message of the parable (verses 41–2). She approached Jesus as a grateful penitent and the Pharisee ought to have known that her actions were a sign of the repentance and transformation that was taking place in her life.[142]

The second part of Jesus's conclusion applies the parable more broadly: 'But whoever has been forgiven little loves little.' Luke tells us nothing about the Pharisee's final response, but Jesus's saying clearly challenges his lack of love for God and concern for the woman. Those who love little and readily dismiss others as hopeless sinners show that they have been forgiven little. They have a limited view of their own need for

---

[141] Nolland, *Luke 1–9:20*, 357.

[142] Nolland, *Luke 1–9:20*, 358, (*hoti ēgapēsen poly*, 'because she loved much'). Tannehill, *Narrative Unity* I, 118, reflects on the complex relationship between experienced forgiveness and love.

God's forgiveness and believe that forgiveness must be earned by doing good (see 18:9–12).[143]

48–50. Jesus confirmed to the woman directly that her sins were forgiven (see verse 47). He also took the opportunity to publicise again his role in God's plan to offer the definitive forgiveness promised by the prophets (see 5:20–24; Jeremiah 31:34; 33:8; Ezekiel 36:25). The woman experienced this by approaching him in faith. 'The other guests began to say among themselves, "Who is this who even forgives sins?"' (see 5:21), but the question was not answered, because Jesus's focus was still on the woman. He went a step further and said to her, 'Your faith has saved you' (*hē pistis sou sesōken se*). The same Greek expression is rendered 'your faith has healed you' in 8:48; 17:19; 18:42, but the healing in 7:50 is not physical. The woman has been restored to a right relationship with God and saved through forgiveness from God's ultimate judgment (see 8:12; 13:23; 19:9–10). 'Go in peace' is a common form of farewell and blessing in Scripture (e.g., Judges 18:6; 1 Samuel 1:17; 1 Kings 22:17), acquiring a deeper significance in association with the themes of forgiveness and eternal salvation (see 1:77–9; 2:14). It points immediately to the possibility of reconciliation with God and ultimately experiencing the complete restoration promised in God's new creation (Isaiah 65:17–25; compare Romans 5:1–11; 8:18–39).

JESUS THE PROPHET

The raising from death of a widow's son led the crowds to declare that 'a great prophet has arisen among us' and 'God has visited his people' (ESV). This claim recalls several biblical expectations. First, God promised to raise up a prophet like Moses for his people to hear and obey (Deuteronomy 18:15–19). Jesus as Son of God fulfils that prediction (9:35; Acts 3:22–3) and speaks about the 'exodus' he was about to bring to fulfilment at Jerusalem (9:31). Second, God promised to send a prophet like Elijah to prepare his people for his coming in judgment (Malachi 3:1; 4:5–6). This role is specifically attributed to John the Baptist (Luke 1:16–17; 7:27), though John speaks of the one who is to come after him in somewhat similar terms (3:16–17), and Jesus raises the dead as Elijah did (7:11–15). Third, in his sermon at Nazareth, Jesus claims to fulfil the role of the Spirit-anointed prophet in Isaiah 61:1–2, announcing and making available the blessings of redemption promised to captive Israel

---

[143] See Robert C. Tannehill, 'Should We Love Simon the Pharisee? Reflections on the Pharisees in Luke', in Robert C. Tannehill, *The Shape of Luke's Story: Essays on Luke–Acts* (Eugene: Cascade, 2005), 267–70; Green, *Luke*, 314–15.

(4:18–21; see 24:19–21). Jesus's answer to the Baptist's question confirms that he has been particularly acting in this last capacity (7:18–23). Tannehill rightly observes, 'Those who speak of Jesus as a prophet in Luke may not understand him completely, but this title does not represent a distortion to be rejected.'[144] Jesus combined different prophetic roles in his earthly ministry as the Son of God, the Messiah and the Suffering Servant (see Isaiah 11:1–4; 50:4–9). Important dimensions to his prophetic ministry are revealed in his encounter with Simon the Pharisee and the woman who came to his house. Jesus discerned the true character of the woman who approached him with tears and extravagant devotion, he acted with divine authority and love in declaring that she was forgiven, and he assured her that her faith had saved her. She was one of 'the poor' to whom the kingdom of God was promised (6:20; 7:22). In this context, Jesus also exposed and challenged the attitude of the Pharisee, who questioned whether Jesus could be a prophet because of his gracious attitude towards such a sinner, and who showed little awareness of his own need for forgiveness.[145] The evaluation of Jesus as a prophet may be a helpful starting point for understanding his ministry and character, but his words and his actions call for expressions of faith and devotion more appropriate towards God himself, as the whole of Luke 7 implies.

9. Hearing God's word and putting it into practice (Luke 8:1–21)

Luke provides a further summary of Jesus's itinerant ministry, adding details about the women who provided support 'out of their own means' (verses 1–3). The kingdom of God continues to be the focus of his preaching (as in 4:43; 6:20; 7:28). Luke 8:4–9:50 then broadly follows the sequence of teaching and events in Mark 4:1–9:41. As in the other Synoptic Gospels, Jesus's use of parables is illustrated and explained with reference to a story about a farmer sowing seed (Luke 8:4–15; see Mark 4:1–20; Matthew 13:1–23). However, Luke offers an abbreviated version and adds only three

[144] Tannehill, *Narrative Unity* 1, 97. Tannehill (77–82) points out that Jesus's prophetic calling involved preaching the gospel of the kingdom and healing, which is not explicitly the role of the Son of David in biblical expectations. The theme of rejection, suffering and death as a prophet is revealed subsequently in Luke (Tannehill, 96–9).

[145] Isaak, 'Luke', 1244, discerns that in the logic of this story and of the parable that Jesus tells, love is 'both the cause and the result or sign of divine forgiveness'.

further parabolic sayings of Jesus (verses 16–18), before he concludes with an episode about Jesus's true relatives (verses 19–21; see Mark 3:31–5; Matthew 12:46–50). As Fitzmyer discerns, the effect of this editing is to make the whole section 'one devoted to the preached and accepted word of God'.[146]

The parable of the sower

8 After this, Jesus travelled about from one town and village to another, proclaiming the good news of the kingdom of God. The Twelve were with him, **2** and also some women who had been cured of evil spirits and diseases: Mary (called Magdalene) from whom seven demons had come out; **3** Joanna the wife of Chuza, the manager of Herod's household; Susanna; and many others. These women were helping to support them out of their own means.

4 While a large crowd was gathering and people were coming to Jesus from town after town, he told this parable: **5** 'A farmer went out to sow his seed. As he was scattering the seed, some fell along the path; it was trampled on, and the birds ate it up. **6** Some fell on rocky ground, and when it came up, the plants withered because they had no moisture. **7** Other seed fell among thorns, which grew up with it and choked the plants. **8** Still other seed fell on good soil. It came up and yielded a crop, a hundred times more than was sown.'

When he said this, he called out, 'Whoever has ears to hear, let them hear.'

9 His disciples asked him what this parable meant. **10** He said, 'The knowledge of the secrets of the kingdom of God has been given to you, but to others I speak in parables, so that,

' "though seeing, they may not see;
though hearing, they may not
understand." [a]

11 'This is the meaning of the parable: the seed is the word of God. **12** Those along the path are the ones who hear, and then the devil comes and takes away the word from their hearts, so that they may not believe and be saved. **13** Those on the rocky ground are the ones who receive the word with joy when they hear it, but they have no root. They believe for a while, but in the time of testing they fall away. **14** The seed that fell among thorns stands for those who hear, but as they go on their way they are choked by life's worries, riches and pleasures, and they do not mature. **15** But the seed on good soil stands for those with a noble and good heart, who hear the word, retain it, and by persevering produce a crop.

A lamp on a stand

16 'No one lights a lamp and hides it in a clay jar or puts it under a bed. Instead, they put it on a stand, so that those who come in can see the light. **17** For

---

[146] Fitzmyer, *Luke I–IX*, 700.

there is nothing hidden that will not be disclosed, and nothing concealed that will not be known or brought out into the open. **18**Therefore consider carefully how you listen. Whoever has will be given more; whoever does not have, even what they think they have will be taken from them.'

Jesus' mother and brothers
19Now Jesus' mother and brothers came to see him, but they were not able to get near him because of the crowd. **20**Someone told him, 'Your mother and brothers are standing outside, wanting to see you.'

21He replied, 'My mother and brothers are those who hear God's word and put it into practice.'

_____

a 10 Isaiah 6:9

1–3. A simple time reference (*Kai egeneto en tō kathexēs*, 'It happened soon afterward' [see 7:11]) introduces the next phase of itinerant ministry ('Jesus travelled about from one town and village to another'). This involved an extensive proclamation of 'the good news of the kingdom of God' (see 4:43–44).[147] Following their calling in 6:12–16, the Twelve were with him, together with some women 'who had been cured of evil spirits and diseases' (see 4:40–41; 6:17–19). Three are named for different reasons: Mary (called Magdalene) was known for her deliverance from a severe form of demonic possession ('from whom seven demons had come out'); Joanna had a surprising link with the tetrarch of Galilee ('the wife of Chuza, the manager of Herod's household'); and Susanna was simply one of many others. Jesus's care for women (see 4:38–9; 7:36–50; 8:40–56; 10:38–42; 13:10–17) and his willingness to have them join the inner core of his disciples was novel. As Tannehill says, it involved 'a sharp break with social expectations and normal responsibilities'.[148] Their particular role at this stage was to 'support' (*diēkonoun*, 'serving') Jesus and the Twelve out of 'their own means' (*tōn hyparchontōn autais*, 'what belonged to them'; see 12:15, 33, 44), presumably with food and money. Women supported Jewish rabbis and their disciples in similar ways, but Nolland observes that 'these women are far more intimately caught up in the enterprise in which Jesus is engaged',[149] some even leaving home and family to share in his itinerant ministry.

_____

[147] Luke uses two verbs together to explain this activity here (*kēryssōn kai euaggelizomenos*, 'proclaiming and bringing good news').

[148] Tannehill, *Narrative Unity* I, 138.

[149] Nolland, *Luke 1–9:20*, 367. 'Luke portrays them as recipients of Jesus's gracious ministry but also as benefactors of that ministry' (Green, *Luke*, 318). See also my comment on 10:38–42.

4–8. 'While a large crowd was gathering and people were coming to Jesus from town after town,' he told them a parable. Charles Dodd aptly described a parable at its simplest as 'a metaphor or simile drawn from nature or common life, arresting the hearer by its vividness or strangeness, and leaving the mind in sufficient doubt about its precise application to tease it into active thought'.[150] Some of Jesus's sayings are called 'parables' (4:23; 5:36; 6:39), while parabolic language is used more extensively to explain his mission (5:31–2; 7:41–2) and call for appropriate responses (6:41–4, 47–9). The narrative form of parable in 8:5–8 exposes the way the seed of the gospel is being sown in the ministry of Jesus and producing different responses.

Luke abbreviates Mark 4:3–20 and modifies the wording with his own emphases. He adds 'his seed' to the introductory sentence (ESV, 'A sower went out to sow his seed'), preparing for the identification of the seed as 'the word of God' in the explanation that follows (verse 11; see Mark 4:14; Matthew 13:19 ('the message about the kingdom')). Luke more briefly states that the yield of the good soil was 'a hundred times more than was sown' (see Mark 4:8; Matthew 13:8). The sowing procedure in the parable is unusually extravagant, with the seed being dispersed in places that prove to be unproductive, but the yield in the good soil is impressive and a sign of God's blessing (Genesis 26:12).[151] A note of urgency is added by Luke to the conclusion: Jesus 'called out, "Whoever has ears to hear, let them hear"' (verse 8; see 14:35). Hearing is mentioned also in verses 10, 12, 13, 14, 15, 18, 21, emphasising the need for an appropriate response to his teaching.

Joachim Jeremias famously argued that this parable presents a simple contrast, illustrating 'the ultimate eschatological success that will attend Jesus's preaching, despite all the human obstacles that will be encountered'.[152] Those who take this view regard the interpretation in verses 11–15 as a later church creation, missing the main point of the original parable, and turning it into 'a warning to the converted against a failure to

---

[150] Charles H. Dodd, *The Parables of the Kingdom* (London: Nisbet, 1936), 5. G. P. Anderson, 'Parables', *DJG,* 653, considers biblical precedents and analogies to Jesus's parables in the rabbinic literature of Judaism. Craig L. Blomberg, *Interpreting the Parables* (2nd edition; Downers Grove: IVP Academic; Nottingham: Apollos, 2012), 17–192, discusses different approaches to interpreting the parables. See also Bock, *Luke 1:1–9:50,* 945–9.

[151] Nolland *Luke 1–9:20,* 372, observes that 'the yield is not typical of Palestinian agriculture, but neither is it beyond one's wildest imaginings'.

[152] Fitzmyer, *Luke I–IX,* 701, summarising Jeremias, *The Parables of Jesus* (3rd edition; London: SCM, 1972), 149–51.

stand fast in time of persecution and against worldliness'.[153] However, the focus of the parable is not simply on the end of human history, but on the immediate or short-term fate of the seed among the soils. Moreover, there is a complexity about the parable that requires explanation.

9–11. The other Gospels record that Jesus was alone when 'the Twelve and the others around him asked him about the parables' (Mark 4:10; compare Matthew 13:10–17). Luke, however, simplifies the account and has them ask in a more public way 'what this parable meant'. Responding to their request, Jesus first affirms the privileged status of his disciples ('the knowledge of the secrets of the kingdom of God has been given to you'). The passive verb 'has been given' (*dedotai*) suggests the action of God in revealing this knowledge to them, though Jesus is the channel (see 10:22).[154] Disciples have come to 'know' in the sense of seeing, hearing and understanding in ways that others have not (see 10:23–4). 'The secrets' (*mystēria*) of the kingdom appear to be different aspects of God's kingdom plan that are being revealed to those who seek understanding (see Matthew 13:11).[155]

Jesus's claim to speak 'to others' in parables cannot be taken in an absolute sense, since he has previously used parables to instruct his disciples (5:36; 6:39). The issue here is why he speaks to the crowds in this way. The purpose clause that begins with 'so that' (verse 10, *hina*) introduces a paraphrase of Isaiah 6:9:[156] 'though seeing, they may not see; though hearing, they may not understand.' Jesus explains his purpose in terms of God's calling of Isaiah to preach to hard-hearted Israelites about approaching judgment. The prophet used both plain and parabolic speech to arouse repentance and faith, but God warned him from the beginning that this would further harden many who heard him. The parables of Jesus were not designed to obscure the truth, but to state it in a way that provoked further inquiry (see 2 Samuel 12:1–10; Isaiah 5:1–7). Nevertheless, a parable may fail, as Hauck discerns, 'if there is no spiritual power to

---

[153] Jeremias, *Parables*, 150. Contrast Bock, *Luke 1:1–9:50*, 731–2; Blomberg, *Parables*, 289–90.

[154] The perfect tense of the verb could suggest a present activity with heightened proximity ('is being given'). See Campbell, *Verbal Aspect, the Indicative Mood, and Narrative*, 210.

[155] The singular form in Mark 4:11 ('the secret of the kingdom of God') refers to 'the whole plan as a unit' (Bock, *Luke 1:1–9:50*, 730). Compare Daniel 2:18, 19, 27–30 ('mystery'); Wisdom 2:22 ('the secret purposes of God'). See my comments on 4:43; 6:20–22 regarding the kingdom of God.

[156] Matthew 13:13–15 cites Isaiah 6:9–10 LXX in full and Mark 4:12 gives an abbreviated version.

grasp its heart or if the revelation of God which it contains is rejected. Jesus experienced both these things.'[157] The disciples are distinguished by their persistence in seeking explanations of his teaching.

11–12. 'The seed is the word of God,' which Jesus has been widely dispersing and which disciples will soon be called to sow (9:1–6; 10:1–12; 24:45–9).[158] The four soils can be understood in relation to this context but may also be applied to ongoing church situations, as Luke's first readers no doubt understood. The sowing of the seed on different soils speaks of evangelism and of the need for the gospel to be deeply rooted in the lives of those who hear it. 'Those along the path are the ones who hear, and then the devil comes and takes away the word from their hearts.' They hear with their ears, but the truth of the message does not captivate 'their heart' (see 4:22–9). They are easy prey for 'the devil' (see 22:3–6), whose aim is 'that they may not believe and be saved'.[159] Consistent with his interest in the theme of salvation, Luke clarifies that the message of Jesus offers the hope of escaping final judgment and the prospect of eternal life in God's presence. But the devil's intention is to keep people from believing this.

13. 'Those on the rocky ground are the ones who receive the word with joy when they hear it, but they have no root.' Receiving the word with joy implies genuine belief (Acts 8:14; 11:1; 17:11), but the response envisaged here is temporary: 'They believe for a while, but in the time of testing they fall away.' Jesus warned his disciples on several occasions about persecution (6:22–3; 12:4–12; 21:12–19) and 'testing' (as in 22:40, 46), highlighting the need for endurance (as in verse 15; 21:19). As Nolland concludes, 'If the rootedness is not there, the new life will wither away. Apostasy is the outcome.'[160]

---

[157] F. Hauck, 'παραβολή', *TDNT* 5:756. Hauck observes that this was so because 'Jesus's ideas on the coming kingdom and the nature of God were quite different from those current in Judaism.'

[158] This parable appears to have been influential in Luke's presentation of the word of the gospel 'growing' and 'multiplying' in Acts 6:7; 12:24; 19:20. See Peterson *Acts*, 32–6.

[159] Nolland, *Luke 1–9:20*, 384, comments, 'That the birds should signify the Devil is not arbitrary allegory': see Jubilees 11:11; Apocalypse of Abraham 13:3–7; 1 Enoch 90:8–13.

[160] Nolland, *Luke 1–9:20*, 388. Bock, *Luke 1:1–9:50*, 734, argues that only the fourth seed really achieves the goal that the word is intended to produce: 'The second and third groups are viewed tragically since opportunity for fruitfulness was present and lost.'

14. 'The seed that fell among thorns stands for those who hear, but as they go on their way they are choked by life's worries, riches and pleasures, and they do not mature.' Temporary discipleship is indicated in this case by saying that 'they are choked,' meaning that their growth is stopped and 'their fruit does not mature' (ESV). The seed of the gospel does not come to fruition because they become absorbed with 'life's worries, riches and pleasures'. Jesus deals with these matters extensively in Luke's narrative: the dangers of riches (6:24; 12:13–21), expensive clothes and luxury (7:25; 16:19) and worry about daily needs (12:22–6; 21:34). These preoccupations prevent some from becoming disciples in the first place (18:18–25) and others from persevering with Jesus.

15. 'The seed on good soil stands for those with a noble and good heart [see 6:45], who hear the word, retain it, and by persevering produce a good crop' (ESV, 'bear fruit with patience'). The contrast is first with the hearts mentioned in verse 12 which are not changed by the gospel. The second contrast is with those whose 'fruit' does not mature (verse 14). The emphasis in verse 8 was on the fruitfulness that the gospel achieves in the right soil, but in verse 15 it is on the response that makes perseverance as a Christian possible (hearing the word, holding fast to it and bearing fruit). These notions are complementary: the gospel of the kingdom calls for a continuing response of faith and, rightly received, the gospel enables the fruitfulness it promises.

16–18. Three parabolic sayings follow, apparently adapted from Mark 4:21–5, but also repeated in slightly different forms in Luke 11:33; 12:2; 19:26 (compare Matthew 5:15; 10:26; 25:29). Here, they continue the challenge to hear the word of Jesus appropriately (verses 4–15). The first saying suggests that 'the light' that he has shown to disciples needs to be shared with others ('No one lights a lamp and hides it in a clay jar or puts it under a bed. Instead, they put it on a stand, so that those who come in can see the light').[161] The second saying more specifically implies that 'the secrets of the kingdom' have been disclosed by Jesus (verses 9–10) so that they can be made known ('For there is nothing hidden that will not be disclosed, and nothing concealed that will not be known or brought out into the open'). The conclusion to this sequence is a further challenge about listening to the message of Jesus in a way that bears fruit ('Therefore consider carefully how you listen'). A promise and a warning

---

[161] Nolland, *Luke 1–9:20*, 391, suggests, 'Since the word of God can not only be spoken and heard but also done (v. 21), the lamp in place on the lampstand will be the person living out and therefore making visible the word of God.'

are attached ('Whoever has will be given more; whoever does not have, even what they think they have will be taken from them'). This parable really summarises the message of verses 12–15. Those who respond to the word of God rightly will receive more insight and become more fruitful; those who fail to persevere will lose even what they thought they had.

19–21. When Jesus' mother and brothers came to see him, 'they were not able to get near him because of the crowd. Someone told him, "Your mother and brothers are standing outside, wanting to see you."' Luke abbreviates and adapts Mark 3:31–2, which occurs in an earlier context in that Gospel (compare Matthew 12:46–50). Fitzmyer's contention that Luke has 'radically changed the meaning' of this incident is an exaggeration.[162] Jesus's conclusion in verse 21 is a modification of Mark 3:34–5 ('My mother and brothers are those who hear God's word and put it into practice'), using language that explicitly recalls the challenge of verses 12–15. Nolland rightly argues, 'Family bonds are not so much negated as other bonds are affirmed and focused upon.'[163] Those who respond appropriately to the message of Jesus find themselves in a spiritual family that transcends natural family ties (see 9:59–62; 11:27–8; 14:26; 18:29–30).

SEEING, HEARING AND BELIEVING

The allusion to Isaiah 6:9 in Luke 8:10 draws attention to the fact that many had seen the mighty works of Jesus but not perceived their significance, and heard his preaching about the kingdom of God but not responded with faith (4:40–44; 6:17–7:23). Only some had turned to Jesus and been forgiven (5:27–32; 7:36–50). Jesus's parable of the soils and his claim that the secrets of the kingdom are given to those who seek them imply that a gracious work of God must take place in human hearts for faith to be genuine and persist. The challenge of the parable is for people in the crowd to evaluate their response to Jesus as he sows the seed of the gospel. The promise of the parable is that his message will prove abundantly fruitful, despite the diversity of responses. Hardness of

---

[162] Fitzmyer, *Luke I–IX*, 722. He concludes this from Luke's pronouncement in verse 21 and his omission of a related Marcan passage (3:20–21). Bock, *Luke 1:1–9:50*, 748–53, and Tannehill, *Narrative Unity* 1, 212–13, argue against this. See also Edwards, *Luke*, 243–4.

[163] Nolland, *Luke 1–9:20*, 395. Fitzmyer, *Luke I–IX*, 723, thinks that Luke presents Jesus's mother and brothers as model disciples here, but Nolland rightly concludes, 'The place left for Mary and the others is in the end based upon their obedience to God rather than upon their physical relationship to Jesus.'

heart will leave some without understanding or any desire to know more. Two obstacles to faith (times of testing and being choked by life's worries, riches and pleasures) are so important that Jesus teaches extensively about them elsewhere. The desired response is to hear the word of God, 'hold it fast in an honest and good heart, and bear fruit with patience' (8:15, ESV). As with the blessings and woes in 6:20–26, encouraging promises associated with Jesus's preaching about the kingdom need to be heard together with the warnings about complacency, self-indulgence and unbelief. The gospel itself is the means of encouraging and nurturing the faith that bears fruit for eternal life. Those who respond with genuine faith are linked together as a family with Jesus and share the task of bringing into the open the things he has revealed to them.

10. Further examples of Jesus's power over life and death (Luke 8:22–56)

Luke reports a series of miracles that shed light on each other, illustrating the power of Jesus and the responses that people made to him. Mark 4:35–5:43 is shortened and modified to bring out Luke's emphases. Jesus calms the storm, moving his disciples to fear and amazement (verses 22–5). He restores a demon-possessed man, exciting fear in the people of that region, but grateful obedience on the part of the man himself (verses 26–39). He raises a little girl from death, to the astonishment of her parents, and heals a woman subject to bleeding for twelve years, encouraging an open confession of the faith that had secretly brought healing to her (verses 40–56).

Stilling a storm (8:22–5)

Jesus calms the storm

22 One day Jesus said to his disciples, 'Let us go over to the other side of the lake.' So they got into a boat and set out. 23 As they sailed, he fell asleep. A squall came down on the lake, so that the boat was being swamped, and they were in great danger.

24 The disciples went and woke him, saying, 'Master, Master, we're going to drown!'

He got up and rebuked the wind and the raging waters; the storm subsided, and all was calm. 25 'Where is your faith?' he asked his disciples.

In fear and amazement they asked one another, 'Who is this? He commands even the winds and the water, and they obey him.'

22–3. A vague temporal reference introduces this event (ESV, 'One day he got into a boat with his disciples'), and Jesus said to them, 'Let us go over to the other side of the lake.' According to verse 26, they were heading for the region of the Gerasenes, which may have been a deliberate move to visit Gentile territory. However, there were many Jewish communities in the Decapolis and a Jewish settlement on the eastern shore of the Sea of Galilee. Lloyd concludes that 'Jesus had every incentive to visit the region and to minister among the Jewish population there'.[164] They set out and, 'As they sailed, he fell asleep.' Fitzmyer observes that Jesus's falling asleep 'stands in contrast to the power he will manifest; he is subject to human fatigue'.[165] 'A squall came down on the lake, so that the boat was being swamped, and they were in great danger.' The boat must have been relatively large to accommodate Jesus and his disciples, but the storm was severe enough to swamp it.[166]

24. Luke substitutes the cry, 'Master, Master, we're going to drown!' for the disciples' more aggressive question in Mark 4:38 ('Teacher, don't you care if we drown?'). The miracle is described in simple terms: 'He got up and rebuked the wind and the raging waters; the storm subsided, and all was calm.' As noted in connection with 4:35, 39, 41, the verb 'rebuked' can express strong disapproval or censure (see 9:55; 17:3; 18:15, 39; 19:39; 23:40), but addressed to demons, a high fever and the forces of nature it indicates a stern command (see also 9:21, 42). The power that was with Jesus to exorcise demons and heal the sick (5:17) was supremely demonstrated in his word to the wind and the waves (Mark 4:39, 'Quiet! Be still!'). This was the power of God as creator (Psalms 29:3–4; 65:7; 104:6–7; Nahum 1:4) and rescuer of his people (Exodus 14:21–31; Psalms 106:9; 107:23–30).[167]

25. Jesus's question to his disciples ('Where is your faith?') meant that their faith was inadequate for this crisis (Mark 4:40, 'Why are you so afraid? Do you still have no faith?'). In terms of the parable about the

---

[164] Lloyd, *Itinerant Jesus*, 377. Lloyd examines Mark 6:45–8:26, which mentions several journeys across the lake not mentioned by Luke, and he argues that Jesus's ministry to Gentiles in this context is incidental.

[165] Fitzmyer, *Luke I–IX*, 729.

[166] Edwards, *Luke*, 244–5, gives details about the occurrence of such storms on the Sea of Galilee and reports the discovery of a large fishing boat from that era.

[167] Nolland, *Luke 1–9:20*, 398, also notes links with Joshua 3:10–13; 2 Kings 2:8; Jonah 1. Although ancient sources speak of kings and wise men exercising power over nature, none depicts a figure using his own supernatural power to still a storm (Nolland, 401).

seed among the soils, they had heard the word, but their faith had not been proven in testing (verse 13).[168] They had called for Jesus to help them (verse 24), but they did not really believe he could deliver them from drowning. When all was calm, 'in fear and amazement they asked one another, "Who is this? He commands even the winds and the water, and they obey him."' God was being directly encountered in the person of Jesus and his actions (see 4:36; 5:9–10, 26; 9:43).

Curing a man with multiple demons (8:26–39)

Jesus restores a demon-possessed man

26 They sailed to the region of the Gerasenes,[b] which is across the lake from Galilee. 27 When Jesus stepped ashore, he was met by a demon-possessed man from the town. For a long time this man had not worn clothes or lived in a house, but had lived in the tombs. 28 When he saw Jesus, he cried out and fell at his feet, shouting at the top of his voice, 'What do you want with me, Jesus, Son of the Most High God? I beg you, don't torture me!' 29 For Jesus had commanded the impure spirit to come out of the man. Many times it had seized him, and though he was chained hand and foot and kept under guard, he had broken his chains and had been driven by the demon into solitary places.

30 Jesus asked him, 'What is your name?'

'Legion,' he replied, because many demons had gone into him. 31 And they begged Jesus repeatedly not to order them to go into the Abyss.

32 A large herd of pigs was feeding there on the hillside. The demons begged Jesus to let them go into the pigs, and he gave them permission. 33 When the demons came out of the man, they went into the pigs, and the herd rushed down the steep bank into the lake and was drowned.

34 When those tending the pigs saw what had happened, they ran off and reported this in the town and countryside, 35 and the people went out to see what had happened. When they came to Jesus, they found the man from whom the demons had gone out, sitting at Jesus' feet, dressed and in his right mind; and they were afraid. 36 Those who had seen it told the people how the demon-possessed man had been cured. 37 Then all the people of the region of the Gerasenes asked Jesus to leave them, because they were overcome with fear. So he got into the boat and left.

38 The man from whom the demons had gone out begged to go with him, but Jesus sent him away, saying, 39 'Return home and tell how much

---

[168] Green, *Luke*, 333. Compare the faith of Paul in Acts 27:13–44.

God has done for you.' So the man
went away and told all over the town
how much Jesus had done for him.

b 26 Some manuscripts *Gadarenes*; other
manuscripts *Gergesenes*; also in verse 37

26. 'They sailed to the region of the Gerasenes, which is across the lake from Galilee,' where Jesus used his power to heal what Fitzmyer calls 'an unfortunate demented human being, an outcast of society, thus restoring him to soundness of mind and wholeness of life'.[169] The site of this meeting is disputed: the best attested manuscripts of verse 26 refer to 'the Gerasenes' (as in Mark 5:1), but some read 'the Gadarenes' (as in Matthew 8:28), and others read 'the Gergesenes'.[170] Gerasa was a prosperous city of the Decapolis (Mark 5:20), which was more than thirty miles to the southeast of the lake (50km). Gadara was another city of the Decapolis, which was closer and whose territory reached to the lake. Perhaps the expression 'the region of the Gerasenes' was used because the influence of Gerasa and its culture was dominant in this location. 'The town' from which the demon-possessed man came is not actually identified, nor is his ethnicity clarified, but he certainly lived 'across the lake from Galilee'.

27. Luke states the man's condition briefly ('For a long time this man had not worn clothes or lived in a house, but had lived in the tombs'). Further details from Mark 5:2–5 are represented in verse 29. The man was controlled by multiple demons (*echōn daimonian*, 'having demons', see 11:26), although a singular expression ('the impure spirit') is used in verse 29 to describe the same overpowering force. The man's desperate need is expressed in terms of his physical, social, psychological and spiritual suffering. He kept company with the dead, because his human life was marred in every respect. He was probably living among pagan tombs, which were a source of ritual uncleanness for a Jew, but Jesus did not hesitate to help him.[171]

---

[169] Fitzmyer, *Luke I–IX*, 735. Fitzmyer is unnecessarily sceptical about the details of Luke's shortened version of Mark 5:1–20 (Matthew 8:28–34 is even shorter).

[170] Metzger, *Textual Commentary*, 18–19, 72, 121, lists all the options and explains why 'the Gerasenes' is the preferred reading of Mark 5:1 and Luke 8:26, while 'the Gadarenes' is the preferred reading of Matthew 8:28, 'The Gergesenes' is a later alternative in each case. See also Bock, *Luke 1:1–9:50*, 782–4; Lloyd, *Itinerant Jesus*, 375–7.

[171] Green, *Luke*, 335–6, says this passage fundamentally concerns 'the crossing of boundaries in Jesus' mission and more particularly the offer of salvation in the Gentile world'. But the possessed man could have been a Jew who had been

28. 'When he saw Jesus, he cried out and fell at his feet, shouting at the top of his voice.' As in 4:33–4, it is the man who cries out to Jesus in this way, but 'the impure spirit' speaks through him. He has a supernatural perception of Jesus's identity as 'Son of the Most High God' (4:34, 'the Holy One of God'),[172] but he expresses a sense of alienation from Jesus when he says, 'What do you want with me?' (compare 4:34, 'What do you want with us?'). Plural pronouns are used once it is revealed that he is possessed by a host of demons (verse 30, 'Legion'). A perception that Jesus has come to defeat the forces of evil is expressed in the pathetic cry, 'I beg you don't torture me!' The man himself feels threatened by the impending judgment of the spirits that bind him (see below on verse 31).

29–31. In 4:35–7, the exorcism of an unclean spirit and the positive impact on the man and others present was simply described. In 8:29–37, however, Luke gives a more elaborate account of the process, suggesting that it was a more serious case. First, there is a declaration that Jesus had already 'commanded the unclean spirit to come out of the man' (see Mark 5:8). Some resistance to the command of Jesus is implied. The adjective 'unclean' (*akathartos*) is used frequently in the LXX to denote physical, moral or ritual contamination. Jesus was the enemy of contamination in all its forms but, as DeSilva says, he was 'willing to cross lines of purity to bring the unclean, the defiled and the sinner back to a state of cleanness, wholeness and integration into the community'.[173] Second, the man's condition is described again in more detail, emphasising his need for deliverance: 'Many times [the unclean spirit] had seized him, and though he was chained hand and foot and kept under guard, he had broken his chains and had been driven by the demon into solitary places.'[174] Third, Jesus asked him, 'What is your name?', engaging in a more direct confrontation with the unclean spirit. The extent of this man's captivity is indicated by the fact that he answered, 'Legion'. A Roman legion could contain up to six thousand soldiers, so the name here represents a large

---

driven into this unclean space (compare 15:13–16) and needed to experience the Messiah's restorative power.

[172] 'The Son of the Most High' is the angel's term in 1:32 and 'the Most High' is a description of Israel's God in 1:35; 76; 6:35; Acts 7:48. However, the term is used by a Gentile in Acts 16:17 in a way that parallels Genesis 14:19–20; Numbers 24:16; Isaiah 14:14; Daniel 3:26.

[173] D. A. deSilva, 'Clean, Unclean', *DJG*, 146.

[174] Bock, *Luke 1:1–9:50*, 773, observes that 'the possession seems to have come and gone in cycles'.

number of demons. 'Many demons had gone into him' and worked as one to defeat him. Fourth, the demonic fear of torture (verse 28) is explained as they beg Jesus repeatedly 'not to order them to go into the Abyss' (Mark 5:10 simply reads 'out of the area'). 'The Abyss' ('an immensely deep space', BDAG) is sometimes used in Scripture as a metaphor for death (e.g., Psalms 71:20 [70:20 LXX]; 107:26 [106:26 LXX]; Romans 10:7), and sometimes more specifically for the place where evil forces are held and finally punished (Isaiah 24:21–2; Revelation 9:1–2, 11; 11:7; 17:8; 20:1, 3).[175] Matthew 8:29 expresses their fear with the question, 'Have you come here to torture us *before the appointed time*?' (my emphasis).

32–3. Since Jews regarded pigs as unclean (Leviticus 11:7; Deuteronomy 14:8), a Gentile location is confirmed by the fact that a large herd of pigs was feeding there on the hillside.[176] The demons begged Jesus to let them go into the pigs to escape immediate banishment to the Abyss, and 'he gave them permission', doubtless knowing what would happen next. 'When the demons came out of the man, they went into the pigs, and the herd rushed down the steep bank into the lake and was drowned.' As Nolland observes, 'The demons unleash the same destructive powers upon the pigs that have up to that point brought misery to the possessed man.'[177] Although the destruction of the pigs poses moral questions about the loss of animal life and the loss of income for their owners, Jesus's priority was the rescuing of a human being from the oppression of evil forces.[178] Even the witnesses focus on the cure of the man rather than the loss of the pigs.

34–7. Those tending the pigs ran off and reported in the town and countryside what had happened. When the people from the region went out to see for themselves, 'they found the man from whom the demons had gone out, sitting at Jesus' feet, dressed and in his right mind'. His condition was completely reversed (see verses 27, 29): he was sitting as a learner at the feet of Jesus, sane, sensible, and self-controlled (BDAG, *sōphroneō*). The local inhabitants, however, were afraid. Those who had witnessed the event told them how the demon-possessed man had been cured, but instead of being amazed and keen to spread the wonderful news throughout the surrounding area (see 4:36), 'all the people of the region of the Gerasenes asked Jesus to

---

[175] Nolland, *Luke 1–9:20*, 410; J. Jeremias, 'Άβυσσος', *TDNT* 1:9–10; Bock, *Luke 1:1–9:50*, 775. Parallel terms are used in 2 Peter 2:4; Jude 6.

[176] Lloyd, *Itinerant Jesus*, 379, agrees with this but argues that 'the ethnicity of this severely disturbed individual cannot be determined on the basis of his proximity to a herd of pigs or to a graveyard'.

[177] Nolland, *Luke 1–9:20*, 411.

[178] Edwards, *Luke*, 250; Bock, *Luke 1:1–9:50*, 776–7.

leave, because they were overcome with fear'. So, Jesus got into the boat and left, seeing no further opportunity for ministry in that area.

38–9. 'The man from whom the demons had gone out begged to go with him, but Jesus sent him away.' Instead of joining the travelling body of disciples, Jesus told him to 'return home and tell how much God has done for you'. This anticipated his later call for disciples to proclaim his name among the nations (24:47; Acts 1:8). The man did as he was told but, significantly, 'went away and told all over the town how much *Jesus* had done for him' (my emphasis). His previous naming of Jesus as 'Son of the Most High God' (verse 28) may have been an attempt to control him, but now he gratefully proclaimed him as the agent of God's saving power in his life (verse 36).

Raising a dead girl and healing a sick woman (8:40–56)

Jesus raises a dead girl and heals a sick woman

40 Now when Jesus returned, a crowd welcomed him, for they were all expecting him. **41** Then a man named Jairus, a synagogue leader, came and fell at Jesus' feet, pleading with him to come to his house **42** because his only daughter, a girl of about twelve, was dying.

As Jesus was on his way, the crowds almost crushed him. **43** And a woman was there who had been subject to bleeding for twelve years,[c] but no one could heal her. **44** She came up behind him and touched the edge of his cloak, and immediately her bleeding stopped.

45 'Who touched me?' Jesus asked.

When they all denied it, Peter said, 'Master, the people are crowding and pressing against you.'

46 But Jesus said, 'Someone touched me; I know that power has gone out from me.'

47 Then the woman, seeing that she could not go unnoticed, came trembling and fell at his feet. In the presence of all the people, she told why she had touched him and how she had been instantly healed. **48** Then he said to her, 'Daughter, your faith has healed you. Go in peace.'

49 While Jesus was still speaking, someone came from the house of Jairus, the synagogue leader. 'Your daughter is dead,' he said. 'Don't bother the teacher anymore.'

50 Hearing this, Jesus said to Jairus, 'Don't be afraid; just believe, and she will be healed.'

51 When he arrived at the house of Jairus, he did not let anyone go in with him except Peter, John and James, and the child's father and mother. **52** Meanwhile, all the people were wailing and mourning for her. 'Stop wailing,' Jesus said. 'She is not dead but asleep.'

53 They laughed at him, knowing that she was dead. 54 But he took her by the hand and said, 'My child, get up!' 55 Her spirit returned, and at once she stood up. Then Jesus told them to give her something to eat. 56 Her parents were astonished, but he ordered them not to tell anyone what had happened.

___

c 43 Many manuscripts *years, and she had spent all she had on doctors*

40–42. Jesus returned to the western side of the lake, where there was more intense Jewish settlement, and 'a crowd welcomed him, for they were all expecting him'. Jairus is mentioned by name as 'a synagogue leader', who unusually 'came and fell at Jesus' feet, pleading with him to come to his house' (see 7:1–10). Despite his dignified office, he made this humble approach to Jesus 'because his only daughter, a girl of about twelve, was dying'. Her age signified that she was near to betrothal and preparation for marriage.[179] This narrative continues in verses 49–56, where there is a parallel to the raising of a widow's only son (7:11–15). The enthusiasm of the crowd is mentioned again when Luke says, 'As Jesus was on his way, the crowds almost crushed him.'

43–4. Meanwhile, Jesus's encounter with a woman 'who had been subject to bleeding for twelve years' interrupted his journey to the home of Jairus. Nolland argues that this pause 'heightens the suspense of the narrative and provides a crescendo which moves from healing to restoration to life'.[180] Jesus demonstrates his concern for her spiritual, as well as her physical, condition (see 5:17–26). She had suffered for the twelve years that the daughter of Jairus had lived, and 'no one could heal her'.[181] Moreover, because of the issue of blood, she was 'unclean' according to the Law (Leviticus 15:19–31) and unable to participate fully in Jewish community life and worship. In this degraded condition, she sought to approach Jesus anonymously and secretly ('She came up behind him and touched the edge of his cloak'). And her bleeding immediately stopped!

45–6. Jesus asked, 'Who touched me?', seeking to draw the woman

---

[179] Fitzmyer, *Luke I–IX*, 742–4, outlines the way Luke has shortened Mark 5:21–43 and brought out certain emphases in his account. Compare Matthew 9:18–26, which is even briefer.

[180] Nolland, *Luke 1–9:20*, 418.

[181] The longer version of verse 43 (NIV note c, 'and she had spent all that she had on doctors') looks like a condensation of Mark 5:26, which Luke the physician could have written, but the shorter version is better attested by early textual witnesses. See Metzger, *Textual Commentary*, 121.

out of the crowd and make face-to-face contact with her.[182] 'When they all denied it, Peter said, "Master the people are crowding and pressing against you,"' offering a simple explanation for what had happened.[183] But Jesus replied, 'Someone touched me; I know that power has gone out from me' (see 6:19). This refers to 'the power of the Spirit' mentioned in 4:14 or 'the power of the Lord' (5:17) which was operative in his healing ministry, even when it was not sought (verses 28–33) or only timidly pursued.

47–8. 'Then the woman, seeing that she could not go unnoticed, came trembling and fell at his feet.' She wanted to avoid attention and was perhaps expecting a reprimand from Jesus. In the presence of all the people, she had to explain 'why she had touched him and how she had been instantly healed'. Her concern about breaking the Law seems to have been paramount and she needed to assure everyone that she would not defile them with her bleeding. Jesus's approach was affectionate ('Daughter'), implying that she belonged to the family of God he had come to save (see 13:16; 19:9). When he said, 'your faith has healed you', he clarified that nothing magical had taken place, but that she had experienced his healing power through faith (see 17:11–19). As Green suggests, genuine faith had been expressed 'in her willingness to cross the barriers of acceptable behavior in order to obtain salvation'.[184] She had been physically healed (verse 47, *iathē*) and restored to the community of believers. But the verb translated 'healed' in verse 48 (*sesōken*) and 'cured' in verse 36 was previously rendered 'saved' in relation to the woman whose sins were forgiven (7:50). Healing, exorcism and forgiveness all pointed to the end-time salvation that Jesus was proclaiming (5:23–4).[185] 'Go in peace' was an encouragement to enjoy the blessings of her new confidence in God through Jesus (as in 7:50).

49–50. While Jesus was still speaking, someone came from the house of Jairus the synagogue leader with bad news. 'Your daughter is dead,' he

---

[182] Isaak, 'Luke', 1246, suggests that Jesus called this woman to come to him 'because she herself, as a person, had not been healed'. More than physical restoration was necessary.

[183] Mark 5:30 has the disciples asking this question somewhat more rudely. Some less-significant manuscripts of Luke 8:45 add 'and those with him' to harmonise more with Mark.

[184] Green, *Luke*, 349.

[185] See Nolland, *Luke 1–9:20*, 420. The same verb (*sōzō*) is applied to the healing of the demon-possessed man (8:36) and the raising of the girl from death (8:50), but the spiritual sense is clear from the context again in 9:24; 13:23; 18:26; 19:10.

said. 'Don't bother the teacher anymore.' When Jesus heard this, he was not deterred, but said to Jairus,[186] 'Don't be afraid; just believe, and she will be healed.' This third use of the Greek verb *sōzō* to describe the healing activity of Jesus (see verses 36, 48) points to the possibility of resurrection from death as another aspect of the salvation he came to achieve.

51–2. 'When he arrived at the house of Jairus, he did not let anyone go in with him except Peter, John and James, and the child's father and mother.' His concern for privacy, rather than secrecy, is explained by what was going on outside the house ('all the people were wailing and mourning for her'). A large group had gathered to begin the customary practice of mourning. Jesus also had a particular desire to share this moment with Peter, John and James as witnesses (see 9:28). He told those outside to 'stop wailing', assuring them, 'She is not dead but asleep.' This did not mean that her death was only apparent, but that she would soon awake from the sleep of death. As Fitzmyer observes, 'With his coming death is seen to be like sleep, not a permanent state, but transitional.'[187]

53–6. The mocking of the crowd ('They laughed at him, knowing that she was dead') confirmed the reality of her death and highlighted the enormity of the miracle. Jesus took the girl by her hand and cried out, 'My child, get up!' The Aramaic words that Jesus used are recalled in Mark 5:41. Once again, his word of command is the means of healing and restoration (see 7:14; 8:24, 29, 54, and contrast 1 Kings 17:19–22). Luke adds that 'her spirit returned, and at once she stood up', emphasising that this was a resumption of her earthly life, not resurrection with a new body.[188] Consequently, Jesus's immediate concern was that her parents should 'give her something to eat'. They were naturally 'astonished, but he ordered them not to tell anyone what had happened'. Jesus's call for secrecy enabled him to withdraw quietly, before the truth came out and he was overwhelmed by those who were simply drawn to the miraculous.

THE DIVINE CHARACTER OF JESUS'S
WORDS AND ACTIONS

In this section of Luke's narrative, the focus is once again on the divine character of Jesus's words and actions. In the first instance (verses 22–5),

---

[186] The Greek (*autō*) simply translates 'to him' (see ESV), but the NIV specifically identifies Jairus, rather than the messenger, as the object of Jesus's comforting words.
[187] Fitzmyer, *Luke I–IX*, 749. See 1 Corinthians 15:20, 51–2; 1 Thessalonians 4:13–17; 5:10. Nolland, *Luke 1–9:20*, 421, agrees that 'with the presence of Jesus, the eschatological abolition of the death barrier begins to take effect'.
[188] 'Spirit' (*pneuma*) here means 'breath' or 'life force' (Nolland, *Luke 1–9:20*, 422).

his power to still the storm delivers the disciples from faithlessness and drowning, causing them to question his true identity with reverent fear and amazement. In the second incident (verses 26–39), the power of Jesus is manifested in his triumph over the supernatural forces controlling a demon-possessed man. Klutz discerns that the demons cannot resist his command, but 'find themselves ripped from their human host and trapped in the swine, who promptly take them precisely where they had hoped not to go'.[189] The man is dramatically transformed and obeys the command to go and tell others how much Jesus has done for him. His release from all the consequences of demon possession is absolute, and his words testify to Jesus as the agent of this deliverance.

Jesus's actions with reference to the storm, the demon-possessed man, the woman who touched him and the daughter of Jairus collectively point to the end-time salvation he proclaimed. Taken together, as Green observes, these stories also 'document the sort of faith for which Jesus has been looking'.[190] Those who are sceptical about the miraculous element in the ministry of Jesus should note that these narratives are paralleled in each of the Synoptic Gospels and contribute significantly to the portrayal of his divine power and authority. The words and works of Jesus cannot be legitimately separated. He is not merely a great teacher and prophet: Jesus saves and restores human beings to a better life in this age by his word of command. Those who experience his grace are drawn to sit at his feet, where they learn to understand, live by his words of promise and warning, and anticipate the consummation of God's plan in the coming kingdom.

11. The mission of the Twelve and its sequel (Luke 9:1–17)

The sending out of the Twelve came after an extended period of watching and listening to Jesus.[191] He had called Peter and his associates to follow him with the promise that they would be fishing for people (5:8–11). They were the first of the Twelve whom he later designated as his apostles (6:13). 'The knowledge of the secrets of the kingdom' had been given to them (8:10) and they had been told that this revelation must be brought

---

[189] Klutz, *Exorcism Stories*, 105.
[190] Green, *Luke*, 344.
[191] Luke has already dealt with Jesus's rejection in Nazareth (4:16–30), omitting Mark 6:1–6 at this point (compare Matthew 13:53–8) and adapting Mark 6:7–13 for his purpose. A more complex discourse on mission and martyrdom is developed in Matthew 10.

out into the open (8:16–17). His commissioning of them to heal and proclaim the kingdom of God was accompanied by specific instructions concerning the way they should approach Israelite households and towns (9:1–5). Luke briefly summarises how the mission unfolded (9:6) and gives a brief report of how Herod the tetrarch of Galilee reacted to this expansion of the ministry of Jesus (9:7–9; compare Mark 6:14–29; Matthew 14:1–12).

Sharing in the ministry of Jesus (9:1–6)

Jesus sends out the Twelve

9 When Jesus had called the Twelve together, he gave them power and authority to drive out all demons and to cure diseases, **2** and he sent them out to proclaim the kingdom of God and to heal those who were ill. **3** He told them: 'Take nothing for the journey – no staff, no bag, no bread, no money, no extra shirt. **4** Whatever house you enter, stay there until you leave that town. **5** If people do not welcome you, leave their town and shake the dust off your feet as a testimony against them.' **6** So they set out and went from village to village, proclaiming the good news and healing people everywhere.

1–2. In an unspecified context, Jesus called the Twelve together and gave them 'power and authority to drive out all demons and to cure diseases', sharing his God-given power (4:14, 36; 5:17; 6:19; 8:46) and authority (4:32, 36; 5:24) with those he commissioned as his emissaries (6:13, 'apostles'). But Luke indicates the priority of preaching when he states that Jesus 'sent them out to proclaim the kingdom of God and to heal those who were ill'. As in his own ministry, exorcisms and healings would be signs of the coming kingdom, but proclamation of the kingdom would be the main aim (4:42–4; compare Acts 3). See also my comments on the mission of the seventy-two (10:1–20).

3–5. Jesus's first instruction ('Take nothing for the journey') is amplified in terms of 'no staff, no bag, no bread, no money, no extra shirt'. Minor variations in the parallel accounts (Mark 6:8–9; Matthew 10:9–10) indicate a broad pattern for 'ongoing missionary endeavour', as Nolland suggests.[192] The manner of their ministry was to demonstrate the urgency of proclaiming the message about the kingdom of God without appearing to be beggars. Jesus's second instruction ('Whatever house you enter, stay there until you leave that town') means that they should depend on

---

[192] Nolland, *Luke 1–9:20*, 427.

God's provision for their daily needs through the generosity of households that welcomed them (see 10:7, 'for the worker deserves his wages') and base their ministry there.[193] However, Jesus's third instruction indicates that a whole town might oppose them ('If people do not welcome you, leave their town') and that they should leave with a clear indication of the seriousness of this response ('and shake the dust off your feet as a testimony against them'). Rejecting the messengers meant rejecting their message. Shaking the dust off their feet implied separation from those who rejected the message, as a sign of God's inevitable judgment for this (see 10:11–12; Acts 13:50–51).

6. Luke's summary of what happened is brief: 'they set out and went from village to village, proclaiming the good news and healing people everywhere'. This period of mission was limited, and the apostles soon returned (verse 10). The manner of their ministry was specifically relevant to their brief foray into Galilean towns and villages. The instructions given to them cannot simply be applied to the range of situations in which Christian mission takes place today. The Twelve would have an expanded role as witnesses of Jesus after his resurrection (24:48; Acts 1:1–8), but the rest of Luke's Gospel focuses on a further period of instruction and involvement with Jesus before that could happen.

The response of Herod the tetrarch (9:7–9)

7 Now Herod the tetrarch heard about all that was going on. And he was perplexed because some were saying that John had been raised from the dead, **8** others that Elijah had appeared, and still others that one of the prophets of long ago had come back to life. **9** But Herod said, 'I beheaded John. Who, then, is this I hear such things about?' And he tried to see him.

7–9. Luke adds his own details to this abbreviation of Mark 6:14–16 (compare Matthew 14:1–2). First, he clarifies that it was Herod 'the tetrarch' of Galilee (3:1), who had heard about 'all that was going on', pointing to the mission of the Twelve as well as the ministry of Jesus himself. Second, Herod was 'perplexed' because of what people were generally saying about Jesus: 'some were saying that John had been raised from the dead, others that Elijah had appeared, and still others that one of the prophets of long

---

[193] Staying in the one place would have enabled them to have a continuing ministry to people in that house and to use it as a base for reaching out to others. See also my comment on 10:7.

ago had come back to life'. These were strange answers to the question of Jesus's identity, but each one acknowledged the prophetic character of his ministry. Third, Herod recalls, 'I beheaded John,' but then he asks the question that the rest of this chapter seek to answer: 'Who, then, is this I hear such things about?'[194] Finally, Luke adds that Herod 'tried to see him', foreshadowing 13:31–3 and 23:6–12 (episodes in which Herod's malevolence and curiosity about Jesus are emphasised).

Feeding the crowds (9:10–17)

Jesus feeds the five thousand

10 When the apostles returned, they reported to Jesus what they had done. Then he took them with him and they withdrew by themselves to a town called Bethsaida, 11 but the crowds learned about it and followed him. He welcomed them and spoke to them about the kingdom of God, and healed those who needed healing.

12 Late in the afternoon the Twelve came to him and said, 'Send the crowd away so they can go to the surrounding villages and countryside and find food and lodging, because we are in a remote place here.'

13 He replied, 'You give them something to eat.'

They answered, 'We have only five loaves of bread and two fish – unless we go and buy food for all this crowd.' 14 (About five thousand men were there.)

But he said to his disciples, 'Make them sit down in groups of about fifty each.' 15 The disciples did so, and everyone sat down. 16 Taking the five loaves and the two fish and looking up to heaven, he gave thanks and broke them. Then he gave them to the disciples to distribute to the people. 17 They all ate and were satisfied, and the disciples picked up twelve basketfuls of broken pieces that were left over.

10–11. Luke's account of the feeding of the five thousand is an abbreviation of Mark 6:30–44 (compare Matthew 14:13–21) and is closely linked to the mission of the Twelve ('When the apostles returned, they reported to Jesus what they had done'). Jesus's care for the returning missionaries is briefly stated: 'Then he took them with him and they withdrew by themselves to a town called Bethsaida.' According to John 1:44; 12:21, Philip, Andrew and Peter came from there. Bethsaida was situated north

---

194 Mark 6:17–29 continues with a lengthy explanation of John's denunciation of Herod's marriage, his imprisonment, Herod's fear of him and ultimately his willingness to put him to death. Luke 3:19–20 records John's imprisonment, but not his death. Compare Josephus, *Antiquities* 18.5,2.

of Lake Gennesaret (5:1), also called the Sea of Galilee and the Sea of Tiberius, east of the Jordan River, 'not far from where it empties into the lake'.[195] Jesus's ministry in that region is mentioned in the 'woe' of 10:13 and elsewhere in the Gospels. At this stage, the enthusiasm of the crowds is highlighted: they 'learned about it and followed him'. Although Jesus may have wished to be alone with his apostles, he 'welcomed [the crowds] and spoke to them about the kingdom of God, and healed those who needed healing'.

12. 'Late in the afternoon' (ESV, 'the day began to wear away', see 24:29–30) and the time for an evening meal approached, 'the Twelve came to him and said, "Send the crowd away so they can go to the surrounding villages and countryside and find food and lodging, because we are in a remote place here."' The size of the crowd had made it necessary for Jesus to withdraw from Bethsaida to an isolated place, where he could continue teaching and healing. Luke alone identifies 'the Twelve' at this point, reflecting their increased significance in the ministry of Jesus (9:1–6).

13–15. Jesus's reply ('You give them something to eat') challenged the apostles to provide what seemed an impossible amount of food for that crowd. This echoed Elisha's instruction to a man with twenty barley loaves to feed a hundred men (2 Kings 4:42–4) and God's promise, 'They will eat and have some left over.' The Twelve might also have recalled God's miraculous feeding of their ancestors in the wilderness (Exodus 16; compare John 6:31–2), but they could only focus on their limited resources ('We have only five loaves of bread and two fish – unless we go and buy food for all this crowd') and the number of those present ('about five thousand men were there').[196] Jesus prepared to meet the need of the crowd by instructing his apostles (now called 'his disciples'), 'Make them sit down in groups of about fifty each.' Luke's expression 'fifty each' recalls Obadiah's words to Elijah in 1 Kings 18:13 about supplying food and water to the Lord's prophets when they were persecuted by

---

[195] Fitzmyer, *Luke I–IX*, 765. Luke omits all the material in Mark 6:45–8:26 in which Bethsaida is mentioned twice (6:45; 8:22). Luke may have introduced it in 9:10 as an indication of Jesus's general location in the period before he asked his disciples the critical question about his identity (9:18–20). Luke gives the impression that this was Galilean territory, as does John 12:21; Josephus, *Antiquities* 18.23. See Lloyd, *Itinerant Jesus*, 207–14, 231–43, 256–7.

[196] The word *andres* ('males') is used in each of the four accounts of this incident, Matthew 14:21 adding, 'besides women and children'. So there were more than five thousand people present. No obvious biblical significance in the mention of fish here is obvious (Nolland, *Luke 1–9:20*, 442).

Ahab and Jezebel. But Obadiah was not himself a prophet, and the link between his action and Jesus's feeding miracle is slight.[197]

16. 'Taking the five loaves and the two fish and looking up to heaven, [Jesus] gave thanks and broke them.' These five actions are recorded in each of the Synoptic accounts (John 6:11 mentions only three). Four of the actions are repeated at the Last Supper (Matthew 26:26; Mark 14:22; Luke 22:19), though Luke uses the verb *eucharistēsas* ('give thanks') in that context and *eulogēsen* ('blessed') here. The NIV has translated the latter 'gave thanks', because these verbs are used interchangeably in the Greek Bible. In both contexts, Jesus blesses God for the food and initiates the meal by breaking the bread (see 24:30, 35; Acts 2:42, 46).[198] Although Luke adds the pronoun *autous* ('them') after 'gave thanks', it is unlikely to mean that Jesus blessed the food in the sense of consecrating it.[199] The unique action that distinguished this event from the Last Supper was his 'looking up to heaven'. In this way, he expressed his dependence on God for a miraculous provision (see Job 22:26; Mark 7:34; Luke 18:13; John 11:41), as he sought to meet the needs of the crowds. Then he began to give what he had to his closest disciples to distribute to the people. Multiplication of the loaves and fishes apparently took place in a way that they alone witnessed. Each of the meal narratives in Luke's Gospel reveals something more about Jesus and his mission to those intimately involved (5:27–32; 9:12–17; 22:7–38; 24:28–32).

17. By way of conclusion, the enormity of the miracle is stressed in two ways. First, 'they all ate and were satisfied'. Second, 'the disciples picked up twelve basketfuls of broken pieces that were left over', showing the extravagant provision of God through his Son (see 2 Kings 4:43–4). Edwards observes, 'The meal is so sufficient and satisfying that a basket of leftovers remains for each of the disciples.'[200] The discourse in John 6:25–59 draws out the ultimate implications of this miracle. As 'the bread of life', Jesus offers the satisfaction of an eternal relationship with God to those who believe in him.

---

[197] Contrast Edwards, *Luke*, 266.

[198] See J. Behm, 'κλάω', *TDNT* 3:728–9. Despite the formal similarities, Marshall (*Luke*, 361–2) outlines key differences between this event and the Last Supper.

[199] See Marshall, *Luke*, 362. God was thanked with respect to the food, as in the Mishnah, 'Blessed are you O Lord our God, king of the world, who cause bread to come forth from the earth' (*Berakot* 6:1). See J. Schneider, 'εὐλογέω', *TDNT* 2:762–3.

[200] Edwards, *Luke*, 267. The significance of the number twelve is not revealed until 22:30, where 'judging the twelve tribes of Israel' means sharing in the Messiah's rule over a restored or renewed Israel (compare Matthew 19:28). The Twelve are foundational to God's plan of salvation.

THE DISTINCTIVE ROLE OF THE TWELVE

As noted in connection with 6:13, the Twelve were first chosen to share in Jesus's ministry to Israel (9:1–6), and then be his foundational witnesses to the nations (24:45–9; Acts 1:6–8, 21–6). They were prepared for this role by listening to his teaching, observing his actions and asking questions. Their question in 8:25 ('Who is this?') was progressively answered in the events they then witnessed: the restoration of a demon-possessed man, the healing of a woman subject to bleeding for twelve years, the raising of the daughter of Jairus from death and the feeding of more than five thousand people in a remote place. Jesus exercised the power of God in healing and saving his people like one of the great prophets of Israel. But Luke shows him to be someone greater and more significant: the unique Son of God and Son of David, who came to inaugurate the end-time rule of God. The Twelve were sent out by him to proclaim his message and to share his power and authority 'to drive out all demons and to cure diseases' (9:1). In time, they became the authorised interpreters of Jesus and his mission, but their commissioning in 9:1–6 simply prepared them for a brief incursion into the homes and villages of Galilee. The manner in which they exercised their ministry reflected the urgency of proclaiming the message about the kingdom of God. It also expressed their dependence on God's provision for them through those who received their message with faith. The manner of gospel ministry portrayed in Acts is more diverse, but the message about the kingdom remains foundational (1:3, 6; 8:12; 14:22; 19:8; 20:25; 28:23, 31), and the need for messengers of the gospel to receive hospitality and care from those who believe is variously illustrated (9:18, 27–8, 43; 10:48; 11:3; 14:28; 16:15, 34; 18:26; 20:11; 21:7, 16; 27:3; 28:10, 14). Acts also emphasises the extent to which faithful gospel ministry is dependent on the foundational witness of the Twelve, whose testimony to Jesus was conveyed to subsequent generations by those who were 'eye witnesses and servants of the word' (1:1–2; 24:48; Acts 1:8, 21–6).

12. Confessing and following the Messiah (Luke 9:18–50)

As in 6:12, a new phase in Jesus's ministry is introduced with him praying. Luke then follows Mark 8:27–9:41 with some abbreviation. Jesus asks his disciples, 'Who do the crowds say I am?', and then, 'Who do you say I am?' Peter responds, 'God's Messiah' (verses 18–20). Jesus then surprisingly

THE GALILEAN MINISTRY OF JESUS

predicts his suffering, death and resurrection, and calls for a pattern of discipleship reflecting this expectation (verses 21–7). About eight days later, Peter, John and James experience something of the glory awaiting Jesus, while a voice from the cloud confirms, 'This is my Son, whom I have chosen; listen to him' (verses 28–36). When they come down from the mountain, Jesus heals a boy with an impure spirit that his disciples could not drive out (verses 37–43a). Jesus again predicts that he will be 'delivered into the hands of men', but the disciples do not understand what this means or perceive the implications for themselves (verses 43b–50). Their failure to respond appropriately shows why they need to hear the extensive teaching of Jesus on his way to Jerusalem (9:51–19:27).

Peter's confession (9:18–20)

Peter declares that Jesus is the Messiah

18 Once when Jesus was praying in private and his disciples were with him, he asked them, 'Who do the crowds say I am?'

19 They replied, 'Some say John the Baptist; others say Elijah; and still others, that one of the prophets of long ago has come back to life.'

20 'But what about you?' he asked. 'Who do you say I am?'

Peter answered, 'God's Messiah.'

18–19. In each of the Synoptic Gospels, Peter's confession and Jesus's response represent a significant turning-point or watershed. But Luke omits any reference to the location of this event,[201] simply introducing it with the words, 'Once when Jesus was praying in private and his disciples were with him'. Although this omission and the brevity of Luke's account may seem to play down the significance of what follows, Luke's way of highlighting the moment is to refer to Jesus 'praying in private' (see 3:21; 6:12; 9:28–9; 11:1; 22:41). Luke omits all of the material found in Mark 6:45–8:26, so that his report of this event immediately follows Herod's question about the identity of Jesus and the feeding of the five thousand (verses 7–17).[202] In answer to his question, 'Who do the crowds

---

[201] According to Mark 8:26; Matthew 16:13, they were in the region of Caesarea Philippi, about twenty-five miles (40km) to the north of the sea of Galilee, at the base of Mount Hermon. See Lloyd, *Itinerant Jesus*, 259–60.

[202] Although there may have been other reasons why Luke omitted this block of episodes (see Fitzmyer *I–IX*, 770–71), his briefer sequence of events shows more immediately how the disciples came to a different conclusion about Jesus than the popular views reported to Herod.

say that I am?', the disciples replied, 'Some say John the Baptist; others say Elijah; and still others, that one of the prophets of long ago has come back to life,' echoing the same opinions that had been reported to Herod (see 7:16; 9:7–8).

20. Jesus made no comment about the view that he was a resurrected prophet, but asked his disciples, 'What about you? . . . Who do you say I am?' Peter answered on behalf of the others, 'God's Messiah' (*ton christon tou theou*). The angelic proclamation in 2:11 (*christos kyrios*, 'the Messiah, the Lord') had identified him as the promised 'Son of the Most High' who would reign for ever on the throne of his father David (2:32–3). Peter's confession emphasised in a different way the special relationship of Jesus as Messiah to God (see 2:26, *ton christon kyriou*, 'the Lord's Messiah'; 23:35, *ho christos tou theou ho eklektos*, 'God's Messiah, the Chosen One').[203] The progress of Luke's narrative suggests that the disciples came to this conviction as they witnessed Jesus's actions and heard his various claims (especially 5:24; 6:20–26; 7:18–23, 48–50). A range of biblical expectations encouraged this simple confession. Jesus later indicates that the Father had been at work in all this, revealing the Son to his disciples in a personal way (10:21–4, compare Matthew 11:25–7; 16:17).[204]

Jesus predicts his suffering and its implications (9:21–7)

Jesus predicts his death

21 Jesus strictly warned them not to tell this to anyone. 22 And he said, 'The Son of Man must suffer many things and be rejected by the elders, the chief priests and the teachers of the law, and he must be killed and on the third day be raised to life.'

23 Then he said to them all: 'Whoever wants to be my disciple must deny themselves and take up their cross daily and follow me. 24 For whoever wants to save their life will lose it, but whoever loses their life for me will save it. 25 What good is it for someone to gain the whole world, and yet lose or forfeit their very self? 26 Whoever is ashamed of me and my words, the Son of Man will be ashamed of them when he comes in his glory and in the glory

---

[203] Mark 8:29 simply records, 'You are the Messiah,' but Matthew 16:16 has, 'You are the Messiah, the Son of the living God,' which is closer to the formulation in Luke 9:20. This is not yet a confession of Jesus's divinity, but an acknowledgement that he is the anointed agent sent by God to establish the kingdom promised to the Son of David (see 2 Samuel 7:12–16; Isaiah 9:6–7; 11:1–12; Jeremiah 23:5–6). See Edwards, *Luke*, 271–3.

[204] Green, *Luke*, 367–9, sees this supernatural insight as an answer to Jesus's prayer in verse 18.

of the Father and of the holy angels. | standing here will not taste death
27 'Truly I tell you, some who are | before they see the kingdom of God.'

21–2. In response to Peter's confession, 'Jesus strictly warned them not to tell this to anyone' (compare Mark 8:30; Matthew 16:20). The title 'Messiah' could have been understood in purely political terms, and Jesus wanted the opportunity to explain further the true nature of his messiahship and his kingdom.[205] His explanation began when he said, 'The Son of Man must suffer many things and be rejected by the elders, the chief priests and the teachers of the law, and he must be killed and on the third day be raised to life.' This prediction combined at least two different strands of Old Testament expectation. As noted in connection with 5:24, the enigmatic self-designation of Jesus as 'the Son of Man' most likely alluded to the vision in Daniel 7:13–14, where a man-like figure is given by God 'authority, glory and sovereign power; all nations and peoples of every nation worshipped him. His dominion is an everlasting dominion that will not pass away, and his kingdom is one that will never be destroyed.' Daniel's vision has messianic overtones, but it contains no specific indication that the figure is Davidic or that he must suffer (God's holy people suffer in Daniel 7:23–5). Jesus saw himself as destined to exercise that heavenly rule (Luke 9:26; 12:40; 17:22, 24, 26, 30; 18:8; 21:27, 36; 22:69), but only by way of rejection, death and resurrection to life again (9:22, 44; 18:31; 22:22; 24:7). The divine necessity for this is indicated by the verb 'must' (*dei*, as in 2:49; 4:43; compare 13:33; 17:25; 22:37; 24:7, 26, 44).

Jesus most likely drew on the portrayal of the Servant's victory through suffering in Isaiah 52:13–53:12 and combined this with his claim that as Son of Man he would ultimately be glorified.[206] In Luke 22:37, Jesus says that Isaiah 53:12 must be fulfilled in him, viewing his approaching death as redemptive and implying that others might share in the benefits. Luke 13:33–4 presents Jesus's more public revelation that he must die as a prophet in Jerusalem, because of Israel's history of killing the prophets (see also 20:9–19). Jesus may also have had in mind some of the psalms of lament, where the righteous sufferer experiences rejection and

---

[205] See Nolland, *Luke 1–9:20*, 449–51; Tannehill, *Narrative Unity* 1, 219–21; M. J. Bird, 'Christ', *DJG*, 115–25. The Greek participle *eipōn* ('and he said') links the new teaching in verse 22 directly with the warning not to tell anyone that he was the Messiah.

[206] See H. Beers, 'Servant of Yahweh', *DJG*, 855–9; J. Dennis, 'Death of Jesus', *DJG*, 172–93. Note the way the expected exaltation of the Servant after suffering begins and ends Isaiah's prophecy (52:13–15; 53:10–12).

mistreatment at the hands of God's own people (e.g., Psalms 22:1–21; 35:1–28; 69:1–29). The three groups that made up the Jewish Council in Jerusalem ('the elders, the chief priests and the teachers of the law', see 22:66; 24:20) are identified specifically. Resurrection 'on the third day' could allude to Hosea 6:2, which promised Israel's political and spiritual restoration in a short while, using the conventional time-reference 'two days and on the third day' to convey this (see Luke 13:32).[207] However, Jesus's prediction proved to be exact, as the apostolic tradition in 1 Corinthians 15:4 records.

23. In the parallel accounts, Peter rejects Jesus's prediction and he responds, 'Get behind me, Satan! You do not have in mind the concerns of God, but merely human concerns' (Mark 8:32–3; compare Matthew 16:22–3). Luke faces his readers immediately with the implications of Jesus's approaching suffering and death. The challenge is addressed to 'them all', meaning all who were with Jesus at that moment.[208] The introductory expression ('Whoever wants to be my disciple') brings out the need for an individual response. 'Be my disciple' translates a present-tense expression indicating continuous action (opisō mou erchesthai, 'to come after me'). Since those addressed were already following Jesus, a new dimension to their relationship with him is signalled, determined by his forthcoming journey to Jerusalem. The expression arnēsasthō heauton ('deny himself') calls for a renunciation of self as the determiner of personal goals, aspirations and desires. The NIV translates this in a plural way ('deny themselves') to bring out the general applicability of the saying. Similarly, the associated challenge ('take up their cross daily') is rendered in the plural, although the Greek is in a singular form.[209] Jesus's pathway to the cross establishes a pattern of discipleship that is set forth in the teaching that follows. Although discipleship is associated

---

[207] The third day is a day of deliverance in Genesis 22:4; 42:17–18; Jonah 1:17–2:1. Bock, *Luke 9:51–24:53*, 1894, notes that the three days in the Gospel tradition were counted in an inclusive way: Friday was day one, Saturday day two and Sunday day three.

[208] Mark 8:34 includes 'the crowd', but Luke 9:1–17 narrows the focus to the smaller circle of the Twelve (compare also verses 28, 32, 33, 49), functioning here as 'representative of the larger group of those who follow (and will follow) Jesus' (Green, *Luke*, 367). Compare 14:25–33.

[209] Two aorist imperatives in the Greek (arnēsasthō, 'deny', and aratō, 'take up') call for specific actions that are a prerequisite for following Jesus (Campbell, *Verbal Aspect and Non-Indicative Verbs*, 89), but Luke's addition of 'daily' indicates the need for repetition.

with joy and praise in many contexts, it is also, as Isaak suggests, 'a most painful task because it is a self-giving and a self-forgetting, like dragging a cross for one's own execution'.[210]

Crucifixion was a form of punishment much favoured by the Romans, for which the condemned customarily carried the beam of their cross to the place of execution.[211] Jesus's prediction that he would be 'handed over to the Gentiles' (18:32–3) explains why he could be certain of that kind of death. Announcing this as his fate, he called for disciples to be willing to die with him (see 14:26–7; Matthew 10:37–9; John 12:24–6), but the word 'daily' signifies an ongoing pattern of service to God like this. If the cross was God's will for Jesus in the establishment of his kingdom, no one else could die to achieve the promised salvation, but disciples could suffer because of their commitment to him and his cause (see Acts 5:41; 14:22; 1 Peter 2:18–25; 4:16).

24. A further saying teases out the implications of the previous one. Paradoxically, 'whoever wants to save their life will lose it, but whoever loses their life for me will save it'. The NIV has rightly translated *psychē* as 'life' (as in 6:9), because Jesus is speaking about the salvation of the whole person (verse 25, *anthrōpos*, 'a person'; *heauton*, 'himself'), not simply the inner person or 'soul'. Jesus warns against holding on to life as presently experienced and missing out on the life of the coming kingdom of God (see 6:20–26; 12:13–21; 16:19–31; 18:18–30).[212] Luke omits 'and the gospel' (Mark 8:35) but includes 'for me'. The missional dimension to discipleship has already been clarified (5:8–11; 9:1–6; compare 10:1–20), and being ashamed of Jesus and his words carries that sense in verse 26.

25. Jesus's rhetorical question raises the stakes: 'What good is it for someone to gain the whole world, and yet lose or forfeit their very self?'[213] Gaining the whole world is an extreme way of speaking about accumulating possessions, influence or fame. The verb 'lose' is used here in contrast with 'gain' and the commercial metaphor is enhanced by

---

[210] Isaak, 'Luke', 1248.

[211] See Fitzmyer, *Luke I–IX*, 787; Plutarch, *Moralia* 9:554A; Luke 23:26.

[212] Losing one's life is first presented in negative terms, as the outcome of self-preservation. But Jesus then uses the expression positively in terms of letting go of self in order to obtain the salvation he offers and to follow him. See Edwards, *Luke*, 276–7, and my Introduction, pages 14–17.

[213] The NIV unfortunately does not translate the conjunction *gar* ('for') at the beginning of verses 25 and 26, which shows that each saying builds on the previous one and intensifies the appeal.

adding 'forfeit'.[214] The temptation is to be satisfied with what the material world offers and reject the eternal benefits of living under Jesus's rule (see 6:24–6; 8:14). Like a wise trader or investor, the challenge is to weigh carefully the costs and benefits.

26. Luke omits Mark 8:37, which echoes Psalm 49, and moves straight to the issue of being ashamed of Jesus and his words in times of testing (see Luke 8:13; 22:54–62). In 12:8–9, being ashamed means disowning him rather than acknowledging him. Mark 8:38 adds 'in this adulterous and sinful generation' to characterise the world in which disciples must live and testify to Jesus. Once again, Jesus associates himself with the mysterious figure of 'the Son of Man' (see 5:24; 6:5, 22; 7:34; 9:22), echoing Daniel 7:13 more explicitly here. However, Jesus portrays the Son of Man's coming not as a reference to his heavenly ascension and enthronement (as in 22:69), but as an earthly appearance 'in his glory and in the glory of the Father and of the holy angels' (as in 12:40; 21:27). Judgment is implied by the reference to being 'ashamed of them when he comes'. Jesus makes this extraordinary connection between himself and the coming Son of Man to make the point that a commitment to him and his teaching in the present is 'eschatologically decisive', as Nolland describes it.[215]

27. Jesus's final challenge in this sequence is linked to the preceding one by the expression, 'Truly I tell you'.[216] The coming of the Son of Man in glory is associated now with the advent of the kingdom of God: 'some who are standing here will not taste death before they see the kingdom of God' (Mark 9:1, 'that the kingdom of God has come with power'). The Son of Man's heavenly rule will be inaugurated by Jesus's death, resurrection and heavenly exaltation (22:69; compare 24:26; Acts 2:32–6), but his triumph will not be apparent to all until his return in glory (12:40; 17:24, 30; 21:27, 36). Contextually, the enigmatic expression in verse 27 implies that some of his disciples will soon see proof of the coming kingdom and the glory of the Son of Man by witnessing his transfiguration, though they will not understand or tell anyone at that time what they see.

---

[214] Green, *Luke*, 375, observes that 'forfeit' is not fully synonymous with 'lose'.

[215] John Nolland, *Word Biblical Commentary 35B Luke 9:21–18:34* (Nashville: Nelson, 1993), 485. Compare Green, *Luke*, 366. In 21:27–8, 36, the Son of Man's coming is also to bring redemption for the faithful who stand before him as judge.

[216] Mark 9:1 includes the Semitic affirmation *Amēn*, which Luke retains in 4:24; 12:37; 18:17, 29; 21:32; 23:43. Luke has *alēthōs* ('truly') in 9:27; 12:44; 21:3. In each case, Jesus is making a significant assertion. See Fitzmyer, *Luke I–IX*, 536–7.

Jesus's glory is partially revealed (9:28–36)

The transfiguration

28 About eight days after Jesus said this, he took Peter, John and James with him and went up onto a mountain to pray. 29 As he was praying, the appearance of his face changed, and his clothes became as bright as a flash of lightning. 30 Two men, Moses and Elijah, appeared in glorious splendour, talking with Jesus. 31 They spoke about his departure,ᵃ which he was about to bring to fulfilment at Jerusalem. 32 Peter and his companions were very sleepy, but when they became fully awake, they saw his glory and the two men standing with him. 33 As the men were leaving Jesus, Peter said to him, 'Master, it is good for us to be here. Let us put up three shelters – one for you, one for Moses and one for Elijah.' (He did not know what he was saying.)

34 While he was speaking, a cloud appeared and covered them, and they were afraid as they entered the cloud. 35 A voice came from the cloud, saying, 'This is my Son, whom I have chosen; listen to him.' 36 When the voice had spoken, they found that Jesus was alone. The disciples kept this to themselves and did not tell anyone at that time what they had seen.

_____

ᵃ 31 Greek *exodos*

28. A close link with the predictions in verses 21–7 is made with Luke's introduction to this event: 'About eight days after Jesus said this', he took Peter, John and James with him (as in 8:51) and went up onto a mountain to pray (as in 6:12).[217] If Jesus was in the region of Caesarea Philippi (Mark 8:26; Matthew 16:13), it is highly likely that this next event took place on Mount Hermon. Jesus presumably prayed about his upcoming journey to Jerusalem and asked the Father to convince his disciples about its meaning and significance.

29. 'As he was praying, the appearance of his face changed,' recalling the description of Moses coming down from Sinai after speaking with God (Exodus 34:29–35), and his clothes 'became as bright as a flash of lightning'. Luke explains in more simple terms what the other evangelists mean by saying that Jesus was 'transfigured before them' (Mark 9:2; Matthew 17:2, *metemorphōthē*).[218] This was an anticipation of what would

_____

[217] Fitzmyer, *Luke I–IX*, 792, lists the changes Luke makes to Mark 9:2–9 and suggests that the change from 'six days later' to 'eight days' 'may be nothing more than a rounded-off way of saying "about a week later"' (797). Compare Nolland, *Luke 9:21–18:34*, 497.

[218] Green, *Luke*, 380, argues that in the Old Testament and Jewish tradition, 'one's countenance is a mirror of one's heart and a manifestation of one's relationship to

be more fully seen at the Son of Man's coming 'in the glory of the Father and of the holy angels' (9:26). Before that, he would have to suffer many things 'and then enter his glory' (24:26).

30–31. Luke gives a more elaborate introduction to the second phase of this supernatural event when he says, 'Two men, Moses and Elijah, appeared in glorious splendour [*en doxē*, 'in glory'], talking with Jesus.' This vision links Jesus with two key biblical prophets, who already shared in the glory of the kingdom that he was about to enter and open to all believers (23:43; compare 20:37–8). Their appearance affirms that what the Law and the Prophets foreshadowed is taking place in the person and ministry of Jesus.[219] The barriers of time and space are broken as they speak about his 'departure, which he was about to bring to fulfilment at Jerusalem'. 'Departure' (*exodos*) can simply be a euphemism for death (BDAG; 2 Peter 1:15), but it also recalls the rescue of Israel from captivity in Egypt (Exodus 19:1; Numbers 33:38 LXX; Hebrews 11:22) and the revelation of God's glory in that event (Exodus 13:20–22; 14:13–31; 15:11). The redemptive significance of the term 'departure' is enhanced by the expression 'bring to fulfilment at Jerusalem' (see the use of 'fulfil' in 1:20; 21:24; 22:16). As the Servant–Messiah, Jesus achieves through his suffering and exaltation the ultimate 'exodus' for God's people anticipated in the Law and the Prophets and brings them into their heavenly inheritance (see 24:44–7). See also my Introduction, pages 25–6.

32–3. Luke makes the special point that 'Peter and his companions were very sleepy' (*bebarēmenoi hypnō*, 'heavy with sleep'), suggesting that it was night (see 9:37; 22:39) and that they only gradually became aware of what was happening. But 'when they became fully awake, they saw his glory and the two men standing with him'. Their lack of understanding about the significance of the event continues in what follows. 'As the men were leaving Jesus, Peter said to him, "Master, it is good for us to be here. Let us put up three shelters – one for you, one for Moses and one for Elijah."'[220] Peter's suggestion treats Jesus as a heavenly figure like Moses and Elijah, and he vainly attempts to capture the moment, forgetting what he has just been taught. Jesus had already told them that he

---

God' (compare Acts 6:15). Jesus at prayer appeared to have been in the glorious presence of the Father.

[219] Compare Nolland, *Luke 9:21–18:34*, 503; Green, *Luke*, 381.

[220] The word 'shelter' (*skēnē*) is used in the LXX for the tabernacle (Exodus 25:9), which was regarded as God's dwelling-place on earth. The term was also used in connect with the Feast of Tabernacles (booths, tents), celebrating the Exodus (Leviticus 23:34–6; Numbers 29:12–38).

must suffer before entering his glory, and Luke makes it clear that Peter 'did not know what he was saying'.

34–5. In the third phase of this event, as Peter was speaking, 'a cloud appeared and covered them, and they were afraid as they entered the cloud'. The overshadowing of the cloud suggests a theophany: God was drawing near to speak to his people, as at Sinai (Exodus 19:9, 16). Then a voice from the cloud came, which Tannehill takes to be 'a correction of Peter's inappropriate proposal and a clarification of what the transfiguration reveals about Jesus'.[221] The heavenly voice echoed some of the Father's words to the Son at his baptism (3:22), though the disciples are addressed here. The identification of Jesus as 'my Son' reflects Psalm 2:7 and recalls the angelic prediction that he would be the messianic 'Son of the Most High' (Luke 1:32–3). The words 'whom I have chosen' recall Isaiah 42:1 and suggest his destiny to fulfil the role of the Servant of the Lord, including the suffering predicted in Isaiah 53.[222] The command, 'listen to him', relates to Jesus's teaching just given (verses 21–6), as well as to what he will continue to give them as the prophet like Moses (see Deuteronomy 18:15; Acts 3:22–3; 7:37–8). What they have witnessed they cannot comprehend without listening to Jesus and believing his word. Fitzmyer concludes, 'Instead of trying to hold on to the figures of old, the heavenly voice charges the disciples to listen to Jesus. The implication is that he now speaks with greater authority than Moses and Elijah.'[223]

36. 'When the voice had spoken, they found that Jesus was alone,' thus confirming the visionary nature of the experience. Although the other Gospels state that Jesus commanded the three witnesses not to disclose what they had experienced, Luke simply indicates that 'the disciples kept this to themselves and did not tell anyone at that time what they had seen'.

The disciples fail to understand and believe (9:37–50)

Jesus heals a demon-possessed boy
37 The next day, when they came down from the mountain, a large crowd met him. **38** A man in the crowd called out, 'Teacher, I beg you to look at my son, for he is my only child. **39** A spirit

---

[221] Tannehill, *Narrative Unity* 1, 224.
[222] The designation *ho eklelegmenos* ('the chosen') is only found here in the New Testament, though *ho eklektos* is used in Luke 23:35; John 1:34. Isaiah 42:1 LXX has *ho eklektos mou* ('my chosen one').
[223] Fitzmyer, *Luke I–IX*, 803.

seizes him and he suddenly screams; it throws him into convulsions so that he foams at the mouth. It scarcely ever leaves him and is destroying him. **40** I begged your disciples to drive it out, but they could not.'

41 'You unbelieving and perverse generation,' Jesus replied, 'how long shall I stay with you and put up with you? Bring your son here.'

42 Even while the boy was coming, the demon threw him to the ground in a convulsion. But Jesus rebuked the impure spirit, healed the boy and gave him back to his father. **43** And they were all amazed at the greatness of God.

Jesus predicts his death a second time

While everyone was marvelling at all that Jesus did, he said to his disciples, **44** 'Listen carefully to what I am about to tell you: the Son of Man is going to be delivered into the hands of men.' **45** But they did not understand what this meant. It was hidden from them, so that they did not grasp it, and they were afraid to ask him about it.

46 An argument started among the disciples as to which of them would be the greatest. **47** Jesus, knowing their thoughts, took a little child and made him stand beside him. **48** Then he said to them, 'Whoever welcomes this little child in my name welcomes me; and whoever welcomes me welcomes the one who sent me. For it is the one who is least among you all who is the greatest.'

49 'Master,' said John, 'we saw someone driving out demons in your name and we tried to stop him, because he is not one of us.'

50 'Do not stop him,' Jesus said, 'for whoever is not against you is for you.'

37–8. Omitting any reference to the discussion Jesus had with his three disciples when they came down from the mountain (Mark 9:9–13; Matthew 17:10–13), Luke uses a simple time reference ('the next day') to link this next incident with the previous one.[224] 'A large crowd met him', though they remain silent until the end of the account (verse 43; see Mark 9:14–15). Luke's abbreviated account focuses first on a man in the crowd, who called out, 'Teacher, I beg you to look at my son, for he is my only child.' Even before the condition of his severely disabled son is described, the fact that he has only one child points to the desperate need of this father (see 7:12; 8:42).

39–40. The symptoms here are reminiscent of 4:35; 8:29: 'A spirit seizes him and he suddenly screams; it throws him into convulsions so that he foams at the mouth. It scarcely ever leaves him and is destroying him.'

---

[224] Luke 9:37–50 is tightly bound together 'topically and in terms of structure and setting' (Green, *Luke*, 385–6).

But no supernatural recognition of Jesus's identity or challenge by this spirit is noted (see 4:33–4, 41; 8:28). The disorder may have been a form of epilepsy, but the convulsions are clearly attributed to a demon (also called 'the impure spirit' in verse 42) and the healing involves exorcism.[225] The seriousness of the case is further emphasised when the father says, 'I begged your disciples to drive it out, but they could not.' Presumably, these were the nine disciples left behind when Peter, John and James went up the mountain with Jesus. Each had been given power and authority 'to drive out all demons and to cure diseases' (9:1), so what had gone wrong?

41. Jesus's first response was to link the failure of the disciples with the unbelief of their contemporaries: 'You unbelieving and perverse generation' (see 'generation' in 7:31; 11:30, 31, 32, 50, 51; 17:25; 21:32). Luke includes the adjective 'perverse' (*diestrammenē*, as does Matthew 17:17), which echoes Moses' description in Deuteronomy 32:5 LXX ('crooked'); 32:20 ('perverse') of those who came out of Egypt with him. Peter later uses a similar expression in urging fellow Jews to respond to the gospel (Acts 2:40) and Paul speaks about unbelievers more generally in this fashion (Philippians 2:15). The disciples had seen the power of God at work in their ministry (9:6), but they were overwhelmed with the difficulty of this boy's illness.[226] Jesus's second response ('How long shall I stay with you and put up with you?') echoes God's challenge to Israel on the borders of the Promised Land in Numbers 14:11. Jesus's third response is a gracious invitation to the father ('Bring your son here'), whose faith that his son could be healed had not wavered (verse 38).

42–3a. A brief description of the cure recalls several aspects of previous exorcisms and healings. First, there was a final attempt by the evil spirit to demonstrate the power it had exercised in the life of this boy ('Even while the boy was coming, the demon threw him to the ground in a convulsion'). Second, the boy was healed with a simple command ('Jesus rebuked the impure spirit').[227] Third, family relationships were restored (he 'gave him back to his father'). Fourth, the bystanders 'were all amazed at the greatness of God'.

43b–45. Jesus's second passion prediction is closely linked with what

---

[225] Here and in 13:10–17 there is an overlap of medical and spiritual factors in the description (see Green, *Luke*, 387, note 118; Edwards, *Luke*, 87–8). Matthew 17:15 actually uses the technical term for an epileptic seizure.

[226] In Mark 9:28–9, Jesus implies that they failed to pray (and 'fast' in some manuscripts) and express their utter dependence on God for healing.

[227] The verb 'rebuked' is used here as in 4:35, 41. Compare also 4:39 (fever) and 8:24 (the storm).

had just taken place ('While everyone was marvelling at what Jesus did'), although his teaching on this subject was clearly for the disciples alone.[228] Luke's account begins emphatically ('Listen carefully to what I am about to tell you') and then focuses on the prospect of betrayal ('the Son of Man is going to be delivered into the hands of men').The verb used here reappears in a third passion prediction in relation to Jesus being 'handed over to the Gentiles' (18:32; compare 23:25; 24:7, 20),[229] but significantly also in relation to his betrayal by Judas to the Jewish authorities (22:4, 6, 21, 22, 48). Jesus was not deceived by the popular responses he received and challenged his disciples to be ready for the opposition that was coming to them too (21:12, 16). Luke emphasises that 'they did not understand what this meant'. On the one hand, 'it was hidden from them, so that they did not grasp it'. On the other hand, they perceived enough to be 'afraid to ask him about it'. Although God's sovereignty could be implied by saying 'it was hidden from them', the secrets of the kingdom had been revealed to them (8:10), and Jesus expected that this new secret could be understood.[230] Fear of the implications kept them from pursuing the issue (Matthew 17:23, 'the disciples were filled with grief').

46–8. The faithlessness of the disciples and their inability to grasp the implications of Jesus's predictions (verses 22–7, 43b–5) left them sadly arguing among themselves 'as to which of them would be the greatest'. Their natural inclination to make comparisons and seek prominence over others may have been excited by false expectations concerning the kingdom of God (see 22:24–7). 'Jesus, knowing their thoughts' (*ton dialogismon tēs kardias autōn*, 'the reasoning of their hearts'), 'took a little child and made him stand beside him', in the place of honour. Jesus said to them, 'Whoever welcomes this little child in my name welcomes me,' challenging their value-system and encouraging them to show hospitality to someone 'at the bottom of the ladder of esteem', as Green puts it.[231] Doing this in Jesus's name would be a reflection of their relationship with him and their adoption of his values. Jesus also challenged their understanding of his relationship with God ('and whoever welcomes

[228] Compare 9:21–7; 18:31–4; Mark 9:30–32. Luke's syntax allows for God to be the continuing subject in verse 43, but the NIV has inserted 'Jesus'. Luke may be making an indirect identification of Jesus as God at this point.
[229] The passive infinitive 'to be handed over' could certainly refer to God (Edwards, *Luke*, 289), but the prior prediction puts the emphasis on human agency (verse 21).
[230] The introductory challenge can be more literally rendered 'put these words into your ears' (ESV, 'Let these words sink into your ears').
[231] Green, *Luke*, 391. Compare Edwards, *Luke*, 290–91.

me welcomes the one who sent me'). In coming to serve and to save God's people, he made himself 'least' among them and thereby showed himself 'the greatest': 'For it is the one who is least among you all who is the greatest.'

49–50. John speaks for the other disciples when he says, 'Master . . . we saw someone driving out demons in your name and we tried to stop him.' Although exorcism in the name of Jesus implied belief in his power over the demonic world, the disciples were worried about an independent outsider misusing his name. This person's orthodoxy was in question because he did not belong to the apostolic group. Jesus, however, was more generous and said, 'Do not stop him . . . for whoever is not against you is for you.' As those called to the way of the cross, Nolland says the disciples were 'really in no position to be acting out of self-importance to secure their own domain of influence'.[232] Many would be needed to share in his ministry (10:1–2; Acts 6–9; 11:19–30), and those who were genuine disciples would be known by their fruit (6:43–5; Acts 19:1–20). Compare Jesus's more extensive response in Mark 9:39–41 and the complementary saying about being against him and not gathering with him in Luke 11:23; Matthew 12:30.

UNDERSTANDING AND FOLLOWING

Peter's confession of Jesus as God's Messiah leads to a new phase in Jesus's teaching about his mission and the true cost of discipleship. As Nolland concludes, 'Now "to follow him" is not just a Jewish way of talking about being a disciple of a master, but a challenge to have one's whole existence determined by and patterned after a crucified messiah.'[233] Self-denial, not self-fulfilment in this life is the path to eternal life. Different versions of the sayings in 9:23–6 appear in 12:8–9; 14:27; 13:33, revealing 'a broad range of concerns, not only the willingness to give one's life but also to renounce family and possessions', as Tannehill discerns.[234] Disciples are called to reflect the values and priorities of Jesus, which express his teaching about the kingdom of God and his own commitment to do the will of God. Green concludes that 'one cannot cling to this life and also serve the redemptive plan of God'.[235]

---

[232] Nolland, *Luke 9:21–18:34*, 525.
[233] Nolland, *Luke 9:21–18:34*, 482. See also Tokunboh Adeyemo, 'Discipleship', *Africa Bible Commentary*, 1249.
[234] Tannehill, *Narrative Unity* 1, 222.
[235] Green, *Luke*, 374. See also my summary of Luke's teaching on discipleship on pages 14–17.

Jesus continues to reveal the nature of his messiahship in association with the term 'Son of Man', linked in this passage for the first time with the necessity for his suffering, rejection by the leaders of Israel, crucifixion and resurrection (9:22, 44). At the same time, he introduces the idea that the Son of Man will be ashamed of those who deny him 'when he comes in his glory and in the glory of the Father and of the holy angels' (9:26). An anticipation of this glory is experienced in his transfiguration (9:28–36), where the heavenly voice echoes to the three disciples what was said to Jesus at his baptism (3:22). He is the unique Son of God, the Davidic Messiah, God's Chosen One, the Servant of the Lord. Moreover, Jesus stands in the prophetic tradition with Moses and Elijah. The instruction to 'listen to him' (9:35) implies that he is the expected end-time prophet like Moses (Deuteronomy 18:15, 18–19; compare Acts 3:22–6). Despite this challenge, however, all his disciples fail to understand the significance of what they have seen and heard and respond appropriately (9:37–50). Their failure shows the need for the extensive instruction and modelling that Jesus gives in the next main section of Luke's narrative (9:51–19:48).

5

Jesus's Final Journey to Jerusalem

LUKE 9:51–19:27

Luke's travel narrative begins at 9:51 and ends when Jesus comes down the Mount of Olives, enters the city and briefly visits the Temple (19:28–46). Then the evangelist introduces an account of Jesus's daily teaching in the Temple (19:47–21:38), with similar editorial notes in 19:47–8 and 21:37–8 clearly demarcating that section. However, since the entry into Jerusalem sets the scene for the next phase of his ministry, 19:28–46 will be treated as part of the next section.[1] The Lukan parable about 'a man of noble birth' going to a different country 'to have himself appointed king and then to return' (19:11–27) forms a significant climax to Jesus's teaching on the way. Luke observes that this was told 'because he was near Jerusalem and the people thought that the kingdom of God was going to appear at once' (19:11).

John's Gospel records several visits to Jerusalem and the Temple (2:13; 5:1; 7:10; 12:12), but Luke follows Mark 10:1–52 in featuring only this final journey (so also Matthew 19:1–20:34).[2] Luke provides regular indications of movement and of Jerusalem as the destination (9:52–5, 56, 57, 59; 10:1, 38; 11:53; 13:22, 33, 34; 14:25–7; 17:11; 18:31, 35; 19:1, 11, 28), but it is impossible to reconstruct an itinerary that runs clearly through the whole section. The material in 18:15–43 closely follows Mark's account, but the rest of the journey section contains teaching and narrative exclusive to Luke or segments paralleled in different contexts in Matthew. Many attempts have been made to explain why the material has been arranged this way. Broadly speaking, there are alternating blocks of instruction to disciples and opponents, continuing to develop themes from the Galilean period of Jesus's ministry, but not always linked to the journey theme or

---

[1] Bock, *Luke 9:51–24:53*, 958–9, argues that 19:44 is the end of the journey, though he acknowledges that 19:28–44 serves as a bridge into the final ministry events in Jerusalem.

[2] Luke omits Mark 9:41–10:12, though he picks up the journey motif from Mark 10:1 ('into the region of Judea and across the Jordan') and parallels Mark 9:42–50 in 17:1–3; 14:34–5.

the approaching suffering of Jesus.[3] Luke seems intent on reinforcing two previous emphases: first, the need for the disciples to be further taught in readiness for the approaching crisis; and second, the need to account for the hostility that finally brought Jesus to the cross.[4] Both of these themes were considered important by the evangelist to fulfil his purpose in writing (1:4; see Introduction pages 2–4).

1. Opposition and opportunity (Luke 9:51–10:24)

Luke's travel narrative commences with a dramatic announcement about Jesus's setting out for Jerusalem and his experience of rejection by a Samaritan village (9:51–6). This excited a reaction from James and John, which brought a rebuke from Jesus. An encounter with three would-be disciples then highlights the challenges associated with following him, not simply on the road to suffering, but also more generally in service to the kingdom of God (9:57–62). A lengthy description of the commissioning of the seventy-two (10:1–16) and the sequel to their mission climaxes this first major segment (10:17–24). Despite the woes pronounced by Jesus on towns that rejected him, his concluding emphasis is on joy, thanksgiving for divine revelation and assurance of eternal salvation.

Dealing with rejection (9:51–6)

Samaritan opposition

51 As the time approached for him to be taken up to heaven, Jesus resolutely set out for Jerusalem. 52 And he sent messengers on ahead, who went into a Samaritan village to get things ready for him; 53 but the people there did not welcome him, because he was heading for Jerusalem. 54 When the disciples James and John saw this, they asked, 'Lord, do you want us to call fire down from heaven to destroy them[b]?' 55 But Jesus turned and rebuked them. 56 Then he and his disciples went to another village.

b 54 Some manuscripts *them, just as Elijah did*

---

[3] See Nolland, *Luke 9:21–18:34*, 527–8. Nolland, 529, observes, 'The materials that sustain the journey motif, especially 9:51; 13:31–35; 18:31–34, but also other materials, reiterate, and in some cases, develop further the thrust of 9:21–50.'
[4] Various attempts to explain the structure and purpose of Luke's journey narrative are discussed by Nolland, *Luke 9:21–18:34*, 529–31; Bock, *Luke 9:51–24:53*, 961–4; and Green, *Luke*, 394–9.

51. A significant change in the narrative is marked by the introduction, 'As the time approached for him to be taken up to heaven'. Luke's expression (*tas hēmeras tēs analēmpseōs autou*, 'the days of his being taken up') identifies this as the period leading up to Jesus's ascension (*analēmpsis*).[5] The related verb is employed in Acts 1:2, 11, 22, and parallel terms are used in Luke 24:51 ('carried up') and Acts 1:9 ('lifted up') to describe how the crucified and resurrected Jesus was exalted to reign at God's right hand as Lord and Messiah (Acts 2:33–6).[6] The joyful prospect of being 'taken up' in this way explains how Jesus could 'resolutely set out for Jerusalem', despite his conviction that betrayal, rejection and death awaited him there (9:22, 44; compare Hebrews 12:2). More literally, Luke's second expression (*autos to prosōpon estērisen tou poreuesthai eis Ierousalēm*) translates 'he set his face to go to Jerusalem' (ESV). This reflects the Servant's determination in Isaiah 50:7 to do the will of God ('Therefore have I set my face like flint').

52–3. 'And he sent messengers on ahead, who went into a Samaritan village to get things ready for him.' Luke's interest in Samaritans emerges with this incident, which he alone records (see 10:30–37; 17:11–19; John 4:4–42). In Acts, Samaritans are among the first to believe the gospel and be baptised in the name of the Lord Jesus (8:1–13, 14–25; 9:31; 15:3). 'Samaritan' was a name for the inhabitants of the area between Judea and Galilee, west of the Jordan, who had developed their own form of the Torah/Pentateuch, built their own temple on Mount Gerizim and devised their own pattern of worship. Jewish tradition identifies them with those who occupied Samaria when the Jews were deported from the region by the Assyrians (2 Kings 17:24–41; Ezra 4:2–24; Nehemiah 2:19; 4:2–9), but Samaritan sources view them as descendants of the original inhabitants of Israel's northern kingdom.[7] Despite the antipathy between Jews and Samaritans that existed at the time, Jesus did not go by a circuitous route to Jerusalem, but he planned to travel through Samaria and stay

---

[5] The temporal construction *en tō symplērousthai* ('in the filling up') is used again in Acts 2:1 to highlight the importance of another moment of completion in the plan of God. Similar terms are used in Luke 1:23; 2:6, 21, 22; 21:24 for the fulfilment of time.

[6] See also Ephesians 4:8; Philippians 2:9; 1 Timothy 3:16 ('taken up in glory'), and the allusions to Psalm 110:1 in Luke 22:69 par.; Romans 8:34; 1 Corinthians 15:25; Ephesians 1:20; Colossians 3:1; Hebrews 1:3, 13; 8:1; 10:12; 12:2; 1 Peter 3:22. See Peterson, *Acts*, 113–15.

[7] H. G. M. Williamson and M. Kartveit, 'Samaritans', *DJG*, 832–6, argue that the Samaritans separated from mainline Judaism in the later Hellenistic period.

there along the way. The failure of the inhabitants of this village to show hospitality and 'welcome him' related to the fact that 'he was heading for Jerusalem'. Rather than being a personal affront to Jesus, this reflected a longstanding cultural and religious animosity.

54–6. 'When the disciples James and John saw this,' they were offended that Jesus had been treated so badly and asked, 'Lord, do you want us to call fire down from heaven to destroy them?' Their reaction echoed the words of Elijah (2 Kings 1:10, 12, 14), when the apostate king in Samaria tried to have him arrested.[8] But Jesus was not yet facing the same explicit rejection of his message and would not allow his disciples to call down God's immediate judgment on those who were so inhospitable. He 'turned and rebuked them', showing himself to be more gracious than they were (see 6:27–36). Then he and his disciples left that place without any warning of impending judgment (contrast 9:5; 10:10–12) and went to another village. This implied a continuing desire to connect with Samaritans and preach to them, despite the rejection of this one village.[9]

Three would-be followers (9:57–62)

The cost of following Jesus

57 As they were walking along the road, a man said to him, 'I will follow you wherever you go.'

58 Jesus replied, 'Foxes have dens and birds have nests, but the Son of Man has nowhere to lay his head.'

59 He said to another man, 'Follow me.'

But he replied, 'Lord, first let me go and bury my father.'

60 Jesus said to him, 'Let the dead bury their own dead, but you go and proclaim the kingdom of God.'

61 Still another said, 'I will follow you, Lord; but first let me go back and say goodbye to my family.'

62 Jesus replied, 'No one who puts a hand to the plough and looks back is fit for service in the kingdom of God.'

---

[8] The longer reading 'just as Elijah did' (NIV note b) is widely attested, though the earliest and best witnesses do not contain this gloss. There are also additions to verses 55 and 56 in some texts (reflected in KJV), one of which is a variant of Luke 19:10, but these are not in the best manuscripts. See Metzger, *Textual Commentary*, 124–5.

[9] In Matthew 10:5–6, Jesus prohibits any ministry to Gentiles or Samaritans because of the priority of bringing the gospel to Israel. However, as he moves towards Jerusalem and his predicted rejection by the leaders of Israel, he begins to engage with Samaritans.

57–8. Luke locates these three encounters on the road to Jerusalem ('as they were walking along the road'), whereas Matthew 8:19–22 records only the first two and places them in an earlier context.[10] Matthew records that the person who approached Jesus and said, 'I will follow you wherever you go,' was a teacher of the law, but Luke is not so precise. The man's enthusiastic and unconditional offer was greeted with an answer that reinforces the challenge of Jesus's lifestyle (see 9:23–6): 'Foxes have dens and birds have nests, but the Son of Man has nowhere to lay his head.' Once again, 'the Son of Man' is an indirect form of self-reference applied to Jesus's earthly life and ministry (see 5:24; 6:5; 7:34; 11:30; 12:10; 19:10; 22:48), but with a tantalising allusion to Daniel 7:13–14. Paradoxically, as the one destined to reign at God's right hand and return in great power and glory to judge and to save, Jesus lived as a homeless wanderer, 'having no shelter, no home, no family – none of the things most people usually consider requisite for ordinary life'.[11] Those who want to follow him must also be prepared to suffer deprivation in various ways. Jesus abruptly challenged this man to count the cost (see 14:28–33), though in 18:28–30 he reassures disciples about the material and relational blessings that commitment brings.

59–60. Jesus took the initiative with another man and said, 'Follow me' (see 5:27; Matthew 8:21–2). This man had good intentions ('Lord, first let me go and bury my father'), since the burial of his father was clearly a way of honouring him and fulfilling the fifth commandment (Exodus 20:12; Deuteronomy 5:16).[12] Most likely, his father was on the point of death or had just died, but Jesus claimed a higher loyalty to himself and his mission ('Let the dead bury their own dead, but you go and proclaim the kingdom of God'). This saying appears harsh in comparison with the generous spirit Jesus displayed in verses 54–6, but he apparently spoke with insight into the man's hesitation (see 5:22; 6:7–8; 7:39–43; 18:21–3). His aphorism contrasted the obligation of the spiritually dead to bury their own dead with the obligation of his disciples to 'go and proclaim the kingdom of God'. By implication, this could bring spiritual life to many.

61–2. Luke alone records this third interaction. 'Still another said,

---

[10] Bock, *Luke 9:51–24:53*, 974–5, argues that both versions are placed topically in their contexts, rather than with regard to chronological sequence. The setting in each case is vague.

[11] Fitzmyer, *Luke I–IX*, 834. Nolland, *Luke 9:21–18:34*, 540, defends the historicity of this saying.

[12] Rabbinic tradition made much of this obligation, although contact with a dead body was normally considered to be defiling (see Numbers 6:6–7; Leviticus 21:11).

"I will follow you, Lord; but first let me go back and say goodbye to my family." This man also wanted to honour family attachments, echoing Elisha's request when called by Elijah (1 Kings 19:19–20). But Jesus's response was more demanding and urgent than Elijah's: 'No one who puts a hand to the plough and looks back is fit for service in the kingdom of God.' The image is of someone seeking to plough a straight furrow while looking behind him. Jesus questioned the ability of this individual to detach himself sufficiently from family obligations and be 'fit for service' (*euthetos*, 'well suited for', BDAG; Hebrews 6:7). As with the previous saying, the issue here is dedicated service 'in the kingdom of God', proclaimed as an imminent reality (verse 60).

The commissioning of the seventy-two (10:1–16)

Jesus sends out the seventy-two

10 After this the Lord appointed seventy-two[a] others and sent them two by two ahead of him to every town and place where he was about to go. **2** He told them, 'The harvest is plentiful, but the workers are few. Ask the Lord of the harvest, therefore, to send out workers into his harvest field. **3** Go! I am sending you out like lambs among wolves. **4** Do not take a purse or bag or sandals; and do not greet anyone on the road.

5 'When you enter a house, first say, "Peace to this house." **6** If someone who promotes peace is there, your peace will rest on them; if not, it will return to you. **7** Stay there, eating and drinking whatever they give you, for the worker deserves his wages. Do not move around from house to house.

8 'When you enter a town and are welcomed, eat what is offered to you. **9** Heal those there who are ill and tell them, "The kingdom of God has come near to you." **10** But when you enter a town and are not welcomed, go into its streets and say, **11** "Even the dust of your town we wipe from our feet as a warning to you. Yet be sure of this: the kingdom of God has come near." **12** I tell you, it will be more bearable on that day for Sodom than for that town.

13 'Woe to you, Chorazin! Woe to you, Bethsaida! For if the miracles that were performed in you had been performed in Tyre and Sidon, they would have repented long ago, sitting in sackcloth and ashes. **14** But it will be more bearable for Tyre and Sidon at the judgment than for you. **15** And you, Capernaum, will you be lifted to the heavens? No, you will go down to Hades.[b]

16 'Whoever listens to you listens to me; whoever rejects you rejects me; but whoever rejects me rejects him who sent me.'

---

a 1 Some manuscripts *seventy*; also in verse 17

b 15 That is, the realm of the dead

1. The sending out of seventy-two others, with an expanded version of the charge given to the Twelve (9:1–5), is loosely linked by the phrase 'after this' (as in 5:27) to the preceding narratives.[13] The manuscript evidence is fairly evenly divided over the number of those sent out, with some important witnesses recording 'seventy'. The latter is used in a number of Old Testament contexts and has given rise to various symbolic interpretations, while the number seventy-two is less biblically significant and more likely to have been changed by copyists to seventy.[14] When Luke as narrator calls Jesus 'the Lord', he does so from the standpoint of his own post-resurrection faith (see 7:13, 19; 10:39, 41; 12:42; 13:15; 17:5; 18:6; 19:8, 31, 34; 22:61; 24:3, 34), revealing something of the significance of this title to his readers in the charge that follows (verses 2–3).

Nothing is said about the geographical location of the mission, but the statement that he 'sent them two by two ahead of him to every town and place where he was about to go' echoes 9:52 and suggests that this mission was a feature of Jesus's slow progress from Galilee to Jerusalem (see Matthew 10:23). His concern for disciples in general to 'go and proclaim the kingdom of God' (9:60) and be 'fit for service in the kingdom of God' (9:62) is more fully expressed in the appointment and sending out of this larger group of committed representatives. Going 'two by two' implied mutual support, but also the possibility of together giving faithful testimony to the truth of their message (following Deuteronomy 19:15; compare Mark 6:7; Luke 9:5).

2–3. Luke's introduction to Jesus's instructions parallels Matthew 9:37–8, where Jesus tells his disciples, 'The harvest is plentiful but the workers are few.' In some Old Testament passages, the harvest is a figure for God's final judgment of the nations (e.g., Isaiah 63:1–6; Joel 3:13; Micah 4:11–13), but here it more likely refers to the end-time gathering of God's people for salvation (see Isaiah 27:12–13; Hosea 6:11). 'The workers' who participate with Jesus in the preaching of his message are few, and the fields are ripe for harvest ('The harvest is plentiful'; see John 4:34–8). With limited time for bringing in the crop, extra workers are needed. Jesus acts as 'the Lord of the harvest' when he appoints and sends the seventy-two (verses 1, 3),

---

[13] Against Fitzmyer, *Luke X–XXIV*, 842–4, Luke's use of material found also in Matthew 9:37–8; 10:5–16; 11:20–24 in this discourse need not mean that it is an artificial expansion of 9:1–5 and that the event did not happen. See Bock, *Luke 9:51–24:53*, 986–93.

[14] Fitzmyer, *Luke X–XXIV*, 845–6, concludes that seventy could also be an approximation or 'round number' for a more original seventy-two. See Metzger, *Textual Commentary*, 126–7.

but then asks them to pray that God would send others to join them. These sayings point to his unique relationship with God in bringing his elect to salvation (19:9–10). The harvest will be plentiful, because God through his Son will enable many to receive the message and believe (verses 21–2). But Jesus also warns of opposition and danger: 'Go! I am sending you out like lambs among wolves' (see Matthew 10:16).[15]

4. Jesus does not explicitly give the seventy-two 'power and authority to drive out all demons and to cure diseases' (9:1), though this can be assumed from their report back in 10:17. He does, however, commission them to heal the sick and tell them, 'The kingdom of God has come near to you' (verse 9). His other instructions to these emissaries are a modified version of those given to the Twelve in 9:3–5. Provisions for the journey are considered first: 'Do not take a purse or bag or sandals; and do not greet anyone on the road'. Variations in the parallel passages indicate a broad pattern for 'ongoing missionary endeavour', rather than a checklist for the disciples to use.[16] Each of these provisions relates to the urgency and simplicity of the task and suggests the need to depend on God's care through the generosity of welcoming households. The injunction not to greet anyone on the road could mean not getting caught up in the distractions of everyday social interaction.

5–6. Guidelines are given for visiting a house and responding to those who seek peace: 'When you enter a house, first say, "Peace to this house." If someone who promotes peace is there, your peace will rest on them; if not it will return to you.' A formal greeting of peace in that culture provided an opportunity to share the gospel with someone who was genuinely seeking peace (*huios eirēnēs*, 'a son of peace'). The messianic peace might 'rest on them' through the proclamation of Jesus's disciples (1:79; 2:14, 29; 19:38, 42; Acts 10:36), assuring them of forgiveness and acceptance by God (7:50; 8:48; 24:36; Acts 15:33). But if a person was not genuinely seeking peace, the gospel offer would 'return' to the evangelist, not having achieved its goal.

7. The simple instruction to the Twelve in 9:4 ('whatever house you enter, stay there until you leave that town') is expanded to explain its

---

[15] Bock, *Luke 9:51–24:53*, 996, notes Jewish texts where Israel among the nations is represented in these terms, but Jesus is speaking about his disciples being persecuted by fellow Israelites. Of course, the saying is also applicable to disciples in later Gentile contexts.

[16] Nolland, *Luke 1–9:20*, 427. The only overlap with 9:4 is 'bag'. If sandals are taken with a bag this implies taking a spare pair. The lists are 'suggestive rather than exhaustive' (Nolland, 551).

significance: 'Stay there, eating and drinking whatever they give you, for the worker deserves his wages.'[17] 'Wages' paid to the workers in God's harvest come in the form of hospitality given by those who receive their message and want to support them. Such generosity should be gratefully received, but not abused. The warning ('Do not move around from house to house') could envisage seeking better accommodation. According to Green, this would constitute 'a serious breach of conventions governing the social role of the guest that would bring the mission unnecessarily into disrepute'.[18]

8–11. Guidelines for visiting a town are presented in a way that reflects and expands on verses 5–7. First, 'When you enter a town and are welcomed, eat what is offered to you.' In other words, gratefully enjoy the hospitality. Second, 'Heal those who are ill and tell them, "The kingdom of God has come near to you."' This corresponds with the offer of peace in verses 5–6 and means that the imminence of the messianic kingdom is communicated by word and deed. The verb 'come near' in the perfect tense (*ēggiken*, verses 9, 11) highlights the presence of the kingdom and its blessings in the ministry of Jesus and those who share in his mission (see Mark 1:15; Matthew 4:17; 10:7), though final redemption is yet to draw near (Luke 21:28). As Nolland discerns, 'For Luke, the kingdom of God is a future eschatological reality that has broken in upon the world in the coming of Jesus but awaits future consummation.'[19] Third, 'when you enter a town and are not welcomed, go into its streets and say, "Even the dust of your town we wipe from our feet as a warning to you"' (see Acts 13:51; 18:6). Together with this symbolic action, they are to repeat their essential message, 'Yet be sure of this: the kingdom of God has come near.' The nearness of the kingdom signifies grace and peace for believers, but also God's judgment on those who refuse his offer of reconciliation (see 9:5, 'as a testimony against them').

12. Jesus warns that a whole town may reject the gospel and be subject to a judgment worse than Sodom's (Genesis 19:23–8). The saying, 'It will be more bearable on that day for Sodom than for that town' refers to the 'day' of the Lord's judgment (e.g., Zechariah 12:3–4). The men of

---

[17] This proverbial saying echoes Leviticus 19:13; Deuteronomy 24:14–15; Malachi 3:5 LXX and is paralleled in Sirach 34:22 and some non-Jewish sources. See also 1 Corinthians 9:14; Galatians 6:6–10; 1 Timothy 5:18.

[18] Green, *Luke*, 360. See also my comment on 9:4.

[19] Nolland, *Luke 9:21–18:34*, 554. The additional words 'to you' (*eph' hymas*) occur in 10:9 and 11:20 (*ephthasen eph' hymas*, 'has come upon you'). Compare 17:21 (*entos hymōn estin*, 'in your midst').

Sodom refused to show hospitality to the messengers of God and sought to have sex with them (Genesis 19:1–9). The judgment that fell on Sodom and its region was proverbial,[20] but even those who have been judged in this life must face the judgment to come. This is portrayed in verse 15 as suffering in Hades (see also my comments on 12:4–5; 13:28; 16:23–4). The comparative expression 'more bearable' suggests a greater level of punishment in the afterlife for those who reject Jesus and his messengers in this life (see 10:14). However, there is no hint in Jesus's teaching of any 'purgatory' or possibility of moving from one level to another.

13–14. Jesus's warning about eschatological judgment is coupled now with a series of woes pronounced on those who had already refused to respond appropriately to his ministry (see Matthew 11:20–24). Like prophecies against the nations in the Old Testament, the woes against 'Chorazin' and 'Bethsaida' in this interlude hold them up as terrible examples of missed opportunities and God's condemnation. They are based on a comparison with two pagan cities that were notorious for godlessness (Isaiah 23; Ezekiel 26–28): 'For if the miracles that were performed in you had been performed in Tyre and Sidon, they would have repented long ago, sitting in sackcloth and ashes.' 'Miracles' translates *dynameis* ('powerful deeds', as in 19:37; Acts 2:22; 8:13; 19:11), drawing attention to the divine power that Jesus exhibited (4:14, 36; 5:17; 6:19; 8:46) and shared in some measure with his disciples (9:1; 10:19). 'Sitting in sackcloth and ashes' was an ancient way of expressing penitence or mourning (Esther 4:1–3; Isaiah 58:5; Daniel 9:3; Jonah 3:6).[21] Luke provides no detail about Jesus's ministry in Chorazin, though his preaching and feeding miracle in the region of Bethsaida is recorded (9:10–17).[22] The fate of these towns had been decided, and God's final judgment would be severe ('it will be more tolerable for Tyre and Sidon at the judgment than for you'), since they had rejected a God-given opportunity to repent (see 5:31–2).

15. The woe against 'Capernaum' is expressed more simply, but with even more rhetorical force. Jesus's question implies some arrogance on the part of its inhabitants, perhaps because he ministered so extensively

---

[20] Isaiah 1:9, 10; 3:9; Ezekiel 16:48; Jubilees 16:5–6; 20:5. Luke 10:12 more generally applies the comparison between Sodom and Capernaum found in Matthew 11:24, while Luke 10:15 offers a briefer condemnation of Capernaum.

[21] Bock, *Luke 9:51–24:53*, 1003.

[22] Fitzmyer, *Luke X–XXIV*, 853, discusses the difficulties associated with locating Chorazin. Jesus's woes can be compared with passages like Amos 6:1–7; Micah 2:1–5; Habakkuk 2:6–19. Paradoxically, people from Tyre and Sidon were among those who gathered to hear Jesus teach in 6:17.

there (4:23, 31–7; 7:1–10): 'And you Capernaum, will you be lifted to the heavens?' In fact, God's judgment against Capernaum had also been decided: 'No, you will go down to Hades.' This is an echo of Isaiah 14:13–15, which taunts the king of Babylon. The Greek word *Hadēs* came to represent the grave or the realm of the dead, regularly translating the Hebrew *šeʾôl* ('Sheol') in the LXX (see Acts 2:24–32, reflecting on Psalm 16 [15 LXX]:8–11). When convictions about bodily resurrection and retribution after death developed in later Jewish literature, Hades/Sheol came to be regarded as 'a place divided into separate locales'.[23] In line with Daniel 12:2–3, Jesus envisions only two outcomes: some will be resurrected to everlasting life; others to shame, suffering and everlasting contempt. Hades is used to represent both death and subsequent punishment for those who are unrepentant in this life (see Matthew 11:23; 16:18; Luke 12:5 ['hell']; 16:23).[24]

16. Jesus's commissioning of the seventy-two concluded with a clear statement of their role as his representatives: 'Whoever listens to you, listens to me; whoever rejects you rejects me.' Even though the performance of miracles was highlighted as evidence against the towns that Jesus had visited (verses 13–14), the critical issue was their rejection of Jesus and his message. The mission of his disciples would similarly challenge people to hear the gospel and repent. Indeed, this is the focus of Jesus's words in 24:47–9, where the Spirit is promised to make their testimony to the nations effective (see Acts 1:6–8). Rejection of the gospel in any situation has serious consequences, not only because of its contents, but also because it expresses a personal rejection of Jesus and the one who sent him ('whoever rejects me rejects him who sent me').[25] The close link between Jesus and the one who sent him is about to be further explained (verses 21–2).

Reflecting on the mission (10:17–24)

17 The seventy-two returned with joy and said, 'Lord, even the demons submit to us in your name.' **18** He replied, 'I saw Satan fall like lightning from heaven. **19** I have given you authority to trample on snakes

---

[23] Fitzmyer, *Luke X–XXIV*, 855 (e.g., 1 Enoch 22:3–13; 63:10; 99:11). Compare J. B. Green, 'Heaven and Hell', *DJG*, 370–76.

[24] See Williamson, *Death and the Afterlife*, 38–54.

[25] These twin sayings are universalised by the use of 'whoever'. A parallel statement in Matthew 10:40 occurs at the end of the discourse in which Jesus commissions the Twelve. See also John 13:20.

and scorpions and to overcome all the power of the enemy; nothing will harm you. **20** However, do not rejoice that the spirits submit to you, but rejoice that your names are written in heaven.'

21 At that time Jesus, full of joy through the Holy Spirit, said, 'I praise you, Father, Lord of heaven and earth, because you have hidden these things from the wise and learned, and revealed them to little children. Yes, Father, for this is what you were pleased to do.

22 'All things have been committed to me by my Father. No one knows who the Son is except the Father, and no one knows who the Father is except the Son and those to whom the Son chooses to reveal him.'

23 Then he turned to his disciples and said privately, 'Blessed are the eyes that see what you see. **24** For I tell you that many prophets and kings wanted to see what you see but did not see it, and to hear what you hear but did not hear it.'

17–20. Nothing is said about the mission itself, but Green discerns that the report of the seventy-two and Jesus's reaction portray mission in every era as 'the arena of conflict and eschatological engagement with diabolical forces'.[26] The missionaries 'returned with joy', because they had witnessed the release of many from demonic oppression ('Lord, even the demons submit to us in your name'). Exorcism in the name of Jesus meant experiencing his power to heal and deliver from Satan's power (see Acts 3:6; 4:7, 10, 17–18, 30; 16:18; contrast 19:13–16). He responded to this enthusiastic report in visionary terms. First, he viewed the submission of demons in his name as an anticipation of Satan's ultimate defeat: 'I saw Satan fall like lightning from heaven.' 'Satan' renders the Hebrew or Aramaic term for 'the adversary' (*haśśāṭān*), who is portrayed in Scripture as the accuser of God's people (Job 1:6–12; 2:1–7; Zechariah 3:1–2) and the inciter of evil (1 Chronicles 21:1; Luke 22:3, 31; Acts 5:3; 1 Corinthians 7:5; 2 Corinthians 2:11). Here, however, Satan is specifically the ruler of the demonic world, whose dominion is being brought to an end by a series of apocalyptic events (11:17–20; John 12:31–2; Romans 16:20; Revelation 12:9; 20:1–10).[27] Jesus further assured his disciples that the authority he had given them 'to trample on snakes and scorpions and to overcome all the power of the enemy' would keep them from becoming captives

---

[26] Green, *Luke*, 411 (emphasis removed).

[27] The verb 'saw (*etheōroun*)' is regularly used in apocalyptic visions (e.g., Daniel 7:2, 4, 6, 7, 9, 11, 13 LXX). Green, *Luke*, 418–19, notes that Jesus's anticipation of Satan's final defeat is 'consonant with some Second Temple Jewish texts'. Compare Nolland, *Luke 9:21–18:34*, 563–4.

of Satan in this spiritual battle ('nothing will harm you'). 'Snakes and scorpions' symbolically refer to demonic forces encountered in gospel mission: this is not an invitation to put yourself at risk with dangerous animals![28] Finally, Jesus spoke about the assured outcome of this battle for his disciples: 'do not rejoice that the spirits submit to you, but rejoice that your names are written in heaven'. This promise draws on the biblical image of a heavenly book recording the names of those who belong to God and are destined to live in his presence (Exodus 32:32–3; Psalm 69:28; Daniel 12:1; Malachi 3:16–18; Philippians 3:20; 4:3; Hebrews 12:23; Revelation 3:5; 13:8).[29] Those who belong to Jesus are already enrolled in the heavenly city.

21. With a specific time reference ('At that time' (ESV 'In that same hour')), Luke links a moment of significant self-disclosure by Jesus, suggesting that his conversation with the returning missionaries and his previous warnings about unbelief and rejection entitled them to participate in this revelatory moment. However, the authenticity of these verses has been questioned by some, because they record the only saying in the Synoptic Gospels in which Jesus speaks as explicitly about himself as the Son of God as he does in John's Gospel (see also Matthew 11:25–7). Parallels have been sought in Hellenistic and other ancient literature, but the critical question is whether the claims attributed to Jesus here and in the Fourth Gospel derive from his own testimony (see John 3:35; 5:19–23; 6:65; 7:28–9; 10:15; 13:3; 14:7, 9–11; 17:2, 25). In Luke's Gospel, they encapsulate and clarify previous hints about his identity and purpose and explain why some believed in him and others did not.[30] They particularly draw out the meaning of revelations concerning Jesus's divine sonship in Luke 1:31–4; 2:11, 26, 49; 3:22; 9:35 (see also 4:3, 9, 34; 8:28).

Jesus shared the joy of the seventy-two 'through the Holy Spirit', as he began to praise God for what had been happening (see Psalms 9:1 [9:2

---

[28] Snakes and scorpions were identified as sources of physical evil and punishment (e.g., Numbers 21:6–9; Deuteronomy 8:15; 1 Kings 12:11, 14; Sirach 39:29–30) and thus became symbols of moral and spiritual evil (e.g., Genesis 3:1–14; Psalm 58:4; Sirach 21:2; Revelation 9:1–11). Bock, *Luke 9:51–24:53*, 1007–8.

[29] Nolland, *Luke 9:21–18:34*, 566, observes that 'the image here is that of a register of citizens and is to be distinguished from the equally widespread image of God's record book of the deeds of the people upon earth (the images are at times merged)'.

[30] Fitzmyer, *Luke X–XXIV*, 870, regards the substance of verses 21–2 as authentic and relates it to 'an implicit Christology expressed in Jesus's words and deeds in his earthly ministry'. Green, *Luke*, 421, describes this as a Christological peak in Luke's Gospel.

LXX]; 35:18 [34:18 LXX]).[31] He first addressed God as 'Father', employing a term of intimacy appropriate to a parent–child relationship (Aramaic, *'abbâ*; see Mark 14:36; Luke 22:29, 42; 23:34, 46; 24:49). God was designated as Father in various Old Testament contexts, and increasingly in the context of prayer in Jewish literature.[32] Jesus invited his disciples to pray to God as Father (11:2–4) and relate to him as such (6:36; 11:11–12), on the basis of his own unique relationship to God as Son and his ability to reveal the Father (10:22).

The accompanying address ('Lord of heaven and earth') reflects more familiar biblical convictions about God as sovereign creator and ruler of the universe, who has hidden certain things 'from the wise and learned' (see 8:10; Isaiah 29:14; 1 Corinthians 1:18–31; 2:6–13; 3:18–20). This could embrace all who have rejected Jesus (verses 10–16), though it may especially refer to the scribes and Pharisees as the official custodians of Israel's wisdom. Many saw and heard things that should have moved them to seek and discover more about Jesus, but they remained unresponsive to the evidence and became hardened against him (5:17–32; 6:1–11; 7:29–35). What was hidden from them was the meaning and significance of Jesus and his ministry, which God had revealed to 'little children' (meaning 'the simple' or 'the uninstructed,' as in Psalms 19:7 [18:8 LXX]; 116:6 [114:6 LXX]; 119:130 [118:130 LXX]). There is an obvious link with 'the poor' who are the recipients of God's salvation (4:16–30; 6:20).[33] Jesus repeated this claim in a different way when he said, 'Yes, Father, for this is what you were pleased to do.' The wise and understanding had failed to humble themselves in the face of God's self-revelation through his Son, so that the word *eudokia* ('pleasure, favour') in verse 21 highlights God's grace in enabling others to discern the truth (see verses 23–4). 'Hidden' in this context means choosing not to reveal in the personal and compelling way that the disciples have experienced.

22. Jesus develops the implications of what he has just said to his Father in prayer.[34] First, he declares, 'All things have been committed to

---

[31] Marshall reviews the variant readings here and concludes that 'the force is that Jesus is filled with joy and the Spirit before an inspired saying' (*Luke*, 433). Compare 3:21–2; 4:1–19; Metzger, *Textual Commentary*, 128.

[32] D. M. Crump, 'Prayer', *DJG*, 685–7, gives the intertestamental evidence and shows how in biblical usage the fatherhood of God was related to divine lordship in creation and redemption.

[33] Green, *Luke*, 422. See also Bock, *Luke 9:51–24:53*, 1009–10.

[34] The variant reading 'and he turned to his disciples and said' is 'doubtless secondary,

me by my Father.' Ultimate truth comes from the Father through the Son, not through angels or other intermediaries. The verb translated 'committed' (*paredothē*, 'handed over') is used here for the passing on of knowledge (see Luke 1:2; 1 Corinthians 11:23; 15:3). The completeness of this revelation through Jesus is shown by the expression 'all things', and the essence of it is the identity, character and unique relationship of the Father and the Son. On the one hand, 'No one knows who the Son is except the Father,' implying that the Father must reveal 'who the Son is' (see Matthew 16:17; Hebrews 1:1–4; 2:1–4). Jesus refers to himself as 'the Son' absolutely in Matthew 11:27; 24:36; 28:19; Mark 13:32; John 3:35, 36; 5:19–26; 6:40; 8:36; 14:13; 17:1.[35] On the other hand, 'no one knows who the Father is except the Son and those to whom the Son chooses to reveal him'. The revelation of who the Son is has been taking place in the ministry of Jesus, as the Father has opened eyes and ears, and Jesus has revealed 'who the Father is'. The mutual knowledge of the Father and the Son and their mutual engagement in the process of revelation is for the purpose of bringing people to salvation, which can also be described as eternal life arising from a true knowledge of God and his will (10:25; 18:18–30; compare John 17:1–3). The Spirit's work in this process is yet to be clarified (see 12:10, 12; Acts 2:1–21, 33–9). Luke 10:21–2 is clearly a foundational text for understanding God as Trinity – three persons in one God.

23–4. Luke appends a blessing pronounced by Jesus concerning the inner core of his disciples as privileged witnesses of his ministry: 'Then he turned to his disciples and said privately, "Blessed are the eyes that see what you see."'[36] Their enlightenment was clearly a result of the divine initiative just highlighted, but Jesus also makes a salvation–historical comparison to explain their privileged situation: 'For I tell you that many prophets and kings wanted to see what you see but did not see it, and to hear what you hear but did not hear it.' These verses anticipate what

---

derived from ver. 23 and introduced by copyists in order to smooth the abrupt transition from Jesus' prayer (ver. 21)' (Metzger, *Textual Commentary*, 128).

[35] The parallel in Matthew 11:27 calls for a relational knowledge, whereas Luke's version stresses the need to know the identity and character of each one in order to have such a relationship. Nolland, *Luke 9:21–18:34*, 575, suggests that Luke has adapted the saying to answer the questions about Jesus's identity in 8:25; 9:9, 18–20.

[36] The parallel in Matthew 13:16–17 is in a similar context, where Jesus has contrasted the revelation his disciples have received and the failure of the crowds to understand the meaning of his parables. Compare the use of *makarios* ('blessed') in Luke 1:45; 6:20–22; 7:23.

is said about the distinctive role of the apostles as eye- and earwitnesses in Acts 1. However, the seventy-two are included in this blessing and have been given a share in the apostolic privilege of perceiving and proclaiming the significance of Jesus and his coming. Moreover, the form of the saying in verse 23 allows for the possibility that others will see what they see through their preaching about Jesus.

THE DEMANDS AND REWARDS OF DISCIPLESHIP

Those who travel with Jesus must learn how to respond appropriately to rejection (9:51–6). James and John thought that they should react as Elijah did (2 Kings 1:10, 12, 14), but this was not the gracious pattern of the one who was going to Jerusalem to suffer and die for them, and then be taken up to heaven. Those who follow Jesus must reflect his values and priorities in every sphere of life (9:57–62). His call involves a willingness to accept deprivation, while trusting in God's providential care. It takes precedence over family loyalties and obligations and involves a readiness to proclaim the kingdom of God. Jesus's instructions to the Twelve (9:1–5) are expanded in his commissioning of the seventy-two (10:1–12), with added implications for his ongoing mission (10:13–24).[37] There is an urgency about proclaiming his message that should be conveyed in the approach as well as the words of his messengers. Miraculous healing or exorcism may be a significant accompaniment in some religious and cultural contexts, but the focus of his commission is on warning people about the need to repent in view of the approaching kingdom and to accept God's offer of peace. Disciples have a vital role to play in bringing this about, but it is God who reveals the truth through their Spirit-directed testimony (12:12) and enables believers to rejoice that their names are written in heaven (10:20). Jesus's praise to his heavenly Father and words to his disciples at the climax of this passage expose the uniqueness of his own relationship to God as Father and the revelation that he has given believers to share with others (10:21–4). There are important lessons here about the process of conversion and the way God makes himself known to individuals as we pray for them and point them to Jesus.

---

[37] Isaak, 'Luke', 1250, observes 'something quite new in the methods of Jesus' here: this was 'a planned campaign'.

2. Fulfilling the law of love (Luke 10:25–42)

A lawyer's question about inheriting eternal life initiates a memorable dialogue with Jesus (verses 25–37), focusing on the two great commandments in the law about loving God and loving one's neighbour (Deuteronomy 6:5; Leviticus 19:18). The lawyer's further question ('And who is my neighbour?') moves Jesus to tell a story about a Samaritan who acted as neighbour to a Jew in need. The lawyer's response to Jesus's story shows that he gets the point, and Jesus concludes the encounter with the challenge, 'Go and do likewise.' Continuing on his journey to the home of Mary and Martha, he focuses on the priority of sitting at his feet and listening to his teaching (verses 38–42). Following the previous incident, this identifies an essential way of loving God.[38]

Love for God and neighbour (10:25–37)

The parable of the good Samaritan

25 On one occasion an expert in the law stood up to test Jesus. 'Teacher,' he asked, 'what must I do to inherit eternal life?'

26 'What is written in the Law?' he replied. 'How do you read it?'

27 He answered, ' "Love the Lord your God with all your heart and with all your soul and with all your strength and with all your mind"[c]; and, "Love your neighbour as yourself."[d]'

28 'You have answered correctly,' Jesus replied. 'Do this and you will live.'

29 But he wanted to justify himself, so he asked Jesus, 'And who is my neighbour?'

30 In reply Jesus said: 'A man was going down from Jerusalem to Jericho, when he was attacked by robbers. They stripped him of his clothes, beat him and went away, leaving him half-dead. **31** A priest happened to be going down the same road, and when he saw the man, he passed by on the other side. **32** So too, a Levite, when he came to the place and saw him, passed by on the other side. **33** But a Samaritan, as he travelled, came where the man was; and when he saw him, he took pity on him. **34** He went to him and bandaged his wounds, pouring on oil and wine. Then he put the man on his own donkey, brought him to an inn and took care of him. **35** The next day he took out two denarii[e] and gave them

---

[38] See Nolland, *Luke 9:21–18:34*, 579–80. Bock, *Luke 9:51–24:53*, 1025, argues that 11:1–13 further develops the theme of loving God with reference to dependent prayer.

to the innkeeper. "Look after him," he said, "and when I return, I will reimburse you for any extra expense you may have."

36 'Which of these three do you think was a neighbour to the man who fell into the hands of robbers?'

37 The expert in the law replied, 'The one who had mercy on him.'

Jesus told him, 'Go and do likewise.'

---

c 27 Deut. 6:5

d 27 Lev. 19:18

e 35 A denarius was the usual daily wage of a day labourer (see Matt. 20:2).

25–6. No indication is given of when and where this meeting took place ('on one occasion' translates *kai idou*, 'and behold'). The link with the preceding context is thematic, with 'an expert in the law' representing 'the wise and learned' (verse 21), while Martha and Mary (verses 38–42) represent 'the little children' to whom the revelation of the Father and the Son has been given. Luke uses the term *nomikos* ('expert in the law'; 7:30; 10:25; 11:45, 46, 52, 53; 14:3) as a synonym for *grammateus* ('scribe', 'teacher of the law'; 5:30; 6:7; 9:22; 11:53; 15:2). A similar event in Mark 12:28–34, which Luke does not record, has his enquirer ask, 'Of all the commandments, which is the most important?' (see Matthew 22:32–40). Luke either adapted this narrative and included the story about the good Samaritan from his special source, or he more likely took the whole sequence from that source, describing a separate event.[39] The expert in the law 'stood up to test Jesus' (see 4:2, 12; 11:16), though not necessarily in a hostile fashion, asking, 'Teacher . . . what must I do to inherit eternal life?' This question reflects the perspective of Daniel 12:2 and developing Pharisaic expectations about the kingdom of God and end-time salvation.[40] The verb 'do' appears again in verse 28, forming an inclusion with verse 25. It also appears in verse 37 twice ('the one who [did] mercy' and 'do likewise'). The emphasis of the parable is on what was done and not done for the man in need.

26–7. Jesus directed his enquirer to the Law of Moses, which would have been the object of his daily study: 'What is written in the Law . . . How do you read it?' Jesus's appeal to Torah about such matters is echoed in his later debate with the Sadducees, who denied the Pharisaic teaching

---

[39] Fitzmyer, *Luke X–XXIV*, 877–8, argues that this episode in Luke is so different from Mark and Matthew that it should be ascribed to Luke's special source. Contrast Nolland, *Luke 9:21–18:34*, 580.

[40] See R. Bultmann, 'ζάω, ζωή, κτλ.', *TDNT* 2:855–61; G. R. Osborne, 'Life, Eternal Life', *DJG*, 518–22; Bock, *Luke 9:51–24:53*, 1023.

about an afterlife (20:34–8).[41] The lawyer's perceptive response combined a version of Deuteronomy 6:5 ('Love the Lord your God with all your heart and with all your soul and with all your strength') with a portion of Leviticus 19:18 ('Love your neighbour as yourself'). Those who love God and neighbour in the way that God's law directs will inherit eternal life. The so-called *Shema* in Deuteronomy 6:4–5 was to be recited twice a day by every Jew (Deuteronomy 6:7; see Mishnah, *Berakot* 1:1–4), putting love for God first among the many commandments of the law. The Hebrew text identifies three ways in which this love should be expressed ('with all your heart and with all your soul and with all your strength'), but the Greek version adds 'and with all your mind'. Both versions call for complete dedication to God and his will. As Nolland comments, '"Your heart" denotes a response to God from the innermost personal center of one's being; "your life" (soul) conjures up the role of the life force that energizes us; "your strength" introduces the element of energetic physical action; "your mind" signals the inclusion of the thinking and planning processes.'[42]

The command to 'love your neighbour as yourself' is found only in Leviticus 19:18, though there are many instructions to care for and provide for the needs of fellow Israelites in God's law. 'As yourself' (*hōs seauton*) means 'in the manner that you love yourself', not 'as much as you love yourself' (see Luke 6:31). Moreover, this does not imply the need to love yourself appropriately before you can love others. The two commands appear to have been brought together in Jewish tradition prior to the time of Jesus,[43] which would explain the fact that the 'expert in the law' makes the same connection that Jesus does in Mark 12:28–34; Matthew 22:32–40.

28. Jesus commended the lawyer for his answer ('You have answered correctly') and responded, 'Do this and you will live.' This echoed the sort of challenge presented by Moses in Deuteronomy 30:15–16, where 'you will live' is clearly related to being blessed by God in the land he was giving Israel to possess (see also Deuteronomy 11:13–15, 22–5; 19:9). Jesus implied a link with prophetic expectations concerning eternal life in a renewed creation for those who showed themselves to be true children of God in this life (see Isaiah 65:17–25; 66:22–4; Daniel 12:1–3). Salvation

---

[41] See L. Cohick, 'Pharisees', *DJG*, 673–9; M. L. Strauss, 'Sadducees', *DJG*, 823–5; G. Thellmann, 'Scribes', *DJG*, 840–45.

[42] Nolland, *Luke 9:21–18:34*, 584.

[43] Nolland, *Luke 9:21–18:34*, 580–82, concludes that the novelty in the Gospels is the identification of these two commands 'as the fundamental principles of godliness'.

is not earned by human effort, yet only those whose faith issues in love and obedience will inherit eternal life.

29. In Leviticus 19:13–18, 'your neighbour' stands in parallel with 'your people' (fellow Israelites), though care for resident aliens is also enjoined in this chapter (19:10, 33–4). When Jesus spoke about love for enemies (6:27–36), he was making a radical contribution to a contemporary debate about the limits of the duty to love.[44] This debate may have provoked the lawyer to test Jesus by asking, 'And who is my neighbour?' But Luke's explanation that 'he wanted to justify himself' (see 16:15; 18:9, 14) implies that he also wanted assurance that he was personally fulfilling the demands of the law (see 18:21). By implication, he was still asking what he must 'do' to gain eternal life.

30–32. The shape of this well-known parable is significant. Seven scenes may be identified, focusing on four characters.[45] First, 'A man was going down from Jerusalem to Jericho, when he was attacked by robbers. They stripped him of his clothes, beat him and went away, leaving him half dead.' He was most likely a Jew, travelling some 18 miles (29km) through desert and rocky country, descending about 3,300 feet (1,006 metres) to the town of Jericho on the western edge of the Jordan plain.[46] The victim was attacked on the road and left naked, unable to be identified by his clothes, and beaten by robbers near to death. Second, 'A priest happened to be going down the same road, and when he saw the man, he passed by on the other side.' The approach of this priest seemed to offer hope, but he chose not to be involved, possibly to avoid contamination by contact with an apparently dead man and so hinder his ministry in the Temple (Leviticus 21:1–3, 11–12; Numbers 19:11–13). Third, 'So too, a Levite, when he came to the place and saw him, passed by on the other side.' The Levite belonged to a lower social class than the priest and was less constricted by cultic regulations, but he too ignored the wounded man's sufferings.

[44] Jeremias, *Parables*, 202–3, lists all the exceptions to the meaning of 'neighbour' argued in Jewish sources from this era. Sirach 12:1–7 even warns against helping 'sinners'!

[45] Fitzmyer, *Luke X–XXIV*, 883, suggests that the concluding words of Jesus (verse 37) make this story 'indirectly a parable or extended simile'. Kenneth E. Bailey, *Poet and Peasant and Through Peasant Eyes: A Literary–Cultural Approach to the Parables of Luke* (Combined Edition; Grand Rapids: Eerdmans, 1983), 40, calls it 'a seven-scene parabolic ballad'.

[46] This was not the site of the Jericho destroyed in Joshua 6, but a later town founded by Herod the Great (Josephus, *War* 4.8,2). Bailey, *Peasant Eyes*, 41–2, cites examples of similar attacks on this road.

33–5. Scene 4 focuses on the unexpected arrival of 'a Samaritan' in that region, who did what neither of the previous two characters did and 'came where the man was'. Each of the travellers 'saw' the man (verses 31, 32), but only the Samaritan 'took pity on him' (*esplagchnisthē*, 'had compassion', as in 7:13 [see comment]; 15:20) and went to extraordinary lengths to care for him. The antipathy between Jews and Samaritans that existed at the time was noted in connection with 9:52–3. Jesus took a bold step in making a Samaritan the hero of this story! Green rightly suggests that 'what distinguishes this traveller from the other two is not fundamentally that they are Jews and he is a Samaritan, nor is it that they had high status as religious functionaries and he does not. What individualizes him is his compassion, leading to action, in the face of inaction.'[47] Nevertheless, the parable portrays love in the face of religious and racial animosity. As Isaak discerns, it challenges us about barriers to racial harmony and 'what it means to be human and humane'.[48]

The Samaritan's compassion was demonstrated in the three scenes that follow: 'He went to him and bandaged his wounds, pouring on oil and wine' (using things he had with him on his journey). 'Then he put the man on his own donkey, brought him to an inn and took care of him' (taking him to a safer and more comfortable place).[49] 'The next day he took out two denarii and gave them to the innkeeper. "Look after him," he said, "and when I return, I will reimburse you for any extra expenses you may have"' (providing for his basic board and lodging for two weeks).

36–7. This story allows for a simple identification of 'my neighbour' with anyone in need, but Jesus's penetrating question turned the argument in a different direction: 'Which of these three do you think was a neighbour to the man who fell into the hands of robbers?' The issue was not who could be legally considered a neighbour, but rather, as Fitzmyer discerns, 'which one of them *acted as a neighbour* to the unfortunate victim'.[50] The expert in the law answered the question correctly,

---

[47] Green, *Luke*, 431. Green adds that the Samaritan 'participates in the compassion and covenant faithfulness of God, who sees and responds with salvific care' (see 1:76–8; 7:13; 15:20). So also Bailey, *Peasant Eyes*, 49–50.

[48] Isaak, 'Luke', 1251.

[49] The expression 'on his own donkey' could mean that 'the man was a merchant who carried his wares on an ass or mule, and rode a second beast himself' (Jeremias, *Parables*, 204). If so, he walked the rest of the way, leading two animals.

[50] Fitzmyer, *Luke X–XXIV*, 884 (my emphasis). Nolland, *Luke 9:21–18:34*, 596, suggests that the perfect tense of the infinitive *gegonai* means that the Samaritan 'became a neighbour in his compassionate actions'.

highlighting the defining issue: 'The one who had mercy on him' (see what is said about God in 1:50, 54, 58, 72, 78). Jesus's final challenge ('Go and do likewise') picks up the emphasis on 'doing' from verses 25 and 28 and relates this to the example of the Samaritan in verses 33–5. Kenneth Bailey observes, 'The Samaritan is an unknown stranger. Yet, in spite of the cost in time, effort, money, and personal danger, he freely demonstrates unexpected love to the one in need.'[51] Drawing attention to the Christological implications of the parable, Bailey asks, 'Is not this a dramatic demonstration of the kind of love God offers through His unique agent in the Gospel?'[52] Neighbour love should be the reflection of God's love for us in the person and work of his Son Jesus.

The priority of listening to Jesus's teaching (10:38–42)

At the home of Martha and Mary

38 As Jesus and his disciples were on their way, he came to a village where a woman named Martha opened her home to him. **39** She had a sister called Mary, who sat at the Lord's feet listening to what he said. **40** But Martha was distracted by all the preparations that had to be made. She came to him and asked, 'Lord, don't you care that my sister has left me to do the work by myself? Tell her to help me!'

41 'Martha, Martha,' the Lord answered, 'you are worried and upset about many things, **42** but few things are needed – or indeed only one.[f] Mary has chosen what is better, and it will not be taken away from her.'

_____
f 42 Some manuscripts *but only one thing is needed*

38. Luke resumes the journey motif ('As Jesus and his disciples were on their way'), but exactly where Martha and Mary lived is not disclosed. John 11:1–3; 12:1–3 locates them in Bethany, which Jesus reached when he was about to enter Jerusalem (Luke 19:29). There are similarities between the accounts in Luke 10:38–42 and John 12:1–3, though Lazarus is present in the latter and Mary anoints Jesus's feet with expensive perfume. Most likely, Luke records an earlier event and places it here because of thematic links with previous narratives. The first emphasis is on hospitality: 'a woman named Martha opened her home to him' (*hypedexato*

[51] Bailey, *Peasant Eyes*, 54.
[52] Bailey, *Peasant Eyes*, 54. Allegorisation of the details in this parable is inappropriate, as Bock, *Luke 9:51–24:53*, 1033–4 argues, but Bailey's Christological application is defensible.

auton, 'welcomed him').[53] Since Martha is presented as the host, she is likely to have been the older sister. Her welcome recalls the contrasting situations in 9:53; 10:8, 10, where parallel terms are used. Green argues that Jesus's encounter with Martha and Mary 'clarifies the nature of the welcome he seeks not only for himself but also for his messengers – that is, for all who participate in the drawing near of God's dominion'.[54] Jesus sought the kind of hospitality that would provide an opportunity to hear his message.

39. The second emphasis is on listening: Martha's sister Mary 'sat at the Lord's feet listening to what he said'. Whether or not they had previously met, Mary immediately assumed the posture of a disciple, acknowledging the authority of Jesus and wanting to learn from him (see 8:35; 17:16; Acts 22:3). She did what those who were with Jesus on the mountain were commanded to do (9:35) and was listening to his word (see 6:47; 8:15, 21; 11:28). Green observes, 'Jewish women were normally cast in the role of domestic performance in order to support the instruction of men rather than as persons who were themselves involved in study,'[55] but Jesus actively encouraged women to learn from him (see also 8:2–3). Jewish women could attend synagogues and be taught, but it was unheard of for a rabbi to come into a woman's house for personal instruction. So, Ben Witherington concludes, 'Not only the role Mary assumes, but also the task Jesus performs in this story is in contrast to what was expected of a Jewish man or woman.'[56]

40. The third emphasis is on distraction: 'But Martha was distracted by all the preparations that had to be made' (*periespato peri pollēn diakonian,* 'distracted with much service'). She was more anxious about serving Jesus hospitably than seizing the opportunity to sit at his feet and listen to him. In her appeal to Jesus, she sadly engaged in what Green calls 'the irony of self–betrayal':[57] When she says, 'Lord, don't you care that my sister has left me to do the work by myself?' she reveals that her focus is on herself and her feeling of being deserted by her sister. Her question

---

[53] The words 'into (her) house' are added in some later manuscripts. See Metzger, *Textual Commentary,* 129.

[54] Green, *Luke,* 433.

[55] Green, *Luke,* 435.

[56] Ben Witherington, *Women in the Ministry of Jesus: A Study of Jesus' Attitude to Women and Their Roles as Reflected in His Earthly Life* (Cambridge: Cambridge University Press, 1984), 101. See also Rebecca McLaughlin, *Jesus through the Eyes of Women* (Austin: The Gospel Coalition, 2022).

[57] Green, *Luke,* 436. Compare Bock, *Luke 9:51–24:53,* 1041.

('Lord, don't you care?') is manipulative: she wants him to compel Mary to share her load ('Tell her to help me!').

41–2. Jesus's reply is firm, but gently chiding, highlighting the problem of worry and distraction: 'Martha, Martha . . . you are worried and upset about many things.' Her name is said twice for emphasis (see Exodus 3:4), and with a hint of rebuke (see Luke 22:31). The word 'worried' (*merimnas*) recalls the use of a related term in his warning about being 'choked by life's worries' (8:14; compare 12:22–31; 21:34–6). The word 'upset' (verse 41, *thorybazē*) is a synonym for 'distracted' (verse 40, *periespato*). In contrast with the 'many things' that had captured her attention, Jesus said that 'few things are needed – or indeed only one'. Some manuscripts simply have the words 'few things are needed', which could relate to the basic necessities for a meal, while others read 'but one thing is necessary', preparing for the final pronouncement in the rest of the verse (ESV; see also NRSVA; NIV note f). The NIV translates a textual variant that combines these alternatives, but the intrinsic and external evidence favours the shorter reading: 'but only one thing is necessary'.[58] Thus, the final emphasis in the passage is on what should have been Martha's primary concern (see 18:22; Philippians 3:13).

Jesus concluded, 'Mary has chosen what is better, and it will not be taken away from her.' The expression 'what is better' (*tēn agathēn merida*, 'the good portion') uses a term that is sometimes applied to food in the Old Testament (Genesis 43:34; Deuteronomy 18:8; 1 Samuel 1:4), but may also metaphorically describe a relationship with God as an abiding possession (Psalms 16:5; 73:26–8; 119:57).[59] Mary's choice to sit at the Lord's feet 'listening to what he said' (verse 39) showed her commitment to him and his message about the kingdom of God. This relationship and its eternal consequences would 'not be taken away from her' (contrast 8:18; 12:19–21). As Nolland concludes, the implied warning to every disciple is that 'preoccupation with the practical affairs of life, even when apparently given over to the service of the kingdom of God, easily seduces one away from a wholehearted attention to the things of God'.[60]

---

[58] Marshall, *Luke*, 452–54. This is found in the major witnesses p[45] p[75] A C W and others. Nolland, *Luke 9:21–18:34*, 600, points to the difficulty of requiring *chreia* ('needed') to function in two quite different senses in the longer reading, which is found in p[3] ℵ B L and others.

[59] The NIV reads the positive form of the Greek adjective 'good' in a comparative sense ('better').

[60] Nolland, *Luke 9:21–18:34*, 605.

LOVE AND SALVATION
The question, 'What must I do to inherit eternal life?' (10:25; 18:18) can only be satisfactorily answered in the light of Jesus's teaching as a whole. Salvation is the gift of God to those who seek it with repentance and faith (7:50; 8:12; 9:24; 13:23–30; 18:26–30; 19:8–10). Put differently, however, the beneficiaries of God's eternal inheritance identify themselves as true believers by their wholehearted love for God and neighbour (7:44–7). The lawyer knew the central demands of God's law, but he was still unsure of his standing with God and was seeking to justify himself. Jesus's parable showed how to *be* a good neighbour, demonstrating compassion like the Samaritan. Those who have experienced the mercy of God in the forgiveness of their sins and continue to hear and obey the word of Jesus have the incentive to mirror his compassion in their dealings with others.[61] Although the parable challenged the legal expert to look at things from the victim's point of view, this was a perspective that he should have had from knowing the character and will of God in Scripture (see Matthew 9:12–13). Jesus's encounter with Martha and Mary highlights the need to attend specifically to the message of Jesus. The love for God and neighbour taught in Scripture is perfectly fulfilled by Jesus himself and made possible for us through his redemptive work. As the focus turns from interpreting the Law to listening to Jesus, Luke illustrates again the importance of rightly hearing his word and putting it into practice (see 8:1–21). In the culture of his day, Jesus radically offered this opportunity to both men and women.

3. Looking to God in prayer (Luke 11:1–13)

Luke continues to develop the theme of loving God, which was implicit in the challenge to prioritise listening to the message of Jesus. Now he adds a section of teaching for disciples on the nature of God-honouring prayer. A model prayer is first offered in response to their request (verse 1–4). A parable follows, with a series of exhortations encouraging earnestness and persistence in prayer (verses 5–10). Jesus finally returns to the image of God as 'your Father in heaven', previously suggested in the prayer (verse 2), and encourages his disciples to

---

[61] Fitzmyer, *Luke X–XXIV*, 885, rather too readily dismisses the idea that the parable has anything to do with 'the love of Jesus for the afflicted and distressed of humanity'. Compare Luke 6:35–6; 7:13–16; Matthew 5:43–8; Green, *Luke*, 426.

expect good gifts from God, especially 'the Holy Spirit to those who ask him' (verses 11–13).

Jesus' teaching on prayer

11 One day Jesus was praying in a certain place. When he finished, one of his disciples said to him, 'Lord, teach us to pray, just as John taught his disciples.'

²He said to them, 'When you pray, say:

' "Father,ᵃ
hallowed be your name,
your kingdom come.ᵇ
³Give us each day our daily bread.
⁴Forgive us our sins,
    for we also forgive everyone who
        sins against us.ᶜ
And lead us not into temptation." 'ᵈ

⁵Then Jesus said to them, 'Suppose you have a friend, and you go to him at midnight and say, "Friend, lend me three loaves of bread; ⁶a friend of mine on a journey has come to me, and I have no food to offer him." ⁷And suppose the one inside answers, "Don't bother me. The door is already locked, and my children and I are in bed. I can't get up and give you anything." ⁸I tell you, even though he will not get up and give you the bread because of friendship, yet because of your shameless audacityᵉ he will surely get up and give you as much as you need.

⁹'So I say to you: ask and it will be given to you; seek and you will find; knock and the door will be opened to you. ¹⁰For everyone who asks receives; the one who seeks finds; and to the one who knocks, the door will be opened.

¹¹'Which of you fathers, if your son asks forᶠ a fish, will give him a snake instead? ¹²Or if he asks for an egg, will give him a scorpion? ¹³If you then, though you are evil, know how to give good gifts to your children, how much more will your Father in heaven give the Holy Spirit to those who ask him!'

ᵃ 2 Some manuscripts *Our Father in heaven*
ᵇ 2 Some manuscripts *come. May your will be done on earth as it is in heaven.*
ᶜ 4 Greek *everyone who is indebted to us*
ᵈ 4 Some manuscripts *temptation, but deliver us from the evil one*
ᵉ 8 Or *yet to preserve his good name*
ᶠ 11 Some manuscripts *for bread, will give him a stone? Or if he asks for*

1. Once again, Luke portrays Jesus engaged in private prayer (3:21–2; [4:42]; 5:16; 6:12; 9:18, 28; 10:21), though this time in an unspecified context ('One day Jesus was praying in a certain place'). Presumably, his manner of praying was one of the reasons why, 'when he finished, one of his disciples said to him, "Lord, teach us to pray, just as John taught his disciples."' There must have been something distinctive about the way John taught his disciples to pray which bound them together as a group of faithful, expectant believers (see 5:33; 1 QS 10:1–11:22). Jesus's disciples wanted to be identified by praying together as he did.

2–4. A longer form of this prayer is given by Matthew in the context of different teaching (6:5–15).[62] The indefinite form of Jesus's introduction in Luke (*hotan proseuchēsthe*, 'whenever you pray') suggests a regular mode of prayer to unite disciples in the same approach to God. The introduction in Matthew ('This, then, is how you should pray') offers more of an example of how to pray. The prayer in Luke's version is short and simple: God is addressed as 'Father', with two petitions concerning the fulfilment of his saving plan ('hallowed be your name, your kingdom come'), followed by three petitions concerning the present needs of disciples ('Give us each day our daily bread. Forgive us our sins, for we also forgive everyone who sins against us. And lead us not into temptation'). As David Crump concludes, 'This prayer is simultaneously the Lord's prayer, conveying his priorities, and the disciples' prayer, instructing them (and all Christians) in how their prayers become like his.'[63]

When Jesus addressed God as 'Father' (10:21; 22:42; 23:34, 46), he expressed the uniqueness of his own relationship with him (24:49, 'my Father'). Certain parallels in Jewish literature have been noted, but Jesus invited his disciples to share an unusual intimacy with God by praying as he did (Mark 14:36 records his use of the Aramaic term *Abba*). The significance of this is observed by the apostle Paul, when he says that the Spirit of God brings about 'adoption to sonship' and 'by him we cry, "*Abba*, Father"' (Romans 8:15; compare Galatians 4:6–7). Knowing him as 'the God and Father of our Lord Jesus Christ' (Romans 15:6; 2 Corinthians 1:3; 11:31; Ephesians 1:3; 1 Peter 1:3), we can approach him as *our* Father and have the confidence that he will hear our prayers and be gracious to us.

The first petition of Jesus's prayer ('hallowed be your name') echoes the promise of Ezekiel 36:22–3 regarding the return of the Jews from exile ('I will show the holiness of my great name') and their spiritual renewal (36:24–7). God promised to act in this way because his name had been profaned by his own people. Jesus fulfils this vision by his saving work. When Christians pray for God's name to be hallowed, their great desire

---

[62] See Fitzmyer, *Luke X–XXIV*, 897. The version in *Didache* 8:2 is closer to the Matthean form, but with a doxology added (also found in later manuscripts of Matthew 6:13). Luke 11:2–4 could be closer to what Jesus taught, though he might have given different versions on separate occasions. Compare Nolland, *Luke 9:21–18:34*, 610–13; Bock, *Luke 9:51–24:53*, 1045–7.

[63] D. M. Crump, 'Prayer', *DJG*, 686.

should be that people everywhere might acknowledge his Son, receive his Spirit and come under his rule (Acts 2:32–9; 13:46–8).[64]

The second petition ('your kingdom come') is closely related to the first. Although Jesus indicated the presence of the kingdom in his earthly ministry (10:9, 11; 11:20; 17:20–21), he made it clear that the full reality was yet to come (19:11–27; 21:31; 22:16, 18, 29–30). Jesus's death, resurrection and ascension established his heavenly rule as Lord and Messiah, enabling him to pour out the promised Holy Spirit and make possible the spread of the gospel to all nations. When disciples pray, 'your kingdom come,' they ask that the transforming work of Christ might continue on earth and be consummated with his glorious return (9:26; 12:40; 13:22–30; 17:22–37; 18:1–8; 21:25–8; compare Acts 4:23–31).[65]

The next three petitions concern the immediate needs of disciples. 'Give us each day our daily bread' recalls the testing of Jesus (4:3–4) and his citation of Deuteronomy 8:3, concerning the daily feeding of Israel in the wilderness (Exodus 16:4).[66] This petition shows how to seek God's kingdom and rely on him for the provision of everyday requirements (see 12:22–34). Commentators have long been divided about the best way to translate the adjective *epiousios* (NIV, 'daily'). Contextually, it is best understood in a general sense to mean 'necessary for existence, essential', rather than having a specifically future reference such as 'the bread for the coming day' or 'bread for tomorrow'.[67]

The fourth petition ('Forgive us our sins') warns disciples about the need to acknowledge the ongoing presence of sin in their lives and seek God's forgiveness for it (see Psalms 25:11; 32:1–7; 51:5–6; 130:8; 1 John 1:8–2:2). Matthew 6:12 uses 'debts' to portray 'sins' as offences requiring some relational resolution, and Luke uses the related verb (*panti opheilonti*

---

[64] Nolland, *Luke 9:21–18:34*, 614, favours the interpretation that this is a prayer that the people of the world 'might duly honor God in action and praise'. There may be further echoes of Ezekiel 36:25–36 in the petitions for feeding and forgiveness.

[65] Metzger, *Textual Commentary*, 130–32, discusses the substitution in later manuscripts of some form of the petition, 'Let your Holy Spirit come upon us and cleanse us.' 'May your will be done on earth as it is in heaven' (NIV note b) is interpolated from Matthew 6:10 in many ancient manuscripts, but not in key early witnesses.

[66] This is the only petition with a Greek present imperative (*didou*), making it more of a general command in the midst of more specific prayers with aorist imperatives. See Campbell, *Verbal Aspect and Non-Indicative Verbs*, 89–90.

[67] Fitzmyer, *Luke X–XXIV*, 904–6. Nolland, *Luke 9:21–18:34*, 615–17, agrees and translates the whole expression, 'Our bread for the day give us day by day' (609). Contrast Green, *Luke*, 442–3 and Edwards, *Luke*, 333–5.

hēmin, 'everyone who is indebted to us').[68] God's forgiveness is freely available because of the saving work of Jesus (5:20–24; 7:48; 12:10; 23:34; 24:47), but those who have received mercy should also recognise the need to be merciful to those who have sinned against *them* (6:36; 17:3–4; Matthew 6:14–15; 18:21–35). The qualifying clause ('for we also forgive everyone who sins against us') functions as a challenge to the honesty and integrity of those who pray 'forgive us our sins'.[69] Forgiving others is not a requirement for salvation, but it is a sign that we value God's forgiveness and see the need for it to be reflected in all our relationships.

The final petition in Luke's version of the prayer ('And lead us not into temptation') recognises the biblical perspective that for various reasons God sometimes brings his people into testing situations (see Exodus 16:4; 20:20; Deuteronomy 8:2, 16; 13:3; 33:8; Judges 2:22; compare Luke 4:1–2; 8:13).[70] The word *peirasmos* can be translated 'trial' or 'temptation'. Since we know that testing can have good or bad outcomes, it is best to understand this as a request to be kept from or through situations that lead to sin or unfaithfulness.[71] By way of example, Jesus's warning to his disciples to pray that they would not 'fall into temptation' (22:39–46) and their failure to respond appropriately left them unprepared to stand firm in the trial that was coming upon them (22:47–62). But his own prayerful preparation enabled him to endure faithfully to the end. 'Do not bring us to the time of trial' (NRSVA) is less likely to be the meaning of the final clause in the Lord's Prayer.[72]

5–8. Jesus's parable about a friend in need, which only Luke records, functions in this context to encourage a bold approach to God in prayer.

---

[68] NIV note c. See F. Hauck, 'ὀφείλω, κτλ.', *TDNT* 5:559–66, and compare Jesus's use of the debt motif in Luke 7:41–3.

[69] Although the conjunction *gar* ('for') normally indicates cause or reason, the clause that follows expresses an ideal rather than an exemplary pattern that God could follow! In Matthew 6:12 the comparative particle *hōs* ('as') likens divine forgiveness to the manner in which forgiveness operates in human relationships.

[70] A wide range of later manuscripts add 'but deliver us from evil' (Matthew 6:13), but this is not the best attested reading for Luke 11:4 (Metzger, *Textual Commentary*, 132). NIV note d ('deliver us from the evil one') provides an alternative translation of this variant.

[71] Nolland, *Luke 9:21–18:34*, 611, aptly describes this as a petition 'to be spared the testing that could crush the human frailty of our devotion to God'. Compare 1 Corinthians 10:13 ('to bear up under, endure'). Nolland, 618, argues against the view that *peirasmos* is a technical term for 'the ultimate crisis of apocalyptic expectation'.

[72] Nolland, *Luke 9:21–18:34*, 618, argues that *peirasmos* is not a technical term for 'the ultimate crisis of apocalyptic expectation' in the prayer of Jesus.

The introduction ('Suppose you have a friend and you go to him at midnight') immediately establishes an awkward scenario.[73] Jesus uses a similar sort of approach on other occasions, requiring his listeners to make a judgment on what he proposes (11:11; 12:25; 14:5, 28; 15:4; 17:7). Three friends are involved: one goes to another and says, 'Friend, lend me three loaves of bread; a friend of mine on a journey has come to me, and I have no food to offer him.' This journeying friend must be fed, but there is no bread to go with a meal! The friend who is approached for help does not even come to the door, but answers abruptly from inside, 'Don't bother me. The door is already locked, and my children and I are in bed. I can't get up and give you anything' (contrast Proverbs 3:28). A single-room house is envisaged, with the whole family sleeping together. Nevertheless, Jesus says, 'I tell you, even though he will not get up and give you the bread because of friendship, yet because of your shameless audacity he will surely get up and give you as much as you need.' The term *anaideia* ('shameless audacity'; ESV, 'impudence') refers to a 'lack of sensitivity to what is proper' or 'carelessness about the good opinion of others' (BDAG). Seeking help from someone at midnight is a bold thing to do. It demonstrates a willingness to break from convention and seek what is best for someone else in need. Here is a model for the sort of approach to God highlighted in verses 9–10. This fits the context better than Nolland's proposal that the man in bed with his children acts to preserve his own reputation, 'because there is the prospect of the shame to be owned if one were to let down a friend in such a situation'.[74] Either way, as Fitzmyer says, the neighbour who responds becomes 'the foil for the heavenly Father'.[75] A 'how much more' argument in relation to God is implied by his reluctant actions to give his neighbour as much as he needs (see verse 13; 18:6–8).

9–10. Three encouragements to approach God boldly in prayer are linked to the preceding parable with the words, 'So I say to you' (see Matthew 7:7–8). Nolland describes these as images of 'venturing' with God ('ask . . . seek . . . knock').[76] A corresponding response to each of them is implied by the related promises ('it will be given to you . . .

---

[73] The theme of friendship is central to the parable, but Bailey, *Poet and Peasant*, 121–33, also outlines broader hospitality obligations in the culture of the day.

[74] Nolland, *Luke 9:21–18:34*, 625–7 (see NIV note e). The NIV translates this verse with second-person pronouns ('you', 'your') to clarify that *tēn anaideian autou* refers to the person who comes to the door, not the man in bed with his family.

[75] Fitzmyer, *Luke X–XXIV*, 910.

[76] Nolland, *Luke 9:21–18:34*, 629. Compare Jeremiah 29:12–13.

you will find . . . the door will be opened to you'). The same three encouragements are repeated in a more general form: 'For everyone who asks receives; the one who seeks finds; and to the one who knocks, the door will be opened.' Such assurances are an incentive to keep praying and should not be understood mechanistically in terms of always getting what you want! In the sovereignty of God, what one receives, finds and discovers behind closed doors may be unexpected. Petitionary prayer is a means of discovering and aligning oneself with the generous will of our heavenly Father.

11–13. The goodness of God's provision in answer to believing prayer is now emphasised (see Matthew 7:9–11). As in verse 5, Jesus invites his listeners to make a judgment on what he proposes, appealing especially to fathers. Two deceptive and hurtful outcomes are proposed: 'Which of you fathers, if your son asks for a fish, will give him a snake instead? Or if he asks for an egg, will give him a scorpion?'[77] The application of this shocking argument begins with an assumption that, although human beings may be evil and self-centred, they generally know how to give 'good gifts' to their children. The version of this saying in Matthew 7:11 concludes with the proposition, 'how much more will your Father in heaven give good gifts to those who ask him!' Luke's version is more specific: 'how much more will your Father in heaven give the Holy Spirit to those to those who ask him!'[78] Some regard Matthew's version as being what Jesus originally said and Luke's version as being a post-Pentecost adaptation to indicate that the Spirit is the greatest gift that God can give.[79] However, Luke records the descent of the Spirit on Jesus at his baptism (3:22) and highlights the implications for him personally (4:18–19; see also 4:1, 14; 10:21). In view of what is said in 10:19–20 and 11:14–26, it is possible, as Max Turner argues, that 'God's Spirit (or a spirit of power from God) is portrayed as a pre-Pentecost possibility available to some of Jesus' followers'.[80] After Pentecost, anyone who turns to Jesus

---

[77] Matthew 7:9–10 puts a bread–stone contrast before the fish–snake proposal and omits the egg–scorpion example. The sense of the argument is similar, but the sequence in Luke is more threatening. (NIV note f acknowledges the manuscript variations in the text of Luke).

[78] 'Your Father in heaven' (ESV, 'the heavenly Father') recalls Jesus's invitation to address God as Father in verse 2.

[79] Nolland, *Luke 9:21–18:34*, 632.

[80] Max M. B. Turner, *Power from on High: The Spirit in Israel's Restoration and Witness* (Sheffield: Sheffield Academic, 1996), 340. The Spirit is given to earlier characters

and acknowledges him as Lord and Messiah can receive the Holy Spirit (Acts 2:38–9) and pray for the Spirit's direction and transforming power in their lives (see Romans 8:9–17, 22–7).

PRAYER AND THE SOVEREIGNTY OF GOD

Jesus, who prayed 'Father, Lord of heaven and earth' (10:21), invited his followers to address God in a similar fashion. The Lord's Prayer and associated teaching encourages us to acknowledge God's sovereignty and to trust in his fatherly care (11:1–13). We should be particularly passionate about the hallowing of God's name and the coming of his kingdom, which God himself must accomplish. Praying for these things deepens our desire for the fulfilment of his plan of salvation. We are motivated to participate with him in the proclamation of his kingdom (10:1–12) and to seek the Spirit's enabling in the battle against the forces of evil (11:13, 14–26). The request for God to 'give us each day our daily bread' expresses an appropriate dependence on God for the provision of everyday needs. Boldness in asking for such things is encouraged in the parable about the three friends and the three loaves of bread (11:5–8). The possibility that God may sometimes provide for us through the generosity and care of others is highlighted in 10:7–8, 33–7, 38–40. Asking, seeking and knocking are different ways of expressing such dependence and looking for the answers God may provide (11:9–10). Seeking the forgiveness of God for our sins must translate into a willingness to forgive those who sin against us (17:3–4). Praying that God would not lead us into temptation is a way of acknowledging our vulnerability and need for the direction and empowerment of God's Spirit (22:40).[81] If God is sovereign, petitionary prayer is not superfluous, but rather the practical expression of that belief. As we seek to do his will prayerfully, and with a recognition of our own weaknesses, God allows us to participate in the outworking of his purpose for humanity and his world.

4. Signs of the kingdom and mounting opposition (Luke 11:14–54)

There are two major divisions in this section of Luke's narrative. Jesus first

---

in Luke 1:15, 41, 67; 2:25–7 for prophetic ministry, in which the Twelve and others share to some extent.

[81] Isaak, 'Luke', 1253, observes that 'to the one prayer for our physical needs, we must add two for our spiritual and moral needs'.

responds to challenges from the crowd about the meaning and significance of his ministry (verses 14–36). The charge that he drives out demons by 'the prince of demons' exposes a clear division in his audience (verses 17–26) and the demand for a sign from heaven brings forth his call to repent (verses 29–32). Appended sayings about light and darkness express parabolically what takes place when the truth about Jesus is revealed and is either received or rejected (verses 33–6). The second main division presents Jesus's specific criticisms of the Pharisees and experts in the law in the setting of a meal (verses 37–52). After this, they 'began to oppose him fiercely and to besiege him with questions, waiting to catch him in something he might say' (verses 53–4). These two divisions bring together material paralleled in several contexts in Matthew and Mark.[82] Luke's purpose in bringing them together is to show the character and developing strength of the opposition to Jesus, even as the crowds grew and many were amazed at what he did.

Challenges about the meaning and significance of Jesus's ministry (11:14–36)

Jesus and Beelzebul

14 Jesus was driving out a demon that was mute. When the demon left, the man who had been mute spoke, and the crowd was amazed. **15** But some of them said, 'By Beelzebul, the prince of demons, he is driving out demons.' **16** Others tested him by asking for a sign from heaven.

17 Jesus knew their thoughts and said to them: 'Any kingdom divided against itself will be ruined, and a house divided against itself will fall. **18** If Satan is divided against himself, how can his kingdom stand? I say this because you claim that I drive out demons by Beelzebul. **19** Now if I drive out demons by Beelzebul, by whom do your followers drive them out? So then, they will be your judges. **20** But if I drive out demons by the finger of God, then the kingdom of God has come upon you.

21 'When a strong man, fully armed, guards his own house, his possessions are safe. **22** But when someone stronger attacks and overpowers him, he takes away the armour in which the man trusted and divides up his plunder.

23 'Whoever is not with me is against me, and whoever does not gather with me scatters.

24 'When an impure spirit comes out of a person, it goes through arid places seeking rest and does not find it. Then

---

[82] Different views about the sources and relationship between these passages are discussed and evaluated by Bock, *Luke 9:51–24:53*, 1067–71, 1086–90, 1105–10.

it says, "I will return to the house I left." 25 When it arrives, it finds the house swept clean and put in order. 26 Then it goes and takes seven other spirits more wicked than itself, and they go in and live there. And the final condition of that person is worse than the first.'

27 As Jesus was saying these things, a woman in the crowd called out, 'Blessed is the mother who gave you birth and nursed you.'

28 He replied, 'Blessed rather are those who hear the word of God and obey it.'

The sign of Jonah

29 As the crowds increased, Jesus said, 'This is a wicked generation. It asks for a sign, but none will be given it except the sign of Jonah. 30 For as Jonah was a sign to the Ninevites, so also will the Son of Man be to this generation. 31 The Queen of the South will rise at the judgment with the people of this generation and condemn them, for she came from the ends of the earth to listen to Solomon's wisdom; and now something greater than Solomon is here. 32 The men of Nineveh will stand up at the judgment with this generation and condemn it, for they repented at the preaching of Jonah; and now something greater than Jonah is here.

The lamp of the body

33 'No one lights a lamp and puts it in a place where it will be hidden, or under a bowl. Instead they put it on its stand, so that those who come in may see the light. 34 Your eye is the lamp of your body. When your eyes are healthy,^{g} your whole body also is full of light. But when they are unhealthy,^{h} your body also is full of darkness. 35 See to it, then, that the light within you is not darkness. 36 Therefore, if your whole body is full of light, and no part of it dark, it will be just as full of light as when a lamp shines its light on you.'

---

^{g} 34 The Greek for *healthy* here implies *generous*.
^{h} 34 The Greek for *unhealthy* here implies *stingy*.

14–16. The context for these challenges is the exorcism of 'a demon that was mute'. The man who was released from demonic control was able to speak, so that 'the crowd was amazed'. They were awed by the experience and began to question its significance (as in 4:22; 8:25; 9:43; Matthew 12:23). But some had already decided that, 'By Beelzebul, the prince of demons, he is driving out demons' (see 7:33). 'Beelzebul' was a variation of the name of an old Canaanite god, meaning 'Baal the Prince' or 'Baal of the Exalted Abode' (see 2 Kings 1:2, 'BaalZebub'). This had become identified with Satan.[83] According to Mark 3:22, the accusation that Jesus was possessed

---

[83] Fitzmyer, *Luke X–XXIV*, 920–21; Bock, *Luke 9:51–24:53*, 1074. Another name for

by Beelzebul and driving out demons with his authority was made by 'teachers of the law who came down from Jerusalem' (Matthew 12:24, 'the Pharisees'), but Luke provides a less specific identification ('some of them said').[84] Others tested Jesus by 'asking for a sign from heaven' (see Mark 8:11–12), which he addresses in verses 29–32. They demanded indisputable proof that his ministry was empowered by God.

17–19. Whether or not Jesus heard the charge of being possessed by Beelzebul, he 'knew their thoughts' (see 2:35; 5:22; 6:8; 7:39–47; 9:47) and responded with two simple propositions: 'Any kingdom divided against itself will be ruined, and a house divided against itself will fall.' He then applied these images of civil war and domestic division to the charge against him: 'If Satan is divided against himself, how can his kingdom stand?' Rather than Satan's kingdom being divided, a clash of opposing kingdoms was taking place, in which Jesus as the messianic Son of God would ultimately be victorious (1:33, 35; 4:3–13). Jesus also questioned their logic by asking, 'Now if I drive out demons by Beelzebul, by whom do your followers drive them out?' Nolland says that to blacken Jesus's name as an exorcist was 'to cast the same doubt upon all other Jewish exorcists'.[85] They would be 'judges' or witnesses against his accusers in the courtroom of God (see verses 31–2).

20. Despite the comparison with other exorcists, however, Jesus claimed to be doing something radically new and different: 'But if I drive out demons by the finger of God, then the kingdom of God has come upon you.' 'The finger of God' recalls what the magicians of Egypt said to Pharaoh when they experienced the plague of gnats, which they could not duplicate 'by their secret arts' (Exodus 8:18–19; see also Deuteronomy 9:10; Psalm 8:3). God was acting in an even more powerful way through Jesus to oppose the forces of evil and liberate his people.[86] Jesus's exorcisms were a sign that 'the kingdom of God' he announced (4:43; 6:20;

Satan was 'Belial', which is used in the Dead Sea Scrolls and 2 Corinthians 6:15. See R. H. Bell, 'Demon, Devil, Satan', *DJG*, 193–202.

[84] However, the reference to 'your sons' in verse 19 (NIV, 'your followers') suggests that Luke was aware that the debate was with the Pharisees and their scribes (see Matthew 12:27). The Pharisees and experts in the law more clearly emerge as his opponents in verses 37–54.

[85] Nolland, *Luke 9:21–18:34*, 639. Jewish exorcists are mentioned in Mark 9:38; Acts 19:13–14 (in both cases using the name of Jesus) and in several Jewish sources. See R. H. Bell, 'Demon, Devil, Satan', 197–8. Contrast Bock, *Luke 9:51–24:53*, 1077.

[86] The version of this saying in Matthew 12:28 puts the emphasis on the Spirit of God as the means by which Jesus exorcised demons. Luke gives a more

7:28; 8:1, 10; 9:11, 27; 16:16), and invited others to proclaim (9:2, 60, 62; 10:9, 11) was manifestly invading and overpowering Satan's realm. As the promised Messiah, he acted in advance of his heavenly enthronement (Acts 2:33–6) to bring the sort of release promised by the prophets (e.g., Isaiah 61:1–2 in Luke 4:18–21). The expression 'has come upon you' (*ephthasen eph' hymas*) signifies their immediate experience of the kingdom, as do the related terms 'come near to you' (10:9) and 'in your midst' (17:21). Nevertheless, Jesus taught that final redemption was yet to come (21:28), and his disciples were encouraged to pray for the advent of everything embraced by the kingdom of God in his teaching (11:2).[87]

21–2. A linked pair of sayings develops the image of attack and victory from verses 17–20, this time relating to 'a strong man, fully armed' who 'guards his own house' so that 'his possessions are safe'. But 'when someone stronger attacks and overpowers him, he takes away the armour in which the man trusted and divides up his plunder'. Contextually, the strong man is Satan, who takes possession of people until the stronger one comes with the power of God to bind him, remove his protection and release his captives (see 10:17–19). An allusion to Isaiah 53:12 is possible here ('he will divide the spoils with the strong'). Bock observes, 'Luke is most emphatic in stating the victory, since he alone mentions the distribution of the spoils.'[88]

23. This linked saying demands a decision about Jesus's ministry of driving out demons and delivering people from Satan's control: 'Whoever is not with me is against me, and whoever does not gather with me scatters' (see Matthew 12:30). Those who charged him with driving out demons 'by Beelzebul, the prince of demons' had seriously misrepresented the situation and were turning people against him. Since Jesus was engaged in gathering the flock of Israel for salvation in the kingdom of God (12:32; see Ezekiel 34:11–24; John 10:11–18), those who refused to gather with him were contributing to its scattering and demise, as faithless leaders in the past had done.[89] Given the claims of Jesus and the signs of God's

---

salvation–historical perspective, suggesting that Jesus inaugurates 'the New Exodus liberation' (Turner, *Power*, 259).

[87] See J. B. Green, 'Kingdom of God/Heaven', *DJG*, 468–81 (especially 476–9 on Luke); Bock, *Luke 9:51–24:53*, 1079–82. See also Luke 12:31–2; 13:18, 20, 28–9; 18:16–17, 24–9; 19:11–27; 21:25–31; 22:16, 18, 29–30; 23:42–3.

[88] Bock, *Luke 9:51–24:53*, 1083. This is a developed version of the saying in Mark 3:27; Matthew 12:29.

[89] Nolland, *Luke 9:21–18:34*, 644, compares the challenge of Joshua 5:13 to take sides in the battle for Israel's future. Unfaithful leaders were the cause of Israel's exile according to Ezekiel 34:1–10.

power in his ministry, a neutral position is impossible (contrast 9:49–50).

24–6. A further parable provides a negative counterpart to verses 21–2 (see Matthew 12:43–5): 'When an impure spirit comes out of a person, it goes through arid places seeking rest and does not find it.' The image of a spirit seeking a dwelling-place is reflected in some Jewish texts (e.g., Tobit 8:3; Baruch 4:35) and may also lie behind the narrative in Luke 8:29–31. Jesus developed this notion by imagining a demon saying, 'I will return to the house I left.' When the demon arrives, 'it finds the house swept clean and put in order'. Nothing has filled the void left by the spirit's departure. 'Then it goes and takes seven other spirits more wicked than itself, and they go in and live there. And the final condition of that person is worse than the first.' Contextually, this suggests the need for 'the protecting presence of God that comes with faith', as Bock puts it.[90] The departure of an impure spirit does not necessarily bring someone under the rule of God (Acts 16:16–18). Multiple spirits can create an even more dangerous situation for the person concerned. The challenge is to acknowledge the kingdom of God powerfully present in the ministry of Jesus (verse 20), to turn to him as 'someone stronger' (verse 22) and to seek the indwelling presence of the Holy Spirit (verse 13).

27–8. Luke finishes the segment about Jesus and Beelzebul by noting, 'As Jesus was saying these things, a woman in the crowd called out, "Blessed is the mother who gave you birth and nursed you."' She expressed gratitude for Jesus by honouring his mother in what was then a culturally appropriate way (see Genesis 49:25; Proverbs 23:24–5).[91] When Jesus replied, 'Blessed rather are those who hear the word of God and obey it,' he was not rebuking the woman or devaluing his mother, but affirming the way of true blessedness for all (see 6:20–22, 47; 8:15, 21; 10:38–42). Mary was not simply blessed by God because she was the mother of Jesus. Luke's overall portrayal of her, according to Green, is 'as one who hears and reflects on the divine word, who responds to it positively, even as one who proclaims it in prophetic fashion (1:26–38, 46–55; 2:19, 51)'.[92]

29–30. At this point, 'as the crowds increased', Jesus responded to the demand for 'a sign from heaven' (verse 16), saying, 'This is a wicked

---

[90] Bock, *Luke 9:51–24:53*, 1093. Fitzmyer, *Luke X–XXIV*, 924, views this as 'cautioning Christian disciples about too great assurance over manifestations of the defeat of physical or psychic evil'.

[91] ESV translates more literally, 'Blessed is the womb that bore you, and the breasts at which you nursed!' Fitzmyer, *Luke X–XXIV*, 928, cites evidence from Jewish literature for maternal organs being used in expressions of praise like this.

[92] Green, *Luke*, 461. See also 1:45; Acts 1:14.

generation. It asks for a sign, but none will be given it except the sign of Jonah.' Many signs were given in Jesus's ministry, but not acknowledged. In Luke's version of this encounter, Jesus simply offers 'the sign of Jonah' and contrasts his own generation with the Ninevites who believed Jonah's message and repented (verse 32; Jonah 3:4–10).[93] The designation 'a wicked generation' (as in 7:31; 9:41) recalls the biblical portrayal of Israel in the wilderness (Exodus 32:9; 33:3, 5; Deuteronomy 10:16; Acts 7:51–2). References to 'this generation' also occur in verses 30, 31, 32, 50, 51; 17:25; 21:32. 'The sign of Jonah' broadly refers to Jesus and his prophetic ministry as the Son of Man in advance of his coming in glory for final judgment (9:26; 12:40). The expression is used 'with a touch of irony', according to Nolland,[94] since Jesus was offering them something more challenging than the sign they were seeking. His ministry pointed to their impending condemnation.

31–2. Two paired sayings articulate the significance of the warning just given. 'The Queen of the South' was the Queen of Sheba, who 'will rise at the judgment of the people of this generation and condemn them, for she came from the ends of the earth to listen to Solomon's wisdom' (1 Kings 10:1–13; 2 Chronicles 9:1–12). Her humble approach exposed the wickedness of Jesus's generation, especially since 'something greater than Solomon' and his wisdom was in their midst (see 7:31–5). The second saying returns to the example of the men of Nineveh, who 'will stand up at the judgment with this generation and condemn it, for they repented at the preaching of Jonah; and now something greater than Jonah is here'.[95] Jesus rebuked unbelievers in his audience with the prediction that they would be condemned by the positive example of believing Gentiles on the day of judgment.[96]

33–4. Linked to the previous passage, this one warns about the evil

---

[93] In Mark 8:11–12 no sign is offered, whereas in Matthew 16:1–4 Jesus offers 'the sign of Jonah'. This may refer back to Matthew 12:39–40, where the sign of Jonah is his 'three days and three nights in the belly of a huge fish', which is compared with the Son of Man's predicted 'three days and three nights in the heart of the earth', alluding to his burial and resurrection.

[94] Nolland, *Luke 9:21–18:34*, 652.

[95] The word 'men' here (*andres*) is meant to include women: it is 'a linguistic reflection of the male domination of public life in the ancient world' (Nolland, *Luke 9:21–18:34*, 654).

[96] Compare 10:12–15. The verbs 'will rise' and 'stand up' could broadly refer to their resurrection from the dead (Green, *Luke*, 465), or more specifically to their being called as witnesses against unbelieving Israelites at the judgment of God.

dispositions from which sign-seeking arises. At the same time, as Green says, it 'urges those in the crowd to take care lest they stand condemned by such faithful persons as the queen of Sheba and the people of Nineveh'.[97] A form of the first parable was used in 8:16 to suggest that the light Jesus had shown to his disciples needed to be shared with others. The reference here is similarly to the light that Jesus brought, so that many might see and believe ('No one lights a lamp and puts it in a place where it will be hidden, or under a bowl. Instead they put it on its stand, so that those who come in may see the light').[98] Jesus had not hidden the light and so, if it was not seen, the fault lay with the receptors. The second parable addresses this problem by stating that the human body has its own 'lamp' ('Your eye is the lamp of your body'; see Matthew 6:22–3). Jesus uses terms that can have both a medical and an ethical meaning: 'when your eyes are healthy [*haplous*, 'without guile, sincere', BDAG], your whole body also is full of light. But when they are unhealthy [*ponēros*, 'wicked, evil, bad', BDAG, as in verse 29], your body also is full of darkness.' This may reflect ancient views about light from the eye mingling with the light of an object under scrutiny and returning via the eye into the body.[99] Fundamentally, the imagery expresses the widely acknowledged phenomenon that we see what we want to see and sometimes refuse to see what is obvious (see 24:13–24).

35–6. Jesus's challenge ('See to it, then, that the light within you is not darkness') is to consider the moral and spiritual factors that keep us from being inwardly flooded by his light. 'The light' we have may be keeping us in darkness. The positive benefit of being fully exposed to the light that Jesus brings is then declared: 'Therefore, if your whole body is full of light, and no part of it dark, it will be just as full of light as when a lamp shines its light on you' (see 1 John 1:5–10).

---

[97] Green, *Luke*, 465.

[98] This parable is repeated in a different form in 12:2 (compare Matthew 5:15; 10:26; Mark 4:21–5). Jesus apparently applied the same image in different contexts for varying reasons (compare John 8:12; 9:5).

[99] Nolland, *Luke 9:21–18:34*, 657–8. Compare Green, *Luke*, 465–6.

Woes against the Pharisees and experts in the law (11:37–54)

Woes on the Pharisees and the experts in the law

37 When Jesus had finished speaking, a Pharisee invited him to eat with him; so he went in and reclined at the table. **38** But the Pharisee was surprised when he noticed that Jesus did not first wash before the meal.

39 Then the Lord said to him, 'Now then, you Pharisees clean the outside of the cup and dish, but inside you are full of greed and wickedness. **40** You foolish people! Did not the one who made the outside make the inside also? **41** But now as for what is inside you – be generous to the poor, and everything will be clean for you.

42 'Woe to you Pharisees, because you give God a tenth of your mint, rue and all other kinds of garden herbs, but you neglect justice and the love of God. You should have practised the latter without leaving the former undone.

43 'Woe to you Pharisees, because you love the most important seats in the synagogues and respectful greetings in the market-places.

44 'Woe to you, because you are like unmarked graves, which people walk over without knowing it.'

45 One of the experts in the law answered him, 'Teacher, when you say these things, you insult us also.'

46 Jesus replied, 'And you experts in the law, woe to you, because you load people down with burdens they can hardly carry, and you yourselves will not lift one finger to help them.

47 'Woe to you, because you build tombs for the prophets, and it was your ancestors who killed them. **48** So you testify that you approve of what your ancestors did; they killed the prophets, and you build their tombs. **49** Because of this, God in his wisdom said, "I will send them prophets and apostles, some of whom they will kill and others they will persecute." **50** Therefore this generation will be held responsible for the blood of all the prophets that has been shed since the beginning of the world, **51** from the blood of Abel to the blood of Zechariah, who was killed between the altar and the sanctuary. Yes, I tell you, this generation will be held responsible for it all.

52 'Woe to you experts in the law, because you have taken away the key to knowledge. You yourselves have not entered, and you have hindered those who were entering.'

53 When Jesus went outside, the Pharisees and the teachers of the law began to oppose him fiercely and to besiege him with questions, **54** waiting to catch him in something he might say.

37–8. When Jesus had finished speaking to the crowd, 'a Pharisee invited him to eat with him'. This invitation reflected a certain positivity towards

Jesus and the possibility of conversing about the great matters raised in verses 14–36 (compare 7:36–50; 14:1–24). 'So he went in and reclined at the table' (14:10; 17:7; 22:14). But the Pharisee was concerned about Jesus's failure to wash his hands ceremonially before eating, which was one of the ways in which the Pharisees sought to preserve biblical standards of purity (see Mark 7:1–5). The fact that they understood purity on radically different lines 'raises the level of hostility dramatically', as Green suggests.[100] Whether or not the Pharisee's surprise was voiced, Jesus went on to address the issues that were a source of contention between them. These issues were so serious that he was prepared to disregard the conventions of hospitality in doing so.

39–41. Luke refers to Jesus again as 'the Lord' to highlight his authority to speak on this matter (see 10:1, 39, 41; 12:42; 13:15). Jesus first identifies the hypocrisy of being concerned about outward purity while neglecting the biblical demand for inward purity: 'Now then, you Pharisees clean the outside of the cup and dish, but inside you are full of greed and wickedness' (a different word for 'greed' is used in 12:15). Religious activities can become a cover for sin and keep people in moral darkness (verse 34). Jesus then charges them with being 'foolish' and asks, 'Did not the one who made the outside make the inside also?' What God said about cups and dishes (Leviticus 11:32–3; 15:12) also applies to 'what is inside you'. Those who are concerned about outward purity should 'be generous to the poor, and everything will be clean for you'. Greed was a significant issue of disobedience that needed to be addressed by the Pharisees in order to be 'clean' or truly holy (see Deuteronomy 13:7–11; Luke 16:14–15). Jesus taught that the inner and outer life of a person should not be separated. As Nolland puts it, 'The inner life expresses itself in outward actions and is to be contrasted to that which is *only* an outward display.'[101]

42–4. The woes pronounced by Jesus in 6:20–26; 10:13 broadly signal the pain or grief awaiting those who reject him and his message about the kingdom of God. But his woes against the Pharisees (verses 42–4) and 'the experts in the law' (verses 45–52) more specifically address the dangerous example and growing influence of these leaders on the people

---

[100] Green, *Luke*, 469. The verb used here might signify that Jesus's hands were rinsed, but not immersed for ritual purification. See R. P. Booth, *Jesus and the Purity Laws: Tradition History and Legal History in Mark 7* (Sheffield: *JSOT*, 1986), 185.
[101] Nolland, *Luke 9:21–18:34*, 665.

of God (see Matthew 23:1–36).[102] Woes were a form of speech used by the prophets to warn Israel (Isaiah 1:4; Amos 6:1) and foreign oppressors (Jeremiah 48:1) about divine judgment.

Jesus's first woe against the Pharisees resumed his criticism of their meticulous concern for some aspects of the law at the expense of weightier matters: 'Woe to you Pharisees, because you give God a tenth of your mint, rue and all other kinds of garden herbs, but you neglect justice and the love of God.' Obedience to the rules about tithing in Deuteronomy 14:22–9 and other contexts (Leviticus 27:30–33; Numbers 18:12; Deuteronomy 26:12–15) was a significant concern for post-exilic Judaism (Nehemiah 10:37–8; 12:44; 13:5, 12; Malachi 3:8–12), but the Pharisees went beyond the literal requirements of the law by listing the 'garden herbs' that should be tithed and offered to the Lord.[103] Jesus did not speak against tithing but condemned the preoccupation with it that allowed anyone to 'neglect justice and the love of God' (echoing Micah 6:8 and the broader teaching of Deuteronomy): 'You should have practised the latter without leaving the former undone.'

Jesus's second woe condemned the spiritual pride and vanity of the Pharisees: 'You love the most important seats in the synagogues and respectful greetings in the market-places' (see more fully Matthew 23:5–12).

Jesus's third woe implies that the Pharisees did not recognise the danger they were to others. As 'unmarked graves, which people walk over without knowing it', they were actually a source of defilement for their fellow Israelites (see Numbers 19:11–22).

45. Luke indicates that 'experts in the law' (*nomikoi*) were present at the same meal. A different term is used in verse 53 (*grammateis*, 'scribes'), but the NIV still calls them 'teachers of the law'. Thelmann describes these people as 'the keepers, interpreters and teachers of Israel's Scripture and traditions that often led to their prominent roles in society and politics'.[104] As the legal specialists among the Pharisees, they would have been responsible for explaining and enforcing the

---

[102] Matthew and Luke appear to be using common material, but Luke has shortened some of the sayings and eliminated others that would not be readily understood by Gentile readers. Luke has also added certain emphases and framed the material differently. See Fitzmyer, *Luke X–XXIV*, 942–4; Nolland, *Luke 9:21–18:34*, 662.

[103] See Fitzmyer, *Luke X–XXIV*, 948; Nolland, *Luke 9:21–18:34*, 665; Richard E. Averbeck, '*ma'ăśēr*' ('Tithe'), *NIDOTTE* 2, 1035–55.

[104] G. Thelmann, 'Scribes', *DJG*, 840. Compare 5:17. Their role in the death of Jesus is anticipated in 9:22 and articulated in 22:2, 66; 23:10.

multitude of obligations governing Pharisaic piety. One of them respectfully addressed Jesus as 'Teacher,' but he was offended by Jesus's accusations ('when you say these things, you insult us also'). Three woes against the lawyers follow.[105]

46. Jesus returned to the theme of minute regulations designed to prevent the law from being broken in even the slightest manner (verse 42): 'Woe to you because you load people down with burdens they can hardly carry, and you yourselves will not lift one finger to help them.' The Jewish Mishnah exemplifies the development of this tradition by listing thirty-nine classes of work that could not be done on the Sabbath (*Shabbat* 7:2). By the addition of many such regulations, Fitzmyer concludes that 'the Torah, which should have been a source of joyful service to God, became a burden'.[106] The lawyers failed to interpret God's law as a gracious gift for the blessing his people, enabling them to respond with grateful obedience (see the preaching of Moses in Deuteronomy).

47–9. The second woe against the legal experts is the longest and most complicated, beginning with, 'Woe to you, because you build tombs for the prophets, and it was your ancestors who killed them' (see 1 Kings 19:10; Nehemiah 9:26; Jeremiah 2:30; 26:20–24; compare Luke 6:23; Acts 7:52). A collaboration is implied between those who killed the prophets and those who later built their tombs: 'So you testify that you approve of what your ancestors did; they killed the prophets, and you build their tombs.' Prophets should be honoured by obedience to their teaching, not by burying them! Jesus's next words sound like a quote from a Jewish wisdom source (literally, 'because of this the wisdom of God said'), though none can be identified. So the NIV takes it to be a general reference to what 'God in his wisdom said'. In Proverbs, Wisdom herself speaks (1:20–21), but in the intertestamental Wisdom of Solomon, she 'passes into holy souls and makes them friends of God,' enabling them to speak as prophets (7:27 NRSVA). What Jesus goes on to say echoes his words about God's wisdom in sending himself and John the Baptist (7:29–35): 'I will send them prophets and apostles, some of whom they will kill and others they will persecute.' 'Apostles' here most likely refers to those appointed by Jesus (9:1–2, 10; Acts 1:21–5).[107] Like John and Jesus, some

---

[105] In Matthew 23:4, 13, 29–36, similar woes are spoken against the Pharisees in general. Luke distributes six woes between the Pharisees and the lawyers.
[106] Fitzmyer, *Luke X–XXIV*, 949. Compare Acts 15:10.
[107] In Matthew 23:34 Jesus speaks similar words in the place of God, identifying

of them would suffer the fate of divine representatives before them (Jeremiah 2:30; 7:25–6; Acts 4:1–22; 5:17–42; 12:1–4).

50–51. A climax to this tragic history of rejecting God's messengers is now predicted:

> Therefore this generation will be held responsible for the blood of all the prophets that has been shed since the beginning of the world, from the blood of Abel to the blood of Zechariah, who was killed between the altar and the sanctuary. Yes, I tell you, this generation will be held responsible for it all.[108]

The two deaths mentioned here ('the blood of Abel' and 'the blood of Zechariah') suggest a time span between the beginning of the Hebrew Canon and its end (Genesis 4:8–10; 2 Chronicles 24:20–22).[109] Repetition of the words 'this generation will be held responsible' implies a missed opportunity to repent of this terrible history and avert God's judgment on the nation (see 19:41–4; 21:20–24; 23:28–31). They had heard a wisdom greater than Solomon's and had been explicitly warned by the Son of Man who would be their judge (11:29–32; 22:69).

52. The third woe accuses the experts in the law of having 'taken away the key to knowledge'. Since Jesus had criticised their interpretation of the law, this most likely means that they had taken away the key to understanding God's gracious purpose for his people in Scripture, which culminated in the revelation that Jesus brought. In Matthew 23:13 they are accused of having 'shut the door of the kingdom of heaven in people's faces'. Jesus's final condemnation clearly relates to entering the kingdom ('You yourselves have not entered, and you have hindered those who were entering'). However, in Luke's sequence the issue is more abstractly entering into the 'knowledge' that brings people into the kingdom and eternal salvation (see 13:23–5; 18:17, 25).[110]

---

those who are sent as 'prophets and sages and teachers'. Compare Luke 13:34–5, where 'those sent to you' corresponds to 'apostles' in 11:49.

[108] With an emphatic 'Yes, I tell you' (also found in 7:28; 12:5), Jesus 'appropriates Wisdom's message as his own by reiterating its major thrust' (Nolland, *Luke 9:21–18:34*, 669).

[109] Fitzmyer, *Luke X–XXIV*, 951, discusses alternate views about this Zechariah. Abel did not function prophetically as Zechariah the priest did, but his life bore witness to the sort of relationship with God that Scripture commends.

[110] Given the mention of wisdom in verse 49, Fitzmyer, *Luke X–XXIV*, 951, and

53–4. 'When Jesus went outside, the Pharisees and the teachers of the law began to oppose him fiercely and to besiege him with questions.' The courtesies of the meal table were left behind. Since they were angry about his accusations, they acted with extreme hostility towards him (see 16:14). As in other contexts, they were 'waiting to catch him in something he might say' (6:7; 14:1; 15:2; 20:19–26).

EXPERIENCING THE PRESENCE OF THE KINGDOM

Jesus proclaimed that in his public ministry the kingdom of God had 'come' or 'drawn near' to people 'in an initial but not consummative form' (see especially 10:9, 11; 11:20; 17:20–21), as Bock puts it.[111] The signs of the kingdom's presence were both physical and spiritual. Healings and exorcisms were accompanied by proclamations of the end-time rule of God. Those who responded to Jesus with faith recognised the power of God operating through him in these transformative events. However, prophetic and apocalyptic hopes concerning God's ultimate rule on earth meant that there was more to come. This was expressed by Jesus in a variety of ways, most obviously by urging his disciples to pray for God's kingdom to come (11:2), by urging them to stand firm and faithful until the moment of final redemption (21:28), and by constantly warning the crowds about approaching judgment (11:31–2, 50–51). Moreover, the kingdom that Jesus proclaimed demanded his triumph over death and heavenly enthronement as Messiah and Son of Man (9:20–22; 22:67–9). The Spirit who worked through Jesus in his public ministry to bring the blessings of God's kingdom to bear on many lives (4:14, 18–19) would eventually be given to believers to enable the extension of those benefits to people everywhere (24:45–9; Acts 1:4–8; 2:1–21). Then and now, those who experience the blessings of the kingdom in advance of its full realisation 'hear the word of God and obey it' (11:28; compare 8:21) and are full of the light that Jesus shines on them (11:33–6; compare 8:16–18). Others are blind to the light and oppose Jesus, either by misguided interpretations of his ministry (11:17–23), an unwillingness to repent (11:29–32) or captivity to a form of religion that keeps them from hearing his message and obeying him (11:37–54). Although some would claim the continuation

---

Nolland, *Luke 9:21–18:34*, 669, take verse 52 more narrowly as a reference to entering 'the house of Wisdom' (Proverbs 9:1).

[111] Bock, *Luke 9:51–24:53*, 1080. Compare Acts 3:13–21; Stein, *Method and Message*, 60–79.

of Jesus's miraculous activity is necessary for effective gospel ministry today, the narrative of Acts indicates that the rule of God is essentially advanced through the proclamation of Jesus's gospel in the power of the Holy Spirit. Miracles are surprisingly few and far between in Luke's second volume, where the focus is on the progress of 'the word' among the nations.[112]

5. Preparing for judgment (Luke 12:1–13:9)

The scene changes from a private encounter with Pharisees and experts in the law (11:37–54) to a public discourse in the presence of 'a crowd of many thousands' (12:1). Although much of Jesus's teaching is directed to his disciples (12:1, 4, 22), the crowd is listening and shows its presence at critical moments (12:13, 54; 13:1). Green suggests that the topics in this discourse are 'woven together into a frame provided by the leitmotif of vigilance in the face of crisis'.[113] Jesus had indicated to the Pharisees and teachers of the law that a time of persecution and judgment was coming (11:47–51) and their reaction to him showed how it would develop (11:53–4). From this point on the theme of judgment in Luke's presentation of Jesus's teaching is more prominent. The implications for disciples are drawn out in 12:1–12, where the end-time nature of this crisis is revealed with references to hell and judgment in relation to the Son of Man. A challenge from the crowd moves Jesus to talk about possessions, greed and accountability to God (12:13–21). Then he addresses his disciples about worry, faith and seeking God's kingdom (12:22–34). Watchfulness in view of the Son of Man's coming 'at an hour when you do not expect him' is the emphasis in the next phase of the discourse (12:35–48). But Jesus must first 'bring fire on the earth', initiated by his 'baptism' of suffering and even dividing families (12:49–53). Finally, he challenges all present to recognise the significance of the moment and prepare for judgment with genuine repentance (13:1–9).

---

[112] See Peterson, *Acts*, 79–92.
[113] Green, *Luke*, 476.

Enduring persecution (12:1–12)

Warnings and encouragements

12 Meanwhile, when a crowd of many thousands had gathered, so that they were trampling on one another, Jesus began to speak first to his disciples, saying: 'Be[a] on your guard against the yeast of the Pharisees, which is hypocrisy. **2** There is nothing concealed that will not be disclosed, or hidden that will not be made known. **3** What you have said in the dark will be heard in the daylight, and what you have whispered in the ear in the inner rooms will be proclaimed from the roofs.

4 'I tell you, my friends, do not be afraid of those who kill the body and after that can do no more. **5** But I will show you whom you should fear: fear him who, after your body has been killed, has authority to throw you into hell. Yes, I tell you, fear him. **6** Are not five sparrows sold for two pennies? Yet not one of them is forgotten by God. **7** Indeed, the very hairs of your head are all numbered. Don't be afraid; you are worth more than many sparrows.

8 'I tell you, whoever publicly acknowledges me before others, the Son of Man will also acknowledge before the angels of God. **9** But whoever disowns me before others will be disowned before the angels of God. **10** And everyone who speaks a word against the Son of Man will be forgiven, but anyone who blasphemes against the Holy Spirit will not be forgiven.

11 'When you are brought before synagogues, rulers and authorities, do not worry about how you will defend yourselves or what you will say, **12** for the Holy Spirit will teach you at that time what you should say.'

------

a 1 Or *speak to his disciples, saying: 'First of all, be*

1. A temporal link with the previous incident is indicated by the expression *en hois* ('meanwhile'). After being fiercely opposed and besieged with questions by the Pharisees and teachers of the law outside the house where he had dined (11:53–4), Jesus discovered that 'a crowd of many thousands had gathered'. The word *myrias* ('myriad') can either refer to a group of 10,000 or 'a very large number, not precisely defined' (BDAG). The number was so great 'that they were trampling on one another', creating a threatening situation. Jesus began to speak first to his disciples, warning them, 'Be on your guard against the yeast of the Pharisees, which is hypocrisy.' According to Fitzmyer, the word translated 'yeast' (*zymē*) actually referred to 'old, sour dough which had been stored away (see Luke 13:21) and subjected to fermenting juices until it was to be used in new dough as a rising agent (to make the new bread light)'.[114] The metaphor of leaven/

------

[114] Fitzmyer, *Luke X–XXIV*, 954. The fermenting process involved some corruption.

yeast could describe a concealed, penetrative or corrupting influence.[115] Jesus related this to the 'hypocrisy' of the Pharisees, which he had exposed in 11:39–52. The term *hypokrisis* was used in Greek literature to refer to 'play-acting, pretense, outward show, dissembling' (BDAG). This noun only occurs once in the LXX (2 Maccabees 6:25), but other terms more broadly describe wicked deceptions in opposition to the truth of God.[116]

2–3. The teaching in verses 2–9 parallels part of the mission charge to the disciples in Matthew 10:26–33, here more explicitly related to the threat presented by Pharisaic opposition. Jesus's first parabolic saying ('There is nothing concealed that will not be disclosed, or hidden that will not be made known') suggests to Fitzmyer that 'the real core of a person cannot be covered up or kept hidden forever; a time comes when it is ruthlessly exposed'.[117] The hypocrisy of the Pharisees and those deceived by them must eventually be revealed. Jesus's second saying ('What you have said in the dark will be heard in the daylight, and what you have whispered in the ear in the inner rooms will be proclaimed from the roofs') emphasises that even what is spoken in secret must be made known. In view of what follows (verses 4–5, 8–10), both sayings point to the final exposure of human hearts at the end-time judgment of God (see 1 Corinthians 4:5).

4–5. Speaking more intimately to his disciples as 'friends' (see John 15:13–15), Jesus warns them again about the possibility of persecution and death. When he first predicted his own suffering, he mentioned rejection by 'the elders, the chief priests and the teachers of the law' (9:22) and went on to challenge his disciples about losing their lives for his sake (9:23–6).[118] There are several parallels to this in the argument that follows. Focusing on two different kinds of fear, Jesus warns against being 'afraid of those who kill the body and after that can do no more'. But he emphatically adds, 'I will show you whom you should fear: fear him who, after your body has been killed, has authority to throw you into hell. Yes, I tell you, fear him.' The same Greek verb is used four times to contrast the natural

---

[115] Green, *Luke*, 480. Compare Mark 8:15; Matthew 16:6; 16:12. Paul uses the metaphor both positively and negatively (1 Corinthians 5:6; Galatians 5:9).

[116] R. B. Vinson, 'Hypocrite,' *DJG*, 394–5. Fitzmyer, *Luke X–XXIV*, 955, compares the way the Pharisees were described in the Dead Sea Scrolls. See also Edwards, *Luke*, 363–4.

[117] Fitzmyer, *Luke X–XXIV*, 957. In 8:17 a parallel saying refers to the revelation that Jesus gives to his disciples, which must be made known to others.

[118] Compare also 11:49, where the implication is that Jesus and his apostles may suffer at the hands of the teachers of the law.

human fear of being put to death with an appropriate fear or respect for God as creator and judge, who 'has authority to throw you into hell'.[119] 'Hell' is only mentioned here in Luke (compare Matthew 5:22, 29, 30; 10:28; 18:9; 23:15, 33; Mark 9:43, 45, 47; James 3:6), but see my comment on Hades in 10:15. The Greek term *geenna* derives from the Hebrew term meaning 'valley of (the son[s] of) Hinnom' (*gê-Hinnōm*), which is variously translated in the LXX. This was the place where apostate Israelites had once built 'the high places of Baal to burn their children in the fire as offerings to Baal' (Jeremiah 19:4–5; see also 7:31). Jeremiah predicted that this would become 'the Valley of Slaughter' when God acted to punish his people (7:32–4; 19:6–9). By the time of Jesus, this smouldering rubbish dump had come to represent 'the place for torment of sinners after judgment, or at least after death', as Fitzmyer puts it.[120]

6–7. The preceding warning is accompanied by an encouragement about God's care for those who truly fear him. Jesus does not promise deliverance from persecution and death, but he insists that disciples will not be forgotten by God in these circumstances (see Isaiah 49:14–15). He first compares the situation of sparrows sold in the marketplace ('Are not five sparrows sold for two pennies? Yet not one of them is forgotten by God').[121] His second comparison emphasises God's detailed knowledge of every believer ('Indeed, the very hairs of your head are all numbered'). This is the basis for believing that he will continue to look after each one individually (see 21:18; Acts 27:34, following 1 Samuel 14:45; 2 Samuel 14:11; 1 Kings 1:52). Jesus returns to the comparison with sparrows to conclude, 'Don't be afraid; you are worth more than many sparrows.' These sayings imply deliverance *through* death to enjoy eternal life in 'the age to come' (18:30).

8–9. The fear identified in verses 4–5, 7 is now related to either acknowledging or disowning Jesus before others (see 22:34, 57, 61; Acts

---

[119] Fear of God in the Old Testament mostly means reverence or respect for God, involving obedience to his commands (Deuteronomy 6:13–19; Joshua 24:14–15; Job 1:1–2; Proverbs 1:7; Ecclesiastes 12:13–14). Such fear is commended in Acts 9:31; 2 Corinthians 7:1; 1 Peter 1:17; 2:17, but when the prospect of judgment is mentioned, an element of trembling or awe must be envisaged (Romans 11:20; Philippians 2:12; Hebrews 12:28–9).

[120] Fitzmyer, *X–XXIV*, 960. God's judgment had long been associated with fire (Deuteronomy 32:22; Isaiah 31:9; 66:24; Judith 16:21; Jubilees 9:15) and was linked with this valley when its high place was destroyed in the time of Josiah (2 Kings 23:10). Compare Williamson, *Death and the Afterlife*, 148–51.

[121] Greek *assarion* ('penny') reflects the Latin term for a small copper coin equivalent to one sixteenth of a denarius. Sparrows were a cheap source of food for the poor.

3:13–15; 2 Timothy 2:12; Titus 1:16; 2 Peter 2:1; 1 John 2:22–3; Jude 4; Revelation 2:13; 2:8; 3:5). Fear of persecution and death is a major reason for disowning him, but this choice has a terrible consequence: 'whoever disowns me before others will be disowned before the angels of God'. Angels represent the final judgment of God here (see Matthew 10:32–3, 'before my Father in heaven'). In Daniel 7:9–10 God is attended by 'thousands upon thousands' and 'ten thousand times ten thousand' stand before him as the heavenly court is seated and 'the books' are opened. Jesus identifies himself with the key figure in this scene (Daniel 7:13, 'one like a son of man') when he says, 'whoever publicly acknowledges me before others, the Son of Man will also acknowledge before the angels of God' (see also 12:40). Edwards observes, 'A genuine confession of Jesus Christ in this world may have the effect of exposing a believer to opposition and persecution, but it *unites* a believer to Jesus Christ and to the holy company of "the angels of God" in the world to come.'[122]

10. Even a temporary denial of Jesus can be forgiven ('everyone who speaks a word against the Son of Man will be forgiven') – as Peter will learn (22:54–62; 24:33–4, 36) – 'but anyone who blasphemes against the Holy Spirit will not be forgiven'. Blasphemy against the Holy Spirit signifies a greater offence since, as Bock proposes, it seems to involve 'a settled judgment against Jesus despite the testimony and activity of the Spirit on Jesus's behalf'.[123] The longer version of the saying in Mark 3:28–30 emphatically states that they 'will never be forgiven' and adds 'they are guilty of an eternal sin' (Matthew 12:32, 'will not be forgiven, either in this age or in the age to come'). When Jesus's opponents accused him of driving out demons by Beelzebul, they placed themselves beyond the reach of God's forgiveness by categorically denying God's powerful presence in the ministry of his Son.[124] But the saying in Luke is detached from Jesus's claim to drive out demons 'by the finger of God' (11:20; Matthew 12:28, 'by the Spirit of God') and linked with a promise about the Spirit's guidance for those on trial for their faith (verses 11–12). This suggests a broader application of the warning, anticipating scenes in Acts, where every testimony to the work of the Spirit in the preaching and community life

---

[122] Edwards, *Luke*, 367.
[123] D. L. Bock, 'Blasphemy,' *DJG*, 86. Later Jewish accusations about Jesus being a deceiver or sorcerer meant that this dispute had an ongoing significance for the earliest Christians (see Justin, *1 Apology* 30, 108; *Dialogue* 69.7; Origen, *Celsus* 1.28, 71).
[124] Nolland, *Luke 9:21–18:34*, 679–80, relates blasphemy against the Spirit to Jewish reflection on the failure of the Israelites at the time of the Exodus from Egypt (see Isaiah 63:10; Psalm 106:32–3).

of the early church was stubbornly denied or resisted by some.[125]

11–12. Jesus returned to the theme of publicly acknowledging or confessing him before others (verse 8), specifically 'when you are brought before synagogues, rulers and authorities'. These terms cover both Jewish and Gentile contexts (so also Matthew 10:17–20; Luke 21:12–15). The promise is that 'the Holy Spirit will teach you at that time what you should say'. Although the disciples' permanent endowment for this ministry would not take place until after his resurrection and ascension (24:48–9; Acts 1:4–8; 2:1–4), the saying in 11:13 may imply that they could seek the Spirit's aid in particular circumstances before that.

Being rich towards God (12:13–34)

The parable of the rich fool

13 Someone in the crowd said to him, 'Teacher, tell my brother to divide the inheritance with me.'

14 Jesus replied, 'Man, who appointed me a judge or an arbiter between you?' **15** Then he said to them, 'Watch out! Be on your guard against all kinds of greed; life does not consist in an abundance of possessions.'

16 And he told them this parable: 'The ground of a certain rich man yielded an abundant harvest. **17** He thought to himself, "What shall I do? I have no place to store my crops." **18** 'Then he said, "This is what I'll do. I will tear down my barns and build bigger ones, and there I will store my surplus grain. **19** And I'll say to myself, 'You have plenty of grain laid up for many years. Take life easy; eat, drink and be merry.'"

20 'But God said to him, "You fool! This very night your life will be demanded from you. Then who will get what you have prepared for yourself?"

21 'This is how it will be with whoever stores up things for themselves but is not rich towards God.'

Do not worry

22 Then Jesus said to his disciples: 'Therefore I tell you, do not worry about your life, what you will eat; or about your body, what you will wear. **23** For life is more than food, and the body more than clothes. **24** Consider the ravens: they do not sow or reap, they have no storeroom or barn; yet God feeds them. And how much more valuable you are than birds! **25** Who of you by worrying can add a single hour to your life[b]? **26** Since you cannot do this very little thing, why do you worry about the rest?

---

[125] See Fitzmyer, *Luke X–XXIV*, 964; Acts 4:1–22; 5:17–32; 7:57–8; 13:45. Green, *Luke*, 484, narrows blasphemy against the Holy Spirit to 'apostasy in the face of persecution'. Contrast Turner, *Power*, 255–7; Graham A. Cole, *Engaging with the Holy Spirit: Real Questions. Practical Answers* (Nottingham: Apollos, 2007), chapter 1.

LUKE

27 'Consider how the wild flowers grow. They do not labour or spin. Yet I tell you, not even Solomon in all his splendour was dressed like one of these. 28 If that is how God clothes the grass of the field, which is here today, and tomorrow is thrown into the fire, how much more will he clothe you – you of little faith! 29 And do not set your heart on what you will eat or drink; do not worry about it. 30 For the pagan world runs after all such things, and your Father knows that you need them.

31 But seek his kingdom, and these things will be given to you as well.

32 'Do not be afraid, little flock, for your Father has been pleased to give you the kingdom. 33 Sell your possessions and give to the poor. Provide purses for yourselves that will not wear out, a treasure in heaven that will never fail, where no thief comes near and no moth destroys. 34 For where your treasure is, there your heart will be also.

b 25 Or *single cubit to your height*

13–15. A challenge from someone in the crowd ('Teacher, tell my brother to divide the inheritance with me') gave Jesus the opportunity to speak forcefully about greed and the right use of material wealth. Questions about inheritance were normally referred to Jewish teachers or scribes, who interpreted and applied what was written in the Law (Deuteronomy 21:15–17; Numbers 27:1–11; 36:7–9). An older brother was responsible for apportioning what was due to each of the beneficiaries of an inheritance, but no details are given about the dispute in this family. Jesus simply refused to act as an intermediary, saying, 'Man, who appointed me a judge or an arbiter between you?' Then he turned to the crowd and said to them, 'Watch out! Be on your guard against all kinds of greed.' This double warning is the strongest in Luke–Acts, highlighting its importance.[126] Greed is ethically and spiritually destructive because a person's 'life [*zōē*] does not consist in an abundance of possessions' (see Ecclesiastes 2:1–11). Jesus's saying has to do with the quality of life in this world, though he goes on to explore what Seccombe calls 'a new quality of existence lived in fellowship with God'.[127]

16–19. Jesus illustrates his warning with a parable about a rich and successful land-owning farmer, which appears only in Luke. This man's property yielded 'an abundant harvest'. Instead of blessing God for his

---

[126] Greed (*pleonexia*) is also mentioned in Mark 7:22; Romans 1:29; 2 Corinthians 9:5; Colossians 3:5; Ephesians 4:19; 5:3; 2 Peter 2:3, 14. Another term (*harpagēs*) is used in in Luke 11:39; Matthew 23:25; Hebrews 10:34.
[127] Seccombe, *The Poor*, 146. Different words for 'life' are used (*zōē*, verse 15; *psychē*, verses 19, 20) to embrace the physical, emotional and spiritual aspects of life and to show that one's attitude towards material things has an impact on the whole.

254

good fortune and considering how God would have him benefit the poor and needy, he thought to himself, 'What shall I do? I have no place to store my crops.' Focusing on his own future happiness and economic security, he said to himself, 'This is what I'll do. I will tear down my barns and build bigger ones, and there I will store my surplus grain.' He wistfully imagines himself saying, 'You have plenty of grain laid up for many years. Take life easy; eat, drink and be merry.'[128] Compare Isaiah 22:13; 1 Corinthians 15:32.

20. The climax of the parable is God's unexpected challenge: 'You fool! This very night your life will be demanded from you.' Like 'the fool' who says in his heart, 'There is no God' (Psalms 14:1; 53:1), this man acted as if he were free to live self-indulgently for his own gratification. He did not reckon with the sudden approach of death, even as he was about to achieve his life's ambition (see Psalm 49:12–14; Sirach 11:18–20; Wisdom 15:8). The expression 'your life will be demanded from you' implies that in death he would be accountable to God for the way he had lived his life (see verse 5; Sirach 5:1–3). God is the implied subject of the verb 'demanded' (*apaitousin*), as he 'calls in' a person's life like a loan (BDAG).[129] The question, 'Then who will get what you have prepared for yourself?', makes the further point that what was acquired in this life would be left to others to enjoy (see Ecclesiastes 2:18–23).

21. Jesus drew out the essential challenge of the parable when he said, 'This is how it will be with whoever stores up things for themselves but is not rich towards God.' At one level, Jesus was concerned about the use of personal resources to care for the poor and needy (as in 11:40; 12:33; compare Deuteronomy 15:7–11; 24:17–22). More fundamentally, however, he called for generosity flowing from a life that is 'rich towards God', namely a life that recognises and responds wholeheartedly to the generosity of God (see verses 32–6).

22–3. There are verbal links between this passage and the preceding one ('life' in verses 22, 23, [25]; 'barn' in verse 24; eating in verses 22–4). Luke has placed this material immediately after Jesus's parable about the foolish farmer to highlight the possibility of 'a radically reconstructed attitude toward and set of behaviors concerning "the abundance of possessions"',

---

[128] The ESV more literally conveys the personal, self-satisfied way in which the man addresses himself: 'I will say to my soul, Soul, you have ample goods . . .'

[129] The Greek verb is in the present tense ('they are demanding') and uses the indefinite and impersonal third person plural instead of the passive to suggest the action of God (as in 6:38; 16:9; 23:31).

as Green puts it.[130] Jesus's first encouragement to his disciples was, 'Do not worry about your life, what you will eat; or about your body, what you will wear.' The reason for this is that 'life is more than food, and the body more than clothes' (see verse 14b). As in verse 31, there are more important things to be concerned about, and 'worry' will keep you from seeking them. Worry is a key idea in this segment of his teaching (verses 22, 25, 26, 29; see also 8:14; 10:41; 12:11).[131] Food and clothing represent everyday needs and are dealt with in order.

24–6. An argument from nature ('Consider the ravens; they do not sow or reap, they have no storeroom or barn') is backed up with the reminder, 'yet God feeds them,' and the claim, 'how much more valuable you are than birds!' (see verses 6–7). Ravens were regarded as unclean and Jews were forbidden to eat them (Leviticus 11:15), making this claim about God's care for them all the more remarkable. Jesus's second encouragement returned to the theme of worry and exposed the futility of it with a rhetorical question: 'Who of you by worrying can add a single hour to your life?' This saying can be understood in terms of physical growth (NIV note b, 'add a single cubit to your height'), though the temporal meaning ('add a single hour to your life') seems more appropriate to the context (so also ESV, CSB). Life span or extent of life is certainly in view in verse 28. If the physical sense is meant in verse 26, Edwards suggests that Jesus is using hyperbole to inject a note of humour 'as a way of underscoring the absurdity of worry'.[132] Jesus concludes, 'Since you cannot do this very little thing, why do you worry about the rest?'

27–8. Jesus's third encouragement is to trust God about clothing, and once again he uses a comparison with nature ('Consider how the wild flowers grow. They do not labour or spin. Yet I tell you, not even Solomon in all his splendour was dressed like one of these').[133] Sowing and reaping were mentioned in connection with food (verse 24), and now

---

[130] Green, *Luke*, 487. Compare Matthew 6:25–34. Jesus has more to say in Luke about the concerns of this life and how they might keep someone from the kingdom of God (8:14; 9:57–62; 10:38–42; 14:25–34; 16:1–31; 18:18–30).

[131] The same verb (*merimnaō*, 'be anxious, [un]duly concerned', BDAG) is used in verses 22, 25, 26, with a synonym (*meteōrizomai*) in verse 29 ('be anxious'). Seccombe, *The Poor*, 157, contends that the passage is dealing with 'the particular anxiety that arises when a person decides to seek the Kingdom'.

[132] Edwards, *Luke* 374. He notes that whereas *hēlikia* can refer to age or physical stature, *pēchys* ('forearm, cubit') is strictly a linear measurement. Applied to physical stature it would signify enormous growth (about 21 inches or 53cm).

[133] Fitzmyer, *Luke X–XXIV*, 979, notes the difficulty of identifying a particular

labouring and spinning come into focus as a means of gaining clothes. The challenge is not to abandon these ordinary human activities but to recognise that, if God can provide for the natural world in different ways, he can provide for his people beyond their own industry (see 8:3b). The transitory nature of grass is implicitly contrasted with the ordinary span of human life ('If that is how God clothes the grass of the field, which is here today, and tomorrow is thrown into the fire, how much more will he clothe you – you of little faith!'). The accusation of 'little faith' implies a diminished view of God and his willingness to provide and care for his people (see comment on 17:5–6).

29–31. A further warning about worry is prefaced by the challenge, 'And do not set your heart on what you will eat or drink.'[134] Believers are to be different from unbelievers in this respect ('For the pagan world runs after all such things'). But Jesus assures his disciples, 'your Father knows that you need them'. This is a reminder of his encouragement to pray to God as Father and expect him to give good gifts to his children (11:1–11). The climactic challenge in this sequence is to 'seek his kingdom' (Matthew 6:33 adds 'and his righteousness') and the promise is given: 'and these things will be given to you as well'. Seeking God's kingdom will mean embracing the rule of God manifested in the life and teaching of Jesus (11:20) and looking for its consummation in his return as the Son of Man and final redemption (21:27–8, 31). The goodness of God is supremely revealed in the gospel, and its powerful message is the fundamental reason for not worrying!

32–4. Luke's conclusion to Jesus's teaching about worry begins with the challenge, 'Do not be afraid, little flock.' This identifies the disciples as the core group of faithful Israelites whom he is rescuing for eternal life (Isaiah 40:11; Ezekiel 34:11–16; Micah 2:12; compare John 10:11–18, 27–9). The reason for not being afraid (see verse 4) is the assurance that 'your Father has been pleased to give you the kingdom'. God's 'pleasure' in revealing his Son to them (10:21–2) included the promise of an eternal inheritance with him. Their seeking of the kingdom (verse 31) should involve praying as Jesus directed (11:2–4). A radical challenge follows:

---

flower here. The riches of Solomon's court (1 Kings 10:4–5, 21, 23) are the basis of the assumption that he was splendidly dressed.

[134] The warning in verse 29 (*mē zēteite*, 'do not seek'; NIV, 'do not set your heart on') anticipates the emphatic contrast in verse 31 (*plēn zēteite*, 'but seek'). The pronoun 'you' in verse 29 sets up a contrast with verse 30 (*panta ta ethnē tou kosmou*), which the ESV renders more literally 'all the nations of the world'.

'Sell your possessions and give to the poor.'[135] This is not a call for total renunciation and disposal of possessions (as in 18:22), but an encouragement to use wealth wisely and generously for the benefit of those in need (see Acts 2:44–5; 4:32–7; 11:27–30).

Jesus employs two complementary metaphors to reinforce this. 'Provide purses for yourselves that will not wear out' means find a completely safe place for your money! Investment in kingdom priorities and projects is the way to do that, because it yields 'a treasure in heaven that will never fail, where no thief comes near and no moth destroys'. Earthly possessions are not simply given by God for personal benefit, but to advance his kingdom and extend its influence in the present. But Jesus does not mean that people can secure a heavenly future simply by being generous with their money. The final saying ('For where your treasure is, there your heart will be also') explains the connection between the promise of eternal life and the transformation of hearts and lives that Jesus has developed (verses 15, 21, 31). Nolland concludes, 'If one follows the trail marked out by a person's use of money, it will lead to that person's heart. The heart that is with God (in heaven) will thereby demonstrate that it has the kingdom of God as its constant consideration (v. 31).'[136] This is the heart of someone genuinely bound for God's eternal kingdom (see 16:9–13).

HYPOCRISY, GREED, WORRY AND GENEROSITY

A warning about the corrupting influence of hypocrisy leads Jesus to speak of the inevitable exposure of what is hidden behind a person's public image (verses 1–3). Rather than being afraid of human opponents, disciples should fear God, who brings everyone into judgment, but takes care of those who are persecuted and oppressed for their faith. Open confession of Jesus, facilitated by the Holy Spirit, will be acknowledged by the Son of Man before the angels of God, but those who disown him will be rejected on the day of judgment. In particular, Jesus warns about the danger of denying the powerful presence of the Holy Spirit in his ministry. With such blasphemy, people put themselves beyond forgiveness and the possibility of eternal salvation (verses 4–12).

---

[135] 'Gifts of mercy' (*eleēmosynē*) to the poor and needy were required of pious Jews (e.g., Tobit 4:8–9; 1 Enoch 38:2; 2 Enoch 50:5), based on biblical teaching. Jesus offered a new way to fulfil this ideal, setting his ethic within the framework of teaching about the kingdom of God.

[136] Nolland, *Luke 9:21–18:34*, 696.

LUKE
'Sell your possessions

The issue of greed surfaces again when Jesus is asked to solve a family dispute (verses 13–21; compare 11:39). His parable about a rich farmer challenges the crowd to consider the relationship between material wealth and a meaningful life. Jesus calls for a richness towards God in the generous employment of the wealth he has given us. These matters are further explored in the teaching to disciples that follows (verses 22–34). Anxiety about food and clothing is an everyday human preoccupation, but it keeps many from trusting God and seeking his kingdom. God's generous provision for ravens and wild flowers points to his greater purpose to care for humanity. The antidote to worry is to trust in the goodness of God, as revealed in the natural world and supremely in the gospel promises. Those who know themselves to be part of his 'little flock' can be assured that he has already granted them a heavenly inheritance. With this hope, they can be fearlessly generous with their earthly possessions, investing in kingdom values and concerns.

Watchful service (12:35–53)

Watchfulness

35 'Be dressed ready for service and keep your lamps burning, 36 like servants waiting for their master to return from a wedding banquet, so that when he comes and knocks they can immediately open the door for him. 37 It will be good for those servants whose master finds them watching when he comes. Truly I tell you, he will dress himself to serve, will make them recline at the table and will come and wait on them. 38 It will be good for those servants whose master finds them ready, even if he comes in the middle of the night or towards daybreak. 39 But understand this: if the owner of the house had known at what hour the thief was coming, he would not have let his house be broken into. 40 You also must be ready, because the Son of Man will come at an hour when you do not expect him.'

41 Peter asked, 'Lord, are you telling this parable to us, or to everyone?'

42 The Lord answered, 'Who then is the faithful and wise manager, whom the master puts in charge of his servants to give them their food allowance at the proper time? 43 It will be good for that servant whom the master finds doing so when he returns. 44 Truly I tell you, he will put him in charge of all his possessions. 45 But suppose the servant says to himself, "My master is taking a long time in coming," and he then begins to beat the other servants, both men and women, and to eat and drink and get drunk. 46 The master of that servant will come on a day when he does not expect him and at an hour he is not aware of. He will cut him to pieces and assign him a place with the unbelievers.

LUKE

47 'The servant who knows the master's will and does not get ready or does not do what the master wants will be beaten with many blows. 48 But the one who does not know and does things deserving punishment will be beaten with few blows. From everyone who has been given much, much will be demanded; and from the one who has been entrusted with much, much more will be asked.

Not peace but division

49 'I have come to bring fire on the earth, and how I wish it were already kindled! 50 But I have a baptism to undergo, and what constraint I am under until it is completed! 51 Do you think I came to bring peace on earth? No, I tell you, but division. 52 From now on there will be five in one family divided against each other, three against two and two against three. 53 They will be divided, father against son and son against father, mother against daughter and daughter against mother, mother-in-law against daugter-in-law and daughter-in-law against mother-in-law.'

35–8. The focus now is more specifically on being prepared for the coming of the Son of Man (verse 40). There are parallels here with Mark 13:33–4, whereas verses 39–40, 42–6 are closer to Matthew 24:42–51. Luke has placed this material about the end-time appearance of the Son of Man earlier in his Gospel, while retaining a more formal prediction of preceding events with appropriate warnings in 21:5–36 (see also 17:22–37). Readers are twice faced with the tension between being prepared for an imminent end while being told of certain things that must happen first.

In parabolic terms, disciples are to be 'dressed ready for service',[137] with 'lamps burning, like servants waiting for their master to return from a wedding banquet' (see Matthew 25:1–13). The master's attendance at a wedding feast implies that he will return home soon. His servants must be prepared, 'so that when he comes and knocks they can immediately open the door for him'. Jesus's promise that 'it will be good for those servants whose master finds them watching when he comes' is then explained in surprising terms: 'Truly I tell you, he will dress himself to serve, will have them recline at the table and will come and wait on them.' This extraordinary reversal of the normal relationship between masters and servants is a picture of the salvation

---

[137] The translation of *hymōn hai osphyes periezōsmena*, 'with your loins girded for action', may allude to Exodus 12:11, though gathering up long robes to free the feet for action is mentioned in other Old Testament contexts (1 Kings 18:46; 2 Kings 4:29; 9:1; Job 38:3 'Brace yourself'; 40:7).

that the Son of Man will bring (21:27–8). Jesus will serve his disciples by enabling them to share in God's end-time banquet, as portrayed in 13:29; 22:27–30 (see Isaiah 25:6–8; Revelation 19:7–9). The promise is repeated for emphasis ('It will be good for those servants whose master finds them ready'), with the suggestion that their wait could nevertheless be longer than expected ('even if he comes in the middle of the night or toward daybreak').[138]

39–40. A further warning ('But understand this') uses the household image differently. The focus changes to the watchful owner of a house (*oikodespotēs*), who is always prepared for a prowling burglar ('if the owner of the house had known at what hour the thief was coming, he would not have let his house be broken into'). Jesus boldly compares the suddenness of the Son of Man's arrival to the coming of a thief! The reality behind the metaphor is, 'You also must be ready, because the Son of Man will come at an hour when you do not expect him.' So far in Luke's Gospel, Jesus has only once spoken about the Son of Man's coming 'in his glory and in the glory of the Father and of the holy angels' (9:26).[139] Subsequent references associate his coming with judgment (11:30; 12:8–10; 17:22–37; 18:8), but also with the full experience of salvation that his earthly ministry anticipates (19:9–10; 21:27–8).

41–4. Peter's question ('Lord, are you telling this parable to us, or to everyone?') is a reminder that the audience is mixed. Jesus does not answer him directly, though he continues to address his disciples before turning to the crowd again in verse 54. His reply begins with a rhetorical question ('Who then is the faithful and wise manager, whom the master puts in charge of his servants to give them their food allowance at the proper time?'). A different image is introduced with the term 'manager' (*oikonomos*), which refers to a slave appointed by 'the master' (*kyrios*) to supervise and care for other slaves and manage his household (see 16:1–8).[140] Jesus returns to the language of verse 37, affirming once

---

[138] The expression 'even in the second or third watch' reflects the threefold Hellenistic and Jewish pattern of dividing the night into periods.

[139] Jesus's climactic statement about the Son of Man being 'seated at the right hand of the mighty God' (22:69) implies an ascension to heavenly glory and power (see 9:51; 24:51) from which he comes to judge and to save.

[140] See O. Michel, 'οἰκονόμος', *TDNT* 5:149–51. The term *kyrios* is variously used in this passage for 'the master' of the house (verses 36, 37, 42), Jesus as leader/teacher of the disciples (verse 41), and Jesus as 'the Lord' in the full, post-resurrection sense that Luke intends (verse 42). Clearly, the parable points to Jesus as the returning Lord/Son of Man (verse 40).

more that 'it will be good for that servant whom the master finds doing so when he returns'.[141] More responsibility will be given to those who prove trustworthy: 'Truly I tell you, he will put him in charge of all his possessions' (see 19:11–27). Although the language of stewardship is applied to disciples in general here (as in 16:10–12), the warning about accountability to God is particularly applicable to Christian leaders.

45–6. A second possibility is considered: 'But suppose the servant says to himself, "My master is taking a long time in coming," and he then begins to beat the other servants, both men and women, and to eat and drink and get drunk.' The servant's betrayal of his master's trust, his abusive behaviour and his abandonment to self-indulgence warrants the most severe punishment. As in verses 35–40, Jesus emphasises the suddenness of divine judgment ('The master of that servant will come on a day when he does not expect him and at an hour he is not aware of'). The predicted punishment reflects the sort of treatment meted out to disobedient slaves in that era ('he will cut him to pieces'),[142] but it does not refer to temporal punishment here. The warning 'and assign him a place with the unbelievers' recalls the language of being thrown into hell in verse 5. The destiny of apostate disciples will be the same as that of unbelievers!

47–8. Jesus illustrates the problem of unfaithfulness in two further ways. A second servant 'who knows the master's will and does not get ready or does not do what the master wants will be beaten with many blows'. In eschatological terms, this servant is not thrown into hell but experiences some form of discipline or deprivation when the Son of Man comes (see 1 Corinthians 3:12–15). A third servant 'who does not know and does things deserving of punishment will be beaten with few blows'. These verses, which are only in Luke, indicate a proportional degree of punishment for sins committed by disciples in ignorance, but not final exclusion from the kingdom of God.[143] Such images of accountability to God cannot be more precisely defined. Put positively, Jesus asserts, 'From everyone who has been given much, much will be demanded; and from the one who has been entrusted with much, much more will be asked.'

---

[141] Green, *Luke*, 504–6, observes that the master–slave model is developed now with examples of fidelity (verses 43–4), infidelity (verses 45–6) and ignorance (verses 47–8).

[142] Moreover, 'the severity of response here is of a piece with the general extremity that characterizes responses in the parable' (Nolland, *Luke 9:21–18:34*, 704).

[143] This somewhat mirrors the Old Testament distinction between unintentional sins, which could be atoned for, and defiant sins, which necessitated exclusion from the people of God (Numbers 15:27–31).

This serves as a conclusion to the linked sayings in verses 35–47 and points to the privileges and responsibilities of disciples in comparison with the crowd.

49–50. Jesus's final words to his disciples in this sequence concern what must take place before the Son of Man comes in glory (see Matthew 10:34–6; Mark 10:38b). 'I have come' introduces a simple mission statement (see 5:32; Matthew 5:17; 10:34–5; John 5:43; 7:28; 12:27, 47; 16:28; 18:37). 'To bring fire on the earth' recalls the Baptist's prediction in 3:16–17 about the Messiah's baptism 'with the Holy Spirit and fire'. As in the Old Testament, fire implies both purification for the penitent and destruction for the godless.[144] Jesus views 'fire on the earth' as a good outcome ('and how I wish it were already kindled!'), because it will fulfil God's kingdom plan. But in a parallel statement ('I have a baptism to undergo'), he indicates, as Nolland says, that 'he who is to spread a fire upon the earth is himself destined to be overwhelmed by disaster'.[145] Jesus will be immersed in the suffering he has predicted as the necessary pathway to his heavenly enthronement and glorious return as the Son of Man (9:21–2, 26). At this point in his ministry, he was preoccupied with fulfilling this destiny ('and what constraint I am under until it is completed!').[146] That is why, 'as the time approached for him to be taken up to heaven, Jesus resolutely set out for Jerusalem' (9:51; see also 13:31–3). Readers of Luke–Acts will know that the fire has been kindled and is spreading on earth, as the gospel about Jesus's death and resurrection is proclaimed in the power of the Holy Spirit (Acts 2:32–41).

51–3. The Lord's next saying returns to the theme of division implied by fire on the earth (verse 49): 'Do you think I came to bring peace on earth? No, I tell you, but division.' His rhetorical question about peace is not an absolute denial that he came to bring peace, but a dramatic way of reinforcing the need for the 'fire' and the 'baptism' he predicted. Jesus challenged the view that the biblical promises of salvation could be fulfilled without suffering and division. The hope of

---

[144] The refiner's fire destroys the dross, but it purifies the precious metal (see Isaiah 1:25; Zechariah 13:9; Malachi 3:2–3). Destruction by fire is represented in 2 Kings 1:10; Isaiah 66:14–16; Amos 1:4, 7.

[145] Nolland, *Luke 9:21–18:34*, 710. Nolland, 708, notes the metaphorical use of 'baptism' for an experience of being overwhelmed by disaster in Hellenistic sources and later Greek versions of the Old Testament. See also Marshall, *Luke*, 547.

[146] The verb *synechomai* ('constrained') is used here with the sense of being absorbed by something (as in Acts 18:5), rather than being 'distressed' or 'overcome' (as in Luke 8:37).

a messianic peace was announced in 1:79; 2:14 (compare 19:38, 42) and the benefits were offered in advance of its achievement in Jesus's death and resurrection (7:50; 8:48; 10:5–6) and subsequently (Acts 10:36). Yet Simeon predicted that Jesus was 'destined to cause the falling and rising of many in Israel, and to be a sign that will be spoken against' (2:34). Peace would ultimately only be achieved at great cost to the Saviour, and its proclamation would divide families: 'From now on there will be five in one family divided against each other, three against two and two against three.' Alluding to Micah 7:6, Jesus develops this picture of unbelief and resistance to his message of peace: 'They will be divided, father against son and son against father, mother against daughter and daughter against mother, mother-in-law against daughter-in-law and daughter-in-law against mother-in-law.' Such is the spiritual battle that continues, until the messianic peace is fully realised and experienced when the Son of Man returns (see 17:22–37).

Interpreting the present time (12:54–13:9)

Interpreting the times

54 He said to the crowd: 'When you see a cloud rising in the west, immediately you say, "It's going to rain," and it does. **55** And when the south wind blows, you say, "It's going to be hot," and it is. **56** Hypocrites! You know how to interpret the appearance of the earth and the sky. How is it that you don't know how to interpret this present time?

57 'Why don't you judge for yourselves what is right? **58** As you are going with your adversary to the magistrate, try hard to be reconciled on the way, or your adversary may drag you off to the judge, and the judge turn you over to the officer, and the officer throw you into prison. **59** I tell you, you will not get out until you have paid the last penny.'

Repent or perish

13 Now there were some present at that time who told Jesus about the Galileans whose blood Pilate had mixed with their sacrifices. **2** Jesus answered, 'Do you think that these Galileans were worse sinners than all the other Galileans because they suffered this way? **3** I tell you, no! But unless you repent, you too will all perish. **4** Or those eighteen who died when the tower in Siloam fell on them – do you think they were more guilty than all the others living in Jerusalem? **5** I tell you, no! But unless you repent, you too will all perish.'

6 Then he told this parable: 'A man had a fig-tree growing in his vineyard, and he went to look for fruit on it but did not find any. **7** So he said to the man who took care of the vineyard, "For three years now I've been coming to look for fruit on this fig-tree and haven't found any. Cut it down! Why should it use up the soil?" 8'"Sir," the man replied, "leave it alone for one more year, and I'll dig round it and fertilise it. 9If it bears fruit next year, fine! If not, then cut it down."'

54–6. Jesus turned to the crowd again (as in verses 13–21) with a more aggressive challenge: 'When you see a cloud rising in the west, immediately you say, "It's going to rain," and it does. And when the south wind blows, you say, "It's going to be hot," and it is.' Previously, he had accused them of being sign-seekers while failing to see the significance of what was going on in his ministry (11:29–36). Here, he accuses them of being 'hypocrites' like the Pharisees. As Fitzmyer suggests, their problem was 'much more an *unwillingness* to interpret than an inability'.[147] Neither those who were educated in the Scriptures (Matthew 16:1–3) nor everyday people who knew how to 'interpret the appearance of the earth and the sky' were responding appropriately to what he was saying and doing. Jesus implied a missed opportunity when he said, 'How is it that you don't know how to interpret this present time?' The word *kairos* here indicates a significant moment in their history as a people (see 7:31–5; 19:44, 'the time of God's coming to you').

57–9. The imagery changes from the weather to the lawcourt:

Why don't you judge for yourselves what is right? As you are going with your adversary to the magistrate, try hard to be reconciled on the way, or your adversary may drag you off to the judge, and the judge turn you over to the officer, and the officer throw you into prison.

Matthew 5:25–6 uses the same imagery in a different context. This parabolic language provides a further challenge to act wisely in relation to the ministry of Jesus, before being called to account before God, the ultimate judge (12:4–5, 9–10). The punishment for not being 'reconciled on the way' will be severe: 'I tell you, you will not get out until you have paid the last penny.'[148] A penny (*lepton*) was the coin with the lowest value in ancient Palestine.

---

[147] Fitzmyer, *Luke X–XXIV*, 1000 (my emphasis).
[148] Green, *Luke*, 512, sees a reference to the Roman debt system: 'Rather than being indentured until the debt was paid off through slave-labor, the debtor is thrown into prison until the liability could be cleared, for example, through the sale of property.'

13:1–5. This segment, which only Luke records, is linked to the previous one (12:54–9) by the phrase 'at that time'.[149] Some people were present in the crowd 'who told Jesus about the Galileans whose blood Pilate had mixed with their sacrifices'. Pontius Pilate, the Roman governor of Judea (AD 26–36), was last mentioned in 3:1. Since sacrifices could only be offered in Jerusalem, the incident must have taken place when these Galileans were on a pilgrimage to the Temple. No parallel record of this event has so far been uncovered, though the details agree with the picture of Pilate's attacks on the Jewish people in various accounts of Josephus.[150] Jesus presumed that the crowd would evaluate this terrible action as divine judgment on those who were particularly sinful, asking, 'Do you think that these Galileans were worse sinners than all the other Galileans because they suffered this way?' Contradicting this assumption ('I tell you, no!'), he took the opportunity to warn, 'Unless you repent, you too will all perish.' As in 12:4–5, 8–10, the issue is what lies beyond death in the ultimate judgment of God. The verb translated 'perish' can refer to loss of physical or spiritual life (BDAG, *apollymi*; see 9:24–5; 17:27, 29). Jesus repeats this warning after mentioning another example of sudden death, this time accidental ('Or those eighteen who died when the tower in Siloam fell on them – do you think they were more guilty than all the others living in Jerusalem?'). Although this tower is known from a description of the city by Josephus (*War* 5.145), the incident Jesus mentions is not recorded elsewhere. Like John the Baptist, Jesus warned people to 'flee from the coming wrath' and produce 'fruit in keeping with repentance' (3:7–9). The latter is picked up in the parable that follows.

6–9. The fig-tree is used in the Old Testament with reference to Israel's fruitfulness in God's service (Jeremiah 8:13; 24:1–10; Hosea 9:10; Micah 7:1). The owner of the vineyard clearly represents God (see Isaiah 5:1–10), who is disappointed to find the tree in his vineyard without fruit. 'So he said to the man who took care of the vineyard, "For three years now I've been coming to look for fruit on this fig-tree and haven't found any. Cut it down! Why should it use up the soil?"' The issues were lack of fruit, time enough for it to grow and the wisdom of allowing such a tree to use up the soil. But the man who took care of the vineyard called for a

---

[149] The word *kairos* ('time') is used here without the critical significance it has in 12:56.

[150] Fitzmyer, *Luke X–XXIV*, 1006–7. Nolland, *Luke 9:21–18:34*, 717, observes that Josephus fails to report 'at least one much more politically significant act of Pilate', and so it is not surprising that he fails to mention this one.

delay (contrast 3:9): "'Sir,' the man replied, "leave it alone for one more year, and I'll dig around it and fertilise it. If it bears fruit next year, fine! If not, then cut it down.'" Judgment is held back because the ministry of Jesus is an opportunity to bear fruit demonstrating genuine repentance. But ultimate accountability is near at hand.[151]

OVERTURNING WORLDLY VALUES AND EXPECTATIONS

Jesus's call for disciples to be ready for the coming of the Son of Man brings several surprising predictions. First, it will be good for his servants if their master finds them watching when he comes, because 'he will dress himself to serve, will make them recline at the table and will come and wait on them' (12:37). This extraordinary reversal of values and roles portrays the returning Lord as the servant who does everything to bring his people into the joys of the consummate banquet of God (Isaiah 25:6–8; Luke 22:14–28; Revelation 19:7–9). Second, those who prove themselves trustworthy in the master's service will be given greater responsibility on his return (12:42–4; compare 19:11–27), while those who prove culpably unfaithful will be condemned along with unbelievers (12:45–6). Third, those who are ignorant of his will and do things deserving punishment will be treated justly (12:47–8). Fourth, the Messiah must be overwhelmed by suffering to achieve the peace promised by the prophets and purge the earth of sin. Disciples will be caught up in the fiery consequences that divide even families, as the gospel is proclaimed in the power of the Spirit (12:49–53). As Tannehill says, 'Jesus' words require difficult decisions, for they conflict with deep loyalties both for the disciples in the story and for its readers.'[152] Turning to the crowd, Jesus warns about the serious consequences of failing to evaluate the significance of his ministry appropriately (12:54–9). He challenges the view that the deliberate killing of certain Galileans or the accidental death of certain Jerusalemites was because they were more sinful than other people, twice warning, 'Unless you repent, you too will all perish' (13:1–5). Jesus concludes that if someone bears no fruit and continues to be unproductive in the life that God has given them, as Fitzmyer puts it, 'that person should be ready to face the fate of the barren fig tree'.[153]

---

[151] Summarising the message of 13:1–9, Isaak, 'Luke', 1257, says 'tragedy is no sure sign of sinfulness, just as the absence of tragedy is no sure sign of righteousness. All alike – those whose lives are tragic and those whose lives are tranquil – are sinners and all alike must repent before God.'

[152] Tannehill, *Narrative Unity* 1, 253. Compare 9:59–62; 14:26; 18:28–30.

[153] Fitzmyer, *Luke X–XXIV*, 1005.

6. Reversals present and future (Luke 13:10–14:35)

Structurally, this part of Luke's travel narrative contains two parallel segments, each consisting of healings on the Sabbath (13:10–17; 14:1–6), parabolic challenges (13:18–21; 14:7–14), clarification about who will be saved and enter the kingdom of God (13:22–30; 14:15–24) and a prediction about Jesus's fate in Jerusalem (13:31–35), climaxing with a challenge to follow him no matter what the cost (14:25–35). Nolland concludes, 'Luke explores a series of reversals and paradoxical inversions associated with the manifestation of the kingdom of God' in the ministry of Jesus, and then 'at the time for the consummation of all God's purposes'.[154]

Release from Satan's power and the coming of the kingdom (13:10–21)

Jesus heals a crippled woman on the Sabbath

10 On a Sabbath Jesus was teaching in one of the synagogues, 11 and a woman was there who had been crippled by a spirit for eighteen years. She was bent over and could not straighten up at all. 12 When Jesus saw her, he called her forward and said to her, 'Woman, you are set free from your infirmity.' 13 Then he put his hands on her, and immediately she straightened up and praised God.

14 Indignant because Jesus had healed on the Sabbath, the synagogue leader said to the people, 'There are six days for work. So come and be healed on those days, not on the Sabbath.'

15 The Lord answered him, 'You hypocrites! Doesn't each of you on the Sabbath untie your ox or donkey from the stall and lead it out to give it water? 16 Then should not this woman, a daughter of Abraham, whom Satan has kept bound for eighteen long years, be set free on the Sabbath day from what bound her?'

17 When he said this, all his opponents were humiliated, but the people were delighted with all the wonderful things he was doing.

The parables of the mustard seed and the yeast

18 Then Jesus asked, 'What is the kingdom of God like? What shall I compare it to? 19 It is like a mustard seed, which a man took and planted in his garden. It grew and became a tree, and the birds perched in its branches.'

20 Again he asked, 'What shall I compare the kingdom of God to? 21 It is like yeast that a woman took and mixed into about thirty kilograms of flour until it worked all through the dough.'

154 Nolland, *Luke 9:21–18:34*, 721. He identifies 'two sets of units in sequential parallelism'.

10–13. Once more on a Sabbath Jesus was teaching in one of the synagogues, proclaiming the good news of the kingdom of God (see 4:15, 31, 44; 6:6). Given his unofficial status and the growing opposition of the Pharisees and the experts in the law to his teaching, it is remarkable that he still had such opportunities. The controversial issue in this context was again his healing on the Sabbath (see 6:6–11). Luke alone records the terrible condition of a woman 'who had been crippled by a spirit for eighteen years' (*pneuma echousa astheneias*, 'having a spirit of weakness'). This could simply describe the debilitating effect of her condition (ESV, 'a disabling spirit'), though it is later clarified that 'Satan has kept [her] bound for eighteen long years' (verse 16). Physically, 'she was bent over and could not straighten up at all'. A link between spiritual bondage and physical disability is implied (see 8:26–39; Acts 10:38), though the nature of the link is not revealed, and we should not presume this in every case of sickness or disability. When Jesus saw her, he took the initiative, 'called her forward and said to her, "Woman, you are set free from your infirmity."'[155] This was not an exorcism, but an invitation to believe in his power to heal. 'Then he put his hands on her, and immediately she straightened up and praised God' (see 4:40; 5:13; 8:54). When she was healed, Satan's hold on her life was broken; she was able to hold her head high and take her place in the community of God's people.

14–16. Although Jesus had instantaneously healed this woman and drawn attention to his divine authority to do such things, the synagogue leader was 'indignant because Jesus had healed on the Sabbath'. Rather than criticising him directly, however, he addressed 'the people' and effectively blamed the woman for coming to be healed on that day ('There are six days for work. So come and be healed on those days, not on the Sabbath'). Jesus's response to this insensitive and legalistic challenge was first to identify the hypocrisy of the leader and those who thought like him ('You hypocrites!', see 12:1, 56). He exposed this by first asking a question about their regular Sabbath practice: 'Doesn't each of you on the Sabbath untie your ox or donkey from the stall and lead it out to give it water?'[156] The word 'untie' (*lyei*, 'release') prepares for the dramatic claim that follows: 'Then should not this woman, a daughter of Abraham,

---

[155] The verb 'set free' (*apolelysai*) anticipates the use of parallel terms in verses 15–16. It also recalls use of the noun *aphesis* in 4:18 ('release'), making this an obvious fulfilment of the prophecy Jesus read out in the synagogue at Nazareth.

[156] Marshall, *Luke*, 558–9, and Bock, *Luke 9:51–24:53*, 1218, outline provisions in the Jewish Mishnah for meeting the needs of animals on the Sabbath.

whom Satan has kept bound for eighteen long years, be set free (*lythēnai*) on the Sabbath day from what bound her?' Jesus contrasted their care for animals with their care for a woman who was one of their own ('a daughter of Abraham'; see 1:55; 3:8; 16:24; 19:9). Moreover, she had been in physical and spiritual bondage for eighteen years and the Sabbath was precisely the context in which to experience the liberating grace of God (6:9). If Satan's grip on her life had been broken by the power of God working through Jesus, then the kingdom of God was clearly breaking into history (11:20).

17–19. As he was saying these things, 'all his opponents were humiliated', indicating an immediate and decisive impact on them. 'But the people were delighted with all the wonderful things he was doing,' implying that his popularity with the crowds was continuing to grow and spread. Two similitudes are closely linked by Luke with the preceding event, one concerning a man and the other a woman. They appear together in a different context in Matthew 13:31–3, but with the same meaning (see also Mark 4:30–32). Jesus first compared the kingdom of God and its manifestation to 'a mustard seed, which a man took and planted in his garden. It grew and became a tree, and the birds perched in its branches.' A mustard seed was considered proverbially small (Matthew 13:32; Mark 4:31), but a mustard plant could grow to between 2.5 and 3 metres (8 to 10 feet).[157] In Luke's version, the smallness of the seed is contrasted with the greatness of the 'tree' (Matthew 13:32; Mark 4:32, 'the largest of all garden plants'). A tree supporting birds in its branches recalls Old Testament passages where powerful kings and kingdoms are likened to trees 'able to provide a widely used protective canopy of stability and peace'.[158] This is not a parable about the gradual growth of the church throughout the ages, though the final image could point to the presence of people from every nation 'at the feast in the kingdom of God' (verse 29; compare 14:21–4). It simply contrasts the apparent insignificance of Jesus's ministry with the abundant blessings God would ultimately bring through him.

20–21. The parable of the yeast (see 12:1) offers another sharp contrast between small and large, present and future. The kingdom of God is 'like yeast that a woman took and mixed into about thirty kilograms

---

[157] C-H, Hunzinger, 'σίναπι', *TDNT* 7:288–9. See Mishnah, *Niddah* 5:2.
[158] Nolland, *Luke 9:21–18:34*, 728. See Ezekiel 17:22–4; 31:5–6; Daniel 4:11–12, 20–22. Jeremias, *Parables*, 147, observes the way 'touches of eschatological colour' can be seen in both parables.

of flour until it worked all through the dough'. Thirty kilograms (about sixty-six pounds) is a large amount of flour! The NIV obscures the figural significance of the verb *ekrypsen* ('hid') by translating it 'mixed'. Nolland observes that this woman has '"super leaven", which, she is confident, will make its way, without being mixed in through this huge lump of dough (the dough will make enough bread to feed around 150 people!)'.[159] Even though the kingdom is hidden and apparently insignificant in the present, its final manifestation will be unmistakable and world-transforming.

Who will enter the kingdom? (13:22–30)

The narrow door

22 Then Jesus went through the towns and villages, teaching as he made his way to Jerusalem. 23 Someone asked him, 'Lord, are only a few people going to be saved?'

He said to them, 24 'Make every effort to enter through the narrow door, because many, I tell you, will try to enter and will not be able to. 25 Once the owner of the house gets up and closes the door, you will stand outside knocking and pleading, "Sir, open the door for us."

'But he will answer, "I don't know you or where you come from."

26 'Then you will say, "We ate and drank with you, and you taught in our streets."

27 'But he will reply, "I don't know you or where you come from. Away from me, all you evildoers!"

28 'There will be weeping there, and gnashing of teeth, when you see Abraham, Isaac and Jacob and all the prophets in the kingdom of God, but you yourselves thrown out. 29 People will come from east and west and north and south, and will take their places at the feast in the kingdom of God. 30 Indeed there are those who are last who will be first, and first who will be last.'

22–3. Luke resumes the journey motif (9:51, 57; 10:1, 38) as the context for further teaching about the kingdom of God ('Then Jesus went through the towns and villages, teaching as he made his way to Jerusalem'). This final journey and its outcome would enable Jesus to fulfil God's kingdom plan (verses 31–5). An important question from an unidentified person ('Lord, are only a few people going to be saved?') sets the scene. The issue of salvation emerges again in 17:19; 18:26, 42, associated with entering the kingdom of God and receiving eternal life, and it comes back into

---

[159] Nolland, *Luke 9:21–18:34*, 730. See his comment on the Greek expression *sata tria*, which is the measure used in the original text.

view as the Gospel draws to a close (19:9–10; 23:37, 39). The question put to Jesus reflected contemporary debates about end-time salvation in Judaism.[160]

24–5. Jesus did not answer directly, but he warned those present with him, 'Make every effort to enter through the narrow door.' This stressed the need for everyone to make a wise choice and pursue the only way into the kingdom of God (see Matthew 7:13–14).[161] Jesus emphatically insisted that a time would come when the opportunity to enter the kingdom would be removed: 'because many, I tell you, will try to enter and will not be able to'. The reason for this is explained in parabolic terms (see Matthew 25:10–12): 'Once the owner of the house gets up and closes the door, you will stand outside knocking and pleading, "Sir, open the door for us."' The owner of the house is a figure for God. Those outside the house act as if they are invited guests, but God answers, 'I don't know you or where you come from.' Being known by God is the critical issue, and this is restated in verse 27 in terms of being known by Jesus. This recalls the idea that Israel was especially known by God, meaning that he had chosen them to be in an exclusive relationship with himself (Amos 3:2 [LXX], ESV 'known'). By implication, true Israelites would prove their identity by acknowledging their Messiah and expressing their need for him. Gentile believers would also come to be known by God (verses 29–30; compare Galatians 4:8–9; 1 Corinthians 13:12).

26–7. As Jesus developed the illustration, he effectively identified himself with God as the owner of the house. Those refused entrance into the kingdom on the last day will say, 'We ate and drank with you, and you taught in our streets,' claiming to have known Jesus, but having no personal relationship with him or commitment to him.[162] Jesus repeats the expression, 'I don't know you or where you come from,' and adds solemn words of rejection: 'Away from me, all you evildoers!' (*pantes*

---

[160] Fitzmyer, *Luke X–XXIV*, 1022, cites a belief among Palestinian Jews that 'all Israelites have a share in the world to come' (Mishnah, *Sanhedrin* 10:1). But an alternative view is found in 4 Ezra 8:1 ('This age the Most High has made for many, but the age to come for few'). Compare 4 Ezra 8:3; 7:47; 9:15; 2 Apocalypse of Baruch 13:2; 18:1–2; 21:11; 44:15; 48:23, 45; 1QSa 2:5–22.

[161] The verb *agōnizomai* ('make every effort, strive') was commonly used for athletic contests (1 Corinthians 9:25) and fighting (John 18:36). In this context, it means holding fast to the teaching of Jesus and persevering in faithfulness to him (8:11–15; 9:23–6; 14:25–7). Compare Colossians 1:29; 4:12; 1 Timothy 4:10; 6:12; 2 Timothy 4:7.

[162] Matthew 7:21–4 is broadly parallel, speaking of many who prophesied, drove out demons and performed miracles in the name of Jesus.

ergatai adikias, 'all you workers of unrighteousness'; see Psalm 6:9 LXX). By turning away from him and his offer of salvation in the present, his contemporaries would show themselves to be unrighteous and bound for final judgment (see 12:5, 9).

28–30. The concluding warning moves beyond the wording of the parable. Those prevented from entering the kingdom will experience 'weeping there, and gnashing of teeth, when you see Abraham, Isaac and Jacob and all the prophets in the kingdom of God, but you yourselves thrown out'. Weeping and gnashing of teeth express regret and anger. Jesus's portrayal of hell is developed elsewhere with such images.[163] The reference to the patriarchs and prophets makes it clear that those immediately in view here are Israelites who failed to respond appropriately to Jesus and his ministry (see 12:54–6). They rejected the way of God proclaimed by John the Baptist and Jesus (7:29–35) and consequently could not enter into the eternal inheritance promised to Israel (10:10–15; 11:29–32, 47–52: 12:8–10). However, 'People will come from east and west and north and south, and will take their places at the feast in the kingdom of God.' This echoes Isaiah's prediction that God would one day 'prepare a feast of rich food for all peoples' (25:6; compare Isaiah 2:2).[164] Jesus anticipated the salvation of many from different lands, who would come to believe the gospel preached by his messengers and ultimately feast in the kingdom with him. The possibility of Gentiles being invited may be implied in 14:23 and is explicit in 24:47; Acts 1:8.[165] This salvation–historical perspective is reinforced by Jesus's concluding words about the great reversal to come: 'Indeed there are those who are last who will be first, and first who will be last' (see Acts 3:25–6; 13:46–7). Even as he warned his complacent and self-confident contemporaries about missing out on the kingdom, he indicated that many would be saved, thus answering the question in verse 23 in a positive way.

---

[163] In Matthew 13:42, 50; 24:51, these terms are associated with punishment, and in 8:12; 22:13; 25:30 with being thrown into darkness. *Gehenna* ('hell') is mentioned in Matthew 5:22, 29, 30; 10:28; 18:9; 23:15, 33; Mark 9:43, 45, 47; Luke 12:5; James 3:6.
[164] The notion of an eschatological banquet provided by God for his chosen ones is developed in Zephaniah 1:7; 1QSa 2:15–22; 1 Enoch 62:14; 2 Baruch 29:4; *Pirque 'Aboth* 3:20. Luke alludes to it again in 14:15; 22:16, 18, 29–30. See also Revelation 3:20; 19:9.
[165] Matthew 8:10–11 attaches this saying to Jesus's commendation of the Roman centurion's faith.

Jesus and the fate of Jerusalem (13:31–5)

Jesus' sorrow for Jerusalem

31 At that time some Pharisees came to Jesus and said to him, 'Leave this place and go somewhere else. Herod wants to kill you.'

32 He replied, 'Go and tell that fox, "I will keep on driving out demons and healing people today and tomorrow, and on the third day I will reach my goal." **33** In any case, I must press on today and tomorrow and the next day – for surely no prophet can die outside Jerusalem!

34 'Jerusalem, Jerusalem, you who kill the prophets and stone those sent to you, how often I have longed to gather your children together, as a hen gathers her chicks under her wings, and you were not willing. **35** Look, your house is left to you desolate. I tell you, you will not see me again until you say, "Blessed is he who comes in the name of the Lord."ᵃ'

_____

a 35 Psalm 118:26

31. As Fitzmyer observes, 'Precisely at the time when Jesus had warned his contemporaries that they would not be guaranteed access to the kingdom merely because of superficial acquaintance with him (13:26–8), he is warned about a contemporary's desire to do away with him.'[166] The chronological link is precise (*En autē tē hōra*, 'At that very hour' (ESV); see 10:21; 12:12; 20:19; 24:33). The warning is surprisingly given by 'some Pharisees' who were well disposed towards him. They came to Jesus and said, 'Leave this place and go somewhere else. Herod wants to kill you.' Herod Antipas, the tetrarch of Galilee (3:1), had already imprisoned John the Baptist (3:19–20) and put him to death (9:9). He was perplexed about the way people were evaluating Jesus and anxious about another prophet being in his region (9:7–9). The warning in 13:31 could suggest an escalation of Herod's anxieties, but when Jesus was arrested and they finally met (23:8–12), Herod no longer considered him to be a threat and treated him with contempt.

32. Jesus expressed no fear, though he indicated that he was aware of the danger confronting him. 'Go and tell that fox' is a rhetorical challenge rather than a specific instruction to report back his words to Herod.[167] Jesus would determine the course of his ministry, not Herod: 'I will keep on driving out demons and healing people today and tomorrow, and on

_____

[166] Fitzmyer, *Luke X–XXIV*, 1029. Luke alone records the incident in verses 31–3, but the prediction in verses 34–5 is paralleled in Matthew 23:37–9.
[167] 'That fox' implies that the tetrarch was crafty and deceitful (Bock, *Luke 9:51–24:53*, 1247).

the third day I will reach my goal.' His ministry of deliverance and healing would continue together with his preaching. The expression 'today and tomorrow' suggests a little while yet, but 'on the third day' points to a definite moment of conclusion.[168] Both NIV ('I will reach my goal') and ESV ('I finish my course') translate the verb *teleioumai* as middle voice. If it is understood as passive, however, it means that Jesus will be perfected by God as the one appointed to accomplish the salvation of his people ('I will be perfected'; see Hebrews 2:10; 5:9; 7:28).[169] The death of Jesus in Jerusalem would be the climax of God's will for his life and ministry (verse 33) and the pathway to heavenly glory for him (9:31, 51; 24:26, 51). He had already indicated that he was constrained until his baptism of suffering was 'completed' (12:50) and nothing would keep him from fulfilling the Father's plan (see 22:37).

33. The opening word of this verse (*plēn*) could suggest a strong contrast with the preceding one (ESV, 'Nevertheless'). However, NIV ('In any case') implies both continuity and a new dimension to the argument. With a slightly modified time reference ('today and tomorrow and the next day'), Jesus reaffirms the need for the journey he is on ('I must press on').[170] But the reason for this is expressed now in an ironic way: 'For surely no prophet can die outside Jerusalem!' The expression 'for surely' (*hoti ouk endechetai*, 'because it is not possible') invites agreement about Jerusalem's history of rejecting and killing God's prophets (6:23; 11:47–51; compare Jeremiah 2:30; Nehemiah 9:26; Acts 7:52).[171] Jesus anticipated such a fate as he went to proclaim the word of God there, although he later added more positive reasons for submitting to death in Jerusalem (22:15–38).

34–5. Speaking like a prophet, Jesus addressed Jerusalem in a soliloquy,

---

[168] Compare Exodus. 19:10–11; Hosea 6:2. Present tense verbs are used in Jesus's declaration to suggest a continuance of what he was doing into the future.

[169] Nolland, *Luke 9:21–18:34*, 740, translates 'I am finished'. When applied to people, however, the verb *teleioō* means 'make complete', 'fulfil', 'mature' or 'qualify'. Compare Herodotus 3.86; Sophocles, *Electra*, 1508–10; 4 Maccabees 7:15; Philippians 3:12.

[170] The 'third (day)' becomes 'the next' in verse 33, no longer making a sharp distinction from the first two days. The impersonal verb *dei* ('it is necessary') suggests a divine compulsion, as in 9:22 and elsewhere in the Gospel.

[171] Fitzmyer, *Luke X–XXIV*, 1032, notes the death of Uriah in Jerusalem (Jeremiah 26:20–23) and the threat on Jeremiah's life (38:4–6), but he acknowledges that Jewish reflections on this theme do not limit the killing of prophets to Jerusalem. The city 'stands as a cipher for Israel' in Jesus's warning (Green, *Luke*, 537).

accusing it of killing the prophets sent by God: 'Jerusalem, Jerusalem, you who kill the prophets and stone those sent to you.' A notable example of a prophet being stoned is given in 2 Chronicles 24:20–22, where blasphemy (Leviticus 24:14, 16, 23) or apostasy (Leviticus 20:2; Deuteronomy 13:6–10) may have been the charge. God's persistence in sending his prophets is then compared to the loving care of a hen for her chicks ('how often I have longed to gather your children together, as a hen gathers her chicks under her wings, and you were not willing').[172] Speaking from God's perspective, Jesus reviews the sad history of his dealings with Israel over many centuries. This would climax with his final visit to Jerusalem and end with God's judgment on the Temple, the city and its people ('Look, your house is left to you desolate'). 'House' is used comprehensively again in 19:41–4 in this way. Although the expression 'is left to you desolate' signifies that its fate is sealed,[173] the discourse in 21:5–24 indicates a period of time before this desolation takes place. Jesus's final visit to the capital would bring about his own removal from the scene (verse 33), until he returned as the glorified Messiah ('I tell you, you will not see me again until you say, "Blessed is he who comes in the name of the Lord."' The words of Psalm 118:26 (117:26 LXX) would soon be uttered by his disciples when they entered Jerusalem (19:37–8), but he speaks here of that greeting being ultimately used by all who would witness his triumphant return.

The Christology implicit in these utterances is remarkable, especially given that Jesus was in the presence of some Pharisees (verse 31). On the one hand, he identified with the God of Israel in his constant attempts to call his covenant people back to himself through the ministry of his prophets. On the other hand, he claimed to be the final prophet, whose rejection and death in Jerusalem would bring judgment on the city and its inhabitants. Put positively, his return in glory as Messiah and Son of Man would lead to a universal acknowledgement that he is the promised ruler and judge of all, who comes 'in the name of the Lord' (see 9:26; 12:40).

---

[172] Jerusalem is represented as 'mother' of her children in Isaiah 54:1–15. More than the literal inhabitants of the city, these included all who looked to her as 'mother'. God's care is likened to a bird's motherly protection in Deuteronomy 32:11; Ruth 2:12; Psalms 17:8; 36:7.
[173] Nolland, *Luke 9:21–18:34*, 742.

Anticipating the feast in the kingdom of God (14:1–24)

Jesus at a Pharisee's house

14 One Sabbath, when Jesus went to eat in the house of a prominent Pharisee, he was being carefully watched. **2** There in front of him was a man suffering from abnormal swelling of his body. **3** Jesus asked the Pharisees and experts in the law, 'Is it lawful to heal on the Sabbath or not?' **4** But they remained silent. So taking hold of the man, he healed him and sent him on his way.

5 Then he asked them, 'If one of you has a child**ᵃ** or an ox that falls into a well on the Sabbath day, will you not immediately pull it out?' **6** And they had nothing to say.

7 When he noticed how the guests picked the places of honour at the table, he told them this parable: **8** 'When someone invites you to a wedding feast, do not take the place of honour, for a person more distinguished than you may have been invited. **9** If so, the host who invited both of you will come and say to you, "Give this person your seat." Then, humiliated, you will have to take the least important place. **10** But when you are invited, take the lowest place, so that when your host comes, he will say to you, "Friend, move up to a better place." Then you will be honoured in the presence of all the other guests. **11** For all those who exalt themselves will be humbled, and those who humble themselves will be exalted.'

12 Then Jesus said to his host, 'When you give a luncheon or dinner, do not invite your friends, your brothers or sisters, your relatives, or your rich neighbours; if you do, they may invite you back and so you will be repaid. **13** But when you give a banquet, invite the poor, the crippled, the lame, the blind, **14** and you will be blessed. Although they cannot repay you, you will be repaid at the resurrection of the righteous.'

The parable of the great banquet

15 When one of those at the table with him heard this, he said to Jesus, 'Blessed is the one who will eat at the feast in the kingdom of God.'

16 Jesus replied: 'A certain man was preparing a great banquet and invited many guests. **17** At the time of the banquet he sent his servant to tell those who had been invited, "Come, for everything is now ready."

18 'But they all alike began to make excuses. The first said, "I have just bought a field, and I must go and see it. Please excuse me."

19 'Another said, "I have just bought five yoke of oxen, and I'm on my way to try them out. Please excuse me."

20 'Still another said, "I have just got married, so I can't come."

21 'The servant came back and reported this to his master. Then the owner of the house became angry and ordered his servant, "Go out quickly into the streets and alleys of the town and bring in the poor, the crippled, the blind and the lame."

22'"Sir," the servant said, "what you ordered has been done, but there is still room."

23'Then the master told his servant, "Go out to the roads and country lanes and compel them to come in, so that my house will be full. **24**I tell you, not one of those who were invited will get a taste of my banquet."'

_____

a 5 Some manuscripts *donkey*

1–4. Luke's third account of Jesus eating in the house of a Pharisee (see also 7:36; 11:37) identifies him as 'prominent' (*tinos tōn archontōn*, 'one of their rulers'). Since it was the Sabbath, Jesus 'was being carefully watched' (see 13:10–17).[174] No explanation is given for the presence of the man in front of Jesus who was suffering from 'abnormal swelling of his body' (*hydrōpikos*, 'dropsy' or 'edema').[175] He may have been an invited guest but, because Jesus 'healed him and sent him on his way', it appears that he was an intruder who had come to seek Jesus's help (see 7:37–8). In the eyes of the Pharisees, his chronic condition would not have justified breaking the Sabbath law to heal him.[176] As with the synagogue meeting in 6:6–11, Jesus took the initiative and asked the Pharisees and experts in the law, 'Is it lawful to heal on the Sabbath or not?' He knew that this would be an issue for them because of the presence of the man in need, but they were unwilling to engage him in debate and remained silent. 'So taking hold of the man, he healed him.'

5–6. Jesus asked a second question to justify his action and challenge his opponents to a more humane view: 'If one of you has a child or an ox that falls into a well on the Sabbath day, will you not immediately pull it out?' The incongruity of 'a child' (*huios*, 'son') being linked together with 'an ox' apparently led some early copyists to alter the first word to 'donkey' or 'sheep' (as in Matthew 12:11). But 'child' is the harder reading and better attested. A nearly contemporary document forbade the rescue of animals on the Sabbath: 'Let no one assist a beast in giving birth on the Sabbath day. Even if it drops (its newborn) into a cistern or into a pit, one is not to raise it up on the Sabbath.'[177] However, the rescue

[174] The verb used here (*paratēreō*) can take on the meaning 'watch maliciously, lie in wait for' (BDAG).

[175] This term refers to a serious fluid-retention problem, possibly indicative of 'congestive heart failure or kidney disease' (Green, *Luke*, 546).

[176] Structurally, Luke provides a sabbath healing here 'to match that in 13:10–17 and to alert his readers to the parallelism to come' (Nolland, *Luke 9:21–18:34*, 745).

[177] CD 11:13–14 (the Damascus Document among the DSS), translated by Fitzmyer,

of a child in such a circumstance would seem to be a clear obligation. Whatever the precise view of Jesus's critics was, they were unwilling to declare it or reply to either of his questions ('they had nothing to say').

7–11. Two further 'parables' were offered by Jesus, challenging the values and expectations of those gathered for this meal (see 13:18–21). Only the first is called a parable (verses 7–11), though the second is similar in character (verses 12–14). Both are in the form of wise advice, the second more clearly relating this to the ultimate judgment of God.[178] When Jesus noticed how the guests 'picked the places of honour at the table', he first commented on what *not* to do: 'When someone invites you to a wedding feast, do not take the place of honour, for a person more distinguished than you may have been invited.' The term 'wedding feast' (*gamos*, as in 12:36) prepares for the parable about 'a great banquet' (*deipnon mega*, verse 16), representing 'the feast in the kingdom of God' (verse 15). Since a host had the right to determine where people sat, he could come and say, 'Give this person your seat.' Then, humiliated, those invited would have to 'take the least important place'. Jesus's positive advice was, 'When you are invited, take the lowest place, so that when your host comes, he will say to you, "Friend, move up to a better place." Then you will be honoured in the presence of all the other guests.'[179] This is more than a reflection on appropriate behaviour at a human banquet, as indicated by the concluding saying ('For all those who exalt themselves will be humbled, and those who humble themselves will be exalted'). Passive verbs suggest the humbling and exalting activity of God. The deeper issue is how people relate to God (see 18:9–14; Matthew 23:11–12). The behaviour of some in the present may reveal that they are in for a shock when they are humbled before God in the future, but those who humble themselves before him now will be exalted when his kingdom comes. The theme of end-time reversal is also emphasised in 1:52–3; 6:21, 25; 10:15; 18:14.

12–14. Jesus's second piece of wise advice was specifically directed to

---

Luke X–XXIV, 1040. Fitzmyer notes that later rabbinic literature was less strict on this point.

[178] The parables of Jesus include wise sayings as well as simple comparisons (13:18–21), similitudes (15:3–10) and stories (15:11–32). See my comment on 8:4–8.

[179] Compare Proverbs 25:6–7. Green, *Luke*, 542, argues, 'Jesus transgresses Jewish and Greco–Roman dining conventions and reverses wider Mediterranean concerns with honor and shame because he is operating with his own, quite different set of "rules".'

'his host' (literally, 'the one who had invited him').[180] Once again, he used the context of a meal to illustrate the values of the kingdom of God and to urge his hearers to respond appropriately. This parable anticipates the picture of God calling a wide diversity of people to the feast in his kingdom (verses 16–24), but uses the example of an ordinary household meal ('When you give a luncheon or dinner').[181] Jesus provocatively began by detailing who should not be invited: 'do not invite your friends, your brothers or sisters, your relatives, or your rich neighbours; if you do, they may invite you back and so you will be repaid'. This challenged the conventional practice of using hospitality for personal advantage and reciprocity, rather than to express generosity and care for others.[182] Four groups should be invited instead: 'the poor, the crippled, the lame, the blind, and you will be blessed'. These are the sorts of people to whom Jesus ministered (7:22). The reward would not come from the guests themselves (because 'they cannot repay you'), but from God ('you will be repaid at the resurrection of the righteous'). Resurrection to eternal life would be the gracious gift of God, as the language of blessing implies (see 6:20–23). Jesus was addressing Pharisees who believed that God would resurrect the righteous to 'everlasting life', but others to 'shame and everlasting contempt' (Daniel 12:2; compare 2 Maccabees 7:9; Luke 12:5; 13:27; 20:34–6; Acts 23:6–8; 24:15). Jesus's point was that those who were truly righteous and bound for the kingdom would identify themselves in this life by humbling themselves (verse 11) and by acting like God with mercy towards the marginalised and needy (verse 13; see also 17:7–10).

15–17. One of those eating with Jesus responded to what he had just said about 'the resurrection of the righteous' by exclaiming, 'Blessed is the one who will eat at the feast in the kingdom of God.' Jesus answered by telling a parable that hinted at the significance of his own ministry in the fulfilment of God's kingdom plan.[183] 'A certain man was preparing a

---

[180] The word 'parable' is not used in verse 12, but the grammatical structure recalls verse 7 (*Elegen de kai*, 'he said also'), suggesting that a kingdom reference is also intended by this prudential advice.

[181] As in 11:37–8, the first term (*ariston*) refers to a noonday meal, whereas the second term (*deipnon*) refers to 'a main meal, taken toward evening' (Fitzmyer, *Luke X–XXIV*, 1047). The more general word for a 'banquet' (*dochē*) is used in verse 13.

[182] Green, *Luke*, 550, describes the gift-and-obligation system that tied every person in the Roman Empire into 'an intricate web of social relations'.

[183] A similar parable about 'a king who prepared a wedding banquet for his son' (Matthew 22:1–10) is given in the context of Jesus's ministry in Jerusalem and

great banquet [*deipnon mega*] and invited many guests. At the time of the banquet he sent his servant to tell those who had been invited, "Come, for everything is now ready."[184] This pattern of inviting guests and then calling them when the meal was prepared is reflected in Esther 5:8; 6:14. There may also be an echo of Proverbs 9:1–6 here, where Wisdom sends out her servants and calls those invited to come to the feast she has prepared for them. From a salvation–historical perspective, Jesus had been sent to tell those who had received the end-time promises of God that the blessings were now available to be enjoyed (see my comments on 13:28–30; 19:1–10).

18–21. Three last-minute reasons for not attending the meal are given, each of which has the same fundamental character ('they all alike began to make excuses').[185] Whether or not there was a legal obligation to inspect and approve his purchase before settlement, 'The first said, "I have just bought a field, and I must go and see it. Please excuse me."' Completing this transaction meant more to him than sharing in the special privilege of the banquet. 'Another said, "I have just bought five yoke of oxen, and I'm on my way to try them out. Please excuse me."' These animals would have been costly, but the man had paid for them without seeing them. Was it really an urgent necessity to try them out instead of enjoying the hospitality of his generous host? 'Still another said, "I have just got married, so I can't come."' This particularly recalls the provision of Deuteronomy 20:7; 24:5 and may explain why the man does not even bother to excuse himself. Although Jesus stressed the importance of honouring marital obligations, he prioritised the call to follow him and enter the kingdom of God (14:26). Each of these excuses demonstrated a preoccupation with worldly concerns and the offence of using them to reject God's gracious invitation to share eternal life with him.

22–3. The parable finishes with two more initiatives on the part of the master or owner of the house. When the servant came back and reported the excuses to him, 'the owner of the house became angry and ordered his servant, "Go out quickly into the streets and alleys of the town and

---

has a different conclusion (22:11–14). Nolland, *Luke 9:21–18:34*, 754, considers the possibility of a single source for both versions.

[184] The word *panta* ('all') appears to have been copied from Matthew 22:4 in later manuscripts. The shorter readings (*hetoima estin* and *hetoima eisin*, 'things are ready') are more likely to be original. See Marshall, *Luke*, 588; Metzger, *Textual Commentary*, 139.

[185] Fitzmyer, *Luke X–XXIV*, 1055, argues that *apo mias* ('from one') refers to a shared opinion.

bring in the poor, the crippled, the blind and the lame.'" These were the sorts of people whom Jesus said should be invited to a banquet (verse 13). Moreover, they were the sorts of people he ministered to (5:27–32; 7:22). When the servant returned and said to his master, 'What you ordered has been done, but there is still room,' then the master ordered, 'Go out to the roads and country lanes and compel them to come in, so that my house will be full.' This could refer to the offer of salvation to Diaspora Jews and Gentiles, as anticipated in passages such as Isaiah 2:2–3; 25:6; 43:5–7; 49:5–6 (compare Luke 13:28–9; Acts 13:44–8; Romans 15:8–12). However, the compulsion envisaged may still relate to a Palestinian context, embracing people who could not possibly reciprocate such an invitation because, as Green says, they belonged to 'an altogether alien social world, across social–religious barriers one simply did not cross'.[186] Above all, the master's desire that his house should be full reinforces the promise that many would ultimately feast in the kingdom of God (13:28–30).

24. Jesus's final words were an emphatic warning to the Pharisees and teachers of the law who were dining with him: 'I tell you, not one of those who were invited will get a taste of *my* banquet' (my emphasis).[187] Jesus identified himself with the owner of the house whose invitations had been rejected and referred to 'the feast in the kingdom of God' (verse 15) as *his* banquet (see 13:25–30)! By implication, those who refused his call to 'Come, for everything is now ready' (verse 17) would miss out on the ultimate blessing promised to God's faithful people (verse 15).

Counting the cost (14:25–35)

The cost of being a disciple

25 Large crowds were travelling with Jesus, and turning to them he said: 26 'If anyone comes to me and does not hate father and mother, wife and children, brothers and sisters – yes, even their own life – such a person cannot be my disciple. 27 And whoever does not carry their cross and follow me cannot be my disciple.

28 'Suppose one of you wants to build a tower. Won't you first sit down and estimate the cost to see if you have enough money to complete it? 29 For if you lay

---

[186] Green, *Luke*, 562. This reading of the parable supposes that the master is 'working from a transformed understanding of social relationships' (561), consistent with the teaching of Jesus in verses 7–14.

[187] This could refer to the practice of sending portions of food from a banquet to guests who were unable to come (Nehemiah 8:10–12). Even this courtesy will not be extended to those who have turned down the initial invitation (Marshall, *Luke*, 591)

the foundation and are not able to finish it, everyone who sees it will ridicule you, **30** saying, "This person began to build and wasn't able to finish."

31 'Or suppose a king is about to go to war against another king. Won't he first sit down and consider whether he is able with ten thousand men to oppose the one coming against him with twenty thousand? **32** If he is not able, he will send a delegation while the other is still a long way off and will ask for terms of peace. **33** In the same way, those of you who do not give up everything you have cannot be my disciples.

34 'Salt is good, but if it loses its saltiness, how can it be made salty again? **35** It is fit neither for the soil nor for the manure heap; it is thrown out.

'Whoever has ears to hear, let them hear.'

25–7. Once more, Luke draws attention to the journey motif (see 13:22, 31–3) and to the large crowds who were travelling with Jesus (see 12:1). 'Turning to them he said: "If anyone comes to me and does not hate father and mother, wife and children, brothers and sisters – yes, even their own life – such a person cannot be my disciple."' Although the preceding parable suggested that many would be invited to the feast in the kingdom of God, the saying here returns to the theme of entering by 'the narrow door' (13:24). Those who were attracted to Jesus and his teaching were confronted with the demands of genuine discipleship in three ways. The first was a willingness to put him before family (9:59–62), and even one's 'own life' (*tēn psychēn heautou*), which can refer to physical life (6:9; 12:20, 22, 23), inner life or self (1:46; 2:35; 10:27; 12:19), or both together (9:24; 14:26; 17:33; 21:19). Given Israel's understanding of the importance of honouring parents (Exodus 20:12) and nurturing children in the context of a believing family (Deuteronomy 6:7–9), this was radical teaching. Jesus made his challenge in the starkest possible way, using the word 'hate' rhetorically rather than literally.[188] This term was often used in Scripture to mean 'not love' (e.g., Genesis 29:30–33; Deuteronomy 21:15–17), with a focus on actions rather than psychological predisposition or feeling (Proverbs 13:24; Isaiah 60:15; Malachi 1:2–3). Like many of Jesus's parabolic stories and sayings, the aim was to alert his hearers to the urgency of the situation they faced and the priority of following him. Jesus himself illustrated what he meant by hating: Seccombe says,

---

[188] Bock, *Luke 9:51–24:53*, 1284. The parallel challenge to disciples in Matthew 10:37–8 reads 'loves more than me'. It is often argued that Matthew softened the harsh original found in Luke, but it is also possible that different versions of the same challenge were given by Jesus on different occasions.

'In "setting his face" to go to Jerusalem he was in effect turning his back on his obligation to his own kin, just as he was also setting himself in opposition to the demands of his own life.'[189]

As he faced the approaching crisis (13:31–3), Jesus summoned would-be disciples to join him with absolute loyalty and dedication. This was encapsulated in his call for them to carry their own cross, which meant self-denial to the point of being willing to suffer and die with him (verse 27; compare 9:23; 12:4–9). Following Jesus in that context meant more than being a learner, as in the ancient philosophical and rabbinic schools: it involved a life-threatening choice to follow him to Jerusalem. The third challenge (verse 33, 'those of you who do not give up everything you have cannot be my disciples') is discussed below. The situational nature of Jesus's demands at this stage in his ministry provided 'a paradigm of real discipleship', as Seccombe puts it.[190] Luke's second volume illustrates how the earliest believers responded to this call in their life together, when they faced persecution, the need for mutual care and support, and a shared dedication to gospel mission (e.g., Acts 2:42–7; 4:1–37; 11:19–30). Their example is a guide to applying his words in subsequent eras and contexts.

28–30. Two parabolic propositions unique to Luke's Gospel illustrate the need to count the cost of discipleship before making a commitment. Although they lack an explicit formula of comparison, such as, 'What is the kingdom of God like?' (13:18, 20), the concluding words in verse 33 make the point: 'In the same way, those of you who do not give up everything you have cannot be my disciples.' The first concerns a building project ('Suppose one of you wants to build a tower').[191] The wise builder will calculate the full cost before beginning ('Won't you first sit down and estimate the cost to see if you have enough money to complete it?'). Although the money, time and energy would be practically wasted if the project was never finished, Jesus highlights the shame factor: 'For if you lay the foundation and are not able to finish it, everyone who sees it will ridicule you, saying, "This person began to build and wasn't able to finish."'

31–2. The second proposition more distantly considers the example

---

[189] Seccombe, *The Poor*, 114. Compare Deuteronomy 33:9 (with its allusion to Exodus 32:27–9). Zeal for God puts family loyalties and other worldly concerns into perspective.

[190] Seccombe, *The Poor*, 121.

[191] 'Suppose one of you' translates *tis gar ex hymōn* ('which of you', as in 11:5, 11; 14:5; 17:7). Fitzmyer, *Luke X–XXIV*, 1065, suggests that Jesus envisages 'some sort of fortification to protect a house, land, or vineyard'.

of 'a king about to go to war against another king'. A wise king will consider whether he has the resources to defeat his enemy before going into battle ('Won't he first sit down and consider whether he is able with ten thousand men to oppose the one coming against him with twenty thousand?'). In this case, Jesus considers the broader consequences of defeat ('If he is not able, he will send a delegation while the other is still a long way off and will ask for terms of peace'). Humiliation and subjugation to an enemy power would be the result.

33. Jesus's application of the propositions in verses 28–32 is simple: 'In the same way, those of you who do not give up everything you have cannot be my disciples.' He focuses on material possessions, though the saying here could also function more broadly as a summary of verses 26–7. Jesus does not simply idealise an ascetic lifestyle, since his teaching in other contexts indicates the need for good stewardship of material resources and generous use of money and possessions (6:30–36; 12:32–4; 16:1–13). The verb translated 'give up' (*apotassetai*) could mean 'say farewell (to)' or 'renounce interest (in)' (BDAG). Nolland argues, 'The important thing in the present context is the need to be disencumbered (as in v. 26) in order to have the necessary freedom to live out the reality of discipleship.'[192]

34–5. The image of salt that has lost its saltiness provides a third warning about failed discipleship (in Mark 9:50 the image is applied differently). Salt was used in a variety of ways in the ancient world, and Jesus's claim that 'salt is good' could apply to any one of these. The notion that salt could lose its saltiness may simply be hypothetical for the sake of the argument ('how can it be made salty again?'), although various ways in which this could practically happen have been suggested.[193] Salt that has lost its saltiness would not even be fit for agricultural use ('neither for the soil nor for the manure heap; it is thrown out'). Disciples who lose their distinctive character and way of life can no longer serve God's purpose for them.

The practical implication of the three warnings is to pay careful attention to his teaching about the demands of discipleship ('Whoever has ears to hear, let them hear'). This saying appeared previously in connection with the parable of the seed and the soils (8:8b), before the reasons for failed discipleship are explained in some detail (8:11–15).

---

[192] Nolland, *Luke 9:21–18:34*, 764. Compare 8:14; 16:13–15; 18:22–5.
[193] Marshall, *Luke*, 596–7; Bock, *Luke 9:51–24:53*, 1290–91.

KNOWING GOD AND BEING KNOWN BY HIM

Jesus's proclamation of the kingdom of God, combined with his healing ministry and many calls to follow him, raised the question of how many would be saved and experience the ultimate blessings of the kingdom (13:22–3). Nolland observes how his first answer (13:24–30), in parallel with his teaching in 14:15–35, establishes 'a dialectic between human responsibility stressed here and the priority of God's grace and initiative'.[194] Jesus spoke of the narrowness of the way into the kingdom, the limited time before the door to the kingdom is shut, and the sovereign initiative of God in making himself known to those who would experience the messianic banquet with him (see 10:21–4).[195] But his call to 'make every effort to enter through the narrow door' (13:24) emphasised the need to heed his call and follow him into the kingdom. Put differently, Jesus challenged his listeners to respond appropriately to the knowledge of God he was imparting to them. His perspective on the Sabbath, his call for humility before God and generosity towards the poor and needy, and his challenge about putting him before family and personal life ambitions (14:1–14) led to warnings about exclusion from the feast in the kingdom of God (14:15–24) and counting the cost of discipleship (14:25–34). These challenges reach beyond the immediate context of his earthly ministry to address people in every culture who hear his invitation. Jesus links all this to the necessity of his death in Jerusalem, which will put in train God's judgment on everything that Jerusalem stood for (13:31–5; compare 9:21–2, 44; 12:49–53; 19:41–4), but also make possible the eternal salvation of those who believe in him (19:9–10; 23:42–3).

7. Seeking the lost (Luke 15:1–32)

Luke returns to a theme announced in 5:27–32 ('Now the tax collectors and sinners were all gathering round to hear Jesus') and indicates continuing opposition to this ministry ('But the Pharisees and the teachers of the law muttered, "This man welcomes sinners, and eats with them"'; see also 7:34). Jesus responded with three parables explaining why he cared

---

[194] Nolland, *Luke 9:21–18:34*, 734.

[195] God made himself known to the people of Israel so that they might acknowledge him and live in obedience to him (Deuteronomy 4:32–40). He also 'knew' or chose particular individuals and revealed himself to them, so that they might serve as leaders of his people (Genesis 18:19; Exodus 33:12; 2 Samuel 7:20–21; Jeremiah 1:5).

for such people: the stories of the lost sheep (verses 3–7), the lost coin (verses 8–10) and the lost sons (verses 11–32).[196] The first two prepare for the even more challenging and lengthy third one. It is likely that these parables were already linked together in the tradition that Luke received and that he placed them here to introduce a larger unit in his travel narrative extending to 19:10, showing 'God's concern for those human beings whom people tend to despise or condemn', as Fitzmyer says.[197]

Rejoicing in heaven and on earth (15:1–10)

The parable of the lost sheep

15 Now the tax collectors and sinners were all gathering round to hear Jesus. **2** But the Pharisees and the teachers of the law muttered, 'This man welcomes sinners, and eats with them.'

3 Then Jesus told them this parable: **4** 'Suppose one of you has a hundred sheep and loses one of them. Doesn't he leave the ninety-nine in the open country and go after the lost sheep until he finds it? **5** And when he finds it, he joyfully puts it on his shoulders **6** and goes home. Then he calls his friends and neighbours together and says, "Rejoice with me; I have found my lost sheep." **7** I tell you that in the same way there will be more rejoicing in heaven over one sinner who repents than over ninety-nine righteous people who do not need to repent.

The parable of the lost coin

8 'Or suppose a woman has ten silver coins[a] and loses one. Doesn't she light a lamp, sweep the house and search carefully until she finds it? **9** And when she finds it, she calls her friends and neighbours together and says, "Rejoice with me; I have found my lost coin." **10** In the same way, I tell you, there is rejoicing in the presence of the angels of God over one sinner who repents.'

---

a 8 Greek *ten drachmas*, each worth about a day's wages

1–6. Jesus's first response to the grumbling Pharisees and teachers of the law is a similitude, narrating a typical human situation that points to God's joy when one sinner repents (verse 7). This story about a moderately rich shepherd is coupled with a similar story about a poor woman

---

[196] See my comment on 8:4–8 regarding the different forms of 'parable' used by Jesus.
[197] Fitzmyer, *Luke X–XXIV*, 1072. Fitzmyer does not consider that these parables were originally uttered together and discusses the different form of the first parable in Matthew 18:12–14 (applied to wandering disciples). Contrast Nolland, *Luke 9:21–18:34*, 769–70.

LUKE

(compare the parables about a man and a woman in 13:18–21). Since God is portrayed in the Old Testament as the shepherd of his people (Psalm 23:1–3; Isaiah 40:11; Ezekiel 34:11–16), Jesus's use of the first story to justify his own ministry is a way of identifying with God's concern to seek and to save the lost.[198] The word 'lost' occurs seven times in this chapter (verses 4, 6, 8, 9, 17, 24, 32) and is obviously a key theme (see 19:10). Losing one of a hundred sheep 'in the open country' would not have been difficult, but the shepherd's response is exemplary: 'Doesn't he leave the ninety-nine in the open country and go after the lost sheep until he finds it?' Presumably the ninety-nine were left in the care of others. When he finds the lost sheep, Jesus imagines that 'he joyfully puts it on his shoulders and goes home. Then he calls his friends together and says, "Rejoice with me; I have found my lost sheep."' The note of shared joy is picked up in verses 7, 9, 10, 32 ('be glad'), extending to feasting and celebration in verse 22–4, 32.

7. Jesus then applied his similitude to the issue raised by his opponents: 'I tell you that in the same way there will be more rejoicing in heaven over one sinner who repents than over ninety-nine righteous people who do not need to repent.' This echoes his claim in 5:32 ('I have not come to call the righteous, but sinners to repentance'). Those who are truly 'righteous' are spiritually healthy and do not need the kind of radical reorientation of their lives that 'sinners' do.[199] Paradoxically, however, even righteous Israelites were drawn to Jesus, as they came to recognise who he was (2:25–38; 23:50–58; 24:13–35). His welcoming attitude did not condone sinful behaviour, but he offered everyone the opportunity to repent and be forgiven. 'Rejoicing in heaven' is a way of saying that repentance brings joy to God (angels are included in verse 10). Consequently, God's people on earth should share the joy of heaven when someone turns to Jesus for salvation!

8–10. Jesus's second example (which is only found in this Gospel) has the same structure and message as the previous similitude. It begins with a loss ('a woman has ten silver coins and loses one'),[200] continues with

---

[198] However, Nolland, *Luke 9:21–18:34*, 771, thinks the OT background is only significant in 'the move from the story world to the world of application and needs to be kept strictly out of sight as we seek to identify the inner dynamic of the story'.
[199] It is possible that the term 'righteous' is used ironically here and in 5:32 with reference to Jesus's opponents (see also 18:9–14).
[200] 'Silver coin' translates *drachmē*, the value of which diminished considerably over time (Fitzmyer, *Luke X–XXIV*, 1081). For a poor woman it would certainly have been a significant loss, perhaps a day's wages (Green, *Luke*, 576).

288

a careful search ('Doesn't she light a lamp, sweep the house and search carefully until she finds it?') and concludes with an invitation for others (in this case, female friends, *philai*) to rejoice ('And when she finds it, she calls her friends and neighbours together and says, "Rejoice with me; I have found my lost coin"). Jesus's pronouncement is briefer, because he makes no comparison between the single coin and the nine others, but the application is the same ('In the same way, I tell you, there is rejoicing in the presence of the angels of God over one sinner who repents'). This similitude is given to reinforce the message of the previous one, that those who truly know God will seek for the lost as he does and rejoice with him when they are found.[201]

Welcoming them home (15:11–32)

The parable of the lost son

11 Jesus continued: 'There was a man who had two sons. **12** The younger one said to his father, "Father, give me my share of the estate." So he divided his property between them.

13 'Not long after that, the younger son got together all he had, set off for a distant country and there squandered his wealth in wild living. **14** After he had spent everything, there was a severe famine in that whole country, and he began to be in need. **15** So he went and hired himself out to a citizen of that country, who sent him to his fields to feed pigs. **16** He longed to fill his stomach with the pods that the pigs were eating, but no one gave him anything.

17 'When he came to his senses, he said, "How many of my father's hired servants have food to spare, and here I am starving to death! **18** I will set out and go back to my father and say to him: Father, I have sinned against heaven and against you. **19** I am no longer worthy to be called your son; make me like one of your hired servants." **20** So he got up and went to his father.

'But while he was still a long way off, his father saw him and was filled with compassion for him; he ran to his son, threw his arms round him and kissed him.

21 'The son said to him, "Father, I have sinned against heaven and against you. I am no longer worthy to be called your son."

22 'But the father said to his servants, "Quick! Bring the best robe and put it on him. Put a ring on his finger and sandals on his feet. **23** Bring the

---

[201] Isaak, 'Luke', 1259–61, offers an extensive reflection on what it might mean to seek for the lost in the complexities of African culture today. This provides a model for people in other cultures to consider what it might mean for them to be moved to action by these parables.

fattened calf and kill it. Let's have a feast and celebrate. 24 For this son of mine was dead and is alive again; he was lost and is found." So they began to celebrate.

25 'Meanwhile, the elder son was in the field. When he came near the house, he heard music and dancing. 26 So he called one of the servants and asked him what was going on. 27 "Your brother has come," he replied, "and your father has killed the fattened calf because he has him back safe and sound."

28 'The elder brother became angry and refused to go in. So his father went out and pleaded with him. 29 But he answered his father, "Look! All these years I've been slaving for you and never disobeyed your orders. Yet you never gave me even a young goat so I could celebrate with my friends. 30 But when this son of yours who has squandered your property with prostitutes comes home, you kill the fattened calf for him!"

31 ' "My son," the father said, "you are always with me, and everything I have is yours. 32 But we had to celebrate and be glad, because this brother of yours was dead and is alive again; he was lost and is found." '

11–12. Jesus's third similitude is often called 'the parable of the prodigal son' (Luke only), though it tells of *two* lost sons. The first part of the story (verses 11–24) broadly follows the structure of the preceding parables, though the focus in verses 17–19 is on the younger son's repentance rather than on the father's search for him. There is also an escalation of loss from one sheep in a hundred to one coin in ten and then to one of only two sons.[202] The second part (verses 25–32) focuses on the resentment of the older son and his unwillingness to rejoice with his father over the return of his brother. Jesus most tellingly challenges the attitude of the Pharisees and teachers of the law, who cannot rejoice when sinners genuinely repent (verse 2). Despite these developments, and even though it is 'a two-peaked parable', Fitzmyer contends that 'the central figure in it is the father'.[203] Jesus points to the unconditional love of God in welcoming home repentant sinners and identifies himself with God by the manner of his ministry.

The main characters are briefly introduced ('There was a man who had two sons') and the request of the younger son is simply stated ('Father, give me my share of the estate'; *ousia*, 'means of living'). A Jewish father would normally dispose of his property by a will to be executed after

---

[202] Green, *Luke*, 578.

[203] Fitzmyer, *Luke X–XXIV*, 1085. Hence the title and focus of Helmut Thielicke, *The Waiting Father: Sermons on the Parables of Jesus* (London: James Clarke, 1966).

his death (Numbers 27:8–11; 36:7–9). The possibility that he might divide his estate before his death is reflected in Tobit 8:21 and Sirach 33:19–23 (where it is advised against). The Mishnah also allowed for this, but it gives no hint that a father could make such a disposition under pressure from a younger son.[204] In short, Jesus imagines an extreme situation that would make the Pharisees shake their heads in dismay! The younger son's request was disrespectful, arrogant and simply designed to enable a self-indulgent life. Nevertheless, his father graciously divided his 'property' (*bios*, 'means of living', as in verse 30) between his sons, showing extraordinary love. After doing this, he might have expected to continue benefiting from the produce of the transferred land.

13–16. 'Not long after that,' however, 'the younger son got together all he had.' Perhaps he converted his inheritance into cash, though the purchaser may not have been able take possession of that portion of the property until the father died. Separating himself from his father as much as he could, he 'set off for a distant country', and there he 'squandered his wealth in wild living' (*zōn asōtōs*, 'living wastefully' or 'prodigally').[205] In this way, he further disgraced his father (Proverbs 28:7). 'After he had spent everything, there was a severe famine in that whole country, and he began to be in need.' So he humbled himself and 'went and hired himself out to a citizen of that country, who sent him to his fields to feed pigs.' Since pigs were considered unclean in Jewish law (Leviticus 11:7; Deuteronomy 14:8) and he was working for a Gentile in a foreign country, his alienation from God and his people was complete. Moreover, he was so hungry that 'he longed to fill his stomach with the pods that the pigs were eating'.[206] When he tried begging for help in the midst of the famine, 'no one gave him anything'. He was trapped in a death spiral.

17–19. The younger son's return to his father began when he 'came to his senses' (*eis heauton de elthōn*, 'when he came to himself'). He acknowledged the foolishness that had led him into such a dire situation ('How many of my father's hired servants have food to spare, and here I am starving to death!') and the need to go back to his father with genuine remorse. He would confess his sin against God ('heaven' as in

---

[204] Bailey, *Poet and Peasant*, 163–4. Compare Nolland, *Luke 9:21–18:34*, 782–3.

[205] The verb translated 'squandered' (*diaskorpizō*) is normally used with the meaning 'scatter, disperse' (BDAG). Another verb is translated 'squandered' in verse 30. Compare 16:1.

[206] Bailey, *Poet and Peasant*, 173, argues that the wild carob is in view here, which is 'more of a shrub, and pigs could grub for its berries. It *can* be eaten by humans, but is bitter and without nourishment.'

Daniel 4:26) and his earthly father ('Father, I have sinned against heaven and against you') and ask to be received back home in a menial role ('I am no longer worthy to be called your son; make me like one of your hired servants'). A hired servant or day-labourer lived a very insecure life, as Green says, 'vulnerable to the full range of natural forces, the seasonal needs of the production of crops, and the whims of the estate manager'.[207]

20–21. The younger son got up and went to his father, taking the first practical step of repentance. 'But while he was still a long way off, his father saw him and was filled with compassion for him.'[208] The father was ready to welcome him back and expressed unconditional forgiveness when he 'ran to his son, threw his arms round him and kissed him' (see Genesis 33:4; 45:14–15; 2 Samuel 14:33). The genuineness of the son's repentance is stressed by the repetition of the words he had prepared to say ('Father, I have sinned against heaven and against you. I am no longer worthy to be called your son'), but the father interrupted him before he finished. The son may have felt unworthy to be called his son, but the father signified by his actions that he had truly, in Nolland's words, 'regained a son'.[209]

22–4. The father's instruction to his servants begins the application that Jesus makes to his hearers (see verses 31–2). The first ('Bring the best robe and put it on him. Put a ring on his finger and sandals on his feet') meant that the prodigal should be treated as a much-loved son, not in the lowly way he asked to be treated (see Genesis 41:42; Esther 6:6–11; 8:2). The second ('Bring the fattened calf and kill it. Let's have a feast and celebrate', compare Genesis 18:7–8; 1 Samuel 28:24–5) meant, 'Let's have a sumptuous welcome home and rejoice together at his return!' This acknowledged the son's deliverance from physical, moral and spiritual alienation: 'For this son of mine was dead and is alive again; he was lost and is found.' The young man never stopped being the father's son, even when his behaviour indicated otherwise, but his condition showed the need for the sort of comprehensive rescue that God was providing

---

[207] Green, *Luke*, 581. Bailey, *Poet and Peasant*, 173–9, questions the son's sincerity and detects continuing pride in his bid to become an independent employee, but Nolland, *Luke 9:21–18:34*, 784, rightly argues against this.

[208] The same verb *esplagchnisthē* in 7:13 is translated 'his heart went out to her' and in 10:33 'he took pity on him'. God's yearning and compassion for disobedient Israel is an interesting parallel in Jeremiah 31:20.

[209] Nolland, *Luke 9:21–18:34*, 785. Some manuscripts have the full form of the confession in verses 18–19 repeated in verse 21, but the shorter reading in verse 21 is intrinsically more likely to be original here.

through Jesus.[210] A full account of God's plan of salvation is not given here, but Luke portrays the dramatic change in the lives of 'tax collectors and sinners' who came to Jesus with repentance and faith (climactically, 19:1–10: Zacchaeus was 'a son of Abraham' who was 'lost'). He also illustrates the sort of welcome they should receive ('they began to celebrate'), emphasising shared joy (as in verses 5–6) in the context of feasting.[211]

25–7. 'The elder son' becomes the focus in the second part of the parable. He is first located 'in the field', suggesting that he had been diligently working for his father in the absence of his brother. But 'when he came near the house, he heard music and dancing',[212] which was doubtless a rare sound since his brother had gone away. 'So he called one of the servants and asked him what was going on. "Your brother has come," he replied, "and your father has killed the fattened calf because he has him back safe and sound."' This servant reflected the father's perspective when he described the younger brother as 'safe and sound' ('healthy', as in 5:31).

28–30. 'The elder brother became angry and refused to go in. So his father went out and pleaded with him.' The anger of this son contrasts with the compassion of his father, who showed love for both sons in different ways (see verse 20). The older son answered his father, 'All these years I've been slaving for you and never disobeyed your orders.' The verb 'slave' (*douleuō*) could express willing obedience to parents (Sirach 3:7), but contextually it suggests resentment at being in such a constrained role (see Genesis 31:41).[213] This is clarified when he says, 'You never gave me even a young goat so I could celebrate with my friends.' The implication is that such loyal service demanded some recognition and reward from his father (see Matthew 20:11–12). He accuses his father of unfairly favouring

---

[210] Nolland, *Luke 9:21–18:34*, 786, observes that, while the language here does not 'actually break the bounds of the story, it comes closer to being immediately symbolic than at other points of the parable'. In other words, a spiritual significance is indicated.

[211] A different verb for rejoicing (*euphrainō*) is introduced in verses 23, 24, 32, which is often used with the particular sense of 'observe a special occasion with festivity, celebrate' (BDAG).

[212] The word *symphōnia* can refer to 'the sound produced by several instruments, music' or 'a group of performing musicians, band', or specifically 'a wind instrument' (BDAG). The word *choros* can refer to a group of singers or dancers or 'rhythmic movements to the accompaniment of music, (choral) dance' (BDAG).

[213] The related noun (*doulos*) is regularly used for a household servant (7:2; 12:37; 14:17; 17:7–10) and the image is easily applied to believers (2:29). The verb is used again in 16:13 in relation to serving God or Money.

his younger brother: 'But when this son of yours who has squandered your property with prostitutes comes home, you kill the fattened calf for him!' He scornfully identifies his brother as 'this son of yours', perhaps implying that he is no true son, and describes him as having literally 'devoured your living' (*kataphagōn sou ton bion*), meaning that he has wasted a significant portion of his father's means of subsistence.[214] The reference to 'prostitutes' specifically defines how he squandered his father's wealth in 'wild living' (verse 13; compare Proverbs 29:3b).

31–2. Despite the elder brother's resentful words, the father continued to address him affectionately ('My son'; *teknon*, 'child') and to assure him that nothing had changed in their relationship ('You are always with me'). In the custom of the day, when his father died, what remained of the property after one-third had been given to his younger brother would be his ('and everything I have is yours').[215] But what mattered most was the restoration of his brother to the life of the family and to God: 'But we had to celebrate and be glad, because this brother of yours was dead and is alive again; he was lost and is found.' The need for outward and inner expressions of joy is stressed again, as the father repeats what was said to his servants in verses 23–4. A gentle rebuke is implied by 'this brother of yours' (see 'this son of yours,' verse 30): his only brother had effectively been brought back to life!

LOVING AS GOD DOES

The third parable in this sequence has been applied in different ways. Isaak follows the tradition of focusing on 'the waiting, running, embracing, kissing and partying One who has compassion for the lost who are *still a long way off* (15:20) and for those who have always been near (15:31)'.[216] Nolland gives attention to both sons as well as to the father, particularly expounding the implications for Jesus's opponents and those like them: 'Their inheritance is undisturbed. But they should not imagine that they have a claim upon God that excludes others. Nor should they imagine that their faithful efforts place God in their debt (see 17:7–10), or oblige

---

[214] BDAG, *bios* (compare 21:4, 'all she had to live on'). This word parallels *ousia* ('means of living') in 15:12 (NIV 'property'). Green, *Luke*, 584–5, outlines the ways in which the elder brother acted outside cultural norms and offended his father.
[215] Fitzmyer, *Luke X–XXIV*, 1087, notes that 'the firstborn son was to inherit or receive a "double portion" i.e. twice the amount that would be given to each of the other sons. See Deut. 21:17. In this case, since there were only two sons, the elder would receive two thirds and the younger one third.'
[216] Isaak, 'Luke', 1262 (author's emphasis).

him to give them some distinctive recognition.'[217] In its immediate context, the conclusion to this parable offers a challenge to anyone who claims to be a child of God yet does not have God's heart for the lost, resisting the need to share the gospel with others or being reluctant to welcome into the fellowship of believers those who genuinely turn to Christ. But does the extravagance of the language in verses 24 and 32 further suggest a connection between the younger son and Jesus? Peter Baker observes, 'The re-reader, who already knows how the narrative of Luke's Gospel will end, can hardly fail to be struck by the mention of a son who was dead and is alive.'[218] Those who have turned away from God find repentance, forgiveness and salvation through the incarnation, death and resurrection of this Son. He was prodigal in his love for sinners, but not in condoning their sinfulness.

8. Prudent and compassionate use of wealth (Luke 16:1–31)

Two lengthy stories about the use of wealth occupy most of this chapter and are found only in this Gospel. The parable of the dishonest manager (verses 1–8a) is followed by three applications for disciples (verses 8b–13).[219] The parable of the rich man and Lazarus (verses 19–31) concludes the chapter without further comment from Jesus. In between, however, there are sayings addressed to the Pharisees (verses 14–18, compare Matthew 11:12–13; 5:18, 31–2), which suggest that the second parable was specifically directed at them.

Worldly wisdom and the kingdom of God (16:1–13)

The parable of the shrewd manager

16 Jesus told his disciples: 'There was a rich man whose manager was accused of wasting his possessions. **2** So he called him in and asked him, "What is this I hear about you? Give an account of your management, because you cannot be manager any longer."

---

[217] Nolland, *Luke 9:21–18:34*, 788–9. Jesus is more generous to the Pharisees and teachers of the law than might have been expected.

[218] Peter Baker, 'The Prodigal Returns? Karl Barth's Christological Interpretation of Luke 15:11–32', *Journal of Theological Interpretation* 16 (2022), 57–73 (70).

[219] Fitzmyer, *Luke X–XXIV*, 1096–7, assesses four different views of where the parable ends and the applications begin, arguing for verse 8a to be the conclusion of the parabolic story.

3 'The manager said to himself, "What shall I do now? My master is taking away my job. I'm not strong enough to dig, and I'm ashamed to beg – **4** I know what I'll do so that, when I lose my job here, people will welcome me into their houses."

5 'So he called in each one of his master's debtors. He asked the first, "How much do you owe my master?"

6 ' "Three thousand litres of olive oil," he replied.

'The manager told him, "Take your bill, sit down quickly, and make it fifteen hundred."

7 'Then he asked the second, "And how much do you owe?"

' "Thirty tons of wheat," he replied.

'He told him, "Take your bill and make it twenty-four."

8 'The master commended the dishonest manager because he had acted shrewdly. For the people of this world are more shrewd in dealing with their own kind than are the people of the light. **9** I tell you, use worldly wealth to gain friends for yourselves, so that when it is gone, you will be welcomed into eternal dwellings.

10 'Whoever can be trusted with very little can also be trusted with much, and whoever is dishonest with very little will also be dishonest with much. **11** So if you have not been trustworthy in handling worldly wealth, who will trust you with true riches? **12** And if you have not been trustworthy with someone else's property, who will give you property of your own?

13 'No one can serve two masters. Either you will hate the one and love the other, or you will be devoted to the one and despise the other. You cannot serve both God and Money.'

1–2. Jesus turns his attention to his disciples again, continuing to develop the theme of faithfully employing material wealth (12:13–21, 32–4; 14:25–7). Two main characters are introduced in this parabolic story: 'a rich man' and his 'manager' (*oikonomos*).[220] The manager was accused of 'wasting' his master's possessions (*diaskorpizōn*, as in 15:13). Since he is later called 'the dishonest manager' (verse 8), this waste most likely involved a deceitful action such as 'siphoning off funds for his own consumption from transactions made in the name of the master', as Nolland proposes.[221] The master called him in and asked him, 'What is this I hear about you? Give an account of your management, because you cannot be manager any longer.' 'Give an account' in this context means, 'Give me a record of the transactions you have made on my behalf' (see the use of this expression in Matthew 12:36).

---

[220] Such a manager or steward was often a slave born in the household, 'who was especially trained and tested in the supervision of a farm-estate' (Fitzmyer, *Luke X–XXIV*, 1099). See O. Michel, 'οἰκονόμος', *TDNT* 5:149–50.
[221] Nolland, *Luke 9:21–18:34*, 797.

3–4 'The manager said to himself, "What shall I do now? My Master is taking away my job. I'm not strong enough to dig, and I am ashamed to beg – I know what I'll do so that, when I lose my job here, people will welcome me into their houses."'[222] With the loss of his position, he would have no income or place to live. But by shrewdly settling accounts with his master's debtors, he would become their benefactor and could be welcomed as a guest 'into their houses'. Jesus previously used a soliloquy like this to reveal someone's thoughts in 12:17–19, 45; 15:17–19.

5–6. 'So he called in each one of his master's debtors,' though only two are mentioned by way of example. Marshall suggests that these debtors were 'merchants who had received goods on credit from the estate and had given promissory notes in their own handwriting' (Philemon 18).[223] In each case the manager asked, 'How much do you owe my master?' The first one answered, 'Three thousand litres of olive oil,' and the manager told him, 'Take your bill, sit down quickly, and make it fifteen hundred.' Since there is uncertainty about the contemporary equivalents of these measures, it is better to translate more literally 'a hundred measures of oil' and 'fifty' (ESV).[224] 'Take your bill' could refer to a promissory note or an IOU.[225] The manager was not cheating his master by making this generous settlement, because the master went on to commend him for this action (verse 8). The debtor strictly owed the master for the supply of fifty 'baths' of oil: the other fifty could either be described as 'interest' or 'the manager's commission'.[226] Depriving himself of the amount he may have expected to keep for himself, the manager acted shrewdly, making sure that his master received what was owed to him before leaving his employ.

7. The second illustration ('thirty tons of wheat') involved interest or

---

[222] The Greek (*aphaireitai tēn oikonomian ap' emou*) is more literally rendered 'taking the management away from me' (ESV).

[223] Marshall, *Luke*, 618. He observes, 'The bills may have been for the receipt of the goods specified, or they may have been for amounts of money that had been restated in terms of amounts of oil and wheat, so as to get round the Jewish laws on usury.' Compare Nolland, *Luke 9:21–18:34*, 798–9.

[224] 'A hundred baths of oil' may have been about 900 US gallons, equating to roughly 3,300 litres. This would be the yield of 'nearly 150 olive trees' (Bock, *Luke 9:51–24:53*, 1331).

[225] Josephus, *Antiquities* 18:6.3.

[226] Marshall, *Luke*, 619, argues for interest, while Fitzmyer, *Luke X–XXIV*, 1101, argues for commission. Jesus presumably mentioned interest or commission of 100 per cent to emphasise what the manager had to forgo.

a commission of 25 per cent, making possible a smaller reduction in the amount owed ('Take your bill and make it twenty-four'). Since there is debate about the volume of 'a hundred kor of wheat', it would be better to translate 'a hundred measures of wheat' and 'eighty' (ESV) to preserve the proportions in the original text.[227]

8. The story ends with the statement, 'The master commended the dishonest manager because he had acted shrewdly [*phronimōs*].' Although some have argued that the master refers to Jesus, more likely this is the rich man expressing his approval of the actions of his manager, who is nevertheless described as 'dishonest' (*adikia*, 'unjust'). In worldly terms, his actions were prudent or wise in dealing with the crisis caused by his own unrighteousness. Only in a limited way is he 'a model for the Christian disciple faced with the crisis which Jesus's kingdom/judgment preaching brings into his/her life', as Fitzmyer puts it.[228] Jesus began to clarify this with his first application of the parable. The unjust manager was typical of 'the people of this world' (*hoi huioi tou aiōnos toutou*, 'the sons of this age'), who are shrewder than 'the people of the light' in dealing with 'their own kind' (*genea*, 'generation'). Robert Brawley discerns, 'All of the personages in the parable – the rich man, the manager and the three debtors – are players in the extractive system of "this age".'[229] Those who live without the hope of eternal life have clever ways of establishing beneficial relationships and securing their wellbeing in this world. The specific lesson for Christian disciples is developed in the next saying.

9. Addressing his disciples directly ('I tell you'), Jesus continued to make the connection between wealth and relationships ('use worldly wealth to gain friends for yourselves'). The NIV 'worldly wealth' translates *mamōna tēs adikia* ('mammon of unrighteousness'), which means that material wealth belongs to the realm of unrighteousness,[230] but it can be used to make friends

---

[227] In earlier times, a hundred kor might have amounted to 4,000 litres, but Josephus records a later standard that may have been in view here, equivalent to almost 40,000 litres or forty tons (Bock, *Luke 9:51–24:53*, 1331).

[228] Fitzmyer, *Luke X–XXIV*, 1102. Against Fitzmyer, 1105, the first application by Jesus (verses 8b–9) is intimately linked with the language and sense of the parable and need not be a later addition.

[229] Robert L. Brawley, *Luke: A Social Identity Commentary* (London; New York: Clark, 2020), 153. Similar expressions in the DSS are used to differentiate outsiders from insiders, unbelievers from believers (Fitzmyer, *Luke X–XXIV*, 1108). See also Luke 20:34–6; John 12:36; Ephesians 5:8; 1 Thessalonians 5:5.

[230] 'Mammon' is formed from an Aramaic word, possibly originally meaning 'that in which one puts one's trust', and so 'wealth' (F. Hauck, 'μαμωνᾶς', *TDNT* 4:388–90).

for eternity. Jesus's saying develops the idea that possessions can be sold and given to the poor as a way of securing 'a treasure in heaven that will never fail' (12:33). This does not mean earning your way to eternal life by generous giving! Luke earlier mentioned another use of wealth by the women who were helping to support the mission of Jesus and the Twelve 'out of their own means' (8:3). Care for the poor and needy and generosity towards those engaged in frontline gospel work will gain friends who cannot pay you back. Seccombe observes that disciples cannot 'separate themselves from the realm of evil and establish a community with its own internal system of purified mammon', but they can convert their money and possessions into 'the kind of wealth which is appropriate to the Kingdom of God'.[231]

The end-time significance of this is revealed when Jesus says, 'so that when [worldly wealth] is gone, you will be welcomed into eternal dwellings'. The NIV translates the verb *dexōntai* as passive ('You will be welcomed'), which could be a circumlocution for God. However, understood as middle voice (ESV, 'they may receive you'), the verb indicates that friends gained though such generosity may be there to welcome you into the kingdom, here represented as 'eternal dwellings'. Although the parable reflects the Graeco–Roman expectation of reciprocity for good deeds done to another, this is not explicit in the application. The kingdom is God's gift, and the servants of the kingdom should act with similar grace towards those in need. Seccombe concludes, 'Value in the new age is measured in terms of relationships, and those who belong to it must begin to accumulate that sort of wealth now.'[232]

10–11. Jesus's third application begins with the need for faithfulness in stewardship: 'Whoever can be trusted with very little can also be trusted with much' (see 12:42; 19:17; 1 Corinthians 4:2). The parallel claim ('whoever is dishonest [*adikos*, 'unjust' or 'unrighteous'] with very little will also be dishonest with much') recalls the example of the dishonest manager. Disciples are encouraged to break the cycle of greed that is endemic in human life and prove trustworthy with everything they are given. Jesus then moves the focus from faithfulness with money and possessions to being entrusted with something else: 'So if you have not been trustworthy in handling worldly wealth' ('mammon', as in verse 9), 'who will trust you with true riches?' It is tempting to think of 'the true riches' (*to alēthinon*, 'the real thing') as the gospel entrusted to Jesus's disciples (9:2, 6; 10:8–12), but the future tense suggests that the thought

---

[231] Seccombe, *The Poor*, 172.
[232] Seccombe, *The Poor*, 178.

is 'of the bestowal of heavenly treasure in the age to come', as Marshall suggests.[233] Disciples confirm and express their eternal hope by the way they handle money and possessions in the present (12:22–4).

12. The same point is made with different imagery: 'And if you have not been trustworthy with someone else's property, who will give you property of your own?' 'Someone else's property' most likely refers to temporal blessings given by God, which disciples must use appropriately in this life. 'Property of your own' will then be a way of speaking about the heavenly treasure, which will be, in Marshall's words, 'their own inalienable possession'.[234] The faithful will share a portion of the inheritance that God will give to all who enter his eternal kingdom.

13. Jesus's final challenge in this sequence is paralleled in Matthew 6:24 ('No one can serve two masters'), making a clear link with the parable in verses 1–8a.[235] This general principle is applied with two parallel predictions: 'Either you will hate the one and love the other, or you will be devoted to the one and despise the other.' The verb 'hate' is used rhetorically in parallel with 'despise', while 'love' is paralleled with 'be devoted'. Mammon is a potential rival for God, because the love of money can master us (see 1 Timothy 6:9–10). As in 14:26, emotive language is used to describe the choice of one lifestyle or commitment over another. A genuine love for God will mean devoted service to him in preference to the pursuit and enjoyment of material wealth and pleasure. Enslavement to the latter engenders a practical hatred or rejection of God (as illustrated in verses 19–31), even if God is merely treated with indifference. 'You cannot serve both God and Money' (*mammon*, as in verses 9, 11).

Challenging the lovers of money (16:14–18)

14 The Pharisees, who loved money, heard all this and were sneering at Jesus. **15** He said to them, 'You are the ones who justify yourselves in the eyes of others, but God knows your hearts. What people value highly is detestable in God's sight.

Additional teachings

16 'The Law and the Prophets were proclaimed until John. Since that time, the good news of the kingdom of God is

---

[233] Marshall, *Luke*, 623.
[234] Marshall, *Luke*, 624.
[235] Luke adds the general term *oiketēs* ('house slave') to the saying, putting all disciples into the same category as servants or slaves in the household of God. Contrast the more distinctive role implied by *oikonomos* (verse 1, 'manager').

being preached, and everyone is forcing their way into it. **17** It is easier for heaven and earth to disappear than for the least stroke of a pen to drop out of the Law.

18 'Anyone who divorces his wife and marries another woman commits adultery, and the man who marries a divorced woman commits adultery.

14–15. A link between the preceding parable and the next one is provided by the intervening verses. Luke first records the reaction of some Pharisees to the teaching just given: 'The Pharisees, who loved money, heard all this and were sneering at Jesus.' Their grumbling against him (15:2) turned to scorn (*exemyktērizon auton*, 'turning up their noses at him', as in 23:35; see also Jeremiah 20:7). They may not have been particularly rich, but they were 'money-loving'. Moreover, Jesus accused them of being 'the ones who justify yourselves in the eyes of others' (see 10:29; 18:9–14). Jesus had previously accused them of being obsessed with outward piety while being inwardly 'full of greed and wickedness' (11:39; compare 20:46–7). In that context he urged them to be 'generous to the poor, and everything will be clean for you' (11:41). Their reaction to his teaching about money showed what was in their hearts, and Jesus reminded them that 'God knows your hearts' (see 1 Samuel 16:7; 1 Kings 8:39; Proverbs 21:2; Acts 1:24; 8:21; 15:8). He therefore warned them, 'What people value highly is detestable in God's sight.' Greed is 'an abomination' in God's eyes (as in 1 Kings 11:5; Daniel 9:27), because it is a form of idolatry (Colossians 3:5).[236]

16. At first glance, verses 16–18 seem unrelated to the preceding ones, but Luke's purpose is not obscure. Foundationally, they point to the end of the era in which the Pharisees live ('The Law and the Prophets were proclaimed until John') and the beginning of a new era in which many are pressing to enter the kingdom of God in response to the message of John and his successor Jesus ('Since that time, the good news of the kingdom is being preached, and everyone is forcing their way into it'). John the Baptist was a transitional figure, whose ministry marked the end of the old era and the beginning of the new (3:1–18; 7:24–35).[237] Jesus and his disciples preached 'the good news of the kingdom' as a present reality,

---

[236] Green, *Luke*, 604, notes the LXX application of the term 'abomination' (*bdelygma*) to immoral financial dealings (Deuteronomy 25:16) and the act of remarrying a divorced woman (Deuteronomy 24:4), which explains the linking of these things in Luke 16:15–18.

[237] The parallel verses in Matthew 11:12–13 are in the same context as Luke 7:24–35, commending John's ministry and linking it closely to the ministry of Jesus. Luke appears to have simplified the language of his source for the benefit of his Gentile readers (Fitzmyer, *Luke X–XXIV*, 1114–15).

while continuing to stress the approaching judgment, as John did (see 4:16–27; 7:18–23; 9:1–2; 10:5–12). The translation 'forcing their way' renders the verb *biazetai* in a middle sense, but it could be understood passively ('everyone is being pressed [to enter it]'), especially since the preceding verb is clearly passive ('the good news of the kingdom is being preached').

17. The ministry of Jesus challenged the authority of the Pharisees and their way of reading and responding to Scripture. Nevertheless, he did not come to abolish the Law or the Prophets, but 'to fulfil them' (Matthew 5:17). This claim is not recorded by Luke, though his overall presentation affirms its message. He simply attaches a version of the following proposition in Matthew 5:18 to make his point: 'It is easier for heaven and earth to disappear than for the least stroke of a pen to drop out of the Law.'[238] In this new era, the Law has continuing authority and relevance as the word of God, but it must be understood and applied in the light of Jesus's teaching and fulfilment of it. For, as Fitzmyer says, 'in the demands of the kingdom itself the law is vindicated'.[239] This saying prepares for the challenge in verses 29–31.

18. The third saying in this sequence is the shortest statement of Jesus's position on divorce and remarriage in the Gospels (see Matthew 5:31–2; 19:3–9; Mark 10:2–12). Jesus consistently challenged Pharisaic teaching on the meaning and application of Deuteronomy 24:1–4. The version here forbids a man to divorce his wife and marry another under any circumstance (compare Matthew 5:32; 19:9, 'except for sexual immorality'). The warning, 'Anyone who divorces his wife and marries another woman commits adultery,' may have been addressing the specific issue of 'divorce for the sake of remarriage', as Nolland suggests.[240] Jesus does not argue the case, but he warns about easing the demands of the Law and effectively condemns his opponents for their handling of the issue. Boldly describing remarriage as adultery, he goes beyond the provision of Deuteronomy by suggesting that the divorced man is still effectively married to his first partner. He goes a step further and warns, 'The man who marries a divorced woman commits adultery.' Elsewhere, he relates his teaching to the 'one flesh' relationship described in Genesis 2:24 (Matthew 19:4–6;

---

[238] Nolland, *Luke 9:21–18:34*, 821, understands 'the least stroke of a pen' to include 'projections (probably both ornamental and those that distinguish similar letters) in the formation of letters in writing, and also to accents and breathings' in the Hebrew.
[239] Fitzmyer, *Luke X–XXIV*, 1116.
[240] Nolland, *Luke 9:21–18:34*, 821. The linking word *kai* ('and') could be used in a final sense ('in order to'). It is important to remember that adultery was a capital offence in the law of Moses.

Mark 10:6–9). Jesus affirmed the biblical ideal for marriage in terms of God's purpose in creating us male and female and urged his hearers to pursue marital faithfulness at all costs.[241] In the flow of the argument in Luke, the implication for Nolland is that 'the demands of the kingdom of God take up and confirm the imperatives of the law and the prophets (Exodus 20:14; Leviticus 18:20; Deuteronomy 5:18; Malachi 2:14–16), but go on to be yet more demanding in very specific ways.'[242]

The fate of money-lovers (16:19–31)

The rich man and Lazarus

19 'There was a rich man who was dressed in purple and fine linen and lived in luxury every day. 20 At his gate was laid a beggar named Lazarus, covered with sores 21 and longing to eat what fell from the rich man's table. Even the dogs came and licked his sores.

22 'The time came when the beggar died and the angels carried him to Abraham's side. The rich man also died and was buried. 23 In Hades, where he was in torment, he looked up and saw Abraham far away, with Lazarus by his side. 24 So he called to him, "Father Abraham, have pity on me and send Lazarus to dip the tip of his finger in water and cool my tongue, because I am in agony in this fire."

25 'But Abraham replied, "Son, remember that in your lifetime you received your good things, while Laza-rus received bad things, but now he is comforted here and you are in agony. 26 And besides all this, between us and you a great chasm has been set in place, so that those who want to go from here to you cannot, nor can anyone cross over from there to us."

27 'He answered, "Then I beg you, father, send Lazarus to my family, 28 for I have five brothers. Let him warn them, so that they will not also come to this place of torment."

29 'Abraham replied, "They have Moses and the Prophets; let them listen to them."

30 ' "No, father Abraham," he said, "but if someone from the dead goes to them, they will repent."

31 'He said to him, "If they do not listen to Moses and the Prophets, they will not be convinced even if someone rises from the dead." '

19–21. This second parable about wealth is contextually directed to the Pharisees as those who are lovers of money. It illustrates what is meant by

---

[241] Further reflection on divorce and remarriage can be found in Jesus's teaching in Matthew 19:7–12 and Paul's teaching in 1 Corinthians 7:10–16. See also D. Instone-Brewer, 'Divorce', *DJG*, 212–16.

[242] Nolland, *Luke 9:21–18:34*, 822. Compare Matthew 5:21–48.

being 'welcomed into eternal dwellings' (verse 9) and reinforces the claim, 'What people value highly is detestable in God's sight' (verse 15). It concludes with an emphasis on taking Moses and the Prophets seriously (verses 29–31). The first character to be introduced is a rich man, who is not named, although he has sometimes been called Dives (Latin, 'rich').[243] He dressed like a king 'in purple and fine linen' (see 1 Maccabees 8:14) and 'lived in luxury every day' (ESV, 'feasted sumptuously'; see 12:19). 'At his gate was laid a beggar named Lazarus.' No other character in Jesus's parables is given a personal identity like this. Lazarus is the shortened form of the Hebrew or Aramaic 'Eleazar' (Genesis 15:2; Exodus 6:23), which means 'God helps/has helped'. This was a fitting name for someone ignored by many but blessed by God in the great reversal of the afterlife. There is no basis for connecting him with the Lazarus whom Jesus raised from death in John 11. His desperate situation is portrayed in detail: he was 'covered in sores' (ulcerated, rather than leprous) 'and longing to eat what fell from the rich man's table'.[244] 'Even the dogs came and licked his sores,' aggravating his distress.

22–4. The earthly scene is short and the ultimate fate of the two men is also briefly described. 'The time came when the beggar died and the angels carried him to Abraham's side,' signifying immediate access to the presence of God with the patriarchs and prophets of Israel (see 13:28–9).[245] Nothing is said about the beggar's faith, but a genuine relationship with God should be understood as the reason for this exaltation, rather than the fact that he was poor and destitute (see 13:23–7). 'The rich man also died and was buried,' but he found himself in the place of ultimate punishment, here identified as 'Hades' (see my comment on 10:15). Although some Jewish literature used this term quite generally for the place of the dead, Nolland observes that 'it comes increasingly to include the idea of a preliminary experience of what is to be the individual's ultimate fate at the final judgment (see 2 Esdras 7:80; 1 Enoch 22:11; Jude 6–7; 1 Peter 3:19–20)'.[246] In this parable,

---

[243] Fitzmyer, *Luke X–XXIV*, 1130, discusses the emergence of other names for this character.

[244] The best attested reading is 'from the things falling from', but some ancient manuscripts and versions add *tōn psichiōn* ('the crumbs'), reflecting Matthew 15:27 (see KJV). A few ancient sources add 'and nobody would give him anything'. The shortest reading is more likely to be the original (see Metzger, *Textual Commentary*, 141).

[245] Fitzmyer, *Luke X–XXIV*, 1132, notes that Abraham's 'side' (*kolpos*, 'breast, chest') suggests either 'a place of honor for a guest at a banquet at the side of the host (see John 13:23) or an association of intimacy (see John 1:18)'.

[246] Nolland, *Luke 9:21–18:34*, 829. Compare J. B. Green, 'Heaven and Hell,' *DJG*,

Hades seems to be more specifically what is meant by Hell (*geenna*) in other contexts (see my comment on 12:5). Although it was not told to reveal details about the afterlife, the parable vividly portrays the finality of the situation into which both characters passed.

The image of separation from God and his saved people is conveyed by saying, 'He looked up and saw Abraham far away, with Lazarus by his side.' The notion that the dead in one place can see those in the other is reflected in 2 Esdras 7:85, 93; 2 Baruch 51:3–6, but Jewish views about the afterlife varied considerably in this period. Torment or severe distress is expressed by his cry, 'Father Abraham, have pity on me and send Lazarus to dip the tip of his finger in water and cool my tongue, because I am in agony in this fire.'[247] Abraham as the father of Israel (1:73; 3:8) is asked to be merciful and send Lazarus to relieve his pain and distress.[248] The man who showed no mercy in this life expects to receive it in the next! When he mentions Lazarus by name, he confirms that he knew him personally, although he did nothing to help him. Even in Hades, he remains unrepentant for his neglectful self-indulgence and wants Lazarus to serve *his* needs (see also verse 27).

25–6. Abraham replies in a way that identifies the rich man as a faithless and lost son, whose opportunity for doing good has passed: 'Son, remember that in your lifetime you received your good things, while Lazarus received bad things, but now he is comforted here and you are in agony.' In the teaching of Jesus, Hades is not a state where people are purged of their sin so that they can finally pass into the presence of God. There is an unbridgeable gap between these two modes of existence and no possibility of passing from one to the other: 'And besides all this, between us and you a great chasm has been set in place, so that those who want to go from here to you cannot, nor can anyone cross over from there to us.' God's final judgment is irrevocable, and it is based on what is in our hearts and displayed in our lives (verses 13–15; compare Matthew 25:31–46; Romans 2:6–11).[249]

370–73.

[247] The verb *odynōmai* ('I am in agony') could express mental pain (as in 2:48), but 'in this fire' suggests the physical nature of the punishment. The mental and spiritual aspect of the torment is expressed by the image of separation from God and his people.

[248] Flames are associated with Hades in Sirach 21:9–10; 1QH 17:13; 1 Enoch 10:13; 63:10, perhaps derived from Isaiah 66:24. Thirst is an aspect of the torment in 2 Esdras 8:59.

[249] The perfect passive *estēriktai* ('has been set in place') implies the irreversible action of God.

27–8. The final part of the story begins with the appeal of the rich man for Abraham to see Lazarus with a message for his family: 'Then I beg you, father, send Lazarus to my family, for I have five brothers. Let him warn them, so that they will not also come to this place of torment.' They needed someone to testify to the awful judgment awaiting them. Some would argue that, like the other 'double-edged' parables of Jesus (Matthew 20:1–16; 22:1–14; Luke 15:11–32), this one also has its stress on the second point. Jeremias, for example, says, 'Jesus does not want to comment on a social problem, nor does he intend to give teaching about the after-life, but he relates the parable to warn men who resemble the brothers of the rich man of the impending danger.'[250] But this argument downplays the significance of the context (verses 1–18) and the lengthy comparison of the two men in the first section of the parable. Both segments of the story are equally important, showing the need to take the warnings of Scripture about divine judgment seriously and show compassionate generosity to the poor and needy.

29–31. Abraham's warning endorses Jesus's claim about the continuing validity of the Law and the Prophets, even as the good news of the kingdom of God is being preached (verses 16–17): 'They have Moses and the Prophets; let them listen to them.' The Old Testament provides enough evidence about life after death and God's ultimate judgment to convince those with ears to hear that they should repent and live faithfully before him in the present (see 20:27–38). As Seccombe concludes, Jesus's parable deals with 'a flagrant outrage of "the Law and the Prophets"'.[251] The rich man and his brothers should have been convinced by Scripture of their guilt before God. However, knowing the hardness of heart of his brothers, the rich man said, 'No, father Abraham . . . but if someone from the dead goes to them, they will repent.' Surely an infallible sign would persuade them (see 4:23; 11:16, 29–32; 23:8–9)! But Abraham replied, 'If they do not listen to Moses and the Prophets, they will not be convinced even if someone rises from the dead.' The language changes here from the possibility of a visitation by someone from the dead (verse 30), which could have involved a dream or vision, to the

---

[250] Jeremias, *Parables*, 186. Both Marshall, *Luke*, 633, and Fitzmyer, *Luke X–XXIV*, 1128–9, challenge this.

[251] Seccombe, *The Poor*, 182. 'Luke is saying in no uncertain terms that the Kingdom is forever closed to those who close their hearts against the needy' (Seccombe, *The Poor*, 187).

possibility that someone *rises* from death. As Fitzmyer observes, 'For the Christian reader of the Lucan Gospel, the reference to Jesus's own death and resurrection is obvious.'[252]

DEATH AND BEYOND

In the Old Testament, death is portrayed as both the natural ending of mortal life and the punishment for sin. Although some texts express the hope that individual believers had of life beyond the grave (e.g., Psalms 16:9–11; 73:18–20), Tom Wright observes that the Old Testament mostly focuses on 'the fate of Israel and her promised land'.[253] The resurrection of God's people in this sense is especially portrayed in Isaiah 26:19; Ezekiel 37:1–14; Hosea 13:14. Perhaps particularly inspired by Daniel 12:1–2, by the time of Jesus most Jews either believed in some form of personal resurrection 'or at least knew that it was standard teaching'.[254] Wright suggests that the parabolic nature of the story in Luke 16:19–31 'prevents us from treating it as Jesus' own description of how the afterlife is organized', but it does indicate, in standard Jewish style, 'a clear belief in continuity between the present life and the future one'.[255] Moreover, the parable ends by linking biblical expectations about ultimate judgment and salvation with the immediate possibility that someone might rise from the dead to fulfil them. Luke continues this emphasis in his record of the apostolic preaching in Acts 4:1–12; 5:30–32; 12:39–43; 13:32–41; 17:30–31; 23:6; 24:14–16; 26:6–8; 28:20 ('the hope of Israel'). With the resurrection of Jesus, the predicted future has come into the present and determines the outcome for all – some to eternal life in God's presence and others to eternal judgment.[256]

---

[252] Fitzmyer, *Luke X–XXIV*, 1134. In narrative terms, this functions as an implicit prediction of Jesus's resurrection, following 9:22 and soon to be confirmed in 18:33.
[253] N. T. Wright, *The Resurrection of the Son of God* (Minneapolis: Fortress, 2003), 99. Compare Williamson, *Death and the Afterlife*, 74–83.
[254] Wright, *Resurrection*, 129. Wright goes on to discuss the many different perspectives on resurrection and life after death in Jewish literature from 200 BC to AD 200. See more briefly Williamson, *Death and the Afterlife*, 68–74.
[255] Wright, *Resurrection*, 438.
[256] See also my comments on Luke 20:34–8; 23:42–3, and my Introduction, pages 18–22.

9. The daily demands of discipleship (Luke 17:1–10)

This brief segment of Jesus's teaching presents a contrast with commitments and practices previously identified with the Pharisees. Green summarises these as 'lack of regard for the "little ones" and sinners in their midst, faithlessness, and a heightened, problematic concern for recognition and status'.[257] In positive terms, these sayings describe four ideal characteristics of the community that Jesus is forming around himself, first in relation to one another – no stumbling blocks and a readiness to forgive (verses 1–4) – and second in relation to God – expectant faith and obedient service (verses 5–10).

No stumbling blocks (17:1–2)

Sin, faith, duty

17 Jesus said to his disciples: 'Things that cause people to stumble are bound to come, but woe to anyone through whom they come. **2** It would be better for them to be thrown into the sea with a millstone tied round their neck than to cause one of these little ones to stumble.

1. 'Jesus said to his disciples: "Things that cause people to stumble are bound to come, but woe to anyone through whom they come."' This woe is an abbreviated form of the warning in Matthew 18:6–7, where Jesus goes on to talk about removing the causes of stumbling in one's own life (Matthew 18:8–9 (compare 5:29–30); Mark 9:42–8). The Lucan version focuses on the possibility of causing other people to stumble. 'Things that cause people to stumble' (*skandala*) could refer to trouble and persecution that provoke apostasy (Mark 4:17; Matthew 13:21, 'they quickly fall away'), but the ESV translation ('temptations to sin') rightly suggests a broader meaning.[258] Similar language is used elsewhere in the New Testament in relation to the dangers of false and divisive teaching (Acts 20:29–30; Romans 16:17–18), a judgmental attitude (Romans 14:13) and behaviour that causes other believers to sin (Romans 14:20–23; 1 Corinthians 8:9–13). Christians are to be

---

[257] Green, *Luke*, 611. Although these sayings may at first seem disconnected, they relate together in presenting a different set of community values.

[258] Fitzmyer, *Luke X–XXIV*, 1138. See also G. Stählin, 'σκάνδαλον, σκανδαλίζω', *TDNT* 7:339–58.

aware of such dangers and to avoid being the cause of someone else's spiritual collapse.

2. Woes are pronounced by Jesus against different groups of people in Luke's Gospel (6:24–6; 10:13; 11:42–52; 17:1; 21:23; 22:22), here specifically against those who 'cause one of these little ones to stumble'. 'These little ones' (*mikroi*) most likely refers to Jesus's disciples (see 12:32; Matthew 10:42; 18:6–14) rather than specifically little children (9:46–8 [*paidion*]; 18:15–17 [*brephē*]). The image of smallness and weakness, according to Edwards, is a reminder of their 'inability to be what they should be in Christ, and the ease with which they are led astray'.[259] The enormity of the judgment facing those who cause disciples to stumble is such that 'it would be better for them to be thrown into the sea with a millstone tied around their neck'. A horrible drowning would be better than the judgment of hell (12:5; 13:28; 16:23–6). If the warning 'So watch yourselves' (verse 3a) concludes the sayings in verses 1–2 (NIV), the focus is on causes of stumbling that might arise from among believers themselves.[260]

A readiness to forgive (17:3–4)

3 So watch yourselves.

'If your brother or sister[a] sins against you, rebuke them; and if they repent, forgive them.

4 Even if they sin against you seven times in a day and seven times come back to you saying "I repent," you must forgive them.'

_____

a 3 The Greek word for *brother or sister* (*adelphos*) refers here to a fellow disciple, whether man or woman.

3–4. If the warning, 'So watch yourselves,' is meant to introduce the next set of sayings (ESV), it highlights the importance of earnestly seeking reconciliation with fellow believers (Matthew 18:15–18 offers an expanded version of this advice). Failure to act like this may perpetuate a situation of conflict or cause some to fall away (verse 1). Jesus's solution ('If your brother or sister sins against you, rebuke them')[261] involves frankly stating

[259] Edwards, *Luke*, 476.
[260] There are no conjunctions in the Greek text indicating whether this command relates to the preceding or following text. In 12:1; 21:34, the phrase clearly begins a new piece of instruction, and it seems best to view it that way here (as the ESV does).
[261] The term *adelphos* ('brother') is rightly understood by the NIV as inclusive

the problem and revealing the hurt (see Leviticus 19:17). The goal is to encourage repentance for the forgiveness of sins ('and if they repent, forgive them'), expressing a change of mind, heart and behaviour (see 15:18–24). Elsewhere in Luke, forgiveness is offered for sins committed against God (1:77; 3:3, 8; 5:20–24, 32; 7:47–9; 12:10; 23:34; 24:47). Here, however, believers are called to mirror the attitude of God by forgiving those who sin against them (see 6:36; 11:4). Jesus allows for the possibility of continuing difficulties in Christian relationships when he emphasises the need for boundless forgiveness (see Matthew 18:21–35, where 'seven times' becomes 'seventy-seven times'): 'Even if they sin against you seven times in a day and seven times come back to you saying "I repent," you must forgive them.' This should be second nature for those who have experienced the liberating power of forgiveness themselves.[262] However, Jesus's injunction is no ground for saying that someone should stay in a dangerous or abusive relationship, where requests for forgiveness become an excuse for continuing to sin.

Expectant faith (17:5–6)

5 The apostles said to the Lord, 'Increase our faith!' **6** He replied, 'If you have faith as small as a mustard seed, you can say to this mulberry tree, "Be uprooted and planted in the sea," and it will obey you.

5–6. Presumably, the apostles are the focus of attention here because of their leadership among the disciples. Their dependence on Jesus for help is highlighted by Luke's identification of him as 'the Lord'. What they asked for (*prosthes hēmin pistin*) more likely means 'give us faith' to do what you have commanded, rather than 'add faith' to what we already have (BDAG). The Lord's response is in the form of a mixed conditional statement. The first part suggests a real possibility: 'If you had faith like a grain of mustard seed . . .' The second part expresses an unrealised outcome: '. . . you could say to this mulberry tree, "Be uprooted and planted in the sea", and it would obey you' (ESV). What is needed is not an increase of faith but, as Nolland insists, 'the exercise

---

('brother or sister'; see 8:21). The best manuscripts do not include *eis se* ('against you'), but the personal nature of the offence is indicated in verse 4 and should be understood in verse 3. Compare Matthew 18:15.

[262] Nolland, *Luke 9:21–18:24*, 838, observes that the number seven is meant to be 'sufficiently high to place the burden of responsibility on the person forgiving rather than on the person repenting'.

of faith'.[263] Jesus uses an exaggerated example to make his point. The mustard seed is small (13:19) and the mulberry tree is relatively large and deeply rooted,[264] but there would be no purpose in planting a mulberry tree in the sea! Similar sayings in the other Gospels speak about moving a mountain (Matthew 17:20; 21:21; Mark 11:22–23). The challenge is to expect great things from God in answer to prayer, but not the bizarre, the fanciful or the magical. Moreover, it would be a dangerously literalistic reading of verse 6 to suggest that commanding inanimate objects is a form of prayer encouraged by Jesus. Contextually, the meaning is that God can enable the miracle of faithful living commended in verses 1–4.

Obedient service (17:7–10)

7 'Suppose one of you has a servant ploughing or looking after the sheep. Will he say to the servant when he comes in from the field, "Come along now and sit down to eat"? 8 Won't he rather say, "Prepare my supper, get yourself ready and wait on me while I eat and drink; after that you may eat and drink"? 9 Will he thank the servant because he did what he was told to do? 10 So you also, when you have done everything you were told to do, should say, "We are unworthy servants; we have only done our duty."'

7–10. Jesus deals with this new topic in a similitude (found only in Luke), inviting his disciples to identify with a wealthy property owner: 'Suppose one of you has a servant ploughing or looking after the sheep. Will he say to the servant when he comes in from the field, "Come along now and sit down to eat"?' Although the Lord suggests this radical possibility in 12:37 and portrays his ministry in such terms (22:37), here he appeals to the simple fact that a servant is normally appointed to serve his master: 'Won't he rather say, "Prepare my supper, get yourself ready and wait on me while I eat and drink; after that you may eat and drink"?' Jesus focuses on one aspect of the master–servant relationship to illustrate how believers ought to relate to God: 'Will he thank the servant because he did what he was told to do?' The application is then

---

[263] Nolland, *Luke 9:21–18:24*, 838.

[264] Fitzmyer, *Luke X–XXIV*, 1144, notes that in the Jewish Mishnah 'such a tree was not to be planted within twenty-five cubits of a cistern, i.e., about thirty-seven feet'. Greek *sycaminos* refers to the 'the sycamore-fig' in 1 Kings 10:27; 1 Chronicles 27:28; 2 Chronicles 1:15 LXX, but Luke uses *sykamoria* for the latter in 19:4, suggesting that 'mulberry tree' is intended here (Marshall, *Luke*, 644).

made to the disciples: 'So you also, when you have done everything you were told to do, should say, "We are unworthy servants; we have only done our duty."' The word *achreioi* can mean 'unprofitable' or 'useless', but the expectation that they might do everything they are told to do suggests the meaning 'unworthy of any praise' (BDAG).[265]

Although Jesus spoke about God rewarding the faithful 'at the resurrection of the righteous' (14:14), the warning in the present context is about any attempt to earn God's favour and put him under obligation. The kingdom of God is his gracious gift and those who desire to enjoy its blessings serve him with grateful anticipation and faithful obedience. A Christian's voluntary submission to God and his will arises from the experience of God's grace. God's demands include the instructions of Jesus in verses 1–6, but even good works over and above God's commandments do not merit his special favour.[266] Modern readers may be uncomfortable about the use of slavery as an image for our relationship with God. However, Jesus's parables do not amount to an endorsement of the oppressive system of slavery that was current in the Roman Empire at that time (see 12:35–48; 16:1–9; 22:24–7). Nolland rightly concludes, 'As the one who is unimaginably supreme over us, he deserves our total loyalty and unstinting obedience. There is nothing meritorious in such obedience: it is merely the fulfillment of a natural obligation.'[267]

10. When and where is the kingdom? (Luke 17:11–37)

At this point in Luke's narrative, references to the journey of Jesus to Jerusalem start to appear again (17:11; 18:31, 35; 19:1, 11) and, as Green says, 'the reality of the journey and the threads of its principal motifs are drawn together'.[268] Luke's last mention of the journey was in 14:25. The healing of ten leprous men recalls an earlier event (5:12–14), which pointed to Jesus as 'the one who is to come' (7:18–23). But the focus this

[265] Nolland, *Luke 9:21–18:24*, 840, translates 'we are slaves to whom no favour is owed; we have done (only) what we ought to do'.
[266] Article XIV of the Articles of Religion in *The Book of Common Prayer* (1662) speaks against the notion of such 'works of supererogation', describing this medieval doctrine as arrogant and impious, and citing Luke 17:10 to counter it.
[267] Nolland, *Luke 9:21–18:24*, 843. Brawley, *Luke*, 158–60 disputes this interpretation.
[268] Green, *Luke*, 615. Green notes in particular the references to 'Samaria' and 'Samaritan' (17:11, 16; compare 9:52–4; 10:25–37) and 'to seek and to save the lost' (19:10; compare 15).

time is on the response of a single Samaritan, who comes back praising God, while throwing himself at Jesus's feet and thanking him (17:11–19). A question from the Pharisees about when the kingdom of God will come is answered by Jesus in a way that points to its manifestation in his ministry (17:20–21; compare 11:20). Exploring this further with his disciples, however, Jesus predicts a delay before they see the Son of Man coming in glory and judgment, during which 'he must suffer many things and be rejected by this generation' (17:22–5). A related theme is the need to be ready, despite the predicted delay (17:26–37). Thus, the tension between the 'now' and the 'not yet' of the kingdom portrayed in 12:32–59 is revisited.

The healing of ten leprous men (17:11–19)

Jesus heals ten men with leprosy

11 Now on his way to Jerusalem, Jesus travelled along the border between Samaria and Galilee. **12** As he was going into a village, ten men who had leprosy[b] met him. They stood at a distance **13** and called out in a loud voice, 'Jesus, Master, have pity on us!'

14 When he saw them, he said, 'Go, show yourselves to the priests.' And as they went, they were cleansed.

15 One of them, when he saw he was healed, came back, praising God in a loud voice. **16** He threw himself at Jesus' feet and thanked him – and he was a Samaritan.

17 Jesus asked, 'Were not all ten cleansed? Where are the other nine? **18** Has no one returned to give praise to God except this foreigner?' **19** Then he said to him, 'Rise and go; your faith has made you well.'

—

b 12 The Greek word traditionally translated *leprosy* was used for various diseases affecting the skin.

11. Luke alone includes this narrative, which somewhat parallels 5:12–14 (Matthew 8:1–4; Mark 1:40–44; see also 2 Kings 5:1–19). The introductory verse recalls 9:51–2, re-establishing the journey motif. Debate surrounds the meaning of the Greek, translated by the NIV as 'Jesus travelled along the border between Samaria and Galilee' (*autos diērcheto dia meson Samareias kai Galilaia*). More literally, he was 'passing through between Samaria and Galilee'. The use of *dia meson* to mean 'between' is unusual (see *dia mesou* in 4:30), and the geographical implications are not clear.[269] Jesus may have returned to the border between Samaria and

—

[269] Fitzmyer, *Luke X–XXIV*, 1152–3, notes various attempts to remedy the confusion

Galilee after the incident in 9:52–6 and continued east until he reached the Jordan Valley and Jericho. We know little about the details of the journey and the extent to which Jesus and his disciples followed the path normally taken by pilgrims travelling from Galilee to Jerusalem. Nolland suggests that the location of their travel at this point may simply account for 'the mixed Jewish and Samaritan makeup of the group of lepers'.[270]

12–13. As Jesus was going into an unnamed village, 'ten men who had leprosy met him'. They were probably afflicted with an inflammatory or scaly skin disease, not the malignant form of leprosy known to modern medicine as Hansen's disease (see my comment on 5:12).[271] Jews who were defiled in this way had to separate themselves from everyday life until a priest could declare them clean again (Leviticus 13:1–46). Therefore, these men 'stood at a distance and called out in a loud voice, "Jesus, Master, have pity on us!"' Their address to him as 'Master' (*epistata*) was unusual, since it was normally used by disciples as a personal recognition of his authority (5:5; 8:24, 45; 9:33, 49). Their cry for mercy expressed the confidence that he could heal them (see 18:38–9). Although not revealed until verse 16, the surprising factor in this episode is that one of them was a Samaritan.

14. Healing is implicitly promised when Jesus says, 'Go, show yourselves to the priests' (alluding to Leviticus 13:39; 14:1–7, as in 5:14). However, whereas in 5:13 he cleansed an individual with a skin disease before sending him to the priests, here he tests the faith of the ten by cleansing them as they set off in obedience to his command ('as they went, they were cleansed', *ekatharisthēsan*).[272] The rest of the narrative focuses on the aftermath.

15–16. 'One of them, when he saw he was healed, came back, praising God in a loud voice.' This man's faith moved him to obey Jesus like the others, but also to glorify God in a public way (*doxazōn*, 'praising'; see 2:20; 5:25, 26; 7:16; 13:13; 18:43; 23:47) for his cleansing. Moreover, 'He threw himself at Jesus's feet and thanked him' (*eucharistōn*, 'thanking';

---

in the textual tradition. He unnecessarily proposes that this sentence exposes Luke's 'geographical ineptitude'.

[270] Nolland, *Luke 9:21–18:24*, 846. See also Lloyd, *Itinerant Jesus*, 349, note 18.

[271] The Greek expression allows for a broader understanding of their condition.

[272] Commands to act with the expectation of healing also occur in 5:25; 6:10; 7:14; 8:54 (see also 7:7–10; John 4:50; 2 Kings 5:10). Nolland, *Luke 9:21–18:24*, 846, notes that 'as they went' (*en tō hypagein autous*) is likely to mean 'as they set off' (as in 8:42).

see 5:12; 7:38, 44–6; 8:35, 41; 10:39). Elsewhere in the New Testament, thanksgiving is offered to God. This man perceived God's powerful presence in his healing by Jesus, conveying what Nolland calls 'an implied Christology that Luke is keen to exploit and develop'.[273] When it is revealed that this Christocentric confession was made by a Samaritan, the reader is being invited to remember the animosity expressed against Jesus by Samaritans (9:52–3), but also the remarkable compassion of the Samaritan in his parable (10:29–37). Luke later shows a special interest in the way the gospel impacted Samaritans and brought them into the fellowship of believers (Acts 8:4–25).

17–18. Jesus's three rhetorical questions emphasise the contrast between the Samaritan and the others who were healed: 'Were not all ten cleansed? Where are the other nine? Has no one returned to give praise to God except this foreigner?' The other nine were apparently Jews, but they failed to praise God and thank Jesus. They had faith enough to ask Jesus for help, but they did not acknowledge him as God's agent or see that their lives should be reoriented towards him in any way. God is glorified when Jesus is acknowledged as the channel of divine mercy. The term 'foreigner' (*allogenēs*) only occurs here in the New Testament, though a parallel word is used in Acts 10:28 for 'a Gentile'.[274]

19. Jesus's final message to the Samaritan expresses an important theme in Luke's Gospel: 'Rise and go; your faith has made you well.' The perfect tense of the verb used here stresses the present reality of physical healing (*sesōken*, as in 8:48; 18:42). However, the same expression in 7:50 is translated 'your faith has *saved* you', because the woman in that context was forgiven and brought into a grateful relationship with Jesus. Both senses could be understood in 17:19, since the Samaritan's experience of healing brought him into a similar relationship (so also Zacchaeus in 19:9–10). Saving faith is here linked with obedience to the command of Jesus and grateful recognition of his authority to restore and transform (see the link between thanksgiving and salvation in Psalm 50:22–3).

---

[273] Nolland, *Luke 9:21–18:24*, 847. Compare 5:8.

[274] Nolland, *Luke 9:21–18:24*, 847, observes that the term was used in the inscription that forbade the entry of foreigners into the Jerusalem Temple: 'more strictly, the Samaritans were viewed as half-foreign, Israelites of doubtful descent'. Compare John 4:7–26.

The kingdom present and still to come (17:20–37)

The coming of the kingdom of God

20 Once, on being asked by the Pharisees when the kingdom of God would come, Jesus replied, 'The coming of the kingdom of God is not something that can be observed, **21** nor will people say, "Here it is," or "There it is," because the kingdom of God is in your midst.'[c]

22 Then he said to his disciples, 'The time is coming when you will long to see one of the days of the Son of Man, but you will not see it. **23** People will tell you, "There he is!" or "Here he is!" Do not go running off after them. **24** For the Son of Man in his day[d] will be like the lightning, which flashes and lights up the sky from one end to the other. **25** But first he must suffer many things and be rejected by this generation.

26 'Just as it was in the days of Noah, so also will it be in the days of the Son of Man. **27** People were eating, drinking, marrying and being given in marriage up to the day Noah entered the ark. Then the flood came and destroyed them all.

28 'It was the same in the days of Lot. People were eating and drinking, buying and selling, planting and building. **29** But the day Lot left Sodom, fire and sulphur rained down from heaven and destroyed them all.

30 'It will be just like this on the day the Son of Man is revealed. **31** On that day no one who is on the housetop, with possessions inside, should go down to get them. Likewise, no one in the field should go back for anything. **32** Remember Lot's wife! **33** Whoever tries to keep their life will lose it, and whoever loses their life will preserve it. **34** I tell you, on that night two people will be in one bed; one will be taken and the other left. **35** Two women will be grinding corn together; one will be taken and the other left.' **[36]**[e]

37 'Where, Lord?' they asked.

He replied, 'Where there is a dead body, there the vultures will gather.'

---

c 21 Or *is within you*

d 24 Some manuscripts do not have *in his day.*

e 36 Some manuscripts include here words similar to Matt. 24:40.

20. A question from certain Pharisees about 'when the kingdom of God would come' (recorded only by Luke) connects with the previous narrative thematically, but not chronologically. This is one of several places in Luke–Acts where, as Green suggests, 'a request for clarity regarding the kingdom leads to the correction of misunderstanding about the eschatological timetable and, then, about the nature of God's dominion'.[275] Their question was doubtless provoked by the preaching of Jesus and his disciples (4:43; 6:20; 7:28; 8:1; 9:2, 11, 60, 62; 10:9, 11; 11:20; 13:18, 20,

---

275 Green, *Luke*, 628. See 12:41–53; 19:11–27; 21:7–36; Acts 1:6.

28, 29; 16:16). Although the term is not used in the Old Testament, the concept of the kingdom of God is clearly present and developed in the literature of Second Temple Judaism.[276] Jesus developed familiar themes and transformed them in the light of his understanding of God's plan to establish his eternal rule over Israel and the nations (e.g., Psalm 2; Isaiah 33:20–22; 52:7–10). The Pharisees did not express unbelief or test him on this occasion, but they simply asked how they would know when the kingdom had come. Jesus first replied that 'the coming of the kingdom of God is not something that can be observed'. According to Nolland, the expression *meta paratēreseōs* means 'with close observation' and was primarily used in Greek 'in connection with medical diagnosis, treatment and prognosis, as well as in connection with various kinds of scientific observation'.[277] People will also not be able to say, 'Here it is,' or, 'There it is,' as if the kingdom could be localised in one place or another (see verses 23–4). This probably relates to contemporary debates about where on earth the kingdom of God might be manifested (see 19:11; Acts 1:8).

21. The reason Jesus gives for his answer is that 'the kingdom of God is in your midst'. The possibility that this last expression (*entos hymōn*) means 'within you' (as an inward, invisible power) must be rejected, because it implies that unbelieving Pharisees were already experiencing the kingdom within themselves, and it leaves no room for a future intervention of God to consummate his plan in history (see verses 24, 26–37). The most likely meaning is 'among you' (NIV, 'in your midst'), alluding to the person of Jesus and his ministry. This recalls Jesus's saying in 11:20 and allows for the incident in 17:11–19 to be viewed as an expression of the healing associated with the coming of God to redeem his people (see Isaiah 35:3–6; Luke 7:18–23). A third possible translation ('within your reach, grasp or possession') implies that the kingdom is already present in the person of Jesus and his ministry, but the Pharisees have failed to notice this.[278]

22. Jesus turned from engaging with the Pharisees about the kingdom of God to instruct his disciples about the coming of the Son of Man (see my comments on his use of this title in 5:24; 9:26; 12:40). Having already implied that the kingdom was active in his person and ministry

---

[276] See J. B. Green, 'Kingdom of God/Heaven', *DJG*, 468–73.
[277] Nolland, *Luke 9:21–18:24*, 852.
[278] Fitzmyer, *Luke X–XXIV*, 1161–2, prefers this but questions whether the term can be understood in this way. Nolland, *Luke 9:21–18:24*, 853–4, reads *estin* in a futuristic way and interprets *entos hymōn* in the light of verses 22–37 to mean, 'When the kingdom of God is due to come it will just be there, right in our midst, with no advance warning and no localized beginning.'

(11:20; 17:21), he taught about its consummation in terms of his return as Son of Man.[279] However, he emphasised that there would a difficult period when he would be absent from his disciples and that the Son of Man would not come as soon as they would like: 'The time is coming when you will long to see one of the days of the Son of Man, but you will not see it.' 'The time is coming' (*eleusontai hēmerai*, 'days are coming') is an expression often used by the prophets when predicting future events (e.g., Jeremiah 7:32; 16:14; compare Luke 5:35; 21:6), but 'one of the days of the Son of Man' only occurs here. The plural 'days of the Son of Man' forms a parallel with 'the days of Noah' (verse 26) and 'the days of Lot' (verse 28), when divine judgment suddenly came upon the people of their generation. But the singular 'day' is used for the Son of Man's actual coming in verse 24 in some manuscripts and in verse 30. The longing of disciples 'to see one of the days of the Son of Man' is best understood as a way of referring to the period of final judgment and redemption (21:28).[280] Nolland observes that the era of unfulfilled longing that Jesus speaks about 'corresponds to what in 18:1–8 is the period in which vindication has not yet been experienced.'[281] This will be a time of suffering and persecution for those who seek to live by and testify to the message of Jesus (6:22–3; 12:8–12, 52–3; 21:12–19).

23–5. The longing of disciples for the coming of the Son of Man could make them vulnerable to misleading information, such as, 'There he is!' or, 'Here he is!' (as in verse 22; compare 21:8).[282] Jesus therefore warns, 'Do not go running off after them.' The Son of Man will not appear in some remote place! 'For the Son of Man in his day will be like the lightning which flashes and lights up the sky from one end to the other.' No one will miss the immediate, worldwide sign of the Son of Man's coming, 'but first he must suffer many things and be rejected by this generation', This fifth passion prediction (see 9:22, 44; 12:50; 13:33) is worded in a way that

---

[279] Parallels may be found in Matthew 24:26–7, 37–8; 10:39; 24:40–41, 28. The eschatological discourse here anticipates in some respects the one found in chapter 21, suggesting the importance of the topic for Luke and his readers.

[280] Marshall, *Luke*, 658–9, observes that 'one of the days' could mean 'the first day of a period'. See, however, Fitzmyer, *Luke X–XXIV*, 1168–9.

[281] Nolland, *Luke 9:21–18:24*, 858. The verb *epithymēsete* ('long') expresses a strong desire.

[282] Metzger, *Textual Commentary*, 142, discusses the variant readings in verse 23, which give different arrangements of the words translated 'There he is!' and 'Here he is!' Although many texts include 'in his day' (verse 24), the best-attested reading in both Alexandrian and western manuscripts omits these words.

links the suffering and rejection of the Son of Man with the anticipated experience of his disciples. The divine necessity of this is stressed with the term *dei* ('must' as in 9:22; 13:33; 24:7, 26, 44). God's kingdom plan can only be fulfilled through the redemptive suffering of the Son of Man (see 22:15–20, 37; 24:45–9). But disciples must also be willing to follow in the way of the cross in their desire to be with Jesus and to propagate his message (9:23–6; 12:8–12; 14:26–7; 21:12–19; Acts 14:22).

26–7. The coming of the Son of Man in judgment is likened to 'the days of Noah' (see also Matthew 24:37–9). The biblical warning about the Son of Man's 'day' (verse 30; compare Daniel 7:13–14) casts its shadow over the present, just as God's warning about the flood hung over the heads of people in Noah's time (Genesis 6:6–7).[283] In that era, 'people were eating, drinking, marrying and being given in marriage up to the day Noah entered the ark'. Surprisingly, Jesus does not mention the gross wickedness of that generation (Genesis 6:5). Rather, he focuses on the complacency and indifference of people to God and his will in the pursuits of everyday life. 'Then the flood came and destroyed them all' (Genesis 7:17–23).

28–9. Luke alone presents an abbreviated version of the same challenge in relation to 'the days of Lot': 'People were eating and drinking, buying and selling, planting and building.' A different selection of everyday activities is given to portray life without God, and no mention is made of the particular evil of the men of Sodom (Genesis 19:4–9). Lot's angelic visitors warned him to escape with his family from imminent judgment (Genesis 19:12–22). 'The day Lot left Sodom, fire and sulphur rained down from heaven' and destroyed all who remained in the region (Genesis 19:24–5).

30–31. The parallel with this is developed by saying, 'It will be just like this on the day the Son of Man is revealed.' What disciples long to see (verse 22) will be revealed to them, their persistent faith will be vindicated and they will be delivered from judgment as Noah and Lot were. However, a warning is added about last-minute failure. Nolland summarises, 'As did Noah and Lot, individuals will need to cooperate in their own immediate removal if they are not to be engulfed in the judgment to fall.'[284] Jesus portrays the coming of judgment in this-worldly terms, precisely related to his first-century Judean context:

---

[283] Fitzmyer, *Luke X–XXIV*, 1168, says, 'Luke appears to have made "the day" of the Son of Man into a phrase to parallel "the days of Noah" (v. 26) and "the days of Lot" (v. 28).' The rhetorical effect is to characterise the whole period between the cross and the return of Jesus as one of imminent judgment.

[284] Nolland, *Luke 9:21–18:24*, 861.

'On that day no one who is on the housetop, with possessions inside, should go down to get them.' Wherever believers are found, this will not be the time to worry about securing material possessions! 'Likewise, no one in the field should go back for anything' (*mē epistrepsatō eis ta opisō*, 'not turn back for what is behind'). This will be a time to trust God for every need!

32–3. 'Remember Lot's wife!' is a challenge to recall the biblical narrative in which she 'looked back' as she fled from Sodom (Genesis 19:26). This implied her attachment to life in that city. By disobeying a critical instruction from God (19:17), Gordon Wenham discerns that 'she forfeited her God-offered salvation'.[285] The lesson for disciples is drawn out in terms recalling 9:24: 'Whoever tries to keep their life will lose it, and whoever loses their life will preserve it.' In this context, their 'life' (*psychē*) initially refers to life as people desire it to be, physically, emotionally and spiritually. But the second part of the saying suggests that a willingness to let go of life conceived in this way will actually lead to the preservation of life through judgment and into the eternal sphere of the kingdom of God. Green concludes, 'Only those whose lives are built on the values of the kingdom of God, and whose case for respectable identity in the world is thus lost, will be ready for the end.'[286]

34–[36]. The image of being removed from the scene of judgment in order to be saved is continued: 'I tell you, on that night two people will be in one bed; one will be taken and the other left. Two women will be grinding corn together; one will be taken and the other one left.'[287] This sudden separation of family members and co-workers is not explained, but it should be understood in relation to Jesus's bringing together teaching about God's electing grace and the need to enter the kingdom by faith 'through the narrow door' (13:23–30). Unbelievers are not left behind to live in this world without believing friends and relatives, as some have taught, since Jesus clearly links the coming of the Son of Man with their immediate

---

[285] Gordon J. Wenham, *Word Biblical Commentary, Volume 2, Genesis 16–50* (Dallas: Word, 1994), 59. According to Wisdom 10:7, she became 'a pillar of salt standing as a monument to an unbelieving soul' (NRSVA).

[286] Green, *Luke*, 635–6. See also the helpful comments of Edwards, *Luke*, 495–6, on the relevance of Jesus's eschatological teaching to everyday life.

[287] The Greek indicates that two men are mentioned in the first illustration (a family sleeping together in one bed) and two women in the second (grinding corn together). Compare Matthew 24:40–41. Commenting on Palestinian sleeping arrangements, Edwards, *Luke*, 493–4, rightly concludes that no hint of a homosexual relationship can be inferred from this image.

judgment (compare 1 Thessalonians 4:16–18 with 2 Thessalonians 1:6–10). Some manuscripts and ancient versions include as verse 36 a version of the saying in Matthew 24:40 ('Two men will be left in the field; one will be taken and the other left'), but the best Lucan texts do not.[288]

37. The disciples asked, 'Where, Lord?', presumably meaning, 'Where will this happen?' Jesus replied with a graphic image: 'Where there is a dead body, there the vultures will gather' (see Matthew 24:28). In other words, just as birds of prey know where to gather for food, the Son of Man will know those who are truly his and where to find them. A more extensive presentation of Jesus's teaching about matters related to the coming of the Son of Man is given in Luke 21.

THE KINGDOM AND THE CROSS

The kingdom of God is mentioned three times in the pivotal passage that links the healing narrative (17:11–19) and the discourse concerning the coming of the Son of Man (17:22–37). Luke uses this sequence, together with the combination of events and teaching in 18:1–19:44, to clarify how and when the kingdom is consummated. The presence of the kingdom in Jesus's ministry is revealed in the miracle story about the return of the Samaritan, who praises God in a loud voice while throwing himself at Jesus's feet and thanking him (verses 15–16). This man recognises the healing power of God operating through Jesus and so is 'saved' by faith (verse 19).

But salvation in the full sense that Luke understands it has not yet been accomplished. In the discourse that follows, the saving and judging activity of God in the past becomes a paradigm for the end-time coming of the Son of Man. Paradoxically, however, Jesus once more predicts that 'first he must suffer many things and be rejected by this generation' (verse 25; compare 9:22, 44). He is on his way to Jerusalem to experience suffering, rejection and death (verse 11), and then to be 'taken up to heaven' (9:51). This is the God-ordained way in which the Messiah must 'enter his glory' (24:26) and be 'exalted to the right hand of God' as 'both Lord and Messiah' (Acts 2:33–6). His death, resurrection and ascension will be the means by which God makes available the benefits of the promised 'new covenant' (22:20; compare Jeremiah 31:31–4) and opens his kingdom to believers from every nation (24:46–7). But the interval between Jesus's heavenly exaltation and his glorious return will

---

[288] See Fitzmyer, *Luke X–XXIV*, 1173, for details. Poor manuscript evidence rules out the possibility that the longer reading is original. The variant also spoils the symmetry of verses 34–5.

be a period of longing for disciples and alienation from a world where people are preoccupied with everyday life, have no time for God and no fear of imminent judgment (17:22–9). The way of faithful disciple-ship is demonstrated and empowered by the single-minded perseverance of Jesus himself, as he goes to the cross to save his people. As Tannehill concludes, disciples need to recognise that 'God's way of working in the world requires suffering from God's servants because they are exposed to rejection.'[289] Moreover, as Luke repeatedly demonstrates in Acts, and Green observes, 'struggle and opposition do not contradict or impede but seem actually to promote the progress of the gospel'.[290]

11. Depending on God (Luke 18:1–30)

A parable unique to this Gospel about a persistent widow and an unjust judge fittingly concludes the warning about being ready for the coming of the Son of Man (17:22–37). However, the mention of prayer in verse 1 also prepares for another parable unique to this Gospel about the prayers of a Pharisee and a tax collector (18:9–14). This parable in turn prepares for a narrative sequence paralleled in Mark 10:13–34, 46–52; Matthew 19:13–30, 20:17–19, 29–34. Jesus speaks about receiving the kingdom of God like a child (18:15–17), engages with a rich ruler (18:18–25) and then teaches about the renunciation necessary to enter the kingdom of God and be saved (18:26–30). The childlikeness Jesus calls for involves self-humbling (18:14), which is further explained in the challenge to 'abandon material supports for the sake of the kingdom of God', as Nolland suggests.[291] So, the whole sequence shows the need for reliance on God for justice, mercy, daily provision and eternal salvation.

[289] Tannehill, *Narrative Unity* 1, 257. In 9:44–5; 19:31–4 there is a connection between the disciples' failure to understand Jesus's passion announcements and 'their premature hopes, doomed to disappointment' (Tannehill, 258).
[290] Green, *Luke*, 634.
[291] Nolland, *Luke 9:21–18:34*, 880. Compare Mark 10:13–31; Matthew 19:13–30.

Praying for justice (18:1–8)

The parable of the persistent widow

18 Then Jesus told his disciples a parable to show them that they should always pray and not give up. **2** He said: 'In a certain town there was a judge who neither feared God nor cared what people thought. **3** And there was a widow in that town who kept coming to him with the plea, "Grant me justice against my adversary."

4 'For some time he refused. But finally he said to himself, "Even though I don't fear God or care what people think, **5** yet because this widow keeps bothering me, I will see that she gets justice, so that she won't eventually come and attack me!" '

6 And the Lord said, 'Listen to what the unjust judge says. **7** And will not God bring about justice for his chosen ones, who cry out to him day and night? Will he keep putting them off? **8** I tell you, he will see that they get justice, and quickly. However, when the Son of Man comes, will he find faith on the earth?'

1. Jesus told this parable 'to show them that they should always pray and not give up'. As indicated in verses 7–8, a specific kind of prayer is encouraged (see 11:3–10): disciples should not give up praying to God for vindication, especially as they 'long to see one of the days of the Son of Man' (17:22; compare 11:2). The nature of this vindication will be considered below. An unspecified interval before it comes is presupposed, while the adverb 'always' emphasises the need for continual, periodic petition throughout this period.[292]

2–3. Two characters are briefly introduced. First the judge, who 'neither feared God nor cared what people thought'. No one told him what to do, not even God! Second the widow, who was needy and vulnerable: she 'kept coming to him with the plea, "Grant me justice against my adversary."'[293] The precise nature of her dilemma is not revealed, but if anyone in Israel took advantage of a widow or the fatherless and cried out to God for help, he promised to act in judgment against their oppressors

---

[292] Marshall, *Luke*, 671. The same verb *egkakein* ('give up') is rendered 'lose heart' in 2 Corinthians 4:1, 16; 'become weary' in Galatians 6:9; 'be discouraged' in Ephesians 3:13; and 'tire' in 2 Thessalonians 3:13. Compare verse 7 ('who cry out to him day and night').

[293] The Greek (*ekdikēson me*) could mean 'give me vengeance', but the context suggests that this is more a call for justice in the sense of equity or deliverance from oppression. 'What the widow wants is not punishment of her opponent but the payment of whatever is due to her' (Marshall *Luke*, 672, citing Plummer).

(Exodus 22:22–4). God was known as 'a father to the fatherless, a defender of widows' (Psalm 68:5), and he expected his people to have the same commitment (Isaiah 1:17, 23; James 1:27), especially rulers and judges (Isaiah 10:1–3). Luke shows a special concern for widows (2:36–8; 4:25–6; 7:12–15; 18:3–5; 20:47; 21:2–3; Acts 6:1; 9:39, 41). This woman's opponent had been aggressive against her, leaving her helpless and hopeless.

4–5. 'For some time' the judge refused to respond to the widow's pleas, but finally he acted. His reason is revealed in a soliloquy ('he said to himself'; see 12:17–19; 15:17–19; 16:3–4), acknowledging his own weaknesses ('Even though I don't fear God or care what people think'), but deciding to help the widow because she annoys him ('yet because this widow keeps bothering me, I will see that she gets justice'). This image recalls 11:7, but a deeper issue is disclosed by the judge's further statement ('so that she won't eventually come and attack me'). The NIV conveys the idea of some force being used, because the verb *hypōpiazeō* literally means 'blacken an eye, strike in the face' (BDAG). But it is hard to imagine how a widow in that culture could have had physical or institutional means of wounding a judge. The verb was also employed figuratively to mean 'wear down', and this is more likely the sense here (NRSVA, 'wear me out'; ESV, 'beat me down'). The sense of a gradual process of shaming by constantly coming for help is also possible.[294]

6–7. Jesus challenged his disciples to 'listen to what the unjust judge says'. The judge's reluctant response invites a 'how much more' comparison with God: 'And will not God bring about justice for his chosen ones, who cry out to him day and night?' God does not need to be worn down by our prayers or shamed into action by our persistence. Parallels with Sirach 35:21–2 have been noted, where it is asserted that 'the prayer of the humble pierces the clouds, and it will not rest until it reaches its goal; it will not desist until the Most High responds and does justice to the righteous, and executes judgement' (NRSVA). In Jesus's rhetorical question, 'his chosen ones' are the humble and righteous, who continually seek God's help. They manifest their divine calling by persistently praying for his kingdom to come, and they will see his justice fully manifested when the Son of Man comes.[295] The NIV supplies a second

---

[294] Nolland, *Luke 9:21–18:34*, 868, argues this and draws a parallel with 11:8.

[295] God's choice is mentioned in Matthew 22:14 and his elect in Matthew 24:22, 24, 31; Mark 13:20, 22, 27. The idea of God's choice of some for eschatological blessing gained prominence in post-biblical Jewish literature. See G. Schrenk, 'ἐκλεκτός', *TDNT* 4:181–92.

rhetorical question ('Will he keep putting them off?'; ESV, 'Will he delay long over them?'), but the Greek could be read as a qualifying statement (*kai makrothymei ep' autois*, 'though he bear long with them', KJV). Jesus contrasts the attitude of God with that of the judge and implies that he will not be annoyed by the persistent cries of his people. God's patience is expressed with the use of a related term in the LXX ('slow to anger' in Exodus 34:6; Numbers 14:18; Psalm 103[102]:8).[296]

8. Jesus's answer to his own question is decisive: 'I tell you, he will see that they get justice, and quickly.' The phrase *en tachei* ('quickly') means 'soon' here (as in Acts 25:4; Romans 16:20; Revelation 1:1; 22:7), rather than 'suddenly' (as in Acts 12:7).[297] As in 21:5–36, Jesus teaches his disciples to expect imminent justice and deliverance with the coming of the Son of Man, even as he warns them about the need for endurance and faithfulness during an indefinite period of delay. These twin perspectives, which are also found in the Lord's Prayer (11:2–4), should govern the lives of believers until he returns.

Jesus concludes with another rhetorical question: 'However, when the Son of Man comes, will he find faith on the earth?' Although God's intention to vindicate his people 'quickly' is a major emphasis in the parable, the need for faith expressed in persistent prayer is another. Both the woman and the judge have something to teach us. The era before the coming of the Son of Man will be one of tribulation, persecution and the need to call upon God for vindication. This will be a time to demonstrate God's character and concerns in seeking justice for the oppressed – including fellow believers – while waiting prayerfully for his kingdom to come.

Asking for mercy (18:9–14)

The parable of the Pharisee and the tax collector

9 To some who were confident of their own righteousness and looked down on everyone else, Jesus told this parable: **10** 'Two men went up to the temple to pray, one a Pharisee and the other a tax collector. **11** The Pharisee stood by himself and prayed: "God, I thank you that I am not like other

---

[296] Nolland, *Luke 9:21–18:34*, 865, translates, 'He will indeed show himself long-suffering with them.' Bock, *Luke 9:51–24:53*, 1452–4, surveys twelve possible interpretations and seems to favour the view that 'God is patient with his elect in lightening the intensity of their suffering until he comes.'

[297] Marshall, *Luke*, 676; Nolland, *Luke 9:21–18:34*, 870.

people - robbers, evildoers, adulterers - or even like this tax collector. **12**I fast twice a week and give a tenth of all I get."

13'But the tax collector stood at a distance. He would not even look up to heaven, but beat his breast and said,

"God, have mercy on me, a sinner." **14**'I tell you that this man, rather than the other, went home justified before God. For all those who exalt themselves will be humbled, and those who humble themselves will be exalted.'

9–10. The introduction to Jesus's next parable, which only Luke records, clearly links it with what has gone before (*Eipen de kai*, 'he also said', not translated by the NIV). Disciples remain present, but the parable is specifically directed 'to some who were confident of their own righteousness and looked down on everyone else'. Although Pharisees are often identified this way by Luke (5:30; 7:39; 16:14–15), the parable has a broader application.[298] 'Two men went up to the temple to pray, one a Pharisee and the other a tax collector.' Both appear to be pious Jews, intent on praying, but the second is 'a toll collector' (*telōnēs*), who mixed with Gentiles and collected indirect taxes for the Roman authorities (see my comment on 3:12). This man willingly classified himself as a sinner (verse 13). Most likely, they both went to the Temple at nine in the morning (Acts 2:15) or at three in the afternoon (Acts 3:1), when private prayer could be offered in the temple courts while sacrifices were being offered by the priests.[299]

11–12. 'The Pharisee stood by himself and prayed' (NIV) portrays a sense of superiority and separation from others (so also ESV). But the manuscript evidence favours the reading 'stood and prayed these things to himself', emphasising that he prayed silently (CSB, 'standing and praying like this about himself').[300] He began his prayer with thanksgiving ('God, I thank you'), but he was not thankful for what *God* had done in his life. Rather, the Pharisee rejoiced in the way he was different from others ('not like other people – robbers, evildoers, adulterers – or even like this tax collector') and scrupulous in the practice of his religion, going well beyond the legal requirements of the Law ('I fast twice a week and give a tenth of all I get'). Fasting was required on the Day of Atonement (Leviticus

---

[298] The verb *exoutheneō* ('look down on') means treating someone as beneath consideration and without merit (BDAG, 'reject disdainfully'; compare 23:11).
[299] See Bailey, *Poet and Peasant*, 144–7; Edwards, *Luke*, 503.
[300] The NIV follows the less well attested variant *statheis pros heauton tauta proseucheto*, but the better manuscripts favour the order *statheis tauta pros heauton proseucheto*. Several ancient witnesses omit the phrase entirely. See Metzger, *Textual Commentary*, 143; Marshall, *Luke*, 679; Nolland, *Luke 9:21–18:34*, 875–6.

16:29–30) and at other times in the year (Esther 9:31; Zechariah 8:19), but Pharisees apparently fasted every Monday and Thursday (*Didache* 8:1). They also exceeded the biblical demand for tithing (Deuteronomy 14:22–3; Luke 11:42). 'All I get' could mean that he paid tithes on everything he acquired, even though the producer of the goods might already have paid the necessary tithes.[301] This man showed little dependence on the grace of God and was unwilling to express grace towards others.

13. 'The tax collector stood at a distance,' expressing his alienation and shame. Lifting one's eyes to heaven was associated with seeking God's mercy (as in Psalm 123), but the tax collector could not do that ('he would not even look up to heaven'; see Ezra 9:6). His only gesture was to 'beat his breast' – as an indication of humility, grief and contrition (see Luke 23:48) – and to say, 'God, have mercy on me, a sinner' (recalling Psalm 51:1–2). His prayer for mercy literally asked for God to be propitiated and willing to forgive him.[302] Praying for forgiveness in that sacrificial context was especially meaningful.

14. Both the Pharisee and the toll collector went up to the Temple to pray (verse 10), but Jesus concluded that only the latter 'went down to his house justified (*katebē houtos dedikaiōmenos eis ton oikon autou*)'. The NIV rightly adds 'before God' (see 2 Esdras 12:7). The toll collector models for Luke's readers the approach of those seeking the mercy of God expressed in the gospel.[303] Previously, the Pharisees were accused of justifying themselves 'in the eyes of others' (16:15; compare 10:29). The difference between the characters in the parable is expressed in their prayers. Jesus used this comparison, as Green says, 'to speak to the issue of what sort of people, with what sort of character and commitments as well as behaviors, are fit for the kingdom of God'.[304] Jesus went on to identify the serious consequences of the two different approaches: 'For all who exalt themselves will be humbled, and those who humble themselves

---

[301] Marshall, *Luke*, 679–70. See Jeremias, *Parables*, 140, for other possibilities.

[302] The verb used here (*hilaskomai*) has that meaning in some LXX passages (e.g., Exodus 32:14; Psalm 78[ET 79]:9; Lamentations 3:42). It was normally used with reference to rituals of atonement. See F. Büchsell, 'ἱλάσκομαι', *TDNT* 3:314–17; Hebrews 2:17.

[303] In the Pauline letters, justification by/through faith is specifically related to the death and resurrection of Jesus (e.g., Romans 3:24–6; 5:1, 9). See Edwards, *Luke*, 502, 506–7.

[304] Green, *Luke*, 644. He notes that 'Luke has structured this account so as to render the choices starkly and ensure that the toll collector will be viewed, however paradoxically, as the positive model' (645).

will be exalted' (restating 14:11; compare 1:52; Psalm 75:6–7). The saying in this context lays a foundation for understanding the significance of the next two narratives.

Seeking salvation (18:15–30)

The little children and Jesus

15 People were also bringing babies to Jesus for him to place his hands on them. When the disciples saw this, they rebuked them. **16** But Jesus called the children to him and said, 'Let the little children come to me, and do not hinder them, for the kingdom of God belongs to such as these. **17** Truly I tell you, anyone who will not receive the kingdom of God like a little child will never enter it.'

The rich and the kingdom of God

18 A certain ruler asked him, 'Good teacher, what must I do to inherit eternal life?'

19 'Why do you call me good?' Jesus answered. 'No one is good – except God alone. **20** You know the commandments: "You shall not commit adultery, you shall not murder, you shall not steal, you shall not give false testimony, honour your father and mother."[a]'

21 'All these I have kept since I was a boy,' he said.

22 When Jesus heard this, he said to him, 'You still lack one thing. Sell everything you have and give to the poor, and you will have treasure in heaven. Then come, follow me.'

23 When he heard this, he became very sad, because he was very wealthy. **24** Jesus looked at him and said, 'How hard it is for the rich to enter the kingdom of God! **25** Indeed, it is easier for a camel to go through the eye of a needle than for someone who is rich to enter the kingdom of God.'

26 Those who heard this asked, 'Who then can be saved?'

27 Jesus replied, 'What is impossible with man is possible with God.'

28 Peter said to him, 'We have left all we had to follow you!'

29 'Truly I tell you,' Jesus said to them, 'no one who has left home or wife or brothers or sisters or parents or children for the sake of the kingdom of God **30** will fail to receive many times as much in this age, and in the age to come eternal life.'

---

a 20 Exodus 20:12-16; Deut. 5:16-20

15–16. Luke follows Mark for the first time since 9:50 to record a series of incidents on the last stage of Jesus's journey to Jerusalem (Mark 10:13–52; Matthew 19:13–30). The story of his encounter with little children has two surprising outcomes. First, it shows his desire to welcome them into the kingdom of God on an equal footing with adults. The strangeness of the situation is highlighted by Luke's distinctive introduction: 'Now they were bringing even infants [*kai ta brephē*] to him' (ESV).[305] Their desire for him to place his hands on them may have been for healing, but Mark more broadly relates this action to blessing (10:16) and Matthew to prayer (19:13). 'When the disciples saw this, they rebuked them,' perhaps considering it a waste of Jesus's time. However, 'Jesus called the little children to him and said, "Let the little children come to me, and do not hinder them, for the kingdom of God belongs to such as these."' At one level, this was a challenge to the disciples about whether his teaching in 9:47–8 was being observed. At another level, he was saying something radically new. Infanticide and child abandonment were common in the ancient world, but children were valued and cared for in the context of Jewish family life (Deuteronomy 6:6–9; Psalms 127:3–5; 128:3–4; Luke 2:51–2). Jesus went a step further in suggesting that they could inherit the kingdom as children, even babies.[306] Christians later used this passage to justify the practice of infant baptism, as an expression of parental confidence in Jesus's willingness to receive their children and save them.

17. The second outcome of Jesus's blessing the children was his use of them as models for adults in relation to the kingdom: 'Truly I tell you, anyone who will not receive the kingdom of God like a child will never enter it' (see verses 24–5). Especially in relation to the preceding parable (verses 9–14) and the narrative to follow (verses 18–30), it is clear that the message of the kingdom is for the helpless, the needy, the powerless and the weak. Receiving the kingdom of God 'like a little child' means receiving it with total dependence on the goodness and grace of God. Nolland concludes, 'Children are free from all the barriers that adult self-importance and self-sufficiency place between an individual and the approach of the kingdom of God, so the kingdom of God is for them and for those who will become childlike.'[307]

18–20. Luke moves immediately to record an encounter with someone at the other end of the social spectrum to children ('a certain ruler'). The

---

[305] Mark uses the more general term *paidia* ('children'), which Luke employs in verses 16, 17. This could refer to those between birth and age seven.

[306] C. Reeder, 'Child, Children', *DJG*, 109–13, helpfully compares the treatment of children in ancient Roman society with those in Jewish families, but he fails to consider the covenantal status of children within Judaism. Solomon Gacece, 'Street Children', *Africa Bible Commentary*, 1266, envisages a Christian response to destitute children in Africa today.

[307] Nolland, *Luke 9:21–18:34*, 872.

term *archōn* was previously applied to a synagogue leader (8:41), a magistrate (12:58) and 'a prominent Pharisee' (14:1). Here it probably describes
someone belonging to the Jewish lay leadership, soon to participate in
the trial and execution of Jesus (23:13, 35; 24:20; Acts 3:17; 5:26).[308] This
man, however, asked the burning question, 'Good teacher, what must I
do to inherit eternal life?' (10:25; 13:23). Jesus first replied with another
question ('Why do you call me good?') and then insisted, 'No one is
good – except God alone.' Although this could raise the question of his
own unique relationship with God, contextually it has another purpose.
It introduces a selection of God's commandments, which express his
goodness in revealing his will for his people: 'You shall not commit
adultery, you shall not murder, you shall not steal, you shall not give false
testimony, honour your father and mother' (see 10:26).[309] Omission of the
commandment against coveting in each of the parallel accounts seems
to be a deliberate preparation for the challenge to follow. Jesus was not
suggesting that eternal life can be earned by keeping God's commandments. Rather, he was saying that those who know the goodness of God
and desire to live in his presence will seek to discover from Scripture
what pleases him and do it. In this way they will show themselves to be
genuine children of God, destined for eternal life.

21–2. The ruler's reply could suggest a life of pious obedience (see
1:6), but he expressed no remorse or sense of failure ('All these I have
kept since I was a boy'). Without the tender words at the beginning of
Mark 10:21 ('Jesus looked at him and loved him'), Luke simply records,
'When Jesus heard this, he said to him, "You still lack one thing. Sell
everything you have and give to the poor, and you will have treasure in
heaven. Then come, follow me."' Jesus understood the inadequacies and
failures of this wealthy and influential man (see verses 23–4). The 'one
thing' he called for was not simply an ascetic lifestyle or the renunciation of possessions as an end in itself. Rather, this man needed to divest
himself of everything that would hinder him from following Jesus and
inheriting eternal life (verse 18). Selling his possessions would be for
the purpose of investing in the kingdom and its priorities (see 5:27;
9:23; 12:33; 14:27, 33). Nolland observes, 'The coming of the kingdom

---

[308] Nolland, *Luke 9:21–18:34*, 885. Mark 10:17 and Matthew 19:16 do not specify
that he was a ruler. Matthew 19:20 adds that he was young.
[309] Perhaps the fifth commandment is placed after the four prohibitions to emphasise
the positive challenge of God's Law (Matthew 19:19 adds 'and love your neighbour
as yourself'). Mark 10:19 includes 'you shall not defraud'.

makes its own fresh demands and sets in a new and radical light the old commandments of God.'[310]

23–5. 'When he heard this, he became very sad, because he was very wealthy.' His sadness suggests a desire to do what Jesus said, but also reveals that he was hindered by his wealth from taking such a radical step.[311] Luke omits any reference to his departure from the scene (see 10:22; Matthew 19:22), and has Jesus address him with words directed to the disciples in the other Gospels: 'Jesus looked at him and said, "How hard it is for the rich to enter the kingdom of God!"' The expression translated 'the rich' (*hoi ta chrēmata echontes*, 'those who have possessions') broadens the application of his warning. This is driven home with an extreme example (see 6:41–2): 'Indeed, it is easier for a camel to go through the eye of a needle than for someone who is rich to enter the kingdom of God.' The absurdity of this image emphasises the enormous difficulty faced by anyone who is captivated by materialism and greed (see 6:24; 8:14; 11:41; 12:13–21, 33–4; 16:1–31).[312]

26–7. Jesus's warning disturbed those who heard it, and one of them asked, 'Who then can be saved?' This question links the parallel concepts of inheriting eternal life (verse 18) with being saved and entering the kingdom of God (verse 25). Salvation in this context means being rescued from divine judgment to enjoy the eternal life of God's kingdom (see 13:23–30). Jesus replied, 'What is impossible with man is possible with God.' Even the wealthy can be saved, as illustrated in 19:1–10, but they must be willing to humble themselves and express their need. Only God can break what Nolland calls 'the mesmerizing effect through which riches control those who possess them'.[313] Mark 10:27 adds that 'all things are possible with God' (see Luke 1:37).

28–30. Peter spoke up and said, 'We have left all we had to follow you!' The expression 'all we had' echoes 5:11, 28 and prepares for the details unfolded in verse 29 ('home or wife or brothers or sisters or parents or children'). They had done what Jesus asked them to do 'for the sake of the kingdom of God', meaning to enter the kingdom themselves, but also

---

[310] Nolland, *Luke 9:21–18:34*, 888.

[311] Green, *Luke*, 655–6, adds 'status honor' to the problem posed by this man's wealth and position in society, though this is not explicit in the account.

[312] Bailey, *Poet and Peasant*, 165–6, rightly dismisses attempts to soften the image, such as reading *kamilon* ('rope') instead of *kamēlon* ('camel') or identifying 'the eye of a needle' as a small door or gate. A later rabbinic saying similarly emphasises the impossibility of an elephant going through the eye of a needle.

[313] Nolland, *Luke 9:21–18:34*, 891.

to propagate the message of the kingdom (9:59–62; 14:26; compare Mark 10:29, 'for me and the gospel'). Jesus emphatically assured them ('Truly I tell you') of God's gracious provision for their immediate future – they would 'receive many times as much in this age' – and ultimately, 'in the age to come eternal life.' The former relates to the family of believers, which becomes a new source of *relational wealth* for them (see Matthew 19:29; Mark 10:30). The distinction between this age and the age to come reappears in 20:34–5.

12. The journey's end (Luke 18:31–19:27)

Luke's travel narrative draws to a close as he records Jesus's most explicit passion prediction so far and the disciples' lack of comprehension (18:31–4). This amplifies the predictions that prepared for the journey (9:21–2; 43b–5). Luke does not mention the request of James and John for prominence in Jesus's kingdom (Mark 10:35–40; compare Matthew 20:20–23), though he later parallels the sequel to this encounter (22:24–7; compare Mark 10:41–45; Matthew 19:24–8).[314] A modified version of the healing narrative in Mark 10:46–52 (compare Matthew 20:29–34) follows, involving a messianic confession (18:35–43). Luke alone presents the climactic story of Zacchaeus the wealthy chief tax collector, who welcomes Jesus into his home and learns that he came to seek and to save even people like himself (19:1–10). A lengthy parable is finally told, because Jesus was near Jerusalem 'and the people thought that the kingdom of God was going to appear at once' (19:11–27).[315]

A final prediction (18:31–4)

Jesus predicts his death a third time
31 Jesus took the Twelve aside and told them, 'We are going up to Jerusalem, and everything that is written by the prophets about the Son of Man will be fulfilled. **32** He will be handed over to the Gentiles. They will mock him, insult him and spit on him; **33** they will flog him and kill him. On the third day he will rise again.'

---

[314] Luke's omission of the 'ransom' saying in Mark 10:45 (*lytron*) is strange, given the fact that he uses the related noun 'redemption' (1:68; 2:38, *lytrōsis*) and the verb 'redeem' (24:21, *lytrousthai*) with reference to the work of Christ. The redemptive nature of Jesus's death is implied by 22:20–22, 37.
[315] Nolland, *Luke 18:35–24:53*, 910–12, argues that this is a variant of the parable in Matthew 25:14–30.

34 The disciples did not understand any of this. Its meaning was hidden from them, and they did not know what he was talking about.

31–3. Luke records six predictions of Jesus's suffering and death (9:22, 44; 12:50; 13:33; 17:25; 18:31–3), this one being closest in form to the first. 'Jesus took the Twelve aside' and shared more alarming details with them privately (see Mark 10:32; Matthew 20:17). He began by saying, 'We are going up to Jerusalem, and everything written by the prophets about the Son of Man will be fulfilled.' This confident prediction amplifies the 'must' (*dei*) of 9:22; 17:25 in terms of God's revealed will for his Messiah. Jesus would soon draw attention to the inevitable fulfilment of Isaiah 53:12 (Luke 22:37). After his resurrection he would speak more broadly in terms of fulfilling what 'Moses and all the prophets' taught (24:25–7) and what 'the Law of Moses, the Prophets and the Psalms' revealed (24:44–9). Daniel 7:13 must have been particularly in mind concerning his heavenly exaltation as 'the Son of Man', but that prophecy does not indicate any prior need for him to suffer (see my comment on 5:24).[316] Involvement by 'the elders, the chief priests and the teachers of the law' (9:22) is presumed when Jesus adds, 'he will be *handed over* to the Gentiles' (my emphasis; compare Mark 10:33; Luke 23:1, 11, 14; Acts 2:23). A series of terms describe the demeaning and extreme pain he will suffer before death: 'They will mock him, insult him and spit on him; they will flog him and kill him.'[317] The ultimate prediction ('On the third day he will rise again') presents the outcome as his own victory over death (as in 24:46; Acts 17:3) rather than as the implied action of God (9:22; 24:7; Acts 10:41). But these are complementary ways of describing the same supernatural event.

34. The failure of the disciples (meaning 'the Twelve' here (verse 31)) to 'understand any of this' teaching mirrors 9:45. As previously, 'Its meaning was hidden from them, and they did not know what he was talking about.' Given the clarity of Jesus's prediction and the number of times he had spoken previously about his approaching suffering, their ignorance was

---

[316] The title 'Son of Man' is used paradoxically in the passion predictions. It can function in a summary way when Jesus is reflecting on various aspects of prophetic teaching about the Messiah and the Suffering Servant.

[317] Jewish guards mock and insult him in 22:63–5. Then Herod and his soldiers ridicule and mock him in 23:11. In 23:36–7, the mocking is by Roman soldiers, and in 23:39 insults are hurled at Jesus by one of the criminals crucified with him. Even before Jesus is handed over to the Gentiles, he suffers these indignities from his own people.

culpable (see 24:16, 25–32). Presumably, they were fearfully resistant to the implications of what they were being told.

A surprising confession (18:35–43)

A blind beggar receives his sight

35 As Jesus approached Jericho, a blind man was sitting by the roadside begging. **36** When he heard the crowd going by, he asked what was happening. **37** They told him, 'Jesus of Nazareth is passing by.'

38 He called out, 'Jesus, Son of David, have mercy on me!'

39 Those who led the way rebuked him and told him to be quiet, but he shouted all the more, 'Son of David, have mercy on me!'

40 Jesus stopped and ordered the man to be brought to him. When he came near, Jesus asked him, **41** 'What do you want me to do for you?'

'Lord, I want to see,' he replied.

42 Jesus said to him, 'Receive your sight; your faith has healed you.'

43 Immediately he received his sight and followed Jesus, praising God. When all the people saw it, they also praised God.

35–7. Jesus was on the move again and approaching Jericho in the Jordan Valley, which was about 29km (18 miles) east of Jerusalem.[318] 'A blind man was sitting by the roadside begging.' Mark tells us that his name was Bartimaeus and that Jesus met him when he was leaving Jericho (10:46; see Matthew 20:29–30, 'two blind men'). Luke, however, portrays Jesus approaching Jericho, possibly to allow for the meeting with Zacchaeus to be the narrative climax to a series of encounters (18:18–19:10). Forced by his blindness to sit in a prominent place and beg for help, Green observes, 'This man would have had no attachments to possessions or kin, his existence would have been an embarrassment (see 16:3), marginal to the daily lives of others, and, if not for the premium placed on almsgiving in Jewish circles, short-lived.'[319] 'When he heard the crowd going by, he asked what was happening. They told him, "Jesus of Nazareth is passing

---

[318] This implies that Jesus journeyed from 'the border between Samaria and Galilee' (17:11) through Perea to Jericho. Note the repetition of the verb 'draw near' in 18:35; 19:29, 37, 41, as a way of highlighting his steady approach to Jerusalem and the Temple.

[319] Green, *Luke*, 663. Recovery of sight for the blind is proclaimed in 4:18, and it is mentioned in 7:21–2 among other forms of healing that Jesus accomplished, but the only example of it in Luke's account is here. See also Matthew 9:27–31; Mark 8:22–6.

by,'"[320] which was enough for him to cry out in faith for Jesus's help, suggesting some prior knowledge of his grace and power.

38–9. Somewhat like the lepers in 17:13, the blind man asked Jesus to have mercy on him, though he is the first person in this Gospel to use the title 'Son of David' openly. The political role of the Messiah in biblical prophecy is emphasised in later Jewish texts, but Luke progressively reveals a different picture. Jesus's Davidic descent is highlighted in 1:27, 32; 2:4; 3:31, but he first appears in public as the end-time prophet and healer of God's people (4:16–27; 7:18–23; compare Isaiah 61:1–2; 35:5–6).[321] The disciples eventually confess him as Messiah, perceiving him to be greater than any of the prophets (9:18–20). Given this sequence of events, the blind man's appeal for the Son of David to heal him reflects a surprisingly insightful understanding of his role. 'Those who led the way' probably refers to those at the front of the crowd, who were in a hurry to reach Jerusalem for Passover. Like the disciples in verse 15, they were impatient with this interruption, and so they 'rebuked him and told him to be quiet'. However, the man would not pass up this opportunity for healing and 'he shouted all the more, "Son of David, have mercy on me!"'

40–43. Jesus stopped and ordered the man to be brought to him. When he came near, he asked him, 'What do you want me to do for you?' As on previous occasions, Jesus sought to engage personally with someone seeking his help and called upon him to articulate what he needed. His reply ('Lord, I want to see') was met with a simple command ('Receive your sight'),[322] and a declaration highlighting the significance of his faith ('your faith has healed you', *sesōken,* as in 17:19). 'Immediately he received his sight and followed Jesus, praising God.' Like the Samaritan who returned to give praise to God and thank Jesus, this man expressed his gratitude openly and caused others to rejoice with him ('When all the people saw it, they also praised God'). The healing miracle and the praise it engendered was a momentary realisation of the promised messianic renewal and restoration of all things (Acts 3:19–21; compare Isaiah 11:6–9; 32:1–4; 35:1–10; 65:17–25).

---

[320] Greek *ho Nazōraios* ('the Nazorean') most likely reflects the fact that Jesus came from Nazareth, though some have argued for messianic overtones derived from Isaiah 11:1 (Hebrew *nēṣer,* 'shoot'). See Nolland, *Luke 18:35–24:53,* 899–900.

[321] See Y. Miura, 'Son of David', *DJG,* 88186.

[322] Given his confession that Jesus was the Son of David, 'Lord' probably meant more than 'Sir' or 'Master' here (Edwards, *Luke,* 526). Note the way the healing of the blind man in John 9:35–8 unfolds.

An unexpected disciple (19:1–10)

Zacchaeus the tax collector

19 Jesus entered Jericho and was passing through. **2** A man was there by the name of Zacchaeus; he was a chief tax collector and was wealthy. **3** He wanted to see who Jesus was, but because he was short he could not see over the crowd. **4** So he ran ahead and climbed a sycamore-fig tree to see him, since Jesus was coming that way.

5 When Jesus reached the spot, he looked up and said to him, 'Zacchaeus, come down immediately. I must stay at your house today.' **6** So he came down at once and welcomed him gladly.

7 All the people saw this and began to mutter, 'He has gone to be the guest of a sinner.'

8 But Zacchaeus stood up and said to the Lord, 'Look, Lord! Here and now I give half of my possessions to the poor, and if I have cheated anybody out of anything, I will pay back four times the amount.'

9 Jesus said to him, 'Today salvation has come to this house, because this man, too, is a son of Abraham. **10** For the Son of Man came to seek and to save the lost.'

1–2. Luke pairs the healing of the blind man with a story from his own unique source about another outcast of Jewish society, who came to Jesus and experienced salvation (verse 9). Drawing together the themes of healing and salvation, the evangelist portrays Jesus as the Son of Man who 'came to seek and to save the lost' (verse 10). Fitzmyer argues, 'The two episodes are fitting scenes at the end of the lengthy Lucan travel account, for they prepare for Jesus' approach to Jerusalem as "the Son of David" and the one who brings salvation to "the lost".'[323] 'Jesus entered Jericho and was passing through', where he met Zacchaeus, who was 'a chief tax collector and was wealthy'. His name was a Greek form of the Hebrew Zakkai or Zaccai (Ezra 2:9; Nehemiah 7:15; 2 Maccabees 10:19), which paradoxically meant 'clean, innocent'.[324] Although the term 'chief tax collector' (*architelōnēs*) is without parallel in ancient texts, it suggests the likely possibility that he was responsible for the management of several agents in the region, who collected indirect taxes or tolls for the Roman government (see 3:12; 5:27–30; 7:34; 18:10–13). He was 'wealthy'

[323] Fitzmyer, *Luke X–XXIV*, 1222. Note also links with the wealthy ruler (18:18–23). Luke has carefully framed 18:9–19:10 'to represent various sides of the question of individual salvation' (Seccombe, *The Poor*, 137). The Zacchaeus story shows how a rich man can be saved.
[324] Fitzmyer, *Luke X–XXIV*, 1223.

because of the financial benefits of this role,[325] but this did not put him beyond salvation.

3–4. Like the wealthy ruler (18:18–23) and the blind beggar (18:36–7), Zacchaeus already knew something about Jesus. He had no need for physical healing, but 'he wanted to see who Jesus was' (see 10:21–2). The rest of the narrative reveals that he was driven by more than curiosity. Since he was short, 'he could not see over the crowd', but this impediment did not stop him, 'So he ran ahead and climbed a sycamore-fig tree to see him, since Jesus was coming that way.'[326] Zacchaeus humbled himself in a very public way in order to achieve his goal.

5–6. 'When Jesus reached the spot, he looked up and said to him, "Zacchaeus, come down immediately. I must stay at your house today."' As in previous encounters with those in need, Jesus responded to the initiative of Zacchaeus by drawing him into a more personal engagement than he expected. We are not told how Jesus knew his name, but addressing him in this way was significant, especially since the blind man in 18:35 was not named. The word 'must' (*dei*) suggests a divine necessity for this meeting, and 'immediately' stresses the urgency of taking up the offer.[327] Jesus's self-invitation to stay at his house expressed acceptance and the possibility of forgiveness. In response, Zacchaeus 'came down at once and welcomed him gladly'. His joyful obedience was a recognition of the grace that Jesus was showing towards him, enabling him to listen to his teaching and become a disciple (see 10:38–42).

7–8. 'All the people saw this and began to mutter, "He has gone to be the guest of a sinner!"' The grumbling of the crowd contrasts with the joy of Zacchaeus. Adopting the attitude of the Pharisees reflected in 5:27–30; 15:1–2, they considered that it was unworthy of Jesus to eat with such a person. However, reacting to their description of him as a sinner, 'Zacchaeus stood up and said to the Lord, "Look, Lord! Here and now

---

[325] The Roman method of revenue collection was open to abuse because collectors could add expenses and profits to the authorised amount. Zacchaeus was guilty of imperial collaboration and exploiting his own people (Brawley, *Luke*, 170).

[326] Nolland, *Luke 18:35–24:53*, 905, observes that the sycamore-fig, which is only mentioned here in the New Testament (compare my comment on 17:11), is 'a large evergreen, said to be easy to climb'.

[327] As in 2:11; 4:21; 19:9, 'Today' is used to communicate 'the immediacy of salvation' (Green, *Luke*, 670). Tannehill, *Narrative Unity* I, 122, describes this as a 'quest story' in which 'the results progressively overshoot Zacchaeus' limited expectations at the beginning'.

I give half of my possessions to the poor, and if I have cheated anybody out of anything, I will pay back four times the amount.'" As in 18:41, addressing Jesus as 'Lord' indicates some recognition of his identity and authority. The NIV adds 'Here and now' to bring out the meaning of the present tense of the verb 'give' in this context. Zacchaeus was not expressing his customary pattern of life (see 18:11), but his intention to act in a radically new way with his wealth.[328] Although 'half of my possessions' falls short of Jesus's challenge to the rich ruler (18:22), it was a voluntary commitment by Zacchaeus in response to what he knew of the teaching of Jesus. It showed his willingness to adopt Jesus's kingdom values and use his money in the way that Jesus directed (see 12:32–4; 16:11–13). In retrospect, it confirms that the demand of Jesus in 18:22 to sell everything and give to the poor was not an absolute requirement for all would-be disciples. Nevertheless, Zacchaeus continued to express his repentance in a dramatic way ('If I have cheated anyone out of anything, I will pay back four times the amount').[329] In biblical law, restitution in connection with theft normally required the addition of one-fifth to the value stolen (Leviticus 6:1–5), but greater restitution was demanded after the theft and disposal of oxen and sheep (Exodus 22:1, fivefold and fourfold respectively). Nolland concludes, 'Against this general background, Zacchaeus' scale of restoration appears to more than compensate for any of his misdeeds.'[330]

9. Speaking to the crowd, but looking at Zacchaeus, Jesus said, 'Today salvation has come to this house.' The word 'today' recalls Jesus's previous use of the term (verse 5; compare 4:21) and confirms the immediate significance of his visit to the house of Zacchaeus (*oikos* could mean 'household', as in Acts 10:2; 11:14; 16:15, 31; 18:8). 'Salvation' in Luke's Gospel embraces everything that the prophets predicted in connection with the coming of the Messiah and the kingdom of God (1:68–79;

---

[328] Fitzmyer, *Luke X–XXIV*, 1220–21, and Green, *Luke*, 671–2, read the present tense verb *didōmi* in an iterative sense, arguing that Zacchaeus sought vindication for his *regular practice* as a pious Jew, rather than salvation. But the context speaks otherwise, and the Greek tense should be read in a futuristic or progressive way to express intention (so also Brawley, *Luke*, 171).

[329] Green, *Luke*, 672, argues that repentance 'lies outside the narrative', but the conditional clause clearly expresses an intended change of attitude and behaviour. Tannehill, *Narrative Unity* I, 123–4, rightly regards Zacchaeus as an example of radical repentance.

[330] Nolland, *Luke 18:35–24:53*, 906. He notes that Roman also law required fourfold restoration in certain circumstances.

2:30–32; 3:6). The verb 'save' is sometimes used in connection with Jesus's healings and exorcisms (6:9; 8:36, 48, 50; 17:19; 18:42). In other contexts, it relates to forgiveness (7:50), rescue from divine judgment (8:12; 9:24; 13:23) and eternal life (18:26–30). When Jesus acts to heal and release people from Satan's bondage, this anticipates the renewal of creation when he comes again in glory (Acts 3:16–21). But when he restores people to a right relationship with God, salvation in terms of forgiveness and transformation through repentance and faith is immediately experienced.

When Zacchaeus encountered Jesus, he was assured that the messianic salvation was for *him*, even though he had strayed from the path of faith and obedience to God. Jesus's explanation ('because this man, too, is a son of Abraham') relates to the biblical promises about God blessing the offspring of Abraham (Genesis 12:1–3; 15:12–19; 22:15–18). Despite his history as a toll collector and sinner, Zacchaeus had not cut himself off irrevocably from the possibility of end-time salvation. Fitzmyer concludes, 'As much as any other Israelite, he is entitled to the blessings of Abraham, and especially to the form of those blessings now coming through Jesus.'[331] Zacchaeus demonstrated by his words and actions that he was a true son of Abraham. In his second volume Luke shows how the promised blessings have been extended to believers in every nation through the preaching of the gospel about Jesus and his saving work (Acts 10–11; 13–19; 28; see also Galatians 3:7–9).

10. This scene finishes with a comprehensive statement about why Jesus came (see 5:32): 'For the Son of Man came to seek and to save the lost.' Zacchaeus was one of 'the lost sheep of Israel' (Matthew 10:6), and Jesus was the Davidic ruler appointed by God to heal, save, and care for his people (Ezekiel 34:16, 22–4). Use of the title 'the Son of Man' in this context may relate especially to his claim to have authority to forgive sins (5:24). His mission 'to seek and to save the lost' certainly recalls the parables in chapter 15. This narrative is not simply about Zacchaeus seeking Jesus, but about Jesus seeking Zacchaeus.

A timely warning (19:11–27)

The parable of the ten minas

11 While they were listening to this, he went on to tell them a parable, because he was near Jerusalem and the people thought that the kingdom of God was going to appear at once. **12** He said: 'A man of noble birth went to a distant country to have himself appointed king and then to return. **13** So he called ten of his servants

331 Fitzmyer, *Luke X–XXIV*, 1226.

and gave them ten minas.ᵃ "Put this money to work," he said, "until I come back."

14 'But his subjects hated him and sent a delegation after him to say, "We don't want this man to be our king."

15 'He was made king, however, and returned home. Then he sent for the servants to whom he had given the money, in order to find out what they had gained with it.

16 'The first one came and said, "Sir, your mina has earned ten more."

17 ' "Well done, my good servant!" his master replied. "Because you have been trustworthy in a very small matter, take charge of ten cities."

18 'The second came and said, "Sir, your mina has earned five more."

19 'His master answered, "You take charge of five cities."

20 'Then another servant came and said, "Sir, here is your mina; I have kept it laid away in a piece of cloth. 21 I was afraid of you, because you are a hard man. You take out what you did not put in and reap what you did not sow."

22 'His master replied, "I will judge you by your own words, you wicked servant! You knew, did you, that I am a hard man, taking out what I did not put in, and reaping what I did not sow? 23 Why then didn't you put my money on deposit, so that when I came back, I could have collected it with interest?"

24 'Then he said to those standing by, "Take his mina away from him and give it to the one who has ten minas."

25 ' "Sir," they said, "he already has ten!"

26 'He replied, "I tell you that to everyone who has, more will be given, but as for the one who has nothing, even what they have will be taken away. 27 But those enemies of mine who did not want me to be king over them – bring them here and kill them in front of me." '

_____

a 13 A mina was about three months' wages.

11. This parable is clearly related to the preceding incident ('While they were listening to this').³³² The crowd who muttered about Jesus being 'the guest of a sinner' (verse 7) included those who were on their way to Jerusalem with him (18:39). When Jesus spoke about salvation coming to Zacchaeus and his household and made his declaration about the Son Man coming 'to seek and to save the lost' (19:9–10), some overheard what he was saying and were disturbed. Luke also indicates that the

_____

³³² Matthew 25:14–30 has a different version of the story in the context of teaching in Jerusalem about the destruction of the Temple, Jesus's coming in glory and 'the end of the age' (24:3). Fitzmyer, *Luke X–XXIV*, 1228–31, argues that both evangelists used a common source and that Luke's modifications flow from the setting he gives it in 19:11. Edwards, *Luke*, 535, sees the parable in Luke 19:11–27 as an expansion of the one in 12:36–46.

parable was provoked by the fact that Jesus was 'near Jerusalem and the people thought that the kingdom of God was going to appear at once'. The prophets often spoke of Jerusalem, Zion or the Temple as the place from which the saving grace of God would extend to the whole nation and beyond (e.g., Isaiah 2:1–5; 4:2–6; 51:17–52:3). Jesus had proclaimed the imminence of the kingdom and the need for an urgent response (11:20; 13:22–30; 17:20–37). He had also predicted that Jerusalem would be the place where he would be put to death (13:31–3) and rise again (18:31–3). How were these expectations related and what would be the implications for his disciples?

12–13. 'A man of noble birth went to a distant country to have himself appointed king and then to return.' Jesus introduces a political scenario to articulate the eschatological timetable implicit in much of his teaching. Although the Romans avoided the title 'king' for their own rulers at that time, Fitzmyer says they granted it occasionally 'to certain ethnic rulers in the eastern provinces of the empire'.[333] The ethical dimension of the parable is introduced when 'he called ten of his servants and gave them ten minas'. A mina was worth about one-sixtieth of a talent (Matthew 25:15 [NIV, 'bag of gold']) or 'roughly four months' wages for a day labourer'.[334] The emphasis in what follows is not on the size of the gift, but on appropriate stewardship (as in 12:35–46). Each of the ten is given the same amount and told, 'Put this money to work . . . until I come back.'[335]

14–15. A new feature in the plot emerges: 'his subjects hated him and sent a delegation after him to say, "We don't want this man to be our king."' When Archelaus the son of Herod the Great inherited half of his father's kingdom in 4 BC, he travelled to Rome to be made king by Caesar Augustus. But a delegation of fifty Palestinians was sent to oppose this and appeal for self-rule.[336] Jesus may have alluded to that event to illustrate his

---

[333] Fitzmyer, *Luke X–XXIV*, 1235. Herod the Great was an example of this. The Greek expression in 19:11 (*labein heautō basileian*) more literally translates 'to receive for himself a kingdom' (ESV).

[334] Green, *Luke*, 678. Marshall, *Luke*, 704, supports the reading 'about three months' wages'.

[335] The verb *pragmateusasthe* ('Put this money to work') is rendered by the ESV 'Engage in business'. The expression *en hō erchomai* ('until I come back') could be rendered 'while I am gone' (Fitzmyer, *Luke X–XXIV*, 1235; Edwards, *Luke*, 537, note 65).

[336] Josephus, *War* 2.14–100; *Antiquities* 17.224–340, records that Caesar appointed Archelaus ethnarch, rather than king.

point, but the scenario he envisaged for himself was different: rejection by his own people in Jerusalem (9:22, 44), enthronement as Messiah by his heavenly Father through resurrection and ascension (20:41–4; 22:69) and ultimate return in glory (21:27). Green observes, 'Jesus often used recognizably realistic anecdotes in order to score important points about the nature of God, the kingdom, and faithful comportment among those oriented toward the purpose of God, without insisting on point-for-point, allegorizing correspondence.'[337] The parable now focuses on what happened when the noble was made king and returned home: 'Then he sent for the servants to whom he had given the money, in order to find out what they had gained with it.'

16–19. 'The first one came and said, "Sir, your mina has earned ten more."' As Brawley observes, this increase of 1,000 per cent 'could hardly be achieved except by some kind of exploitative behavior'.[338] Nevertheless, the servant is commended by the king ('Well done, my good servant') and is given an extremely generous reward ('Because you have been trustworthy in a very small matter, take charge of ten cities' [see 12:32; 22:30]). Jesus did not shrink from using worldly examples to shock his audience and make his point. Brawley notes that the king's commendation is for his servant's success as 'a manipulator in an extractive economy'.[339] He is like the dishonest manager who uses 'worldly wealth' to secure his future (16:8–9).

'The second came and said, "Sir, your mina has earned five more."' His achievement was less impressive (a 500 per cent increase), but the master rewarded him in a similar way, answering, 'You take charge of five cities.' As in 16:1–12, Jesus uses a confronting example of stewardship to challenge his listeners. The details of the parable should not be applied with simplistic spiritual parallels.

20–23. Attention turns to a third servant among the ten (*ho heteros*, 'the other', denoting 'the odd man out'), who said to his master, 'Sir, here is your mina; I have kept it laid away in a piece of cloth. I was afraid of you because you are a hard man. You take out what you did not put in and reap what you did not sow.' In view of the instruction to 'put this money

---

[337] Green, *Luke*, 676. Compare 11:5–8; 16:1–9; 18:1–8.

[338] Brawley, *Luke*, 172. Marshall, *Luke*, 705, notes the possibility of such a profit 'under ancient conditions with enormous interest and commission rates'. The commendations in Matthew 25:21, 23 are more fulsome and invite the servants to 'come and share your master's happiness', thus providing a more positive model for disciples to follow.

[339] Brawley, *Luke*, 172.

to work' (verse 13), this servant was disobedient and careless.[340] His fear that his master was exacting (*austēros*) and exploitative was correct, but his response was not consistent with this understanding. Consequently, the king replied, 'I will judge you by your own words, you wicked servant!' If the servant viewed his master that way, he should have acted more shrewdly: 'You knew, did you, that I am a hard man, taking out what I did not put in and reaping what I did not sow?' The king accepts this evaluation of his character and behaviour and asks, 'Why then didn't you put my money on deposit, so that when I came back, I could have collected it with interest?' The expression 'put my money on deposit' (*epi trapezan*, 'on the table') suggests a less effective method of increasing the value of his money, perhaps with money lenders. Given the prohibition against charging interest on loans to fellow Israelites (Deuteronomy 23:19–20), this may be ironical and mean, 'You could have at least lent the money to non-Jews and earned interest on it!'[341] This king is nothing like Jesus, but his call for a stewardship consistent with his character and expectations provides the basis for a 'how much more' application.

24–6. Then the master instructed 'those standing by' (presumably his attendants), 'Take his mina away from him and give it to the one who has ten minas.' They objected, 'Sir . . . he already has ten,' but he replied, 'I tell you that to everyone who has, more will be given, but as for the one who has nothing, even what they have will be taken away.' This restates a principle enunciated by Jesus in 8:18, where it refers to the teaching given to his disciples, so that they might share it with others. The economic focus of the parable broadens the application of the stewardship principle to the faithful employment of everything given by God for disciples to use in his service. The third servant does not lose his place in the household,[342] but even the small gift that he received from his master has to be taken away and given to someone who will put it to better use and make a profit with it.

27. The final words of the master return to the royal framework established in verses 12 and 14: 'But as for those enemies of mine who did not want me to be king over them – bring them here and kill them

---

[340] Bock, *Luke 9:51–24:53*, 1538, notes that 'hiding money in this fashion is attested in Jewish sources, but it was not regarded as safe as burying it in the ground'.
[341] Following Fitzmyer, *Luke X–XXIV*, 1237, Nolland, *Luke 9:21–18:34*, 798–9, discusses the complexities of the first-century loan market. Laws prohibiting interest to Jews on personal loans may not have been regarded as applicable to business loans (see also Exodus 22:25; Leviticus 25:35–8).
[342] Bock, *Luke 9:51–24:53*, 1542–3, argues differently on the basis of Matthew 25:30.

in front of me.' This possible allusion to the slaughter of Jesus's enemies has been unfairly taken as a sign of Luke's anti-semitism. The theme of rejection has been present since 4:16–30, but Jesus does not enter Jerusalem at this time to destroy his enemies. Rather, Luke draws attention to the meekness of his approach (19:28–40) and the injustice that he must suffer. Judgment will come (19:41–4; 21:20–28), but Jesus must first be treated like the enemies of the king in his parable (22:47–23:49)! Only thus will he save those who acknowledge him as their Lord and Master and reconstitute the people of God around himself.

6

Jesus's Ministry in Jerusalem

LUKE 19:28–21:38

Three episodes set the scene for a teaching ministry in Jerusalem. First, Jesus prepares to enter the city as 'the king who comes in the name of the Lord' (19:28–40). Second, as he approaches, he weeps over Jerusalem and predicts its destruction, because its inhabitants will not recognise 'the time of God's coming' (19:41–4). Third, he enters the temple courts and drives out those selling there, claiming that they had made God's house 'a den of robbers' (19:45–6). Then a narrative summary in 19:47–8 outlines his daily pattern of teaching at the Temple, highlighting the desire of the Jewish authorities to kill him and their difficulty in finding a way to do it, 'because all the people hung on his words'.

A particular day of teaching in the face of opposition is described in 20:1–40, during which Jesus's authority is openly challenged, the issue of paying taxes to Caesar is raised and a question from some of the Sadducees about the resurrection of the dead is answered. Then Jesus takes the initiative in questioning what David meant in Psalm 110:1 about the Messiah being his lord, warns his disciples about the behaviour of the teachers of the law and compares the gifts of the wealthy put into the temple treasury with that of a poor widow (20:41–21:4). A final segment of teaching develops his prediction about the destruction of the Temple and its end-time significance (21:5–36). Luke concludes this section of his Gospel with another narrative summary about Jesus's daily teaching at the Temple, emphasising the eagerness of the people to come early in the morning to hear him (21:37–8).

1. *The coming of the king (19:28–48)*

Entering Jerusalem (19:28–44)

Jesus comes to Jerusalem as king

28 After Jesus had said this, he went on ahead, going up to Jerusalem. **29** As he approached Bethphage and Bethany at the hill called the Mount of Olives, he sent two of his disciples, saying to them, **30** 'Go to the village ahead of you, and as you enter it, you will find a colt tied there, which no one has ever ridden. Untie it and bring it here. **31** If anyone asks you, "Why are you untying it?" say, "The Lord needs it." '

32 Those who were sent ahead went and found it just as he had told them. **33** As they were untying the colt, its owners asked them, 'Why are you untying the colt?'

34 They replied, 'The Lord needs it.'

35 They brought it to Jesus, threw their cloaks on the colt and put Jesus on it. **36** As he went along, people spread their cloaks on the road.

37 When he came near the place where the road goes down the Mount of Olives, the whole crowd of disciples began joyfully to praise God in loud voices for all the miracles they had seen:

38 'Blessed is the king who comes in the name of the Lord!'**b**

'Peace in heaven and glory in the highest!'

39 Some of the Pharisees in the crowd said to Jesus, 'Teacher, rebuke your disciples!'

40 'I tell you,' he replied, 'if they keep quiet, the stones will cry out.'

41 As he approached Jerusalem and saw the city, he wept over it **42** and said, 'If you, even you, had only known on this day what would bring you peace – but now it is hidden from your eyes. **43** The days will come upon you when your enemies will build an embankment against you and encircle you and hem you in on every side. **44** They will dash you to the ground, you and the children within your walls. They will not leave one stone on another, because you did not recognise the time of God's coming to you.'

_____

b 38 Psalm 118:26

28. All four Gospels record Jesus's entrance into Jerusalem and its sequel, but with different emphases and details (compare Matthew 21:1–22; Mark 11:1–25; John 12:12–36). Luke begins with a statement that, after Jesus had told the preceding parable, 'he went on ahead, going up to Jerusalem' (see Mark 10:32). This recalls the opening words of the travel narrative, where 'Jesus resolutely set out for Jerusalem' (9:51), and several declarations that he was determined to face what awaited him there (9:22, 44; 12:50; 13:32–3; 18:31–3). 'Going up to Jerusalem' from Jericho meant walking about 29km (18 miles) along the Roman road and climbing about a thousand metres (3,300 feet)!

29–31. 'As he approached Bethphage and Bethany at the hill called the Mount of Olives,' he was moving west towards the city and its temple.[1] At this point in the journey, 'he sent two of his disciples, saying to them, "Go to the village ahead of you, and as you enter it, you will find a colt tied there, which no one has ever ridden."' Although these details might suggest a prior arrangement that Jesus had made with the owner of the colt, they more likely indicate his foreknowledge of how a suitable animal might be obtained (see Jesus's knowledge about the fish in 5:4–7). Two disciples would confirm the fulfilment of his prediction 'according to the OT requirements for legally valid witness'.[2] Two other features of this narrative indicate Jesus's complete control over the situation. First, he declares his intention to ride into the city on 'a colt . . . which no one has ever ridden'.[3] The messianic significance of this method of arrival is highlighted in Matthew 21:4–5 with the assertion that 'this took place to fulfil what was spoken through the prophet' and a quote from Zechariah 9:9. Luke only alludes to this text, but Jesus's choice of this mode of transport constituted, as Watts says, 'his most direct claim to being God's promised humble Davidic Messiah (Zechariah 9:9), whose trust is in the Lord (Psalm 20:7; Isaiah 31:1; 43:17; compare Deuteronomy 11:4; 20:1; *Psalms of Solomon* 17:33)'.[4] Second, Jesus instructs the two messengers, 'If anyone asks you, "Why are you untying it?" say, "The Lord needs it."' Jesus's self-reference as 'the Lord' (*ho kyrios*) could simply mean 'the Master', though intimations of divinity are present in the broader narrative.

32–5. Luke emphasises the fulfilment of Jesus's prediction about the colt even more emphatically than the other evangelists by adding that those who were sent ahead went and found it 'just as he had told them'.

---

[1] There is uncertainty about the exact location of Bethphage, but Bethany is located about 2.7km east of Jerusalem (Fitzmyer, *Luke X–XXIV*, 1247–8)

[2] Nolland, *Luke 18:35–24:53*, 928. Marshall, *Luke*, 713, argues for a prior arrangement, but Fitzmyer, *Luke X–XXIV*, 1249, opts for Jesus's 'superior foreknowledge'.

[3] The word *pōlon* could refer to the foal of a horse (BDAG), but the echo of Zechariah 9:9 here points to the likelihood of a donkey (Nolland, *Luke 18:35–24:53*, 924).

[4] R. E. Watts, 'Triumphal Entry', *DJG*, 980–85. Watts contrasts accounts of 'triumphal entries' in Graeco–Roman and Jewish sources and relates Jesus's entry to biblical precedents.

Luke also notes that it was the colt's 'owners' (*ho kyrioi*) who asked them, 'Why are you untying the colt?' (Mark 11:5, 'some people standing there'). As instructed, the disciples replied, 'The Lord needs it,' and the owners made no objection to this sudden appropriation of their animal. This suggests some recognition of his identity and authority. So the two disciples 'brought it to Jesus, threw their cloaks on the colt and put Jesus on it'. In further acts of homage, 'as he went along, people spread their cloaks on the road' (see 2 Kings 9:13). Surprisingly, Luke says nothing about those who 'spread branches they had cut in the fields' (Mark 11:8; compare Matthew 21:8), omitting the detail that has captured the imagination of Christians celebrating Palm Sunday ever since!

37–8. Although Luke indicates that a wider group of people was involved in honouring Jesus, he emphasises that disciples were responsible for the praise that was uttered. 'When he came near the place where the road goes down the Mount of Olives, the whole crowd of disciples began joyfully to praise God in loud voices for all the miracles they had seen.' Those who had followed him from Galilee and had witnessed the mighty works he had done there were doubtless joined by others along the way. Luke uses two of his favourite verbs here – 'praise' (see 2:13, 20; 24:53; Acts 2:47; 3:8, 9) and 'rejoice' (see 1:14, 28; 6:23; 10:20; 13:17; 15:5, 32; 19:6; 22:5; 23:8) – implicitly inviting his readers to share in this response to Jesus. What they were saying in praise to God was, 'Blessed is the king who comes in the name of the Lord!' This greeting comes from Psalm 118:26 (117:26 LXX), where it relates to a royal figure who comes to visit 'the house of the Lord' and give thanks for his God-given victory in battle.[5] This psalm came to be used in welcoming pilgrims to Jerusalem for great festivals like Passover.[6] On this occasion, however, the greeting was specifically applied to Jesus, acknowledging him as 'the king' (see Mark 11:10, 'Blessed is the coming kingdom of our father David!'), whose victory was yet to be accomplished.

A further acclamation reminiscent of the angelic revelation at the birth of Jesus (2:13) proclaimed, 'Peace in heaven and glory in the highest!' This was both an expression of praise to God and a promise of blessing to his people. Universal peace is associated with the rule of the coming king in Zechariah 9:10 (see also Isaiah 9:6–7; Luke 1:79). Jesus's birth was announced in terms of peace on earth, and his advent into Jerusalem

---

[5] See Allen, *Psalms 101–150*, 124–5. Metzger, *Textual Commentary*, 144–5 evaluates different textual variants of this acclamation in verse 38.

[6] Mishnah, *Pesach* 10:6.

signified that heaven's peace and glory were now available for its people to experience.[7] Luke omits the Aramaism 'Hosanna' (Mark 11:9), which is expanded in Matthew 21:9 to 'Hosanna to the Son of David!' Originally a form of prayer in Psalm 118:25 ('Lord, save us!' (Hebrew, *Hoši'â nā'*)), this became part of the welcome offered to Jesus in those Gospels.

39–40. 'Some of the Pharisees in the crowd said to Jesus, "Teacher, rebuke your disciples!"' This is the last time Pharisees appear by name in Luke's narrative, though see my comment on 20:39.[8] They show respect for Jesus by calling him 'Teacher', but they are appalled by the claim that he is the promised messianic ruler. They exemplify those who say, 'We don't want this man to be our king' (verse 14) and who do not recognise 'the time of God's coming' to them (verse 44). In Nolland's words, 'They see in what Jesus does only the fracturing of their piety and therefore the insulting of God.'[9] Jesus responds by saying that the joyful news his disciples proclaim cannot possibly remain a secret. '"I tell you," he replied, "if they keep quiet, the stones will cry out."' A similar image in Habakkuk 2:11 speaks of stones crying out in judgment, but Psalm 96:11–13 might be a better comparison, where the natural world rejoices in the coming of the Lord to judge and to save (see also Isaiah 55:12; Luke 3:8).

41–2. 'As he approached Jerusalem and saw the city, he wept over it.' This passage, which only occurs in Luke, picks up and develops the themes of a previous lament (13:34–5; see also 23:28–31).[10] Jesus's weeping expressed his grief about the oracle against the city and its inhabitants he was about to deliver (see 2 Kings 8:11; Jeremiah 9:1; 14:17). The only other time he is recorded as weeping is in John 11:35 (at the grave of Lazarus). With deep pathos, and using the singular pronoun 'you' twelve times in three verses in a personal address to the city and its people, Jesus says, 'If you, even you, had only known on this day what would bring you peace.'[11] Many failed to understand the significance of the 'day'

---

[7] If 10:18 is recalled, the implication could be that the Messiah comes to defeat every evil force in the spiritual realm, establishing peace in heaven so that there can be peace on earth. See Gladd, *From the Manger to the Throne*, chapter 3.

[8] In Matthew 21:15–16 the objection is attributed more broadly to 'the chief priests and the teachers of the law'. Pharisees could be included among the latter.

[9] Nolland, *Luke 18:35–24:53*, 927.

[10] Jesus's prophetic foresight is illustrated in a number of ways by Luke, and Old Testament imagery is used to reinforce his central claims. See Fitzmyer, *Luke X–XXIV*, 1254–5; Nolland, *Luke 18:35–24:53*, 930.

[11] An unfulfilled wish is expressed in the Greek first clause, echoing the sentiment of

when Jesus entered the city and the 'peace' he would bring (see Jeremiah 6:9–15). This last term recalls the proclamation, 'Peace in heaven and glory in the highest!' (verse 38) and earlier predictions of the peace that the Messiah would bring (1:78–9; 2:14). In narrative terms, as Tannehill puts it, 'The great expectations in the birth narrative for the redemption of Israel and Jerusalem are not being realized in the anticipated way and with the anticipated fullness, because Jerusalem is failing to recognize the time of its visitation.'[12] 'But now it is hidden from your eyes' implies a divine judgment already being experienced because of the city's resistance to God's revelation. The blindness of Jesus's disciples was temporary (9:45; 18:34; 24:16), but the blindness of Jerusalem was entrenched (8:9–10; 11:47–51; Acts 4–7). The peace that God provides continues to remain hidden from those who seek peace on their own terms.

43–4. Jesus's lament continues with a prediction of enemy attack and destruction, paradoxically reversing the expectation in 1:71, 74. 'The days will come upon you' reflects the sort of language used by Old Testament prophets when speaking about imminent judgment or salvation (e.g., Isaiah 39:6; Hosea 9:7; Amos 4:2; Zechariah 14:1). Five descriptions are given: 'your enemies will build an embankment against you and encircle you and hem you in on every side. They will dash you to the ground, you and the children within your walls. They will not leave one stone on another.' This language reflects prophecies and descriptions of the sack of Jerusalem by the Babylonians in the sixth century BC (e.g., Isaiah 29:1–4; Jeremiah 6:6–8; 52:4–5; Ezekiel 4:1–3; Micah 3:12; Nahum 3:10). Similar things happened when the Romans destroyed Jerusalem and its temple in AD 70.[13] Jesus broadly links the city's past experience of judgment with what is to come, explicitly 'because you did not recognise the time of God's coming to you'. This parallels the first clause of Jesus's utterance in verse 42 in two ways: the verb 'know' is repeated, but is here translated 'recognise', while 'the time of God's coming to you' (ESV, 'the time of your visitation') parallels 'this day'. The whole ministry of Jesus was a

---

13:34. Variants in the text of verse 42 are discussed by Metzger, *Textual Commentary*, 145.

[12] Tannehill, *Narrative Unity* 1, 160. Fitzmyer, *Luke X–XXIV*, 1256, suggests that there may also be a play on words here: 'The city, whose very name is associated with peace, fails to recognize what makes for its own peace.'

[13] Josephus, *War* 7.1–4. However, 'since in precise detail what actually happened when Jerusalem met its doom in AD 70 does not agree with this description, we can be reasonably confident that this is not prophecy after the event' (Nolland, *Luke 18:35–24:53*, 933).

visitation from God (see 1:68, 78; 7:16, where a related verb is translated 'come to'), but his arrival in Jerusalem was the climax of this.

Entering the Temple (19:45–8)

Jesus at the temple

45 When Jesus entered the temple courts, he began to drive out those who were selling. **46** 'It is written,' he said to them, ' "My house will be a house of prayer"**c**; but you have made it "a den of robbers".**d'**

47 Every day he was teaching at the temple. But the chief priests, the teachers of the law and the leaders among the people were trying to kill him. **48** Yet they could not find any way to do it, because all the people hung on his words.

c 46 Isaiah 56:7
d 46 Jer. 7:11

45–6. Luke offers the briefest account of Jesus's visit to the Temple (compare Matthew 21:12–13; Mark 11:15–17; John 2:13–22).[14] He simplifies the story, so that only one action is described ('When Jesus entered the temple courts, he began to drive out those who were selling').[15] Although animals were needed for sacrifice in obedience to God's command, selling them in this context hindered the function of the Temple as a place of prayer. No mention is made of Jesus overturning the tables of the money-changers and the benches of those selling doves or preventing anyone from carrying merchandise through the temple courts. Luke's simplification has the effect of emphasising what Jesus *said* to them, quoting Scripture ('It is written'). First, he rephrases a portion of Isaiah 56:7 ('My house will be a house of prayer'). The full text in Isaiah reads, 'my house will be called a house of prayer for all nations', but the abbreviation simply emphasises that the Temple's chief function as 'a house of prayer' had been obscured by commerce. Second, Jesus quotes from Jeremiah 7:11 ('but you have made it "a den of robbers"'), identifying his action with Jeremiah's protest about the misuse of the Temple in his day.[16] Jesus's

---

[14] It is difficult to decide whether John describes another event early in Jesus's ministry or whether this is a displaced version of the account located at the end of his ministry in the Synoptics. Compare Fitzmyer, *Luke X–XXIV*, 1264–5; Bock, *Luke 9:51–24:53*, 1576–7.

[15] Greek *hieron* can refer to the whole temple precinct (BDAG). Nolland, *Luke 18:35–24:53*, 935–6, records nine different interpretations that have been offered to explain this episode and makes four suggestions about its meaning.

[16] Jeremiah complained that those coming to worship at the Temple were desecrating

prophetic action cleared the way for him to teach in the temple courts and enabled people to pray there more easily. Malachi 3:1–4 predicted the coming of God to his Temple in association with 'the messenger of the covenant' to purify the worship of his people. Jesus fulfils that role as 'the king who comes in the name of the Lord' (verse 38) and takes possession of the Temple as if it belonged to him! His teaching would be God's way of purifying and reforming the people who gathered there.

47–8. This narrative summary expands Mark 11:18 and sets the scene for what follows (see 4:14–15). Jesus's public ministry in Jerusalem was confined to the temple courts ('Every day he was teaching at the temple'; see 21:37–8). His action in taking possession of this sacred location and teaching the people aroused the opposition of the Jewish authorities ('the chief priests, the teachers of the law and the leaders among the people were trying to kill him'). They represented the Sanhedrin (20:1; 22:66), which Twelftree describes as 'the supreme Jewish religious, political, and legal council in Jerusalem in NT times'.[17] 'The chief priests' probably included former high priests and members of the priestly aristocracy. 'Teachers of the law' were biblical scholars, who challenged the ministry of Jesus from its earliest days in Galilee to its end (see my comment on 5:17). 'Leaders among the people' (*hoi prōtoi tou laou*) could be a summary term like 'the elders' (20:1, *presbyteroi*), embracing priests and lay members of the nobility.[18] Their approach foreshadowed Jesus's arrest and trials, but for the moment, 'they could not find any way to do it, because all the people hung on his words'. Leaders and people continued to differ about Jesus (20:1–6, 19, 26, 45–7; 22:2; 23:5), until the leaders finally prevailed (23:11–18). The success of their plot depended on undermining the support of the people.

A DIVINE VISITATION

Jesus's messianic status was confirmed by his entrance into Jerusalem in a manner recalling the prophecy of Zechariah 9:9. His disciples acknowledged him as king and celebrated the coming of heaven's peace and glory. When some of the Pharisees were indignant about this, Jesus warned that God's judgment would fall on those who refused to acknowledge him

---

it by their idolatry and lawlessness and were falsely confident that they would escape God's judgment.

[17] G. H. Twelftree, 'Sanhedrin', *DJG*, 836.

[18] The Greek expression at the end of 19:47 (*kai hoi prōtoi tou laou*) could be translated 'even the leaders of the people'. Compare 22:66, where *to presbyterion tou laou* ('the elders of the people') appears to be a summary term for 'both the chief priests and the teachers of the law'. See, however, my comment on 20:1.

and recognise the significance of the moment.[19] His lament over Jerusalem concluded with the assertion that his coming to the city as Messiah was in fact a divine visitation (19:41–4; see his identification with God in 13:34–5). This continued a theme first announced with the promise to Mary that her son would be both the promised Son of David and the Son of God (1:31–5). A close link between these identities is also implicit in the account of Jesus's visit to the Temple. As 'the king who comes in the name of the Lord' (verse 38), he set out to purify the worship of God's people in fulfilment of Malachi 3:1. This happened symbolically with the driving out of those who were selling animals for sacrifice, but morally and spiritually with his teaching in the Temple courts. Jesus claimed the Temple as his own and brought his word to bear on those who gathered to hear him. In the context of proclaiming God's judgment on Jerusalem, he offered the hope that a believing remnant might be saved through him (19:9–10, 38). Although Luke is not as explicit as John in expressing incarnational theology, he illustrates how the divine Lord 'came to that which was his own, but his own did not receive him' (John 1:11). Put positively, Luke emphasises that God's coming to Israel in the person of Jesus was a unique event in human history, offering a continuing challenge to people everywhere to receive him, believe in his name and become 'children of God' (John 1:12). The letters to the seven churches in Revelation 2–3 suggest that the exalted Lord Jesus continues to reform and purify his people though the ministry of his word and his Spirit. The warnings in these letters are accompanied by promises of ultimate victory for those who persevere in the way of Christ.

2. The authority of Jesus challenged (20:1–19)

Jesus's origin (20:1–8)

The authority of Jesus questioned

20 One day as Jesus was teaching the people in the temple courts and proclaiming the good news, the chief priests and the teachers of the law, together with the elders, came up to him. **2** 'Tell us by what authority you are doing these things,' they said. 'Who gave you this authority?'

3 He replied, 'I will also ask you a

---

[19] The parable in 19:11–27, the lament in 19:41–4 and the parable in 20:9–19 indicate that 'the king will be rejected by his citizens and that this will bring disaster upon the city as a whole, both the leaders and the people' (Tannehill, *Narrative Unity* I, 159).

question. Tell me: **4** John's baptism – was it from heaven, or of human origin?'

5 They discussed it among themselves and said, 'If we say, "From heaven," he will ask, "Why didn't you believe him?" **6** But if we say, "Of human origin," all the people will stone

us, because they are persuaded that John was a prophet.'

7 So they answered, 'We don't know where it was from.'

8 Jesus said, 'Neither will I tell you by what authority I am doing these things.'

1–2. Luke substantially follows Mark 11:27–12:12 with some modifications (compare Matthew 21:13–27, 33–46). He first indicates that 'Jesus was teaching the people in the temple courts and proclaiming the good news' (*euaggelizomenou*), continuing to do what he had done in Galilee and on the road to Jerusalem. However, he was now in the place where the official teachers of Israel were normally found (2:46). Consequently, representatives of the Sanhedrin – 'the chief priests and the teachers of the law, together with the elders' (see 9:22; 19:47) – came up to him and said, 'Tell us by what authority you are doing these things . . . Who gave you this authority?' Jesus was not an authorised rabbi in the usual sense. Was he claiming the immediate authority of God by taking over the Temple courts and teaching there? Moreover, he had ridden into Jerusalem in a kingly fashion and driven out those selling in the Temple courts like one of the prophets.

3–6. Instead of answering them directly, Jesus said, 'I will also ask you a question. Tell me: John's baptism – was it from heaven, or of human origin?' This caused his opponents to pause and discuss the implications of his question among themselves. They recognised that they were trapped: 'If we say, "From heaven," he will ask, "Why didn't you believe him?"' This recalls Luke's comment about the Pharisees and the experts in the law rejecting 'God's purpose for themselves, because they had not been baptised by John' (7:30). But if they denied John's heavenly authority and answered, 'Of human origin,' they were afraid that the general population would stone them, because they were 'persuaded that John was a prophet' (see 7:29). Jesus's words and actions suggested that he was greater still than any prophet sent by God to his people (4:16–30; 7:16–35; 9:18–27; 24:19).

7–8. Jesus's opponents refused to commit themselves, answering, 'We don't know where it was from.' They showed that they were unwilling to consider whether his authority might also have come from God and revealed, as Nolland suggests, 'their own bankruptcy as guides to the truth'.[20] So Jesus replied, 'Neither will I tell you by what authority I am doing these things,' foreshadowing his response to the question put to him at his trial in 22:66–8.

An unmistakable warning (20:9–19)

The parable of the tenants

9 He went on to tell the people this parable: 'A man planted a vineyard, rented it to some farmers and went away for a long time. **10** At harvest time he sent a servant to the tenants so they would give him some of the fruit of the vineyard. But the tenants beat him and sent him away empty-handed. **11** He sent another servant, but that one also they beat and treated shamefully and sent away empty-handed. **12** He sent still a third, and they wounded him and threw him out.

13 'Then the owner of the vineyard said, "What shall I do? I will send my son, whom I love; perhaps they will respect him."

14 'But when the tenants saw him, they talked the matter over. "This is the heir," they said. "Let's kill him, and the inheritance will be ours." **15** So they threw him out of the vineyard and killed him.

'What then will the owner of the vineyard do to them? **16** He will come and kill those tenants and give the vineyard to others.'

When the people heard this, they said, 'God forbid!'

17 Jesus looked directly at them and asked, 'Then what is the meaning of that which is written:

' "The stone the builders rejected
  has become the cornerstone"[a]?

18 Everyone who falls on that stone will be broken to pieces; anyone on whom it falls will be crushed.'

19 The teachers of the law and the chief priests looked for a way to arrest him immediately, because they knew he had spoken this parable against them. But they were afraid of the people.

_____
a 17 Psalm 118:22

9. Jesus went on to tell his parable of the tenants to the *people*, but it was occasioned by the preceding encounter and clearly directed against the Jerusalem *authorities* (verse 19). His story of a man who 'planted a vineyard, rented it to some farmers and went away for a long time' echoes his parable about the man who 'went to a distant country to have himself appointed king and then to return' (19:12). But there are

_____
[20] Nolland, *Luke 18:35–24:53*, 943. Edwards, *Luke*, 562, similarly observes that by suspending judgment they were avoiding the pursuit of truth.

stronger echoes here of songs about God's vineyard in Isaiah 5:1–2; 27:2–6.[21] Commentators often resist the idea that there could be allegorical elements in the parables of Jesus, but the biblical image of Israel being God's vineyard lent itself to the sort of development we find in this one (Israel is God's 'vine' in Psalm 80:8–13; Jeremiah 2:21; Ezekiel 19:10–14; Hosea 10:1).[22] The common first-century practice of absentee landowners contracting tenant farmers to manage their property is the basis for Jesus's application of Isaiah 5:3–4 to his situation. These tenants represent the leaders of Israel appointed by God.

10–12. The refusal of the tenants to honour their contract with the owner is revealed 'at harvest time'.[23] The owner 'sent a servant to the tenants so they would give him some of the fruit of the vineyard'. Fruit is a metaphor for a life reflecting genuine repentance and faith in response to God's word (3:7–9; 6:43–5). 'But the tenants beat him and sent him away empty-handed.' An extended period of sending out further servants is then indicated: 'He sent another servant, but that one also they beat and treated shamefully and sent away empty-handed. He sent still a third, and they wounded him and threw him out.' Once the vineyard is recognised as a reference to Israel, the servants are likely to be prophets, commissioned by God to call the people and their leaders to account (see 11:49; Jeremiah 7:25–6). The owner's persistence in pursuing his contractual arrangement with the tenants represents God's faithfulness in maintaining his covenant with Israel.

13. The parable becomes more challenging when Jesus has the owner of the vineyard say, 'What shall I do? I will send my son, whom I love; perhaps they will respect him.'[24] With this allegorical development, Jesus implies that he is God's beloved Son. Readers of Luke's Gospel will recall that Jesus's birth was announced in such terms (1:31–5) and similarly

[21] Green, *Luke*, 704 note 21, lists three verbal associations with Isaiah 5:1, 4–5, 7, where God pronounces judgment on the vineyard, but not on the tenants (705). Edwards, *Luke*, 563–5, argues that the subject and plot of the parable are wholly determined by Isaiah 5:1–7, but the details by the social circumstances of Jesus's day.
[22] Fitzmyer, *Luke X–XXIV*, 1278–82, is unnecessarily sceptical about whether allegorical elements in the parable go back to Jesus, but Nolland, *Luke 18:35–24:53*, 949, concludes that this parable is 'inalienably semi-allegorical'.
[23] The Greek (*kairō*) could simply mean 'in time', but the NIV has rightly represented this as 'harvest time' (see Matthew 21:34, *ho kairos tōn karpōn,* 'the time for fruit').
[24] This soliloquy 'provides a turning point in the parable as a course of action is decided' (Green, *Luke*, 707). Compare 12:17–19; 15:17–19; 16:3–4.

proclaimed at different stages in the narrative.[25] Indeed, Jesus has just been acknowledged as 'the king who comes in the name of the Lord' (19:38) and has spoken about his coming to Jerusalem as a divine visitation (19:44). But what would his audience in Jerusalem have understood about this aspect of the parable? The notion of a beloved son being the owner's agent and heir would have been familiar to them from their social context, and some might have perceived this as a messianic claim, but its full significance could only have been appreciated after his resurrection.

14. When the tenants saw the son, 'they talked the matter over. "This is the heir," they said, "Let's kill him, and the inheritance will be ours."' These tenants express the full horror of what the leaders of Israel were about to do, killing God's Son to seize for themselves what was rightly his. In this way, Jesus publicly but parabolically predicts his death at their hands (see 13:31–3). Many who heard the parable are likely to have been outraged by this outcome, although they had a limited understanding of its significance.

15–16. Jesus confirmed that the tenants did what they proposed ('So they threw him out of the vineyard and killed him'), and asked the rhetorical question, 'What then will the owner of the vineyard do to them?' The challenge was to consider what God would do in response to the rejection of his Son. Jesus answered his own question in a highly provocative way ('He will come and kill those tenants and give the vineyard to others'), perhaps alluding to his apostles as the 'others' (see 22:28–30). The next verse implies that he will be resurrected as the ultimate ruler of God's people (see Acts 5:31, 'as Prince and Saviour'). Israel would be reconstituted as the community of the Messiah Jesus. As Edwards observes, this parable 'does not lay a blanket of blame on the Jewish people, but on their leaders, particularly the Sanhedrin'.[26] Whatever they understood about the implications of the parable, the people could only respond, 'God forbid!' (*mē genoito*, 'may it not be').

17. Jesus pressed home the message of the parable by first relating it to a biblical text. He looked directly at them and asked, 'Then what is the meaning of that which is written: "The stone the builders rejected has become the cornerstone"?' A proverbial saying in Psalm 118:22 (117:22

---

[25] The expression here (*ton huion mou ton agapēton*) echoes the divine declaration in 3:22 ('my Son, whom I love') and 9:35 ('my Son, whom I have chosen', *ho huios mou ho eklelegmenos*). It also recalls Jesus's claim about his exclusive relationship with God as Father, which was overheard by the disciples in 10:22.

[26] Edwards, *Luke*, 568. Against Edwards, 569–70, however, the focus here is on the future leadership of Israel, not on Gentiles joining the people of God.

LXX) is applied to his rejection, death and resurrection (Mark 12:11 also includes the next verse). Previously, the wording of Psalm 118:26 was used in welcoming Jesus to Jerusalem as 'the king who comes in the name of the Lord' (19:38). In that psalm, 'the stone the builders rejected' refers to the humiliation of a king by his enemies, while God's restoration of his honour and influence is suggested by the words 'has become the cornerstone'.[27] Jesus's use of this text implies that he will become 'the key figure in God's new building, the reconstituted Israel', as Fitzmyer puts it.[28] His hearers are being urged to accept him as the one appointed to this role, soon to be rejected by their leaders, but raised from death by God (see later applications of this text in Acts 4:5–11; 5:31; Romans 9:30–33; 1 Peter 2:4–8).

18. Jesus concluded, 'Everyone who falls on that stone will be broken to pieces; anyone on whom it falls will be crushed.'[29] The image of falling on 'that stone' and being 'broken' recalls the warning in Isaiah 8:14 about God being 'a stone that causes people to stumble and a rock that makes them fall', together with Isaiah 8:15 ('they will fall and be broken'). This prophetic language is applied to those who fail to recognise Jesus as the cornerstone of God's plan for his people. As predicted by Simeon, he was destined 'to cause the falling and rising of many in Israel' (2:34; compare 12:49–53). The image of being crushed by that stone may be derived from Daniel 2:34–5, 44–5, where it represents the coming of the kingdom of God 'that will never be destroyed, nor will it be left to another people'. As the ruler of that kingdom, Jesus will judge the nations, including those in Israel who continue to reject him (see Luke 12:8–9, 40; 17:30–37).

19. 'The teachers of the law and the chief priests looked for a way to arrest him immediately, because they knew he had spoken this parable against them.' They understood something of what he meant, but they could not accept the implications (see Acts 4:5–22). They wanted to arrest Jesus, but they were not yet able to do so because 'they were afraid of the people'. Matthew 21:46 adds 'because the people held that he was a prophet'.

---

27 See Allen, *Psalms 101–150*, 124–5.
28 Fitzmyer, *Luke X–XIV*, 1282. 'The cornerstone' (*kephalēn gōnias*, 'head of the corner') relates to the stone used in antiquity at the corner of a building to bear the weight of the two walls, or as the 'keystone' or 'capstone' in an arch.
29 Note the parallel in Matthew 21:44.

3. Two important questions (20:20–40)

Paying taxes to Caesar (20:20–26)

Paying taxes to Caesar

20 Keeping a close watch on him, they sent spies, who pretended to be sincere. They hoped to catch Jesus in something he said, so that they might hand him over to the power and authority of the governor. 21 So the spies questioned him: 'Teacher, we know that you speak and teach what is right, and that you do not show partiality but teach the way of God in accordance with the truth. 22 Is it right for us to pay taxes to Caesar or not?'

23 He saw through their duplicity and said to them, 24 'Show me a denarius. Whose image and inscription are on it?'

'Caesar's,' they replied.

25 He said to them, 'Then give back to Caesar what is Caesar's, and to God what is God's.'

26 They were unable to trap him in what he had said there in public. And astonished by his answer, they became silent.

20. Luke broadly follows the account of this incident in Mark 12:13–17 (see also Matthew 22:15–22). However, he expands Mark's introduction by specifying that the teachers of the law and the chief priests (verse 19) were 'keeping a close watch on him' (see 6:7; 14:1), and 'they sent spies, who pretended to be sincere' (*dikaios*, 'righteous'; see 16:15). The authorities 'hoped to catch Jesus in something he said, so that they might hand him over to the power and authority of the governor' (recall 18:32). Their fundamental concern was theological, aiming to expose Jesus as a false teacher and messianic claimant, but their chosen method of getting rid of him and avoiding confrontation with the people was political (see 23:1–5).[30]

21–2. The spies approached Jesus with flattery, but ironically stated what was true: 'Teacher [*didaskale*, as in 7:40; 10:25], we know that you speak and teach what is right.' They acknowledged that he was no crowd pleaser ('you do not show partiality') but was committed to teaching 'the way of God in accordance with the truth'. Nevertheless, their question ('Is it

---

[30] Mark 12:13 says they sent 'some of the Pharisees and Herodians to Jesus to catch him in his words'. As supporters of Herodian rule the Herodians would have been concerned to maintain good relations with Rome, while Pharisees would have had reservations about this, but they combined in their determination to get rid of Jesus.

right for us to pay taxes to Caesar or not?') was cunningly designed to force him to make a judgment in conformity with Jewish expectations but contrary to Roman demands.[31] If he answered 'No' to the question, he would be compromised in the eyes of the Romans; if he said 'Yes', he would be compromised in the eyes of many Jews. Luke employs the general term *phoros* (BDAG, 'tribute') to describe 'the direct poll tax levied on inhabitants of Judea'.[32] 'Is it right' (*exestin*) in this context means 'is it lawful' in terms of God's revealed will for his people to pay this tax.

23–5. When Jesus 'saw through their duplicity' (*panourgia*, 'craftiness', BDAG), he said to them, 'Show me a denarius.' This silver coin was the annual amount to be paid to Caesar, equivalent to the average daily wage for a farm labourer (Matthew 20:2). When he asked, 'Whose image and inscription are on it?' they replied, 'Caesar's,' using the family name adopted by every Roman emperor from the time of Gaius Julius Caesar. The image on the coin would have been that of Tiberius (AD 14–37), and the inscription 'Tiberius Caesar, son of the divine Augustus, Augustus'. On the reverse side was the image of his mother as an incarnation of the Roman goddess of peace and a description of Tiberius as high priest. As Marshall puts it, this coin 'symbolised the power of the emperor and made religious claims for him that Jews would consider blasphemous'.[33] Jesus concluded, 'Then give back to Caesar what is Caesar's, and to God what is God's.' The image on the coin indicated that it belonged to Caesar and should be given back to him. More profoundly, however, Jesus encouraged the payment of this tax because of the greater obligation to obey God and honour him in civic life.[34] The second half of Jesus's answer controls the first half, because it expresses God's sovereignty over everything: Jesus does not envisage two parallel and equally authoritative realms. As Brawley concludes, '"Caesar" is always subservient to God's justice and judgment.'[35] Early Christian writers continued to reflect these perspectives (e.g., Romans 13:1–7; 1 Timothy 2:1–6; 1 Peter 2:13–17),

---

[31] Marshall, *Luke*, 733.

[32] Fitzmyer, *Luke X–XIV*, 1296. Mark and Matthew use the Latinism *kēnsos* ('census'), which more specifically refers to the 'head tax' or 'poll tax' that Jews paid to the Romans. They also had to pay the temple tax and other charges to Jewish political authorities. See D. Downs, 'Economics', *DJG*, 381–7.

[33] Marshall, *Luke*, 736.

[34] Although it is an extrapolation from the text, it is true that humanity bears God's image and must therefore render 'ultimate submission to the God in whose image it is made' (Edwards, *Luke*, 575).

[35] Brawley, *Luke*, 179.

but they also discerned that there are situations in which God's demands counter those of earthly rulers, so that believers must be willing to suffer for their allegiance to him (e.g., Acts 4:18–20; 5:29–32; 1 Peter 4:12–19; Revelation 13:1–10).

26. Luke expands Mark's conclusion, noting first that 'they were unable to trap him in what he had said there in public'. Nevertheless, they soon dishonestly accused him before Pontius Pilate of opposing the payment of taxes to Caesar (23:2)! They were astonished by his answer, because it failed to incriminate him, but it also questioned their loyalty to God. Consequently, 'they became silent'.

Resurrection and the afterlife (20:27–40)

The resurrection and marriage

27 Some of the Sadducees, who say there is no resurrection, came to Jesus with a question. 28 'Teacher,' they said, 'Moses wrote for us that if a man's brother dies and leaves a wife but no children, the man must marry the widow and raise up offspring for his brother. 29 Now there were seven brothers. The first one married a woman and died childless. 30 The second 31 and then the third married her, and in the same way the seven died, leaving no children. 32 Finally, the woman died too. 33 Now then, at the resurrection whose wife will she be, since the seven were married to her?'

34 Jesus replied, 'The people of this age marry and are given in marriage. 35 But those who are considered worthy of taking part in the age to come and in the resurrection from the dead will neither marry nor be given in marriage, 36 and they can no longer die; for they are like the angels. They are God's children, since they are children of the resurrection. 37 But in the account of the burning bush, even Moses showed that the dead rise, for he calls the Lord "the God of Abraham, and the God of Isaac, and the God of Jacob".b 38 He is not the God of the dead, but of the living, for to him all are alive.'

39 Some of the teachers of the law responded, 'Well said, teacher!' 40 And no one dared to ask him any more questions.

_____

b 37 Exodus 3:6

27. Luke follows Mark 12:18–27 with some modifications (compare Matthew 22:23–33). The Sadducees rejected popular beliefs about bodily resurrection or any form of post-mortem existence.[36] This denial set them

_____

[36] Wright, *Resurrection*, 131–40, argues from Acts 23:8 that the Sadducees denied

in opposition to the Pharisees and Jesus, whose eschatological teaching must have become known to them in some form. The Sadducees were a priestly party, who favoured a strict interpretation of the written Law. They were disliked by the general population and enjoyed only the confidence of the wealthy. Strauss says, 'Like the Jewish aristocracy in general, they were conservative politically, and thus pro-Roman, supporting the status quo in order to maintain their own position and authority.'[37] Sadducees regarded teaching about resurrection and the age to come as revolutionary and not discoverable in the Five Books of Moses.

28–33. Addressing Jesus as 'Teacher' (see verse 21), the Sadducees presume that he concurs with current beliefs about the resurrection of the dead and ridicule these with a far-fetched argument based on Deuteronomy 25:5–6 (see also Genesis 38:8; Ruth 3:9–4:10): 'Moses wrote for us that if a man's brother dies and leaves a wife but no children, the man must marry the widow and raise up offspring for his brother.' The purpose of this law was to keep property in the family by providing a line of inheritance. An extreme application is proposed: 'Now there were seven brothers. The first one married a woman and died childless. The second and then the third married her, and in the same way the seven died, leaving no children. Finally, the woman died too.' For the sake of the argument, the Sadducees assume the possibility of resurrection and ask, 'Now then, at the resurrection whose wife will she be, since the seven were married to her?'

34–5. Although Luke does not record the challenge found in Mark 12:24, he shows from what follows that the error of the Sadducees was their ignorance of the Scriptures and the power of God. An expanded version of Mark 12:25 is offered first: 'The people of this age [ESV, 'the sons of this age', as in 16:8] marry and are given in marriage. But those who are considered worthy of taking part in the age to come [ESV, 'that age'] and in the resurrection from the dead will neither marry nor be given in marriage.'[38] This pronouncement not only challenged the

---

resurrection from the dead and 'the two current accounts of the intermediate state' (that the dead exist as angels or spirits). See also Peterson, *Acts*, 617.

[37] M. L. Strauss, 'Sadducees', *DJG*, 825. See Josephus, *Antiquities* 13.10.6; Edwards, *Luke*, 576–7. Their name appears to derive from 'Zadok', whose descendants became high priests after the Babylonian Exile (Ezekiel 40:46; 43:19).

[38] The passive participle *kataxiōthentes* ('considered worthy') implies the gracious decision of God (compare Acts 5:41; 2 Thessalonians 1:5). They are worthy because of their confidence in God's promises, which moves them to live in love and obedience.

Sadducees but, as Edwards points out, it also 'cut against the grain of popular Judaism, which assumed conditional continuity between earthly and celestial life, including marriage and sexual relations in the resurrected state'.[39] Marriage between a man and a woman is the gift of God in this life for the procreation and nurture of children, and 'for the mutual society, help and comfort that the one ought to have of the other, both in prosperity and adversity'.[40] 'In the age to come and in the resurrection from the dead,' however, marriage as the means of perpetuating the human race will no longer be necessary. Moreover, the exclusive nature of marriage, which is essential to stable and faithful family life in this age, will be superseded by the perfection of God-centred relationships in the age to come (see Revelation 7).

36. Luke adds that resurrection from the dead means that 'they can no longer die; for they are like the angels'. Alexey Somov points out that this amplification serves to demonstrate 'the glorious and transformed state of the risen ones, and their immortality as a gift of eternal life'.[41] But they are not merely heavenly beings like angels, nor do they replace fallen angels, as some argue. Luke adds that they are transformed and share in the life to come as 'children of the resurrection' (*huioi eisin theou tēs anastaseōs huioi ontes,* 'sons of God, being sons of the resurrection'). God's children are destined to share in the bodily resurrection that he makes possible for all who trust in him. Jesus deals with the fate of the wicked after death elsewhere (12:4–5, 9; 13:24–30; 16:19–31; compare Acts 24:15).

37–8. Jesus's second response to the Sadducees concerns the resurrection implications of Exodus 3:6: 'But in the account of the burning bush, even Moses showed that the dead rise, for he calls the Lord "the God of Abraham, and the God of Isaac, and the God of Jacob."' This apparent modification of Mark 12:26–7 makes the point that the Sadducees had failed to read the Torah properly. Moses as the assumed author of the Book of Exodus believed in God's ongoing relationship with Israel's forefathers. Although the patriarchs could not enjoy the physical inheritance of Canaan, Jesus concluded from Moses's words that they were still alive to God: 'He is not the God of the dead, but of the living.' By implication, they share in the heavenly inheritance which Canaan anticipated

[39] Edwards, *Luke*, 579.
[40] 'The Form of Solemnization of Matrimony', in *The Book of Common Prayer* (1662), reflecting on Genesis 1:27–30; 2:19–24.
[41] Alexey Somov, *Representations of the Afterlife*, 184. Luke uses the unusual term *isangelloi* ('equal to angels') instead of *hōs aggeloi en tois ouranoi* ('like the angels in heaven', Mark 12:25; compare Matthew 22:30).

(see Hebrews 4:1–11; 11:39–40). The additional clause ('for to him *all* are alive', my emphasis) means that what is said about Abraham, Isaac and Jacob relates to all who have enjoyed a genuine relationship with God in this life: even though they die, they literally 'live to him' (*autō zōsin*; see 4 Maccabees 7:19; 16:25).[42]

Jesus adopted the two-age view that was current in different strands of Judaism at the time, but his parable of the rich man and Lazarus pointed to an immediate experience upon death of either life in God's presence (see 13:28–9; 23:43) or judgment (16:22–31). The implication is that, when people die, they move into 'the end' they are destined to experience (see 2 Corinthians 5:1–10 and my comment on 23:43). However, we still await in history a general resurrection with the return of Christ (1 Corinthians 15:20–28), when what is already true for those who have died and risen with him will be manifested in a transformed creation. In the apocalyptic vision of Revelation 21:1–4, this is represented in terms of the descent of the heavenly city and its inhabitants to earth (see 1 Thessalonians 4:13–18).[43]

39–40. 'Some of the teachers of the law' mentioned in verses 1, 19 (ESV, 'scribes') responded, 'Well said, teacher!' They probably belonged to the Pharisaic party (see 5:17) and were consequently enthusiastic about Jesus's answer to the Sadducees about resurrection from death. The Sadducees could be the subject of the next clause (*ouketi gar etolmōn eperōtan auton ouden*), which literally translates 'for they no longer dared to ask him anything'. However, in view of what follows, the NIV broadens the reference ('And no one dared to ask him any more questions'). Faced with no further challenges, Jesus took the initiative in addressing the crowd about the adequacy of their messianic expectations.[44]

---

[42] Anderson, *Jesus' Resurrection in Luke–Acts*, 139, observes that the verb *zōsin* in the present tense ('they live') could indicate that the patriarchs already enjoy resurrection life. Less likely is the view that a futuristic use of the present refers to resurrection at the end of the age. Fitzmyer's argument that this speaks about the immortality of the soul is inconsistent with the focus on resurrection from death in this passage (*Luke X–XIV*, 1301–2).

[43] See Harris, *From Grave to Glory*, 185–256; Somov, *Representations of the Afterlife*, 224–30; and my Introduction, pages 18–22.

[44] Luke omits Jesus's friendly dialogue with one of the teachers of the law about the most important of all the commandments (Mark 12:28–34), presumably because he had included a similar incident in 10:25–9 as a preface to the parable of the Good Samaritan.

4. Three counter challenges (20:41–21:4)

Whose son is the Messiah? (20:41–4)

Whose son is the Messiah?

41 Then Jesus said to them, 'Why is it said that the Messiah is the son of David? **42** David himself declares in the Book of Psalms:

' "The Lord said to my Lord:
  'Sit at my right hand

43 until I make your enemies
  a footstool for your feet.' "c

44 David calls him "Lord." How then can he be his son?'

———

c 43 Psalm 110:1

41. In Luke's slightly abbreviated version of the incident in Mark 12:35–7 (compare Matthew 22:41–5), Jesus apparently speaks to the crowd ('Then Jesus said to them'), questioning them about what the teachers of the law (verses 39, 46) said concerning the Messiah (*pōs legousin,* 'How can they say', ESV).[45] The issue is their identification of 'the Messiah' (*ho Christos*) with 'the son of David', which Jesus does not contradict, but which he uses as a basis for exposing a broader perspective from Scripture. The first term is used by others with reference to Jesus in 2:11, 26; 4:41; 9:20; 22:67; 23:2, 35, 39, and by Jesus with reference to himself in 24:26, 46. The second term recalls the announcement of Jesus's birth in 1:31–3, with its echoes of the promise to David in 2 Samuel 7:12–16 (especially 7:14a) and subsequent prophetic developments of this promise concerning an end-time deliverer of God's people (e.g., Isaiah 9:6–7; 11:1–5; Jeremiah 23:5–6; 33:14–22; Ezekiel 34:22–4). Jesus is only called 'Son of David' in Luke 18:38, 39, but the term was increasingly employed with a messianic sense in contemporary Jewish sources.[46]

42–3. Before anyone had a chance to reply, Jesus quoted what 'David himself declares in the Book of Psalms'. Jesus regarded David as the inspired author of those psalms attributed to him (see 2 Samuel 23:2–3; Mark 12:36) and taught his disciples to regard David as speaking prophetically (see Acts 1:16; 2:30, 34–5; 4:25). The text cited is Psalm 110:1 (109:1 LXX):

———

[45] The NIV obscures this by translating the Greek as an implied passive ('Why is it said that'). Mark 12:35 explicitly mentions 'the teachers of the law' and Matthew 22:42 ('What do you think') clearly relates to the Pharisees in the preceding verse.
[46] See especially *Psalms of Solomon* 17:4, 21 (first century BC) and the DSS references cited by Y. Miura, 'Son of David', *DJG*, 881–6.

The Lord said to my Lord;
  'Sit at my right hand
until I make your enemies
  a footstool for your feet.'

David recounts an oracle from the Lord (meaning from the Lord God), which is addressed to someone whom David calls 'my Lord'. This promises enthronement at God's 'right hand' – the place of ultimate honour and power – with complete victory over his enemies. Scholars often argue that the original setting of this psalm was a royal coronation at some time in Israel's past, and that its author was not David, but another person speaking about David or one of his successors.[47] Jesus, however, appears to have understood that David was reflecting on the promises made to him concerning the *eternal* reign of his son in a special and exclusive relationship with God (2 Samuel 7:12–16). Nolland rightly observes, 'Messianic hope involves for Jesus much more than simply a glorious rerun of the triumphs of the kingdom of David.'[48] On trial before the Sanhedrin, he again alluded to this text in a prediction about his heavenly enthronement as Son of Man (22:69; compare 19:12). Peter's sermon in Acts 2:34–6 develops this further in terms of Jesus's ascension and enthronement as 'both Lord and Messiah'. Psalm 110 is the most frequently quoted Old Testament text in the New Testament.[49]

44. Jesus repeated his first question in a different way, reflecting on the text of the psalm ('David calls him "Lord." How then can he be his son?'). This was a veiled way of suggesting that his Davidic sonship was more than a matter of physical descent and his kingdom 'not of this world' (John 18:36). 'Lord' in the context of heavenly enthronement implied a share in the eternal rule of God. As Edwards concludes, 'The combination of "authority" (vv. 2, 8), "beloved son" (v. 13), "Messiah" (v. 41), and "Lord" (vv. 42, 44) effects an exalted Christology in Luke 20.'[50]

[47] For example, Allen, *Psalms 101–150*, 83, argues that it is a post-exilic composition by a court poet but 'eschatological and messianic from the outset'.
[48] Nolland, *Luke 18:35–24:53*, 972. See also my comment on Luke 1:29–33. Edwards, *Luke*, 582–5, discusses rabbinic interpretations of Psalm 110 in the time of Jesus and later.
[49] A list of quotations and allusions is provided by David M. Hay, *Glory at the Right Hand: Psalm 110 in Early Christianity* (New York; Nashville: Abingdon, 1973), 163–6.
[50] Edwards, *Luke*, 585.

Beware of faulty leadership (20:45–7)

Warning against the teachers of the law

45 While all the people were listening, Jesus said to his disciples, 46 'Beware of the teachers of the law. They like to walk around in flowing robes and love to be greeted with respect in the market-places and have the most important seats in the synagogues and the places of honour at banquets. 47 They devour widows' houses and for a show make lengthy prayers. These men will be punished most severely.'

45–7. 'While all the people were listening,' Jesus's next challenge was specifically for his disciples to 'beware of the teachers of the law' (see Mark 12:38–40). Matthew 23 provides an extended discourse at this point, warning against the hypocrisy of the teachers of the law and the Pharisees. Some of this is paralleled in Luke 11:37–52. Rather than offering a blanket condemnation of them all, he focused on the behaviour of some (ESV, 'the scribes, who . . .'). First, he criticised their ostentation ('They like to walk around in flowing robes') and desire to be treated with respect and honour in every context (they 'love to be greeted with respect in the market-places and have the most important seats in the synagogues and the places of honour at banquets'). Scribes had an important role in Jewish society (see my comment on 5:17), but some were too conscious of their religious and social status.[51] Second, Jesus criticised them for their deceit and hypocrisy ('They devour widows' houses and for a show make lengthy prayers'). Instead of obeying the biblical injunctions to care for widows, they cheated them of 'what was rightly theirs'.[52] Their 'lengthy prayers' were 'for a show', or even 'for a pretext' (BDAG, *prophasei*): displays of piety can be used to gain financial advantage, as many Christian leaders have also sadly discovered. Jesus's final message about such scribes was that 'These men will be punished most severely,' referring to their ultimate judgment by God (*perissoteron krima*, 'the greater condemnation'). This was not the kind of leadership that would inspire and direct God's people in the way of truth and righteousness.

---

[51] See G. Thelmann, 'Scribes', *DJG*, 840–42. Green, *Luke*, 727, notes that 'three major public arenas are mentioned – the marketplace as social center, the synagogue, and the banquet room – together with the symbols relevant to each'.

[52] Fitzmyer, *Luke X–XXIV*, 1318. He follows Derrett in arguing that this could refer to their legal role, 'acting as guardians appointed by a husband's will to care for the widow's estate'.

The widow's offering (21:1–4)

The widow's offering

21 As Jesus looked up, he saw the rich putting their gifts into the temple treasury. **2** He also saw a poor widow put in two very small copper coins. **3** 'Truly I tell you,' he said, 'this poor widow has put in more than all the others. **4** All these people gave their gifts out of their wealth; but she out of her poverty put in all she had to live on.'

1–4. Jesus's warning about the mistreatment of widows by rapacious teachers of the law (20:47) led him to contrast the giving of rich and poor to the work of the Temple (see Mark 12:41–4). First, 'As Jesus looked up, he saw the rich putting their gifts into the temple treasury.' No judgment is made about the amount being contributed, though Jesus concluded, 'All these people gave their gifts out of their wealth.' By implication, they gave in a way that made no difference to their comfortable lifestyle. Second, 'He also saw a poor widow put in two very small copper coins.' The amount she gave was small – a 'lepta' was the smallest coin in use at that time (see 12:59) – but significant for her. Jesus emphatically commended her sacrificial generosity, saying, 'Truly I tell you . . . this poor widow has put in more than all the others.' He went on to clarify that 'she out of her poverty put in all she had to live on'. Her dedication recalls the practical piety of Anna (2:36–8) and Jesus's demand for a radical self-abandonment to himself and his cause, no matter what the cost (9:57–62; 12:22–34). Jesus's praise of this woman is the dominant feature of the narrative, rather than a condemnation of the rich or an implied criticism of the temple system.[53]

5. Living in light of the end (21:5–38)

Luke's version of Jesus's teaching on this subject is largely based on Mark 13, with some additions and subtractions.[54] The tradition inherited from

[53] Green, *Luke*, 728–9, understands Luke to be exposing an unjust system that 'feeds off those who cannot fend for themselves' (so also Fitzmyer, *Luke X–XXIV*, 1321; Brawley, *Luke*, 182–3), but this is not an obvious feature of the narrative.

[54] Fitzmyer, *Luke X–XXIV*, 1323–30, considers different theories about the emergence of the three different versions of Jesus's Jerusalem eschatological discourse. Both he and Nolland, *Luke 18:35–24:53*, 983–7, conclude that Luke 21:5–36 is best viewed as an adaptation of Mark with sayings from other sources.

Mark is refashioned in the light of Jesus's earlier teaching about being ready for the unexpected coming of the Son of Man and final judgment (12:35–48; 17:20–37) and his laments over the future of Jerusalem (13:34–5; 19:41–4; 23:28–31). Luke's aim is to show how these different emphases fit together and provide the basis for both warning and encouragement.

The fate of the Temple (21:5–7)

The destruction of the temple and signs of the end times

5 Some of his disciples were remarking about how the temple was adorned with beautiful stones and with gifts dedicated to God. But Jesus said, 6 'As for what you see here, the time will come when not one stone will be left on another; every one of them will be thrown down.'

7 'Teacher,' they asked, 'when will these things happen? And what will be the sign that they are about to take place?'

5–6. By implication, this discourse took place in the temple precincts (see Mark 13:1, 'leaving the temple'; Matthew 24:1, 'walking away'). It was provoked by the fact that some were 'remarking about how the temple was adorned with beautiful stones and with gifts dedicated to God'. The NIV rendering 'some of his disciples' may be too precise (*tinōn* simply means 'some'). The address to Jesus as 'Teacher' (verse 7) could reflect that this was the view of the crowd.[55] In 20–19 BC, Herod the Great began to refurbish the Second Temple, which was built when the Jews returned from the Babylonian Exile (Ezra 6:13–18; Haggai 1:4–15), providing a larger and more beautiful complex.[56] The work of adornment continued for several decades and may have still been going on when these comments were made. Jesus, however, responded with an alarming prediction: 'As for what you see here, the time will come when not one stone will be left on another; every one of them will be thrown down.' The prophetic expression 'the time will come' (*eleusontai hēmerai*, 'the days will come') recalls 5:35; 17:22; 19:43 and Old Testament precedents (e.g., Isaiah 39:6; Jeremiah 7:32; Hosea 9:7; Amos 4:2; Zechariah 14:1).

7. The follow-up questions in each of the Synoptic Gospels are slightly

---

55 Nolland, *Luke 18:35–24:53*, 988–9. Edwards, *Luke*, 593–4, summarises what Josephus and others in his time wrote about the grandeur of this Temple. 'Teacher' is the address normally used by those who are either not Jesus's disciples or not among the Twelve (7:40; 8:49; 9:38; 10:25; 11:45; 12:13; 18:18; 19:39; 20:21, 28, 39; 21:7; 22:11).

56 See Josephus, *War* 1.21,1; 5.5,6.

different, providing some guidance about the way in which each discourse is constructed. The first question is virtually the same in each account: 'Teacher, when will these things happen?' (Mark specifies that it was asked by Peter, James, John and Andrew). This reference to the predicted destruction of the Temple in Luke is followed by a broader eschatological question: 'And what will be the sign that they are about to take place?' (Mark 13:4, 'And what will be the sign that *they are all about to be fulfilled*', my emphasis). Even more broadly, the disciples in Matthew 24:3 ask, 'And what will be the sign of your coming and of the end of the age?' Fitzmyer suggests that Luke is only concerned in verses 8–24 with the fate of the Temple and 'with events that do not belong to the *eschaton*',[57] but it is more accurate to say with Green that Jesus goes on to interpret the fall of Jerusalem 'as an eschatological event, but not in immediate relation to the coming of the eschaton'.[58] 'Sign' here refers to a decisive indication or portent from God that a predicted sequence of events has begun (11:16, 29, 30; 21:7, 11, 25). Jesus responds to the first question in verses 20–24 and the second question more broadly in the rest of the discourse.

Deceptive signs (21:8–11)

8 He replied: 'Watch out that you are not deceived. For many will come in my name, claiming, "I am he," and, "The time is near." Do not follow them. **9** When you hear of wars and uprisings, do not be frightened. These things must happen first, but the end will not come right away.'

10 Then he said to them: 'Nation will rise against nation, and kingdom against kingdom. **11** There will be great earthquakes, famines and pestilences in various places, and fearful events and great signs from heaven.'

8. Jesus first warned, 'Watch out that you are not deceived.' His immediate concern was that people might come in his name with false end-time messages: 'For many will come in my name, claiming, "I am he," and, "The time is near."' The expression 'in my name' could simply mean pretending to be his authorised representatives, but linked to 'I am he' it more likely means, 'I am the Messiah' (as in Matthew 24:5; compare Mark 13:21–3) or, 'I am Jesus, risen and returned.'[59] As predicted, messianic pretenders

---

[57] Fitzmyer, *Luke X–XXIV*, 1331, 1334–5.

[58] Green, *Luke*, 731.

[59] Marshall, *Luke*, 763, rightly argues that *egō eimi* ('I am he') can hardly mean

in the first decades of the Christian era soon linked emerging political events with expectations about the end of the age.[60] Sadly also, they have been doing so ever since! Anticipating that disciples might be led astray by such pretenders and their false claims, Jesus insisted, 'Do not follow them.'

9. Special mention is made of 'wars' and 'uprisings', which were the sort of threatening events that would make people think the end was near. Jesus warned his disciples not to be frightened by such calamities, adding that 'these things must happen first'. They are part of God's unfolding plan to replace the kingdoms of this world with his eternal and unshakable kingdom (see Daniel 2:44–5; Revelation 6:1–17). Nevertheless, 'the end will not come right away.' Wars and political upheavals continue to arise in human experience, but they are not a sufficient basis for Christian prophets to provide an exact timetable of final events (see Acts 1:6–7).

10–11. 'Then he said to them: "Nation will rise against nation, and kingdom against kingdom,"' repeating and reinforcing his previous warning (there is no break between these announcements in Mark 13:7–8). This focus on human conflict and self-destruction is then paired with a prediction of terrifying disturbances in nature: 'There will be great earthquakes, famines and pestilences in various places.' Although such disasters are a constant feature of life in this fallen world, they sometimes appear in biblical contexts as specific expressions of divine judgment (e.g., 1 Chronicles 21:14; 2 Chronicles 15:6; Isaiah 8:21; 13:13; 14:30; Haggai 2:6; Zechariah 14:4).[61] The accumulation of such events, together with 'fearful events and great signs from heaven', could suggest the beginning of the end. But Luke omits the claim that 'these are the beginning of birth-pains' (Mark 13:8) and moves immediately to the themes of persecution and testimony for disciples (verses 12–19). Natural disasters face us with the fragility of life in this universe, the sovereignty of God over nature and human history and our ultimate accountability to God as human beings made in his image and likeness. The theme of signs in the heavens and distress on earth is resumed when Jesus talks about the immediate indications of the Son of Man's coming 'with power and great glory' (verses 25–8).

'I am God' here, although Jesus implicitly claims to be the ultimate deliverer of God's people.

[60] See Green, *Luke*, 734–5. Edwards, *Luke*, 595, notes that in the second Jewish revolt (AD 132–5), Bar Kokhba claimed to be the Messiah, and 'swept many devout Jews into revolt'. Theudas (Acts 5:36) and an unnamed Egyptian (Acts 21:38) led earlier revolts.

[61] Edwards, *Luke*, 598, notes the use of such apocalyptic imagery in Jewish intertestamental literature.

Persecution and witness (21:12–19)

12'But before all this, they will seize you and persecute you. They will hand you over to synagogues and put you in prison, and you will be brought before kings and governors, and all on account of my name. **13**And so you will bear testimony to me. **14**But make up your mind not to worry beforehand how you will defend yourselves. **15**For I will give you words and wisdom that none of your adversaries will be able to resist or contradict. **16**You will be betrayed even by parents, brothers and sisters, relatives and friends, and they will put some of you to death. **17**Everyone will hate you because of me. **18**But not a hair of your head will perish. **19**Stand firm, and you will win life.'

12–13. Luke adapts Mark 13:9–13, adding the words 'But before all this' to explain why 'the end will not come right away' (verse 9). Before the destruction of Jerusalem and the Temple, a period of persecution for disciples is predicted: 'they will seize you and persecute you. They will hand you over to synagogues and put you in prison, and you will be brought before kings and governors, and all on account of my name.' Luke extensively illustrates such opposition from Jewish and Gentile sources in his second volume (e.g., Acts 4:1–22; 8:1–4; 12:1–5; 13:44–14:6; 16:19–24). But persecution and arrest would enable Jesus's followers to testify to him in critical places and before significant religious and political leaders: 'And so you will bear testimony to me' (e.g., Acts 4:8–12; 5:29–32; 23:1–11; 26:1–32).[62] Some of Luke's first readers may already have experienced these things, as many have ever since. In today's world, one in seven Christians is reportedly persecuted for their faith. Mark 13:10 ('And the gospel must first be preached to all nations') is not paralleled here, but Luke records that charge later (24:45–9).

14–15. In preparation for such opportunities, Jesus urged, 'But make up your mind not to worry beforehand how you will defend yourselves' (see 12:11). The reason for confidence is stated in very personal terms: 'For I will give you words and wisdom that none of your adversaries will be able to resist or contradict.' This implies the continuing presence and influence of the risen Lord in the mission he gives to his disciples (see Matthew 28:20). He had previously said, 'the Holy Spirit will teach you at that time what you should say' (12:12; compare Mark 13:11), but here he promises to be

---

[62] The Greek does not include 'to me' (*apobēsetai hymin eis martyrion*, 'this will be your opportunity to bear witness', ESV). Marshall, *Luke*, 76, argues that *eis martyrion* could mean 'as evidence against' their persecutors. However, 21:13 lacks the expression *ep' autous* (9:5, 'against them').

the giver of those gifts himself. This prepares for the emphasis in Acts on the exalted Jesus continuing his ministry on earth through the empowering of his witnesses by the Holy Spirit (e.g., 1:8; 2:4; 4:8, 31). Luke specifically illustrates this in the case of Stephen, who was 'full of the Spirit and wisdom' (Acts 6:3). When he debated with his opponents, 'they could not stand up against the wisdom the Spirit gave him as he spoke' (6:10). The Holy Spirit is called 'the Spirit of Jesus' in Acts 16:6–7.

16–17. Jesus's warning escalated when he said, 'You will be betrayed even by parents, brothers and sisters, relatives and friends' (see Mark 13:12). This picks up the reference to leaving behind family relationships 'for the sake of the kingdom of God' (18:29; compare 9:57–62; 14:26). It also recalls the prediction of family division in 12:52–3 and the prophecy of Simeon about division in Israel (2:34). Betrayal to arresting authorities implies an intensity of opposition to the gospel and its agents, breaking the ties of family and friendship.[63] The claim that 'they will put some of you to death' relates to the authorities to whom Christians are betrayed, rather than to unbelieving family and friends who might take the law into their own hands. However, mob violence soon became a danger for believers, and sometimes civic authorities actually protected them from such attack (e.g., Acts 19:23–41; 21:30–36). The real issue behind such animosity is simply stated: 'Everyone will hate you because of me' (*dia to onoma mou*, 'because of my name'). The name of Jesus represents his identity, character and claims. Christians are still persecuted because they proclaim Jesus and seek to live by his standards and values (see 6:22), which others see as a threat to their autonomy and cultural or religious norms.

18–19. This section of the discourse finishes with the promise that 'not a hair of your head will perish'. A similar saying in Acts 27:34 relates to physical safety, but the context here suggests something more. Jesus had previously said, 'the very hairs of your head are all numbered' (12:7), assuring believers under attack that they would not be forgotten by God but would be delivered from judgment after death. Following the warning that 'they will put some of you to death' (verse 16), something beyond death must be implied here too.[64] Given the security and hope of his promise, disciples are encouraged to 'Stand firm, and you will win

---

[63] Edwards, *Luke*, 601, draws attention to evidence outside the New Testament for such betrayal in the early years of the Christian era.

[64] Fitzmyer, *Luke X–XXIV*, 1341 dismisses this possibility and supposes a contradiction with verse 16, but the parallel with 12:4–7 should not be ignored. See Green, *Luke*, 737–8.

life' (*en tē hypomonē hymōn ktēsasthe tas psychas hymōn*, 'By your endurance you will gain your lives', ESV).[65] The word 'life' here (*psychē*), as in 9:24; 14:26; 17:33, is used in a comprehensive way for embodied selves. 'You will win life' effectively means 'you will be resurrected to eternal life' (see Mark 13:13, 'the one who stands firm to the end will be saved').

Judgment on Jerusalem (21:20–24)

20 'When you see Jerusalem being surrounded by armies, you will know that its desolation is near. 21 Then let those who are in Judea flee to the mountains, let those in the city get out, and let those in the country not enter the city. 22 For this is the time of punishment in fulfilment of all that has been written. 23 How dreadful it will be in those days for pregnant women and nursing mothers! There will be great distress in the land and wrath against this people. 24 They will fall by the sword and will be taken as prisoners to all the nations. Jerusalem will be trampled on by the Gentiles until the times of the Gentiles are fulfilled.'

20. Luke adapts Mark 13:14–20 with material from his own sources, including restatements of Jesus's earlier teaching about the future of Jerusalem (13:34–5; 19:41–4), but not including the apocalyptic warning in Mark 13:14 ('When you see "the abomination that causes desolation" standing where it does not belong' (see Daniel 9:26–7; 11:31; 12:11); Matthew 24:15). Luke's Jesus speaks more simply about the desolation of the *city*, which would bring the destruction of the *Temple*, but gives no hint that the sanctuary would first be desecrated. He picks up the story from verse 11 and warns, 'When you see Jerusalem surrounded by armies, you will know that its desolation is near.' Similar language was used by the prophets concerning the destruction of Jerusalem by foreign armies, especially the Babylonians (e.g., Isaiah 29:3; Jeremiah 6:6–8; see comments on Luke 13:35; 19:43). Jesus apparently viewed these events as prefiguring the destruction of both city and Temple by the Romans, which took place in AD 70. It is not necessary to suppose that Luke was writing after the event and reading back the details into Jesus's predictions.[66]

---

[65] Both NIV and ESV translate the future tense of the verb 'win' or 'gain' here (*ktēsesthe*), but there is some textual evidence for the aorist imperative (*ktēsasthe*), which Metzger, *Textual Commentary*, 147, considers a slightly preferable reading ('stand firm and win life').

[66] See Josephus, *War* 7.1–4. The desolation of Jerusalem and the surrounding region at the hands of the Babylonians in the sixth century BC is predicted in Jeremiah

21–2. The warning to those who are in Judea is to 'flee to the mountains', presumably meaning the Transjordan region or 'the remoter areas of Judea itself, such as the inaccessible mountains and caves around the Dead Sea'.[67] The warning to those who are in the city is to 'get out, and let those in the country not enter the city'. Elements of the more extended warning in Mark 13:15–19 can be found in Luke 17:31. The reason for escape is to avoid the judgment of God on Jerusalem and its people, as predicted by Jesus (11:47–51; 13:34–5; 19:41–4): 'For this is the time of punishment [hēmerai ekdikēseōs, 'days of vengeance'] in fulfilment of all that has been written.' Relevant Old Testament prophecies could include 1 Kings 9:6–9; Jeremiah 5:29; Daniel 9:26; Hosea 9:7; Micah 3:12.

23–4. The horrors of that time for a particularly vulnerable group in the community are then contemplated: 'How dreadful it will be in those days for pregnant women and nursing mothers!' (see also 23:28–31). More broadly, Jesus declares, 'There will be great distress in the land and wrath against this people.' As with previous invasions, 'They will fall by the sword and will be taken prisoners to all the nations.' No shortening of this period of terror is mentioned here (see Mark 13:20). Luke alone records that 'Jerusalem will be trampled on by the Gentiles until the times of the Gentiles are fulfilled' (see Daniel 8:13–14; 12:5–13). Some argue that 'the times of the Gentiles' has a dual reference to the role of Gentiles in the destruction of Jerusalem and the proclamation of the gospel in all the world.[68] But the Gentile mission began long before the destruction of Jerusalem (Acts 13–28), having been clearly instituted by the resurrected Lord (Luke 24:45–7). It is also unlikely that this saying 'deliberately holds open the future for Jerusalem and Israel', as Tannehill contends.[69] Even the apostle Paul's hopeful words about God saving a hardened portion of Israel (Romans 11:11–14, 25–32) were not a prediction that the nation, its capital and Temple, would one day be restored to their original purpose. 'The times of the Gentiles [nations]' simply marks the whole period from the fall of Jerusalem to the consummation of God's purpose in the coming of the Son of Man.

4:7; 7:34 and described in 2 Chronicles 36:15–21. Fitzmyer, *Luke X–XXIV*, 1343, summarises Josephus's extensive account of the fall of Jerusalem, which was the decisive event of the First Jewish–Roman War (AD 66–73).

[67] Marshall, *Luke*, 772.

[68] Green, *Luke*, 739. See also Edwards, *Luke*, 605–6.

[69] Tannehill, *Narrative Unity* 1, 163. Fitzmyer, *Luke X–XXIV*, 1345, rightly observes that 'the destruction of Jerusalem will mean its "end" in God's salvation-history'.

The coming of the Son of Man (21:25–8)

25 'There will be signs in the sun, moon and stars. On the earth, nations will be in anguish and perplexity at the roaring and tossing of the sea. 26 People will faint from terror, apprehensive of what is coming on the world, for the heavenly bodies will be shaken. 27 At that time they will see the Son of Man coming in a cloud with power and great glory. 28 When these things begin to take place, stand up and lift up your heads, because your redemption is drawing near.'

25–6. Luke omits any further reference to false messiahs and false prophets performing signs and wonders 'to deceive, if possible, even the elect' (Mark 13:22), and focuses on cosmic signs that will immediately precede the coming of the Son of Man: 'There will be signs in the sun, moon, and stars.'[70] 'Fearful events and great signs from heaven' were mentioned in connection with 'earthquakes, famines and pestilences in various places' before the judgment on Jerusalem (verse 11). But the ultimate manifestation of such warnings will bring unprecedented alarm and anxiety everywhere: 'On the earth, nations will be in anguish and perplexity at the roaring and tossing of the sea. People will faint from terror, apprehensive of what is coming on the world, for the heavenly bodies will be shaken.' Marshall observes that, in prophetic terms, 'The shaking of the heavens (Hag. 2:21) is the appropriate prelude to the heavenly coming of the Son of Man.'[71]

27. 'At that time they will see the Son of Man coming in a cloud with power and great glory.' Elements of previous predictions about the Son of Man's coming (9:26; 12:40; 17:24, 30; 18:8) are brought together here, affirming the fulfilment of Daniel 7:13–14. However, the emphasis in Jesus's application of that prophecy is mostly on the Son of Man coming to *earth* for judgment and redemption, whereas Daniel envisaged the coming of 'one like a son of man' as an approach to God in heaven.[72] Luke 22:69 predicts the latter as the first stage in the fulfilment

---

[70] See, however, Luke 17:23; 21:8–9. Mark 13:24–5 expresses the disturbance in the universe with a quote blending words from Isaiah 13:10 and 34:4. Compare Joel 2:30–31.

[71] Marshall, *Luke*, 775. All the biblical images that Jesus uses 'portend the advent of the Day of the Lord and, so, portray the coming of the Son of Man as a theophany' (Green, *Luke*, 740).

[72] Marshall, *Luke*, 776–7, rightly argues against the view that in Luke 21:25–8, 'parousia language is used symbolically to describe the fall of Jerusalem as the vindication of Jesus'.

of this cosmic vision. The singular expression 'in a cloud with power and great glory' suggests that Jesus's ascension and heavenly enthronement will enable him to return to earth to manifest to all what was partially revealed to the chosen few, when he was previously transfigured before them (9:28–36; compare Exodus 40:34). As in 17:24, the imagery relates to a supernatural event visible to everyone on earth, not merely to the fall of Jerusalem in AD 70.

28. The Son of Man's coming in fulfilment of Daniel's prophecy is associated with God's final judgment of humanity (Daniel 7:9–10) and the establishment of 'an everlasting dominion that will not pass away,' a kingdom 'that will never be destroyed' (7:13–14). Jesus portrays his involvement in that process in various ways (e.g., 9:26; 12:8–10, 40–48; 13:23–30; 18:26–37). Judgment is implied by the biblical imagery in 21:25–7, portraying the end of this world and the terror it provokes. However, Jesus's final word on this subject in Luke's account is one of encouragement for disciples: 'When these things begin to take place, stand up and lift up your heads, because your redemption is drawing near.' 'Redemption' (*apolytrōsis*) implies release from captivity to evil powers, affliction, sin and death, in the Son of Man's everlasting kingdom (see Romans 8:23; Ephesians 1:14; 4:30).[73]

Being alert and ready (21:29–38)

29 He told them this parable: 'Look at the fig-tree and all the trees. **30** When they sprout leaves, you can see for yourselves and know that summer is near. **31** Even so, when you see these things happening, you know that the kingdom of God is near.

32 'Truly I tell you, this generation will certainly not pass away until all these things have happened. **33** Heaven and earth will pass away, but my words will never pass away.

34 'Be careful, or your hearts will be weighed down with carousing, drunk- enness and the anxieties of life, and that day will close on you suddenly like a trap. **35** For it will come on all those who live on the face of the whole earth. **36** Be always on the watch, and pray that you may be able to escape all that is about to happen, and that you may be able to stand before the Son of Man.'

37 Each day Jesus was teaching at the temple, and each evening he went out to spend the night on the hill called the Mount of Olives, **38** and all the people came early in the morning to hear him at the temple.

---

[73] See my comment on the use of similar terms in 1:68; 2:38.

29–31. Jesus's parable about 'the fig-tree and all the trees' relates to the signs of the Son of Man's coming.[74] Most Palestinian trees are not deciduous, but the fig-tree loses all its leaves in winter, so that when they reappear in spring, 'you can see for yourselves and know that the summer is near'. The parallel is simply drawn: 'Even so, when you see these things happening, you know that the kingdom of God is near.' 'These things' refers to the immediate signs of the end mentioned in verses 25–6 (so also 'these things' in verse 28), not to the destruction of Jerusalem and the Temple. A time gap between the events described in verses 20–24 and the signs of the end (verses 25–6) is indicated by the need for 'the times of the Gentiles' to be fulfilled.[75] Nevertheless, the events described in verses 20–24 function as an historic guarantee of the end-time judgment of God associated with the coming of the Son of Man. Luke clarifies that 'the kingdom of God' is only fully consummated or realised when the Son of Man appears with power and great glory (contrast 17:21).

32. Jesus characteristically used the word 'Truly' (*amēn*) to affirm the veracity of an important saying (4:24; 12:37; 18:17, 29; 23:43). In this case, two declarations are linked together by a common term ('pass away'), the first promising that 'this generation will not pass away until all these things have happened (*heōs an panta genētai*)'. The term 'this generation' most obviously refers to Jesus's contemporaries (7:31; 9:41; 11:29, 30, 31 32, 50, 51; 17:25). 'All these things' most likely embraces the whole sequence of events in verses 8–28. Without giving a precise timetable, Luke wants us to know that Jesus preached an imminent end (despite the implied time gap between verses 20–24 and 25–6). Like many of the prophets before him, he faced his contemporaries with a foreshortened view of the future, demanding that they live with the expectation that it would all happen soon. Nolland explains this by saying that the prophets 'put together, as though they would happen together, things that belong together in principle but turn out to be separated chronologically by large spans of time'.[76] Another possibility is that 'all these things' refers only to

---

[74] Luke's addition of 'and all the trees' (compare Mark 13:28) is simply a 'rhetorical extension' (Fitzmyer, *Luke X–XXIV*, 1352).

[75] Whereas Mark 13:24 introduces the immediate signs of the Son of Man's coming with the words 'but in those days, following that distress' (compare Matthew 24:29), Luke's timeless introduction is simply factual (verse 25, 'there will be'), but also distant (verse 27, 'they will see').

[76] Nolland, *Luke 18:35–24:53*, 1011. Bock, *Luke 9:51–24:53*, 1688–9, dismisses this view, because 'it makes Jesus manifestly wrong'. But he fails to note that this is the pattern of prophetic preaching in the Old Testament. For example, Joel 1:1–2:27

verses 8–24, so that Jesus is saying that his generation will experience the destruction of Jerusalem, in Bock's words, as 'an event that itself pictures the beginning of end-time events'.[77] Luke does not parallel Mark 13:32 ('about that day or hour no one knows, not even the angels in heaven, nor the Son, but only the Father'), but he does report that the risen Lord said, 'It is not for you to know the times or dates the Father has set by his own authority' (Acts 1:7).

33. Despite the close connection of this saying with the preceding one, it probably refers to more than Jesus's teaching about the end-time. The idea that 'heaven and earth will pass away' is quite shocking and unsettling, but there is security and hope in the teaching of Jesus, which has abiding significance and relevance ('but my words will never pass away'). Jesus puts his teaching on the same level as the Law of God (16:17; compare Psalm 119:89) and the word of the Lord through his prophets (Isaiah 40:6–8; 55:10–11).

34–6. This concluding exhortation replaces the one in Mark 13:33–7, which was earlier paralleled in Luke 12:35–40; 19:12–13.[78] It begins with a warning about hearts being made heavy by self-indulgence and worldly concerns and not prepared for the sudden coming of the Son of Man (see 12:45–6): 'Be careful, or your hearts will be weighed down with carousing, drunkenness and the anxieties of life, and that day will close on you suddenly like a trap' (see Romans 13:11–14; 1 Thessalonians 5:1–9). 'That day' will be inescapable, 'for it will come on all those who live on the face of the whole earth'.[79] The alternative for disciples is to 'be always on the watch, and pray that you may be able escape all that is about to happen, and that you may be able to stand before the Son of Man' (see Ephesians 6:18; 1 Thessalonians 5:23). Standing with confidence before the Son of Man as judge is implied.

37–8. Luke concludes his report of Jesus's teaching in Jerusalem with

---

urges a response to immediate issues in the light of apparently impending eschatological events (2:28–3:21).

[77] Bock, *Luke 9:51–24:53*, 1691. This seems more likely than Bock's preferred view that, when Jesus speaks of the generation that sees these things, he means 'the generation that sees the events of the end' in the destruction of Jerusalem. Compare Fitzmyer, *Luke X–XXIV*, 1353.

[78] Marshall, *Luke*, 781–2, argues that Luke is working from an independent source here.

[79] Some less significant witnesses place *hōs pagis* ('like a trap') at the beginning of the next clause ('for, like a trap, it will come upon you'). See Metzger, *Textual Commentary*, 147.

a summary recalling 19:47–8, but with new information: 'Each day Jesus was teaching at the temple, and each evening he went out to spend the night on the hill called the Mount of Olives' (see 22:39).[80] The antagonism of the chief priests and teachers of the law is not mentioned again until 22:2, but the enthusiasm of the crowd is emphatically noted: 'and all the people came early in the morning to hear him at the temple.'

LIVING WITH CONFIDENCE IN JESUS'S END-TIME TEACHING

Ever since Jesus taught in this manner, cynics have echoed the challenge, 'Where is this "coming" he promised? Ever since our ancestors died, everything goes on as it has since the beginning of creation' (2 Peter 3:4). Jesus proclaimed an imminent end, but he warned that deceptive signs could hinder disciples from living faithfully while they waited. When he talked about the destruction of Jerusalem, he portrayed it as an end-time event, fulfilling many predictions about God's judgment on his stubborn people. This anticipated and guaranteed the Son of Man's ultimate judgment of the nations, functioning as 'a precursor or proto-type of the final eschatological fulfillment', as Edwards argues.[81] It also signalled the need for something to replace the Temple and its provisions for approaching God (see John 2:18–22; 4:19–26). The promised new covenant was inaugurated with Jesus's death, resurrection and ascension (Luke 22:14–20; Acts 2:32–9), but the benefits will only be fully experienced on his return as Son of Man with final redemption (Luke 21:25–8; Acts 3:19–21). Meanwhile, Jesus emphasised the need for his disciples to endure suffering and persecution, while taking every opportunity to bear witness to him and his message. He also highlighted the need to remain spiritually alert, prayerful and morally ready for the coming of the Son of Man (see 12:35–48; 17:25–37). Luke's rhetorical strategy in presenting Jesus's Jerusalem discourse on this subject is to highlight the significance of the city's destruction as a fulfilment of his earlier predictions and as a guarantee of the fulfilment of his promises about the return of the Son of Man and the universal judgment of the nations.

---

[80] Edwards, *Luke*, 614–15, suggests that *ēulizeto* ('spent the night') could refer to lodgings in a town and therefore mean Bethany, some two miles (3km) east of Jerusalem on the far side of the Mount of Olives, as in Matthew 21:17; 26:6; Mark 11:1, 11, 12; 14:3.

[81] Edwards, *Luke*, 598.

7

The Suffering, Death and Burial of Jesus

LUKE 22:1–23:56

The conflict between Jesus and the Jewish authorities comes to its climax here. As Green observes, 'The propagation of the "good news" has attracted both allies and opposition, with some persons working to embrace and serve the divine purpose, others to reject and obstruct it.'[1] Jesus is aligned with God, his disciples and the people who remain largely supportive. The chief priests and teachers of the law are aligned with Satan and one of the Twelve in securing his arrest (22:1–6, 47–53). They then set out to persuade the Roman governor to do their will (23:1–25). Some of the crowd eventually join in their cry for Jesus to be crucified (23:18–25), but Luke also records the public grief of many over his suffering (23:27, 48). Jesus's final Passover meal with his disciples is an important opportunity to reveal more about the significance of his impending death to them (22:7–30). At the same time, he warns of Peter's denial, which soon occurs (22:31–4, 54–62). Jesus prayerfully approaches his suffering and death, but his disciples remain ill-prepared (22:39–46), only able to stand at a distance and watch as he is crucified (23:49). Joseph of Arimathea emerges as a surprising ally at the end, securing his body from the governor and providing a place for his burial (23:50–54). As previously, Luke focuses on the impact that Jesus had on individuals, notably on one of the criminals crucified with him (23:39–43) and the Roman centurion (23:47).

All four Gospels have a passion narrative 'with a certain striking similarity'.[2] Some scholars have argued that a primitive form of this narrative was available to each of the evangelists, who modified it in the light of other sources available to them. However, Luke seems to be particularly dependent on Mark's account, with significant subtractions and additions.[3] Luke omits four Marcan episodes: the anointing of Jesus in Bethany (Mark 14:3–9); Jesus's

---

[1] Green, *Luke*, 744.

[2] Fitzmyer, *Luke X–XXIV*, 1360.

[3] Fitzmyer, *Luke X–XXIV*, 1360, argues against the existence of a pre-Marcan continuous narrative, whereas Nolland, *Luke 18:35–24:53*, 1023, contends that Luke had such a source available to him. Compare Bock, *Luke 9:51–24:53*, 1698–700.

prediction of the disciples' desertion (14:27–8); the flight of the disciples and the young man (14:50–52); and the mocking of the soldiers in the Praetorium (15:16–20). Luke adds a four-part discourse at the end of his account of the Last Supper (22:21–3, 24–30, 31–4, 35–8), and two significant narratives (Jesus sent to Herod, 23:6–12; and Pilate's final judgment, 23:13–16), as well as expanding Mark 14:1–2 in 22:1–6 and Mark 15:27–32 in 23:32–43.

1. The Last Supper (22:1–38)

The chief priests and teachers of the law, who were looking for a way to dispose of Jesus, found an unexpected solution in the willingness of Judas to betray him (verses 1–6). Luke presents this as an initiative of Satan, which is later described by Jesus as their 'hour – when darkness reigns' (verse 53). But before these events unfold, Luke offers an expanded version of Jesus's last meal with his disciples. An explanation of the significance of the occasion for Jesus (verses 15–18, 21–3) and for them (verses 19–20) is followed by a challenge about serving as he serves and sharing in his kingdom (verses 24–30). A prediction about Simon's denial and restoration (verses 31–4) precedes a final warning about the approaching conflict (verses 35–8).

A fateful alliance (22:1–6)

Judas agrees to betray Jesus

22 Now the Festival of Unleavened Bread, called the Passover, was approaching, **2** and the chief priests and the teachers of the law were looking for some way to get rid of Jesus, for they were afraid of the people. **3** Then Satan entered Judas, called Iscariot, one of the Twelve. **4** And Judas went to the chief priests and the officers of the temple guard and discussed with them how he might betray Jesus. **5** They were delighted and agreed to give him money. **6** He consented, and watched for an opportunity to hand Jesus over to them when no crowd was present.

1–2. 'Now the festival of Unleavened Bread, called the Passover, was approaching.'[4] This was an annual opportunity for the Jews to celebrate their redemption from Egypt and its covenant implications (Exodus 12:1–30; 19:1–8). Strictly speaking, Nolland notes that Passover was 'the feast prepared

---

[4] Edwards, *Luke*, 614, notes that the Passover is mentioned with increasing specifications of time: 'the day (verse 7) and 'the hour' (verse 14).

for by the slaughter of the lamb in the late afternoon of 14 Nisan and celebrated in family or wider groupings from after sunset'.[5] Nisan was the first month of the year in the Jewish calendar of festivals. The Feast of Unleavened Bread commenced with this meal (in the Jewish calendar 15 Nisan began at sunset) and continued for seven days, commemorating the eating of unleavened bread on the eve of their departure from Egypt (Leviticus 23:5–6; Numbers 28:16–17; Deuteronomy 16:1–8). Jerusalem would have been filled for the week with pilgrims from many places. In this time of religious and national fervour, the Roman leadership came down from Caesarea to keep the peace. The chief priests and the teachers of the law, as the leading opponents of Jesus and his ministry, were looking for some way to 'get rid' of him (*anelōsin*, 'destroy, kill'; see 19:47; 20:19), but 'they were afraid of the people', because many were attracted to his teaching (19:48; 21:38) and could easily have turned against them (Mark 14:2; Matthew 24:5).

3–4. Luke omits the story of Jesus's anointing at Bethany (Mark 14:2–9; Matthew 26:6–13), possibly because he earlier gave prominence to another anointing event (7:36–50). An expanded record of the betrayal of Jesus is introduced with the perspective that 'Satan entered Judas, called Iscariot, one of the Twelve' (see Mark 14:10–11; Matthew 26:14–16). Luke's account of the testing of Jesus in the wilderness concluded with the note that the devil left him 'until an opportune time' (4:13). Satan's malevolent influence as 'the adversary' reappears in various ways throughout this Gospel (10:18–20; 11:18; 13:16; 22:31; called 'the devil' again in 8:12), but the supreme moment for doing evil occurs when he moves Judas to betray his master (see John 13:2, 27). Luke highlights the tragedy of this with the reminder that Judas was 'one of the Twelve' (see 6:14–16; 22:21). His approach to 'the chief priests and the officers of the temple guard' was deliberate and calculated.[6] Knowing that they were looking for a way to arrest Jesus and put him on trial, 'he discussed with them how he might betray Jesus'. No reason for this is given by Luke, other than the suggestion of financial gain. John's Gospel links Judas with those who did not believe in Jesus (6:64) and highlights his greed and dishonesty (12:6; 13:29).

5–6. The chief priests and Temple officers 'were delighted and agreed

[5] Nolland, *Luke 18:35–24:53*, 1027. During the Roman occupation, this festival was sometimes an occasion for civil disturbance (Josephus, *War* 2.1.3; 2.12.1). See G. H. Twelftree, 'Feasts', *DJG*, 272–4. Eckhard J. Schnabel, *Jesus in Jerusalem: The Last Days* (Grand Rapids: Eerdmans, 2018), 145–7, argues that Galileans were permitted at that time to celebrate Passover a day early because of the crowds.
[6] The noun *stratēgoi* simply means 'officers', but the NIV rightly assumes that they were 'officers of the temple guard' (as in verse 52).

LUKE

to give him money' (Matthew 26:15 specifies 'thirty pieces of silver'). The verb translated 'delighted' (*chairō*) is normally applied by Luke to rejoicing in God and his goodness (1:14; 6:23; 10:20; 13:17; 15:5, 32; 19:6, 37), but a perverse joy is indicated here (see 23:8). The payment Judas received for his wickedness was sufficient for him to buy a field (Acts 1:18). His whole-hearted complicity in the arrest of Jesus is emphasised: 'He consented, and watched for an opportunity to hand Jesus over to them when no crowd was present.' Paradoxically, however, betrayal was part of the divine plan, as previously revealed by Jesus (9:44, *paradidosthai*, 'to be handed over'; see also 22:21–3). Diverse human agendas, with Satan playing his part, inexorably advanced the saving purpose of God (see Acts 2:23–36; 4:23–31).

Preparing for the Passover meal (22:7–13)

The Last Supper

7 Then came the day of Unleavened Bread on which the Passover lamb had to be sacrificed. 8 Jesus sent Peter and John, saying, 'Go and make preparations for us to eat the Passover.'

9 'Where do you want us to prepare for it?' they asked.

10 He replied, 'As you enter the city, a man carrying a jar of water will meet you. Follow him to the house that he enters, 11 and say to the owner of the house, "The Teacher asks: where is the guest room, where I may eat the Passover with my disciples?" 12 He will show you a large room upstairs, all furnished. Make preparations there.'

13 They left and found things just as Jesus had told them. So they prepared the Passover.

7–8. 'Then came the day of Unleavened Bread on which the Passover lamb had to be sacrificed' (see verse 1).[7] Luke follows Mark 14:12 in using the word *pascha* for 'the Passover lamb' (see Exodus 12:21 LXX), rather than the festival. The lamb had to be sacrificed on the afternoon of 14 Nisan by the head of a household in the court of the priests (see Exodus 12:6 and my comment on Nisan with reference to Luke 22:1–2).[8]

---

[7] Nolland, *Luke 18:35–24:53*, 1033, notes the precedence for referring to 14 Nisan as 'the day of Unleavened Bread' in Exodus 12:18. It was the day for removing all leaven from households (Josephus, *War* 5.99).

[8] The Last Supper is presented as a Passover meal in each of the Synoptic Gospels, but more extensively so in Luke. Fitzmyer, *Luke X–XXIV*, 1378–82 discusses the problem of relating this to the meal 'before the feast of the Passover' in John 13:1–2. But it is possible that each of the Gospels records an early, modified Passover, celebrated by Jesus with his disciples on the evening of the Day of Preparation (Nisan 14), before the lambs were sacrificed, to 'form the basis of the remembrance of

The feast of Unleavened Bread began that evening (15 Nisan) and lasted for seven days. Jesus sent Peter and John (named only by Luke here), saying, 'Go and make preparations for us to eat the Passover.' This would involve finding a place to gather, purchasing and sacrificing the lamb, and preparing other elements of the meal.

9–11. The disciples asked, 'Where do you want us to prepare for it?' Jesus's answer could indicate a prior arrangement he had made or demonstrate once more his amazing foreknowledge (see 5:4–7; 19:29–32). The latter seems more likely in view of his apparent control of events in the narrative that follows. Peter and John were to enter the city (having spent the previous night on the Mount of Olives, 21:37), where 'a man carrying a jar of water' would meet them. This man would have stood out, because it was normally the task of women to carry water. The need for secrecy is suggested by the next instruction ('Follow him to the house that he enters'). If Jesus was aware of the possibility of betrayal, he wanted to make sure he could spend these last hours undetected with his disciples. His message to the owner of the house ('The Teacher asks: where is the guest room, where I may eat the Passover with my disciples?' see 'the Lord' in 19:31) presumes that he knows Jesus by reputation at least.

12–13. Jesus finished instructing Peter and John by saying, 'He will show you a large room upstairs, all furnished. Make preparations there.' 'A large room upstairs' describes the sort of 'guest room' (verse 11, *katalyma*, as in 2:7) sufficient for such an occasion. The added description 'all furnished' (*estrōmenon*, 'spread out') probably refers to carpets or cushions suitable for reclining at table. Luke re-emphasises the foreknowledge of Jesus when he concludes that 'they left and found things just as Jesus had told them' (see 19:32). Their role in preparing the Passover illustrates the pattern of service commended to all disciples in verses 25–7.

Experiencing the meal together (22:14–20)

14 When the hour came, Jesus and his apostles reclined at the table. **15** And he said to them, 'I have eagerly desired to eat this Passover with you before I suffer. **16** For I tell you, I will not eat it again until it finds fulfilment in the kingdom of God.'

17 After taking the cup, he gave thanks and said, 'Take this and divide it among you. **18** For I tell you I will not drink again from the fruit of the vine until the kingdom of God comes.'

---

his death as the Lamb of God' (Christopher K. W. Moore, *Mark* (London: Hodder & Stoughton, 2024), 25).

19 And he took bread, gave thanks and broke it, and gave it to them, saying, 'This is my body given for you; do this in remembrance of me.'

20 In the same way, after the supper he took the cup, saying, 'This cup is the new covenant in my blood, which is poured out for you.'[a]

---

a 19,20 Some manuscripts do not have *given for you . . . poured out for you.*

14–16. 'When the hour came, Jesus and his apostles reclined at the table.' Although it is possible that 'the hour' (*hē hōra*) means something like 'critical moment' (as in verse 53), a simple chronological reference is more likely. Instead of 'the Twelve' (Mark 14:17; Matthew 26:20), Luke identifies Jesus's companions as 'his apostles', alluding to their calling (6:13–16) and distinctive role as his emissaries and witnesses (9:10; 11:49; Acts 1:2–8, 21–6). This was to be a revelatory moment in their preparation for that ministry. Jesus solemnly announced, 'I have eagerly desired to eat this Passover with you before I suffer. For I tell you, I will not eat it again until it finds fulfilment in the kingdom of God.'[9] He gave his own end-time perspective to the celebration, viewing it as an anticipation of the meal he would share with them 'in the kingdom of God' (see also verses 18, 29–30; compare 13:28–9; 14:15–24).[10] However, his ardent wish to eat the Passover lamb/meal with them *before his suffering* introduced another perspective. Luke alone records that what the Passover represented in Exodus 12 would be fulfilled 'in the kingdom of God'. The verb 'fulfil' (*plēroō*) is normally used by Luke in connection with the fulfilment of Scripture (4:21; 24:44; Acts 1:16; 3:18), but here it suggests the typological fulfilment of the Passover sacrifice by Jesus's approaching death, achieving his 'exodus' (9:31, 'departure') and their participation in his heavenly rule (22:29–30). Furthermore, as Nolland observes, 'The mention of Jesus' suffering here already prepares for a parallelism between the role of the (sacrificial) blood of the Paschal lamb in Egypt and the new covenant in Jesus' blood of v. 20.'[11] The apostle

---

[9] Luke possibly amplifies Mark 14:25; Matthew 26:29 to form from his own distinctive source an introduction to the meal. Edwards, *Luke*, 623–5, argues that Luke follows 'a separate Passover tradition that is combined with a Pauline tradition'.

[10] Later Jewish texts show that Passover celebrations focused on redemption at the time of the Exodus, but also looked forward to ultimate redemption by the Messiah. Both emphases were probably present in Jesus's time. See Joachim Jeremias, *The Eucharistic Words of Jesus* (London: SCM, 1966), 252, 256–62.

[11] Nolland, *Luke 18:35–24:53*, 1050. When Jesus eats the Passover 'again' with his disciples, it will be in the eternal fellowship of the kingdom that his sacrifice establishes, not a literal Passover meal.

Paul developed this typology when he claimed that 'Christ, our Passover lamb, has been sacrificed. Therefore, let us keep the Festival, not with the old bread leavened with malice and wickedness, but with the unleavened bread of sincerity and truth' (1 Corinthians 5:7–8).

17–18. Luke alone mentions Jesus's words in connection with a preliminary cup of wine: 'After taking the cup, he gave thanks and said, "Take this and divide it among you. For I tell you I will not drink again from the fruit of the vine until the kingdom of God comes."' This could refer to either the first or second cup of wine that was normally shared at the Passover meal. The first cup was drunk as part of the preliminary course, after God was blessed for the occasion. The second was drunk after the leader of the group had recalled the story of the Exodus and invited all to join in a psalm of praise.[12] As in verse 16, Jesus gives an end-time perspective to the celebration, more explicitly viewing it as anticipating the meal to be shared with his disciples when 'the kingdom of God comes' (see 21:31). The sequence of lamb and cup in verses 15–18 prepares for the sequence of bread and cup in verses 19–20.

19. The verbal differences between the accounts of what Jesus said next (Matthew 26:26–8; Mark 14:22–4) are possibly owing to variations in the 'eucharistic' practice of the churches with which the evangelists were associated. 'Eucharistic' is a derivative of 'Eucharist' ('Thanksgiving'), which became a common way of referring to 'the Lord's Supper' (1 Corinthians 11:20) in later Christian literature (e.g., *Didache* 9:1). Luke's wording mostly resembles that of Paul in 1 Corinthians 11:23–5. The Passover context outlined in Luke 22:14–18 particularly helps to illuminate the meaning of Jesus's words about the bread and the cup. The sequence 'he took bread, gave thanks and broke it, and gave it to them' recalls the common Jewish practice of saying grace and initiating a meal (see 9:16; 24:30; Acts 2:42, 46; 20:7, 11).[13] But this was an especially significant feature of the Passover celebration, because elements of the meal were normally interpreted at this moment (the Passover lamb, the unleavened bread and the bitter herbs).[14] On this occasion, however, when Jesus gave thanks for the unleavened bread with which the main course began, he broke it and gave it to those present, saying, 'This is my body given for

---

[12] Details about how the Passover meal was celebrated in the first century are given by Jeremias, *Eucharistic Words*, 84–8. See also Fitzmyer, *Luke X–XXIV*, 1390–91; Green, *Luke*, 758.

[13] Peterson, *Acts*, 161, 557–8; J. Behm, 'κλάω κτλ.', *TDNT* 3:728–30.

[14] Jeremias, *Eucharistic Words*, 56–61.

you.' His action symbolised the possibility of sharing in the benefits of his death, not the breaking of his body on the cross (there is no suggestion of breaking in 23:33–49). Luke alone includes the proleptic term 'given for you', which implies 'the vicarious gift of himself', as Fitzmyer suggests.[15] The parallel use of 'my blood, which is poured out for you' at the end of the meal (verse 20) points independently to his coming death.[16] Together they imply that Jesus was assigning to his disciples the benefits of the sacrifice he was about to offer on their behalf. Eating the bread and drinking from his cup was a way of receiving by faith what he offered. Only Matthew 26:26 contains the full instruction 'Take and eat,' though Mark 14:22 ('Take it') implies this.

'Do this in remembrance of me' (*touto poieite eis tēn emēn anamnēsin*) only occurs here in the Gospels, though 1 Corinthians 11:24 also records it, together with an instruction concerning the cup. The absence of this saying from Matthew and Mark has suggested to some scholars that it was a later development that cannot be attributed to the historical Jesus. However, 'remembrance' was a significant aspect of the Passover meal (Exodus 12:14 LXX, 'this day shall be for you a memorial day', ESV; compare Deuteronomy 16:3; Mishnah, *Pesach* 10:5). Even without the call to repeat the actions of eating and drinking, the Passover context of Jesus's words about the bread and cup could suggest the need for an ongoing appropriation by believers of the benefits they represent.[17] The Greek present imperative (*poieite*) does not necessarily imply repetition, but the challenge to 'do this in remembrance of me' certainly points to an activity continuing beyond the death of Jesus.

20. 'In the same way, after the supper he took the cup.' Most likely this was the third cup of the Passover meal, which was called 'the cup of blessing' in Jewish sources (see 1 Corinthians 10:16). 'In the same way' implies the same pattern as before: taking, giving thanks and sharing it with those present (Mark 14:23; Matthew 26:27). A single cup was used, which was a departure from standard Passover practice. Nolland argues that Jesus offered his own personal cup to the disciples present,

[15] Fitzmyer, *Luke X–XXIV*, 1401. The present participle *didomenon* could be understood as a 'giving' in process or as proleptic ('is about to be given').

[16] Nolland, *Luke 18:35–24:53*, 1053.

[17] Some manuscripts of the 'western' type do not include Luke 22:19b–20, even though these verses are widely attested in other textual traditions. It is likely that the shorter version arose because an ancient editor was puzzled by the mention of two cups in verses 17–20 and removed the reference to a second cup. See Metzger, *Textual Commentary*, 173–7; Fitzmyer, *Luke X–XXIV*, 1388–9.

'rather than having them drink from their own individual cups'.[18] Jesus's words of interpretation reveal more about the significance of doing this in view of his approaching death: 'This cup is the new covenant in my blood, which is poured out for you.'[19] The expression 'my blood of the covenant' is used in Matthew 26:28 and Mark 14:24, recalling Exodus 24:8, where the covenant established by God at Mount Sinai was sealed by means of animal sacrifice. Both Luke and Paul (1 Corinthians 11:25) indicate that Jesus meant 'the new covenant in my blood' (see Jeremiah 31:31–4). Jeremiah said nothing about a blood sacrifice, but he pointed to 'a definitive and permanent solution to the problem of Israel's sin as a basis for the renewal of God's relationship with his people'.[20] The 'pouring out' of his blood (*ekchynnomenon*) suggests a violent death. The phrase 'for you' (*to hyper hymōn*) implies a substitutionary dimension to Jesus's sacrifice (see Isaiah 53:12, 'he bore the sin of many').[21]

The pattern of true service (22:21–30)

21 But the hand of him who is going to betray me is with mine on the table. 22 The Son of Man will go as it has been decreed. But woe to that man who betrays him!' 23 They began to question among themselves which of them it might be who would do this.

24 A dispute also arose among them as to which of them was considered to be greatest. 25 Jesus said to them, 'The kings of the Gentiles lord it over them; and those who exercise authority over them call themselves Benefactors. 26 But you are not to be like that. Instead, the greatest among you should be like the youngest, and the one who rules like the one who serves. 27 For who is greater, the one who is at the table or the one who serves? Is it not the one who is at the table? But I am among you as one who serves. 28 You are those who have stood by me in my trials. 29 And I confer on you a kingdom, just as my Father conferred one on me, 30 so that you may eat and drink at my table in my kingdom and sit on thrones, judging the twelve tribes of Israel.'

---

[18] Nolland, *Luke 18:35–24:53*, 1054. This can be related to 'a Jewish practice in which the host might share his cup with a particular guest as a way of honouring and bestowing a blessing on that individual' (1057).

[19] The verb *estin* ('is') in verse 19 ('this is my body') is understood in verse 20 ('this cup [is] the new covenant in my blood') and means 'represents' in a symbolic way.

[20] Peterson, *Engaging with God*, 122. Matthew 26:28 ('for the forgiveness of sins') makes the link with Jeremiah 31:34 differently. Compare Fitzmyer, *Luke X–XXIV*, 1391.

[21] See Daniel B. Wallace, *Greek Grammar Beyond the Basics* (Grand Rapids: Zondervan, 1996), 383–9; Edwards, *Luke*, 628–30, and my comment on verse 37.

21–3. Jesus then stunned his disciples by predicting that one of them would betray him: 'But the hand of him who is going to betray me is with me on the table.' Judas had received the symbols of Jesus's approaching sacrifice, but he would not experience the benefits. Luke abbreviates Mark 14:18–21 (= Matthew 26:20–24) and places it after the meal, as the first in a series of warnings and encouragements. Readers were told in 6:16 that Judas would be the traitor and his plan was revealed in 22:1–6. Jesus, however, left the other apostles 'to question among themselves which of them it might be who would do this'.[22] The hand on the table image signifies a person close to him who will bring about his demise (Psalm 41:9). Jesus viewed his betrayal as a necessary part of the divine plan, but this in no way excused the wickedness of Judas: 'The Son of Man will go as it has been decreed. But woe to that man who betrays him!' (see 9:44; 24:7; Acts 2:23). God can use those who resist or oppose his will to achieve his good purposes (see Genesis 45:1–8), but divine judgment will come upon all who refuse to repent and seek his mercy, as implied by this woe (see 10:13–15).

24–5. 'A dispute also arose among them as to which of them was considered to be greatest.' Once more, the Twelve appear to be out of step with Jesus's teaching and example.[23] In an earlier context, he drew a little child into their midst and urged them to humble themselves by welcoming the child in his name (9:46–8). Their insensitivity on that occasion to what he had just predicted about himself (9:44–5) is matched in the present context by their failure to consider the implications of his Passover pronouncements and warning of betrayal (22:15–22).[24] Jesus said to them, 'The kings of the Gentiles lord it over them; and those who exercise authority over them call themselves Benefactors.' Graeco–Roman rulers used their power to dominate their subjects, while presenting themselves as benefactors. Private benefaction was also, in Green's words, 'the primary means by which the wealthy were legitimated as those most deserving of public office and prestige in the community'.[25] People in every culture tend to measure greatness in terms

---

[22] Matthew 26:25 records a private conversation between Jesus and Judas, with no reaction from the other disciples or any attempt to stop him. Compare John 13:18–30.
[23] The parallel use of *to tis autōn* ('which of them') in verses 23, 25, shows how preoccupied they were with themselves. Compare Mark 10:35–45; Matthew 20:20–28.
[24] The closest parallels in Mark 10:41–5; Matthew 20:24–8 conclude with a reference to his self-sacrifice as the Son of Man (see also Matthew 23:11–12). But the upper-room narrative in John 13:1–20 may have 'spurred Luke to locate the material here' (Nolland, *Luke 18:35–24:53*, 1062).
[25] Green, *Luke*, 768. Edwards, *Luke*, 633–4, gives evidence for the widespread use of the term 'benefactors' for Jewish and Gentile rulers and leaders.

of power, wealth and sociopolitical influence. By drawing attention to this pattern of self-promotion and control, Jesus indicated the worldly nature of the thinking and behaviour of his disciples.

26–7. The warning, 'But you are not to be like that,' introduces the Christlike alternative: 'Instead, the greatest among you should be like the youngest, and the one who rules like the one who serves.' True greatness involves forgoing honour and status, 'like the youngest' who may have no such aspirations. Jesus's parabolic question ('For who is greater, the one who is at the table or the one who serves?') has an obvious answer: in everyday human experience, 'Is it not the one who is at the table?' However, his own life and death provide a challenge to the norm ('But I am among you as one who serves'). In this way, Luke expresses the essence of the claim in Mark 10:45; Matthew 20:28, that 'even the Son of Man did not come to be served, but to serve, and to give his life as a ransom for many'. The redemptive nature of Jesus's service is reinforced by the citation in verse 37.

28–30. Despite his challenge about the disciples' worldly concern for greatness, Jesus acknowledged, 'You are those who have stood by me in my trials.' They not only observed his manner of life, but they also shared it in various ways (see 'trials' and 'temptation', *peirasmoi*, in 4:13; 8:13; 11:4; 22:40, 46). Their present behaviour was a contradiction of all that they had learned from him! Nevertheless, he declared, 'I confer on you a kingdom, just as my Father conferred one on me.' The messianic kingship of Jesus was announced in 1:32–3, 68–75; 2:11, and it became linked to his teaching about the kingdom of God (9:1–20; 19:11–40). God the Father had conferred this role on his Son before time began, revealing it in various ways through his prophets (e.g., 2 Samuel 7:12–16; Psalms 2:6–9, 110:1; Isaiah 9:6–7). Jesus graciously offers a share in his kingdom to those who demonstrate genuine faith in him (12:32; 23:42–3).[26] Here that promise is expressed in terms of participating in the banquet that is to come: 'so that you may eat and drink at my table in my kingdom' (see 13:28–9; 14:15; 22:15–16). But an additional role is promised to the Twelve, who would 'sit on thrones, judging the twelve tribes of Israel'. In this context, 'judging' means sharing in his rule over 'the twelve tribes of Israel', fulfilling predictions such as Ezekiel 34:20–24; 37:15–28 about the end-time renewal of God's people.[27] The apostles would initially share in

---

[26] The verb *diatithēmi* ('confer') was often used to express a formal arrangement or covenant, such as the making of a will or the disposition of property after someone's death (BDAG).

[27] Nolland, *Luke 18:35–24:53*, 1067, draws attention to 'the judicial function of OT

Jesus's messianic rule over a reconstituted Israel through their teaching and mighty works in his name (Acts 1–12).[28] No mention is made of their mission to the nations until 24:47.

Preparing for the time of trial (22:31–8)

31 'Simon, Simon, Satan has asked to sift all of you as wheat. **32** But I have prayed for you, Simon, that your faith may not fail. And when you have turned back, strengthen your brothers.'

33 But he replied, 'Lord, I am ready to go with you to prison and to death.'

34 Jesus answered, 'I tell you, Peter, before the cock crows today, you will deny three times that you know me.'

35 Then Jesus asked them, 'When I sent you without purse, bag or sandals, did you lack anything?'

'Nothing,' they answered.

36 He said to them, 'But now if you have a purse, take it, and also a bag; and if you don't have a sword, sell your cloak and buy one. **37** It is written: "And he was numbered with the transgressors"[b]; and I tell you that this must be fulfilled in me. Yes, what is written about me is reaching its fulfilment.'

38 The disciples said, 'See, Lord, here are two swords.'

'That's enough!' he replied.

___

b 37 Isaiah 53:12

31–2. Jesus's farewell speech concludes with a further series of warnings (only found in Luke; but compare verse 34 with Mark 14:29–31; Matthew 26:33–5). The first is directed to Simon Peter, using his original name twice, perhaps as a way of chiding him (see 10:41; Acts 9:4; 22:7; 26:14). However, the warning ('Satan has asked to sift all of you as wheat') concerns the welfare of the Twelve ('you', *hymas*, is plural here). A satanic attack on them all is predicted, using the image of a sieve that separates wheat from chaff (see 3:17), genuine disciples from false ones. Satan is not only the accuser here, who detects faithlessness, but, as Green says, 'the one who presents occasions for failure, who is active in resisting God's plan and God's people'.[29] Satan needs God's permission to do this ('Satan has asked'), as in Job 1–2. Jesus has been Simon's advocate with

___

kings (e.g. 2 Sam 15:1–6; 1 Kgs 3:16–28)' and 'the broad sense of judging associated with the judges raised up by God (e.g. Judg 3:9, 15; 6:11–18)'.

[28] The parallel passage in Matthew 19:28 clearly locates this ruling 'at the renewal of all things, when the Son of Man sits on his glorious throne'. Luke sees an anticipation of this in the way the Twelve function in Acts 1–12, with Matthias appointed to make up their number. See Bock, *Luke 9:51–24:53*, 1741; Peterson, *Acts*, 119–29.

[29] Green, *Luke*, 772.

the Father, pleading for him: 'But I have prayed for you [singular], Simon, that your faith may not fail.' This illustrates again the intimacy of Jesus as Son of God with his heavenly Father (10:21–2; compare John 17). Judas has already shown himself to be false and Simon will be the next to be tested (22:34). Jesus has prayed that his faith will not be eclipsed (*eklipē*; see the use of the same verb in 16:9). Put positively, Jesus can say, 'When you have turned back, strengthen your brothers.' Peter's repentance (*epistrepsas*) will enable him to encourage others to stand firm (*stērison*, 'strengthen'; a related verb is similarly used in Acts 14:22; 15:32, 41; 18:23)

33–4. Peter's unqualified self-confidence ('Lord, I am ready to go with you to prison and to death') reveals why he will be vulnerable to Satan's attack. Jesus predicts a threefold denial ('I tell you, Peter, before the cock crows today, you will deny three times that you know me'), which will happen early in the morning of that day (in Jewish reckoning, a day began the night before). Luke's version of this warning highlights the magnitude of the predicted denial with the words 'that you know me'. Peter's recollection of this after the event will enable him to acknowledge his failure with tears (verses 54–62). In this sequence of events, the stress is on God's enabling of those who seek his help to stand firm and resist Satan's accusations and promptings. God will bring them safely through their time of trial.

35–6. Finally, Jesus asked them, 'When I sent you without purse, bag or sandals, did you lack anything?' This recalls the promise of God's provision for them when he first sent them out as his messengers (9:3–4; expanded for the seventy-two in 10:4–8). The Twelve answered, 'Nothing.' As a final warning to them, therefore, he signalled the approach of a much more threatening situation: 'But now if you have a purse, take it, and also a bag; and if you don't have a sword, sell your cloak and buy one.' Buying a sword implied being alert and ready for danger, not that they should attack and kill their opponents (as is made clear in verses 49–51). Two of them already had swords (verse 38), presumably for protection in travel, but these would hardly be enough to resist arrest. Jesus does not abrogate his earlier promise with this challenge, but he dramatically alerts them to the serious crisis that he and they are about to face.[30] There are times for simple reliance on God's providential care and times to prepare for danger.

---

[30] Fitzmyer, *Luke X–XXIV*, 1432, and Green, *Luke*, 774–5, view the change from hospitality to hostility in absolute terms. But Nolland, *Luke 18:35–24:53*, 1078, rightly argues that 'Christian mission takes place between the poles of providential provision and protection and Satanic sifting'.

37. Jesus citates a portion of Isaiah 53:12 ('It is written: "And he was numbered with the transgressors"') predicting a violent and unjust death in the company of convicted criminals. This is the only place in Luke's Gospel where Jesus clearly aligns himself with that prophecy, though intimations that he will fulfil the role of God's Servant in Isaiah 52:13–53:12 have previously been given (9:22, 44; 12:50; 17:25; 18:31–3; 20:13–15). The quotation of a single sentence here, in the context of a broad claim about fulfilment, suggests that the whole oracle anticipates what will happen in his betrayal, arrest, death, resurrection, and heavenly exaltation.[31] Luke's allusions to this passage in the next chapter reinforce the view that he understood the whole Servant Song to apply to Jesus. The language of divine necessity (*dei*) is combined with an unusual term for scriptural fulfilment (*telesthēnai*) when Jesus declares, 'And I tell you that this must be fulfilled in me.' His emphatic conclusion ('Yes, what is written about me is reaching its fulfilment') confirms that he is speaking about the fulfilment of 'what was said in all the Scriptures concerning himself' (24:27).[32]

38. The response of the disciples ('See, Lord, here are two swords') reveals that they were simply thinking literally, rather than being alert to the spiritual struggle that lay ahead. Jesus declines to correct their misunderstanding ('That's enough') and leaves them to reflect on the meaning of his quotation from Scripture as events unfold.

LAST SUPPER AND LORD'S SUPPER

Luke establishes a close link between Jesus's final Passover meal and the practice of what came to be known as the Lord's Supper or Christian Eucharist. He does this by including more introductory material than Matthew and Mark and by recording Jesus's instruction to 'do this in remembrance of me' (22:19; compare the two sayings in 1 Corinthians 11:24–5). A parallel is indicated between the impending suffering of Jesus (verse 15) and the pouring out of his blood to inaugurate the new covenant (verse 20; see Jeremiah 31:34). The Passover sacrifice prefigured his death

---

[31] See David G. Peterson, 'Atonement Theology in Luke–Acts: Some Methodological Reflections', in *The New Testament in its First Century Setting: Essays on Context and Background in Honour of B. W. Winter on his 65th Birthday*, eds. Peter J. Williams, Andrew D. Clarke, Peter M. Head and David Instone-Brewer (Grand Rapids; Cambridge, UK: Eerdmans, 2004), 56–71.

[32] The concluding expression (*to peri emou telos echei*, 'what is [written] about me is reaching its fulfilment') recalls Jesus's prediction in 13:32 about being 'perfected' or 'completed' by death in Jerusalem (*teleioumai*).

as the means of achieving the end-time salvation of God's people. Jesus views this final meal with his disciples as an anticipation of their gathering together in the kingdom of God, which his death and resurrection will make possible. But his giving of the bread to those present with the command to 'do this in remembrance of me' suggests a repeated action beyond his death and before their participation in the messianic banquet.

Luke draws out the ecclesial implications of eating and drinking together with Jesus in this way by highlighting the need for humble service to one another and ongoing faithfulness to Jesus as Lord and Saviour (verses 21–38). The apostle Paul links the Last Supper with the practice of community meals at Corinth by using Passover terminology ('the cup of thanksgiving for which we give thanks', 'the bread that we break', 1 Corinthians 10:16) and by reminding this church of the tradition that he passed on to them about Jesus's words and actions at that final meal (1 Corinthians 11:23–5).[33] Paul draws out the meaning of this tradition when he says, 'whenever you eat *this* bread and drink *this* cup, you proclaim the Lord's death *until he comes*' (1 Corinthians 11:26, my emphasis). His reminder is in the context of a warning to exercise appropriate care for one another as 'the body of Christ' (1 Corinthians 11:17–22, 27–34; compare 10:16–17). The community meals at Corinth may have had a different character than the Passover Jesus celebrated with his disciples, but Paul wanted the Corinthians to perceive the connection. We in turn should reflect on the implications of Paul's teaching for celebrations of the Lord's Supper in our different congregational contexts today.

2. The mounting crisis (22:39–65)

Jesus's struggle on the Mount of Olives is presented by Luke as 'the critical point at which', in Green's words, 'faithfulness to the divine will is embraced definitively in the strenuousness of prayer'.[34] Nevertheless, even more than the parallel accounts in the other Gospels, Luke focuses on the implications for the disciples (verses 39–46). In quick succession, Jesus is betrayed by Judas and arrested (verses 47–53), he is taken to the high priest's house, where Peter denies him three times (verse 54–62), and he is mocked and beaten by his captors (verses 63–5).

---

[33] See Peterson, *Engaging with God*, 152–8; 215–18. This seems to be the tradition that was available to Luke too.

[34] Green, *Luke*, 777.

Praying on the Mount of Olives (22:39–46)

Jesus prays on the Mount of Olives

39 Jesus went out as usual to the Mount of Olives, and his disciples followed him. **40** On reaching the place, he said to them, 'Pray that you will not fall into temptation.' **41** He withdrew about a stone's throw beyond them, knelt down and prayed, **42** 'Father, if you are willing, take this cup from me; yet not my will, but yours be done.' **43** An angel from heaven appeared to him and strengthened him. **44** And being in anguish, he prayed more earnestly, and his sweat was like drops of blood falling to the ground.^c

45 When he rose from prayer and went back to the disciples, he found them asleep, exhausted from sorrow. **46** 'Why are you sleeping?' he asked them. 'Get up and pray so that you will not fall into temptation.'

c 43,44 Many early manuscripts do not have verses 43 and 44.

39. 'Jesus went out as usual to the Mount of Olives, and his disciples followed him.' Luke has a more abbreviated account of this incident than Mark 14:32–42; Matthew 26:36–46, though he adds some significant details.[35] The Mount of Olives was Jesus's customary place of retreat from Jerusalem (21:37). No mention is made here of Gethsemane as the specific location at the foot of that mountain. The note that 'his disciples followed him' emphasises that the Eleven were at this stage willing to go forward with him into the threatening situation he had predicted (verses 31–8). Judas had presumably left their company to lead the authorities to where they might find him (verses 47–8; compare John 13:27–30).

40. 'On reaching the place, he said to them, "Pray that you will not fall into temptation."' Despite the focus on Jesus's personal prayer in verses 41–4, both the beginning and the end of this passage stress the need for disciples to follow his example and teaching. There are echoes here of the prayer Jesus taught them in 11:2–4, especially when he calls God 'Father', asks for his will to be done and urges the disciples to pray that they may not 'fall into temptation' (*eiselthein eis peirasmon*, repeated in verse 46; see comment on 11:4). Knowing that they must share with him in the testing events to follow, Jesus wanted them to pray that they would resist the temptation to deny him, fall away and be scattered (Mark 14:27–9 is not paralleled here).

[35] Fitzmyer, *Luke X–XXIV*, 1437–9, lists the differences and argues that Luke presents 'a stark abridgement of the Marcan account', centring on Jesus's relation to his Father. But Fitzmyer fails to note how much Luke's restructuring emphasises Jesus's concern for his disciples to be prepared for what would follow.

41–2. In Mark 14:33–5, Jesus takes Peter, James and John some distance with him, and then he leaves them to keep watch while he prays. Luke simply records that Jesus 'withdrew about a stone's throw beyond them, knelt down and prayed'.[36] Luke also simplifies the prayer of Jesus. The address, 'Father, if you are willing' replaces the introductory formula in Mark 14:36 ('*Abba*, Father . . . everything is possible for you'). The central request, 'Take this cup from me,' remains the same, using the image of the cup to express God's wrath or punishment (as in Isaiah 51:17, 22; Jeremiah 25:15–16; 49:12; Lamentations 4:21–2). As a human being, the Son of God must have been apprehensive about the agony of crucifixion and the curse that this implied (Deuteronomy 21:23; Acts 5:30). But his obedience made it possible for believers to be saved from God's wrath and share in his eternal kingdom. Later Christian reflection draws out the implications of Jesus's prayer and what it signified (e.g., Romans 5:6–11, 19; Galatians 3:13–14; Hebrews 5:7–10). His overwhelming desire was for his Father's will to be done ('yet not my will, but yours be done') and his people to be delivered from judgment. With that commitment Jesus faced his enemies and submitted to their unjust treatment. Compare John 12:27; 18:11.

43–4. Many Greek manuscripts and ancient versions omit these verses, although a number of witnesses include them (with variations), and they are cited by early Christian writers. They have no exact parallel in Matthew and Mark, and the shorter reading is generally preferred.[37] However, the vivid portrait of Jesus in verse 44 may be Luke's way of summarising the emotional, spiritual and physical struggle that Mark 14:33–4, 37–41 records. The strenuousness of Jesus's prayer reflected the seriousness of the situation he faced: 'being in anguish, he prayed more earnestly, and his sweat was like drops of blood falling on the ground'. Moreover, he was able to persevere in prayer because 'an angel from heaven appeared to him and strengthened him' (see Daniel 10:17–19; Luke 1:11). Perhaps early copyists omitted these verses because they were uncomfortable with the way they expose the vulnerability of Jesus and his need for angelic aid.

45–6. 'When he rose from prayer and went back to the disciples, he found them asleep.' Luke contrasts their behaviour with that of Jesus and adds the explanation that they were 'exhausted from sorrow'. This suggests

---

[36] Kneeling for prayer expresses submissiveness and is mentioned again in Acts 7:60; 9:40; 20:36; 21:5. Mark 14:35 more dramatically records that Jesus 'fell to the ground'.
[37] See Fitzmyer, *Luke X–XXIV*, 1443–4; Nolland, *Luke 18:35–24:53*, 1080–82; Metzger, *Textual Commentary*, 151. Bock, *Luke 9:51–24:53*, 1763–4, answers the objections of Fitzmyer and gives positive reasons for accepting these verses as Lucan. See also Edwards, *Luke*, 642–4.

that they now took seriously the threat of betrayal, arrest and death that was facing Jesus, but their grief did not move them to pray as he had instructed them (verse 40; compare 21:36). Jesus's rebuke ('Why are you sleeping?') is accompanied by a renewed challenge to pray ('Get up and pray so that you will not fall into temptation'). Knowing Satan's intentions (verses 31–2) and Jesus's predictions about what would happen (verses 34–8), they needed to take seriously the possibility that their faith might fail and that they might abandon him out of fear for their own lives. Jesus's encouragement to pray for faithful perseverance is applied more generally in several New Testament contexts (e.g., Ephesians 6:18–20; 1 Peter 4:19; 5:7–11; Jude 20–21).

Betrayed and arrested (22:47–53)

Jesus arrested

47 While he was still speaking a crowd came up, and the man who was called Judas, one of the Twelve, was leading them. He approached Jesus to kiss him, **48** but Jesus asked him, 'Judas, are you betraying the Son of Man with a kiss?'

49 When Jesus' followers saw what was going to happen, they said, 'Lord, should we strike with our swords?' **50** And one of them struck the servant of the high priest, cutting off his right ear.

51 But Jesus answered, 'No more of this!' And he touched the man's ear and healed him.

52 Then Jesus said to the chief priests, the officers of the temple guard, and the elders, who had come for him, 'Am I leading a rebellion, that you have come with swords and clubs? **53** Every day I was with you in the temple courts, and you did not lay a hand on me. But this is your hour – when darkness reigns.'

47–8. Luke apparently abbreviates Mark 14:43–52 (compare Matthew 26:47–56; John 18:2–11) and makes a few distinctive additions of his own. The crowd that 'came up' to Jesus is not identified until verse 52, because the focus is first on 'the man who was called Judas, one of the Twelve'. Luke intensifies the note of personal betrayal by mentioning that Judas was 'leading them' (see Acts 1:16). Judas 'approached Jesus to kiss him' and identify him in the dark (Mark 14:44 indicates that this was the pre-arranged signal to the arresting authorities). Luke alone records Jesus's poignant question: 'Judas, are you betraying the Son of Man with a kiss?' This recalls Jesus's predictions in 9:44; 18:31–2; 22:22, locating the action of Judas clearly within the divine plan of salvation.[38]

---

[38] Fitzmyer, *Luke X–XXIV*, 1449, observes that 'the nadir of infidelity is reached'

49–51. Luke alone records that, when Jesus's followers saw what was going to happen, they said, 'Lord, should we strike with our swords?' (see verse 38). Each of the Gospels, however, mentions that 'one of them struck the servant of the high priest', cutting off his ear (only Luke and John 18:10 specify 'his right ear').[39] Jesus's response was sudden and emphatic ('No more of this!'), curtailing their violence and allowing events to take their course (note the additional response in Matthew 26:52–4; John 18:11). Only Luke records that Jesus 'touched the man's ear and healed him'. This gracious act anticipated his prayer for his enemies in 23:34.

52. Luke finally reveals that the arresting party consisted of 'the chief priests, the officers of the temple guard, and the elders, who had come for him'. The chief priests and the teachers of the law had been looking for some way to get rid of Jesus (19:47; 22:2; compare 9:22), but Judas consulted specifically with the chief priests and 'the officers' (*stratēgoi*, as in verse 4), who are more precisely defined as 'officers of the temple guard' here. Jesus asked his captors, 'Am I leading a rebellion, that you have come with swords and clubs?' The word *lēstēs* ordinarily meant 'robber, highwayman bandit' (BDAG), but it could also be used to describe a 'revolutionary, insurrectionist, guerrilla' (BDAG; see Josephus *War*, 2.13), hence NIV 'Am I leading a rebellion?' Jesus's response in verse 51 showed that he definitely was not a man of violence!

53. The injustice of the arresting process is exposed when Jesus says, 'Every day I was with you in the temple courts, and you did not lay a hand on me.' They had ample opportunity to discover his agenda and seize him openly (see John 18:20), but they were afraid of a popular backlash (Luke 19:47–8; 21:37–8). Jesus concluded, 'But this is your hour – when darkness reigns,' using the word 'hour' in the sense of a significant moment. As Nolland puts it, the darkness of the night was 'a cloak for the evil of the action'.[40] Moral and spiritual darkness was about to triumph, as the leaders of Israel succumbed to its influence (see 11:34–5; John 9:4–5; 12:35–6, 46).

---

with this mark of 'supreme affection, respect, and love'.

[39] John 18:10 adds that it was Simon Peter who did this and that the servant's name was Malchus. Mark 14:46–7 indicates that Jesus had already been seized and arrested, suggesting that the attack on the high priest's servant was an attempt to have Jesus released.

[40] Nolland, *Luke 18:35–24:53*, 1089. Nolland says that Jesus challenges 'the probity of an arrest that could not be made in the light of day'.

Despised and rejected (22:54–65)

Peter disowns Jesus

54 Then seizing him, they led him away and took him into the house of the high priest. Peter followed at a distance. **55** And when some there had kindled a fire in the middle of the court-yard and had sat down together, Peter sat down with them. **56** A servant-girl saw him seated there in the firelight. She looked closely at him and said, 'This man was with him.'

57 But he denied it. 'Woman, I don't know him,' he said.

58 A little later someone else saw him and said, 'You also are one of them.'

'Man, I am not!' Peter replied.

59 About an hour later another asserted, 'Certainly this fellow was with him, for he is a Galilean.'

60 Peter replied, 'Man, I don't know what you're talking about!' Just as he was speaking, the cock crowed. **61** The Lord turned and looked straight at Peter. Then Peter remembered the word the Lord had spoken to him: 'Before the cock crows today, you will disown me three times.' **62** And he went outside and wept bitterly.

The guards mock Jesus

63 The men who were guarding Jesus began mocking and beating him. **64** They blindfolded him and demanded, 'Prophesy! Who hit you?' **65** And they said many other insulting things to him.

54. 'Then seizing [Jesus], they led him away and took him into the house of the high priest.' The four Gospels agree that Peter's denials took place in this context, though John 18:12–13 specifies that Jesus first appeared before Annas, 'who was the father-in-law of Caiaphas, the high priest that year'. Peter followed at a distance, remaining bold for the moment. No mention is made of what happened to the other disciples: Peter is the only defector in Luke's narrative (see Mark 14:50).[41] Luke immediately describes Peter's threefold denial, whereas Mark 14:53–65 says 'the whole Sanhedrin' met at this point to find evidence against Jesus, and then Mark 14:66–72 records Peter's denials.[42] Luke's version aligns Peter's betrayal more closely with that of Judas (verses 47–53) and highlights the immediate fulfilment of Jesus's predictions in verses 31–4.

55–8. Initially, Peter felt safe, and 'when some there had kindled a fire in the middle of the courtyard and had sat together, Peter sat down with them'. His first challenge came when 'a servant-girl saw him seated there in the firelight. She looked closely at him and said, "This man was with

---

[41] John 18:15–16 adds that one of the disciples, who was known to the high priest, accompanied Peter and gained access for them both to the high priest's courtyard.
[42] Fitzmyer, *Luke X–XXIV*, 1454–5, charts the similarities and differences between the Gospels at this point. Matthew 26:57–72 closely follows Mark's order.

him.'" Her accusation was met with Peter's first deceit: 'Woman, I don't know him' (fulfilling Jesus's prediction in verse 34). 'A little later, someone else saw him and said, "You also are one of them."' John 18:19–24 presents the high priest's questioning of Jesus at this point. The time delay gave Peter the opportunity to reflect on what he had just said and be more honest. But lies breed lies, and Peter protected himself even further by rejecting any association with Jesus's disciples, saying, 'Man, I am not!'

59–60. The time delay before the next accusation is even longer ('About an hour later'). Another man asserted more emphatically, 'Certainly this fellow was with him, for he is a Galilean' (Matthew 26:73 adds 'your accent gives you away'; see John 18:26, 'Didn't I see you with him in the garden?). Peter's denial was also more emphatic: 'Man, I don't know what you're talking about!' His instinct for self-protection led him to disassociate himself even from Galilee, because of Jesus's ministry there. Peter had forgotten the warnings about being ashamed of him and disowning him (9:26; 12:8–9) and saw no need to seek God's help in this moment of trial (12:11–12; 21:14–15). Most of all, he had wilfully ignored Jesus's prediction about his imminent denials (verses 31–4) and his urging to all his disciples to 'pray that you will not fall into temptation' (verses 40, 46). Even as he was speaking, 'the cock crowed'.

61–2. Luke alone records that 'the Lord turned and looked straight at Peter'. This look, together with the crowing of the cock, was sufficient to remind Peter of 'the word the Lord had spoken to him: "Before the cock crows today, you will disown me three times."' Luke's language, especially his repetition of the title 'the Lord', points to Jesus as one who 'speaks and acts for God with divine authority', as Green says.[43] His prediction had been sadly fulfilled, but Peter's turning back to the Lord (verse 32) began when 'he went outside and wept bitterly'.

63–5. Luke delays mention of Jesus's examination by the elders, the chief priests and the teachers of the law until verses 66–71. He focuses first on the mistreatment of Jesus by the men who were guarding him: they 'began mocking and beating him'.[44] This recalls the prediction of Jesus in 18:32 and emphasises again the theme of fulfilment (see verses 61–2; Isaiah 50:5–6; 53:3–5). The mockery of his captors included blindfolding him and demanding, 'Prophesy! Who hit you?', deepening his

---

[43] Green, *Luke*, 788. The Greek could be more literally rendered, 'and Peter remembered the word of the Lord'.
[44] In Mark 14:65 and Matthew 26:67 this mistreatment takes place after the trial by the Sanhedrin and before the account of Peter's threefold denial.

humiliation. These Jewish guards scorned the common assessment of Jesus as a prophet (7:16, 39; 9:8, 19), and 'said many other insulting things to him'. Luke's use of the verb 'insulting' (*blasphēmountes*) is especially significant in view of his twofold reference to Jesus as 'the Lord' in verse 61. Luke has consistently portrayed Jesus as more than a prophet, and that picture is filled out dramatically in the next scene.

3. The trials of Jesus (22:66–23:25)

Luke first records an early morning examination of Jesus before the council of the elders of the people in Jerusalem to determine the charge they would bring to the Roman governor (22:66–71; compare Matthew 26:57–68; Mark 14:53–65). Then he presents the trial of Jesus by the governor in two stages (see Matthew 27:11–31; Mark 15:1–20; John 18:28–19:16). From his own unique source, he inserts an account of the examination by Herod Antipas, the puppet ruler of Galilee, who was also in Jerusalem at that time (23:7). The mockery of Herod's soldiers is described before Jesus is sent back to Pontius Pilate. The effect of this Lucan sequence is to clarify the theological and political concerns of the Jewish authorities and provide four indications that Jesus was innocent of the charges against him (23:4, 14, 15, 22). Nevertheless, Pilate accedes to the demands of the accusers, releases a man convicted of murder and insurrection, and allows Jesus to be crucified (verses 18–25).

Tried by the Jewish Sanhedrin (22:66–71)

Jesus before Pilate and Herod

66 At daybreak the council of the elders of the people, both the chief priests and the teachers of the law, met together, and Jesus was led before them. 67 'If you are the Messiah,' they said, 'tell us.'

Jesus answered, 'If I tell you, you will not believe me, 68 and if I asked you, you would not answer. 69 But from now on, the Son of Man will be seated at the right hand of the mighty God.'

70 They all asked, 'Are you then the Son of God?'

He replied, 'You say that I am.'

71 Then they said, 'Why do we need any more testimony? We have heard it from his own lips.'

66. 'At daybreak the council of the elders of the people, both the chief priests and the teachers of the law, met together, and Jesus was led before them.' Matthew and Mark record an evening meeting at which many false

witnesses gave conflicting evidence against Jesus and attention then turned to his identity. Luke briefly mentions that gathering in verse 54 and presents a morning examination as the occasion for the official declaration of guilt against Jesus.[45] Jesus was brought *eis to synedrion autōn* (ESV, 'to their council'). The word *synedrion* can refer to the council itself or to the council's place of meeting. It is sometimes transliterated as 'Sanhedrin' (CSB, 'before their Sanhedrin'). This was the supreme indigenous governing body in Judea at that time, meeting under the presidency of the current high priest Caiaphas. It was the ultimate authority 'not only in religious matters, but in legal and governmental affairs as well, in so far as it did not encroach on the authority of the Roman procurator' (BDAG). 'The elders of the people' (*to presbyterion tou laou*) is a summary term for the body of elders, which included 'both the chief priests and the teachers of the law'. Luke's statement that 'Jesus was led before them' suggests to Green that he was 'held in the courtyard of the high priest throughout the night, then brought to the chambers of the Jewish council the following morning'.[46]

67–8. No witnesses are produced and there is no reference to Jesus having spoken of the destruction of the Temple (see Mark 14:55–9). Since the Romans did not allow the Sanhedrin to impose the death penalty, this could only have been a pretrial designed to establish 'a basis for bringing a case before Pilate', as Nolland concludes.[47] The first challenge ('If you are the Messiah . . . tell us') was probably made by the high priest on behalf of the whole council. Enough has been said and done in Luke's record of Jesus's ministry to justify this inquiry (2:11, 26; 4:41; 7:18–23; 9:20; 18:35–43; 19:28–40; 20:41–4), though Jesus himself has not openly claimed to be the Messiah. With this question they seek to expose him as a political threat, capable of leading an insurrection against the Romans (23:2). Jesus discerns that they have already made up their minds and that they are determined to get rid of him, saying, 'If I tell you, you will not believe me, and if I asked you, you would not answer' (see 20:1–8).

69. Jesus chooses to answer his accusers in his own preferred way: 'But from now on, the Son of Man will be seated at the right hand of the mighty God (*ek dexiōn tēs dynameōs tou theou*, 'at the right hand of the power of God', CSB).' This predicts his heavenly enthronement as Messiah by alluding

---

[45] Bock, *Luke 9:51–24:53*, 1791–4, notes that, according to the Mishnah, *Sanhedrin* 4:1, an evening verdict would have had no weight. He also discusses various historical issues related to the trials of Jesus.

[46] Green, *Luke*, 794. This pattern is repeated in Acts 4:1–5; 5:17–21; 22:30.

[47] Nolland, *Luke 18:35–24:53*, 1112.

to Psalm 110:1 (see also 20:39–44; Acts 2:33–6). He uses the title 'the Son of Man' to link this enthronement with the universal and unending dominion given by God to the man-like figure in Daniel 7:13 (see my comment on Luke 5:24). Jesus brings these biblical expectations together as he answers his accusers and anticipates their imminent fulfilment. Matthew 26:64 and Mark 14:62 add 'and coming on the clouds of heaven', hinting at his return in glory to judge the living and the dead (as in Luke 9:26). However, the phrase 'from now on' signifies that a new stage in God's dealing with his people is about to begin (see 1:48; 5:10; 12:52; 22:18; Acts 18:6). The real power in the universe lies with God and the ascended Lord who sits next to him, here identified as the Son of Man. He will soon be in a position to judge his accusers, even before that final day.[48]

70–71. The second question put to Jesus ('Are you then the Son of God?') may have been another way of asking whether he claimed to be the Messiah (see Matthew 26:63; Mark 14:61), though Luke's sequence suggests that a deeper meaning was intended.[49] The teachers of the law and the chief priests had heard him speak about the owner of the vineyard's beloved son in the parable he spoke against them (20:9–19), and the issue of the Messiah's divine sonship had been raised by Jesus in 20:39–44, when he publicly asked how they understood Psalm 110:1. When Jesus implied that he would soon sit at God's right hand and rule from there as the Son of Man (22:69), he appeared to be profaning the uniqueness and holiness of God.[50] His answer to them now ('You say that I am') was a qualified admission. Those who were previously 'waiting to catch him in something he might say' (11:54) had finally achieved their goal! They saw no need for any more testimony, having heard it 'from his own lips'. Nevertheless, the more-political charge they brought before the secular authority was specifically that he claimed to be 'Messiah, *a king*' (23:2, my emphasis).

Tried by Pontius Pilate (23:1–7)

23 Then the whole assembly rose and led him off to Pilate. [2]And they began to accuse him, saying, 'We have found this man subverting our nation. He opposes payment of taxes to Caesar and claims to be Messiah, a king.'

---

[48] Green, *Luke*, 795, note 17, rightly acknowledges that judgment by the Son of Man is implied in 9:26; 12:8, but unnecessarily narrows the meaning of 22:69 to exaltation.

[49] See Nolland, *Luke 1–9:20*, 163–4; *Luke 18:35–24:53*, 1112.

[50] Bock, *Luke 9:51–24:53*, 1799.

3 So Pilate asked Jesus, 'Are you the king of the Jews?'

'You have said so,' Jesus replied.

4 Then Pilate announced to the chief priests and the crowd, 'I find no basis for a charge against this man.'

5 But they insisted, 'He stirs up the people all over Judea by his teaching.

He started in Galilee and has come all the way here.'

6 On hearing this, Pilate asked if the man was a Galilean. **7** When he learned that Jesus was under Herod's jurisdiction, he sent him to Herod, who was also in Jerusalem at that time.

1. Jesus's trial before the supreme representative of the Roman government in Judea began when 'the whole assembly rose and led him off to Pilate' (see Mark 15:1). There was a united attempt by 'the elders of the people, both the chief priests and the teachers of the law' (22:66) to have Jesus put to death, though Joseph of Arimathea was one member of the Council who did not consent to their decision (Luke 23:51; John 19:38–41 adds Nicodemus). Pontius Pilate as 'governor of Judea' (3:1; 13:1; 20:20, *hēgemonos*) was a prefect appointed by the Roman senate, serving in that capacity from AD 26 to 36,[51] with the authority to impose capital punishment (John 18:31). Green argues that the following account 'coheres with traditional Roman trial proceedings: accusations were made, charges formulated, opportunity for defense given, and judgment rendered'.[52]

2. The Sanhedrin was troubled by Jesus's apparent claim to be Messiah (22:67–71), which had theological and political implications for them. Their essential charge against him was, 'We have found this man subverting our nation,' which is restated in verse 5 ('He stirs up the people by his teaching') and in verse 14 ('one who was inciting the people to rebellion'). 'Subverting our nation' sounds like the accusation against the prophet Elijah in 1 Kings 18:17 ('you troubler of Israel'). The same verb (*diastrephein*) is translated 'turn, pervert, draw away' in Acts 13:8, 10; 20:30. Jesus was viewed as having turned his fellow Jews from the true faith and divided the nation. Moreover, he had jeopardised their relationship with the occupying power by allegedly opposing payment of taxes to Caesar. Jesus's teaching about this was clarified in 20:20–25 and is deliberately misrepresented by these

---

[51] See my note on 3:1. An inscription discovered at Caesarea describes Pilate as *praefectus* ('prefect'). The title 'procurator' was only applied to the governor of Judea at a later date (C. A. Evans, 'Pilate Inscription', *DNTB*, 803–4). Edwards, *Luke*, 663–6, observes that Luke tends to be more sympathetic to Pilate than either of the Jewish historians Philo and Josephus.

[52] Green, *Luke*, 798. See Josephus, *War* 2.8.1 and the caution of Nolland, *Luke 18:35–24:53*, 1117.

witnesses. Most provocatively, they said that he 'claims to be Messiah, a king'. In Nolland's words, 'Luke portrays the Jewish leadership making opportunistic use of Jesus' links with Jewish messianism.'[53]

3–4. Pilate's question ('Are you the king of the Jews?') is the same in all four Gospels (see Matthew 27:11; Mark 15:2; John 18:33) and the title reappears in the inscription he orders to be placed on the cross of Jesus (Matthew 27:37; Mark 15:26; Luke 23:38; John 19:19). Jesus's answer is also the same in each of the Gospels ('You have said so'), though it is developed in John 18:37. His response suggests partial agreement (as in 22:70), but it leaves room for further clarification: he had not come to establish an earthly kingship such as Israel had experienced in the past. The governor's reply probably came after further questions had been asked: 'I find no basis for a charge against this man.' For the first time, Luke mentions the crowd that had gathered with the chief priests to witness the proceedings. Pilate's judgment simply meant that the evidence they had presented for a capital offence was inadequate (see John 18:38). Pilate did not see Jesus as a threat to Roman rule.

5. Jesus's accusers were 'growing stronger' (*epischyon*, BDAG), insisting, 'He stirs up the people all over Judea by his teaching.' However, as verses 18–23 ironically show and Green clarifies, 'It is not Jesus who leads the people astray, but rather the Jewish leaders who stir up the people.'[54] Fitzmyer suggests that the expression 'all over Judea' could be used in a narrowly political way to stress that 'Jesus has already appeared in the territory of Pilate'.[55] However, since Galilee is mentioned in conjunction with Jerusalem ('He started in Galilee and has come all the way here'), 'all over Judea' more likely refers to the whole of Palestine (see 1:5; 4:44; 6:17; 7:17; Acts 10:37, 'the province of Judea').

6–7. On hearing the mention of Galilee, 'Pilate asked if the man was a Galilean. When he learned that Jesus was under Herod's jurisdiction, he sent him to Herod, who was also in Jerusalem at that time.' Although Jesus was born in Bethlehem in Judea (2:4), he was known as a Galilean because he was brought up there (2:39, 51) and began his ministry there (4:14–43). Pilate may have been looking for a second opinion (see Acts 25:23–7) or simply anxious to pass the responsibility for dealing with Jesus to another.

---

[53] Nolland, *Luke 18:35–24:53*, 1118. See C. A. Evans, 'Messianism', *DNTB*, 698–707.
[54] Green, *Luke*, 802.
[55] Fitzmyer, *Luke X–XXIV*, 1476. 'Judea' is used more narrowly in 1:65; 2:4; 21:21; Acts 9:31.

Examined by Herod Antipas (23:8–12)

8When Herod saw Jesus, he was greatly pleased, because for a long time he had been wanting to see him. From what he had heard about him, he hoped to see him perform a sign of some sort. **9**He plied him with many questions, but Jesus gave him no answer. **10**The chief priests and the teachers of the law were standing there, vehemently accusing him. **11**Then Herod and his soldiers ridiculed and mocked him. Dressing him in an elegant robe, they sent him back to Pilate. **12**That day Herod and Pilate became friends – before this they had been enemies.

8. Although this narrative is only found in Luke's Gospel, there are no compelling reasons to doubt its authenticity.[56] Herod personally examines Jesus and his claims, rather than engaging in a formal trial. Upon the death of his father Herod the Great, Herod Antipas received Galilee and Perea as his inheritance, ruling as 'tetrarch' until AD 39 (see 3:1). This Herod was rebuked by John the Baptist because of his evil deeds, so that he eventually imprisoned John (3:19–20) and beheaded him (9:9). Herod was perplexed because of what he heard about the ministry of Jesus and feared what people were saying about him (9:7–8). He tried to 'see' Jesus (9:9) but could not until this moment. Hence, the significance of Luke's claim, 'When Herod saw Jesus, he was greatly pleased, because for a long time he had been wanting to see him.' Although he previously sought to kill Jesus (13:30), he no longer regarded him as a threat to his reputation and rule. Herod's main desire was to experience a miracle: 'From what he had heard about him, he hoped to see him perform a sign of some sort.' But Jesus had previously condemned such faithless sign-seeking (11:29–30).

9–12. So when Herod plied Jesus with many questions, it was not as an honest seeker after the truth. Therefore, 'Jesus gave him no answer' (contrast his response to the Council in 22:67–70 and Pilate in 23:3). There is an echo of Isaiah 53:7 here ('he did not open his mouth'), which is cited in Acts 8:32. Relentlessly pursuing their goal of doing away with Jesus, 'The chief priests and the teachers of the law were standing there, vehemently accusing him.' Presumably, their accusations fuelled many of Herod's questions. 'Then Herod and his soldiers ridiculed and mocked him.' When they dressed him in an elegant robe and sent him back to

---

[56] Fitzmyer, *Luke X–XXIV*, 1478–9, and Bock, *Luke 9:51–24:53*, 1815–7, deal with arguments that this is a Lucan creation. Edwards, *Luke*, 666–8 reviews the life and character of this Herod.

Pilate, they were making fun of the claim that he was 'Messiah, a king' (verse 2).⁵⁷ Luke enigmatically concludes that 'Herod and Pilate became friends with each other that very day' (ESV). There is no extant evidence to illuminate Luke's claim that 'before this they had been enemies', but Fitzmyer suggests that it is reasonable to suppose that 'a tetrarch would be ill at ease with an overlord, especially one that represented an occupying power'.⁵⁸ Herod must have been pleased with Pilate's invitation to participate in the examination of Jesus and glad that Pilate would be responsible for his death (see Acts 4:27).

Tried by Pilate again (23:13–25)

¹³Pilate called together the chief priests, the rulers and the people, ¹⁴and said to them, 'You brought me this man as one who was inciting the people to rebellion. I have examined him in your presence and have found no basis for your charges against him. ¹⁵Neither has Herod, for he sent him back to us; as you can see, he has done nothing to deserve death. ¹⁶Therefore, I will punish him and then release him.' [¹⁷]ᵃ

¹⁸But the whole crowd shouted, 'Away with this man! Release Barabbas to us!' ¹⁹(Barabbas had been thrown into prison for an insurrection in the city, and for murder.)

²⁰Wanting to release Jesus, Pilate appealed to them again. ²¹But they kept shouting, 'Crucify him! Crucify him!'

²²For the third time he spoke to them: 'Why? What crime has this man committed? I have found in him no grounds for the death penalty. Therefore I will have him punished and then release him.'

²³But with loud shouts they insistently demanded that he be crucified, and their shouts prevailed. ²⁴So Pilate decided to grant their demand. ²⁵He released the man who had been thrown into prison for insurrection and murder, the one they asked for, and surrendered Jesus to their will.

_____

a 17 Some manuscripts include here words similar to Matt. 27:15 and Mark 15:6.

---

⁵⁷ Fitzmyer, *Luke X–XXIV*, 1482, suggests the translation 'a bright shining garment' (*esthēta lampra*) and argues that this is chosen to 'mock his guiltlessness'. But the preceding context points to the issue of Jesus's kingship, and this is the significance of the purple robe put on him by Pilate's soldiers in Mark 15:17–18 (compare Acts 12:21). Compare Green, *Luke*, 805–6.

⁵⁸ Fitzmyer, *Luke X–XXIV*, 1482. Green, *Luke*, 806, considers different interpretations of this new-found friendship.

13. The trial before Pilate resumes at the point when Jesus is sent back to the governor by Herod (see Mark 15:1–15).[59] Aiming to bring the matter to a swift conclusion, Pilate called together again 'the chief priests, the rulers, and the people'. The rulers (*archontes*) here appear to be members of the Sanhedrin other than the chief priests. In 22:6, 'the council of the elders' includes 'the chief priests and the teachers of the law', but in 23:35, 'the rulers' appear to be synonymous with 'the elders' (see Acts 3:17; 13:27). Luke obviously uses the terminology in different ways (see also Acts 4:5, 8). 'The people' were those who had previously gathered to witness the trial. The responsibility of the people of Jerusalem and their leaders for the unjust crucifixion of Jesus is emphasised in Acts 2:23; 3:13–14, 17; 4:27; 10:39; 13:27–8, although many individuals lamented what was happening (Luke 23:27).

14–16. Pilate summarises the proceedings so far, acknowledging the essence of the accusation against Jesus ('You brought me this man as one who was inciting the people to rebellion') and restating his original judgment ('I have examined him in your presence and have found no basis for your charges against him'). He then adds the further reason that Herod has found no foundation for the charge of sedition ('for he sent him back to us; as you can see, he has done nothing to deserve death').[60] Pilate therefore concludes, 'I will punish him and then release him.' Matthew 27:26 and Mark 15:15 record that Jesus was flogged and then handed over to be crucified, but Luke includes a prior offer to punish but not crucify him. Edwards observes, 'In his power struggle with the religious leaders, and because of his ultimate indifference to Jesus, Pilate is willing to subject Jesus to extreme cruelty.'[61]

[17.] In some ancient manuscripts and versions, these words prepare for the next segment: 'He had to release someone to them on the feast.' Although this is included in the KJV, it appears to be a gloss based on Matthew 27:15 and Mark 15:6, and it is not found in the earliest texts of Luke.[62] This Passover custom is not mentioned in other ancient sources, but it is implied in verses 18 and 25 and explicit in John 18:39. Nolland

---

[59] It is likely that Luke has used a special source to expand Mark's narrative at this point. Fitzmyer, *Luke X–XXIV*, 1487–8, identifies ten points of Lucan style, but Bock, *Luke 9:51–24:53*, 1824–5, disputes his conclusion that Luke is responsible for the content. Nolland, *Luke 18:35–24:53*, 1126–7, 1129, argues for contacts with John 19.

[60] As a translation of *idou*, NIV ('as you can see') presumes the agreement of Jesus's accusers. ESV ('Look') or CSB ('Clearly') simply express the conviction of Pilate.

[61] Edwards, *Luke*, 676.

[62] Metzger, *Textual Commentary*, 153; Fitzmyer, *Luke X–XXIV*, 1485–6.

draws attention to four historical analogies that provide precedent for such a release of prisoners.[63]

18–19. Pilate's intention to 'release' Jesus (verse 16) aroused the opposition of 'the whole crowd' (*pamplēthei*, 'all together', BDAG). If this is a simple parallel to verse 1 (*hapan to plēthos autōn*, 'the whole company of them', ESV), the reference will be to the members of the Sanhedrin (22:66), but Luke has made it clear that representatives of 'the people' had gathered with them to hear the verdict (verses 4, 13). Their shouting together, 'Away with this man! Release Barabbas to us!' suggests that the leaders had stirred the crowd to respond in this way (see Matthew 27:20; Mark 15:11).[64] They wanted Jesus to be taken away in the sense of being put to death (see Acts 8:13, citing Isaiah 53:8 LXX; 21:36; 22:22). Peter later reflects on the significance of this to a crowd in Jerusalem (Acts 3:13–14). Nothing more is known about Barabbas or the reason for his imprisonment than Luke reveals: 'Barabbas had been thrown into prison for an insurrection in the city, and for murder' (see Mark 15:7; John 18:40). The primary function of Barabbas in the narrative, as Green suggests, is to be 'a foil for Jesus' innocence',[65] which raises the possibility of viewing his death as a substitutionary atonement for the sins of others (see Isaiah 53:5–12).

20–22. Luke makes explicit what has been implicit in the narrative so far, that Pilate was 'wanting to release Jesus'. Consequently, he 'appealed to them again. But they kept shouting, "Crucify him! Crucify him!"'[66] Still unwilling to condemn him to death, for the third time Pilate spoke to them. His final appeal ('Why? What crime has this man committed?') is accompanied by a restatement of his judgment in verse 15 ('I have found in him no grounds for the death penalty') and his solution to the problem in verse 16 ('Therefore I will have him punished and then release him').

23–25. 'But with loud shouts they insistently demanded that he be crucified, and their shouts prevailed.' Given the emphasis in this passage on the fact that Pilate found no grounds for the death penalty, why did

---

[63] Nolland, *Luke 18:35–24:53*, 1130.

[64] In John 18:39–40 Pilate recalls the custom of releasing a prisoner at Passover and offers to release Jesus, motivating his accusers to shout for Barabbas.

[65] Green, *Luke*, 809.

[66] Fitzmyer, *Luke X–XXIV*, 1491, notes that the verb *stauroun* means 'fix a stake' or 'fix on a stake', but in the New Testament it is used exclusively of crucifixion. Green, *Luke*, 810, summarises different practices associated with crucifixion and observes that it was especially reserved for 'those who resisted the authority of Roman occupation'. See also Bock, *Luke 9:51–24:53*, 1830–31.

he submit to this pressure from the crowd and their leaders? If there was a Passover custom that allowed for an exchange of prisoners facing crucifixion, it was a political decision designed to keep the peace. The agitation of the Jewish leaders seems to have aroused the disillusion-ment of the crowd with Jesus, while Barabbas in some ironic way better represented their nationalistic aspirations.[67] Luke repeats the substance of verse 19 (Pilate 'released the man who had been thrown into prison for insurrection and murder'), emphasising again that Barabbas was 'the one they asked for', and implicitly condemns Pilate, because he 'surrendered Jesus to their will'.[68] Some argue that his Jewish opponents are more obvi-ously held responsible for the crucifixion with this conclusion. However, although the trial scene demonstrates that Jesus's fate corresponded to their will, Nolland observes that the following narrative shows how 'the *action* of Roman authorities implements that will'.[69] Both parties were complicit in this miscarriage of justice.

THE SERVANT KING

The opposition of the leaders of Israel towards Jesus is presented in two different stages by Luke. During his Galilean ministry and final journey to Jerusalem, it comes from the Pharisees and teachers of the law (5:21, 30; 6:1–11; 11:53–4). Then, in his final week of teaching in Jerusalem, opposition comes from 'the chief priests, the teachers of the law and the leaders among the people' (19:47; 22:66–23:1–2). Although there are many indications of Jesus's popularity with the crowds (4:14–15; 6:17–19; 7:16–17; 19:48; 21:38), his predictions in 9:22, 44; 18:31–33 and his parable in 19:11–27 warn about leaders and people turning against him. The foundational issue for the leaders in Jerusalem was his apparent claim to be their Messiah (23:2), which had theological and political implications for them. They were afraid of losing their influence and allowing his apparently radical teaching to have its sway. At the same time, they were worried about Roman reactions to the movement associated with Jesus. The leaders stirred up others with these fears and moved them to act in the frenzied way that Luke records. Together, they represent those in every age who resist the claim of Jesus on their lives for different reasons

---

[67] Nolland, *Luke 18:35–24:53*, 1133.

[68] Mark 15:15 and Matthew 27:26 record the flogging that Luke only mentions as a threat. John 19:16 is closer to Luke in sense, suggesting that Pilate handed Jesus over to the soldiers 'to satisfy the demands of the Jews' (D. A. Carson, *The Gospel According to John* (Leicester: InterVarsity; Grand Rapids: Eerdmans, 1991), 606).

[69] Nolland, *Luke 18:35–24:53*, 1138.

and with varying degrees of intensity. The mocking of Jesus as King of the Jews continues in the crucifixion scene, as it does in our world.

The other main feature of this narrative is the proclaimed innocence of Jesus, who is condemned to die, while Barabbas, who is guilty of insurrection and murder, is set free from punishment. There are echoes of Isaiah 52:13–53:12 here, which outlines the path of suffering that God's Servant must tread before he is 'raised and lifted up and highly exalted' (52:13). Luke indicates in 22:37 that this prophecy must be fulfilled in the events that follow. Jesus is despised and rejected, silent before his accusers and punished for the transgressions of others, suggesting that God is making his life 'an offering for sin', in fulfilment of that prediction.[70] Isaiah 53:4–6 signals the way to acknowledge the plan and purpose of God in all this.

4. The predicted end (23:26–56)

Luke abbreviates Mark's record here and adds new material from his own sources: the mourning of the people who followed Jesus and his response to them (verses 27–31); his prayer of forgiveness for those who crucified him (verse 34); his conversation with those who were crucified with him (verses 39–43); his final prayer (verse 46); a concluding note about the response of the witnesses (verses 48–49); and extra details about his burial (verses 50–56).[71] These additions sometimes emphasise the division between those who mourned and wailed for Jesus and those who sneered at him and mocked him. At the same time, Luke continues to demonstrate how Jesus's ministry is 'oriented toward and embraced by those living beyond the margins of the religious inner circle', as Green observes.[72] Jesus maintains a calm trust in God as he predicts the coming judgment (verses 28–31), prays for his enemies (verse 34), offers eternal life to a man dying with him (verse 43) and commits himself into his Father's hands (verse 46).

---

[70] See Steve Jeffery, Mike Ovey and Andrew Sach, *Pierced for our Transgressions: Rediscovering the Glory of Penal Substitution* (Nottingham: InterVarsity Press, 2007), 52–67.

[71] Matthew 27:32–61 follows Mark 15:21–47 more closely, adding further details in 27:51–4, 62–6.

[72] Green, *Luke*, 812.

Crucified (23:26–49)

The crucifixion of Jesus

26 As the soldiers led him away, they seized Simon from Cyrene, who was on his way in from the country, and put the cross on him and made him carry it behind Jesus. **27** A large number of people followed him, including women who mourned and wailed for him. **28** Jesus turned and said to them, 'Daughters of Jerusalem, do not weep for me; weep for yourselves and for your children. **29** For the time will come when you will say, "Blessed are the childless women, the wombs that never bore and the breasts that never nursed!" **30** Then

'"they will say to the mountains,
'Fall on us!'
and to the hills, 'Cover us!' "**b**

31 For if people do these things when the tree is green, what will happen when it is dry?'

32 Two other men, both criminals, were also led out with him to be executed. **33** When they came to the place called the Skull, they crucified him there, along with the criminals – one on his right, the other on his left. **34** Jesus said, 'Father, forgive them, for they do not know what they are doing.'**c** And they divided up his clothes by casting lots.

35 The people stood watching, and the rulers even sneered at him. They said, 'He saved others; let him save himself if he is God's Messiah, the Chosen One.'

36 The soldiers also came up and mocked him. They offered him wine vinegar **37** and said, 'If you are the king of the Jews, save yourself.'

38 There was a written notice above him, which read: THIS IS THE KING OF THE JEWS.

39 One of the criminals who hung there hurled insults at him: 'Aren't you the Messiah? Save yourself and us!'

40 But the other criminal rebuked him. 'Don't you fear God,' he said, 'since you are under the same sentence? **41** We are punished justly, for we are getting what our deeds deserve. But this man has done nothing wrong.'

42 Then he said, 'Jesus, remember me when you come into your kingdom.**d**'

43 Jesus answered him, 'Truly I tell you, today you will be with me in paradise.'

The death of Jesus

44 It was now about noon, and darkness came over the whole land until three in the afternoon, **45** for the sun stopped shining. And the curtain of the temple was torn in two. **46** Jesus called out with a loud voice, 'Father, into your hands I commit my spirit.'**e** When he had said this, he breathed his last.

47 The centurion, seeing what had happened, praised God and said, 'Surely this was a righteous man.' **48** When all the people who had gathered to witness this sight saw what took place, they beat their breasts and went away. **49** But all those who knew him, including the women who had followed him from Galilee, stood at a distance, watching these things.

b 30 Hosea 10:8

c 34 Some early manuscripts do not have this sentence.
d 42 Some manuscripts *come with your kingly power*
e 46 Psalm 31:5

26. Luke omits any reference to the mocking of Jesus by the Roman soldiers here (see Mark 15:16–20a) and proceeds with a longer portrayal than Mark of the journey to the place of crucifixion. The NIV ('As the soldiers led him away') presumes that the ambiguous 'they' in the Greek text refers to the soldiers, who would have been responsible for seizing Simon of Cyrene, putting the crossbeam on him and making him carry it to the place of execution.[73] Each of the Synoptic Gospels names him (Mark 15:21 adds 'the father of Alexander and Rufus', implying that he was known in later Christian circles). Luke follows Mark in describing Cyrene, the capital of the Roman province of Cyrenaica (Libya) in North Africa, as his place of origin, and in stating that he 'was on his way in from the country'. This last expression indicates that he was not part of the crowd that had called for Jesus's crucifixion. Luke alone adds that he was forced to carry the cross 'behind Jesus' (*opisthen tou Iēsou*), echoing the call of Jesus to those who would follow him (9:23, *opisō mou erchesthai*, 'come after me') to take up their cross (see also 14:27). Simon from Cyrene functions as a visual reminder of that challenge.

27–29. Luke uniquely introduces at this point a large group of people who followed Jesus to the place of execution, 'including women who mourned and wailed for him'. Like Simon, they were not part of the crowd intent on doing away with Jesus, but they were also not necessarily disciples. As 'daughters of Jerusalem', the women had come from the city to mourn the injustice of Jesus's sentence and his death.[74] The final expression of their grief is noted in verse 48. His prophetic address to them began when he turned to them and said, 'Do not weep for me; weep for yourselves and for your children.' Despite their concern for him, they did not discern his true identity and the terrible consequences of his rejection for their city and nation (see 13:34–5; 19:41–4; 21:20–24).[75] The

---

[73] Contrast Green, *Luke*, 814.
[74] Edwards, *Luke*, 683, argues that the expression 'daughters of Jerusalem' may be a personification of the city as in 13:34, but Luke has a special interest in roles that women played at the cross and burial of Jesus.
[75] Although there are echoes of Zechariah 12:10–14 here, the prophet envisages a profound repentance for having 'pierced' the one sent to them by God. This is more

need for weeping is then proclaimed in more dramatic terms: 'For the time will come when you will say, "Blessed are the childless women, the wombs that never bore and the breasts that never nursed!"' (see 21:23). As Green observes, 'Children are generally seen as expressions of divine favour, but in the coming catastrophe, it is better to be barren.'[76]

30. Jesus's prophetic warning continued with language drawn from Hosea 10:8: 'They will say to the mountains, "Fall on us!" and to the hills, "Cover us!"' Hosea addressed the northern kingdom of Israel in the eighth century BC, anticipating God's judgment for their foreign alliances and idolatry. Such unfaithfulness to the Lord and his covenant with them would be punished when the Assyrians invaded their land and captured its inhabitants. Hosea envisaged that being suddenly buried under mountains and hills would be preferable to experiencing this divine judgment! Jesus used Hosea's language analogously to emphasise the awfulness of the fate awaiting the city of Jerusalem and its inhabitants in his time.

31. An enigmatic question brings this challenge to a climax: 'For if people do these things when the tree is green, what will happen when it is dry?' Fire as an image of divine judgment is implied here (see Isaiah 10:16–19; Ezekiel 20:45–8; 24:9–10). Green wood does not burn as easily as dry wood. If God allows the innocent Jesus (a green tree) to suffer such a terrible fate, what will be the fate of guilty Jerusalem and those who crucify him (a dry tree)?[77]

32–3. Luke's narrative about Jesus's journey to the cross ends with the statement, 'Two other men, both criminals, were also led out with him to be executed' (see Mark 15:27).[78] These verses specifically recall the prediction of Jesus in 22:37, citing Isaiah 53:12 ('he was numbered with the transgressors'), and prepare for the conversation he will have with them – 'one on his right, the other on his left' (23:39–43). Their crimes are not stated (see verse 25), but the fact that they were to be crucified

---

obviously fulfilled in Acts 2:37–41 and subsequently, when many in Jerusalem come to believe in Jesus and understand the significance of his death in the plan of God.
[76] Green, *Luke*, 816. A similar expression to 'the time will come' (*erchontai hēmerai*, 'days are coming') is used in 5:35; 19:43. Compare Jeremiah 7:32; 16:14; 31:31 (LXX 38:31).
[77] Fitzmyer, *Luke X–XXIV*, 1498–9. Bock, *Luke 9:51–24:53*, 1847–8, argues that *ei . . . poiousin* ('if they do') is an oblique third-person reference to God (compare 12:20).
[78] Mark 15:27 and Matthew 27:38, 44 identify those crucified with Jesus as *lēstai*, which ordinarily meant 'robber, highwayman bandit' (BDAG; Luke 10:30, 36), but it could also describe a 'revolutionary, insurrectionist, guerrilla' (BDAG; see Josephus *War*, 2.13.2–3). Luke uses the more general term *kakourgai* ('criminals' or 'evildoers') in 22:32, 33, 39.

marks them as rebels, 'a threat to the state, perhaps dangerous and violent men', as Green discerns.[79] Crucifixions were normally held outside the gates of a city, in prominent places where the awfulness of the punishment could be readily observed. Nolland records that 'there were many different ways in which victims were crucified: various kinds of preliminary torture, different kinds of crosses, different postures on the cross (impaled, cruciform, upside down)'.[80] The place called 'the Skull' (Mark 15:22, 'Golgotha' in Aramaic) was probably so described because of the shape of the hill.

34. Quite unexpectedly, and only in this Gospel, Jesus prays, 'Father, forgive them, for they do not know what they are doing.' Praying for his enemies exemplified his teaching in 6:27–8 and continued his emphasis on the need of all for divine forgiveness (5:20–24; 7:47–8); 11:4; 17:3; 24:47). Jesus does not pray for God's judgment against the nation to be abandoned but for those who specifically opposed and mistreated him to be pardoned. At one level they knew what they were doing to him, but they did not recognise the extraordinary implications of their actions (see Acts 3:17; 13:27).[81] They were rejecting God's Messiah and any hope of sharing in his eternal kingdom, but repentance for the forgiveness of sins would soon be preached in his name 'to all nations, beginning at Jerusalem' (24:47; Acts 2:38; 5:31; 10:43). Despite some textual uncertainty, Nolland argues that the prayer from the cross has 'good claim to being based upon historical reminiscence'.[82] It is also worth noting, with Marshall, that 'sayings by Jesus are found in each main section of the Lucan crucifixion narrative (23:28–31, 43, 46); the lack of such a saying at this point would disturb the pattern'.[83] There may be another echo of Isaiah 53:12 here (he 'made intercession for the transgressors'), though the prophet indicates that God's Servant intercedes by bearing the sin of many, whereas Jesus simply prays that the benefits of his sacrificial death might be experienced by those who have conspired against him.

---

[79] Green, *Luke*, 819.

[80] Nolland, *Luke 18:35–24:53*, 1145. See also Edwards, *Luke*, 685–6.

[81] The motif of acting in ignorance surfaces again in Acts 14:16; 17:30; 26:9, but in each case the context indicates that this is culpable ignorance.

[82] Nolland, *Luke 18:35–24:53*, 1144. Some important early manuscripts do not include verse 34a (papyrus 75, B, D*, W, Θ, and others), though many do (ℵ, A, C, D², L, Δ, Ψ, and numerous others). Nolland, 1141, notes Luke's conscious paralleling of the deaths of Jesus and Stephen (Acts 7:59–60). Edwards, *Luke*, 687–8, suggests reasons why some copyists may have omitted the prayer of Jesus.

[83] Marshall, *Luke*, 868. Marshall discusses the textual issues quite fully and concludes that the balance of the evidence favours acceptance of the saying as Lucan.

Together with Matthew 27:35 and Mark 15:24, Luke then records that 'they divided up his clothes by casting lots' (see also John 19:23–4). This action recalls Psalm 22:18, suggesting that the shaming and mocking that the psalmist endured prefigured the experience of Jesus in precise ways. Luke does not include the cry recorded in Matthew 27:46; Mark 15:34 and echoing Psalm 22:1 ('My God, my God, why have you forsaken me?'), but he hints at the same apparent abandonment by God in the scene he paints.

35. 'The people stood watching, and the rulers even sneered at him.' The verb 'sneered' (*exemyktērizon*) is used in Psalm 22:7 (21:8 LXX), providing another direct parallel with the psalmist's experience. In that text, the watchers are the mockers, but Luke makes a distinction between the onlookers and the Jewish leaders, who were openly antagonistic (see 16:14). 'He saved others,' they said; 'let him save himself if he is God's Messiah, the Chosen One.' If the word 'save' is used here in the sense of rescue from death, his opponents would have been reflecting claims that he had raised others in that way.[84] This challenge echoes Psalm 22:8 (21:9 LXX), but also recalls the testing of Jesus by the devil in Luke 4:3–12. The title 'the Son of God' in that context is replaced with 'God's Messiah' and combined with 'the Chosen One' here.[85] God's Servant is addressed as 'my chosen one' in Isaiah 42:1, and these words were applied to Jesus by the heavenly voice in Luke 9:35. But how did his opponents understand these claims? Green observes, 'All the requisite categories are present in these words, but they cannot collate them in any way other than to repudiate Jesus' salvific role.'[86]

36–8. The Roman soldiers also 'came up and mocked him', which was what Jesus predicted (18:32) and had already experienced from Jewish guards (22:63; 23:11). Their offering to him of 'wine vinegar' (*oxos*) expressed their disdain because it was a cheap drink, unfit for a king (see Psalm 69:21 [68:22 LXX]). They picked up the challenge of the Jewish leaders (verse 35), expressing it in their own terms: 'If you

---

[84] Luke is silent about their charge that he said he would destroy the Temple and rebuild it in three days (Matthew 27:40; Mark 15:29–30).

[85] Matthew 27:40 ('If you are the Son of God') makes the link with the temptation narrative even more obvious. Matthew also includes the charge that Jesus said he would destroy the Temple and build it in three days (see Mark 15:29–30), but Luke makes no mention of this, focusing on the issue of Jesus's messianic identity (as in Matthew 27:42–3; Mark 15:32).

[86] Green, *Luke*, 821. Green notes evidence for Isaiah 42:1 being used messianically in this period.

are the king of the Jews, save yourself.' Luke reminds us that this was the central issue for both Jews and Romans by recording, 'There was a written notice above him, which read: THIS IS THE KING OF THE JEWS' (see Mark 15:25–6; Matthew 27:37). John 19:19–22 makes more of this notice and the offence it caused to the Jewish leaders.

39–41. Mark 15:32 indicates that 'those crucified with him also heaped insults on him' (Matthew 27:44, 'the rebels who were crucified with him'), but Luke alone records the words spoken by 'one of the criminals who hung there'. This term could be a way of identifying him as someone under the curse of God (see Deuteronomy 21:22–3; Acts 5:30; 10:39; Galatians 3:13). The verb *eblasphēmei* ('was insulting') was previously used in 22:65. Picking up the sneer of the rulers about him being the Messiah and unable to save himself (verse 35), this man says, 'Aren't you the Messiah? Save yourself and us!" (see 4:23, 'Physician, heal yourself!'). This presumed that the three of them needed rescuing in the same way, but the second criminal rebuked him with the challenge, 'Don't you fear God?' All three were 'under the same sentence' of death, though he discerned that, 'We are punished justly, for we are getting what our deeds deserve. But this man has done nothing wrong.' In Nolland's words, this provides 'a "street-level" confirmation of Pilate's conviction that Jesus was innocent'.[87]

42–3. The second criminal reflects a remarkable awareness of the significance of Jesus when he says, 'Jesus, remember me when you come into your kingdom.'[88] He believes that the messianic rule of Jesus will somehow be established through his death and asks to be remembered when it is accomplished. Edwards observes, 'For the unrepentant criminal, Jesus must come down from the cross to save; for the penitent criminal Jesus must remain on the cross and fulfil his divine duty to save.'[89] In biblical usage, the petition 'remember me' is a way of appealing for God's help (e.g., Genesis 40:14; Psalm 106:4; Nehemiah 13:31). With these words, a guilty man effectively acknowledges the divine authority of Jesus to forgive sins, deliver him from judgment after death and

---

[87] Nolland, *Luke 18:35–24:53*, 1151.
[88] The phrase *eis tēn basileian sou* ('into your kingdom') is well attested, though many more witnesses read *en tē basileia sou* ('in your kingly rule'; NIV note d 'come with your kingly power'), referring to the Second Coming. Although the latter 'fits less well into the thought of the passage and into Luke's wider use of kingdom language, it is unlikely to be the original (Nolland, *Luke 18:35–24:53*, 1150). Compare Edwards, *Luke*, 691.
[89] Edwards, *Luke*, 692.

receive him into his heavenly kingdom. Luke presents him as the last in a series of religious and social outcasts who see their need for Jesus and come to share in the kingdom he proclaimed. The answer Jesus gives is both surprising and affirming: 'Truly I tell you, today you will be with me in paradise.' The introductory expression 'Truly I tell you' (*amēn soi legō*) affirms to this man personally the truth of Jesus's promise ('you' is singular here, but plural in parallel expressions, 4:24; 12:37; 18:17, 29; 21:32). 'Today' expresses immediacy, though both will have to suffer death before experiencing the promised outcome.[90] End-time predictions are about to be fulfilled for Jesus and everyone who believes in him. 'With me' means being together with the Messiah in his glorified state.

The Greek word *paradeisos* was derived from an old Persian term for an enclosed garden (BDAG). It was applied to the Garden of Eden in the Septuagint (Genesis 2:8; 13:10; Ezekiel 31:8) and to God's work of restoring his people and their land after the Babylonian Exile (Isaiah 51:3). In some later Jewish literature, paradise came to mean a pleasant resting place for the righteous prior to the great day of resurrection.[91] However, in view of the biblical promises concerning a new creation or restoration of Edenic life that were broadly linked with the establishment of the Messiah's rule (e.g., Isaiah 11:1–9; 35:1–10; 65:17–25; Ezekiel 34:20–31), it is more likely that 'paradise' on the lips of Jesus is equivalent to 'your kingdom', rather than 'some conscious, intermediate state', as Bock suggests.[92] Jesus was speaking about an imminent experience of everything promised in Scripture concerning his victory over death and God's new creation.

44–5. The final moments of Jesus's suffering are briefly recounted. First, there is an indication that his last three hours were shrouded in darkness:

---

[90] Peter speaks about the Messiah not being abandoned to 'the realm of the dead' (Acts 2:31, 'Hades'), 'nor did his body see decay' (applying Psalm 16:10, which is cited in Acts 2:27). Jesus returned from death to the earthly realm in his resurrection, but the man on the cross next to him clearly did not.

[91] Nolland, *Luke 18:35–24:53*, 1152, notes the way an end-time reversal of the expulsion of humanity from the Garden of Eden is expected in *Testament of Levi* 18:10–11; Revelation 2:7, 22. Paradise is predicted to be peopled with the saints of the past in 1 Enoch 60:8; 61:12. In 2 Corinthians 12:4 Paul speaks of the ecstatic experience of being 'caught up to paradise'.

[92] Bock, *Luke 9:51–24:53*, 1858. Williamson, *Death and the Afterlife*, 54–5, 175–92, similarly argues for a temporary heavenly abode, as believers await the resurrection of their bodies. However, see my Introduction, pages 18–22, and comments on Luke 16:19–31; 20:27–38.

'It was now about noon, and darkness came over the whole land until three in the afternoon.' Luke does not mention that Jesus was crucified at nine in the morning (Mark 15:25) or record his cry of anguish at three in the afternoon and its sequel (Matthew 27:46–50; Mark 15:34–7). He simply emphasises the unnatural character of the darkness, adding, 'for the sun stopped shining'.[93] Without explanation, this invites readers to reflect on the biblical association of darkness with the judgment of God (e.g., Amos 8:9; Joel 2:30–32, as cited in Acts 2:19–21). Second, an extraordinary event in the Temple is recalled: 'And the curtain of the temple was torn in two.' Luke does not attribute this to an earthquake (as Matthew 27:51–3 does), and once more leaves his readers to reflect on its significance. Since he has put the two together (contrast Matthew and Mark), he may be signalling that both are signs of imminent judgment on Jerusalem and the Temple. However, especially if the curtain hiding the inner sanctuary of the Temple is meant, its tearing could also suggest the end of the old cultic way of approaching God and the opening of a new way through the death of Jesus (see Hebrews 10:19–22).[94]

46. Third, Luke agrees with Matthew 27:50 and Mark 15:37 that Jesus called out 'with a loud voice' before dying, but clarifies that he said, 'Father, into your hands I commit my spirit.' 'Spirit' here means 'breath' or 'life force' (*pneuma,* as in 8:55), not 'soul'. This is explained by the verb that follows (*exepneusen,* 'he expired, breathed his last'). Jesus's prayer expressed confident resignation, adapting Psalm 31:5 (30:5 LXX). The psalmist prayed for deliverance from his enemies so that he might live and rejoice in God's love. Jesus looked to his Father to resurrect him from death to reign with him in glory (see Hebrews 5:7–10; 12:2). Prayer was an essential aspect of his life and ministry at every stage (3:21; 5:16; 6:12; 9:18; 10:21–2; 22:41–4). This climactic petition is a model for believers facing death and longing to experience with him the joys and blessings of his kingdom (verses 42–3; compare Acts 7:59–60).

47. Each of the Synoptic Gospels gives a slightly different version of what happened next. Mark 15:39 testifies that 'when the centurion, who stood there in front of Jesus, saw how he died, he said, "Surely this man was the

---

[93] A dust storm may have been the natural cause, though the context suggests a supernatural event. An eclipse of the sun at Passover time is unlikely, because there is a full moon at night (Bock, *Luke 9:51–24.53*, 1859). See, however, Fitzmyer *Luke X–XXIV*, 1518.

[94] Nolland, *Luke 18:35–24:53*, 1157, lists numerous possible interpretations, and takes the event in 23:45 to symbolise 'the revealing of the glory of God, hitherto hidden behind the veil of the temple'. Compare Bock, *Luke 9:51–24.53*, 1860–61.

Son of God!'" (expanded in Matthew 27:54). William Lane suggests that this could mean that 'Jesus was a divine man or deified hero who accepted humiliation and death as an act of obedience to a higher mandate'.[95] His thought-world was popular Hellenism, so that what he said was true in a higher sense than he understood. Luke's account differs in two significant ways. First, he notes that the centurion, 'seeing what had happened, praised God'. The language of praise is used extensively throughout this Gospel to describe a believing response to manifestations of God's grace and power. The implication is that this Roman soldier had recognised 'the salvific hand of God at work in Jesus', as Green supposes.[96] We know nothing of his experience of Judaism or the ministry of Jesus, but his response suggests a parallel with the centurion in 7:1–10 (see also Acts 10:1–4). Second, Luke has the centurion say, 'Surely this was a righteous man.' The adjective 'righteous' (dikaios) means more than 'innocent' here.[97] It is used throughout Luke's Gospel with reference to those who demonstrate a right relationship with God by their behaviour (1:6, 17; 2:25; 5:32; 14:14; 23:50) and ironically for those whose righteousness is questionable (15:7; 18:9; 20:20). Frank Matera argues that the centurion's confession means that 'Jesus, and not the religious leaders, stands in the right relationship with God'.[98] The evangelist does not shy away from affirming Jesus as God's Son (1:35; 3:22; 4:41; 8:28; 9:35; 22:70), but has the centurion specifically identify him as a righteous man suffering because of his relationship with God.

48–9. Luke turns attention again to 'all the people who had gathered to witness this sight'. Using language that recalls verse 27, he records that, when they saw what took place, 'they beat their breasts and went away'. The outcome was distressing for them, but they saw no point in staying. However, 'all those who knew him, including the women who had followed him from Galilee, stood at a distance, watching these things'. The other Gospels name some of these women at this point (Matthew 27:55–6; Mark 15:40–41; compare John 19:25). Luke refers to them again in verses 55, 56 and 24:1–10, only identifying them when the full extent of their witness to what happened is revealed. Initially, they dealt with their grief by remaining and reflecting. Green suggests that their standing at a distance indicated that they were 'as yet unwilling to identify too

---

[95] Lane, *Mark*, 576.

[96] Green, *Luke*, 827. The verb here (*doxazō*, 'glorified, praised') is also used in 2:20; 5:25, 26; 7:16; 13:13; 17:15; 18:43; Acts 4:21; 11:18; 21:20.

[97] Contrast Bock, *Luke 9:51–24:53*, 1864.

[98] Frank Matera, 'The Death of Jesus according to Luke: A Question of Sources', *CBQ* 47 (1985), 483. See also Nolland, *Luke 18:35–24:53*, 1159.

closely with Jesus in his humiliation and death',[99] but they could not abandon him completely, as the following narratives show.

SHARING WITH JESUS IN HIS KINGDOM

Luke's crucifixion narrative has much in common with Matthew and Mark, but with distinctive inclusions and emphases. Luke presents a more complex portrait of the witnesses than the other Gospels. The mocking of Jesus is more specifically attributed to the Jewish leaders, the Roman soldiers and one of the criminals crucified with him. Many onlookers follow him to the place of execution, including women who mourn and wail for him (verse 27). When they leave, beating their breasts, only the disciples of Jesus remain, standing at a distance and watching (verse 49).

Two positive reactions to Jesus are recorded: the confession and appeal of the second criminal (verses 40–42) and the judgment of the Roman centurion (verse 47). Luke's version of the latter emphasises the righteousness of Jesus in relation to God and implicitly highlights the unrighteousness of those who pursued him to death. Jesus speaks prophetically again about the judgment to come on Jerusalem and the nation (verses 28–31; compare 13:34–5; 19:41–4; 21:20–24). Nevertheless, he prays for the forgiveness of those who have opposed him and achieved his crucifixion (verse 34). The rulers who sneer at him challenge him to 'save himself if he is God's Messiah, the Chosen One' (verse 35). Their taunt brings together his apparent claim to be the one destined to sit at God's right hand (22:69–70) and the one chosen by God to bring salvation to Israel and the nations (Isaiah 42:1–4). Luke affirms the truth of these claims with allusions to Psalms 22 and 31, implying that Jesus exemplifies and fulfils the role of the righteous sufferer in those texts. Luke further indicates with allusions to Isaiah 52:13–53:12 that Jesus's suffering is redemptive for others. As the one 'numbered with the transgressors' (Isaiah 53:12, cited in Luke 22:37), 'he bore the sin of many, and made intercession for the transgressors'.[100] Jesus specifically anticipates his glorification and the benefit it will bring to others, when he says, 'Truly I tell you, today you will be with me in paradise.'

By means of this narrative, particularly highlighting the response of witnesses, Luke invites readers to consider where they stand in relation to the crucified Jesus and the hope of sharing in his eternal kingdom.

---

[99] Green, *Luke*, 828.
[100] Tannehill's argument, *Narrative Unity* 1, 285–9, that Jesus's death is simply portrayed in Luke–Acts in martyrological terms, fails to grasp all the evidence.

Buried (23:50–56)

The burial of Jesus

50 Now there was a man named Joseph, a member of the Council, a good and upright man, **51** who had not consented to their decision and action. He came from the Judean town of Arimathea, and he himself was waiting for the kingdom of God. **52** Going to Pilate, he asked for Jesus' body. **53** Then he took it down, wrapped it in linen cloth and placed it in a tomb cut in the rock, one in which no one had yet been laid. **54** It was Preparation Day, and the Sabbath was about to begin.

55 The women who had come with Jesus from Galilee followed Joseph and saw the tomb and how his body was laid in it. **56** Then they went home and prepared spices and perfumes. But they rested on the Sabbath in obedience to the commandment.

50–54. As that awful day drew to a close, there was an unexpected intervention by one of the Jewish leaders. Joseph from the town of Arimathea is introduced as 'a member of the Council, a good and upright man [*dikaios*, as in verse 47], who had not consented to their decision and action'.[101] Most importantly, 'he himself was waiting for the kingdom of God' (see 2:25, 38; 24:20–21). John 19:38 goes further and describes him as 'a disciple of Jesus, but secretly because he feared the Jewish leaders' (so also Matthew 27:57). As a member of the Sanhedrin, he could have had easy access to the Roman governor.[102] Going to Pilate, therefore, he asked for the body of Jesus. John 19:39 adds that he was 'accompanied by Nicodemus, the man who earlier had visited Jesus at night' (John 3:1–15), who brought the extraordinary gift of 'a mixture of myrrh and aloes, about thirty-five kilograms'. Both were intent on giving Jesus an honourable burial in accordance with Jewish customs.[103] Luke simply records that Joseph took the body of Jesus down from the cross, 'wrapped it in linen cloth and placed it in a tomb in the rock, one in which no one had yet been laid' (see John 19:41–2). This was done quickly, because 'it was Preparation Day, and the Sabbath was about to begin'. Mark 15:44–6 provides the additional information that Pilate was surprised to hear that Jesus was already dead. He summoned the centurion to learn

[101] Fitzmyer, *Luke X–XXIV*, 1526, lists various suggestions for the location of Arimathea. Edwards, *Luke*, 701, argues for Ramah, some twenty miles (30km) northwest of Jerusalem.
[102] Nolland, *Luke 18:35–24:53*, 1164, considers three reasons why Pilate may have acceded to Joseph's request.
[103] See B. R. McCane, 'Burial Practices, Jewish', *DNTB*, 173–5; Edwards, *Luke*, 702–4.

if this was so, and then he gave the body to Joseph, who took it down from the cross, wrapped it in the linen, placed it in a tomb cut out of rock, and 'rolled a stone against the entrance of the tomb'. This last detail is assumed in Luke 24:2. Matthew 27:57–60 adds that Joseph was a rich man and that he placed Jesus 'in his own new tomb that he had cut out of the rock'.[104] Edwards rightly argues, 'The proper understanding of the resurrection begins with the placement of Jesus' body in a tomb, for the body raised on Easter morning was necessarily understood to be the transformed body that was buried by Joseph of Arimathea three days earlier.'[105]

55–6. A close link between 23:49 and 24:1 is provided here, first with the statement, 'The women who had come with Jesus from Galilee followed Joseph and saw the tomb and how his body was laid in it.'[106] With this information, Luke precludes the possibility that they may have gone to the wrong tomb the next morning. Second, he notes that 'they went home and prepared spices and perfumes', which were used to obscure the smell of a decomposing body. Whether or not Luke was aware of the large amount of myrrh and aloes that Nicodemus brought to the tomb (John 19:39), he emphasises the loving intention of these women to honour the body of Jesus in an appropriate way. Third, the qualification that 'they rested on the Sabbath in obedience to the commandment' presents these initial witnesses to the empty tomb as faithful, law-abiding Jewish women.[107]

[104] Compare Isaiah 53:9. Nolland, *Luke 18:35–24:53*, 1165, suggests that 'a rock-hewn tomb is likely to have fitted the socio-economic standing of Joseph better than that of Jesus himself (see Isa. 22:16)'.
[105] Edwards, *Luke*, 700.
[106] There is no noun after the verb 'followed' in the Greek, but the NIV makes the reasonable assumption that they followed Joseph to the tomb.
[107] The Greek syntax (*men* in 23:56; *de* in 24:1) closely links this clause with the next one, emphasising that they did not go to the tomb on the Sabbath, but on the first day of the week.

8

The Resurrection and Heavenly Ascent of Jesus

LUKE 24:1–53

In this chapter, Jesus's 'departure' (*exodus*, 9:31) is completed, as he is raised from death (24:6), enters his glory (24:26) and is finally parted from his disciples and 'taken up into heaven' (24:51). This takes place in and around Jerusalem, mostly on Easter Day, although the ascension occurs later according to Acts 1:1–11. Each Gospel records the discovery of the empty tomb with different inclusions and emphases (Matthew 28:1–10; Mark 16:1–8; Luke 24:1–12; John 20:1–10). Mary Magdalene is the key witness in each case, but other women who came to anoint the body of Jesus are also mentioned. Bock lists eight points of general agreement between the resurrection narratives in the Gospels and contends that 'their differences are complementary, not contradictory'.[108] Three appearances of the resurrected Jesus are recorded by Luke. The first is to Peter, which is mentioned retrospectively (verse 34), the second is to two disciples on the road to Emmaus (verses 13–35), and the third is to the Eleven and those with them, which becomes a commissioning event (verses 36–49). A brief reference to the heavenly ascension of Jesus and its sequel (verses 50–53) brings the first volume of Luke's 'orderly account' to a dramatic conclusion (1:3) and prepares for the second.

1. The empty tomb (24:1–12)

Luke adapts Mark 16:1–8, which begins by identifying the women who visit the tomb to anoint the body of Jesus when the Sabbath is over. When they arrive at the tomb, they discover that the stone has already been moved.[109] Then Mark and Matthew recount an angel's testimony to Jesus's resurrection and his promise to meet them in Galilee. Luke, however, has the two messengers ask, 'Why do you look for the living

---

[108] Bock, *Luke 9:51–24:53*, 1880–81.
[109] Matthew 28:2–4 explains this in terms of a violent earthquake and the coming of an angel from heaven to roll back the stone.

among the dead?' and proclaim, 'He is not here; he has risen!' Rather than directing them to meet with Jesus in Galilee, they simply challenge the women to remember his predictions (verses 1–8). When the women tell the Eleven and those with them what they have seen and heard, they do not believe them (verses 9–11). Luke then records Peter's visit to the tomb and his wondering at the evidence (verse 12; compare John 20:3–10).[110]

Jesus has risen

24 On the first day of the week, very early in the morning, the women took the spices they had prepared and went to the tomb. **2** They found the stone rolled away from the tomb, **3** but when they entered, they did not find the body of the Lord Jesus. **4** While they were wondering about this, suddenly two men in clothes that gleamed like lightning stood beside them. **5** In their fright the women bowed down with their faces to the ground, but the men said to them, 'Why do you look for the living among the dead? **6** He is not here; he has risen! Remember how he told you, while he was still with you in Galilee: **7** "The Son of Man must be delivered over to the hands of sinners, be crucified and on the third day be raised again." ' **8** Then they remembered his words.

9 When they came back from the tomb, they told all these things to the Eleven and to all the others. **10** It was Mary Magdalene, Joanna, Mary the mother of James, and the others with them who told this to the apostles. **11** But they did not believe the women, because their words seemed to them like nonsense. **12** Peter, however, got up and ran to the tomb. Bending over, he saw the strips of linen lying by themselves, and he went away, wondering to himself what had happened.

1–3. On the first day of the week (Sunday), 'very early in the morning, the women took the spices they had prepared and went to the tomb'. Luke does not name these women until their status as reliable witnesses to the apostles and those with them is challenged (verses 9–11). The phrase 'very early in the morning' (*orthrou batheōs*, 'at deep dawn') suggests that they went as early as possible, when it was light enough to find the tomb (Mark 16:2, 'just after sunrise').[111] Luke has not previously mentioned the

---

[110] Matthew 28:9–15 testifies to a brief encounter that these women had with the risen Lord, before narrating how the guards reported the empty tomb to the chief priests and were paid to say that the disciples of Jesus had stolen his body during the night. Harris, *From Grave to Glory*, 129–39, lists the resurrection appearances of Jesus and discusses their historicity.
[111] Nolland, *Luke 18:35–24:53*, 1188. Codex D and some other manuscripts include an interpolation between verses 1 and 2, partly following Mark 16:3.

stone, but now clarifies that 'they found the stone rolled away from the tomb'. Fitzmyer notes, 'Tombs in the neighbourhood of Jerusalem from the first century A.D. have been found fitted with huge circular stone discs that were set in a transverse channel hollowed out of stone, along which the discs would be rolled in front of a rectangular doorway opening on to the tomb proper.'[1] Matthew 28:2–4 offers a supernatural explanation for this. The surprising consequence is that 'when they entered, they did not find the body of the Lord Jesus'. Although Luke regularly calls Jesus 'the Lord', this is the only place where he uses the full expression 'the Lord Jesus', highlighting the paradox of 'the Lord' being identified with the dead body of Jesus (see Acts 1:21; 4:33; 8:16).[2]

4. 'While they were wondering about this, suddenly two men in clothes that gleamed like lightning stood beside them.' The verb translated 'wondering' conveys the sense of perplexity (*aporeisthai*, 'to be in a confused state of mind', BDAG). Mark 16:5 speaks of 'a young man dressed in a white robe sitting on the right side', while Matthew 28:2 records that an angel of the Lord had come down from heaven, 'rolled back the stone and sat on it'. The messengers are called angels in Luke 24:23; John 20:12. The gleaming robes mentioned in each of these accounts identify them as supernatural beings in human form. As Nolland concludes, 'something of the splendor of God attaches itself to these heavenly visitors'.[3] Luke and John may have used a common source that recognised the significance of two witnesses, rather than the one mentioned by Matthew and Mark. Like the 'two men dressed in white' in Acts 1:10, these two fulfil the requirement of Deuteronomy 19:15 regarding a reliable testimony.

5–7. Each of the Synoptic accounts emphasises the fear of the women in different ways (see Matthew 28:8; Mark 16:8). Luke observes that, immediately upon seeing the men, 'in their fright the women bowed down with their faces to the ground' (see 1:12, 29–30; 2:9). They recognised that they were in the presence of divine messengers. Uniquely in Luke's version, the angels say, 'Why do you look for the living among the dead? He is not here; he has risen!'[4] Instead of the encouragement not to be afraid

---

[1] Fitzmyer, *Luke X–XXIV*, 1544. Nolland, *Luke 18:35–24:53*, 1189, thinks it more likely that there was 'a spherical stone plug that was pushed into the tomb opening'.

[2] Codex D and some Old Latin manuscripts do not include 'of the Lord Jesus', but this reading is well attested by a range of reliable witnesses. See Metzger, *Textual Commentary*, 156–7.

[3] Nolland, *Luke 18:35–24:53*, 1189.

[4] Bock, *Luke 9:51–24:53*, 1895, argues that although Luke conveys the angelic message in his own style, 'it appears to be traditionally based and is not his own

(Matthew 28:5; Mark 16:6), they are rebuked for looking in the wrong place for their Master. The significance of the empty tomb ('He is not here') is explained with the proclamation ('he has risen'). This specifically recalls the prediction of Jesus in 9:22 (where the same verb *ēgerthē*, 'raised to life', is used) and 18:33 (where the verb *anastēnai*, 'will rise again', is used).[5] These are two different but related ways of talking about what happened. Jesus was raised from death by the Father (see verse 34) and by that means 'he has risen' (verse 7). The truth of this claim is asserted with a call to 'Remember how he told you, while he was still with you in Galilee: "The Son of Man must be delivered over to the hands of sinners, be crucified and on the third day be raised again."'[6] 'Sinners' in this context probably refers to 'the Gentiles' (18:32). 'Crucified' specifies the manner of his death in the light of what has just happened. 'On the third day be raised again' expresses the precise timing of his vindication (as in 9:22; 18:33; compare 24:21, 46). The absence of his corpse should be understood in this light.

8. Luke does not include the angelic charge to 'go, tell his disciples and Peter, "He is going ahead of you into Galilee. There you will see him, just as he told you"' (Mark 16:7; abbreviated in Matthew 28:7). Luke wants to focus on resurrection appearances in the vicinity of Jerusalem (as John 20 does), emphasising that this was the place from which the gospel would go to the nations, as predicted in Scripture (Luke 24:44–9; Acts 1:6–8). However, in the forty days that Jesus 'presented himself to them and gave many convincing proofs that he was alive' (Acts 1:3), there was opportunity for appearances in Galilee as well as in Jerusalem (see John 21). Luke's claim that the women 'remembered his words' is pregnant with meaning. Nolland concludes, 'With memory thus restored and with the assistance of the angelic revelation, the women are now ready to explain the empty tomb in terms of the gospel message of the resurrection.'[7]

9–11. 'When they came back from the tomb, they told all these things

---

creation'. Codex D and some other manuscripts do not contain the words 'He is not here; he has risen', but the weight of textual evidence supports their inclusion. See Metzger, *Textual Commentary*, 157.

[5] The NIV, ESV and CSB read the aorist passive verb *ēgerthē* intransitively in 24:6 ('he has risen'), but if it is understood transitively, it implies the agency of God, as in 9:22 (compare Acts 3:15; 4:10; 5:30; 10:40; 13:30, 37). The aorist active infinitive *anastēnai* in 24:7 is more appropriately rendered 'rise' (ESV, CSB), than 'be raised again' (NIV).

[6] The word *dei* ('must') signifies the divine necessity of certain events, as in 2:49; 4:43; 9:22; (11:42;) 12:12; 13:14, 16, 33; (15:32;) 17:25; 18:1; 19:5; 21:9; 22:7, 37; 24:26, 44.

[7] Nolland, *Luke 18:35–24:53*, 1190–91. Nolland observes a parallel in Acts 11:15–17,

to the Eleven and to all the others.' The number of the apostles had been reduced to eleven with the betrayal and suicide of Judas Iscariot (see Matthew 27:3–5). In this context, Luke finally identifies who the women were. Mary Magdalene and Joanna belonged to the inner circle of the disciples (8:2–3), and Mary the mother of James appears to have had an early connection too (5:10; 6:14; compare Mark 15:40; 16:1). Mark 16:1 says that Salome was also present, but Luke simply mentions 'the others with them'. Matthew 28:1 only records the two Marys. The apostles were destined to be the officially appointed witnesses of Jesus's resurrection (Acts 1:21–2), which included the role of explaining its significance (Acts 2:22–36), but the women were the first to report the fact of the empty tomb. Strikingly, 'they did not believe the women, because their words seemed to them like nonsense' (*lēros,* 'that which is totally devoid of anything worthwhile', BDAG). Their failure to understand and believe what Jesus had said to them (9:45; 18:34) blinded them to the evidence they were now receiving and made them quite dismissive.[8]

12. 'Peter, however, got up and ran to the tomb' (compare the more developed narrative in John 20:3–10).[9] Presumably, he wanted to check for himself if the body of Jesus was truly missing. When he bent down to peer into the tomb, 'he saw the strips of linen lying by themselves' – a piece of evidence not previously mentioned by Luke. The term *othonia* (BDAG, 'linen cloths') was often used for burial wrappings (see also John 19:40; 20:5, 6, 7). Although this could be another way of describing the linen cloth or shroud mentioned in 23:53 (*sindōn*), it is more likely that both wrappings and a shroud were used together.[10] The critical point was that they were 'lying by themselves'. If someone had stolen the body, they would surely not have removed the wrappings and left them there.

---

where an act of God is interpreted by remembering what Jesus predicted and leads to a new understanding and commitment.

[8] Nolland, *Luke 18:35–24:53,* 1191, and Green, *Luke,* 839–40, argue that the testimony was dismissed because they were women, but the text more obviously suggests a continuation of the stubbornness previously noted by Luke. Compare Edwards, *Luke,* 713.

[9] Although Luke 24:12 with minor variants is included in many Greek manuscripts and versions, it is missing from Codex D and some Old Latin texts. Metzger, *Textual Commentary,* 164–6, discusses the problem of the non-inclusions in Luke 24:3, 6, 10, 12, 17, 36, 40.

[10] John 20:7 adds that 'the cloth that had been wrapped around Jesus' head' (*soudarion,* 'facecloth') was 'still lying in its place, separate from the linen' (*othnia*). See B. R. McCane, 'Burial Practices, Jewish', *DNTB,* 173–5.

As Peter went away, he was 'wondering to himself what had happened', but still not accepting the angelic testimony passed on to him by the women. Peter's wondering (*thaumazōn*) expressed amazement rather than perplexity (see my comment on verse 4). An appearance of the risen Lord to Peter is retrospectively mentioned in verse 34 (see 1 Corinthians 15:5).

THE SIGNIFICANCE OF THE EMPTY TOMB

Although the significance of the empty tomb was not immediately grasped by those who first encountered it, Luke regarded it as an important piece of evidence for the bodily resurrection of Jesus. Initially, it caused the women to be perplexed, but angelic messengers reminded them of what Jesus himself had predicted and provided the context for understanding and believing that an extraordinary act of God had taken place. Peter was particularly amazed to discover the grave clothes lying by themselves. Even so, none of the witnesses was persuaded that Jesus had risen from death until he manifested himself to them and opened the Scriptures to them. The empty tomb on its own did not prove his resurrection and they were not expecting to see him alive again. The apostle Paul's summary of the gospel he received and passed on to others included the claim that 'Christ died for our sins according to the Scriptures, that he was *buried*, that he was raised on the third day according to the Scriptures' (1 Corinthians 15:3–4, my emphasis). The burial of Jesus confirmed the reality of his death and, in Paul's summary, 'it probably alluded to the reality of the *empty tomb*', as Anthony Thiselton argues.[11] There, the women were challenged to remember the predictions of Jesus. When they later encountered the resurrected Lord in the presence of the other disciples, they were taught by him how to use the Scriptures as 'the frame of reference for understanding'.[12] Luke and Paul provide the same pattern of testimony to the resurrection of Jesus, showing us how to present the evidence and explain its significance to people in our own time.

2. Jesus opens the eyes of two disciples (24:13–35)

This lengthy account of Jesus's appearance to two disciples on their way to Emmaus focuses on *why* they were 'kept from recognising him' (verse 16)

---

[11] Anthony C. Thiselton, *The First Epistle to the Corinthians* (Grand Rapids: Eerdmans; Carlisle: Paternoster, 2000), 1193 (author's emphasis).
[12] Thiselton, *Corinthians*, 1201. See Luke 24:25–7, 44–7.

and *how* 'their eyes were opened' and they finally came to recognise him (verse 31). Many characteristically Lucan expressions can be found here, but this does not mean that Luke simply made up the story.[13] Marshall concludes that, 'despite the difficulty of separating between tradition and redaction, it is most probable that the story has a traditional basis and is not due to Lucan invention'.[14] Mark 16:12–13 provides a brief parallel: 'Jesus appeared in a different form to two of them while they were walking in the country. These returned and reported it to the rest; but they did not believe them either.'[15]

On the road to Emmaus

13 Now that same day two of them were going to a village called Emmaus, about seven miles[a] from Jerusalem. **14** They were talking with each other about everything that had happened. **15** As they talked and discussed these things with each other, Jesus himself came up and walked along with them; **16** but they were kept from recognising him.

17 He asked them, 'What are you discussing together as you walk along?'

They stood still, their faces downcast. **18** One of them, named Cleopas, asked him, 'Are you the only one visiting Jerusalem who does not know the things that have happened there in these days?'

19 'What things?' he asked.

'About Jesus of Nazareth,' they replied. 'He was a prophet, powerful in word and deed before God and all the people. **20** The chief priests and our rulers handed him over to be sentenced to death, and they crucified him; **21** but we had hoped that he was the one who was going to redeem Israel. And what is more, it is the third day since all this took place. **22** In addition, some of our women amazed us. They went to the tomb early this morning **23** but didn't find his body. They came and told us that they had seen a vision of angels, who said he was alive. **24** Then some of our companions went to the tomb and found it just as the women had said, but they did not see Jesus.'

25 He said to them, 'How foolish you are, and how slow to believe all that the prophets have spoken! **26** Did not the

---

[13] Nolland, *Luke 18:35–24:53*, 1198, discusses four main views about Luke's source for the Emmaus narrative.

[14] Marshall, *Luke*, 890. Green, *Luke*, 841–2, notes the role of this narrative in showing a movement from possibility (verses 1–12) to probability (verses 13–35) to actuality (verses 36–49) and resolution (verses 50–53) for the disciples.

[15] Mark 16:9–20, which the NIV prints in italic, is missing in the earliest and best manuscripts. The connection with verse 8 is awkward and the vocabulary and style are non-Marcan. See Metzger, *Textual Commentary*, 102–6. These additions to Mark summarise some of the concluding evidence of the other Gospels and Acts, but also record unparalleled details.

Messiah have to suffer these things and then enter his glory?' **27** And beginning with Moses and all the Prophets, he explained to them what was said in all the Scriptures concerning himself.

28 As they approached the village to which they were going, Jesus continued on as if he were going further. **29** But they urged him strongly, 'Stay with us, for it is nearly evening; the day is almost over.' So he went in to stay with them.

30 When he was at the table with them, he took bread, gave thanks, broke it and began to give it to them. **31** Then their eyes were opened and they recognised

him, and he disappeared from their sight. **32** They asked each other, 'Were not our hearts burning within us while he talked with us on the road and opened the Scriptures to us?'

33 They got up and returned at once to Jerusalem. There they found the Eleven and those with them, assembled together **34** and saying, 'It is true! The Lord has risen and has appeared to Simon.' **35** Then the two told what had happened on the way, and how Jesus was recognised by them when he broke the bread.

a 13 Or about 11 kilometres

13. Luke begins his narrative by emphasising that this incident took place on 'that same day' when the empty tomb was discovered and the resurrection of Jesus was proclaimed by angelic messengers. The 'two of them' who were going to Emmaus had been among 'all the others' who were with the Eleven when they heard what the women had to say about these things (verse 9), but they did not believe them (verse 11). These two, possibly husband and wife, were returning to their own home for the night.[16] Four sites for this village have been proposed, but only two fit the description of being roughly seven miles (11km; Greek, 'sixty stadia') from Jerusalem. Since there are no records earlier than the Middle Ages to confirm that towns existed in these two locations, Luke may have had in mind the Emmaus known to Josephus, which was 3.75 miles (6km) west of Jerusalem. If that is so, 'seven miles' could refer to the round trip for those staying outside the city.[17] A fourth possibility is the Emmaus known from Maccabean times, which was some 17 miles (27km) from Jerusalem. Although a round trip of some 35 miles a day might seem insuperable to modern readers, Edwards argues that such travel would not have been unusual in the first century.[18]

[16] Nolland, *Luke 18:35–24:53*, 1200, raises the possibility of rented accommodation, arguing that Jerusalem could not cope with the number of pilgrims wishing to stay for Passover and the Festival of Unleavened Bread.
[17] See Josephus, *War* 17.1; Marshall, *Luke*, 892–3; Fitzmyer, *Luke X–XXIV*, 1561–2.
[18] Edwards, *Luke*, 714–16.

14–16. Unsurprisingly, these disciples were 'talking with each other about everything that had happened' (the verb *syzētein* could imply dispute or debate, BDAG). They were not completely closed off to the evidence and were still looking for answers! As they spoke in this way, 'Jesus himself came up' (*eggisas*, 'drew near') and 'walked along with them; but they were kept from recognising him' (literally, 'their eyes were kept from recognising him', ESV). The passive verb 'kept' (*ekratounto*, 'hindered', BDAG) could suggest that they were held back by God from acknowledging Jesus, though Luke emphasises that it was their own failure to understand and believe what Jesus had predicted that caused them to reject the evidence of his presence. Unbelief, confusion and grief gripped them (see John 20:14–15), so that Jesus appeared to be just another pilgrim returning home from the celebration of Passover in Jerusalem. His resurrected body was apparently different,[19] but the problem was more than a failure to recognise him physically.

17–18. Jesus began to open their spiritual eyes when he asked them, 'What are you discussing together as you walk along?' Opening their *minds* to understand the significance of what had happened would open their *eyes* to his living presence. Jesus wanted to help them think again about what they had learned and experienced, but they could not even look at the stranger by their side as he spoke to them: 'They stood still, their faces downcast' (*skythrōpoi*, 'sad, gloomy'). Then one of them, named Cleopas, somewhat impatiently asked him, 'Are you the only one visiting Jerusalem who does not know the things that have happened there in these days?'[20] Nolland observes an irony in their accusation that Jesus is the one who does not know what has happened, 'when it is they who *do not know* who is talking with them or that the resurrection has taken place'.[21]

19–21a. A further question was asked by Jesus ('What things?'), inviting these disciples to articulate and explain from their own point of view what had happened. Their first response was to locate 'Jesus of Nazareth' at the centre of recent events and to describe him as 'a prophet, powerful in word and deed before God and all the people' (see Acts 2:22; 7:22 (Moses); 10:37–8). This certainly expressed the viewpoint of many in Luke's Gospel (see especially 7:16, 39; 9:8, 19), but it fell short of the revelation Jesus had

---

[19] Harris, *From Grave to Glory*, 102–4, observes that Jesus 'rose to life in a transformed body whose capacities seemed to outstrip immeasurably a merely physical body'.
[20] Marshall, *Luke*, 894, and Edwards, *Luke*, 717–18, discuss the various attempts to identify Cleopas and his companion, none of which seems convincing.
[21] Nolland, *Luke 18:35–24:53*, 1202, following Tannehill, *Narrative Unity* 1, 282. Nolland, 1201, attributes the blinding effect to Satan.

progressively given of himself as Son of Man, Messiah and Son of God. Cleopas and his companion went on to accuse the leaders of Israel of being ultimately responsible for his betrayal and death: 'The chief priests and our rulers handed him over to be sentenced to death, and they crucified him.' These disciples, however, 'had hoped that he was the one who was going to redeem Israel' (see 1:68; 9:20). This echoes the expectation of earlier characters in Luke's Gospel, who were 'waiting for the consolation of Israel' (2:25) and 'looking forward to the redemption of Jerusalem' (2:38; see also Joseph in 23:51, 'waiting for the kingdom of God'). But this hope had been dashed by Jesus's crucifixion and death. They had not grasped the need for the Messiah to suffer many things and 'then enter his glory' (verse 26).[22]

21b–4. In their gloomy reflection on what had taken place in Jerusalem, Cleopas and his companion apparently recalled the prediction that Jesus would be raised on the third day: 'And what is more, it is the third day since all this took place.' Jesus's promise (9:22; 18:33) was repeated by angels to the women at his tomb (24:7) and was being echoed by these two men. The women had amazed them all when they went to the tomb early in the morning but 'didn't find his body'. Moreover, 'They came and told us that they had seen a vision of angels, who said he was alive.' The final piece of evidence pointing to the possibility of bodily resurrection was that 'some of our companions went to the tomb and found it just as the women had said, but they did not see Jesus' (see verse 12). Others apparently accompanied Peter or went after him to verify the testimony of the women about the empty tomb (see John 20:3–10). From a narrative perspective, the recollection of events recorded in verses 1–12 establishes the compelling nature of the evidence and the culpability of those who failed to believe the promise of Jesus. All the raw materials for making sense of these events were available to them but, in Green's words, they were 'unable to construct a faithful interpretation'.[23] As John 20:9 makes clear, 'They still did not understand from Scripture that Jesus had to rise from the dead.'

25–6. Jesus continued to open the eyes of them both by saying, 'How foolish you are, and how slow to believe all that the prophets have spoken!' (*bradeis tē kardia tou pisteuein*, 'slow of heart to believe', ESV). Their

---

[22] Anderson, *Jesus' Resurrection in Luke–Acts*, 169, observes that Jesus is portrayed in this encounter as 'the one who, through rejection, death, and resurrection, embodies the role of the prophet like Moses who is initiating a New Exodus for the people of God'. Compare Acts 3:17–23.

[23] Green, *Luke*, 847.

dispositions and attitudes kept them from accepting what the prophets had taught. They were rebuked for 'for reading the Scriptures without understanding and belief', as Edwards discerns.[24] Jesus went on to identify their specific failure to grasp what the prophets predicted about the Messiah's role in achieving the redemption of God's people: 'Did not the Messiah have to suffer these things and then enter his glory?' Hints of this had been given in previous pronouncements (9:22, 44; 12:49–53; 13:31–5; 17:22–5; 18:31–3; 22:19–22, 37), with the emphasis on entering his glory particularly reflecting what Tannehill calls 'the scriptural prophecies of his exaltation to which he refers while in Jerusalem (see 20:17, 42–43; 22:69)'.[25] These texts imply that resurrection is the pathway to heavenly enthronement for the Messiah. As Harris observes, in its widest sense, 'The resurrection of Jesus was his rising from the grave in a transformed body to glory at God's right hand.'[26] Compare Acts 2:31–5; 5:30–31; Hebrews 1:3.

27. Jesus's immediate concern was to provide his disciples with an open, comprehensive and detailed exposition of God's plan for the Messiah. Therefore, 'Beginning with Moses and all the Prophets, he explained to them what was said in all the Scriptures concerning himself.' Two parts of the Hebrew canon are mentioned here (as in 16:31; Acts 26:22; 28:23), but 'the Psalms' in verse 44 also refers to the third part known as 'the Writings'. Although scholars have debated whether Judaism at the time had any expectation of a suffering and dying Messiah, Luke indicates that this was the conviction of Jesus himself and that he established a pattern of biblical interpretation that is reflected in early Christian preaching (Acts 3:18; 8:35; 17:3; 20:27–8; 26:23) and later New Testament writings.[27] This involved the use of key texts to identify an unfolding biblical metanarrative and show the role of the Messiah in bringing this to its divinely appointed conclusion.

28–30. 'As they approached the village to which they were going, Jesus continued on as if he were going further.' Their moment of opportunity seemed to be passing by, 'but they urged him strongly, "Stay with us, for it is nearly evening; the day is almost over."' Their offer would make it possible for them to hear more from him (see Acts 16:15), and so 'he went in to stay with them'. 'When he was at the table with them, he took bread, gave thanks, broke it and began to give it to them.' Although this

---

[24] Edwards, *Luke*, 721.

[25] Tannehill, *Narrative Unity* 1, 284.

[26] Harris, *From Grave to Glory*, 103 (emphases removed). See also Anderson, *Jesus' Resurrection in Luke–Acts*, 172–9.

[27] See Edwards, *Luke*, 721–2.

was a familiar way of initiating a meal in first-century Jewish culture,[28] Jesus unexpectedly took charge of the situation by acting as the host. This was reminiscent of meals shared with him in the past, especially his feeding of the five thousand (9:16) and the Last Supper (22:19), though Luke only mentions the presence of his apostles in 22:14. It is going beyond the evidence to suggest that Luke told this story to assure his readers of Jesus's ongoing spiritual presence in their 'eucharistic celebrations'.[29] However, the Emmaus meal, together with the preceding period of instruction and discussion, certainly anticipated the continuity of fellowship with the exalted Lord Jesus that believers have when they share teaching and meals together.[30]

31. 'Then their eyes were opened and they recognised him, and he disappeared from their sight.' The passive verb *diēnoichthēsan* ('were opened') suggests a divine action reversing the closure previously mentioned (verse 16; compare 2 Kings 6:17). The opening of their eyes is related to Jesus's opening of the Scriptures to them in the next verse, but his action in initiating the meal confirmed that they were in the presence of the living Lord. His sudden disappearance from their sight (he became 'invisible', *aphantos*, to them) could be compared with the departure of angelic visitors in 1:38; 2:15; Acts 10:7; 12:10, but does not mean that his resurrection body was in some way transient or less than truly physical (see 24:37–43). He left them suddenly when his self-disclosure was complete (see Acts 8:39–40). Nevertheless, references to his appearances to the disciples behind locked doors (see 24:36; John 20:19–20) suggest that his resurrection body was 'a spiritually transformed body no longer subject to physical properties alone', as Edwards observes.[31] Luke and John provide the evidence for Paul's claim in 1 Corinthians 15:20 that the resurrected Jesus is 'the firstfruits of those who have fallen asleep' (see 15:42–9). Put differently, his resurrection in glory and in power provides assurance that he will 'transform our lowly bodies so that they will be like his glorious body' (Philippians 3:21).

---

[28] See J. Behm, 'κλάω κτλ.', *TDNT* 3:728–30; Green, *Luke*, 851, note 42.

[29] Nolland, *Luke 18:35–24:53*, 1206, rightly concludes that 'there is no sense in which Luke is claiming that Jesus celebrated the eucharist with these disciples', but he argues for an analogous experience in later Christian gatherings.

[30] Tannehill, *Narrative Unity* 1, 290. Green, *Luke*, 843, challenges the view that Luke was particularly interested in the theme of 'eucharistic celebration'. See also Peterson, *Acts*, 161, 557–8; Edwards, *Luke*, 723–4.

[31] Edwards, *Luke*, 724. Harris, *From Grave to Glory*, 130–32, discusses the terminology used to describe the nature of the appearances of the resurrected Jesus. Acts 1:3–4

32. The initial response of the two disciples was to ask each other, 'Were not our hearts burning within us while he talked with us on the road and opened the Scriptures to us?' Those who were 'slow of heart to believe' (verse 25, ESV) experienced a change of heart when Jesus talked with them and their eyes were opened. When they later reported their experience to the Eleven and those with them in Jerusalem, the two added, 'how Jesus was recognised by them when he broke the bread' (verse 35). Marshall suggests, 'The reality of the risen Jesus was already making itself known to the disciples as he spoke to them, struggling to put itself into conscious form, and only being recognised for what it was after the visual revelation of Jesus.'[32]

33–5. Now with burning hearts, the two disciples got up and returned at once to Jerusalem, aiming to tell 'the Eleven and those with them, assembled together' about what they had experienced. Given that it was nearly evening when they had invited Jesus to eat with them (verse 29), their arrival back in Jerusalem must have been at a very late hour! But they found the disciples awake and excited, already convinced and saying, 'It is true! The Lord has risen and has appeared to Simon.'[33] The focus shifts from the Emmaus incident to the primary revelation given to Peter, which must have happened after Peter's visit to the empty tomb (verse 12). This incident is only briefly recalled by Luke and is mentioned in none of the other Gospels, but Peter's testimony had a profound impact on the rest of those gathered there. It was later recalled by the apostle Paul as the first in a series of resurrection appearances to the disciples (1 Corinthians 15:5, 'Cephas'). When the two travellers told what had happened on the way to Emmaus and 'how Jesus was recognised by them when he broke the bread', they linked their experience to that of Simon Peter and confirmed it for the benefit of everyone present. It is noteworthy that Luke uses the expression 'truly' (*ontōs*) for a second time here: the centurion at the cross praised God and said, 'Surely this was a righteous man' (23:47), while the disciples affirmed the certainty of Jesus's resurrection with a similar confidence (CSB, 'The Lord has truly been raised').

---

mentions 'many convincing proofs that he was alive' and specifically recalls one occasion when he was eating with his disciples.

[32] Marshall, *Luke*, 899. Green, *Luke*, 844, observes, 'What has happened with Jesus can be understood only in light of the Scriptures, yet the Scriptures themselves can be understood only in light of what has happened with Jesus. These two are mutually informing.'

[33] The verb 'was seen' or 'appeared' is used with reference to angels in Luke 1:11; 22:43; Acts 7:2, 30, and with reference to Jesus in Luke 24:34; Acts 13:31.

SEEING JESUS NOW

The inability of the two disciples on the road to Emmaus to recognise the risen Lord reveals the inhibiting power of spiritual blindness. They needed to have their minds and hearts opened to the teaching of Scripture to understand the significance of the empty tomb, believe the angelic testimony and discern the presence of Jesus with them. When he initiated a meal with them, as he had done before, 'their eyes were opened and they recognised him' (verse 31). Something was different about his physical appearance, but Luke does not mean that when Jesus became 'invisible' (verse 31) he was merely a ghost or a spirit. The physicality of his body is emphasised in the following narrative (verses 42–3). Peter Orr observes, 'Even in his transformed bodily state, the risen Christ retains his humanity and can be distinguished from other human beings.'[34] The nature of this transformation can be gleaned from the way Jesus himself talked about the Messiah entering his glory (verse 26). When he was resurrected, he was 'exalted to the right hand of God' in fulfilment of Psalm 110:1 (Acts 2:33–5) or 'glorified' (Acts 3:13–15). Jesus appeared to his disciples for forty days as the glorified Messiah from heaven, until he finally parted from them in a decisive way and was 'taken up into heaven' (verse 51; Acts 1:11).[35] His resurrection appearances, culminating in his ascension, were sufficient to convince his disciples of the fulfilment of Scripture and his exalted status. When the Spirit came upon them, they saw this as a further confirmation of his heavenly rule (Acts 2:33). Guided and empowered by the Spirit, they proclaimed him as Lord and Messiah and urged people to 'see' him as living in the heavenly realm (Acts 2:34–6), but still powerfully active in the earthly sphere to heal and to save (Acts 3; 4:8–12; 5:30–32). We too can only 'see' the risen Lord through their testimony. The ascension of Jesus and his pouring out of the Holy Spirit signify that he will not appear in his transformed body again until he finally returns in glory (Acts 1:11).

3. Commissioned to proclaim (24:36–49)

In this encounter with the risen Lord, the Eleven and those with them in Jerusalem were initially 'startled and frightened, thinking they saw a ghost'

[34] Peter Orr, *Christ Absent and Present: A Study in Pauline Christology* (Tübingen: Mohr Siebeck, 2014), 89.
[35] Fitzmyer, *Luke X–XXIV*, 1539. Jesus's ascension was 'the ultimate confirmation of the status that had been his from the moment of his resurrection' (Peterson, *Acts*, 115). See also my comments on the ascension below.

THE RESURRECTION AND HEAVENLY ASCENT OF JESUS

(verse 37).[36] When Jesus showed them his hands and feet, they still did not believe 'because of joy and amazement' (verse 41). While they remained silent, Jesus spoke three times, first with a greeting of peace (verse 36), second with a twofold challenge not to be troubled and doubt (verses 38–9), and third to request something to eat (verse 41). Revelatory actions confirmed the reality of his presence (verses 40, 42–3). When he explained again from the Scriptures the need for his suffering and resurrection, he went on to commission those present to proclaim the implications 'to all nations, beginning at Jerusalem'. But first they were required to wait in the city to be 'clothed with power from on high' (verses 44–9).

Jesus appears to the disciples

36 While they were still talking about this, Jesus himself stood among them and said to them, 'Peace be with you.' 37 They were startled and frightened, thinking they saw a ghost. 38 He said to them, 'Why are you troubled, and why do doubts rise in your minds? 39 Look at my hands and my feet. It is I myself! Touch me and see; a ghost does not have flesh and bones, as you see I have.' 40 When he had said this, he showed them his hands and feet. 41 And while they still did not believe it because of joy and amazement, he asked them, 'Do you have anything here to eat?' 42 They gave him a piece of broiled fish, 43 and he took it and ate it in their presence.

44 He said to them, 'This is what I told you while I was still with you: everything must be fulfilled that is written about me in the Law of Moses, the Prophets and the Psalms.'

45 Then he opened their minds so they could understand the Scriptures. 46 He told them, 'This is what is written: the Messiah will suffer and rise from the dead on the third day, 47 and repentance for the forgiveness of sins will be preached in his name to all nations, beginning at Jerusalem. 48 You are witnesses of these things. 49 I am going to send you what my Father has promised; but stay in the city until you have been clothed with power from on high.'

36–7. The clause, 'While they were still talking about this,' provides a close link with the preceding account, locating this event late in the evening of 'the first day of the week' (see verses 1, 13, 33). Jesus's appearance

---

[36] Fitzmyer *Luke X–XXIV*, 1574–5, notes parallels between the first scene (verses 36–43) and John 20:19–23, though Jesus's breathing of the Holy Spirit upon the disciples anticipates Acts 2:1–3. See also Mark 16:14–16 and my note on the longer ending of Mark above. The second scene (verses 44–9) is remotely related to Matthew 28:16–20 (in Galilee).

is presented in terms reminiscent of angelic manifestations in the Old Testament: 'Jesus himself stood among them' and greeted them with the words 'Peace be with you' (see Judges 6:22–3; Daniel 10:18–19).[37] However, since 'peace' has a more specific meaning in relation to the Messiah's saving work in Luke's Gospel (1:79; 2:14, 29; 7:50; 8:48; 10:5; 12:51; 19:38, 42), it should be understood in that fuller sense here. The reaction of the disciples ('they were startled and frightened') is explained in terms of their perception ('thinking they saw a ghost [*pneuma*]'). The language of fear further recalls angelic appearances (Daniel 8:17; Luke 1:12, 30; 2:9; 24:5), but the word *pneuma* ('spirit, ghost') implies that they viewed this as a ghostly appearance of the dead Jesus.[38]

38. Jesus posed a twofold question to his disciples, which acknowledged their confusion and distress: 'Why are you troubled, and why do doubts rise in your minds?' Although the word *dialogismos* can simply refer to honest deliberation or reflection, the sense of 'evil thoughts', 'anxious reflection' or 'doubt' could apply here.[39] Compare the angelic message to the women at the tomb (verses 4–5) and Jesus's challenge to the Emmaus disciples about being foolish and 'slow to believe all that the prophets have spoken' (verse 25). The original witnesses were not easily persuaded by the evidence of the empty tomb or by his resurrection appearances alone. They needed to be reminded about the predictions of Scripture, to which Jesus had drawn attention in various ways (9:22, 44; 17:25; 18:31–3; 22:37), and to view their experiences in that light. Faith is the choice to believe what we know to be true, even in the face of 'bewilderment, astonishment, and incredulity', as Fitzmyer says.[40]

39–40. Recognising the nature of their fears and doubts, Jesus gave a twofold command. First, he said, 'Look at my hands and my feet.' Face, hands and feet would have been the only visible parts of his body, given what Nolland calls 'the loose and rather full clothing characteristic of ancient Palestine'.[41] But perhaps there was something distinctively recognisable about his hands and his feet, because they bore the marks of crucifixion (see John 20:25, 27). Whatever the case, he needed to confirm the continuity of his physical presence with them before and after his

[37] This greeting is well attested in Greek manuscripts and is paralleled in John 20:19, 21, 26, but it is strangely missing from Codex D and certain Old Latin versions. See Metzger, *Textual Commentary*, 160, 164–6.
[38] Nolland, *Luke 18:35–24:53*, 1213; Green, *Luke*, 853–4; Edwards, *Luke*, 729.
[39] G. Schrenk, 'διαλογισμός', *TDNT* 2:97–8.
[40] Fitzmyer, *Luke X–XXIV*, 1572.
[41] Nolland, *Luke 18:35–24:53*, 1213.

crucifixion ('It is I myself [*egō eimi autos*])!'[42] Second, he said, 'Touch me and see; a ghost does not have flesh and bones, as you see I have.' This challenge emphasised again the physical nature of his resurrection body. The twofold command to look and touch was accompanied by his action in showing them his hands and his feet.[43]

41–3. The disciples were still unbelieving, though Luke emphasises that this was 'because of joy and amazement'. What they were experiencing seemed too wonderful to be true! This prompted Jesus to ask another question ('Do you have anything here to eat?'), and so, 'They gave him a piece of broiled fish, and he took it and ate it in their presence.'[44] This was a reminder of meals previously shared with his disciples (9:16–17; 22:19, 28–32; see also John 21:10–14). Eating alone might not prove his genuine materiality, since angels ate and drank in the presence of Abraham (Genesis 18:1–8; 19:3), but in this context it was certainly a further indication of his physicality.

44–5. Two related utterances by Jesus are introduced with similar expressions in verses 44 ('He said to them ') and 46 ('He told them'). The first recalls the pattern of his teaching to the disciples during his earthly ministry (ESV, 'These are my words that I spoke to you while I was still with you'). In broad terms, he taught that 'everything must be fulfilled that is written about me in the Law of Moses, the Prophets and the Psalms'. Divine necessity is implied by *dei* ('must'), especially in relation to what the Scriptures say about the need for the Messiah to suffer and enter his glory (see 22:37; 24:7, 26–7). Three divisions in the Hebrew Bible are mentioned, with the Book of Psalms representing the third (later called 'the Writings'). This could have been because it was the first in that collection, but it is also noteworthy that Jesus makes special mention of Psalms 118:22 and 110:1 in speaking about his destiny

---

[42] Although it is sometimes suggested that this is a claim to divinity by association with the name of God in Exodus 3:14–15 ('I am who I am' and 'I am has sent me to you'), the Greek syntax in Luke 24:39 is different and serves a more simple purpose.

[43] Harris, *From Grave to Glory*, 145, notes that the risen Jesus sometimes allows and sometimes prohibits disciples from touching him, depending on the needs of those concerned. A wide range of reliable Greek manuscripts and versions include verse 40, but it is omitted by Codex D and some other witnesses. Metzger, *Textual Commentary*, 160–61, argues against the suggestion that it is an interpolation from John 20:20 ('his hands and side').

[44] KJV adds 'and of an honeycomb,' which appears in later manuscripts, but is 'an obvious interpolation' (Metzger, *Textual Commentary*, 161).

in 20:17, 41–44.[45] The following verses indicate that Jesus gave his disciples a broad understanding of the saving plan of God in Scripture, climaxing in the suffering of the Messiah, his heavenly exaltation and the sending out of his message of salvation to all nations in the power of the Holy Spirit. In this manner, Jesus 'opened their minds so they could understand the Scriptures'. This pattern of biblical interpretation is reflected in the apostolic preaching that is recorded in Acts 2:14–36; 3:13–26; 4:8–12; 5:30–32; 10:34–43; 13:16–41.

46–7. Jesus's explanation of 'what is written' about him (verse 44) began with what the Scriptures say about the Messiah having to 'suffer and rise from the dead on the third day' (see verses 6–7, 25–7; 18:31–3). However, the missional consequences of his death and resurrection may also be discerned from a proper understanding of the Law, the Prophets and the Psalms (see Acts 3:17–26; 13:47; 15:13–18; 26:19–23). It was part of the original plan of God that Israel and the nations should share the benefits of the messianic salvation (Luke 2:28–35). God's promise to bless Israel's patriarchs and their offspring included the expectation that 'all peoples on earth' would be blessed through them (Genesis 12:3; 22:18). This hope was developed and articulated in various ways by the prophets (e.g., Isaiah 2:1–4; 11:1–11; 49:5–6; Jeremiah 3:17; Amos 9:11–12; Zechariah 9:9–10) and the psalmists (e.g., Psalms 2; 22:27–31; 98:1–6).[46] Both John the Baptist (3:3) and Jesus preached repentance (5:32; 10:13; 11:32; 13:3, 5; 15:7, 10; 16:30; 17:3, 4) and offered the forgiveness of sins to fellow Israelites (5:24; 7:47–9).[47] However, on the basis of biblical teaching about the Messiah having to 'suffer and rise from the dead on the third day', the proclamation of repentance for the forgiveness of sins would take place in a new and definitive way, 'in his name to all nations'.[48] Acts 2:5–40 records the first example of this, where baptism in the name of Jesus is the means of expressing repentance and receiving by faith the forgiveness of sins and the gift of the Holy Spirit. These new covenant blessings were made available to Jews who had gathered

---

[45] The prologue of the intertestamental book Sirach describes this tripartite division as 'the Law and the Prophets and the others that followed them' (NRSVA).
[46] See Edwards, *Luke*, 735–8.
[47] The noun *aphesis*, which is translated 'forgiveness' in 1:77; 3:3; 24:47, is rendered 'freedom' in 4:18 (citing Isaiah 61:1). The broad purpose of Jesus's ministry was to release captive Israel from the consequences of sin. Forgiveness is also a theme in 11:4; 12:10; 17:3–4; 23:34.
[48] Tannehill, *Narrative Unity* 1, 297–8, notes the way similar terminology in Acts 26:16–23 links Paul to this mission.

in Jerusalem from many parts of the Dispersion for the celebration of
Pentecost (see Jeremiah 31:33–4; Ezekiel 36:25–7). This event anticipated
the outreach to the nations that would soon take place (see Acts 8:12,
36–8; 10:48; 16:15, 33). It involved a call to 'Save yourselves from this
corrupt generation' and join the community of Jesus's disciples (2:40–42;
compare 3:19–23; 22:16).[49]

48–9. Jesus here explains how the gospel would reach the nations and
bring about 'repentance for the forgiveness of sins' in his name (verse
47). The Eleven and those with them are first told, 'You are witnesses of
these things.' This theme is developed in Acts 1:7–8, 21–2; 2:32; 3:15; 5:32;
10:39, 41; 13:31, where the emphasis is on testifying to the reality of Jesus's
resurrection and its implications (see also Acts 22:15; 26:16 in relation to
Paul). The apostles became 'eye' and 'ear' witnesses by virtue of having
been with Jesus from the beginning of his ministry. They had the benefit
of hearing his teaching, before and after his resurrection, observing his
mighty acts and being shown how to interpret Scripture and explain the
significance of these things. Luke's second volume reveals how others came
to rely on their testimony as the foundation for proclaiming the gospel
in ever-widening circles.[50] Second, all those gathered on this occasion are
told that the Holy Spirit will be given to empower them for the work
of proclamation: 'I am going to send you what my Father has promised.'[51]
Jesus earlier spoke about his Father giving the Holy Spirit to those who
ask him (11:13), but here he promises to send the Spirt himself (see Acts
2:33). The nature of this promise is amplified when they are told to 'stay
in the city until you have been clothed with power from on high' (see
Isaiah 32:15; 44:3; Ezekiel 39:29; Joel 2:28). This is the power that was
present in his earthly ministry (4:14). It is further explained in Acts 1:4–8
as being 'baptised with the Holy Spirit' (alluding to the promise of John
the Baptist in Luke 3:16), to be his witnesses 'in Jerusalem, in all Judea
and Samaria, and to the ends of the earth' (Acts 1:8)[52]

---

[49] See Peterson, *Acts*, 135–8, 153–8.

[50] Peterson, *Acts*, 79–83.

[51] The reading reflected by the NIV is well attested and favoured by Metzger,
Textual Commentary, 162. However, some manuscripts have the more solemn and
emphatic introductory expression *kai [idou] egō* ('And behold I').

[52] Although the context in Luke 24 seems to limit the Spirit's role to empowerment for witness and proclamation, a broader function is unfolded in Acts. See
Peterson, *Acts*, 60–65.

TRUSTING THE WITNESSES

The commissioning scene in 24:44–9 overlaps with the parallel account in Acts 1:1–8, so that each version helps to interpret the other. It also recalls 1:1–4, where Luke talks about 'the things that have been fulfilled among us' and commends his orderly account to Theophilus and others seeking certainty about the things they have been taught. In both contexts, Luke draws attention to the witnesses, whose testimony to these great events and their significance formed the basis of his account.[53] In Acts 1:21–2, when a replacement for Judas Iscariot is chosen to be a witness of Jesus's resurrection, the apostles look for someone who has been 'with us the whole time the Lord Jesus was living among us, beginning from John's baptism to the time when Jesus was taken up from us'. Broadly speaking, this covers the span of Luke's first volume. Although it is true that others in the narrative of Acts soon testify to the gospel events in different ways, the witness of the Twelve is presented as foundational. Luke's two-volume work was written to convince those in doubt about the truth of the apostolic message and to encourage their collaboration in the work of bringing it to the nations. It is therefore inadequate to conclude, as Nolland does, that 'the logic of witness in the Christian life is that each witnesses to his or her own gift'.[54] Luke's focus is not so much on testifying to one's own experience of the risen Lord and the spiritual gifts he imparts, but on conveying the primary witness of the apostles in ways that speak to people in different social and cultural contexts. Put differently, we may say that Luke wanted his own 'orderly account' to be a resource and guide for ongoing Christian witness by his readers to the person and work of the Lord Jesus in every nation.

4. The final parting (24:50–53)

Luke provides two narrative descriptions of Jesus's ascent into heaven, with different emphases.[55] The focus of the first is on the way the disciples

---

[53] Anderson, *Jesus' Resurrection in Luke–Acts*, 159, similarly notes that in Luke 24 'the sources for Luke's narrative are authorized'.

[54] Nolland, *Luke 18:35–24:53*, 1221.

[55] Jesus's ascension is briefly mentioned in Mark 16:19, alluded to in John 20:17; Hebrews 4:14; 9:11–12 and assumed in passages such as Acts 2:33; Romans 8:34; Ephesians 1:20–21; Colossians 3:1. Matthew 28:16–20 is not explicitly an ascension scene, though it anticipates his exaltation and involves a commissioning of the eleven disciples on a mountain in Galilee.

finally acknowledged his divine character and authority, worshipping him and returning to Jerusalem and the Temple with great joy to praise God and await the promised gift of the Holy Spirit. The narrative in Acts 1:1–11 presents Jesus's ascension more specifically as the end of his earthly appearances and the beginning of his ministry from heaven as the exalted Lord through his witnesses. There are parallels with the ascent of Elijah in 2 Kings 2:1–18 and the succession of Elisha, but the differences are more significant. Both of Luke's accounts lack the fiery horses and chariots and the whirlwind; the Elijah story lacks the appearances and preparatory teaching over forty days, the worship of Jesus by his followers and his place at God's right hand. Steve Walton points out that, by various means, Luke signals that the exalted Jesus is 'far more than a "new Elijah": he is "Lord of all" (Acts 10:15)'.[56]

The ascension of Jesus

50 When he had led them out to the vicinity of Bethany, he lifted up his hands and blessed them. 51 While he was blessing them, he left them and was taken up into heaven. 52 Then they worshipped him and returned to Jerusalem with great joy. 53 And they stayed continually at the temple, praising God.

50. The events of Easter Day are closely linked by time references (verses 1, 13, 33, 36), but the connection here is loose ('When he had led them out to the vicinity of Bethany'). Luke's vagueness does not imply that Jesus's heavenly ascension took place on the same day as his resurrection. This would be inconsistent with the record of Acts, where Jesus appears to his disciples for forty days before being 'taken up before their very eyes' (1:1–9). Bethany on the eastern slope of the Mount of Olives was the place from which he entered Jerusalem (Luke 19:29–40) and it was the place of his departure from earthly life and ministry (Acts 1:12). With great solemnity, Jesus 'lifted up his hands and blessed them'. This could be interpreted as a priestly action (Leviticus 9:22; Numbers 6:22–7; Sirach 50:20–22), like the blessing of the baby Jesus by Simeon (2:28–32). The farewells of Jacob (Genesis 49) and Moses (Deuteronomy 33) could also provide parallels, the former involving predictions about the future

---

56 Steve Walton, 'Jesus's Ascension through Old Testament Narrative Traditions', in *Ascent into Heaven in Luke–Acts: New Explorations of Luke's Narrative Hinge*, eds. David K. Bryan and David W. Pao (Minneapolis: Fortress, 2015), 39. There is little reason to see an echo of Genesis 5:24 in Luke's account, though later Jewish literature about Enoch shows some parallels.

of Jacob's sons and the latter combining prayers with predictions about Israel's future.

51. 'While he was blessing them, he left them.' This parting was different from the one mentioned in verse 31 in the sense that he was now visibly 'taken up into heaven'.[57] The passive verb here (*anephereto*) signifies an action of God, recalling the prediction in 9:51, where a parallel term is used (*analēmpsis*). Although the glorified Lord had appeared to his disciples from heaven after his resurrection, this event signified a definitive withdrawal from the earthly realm to reign at God's right hand (Acts 2:33), in fulfilment of Psalm 110:1. There is no indication here or in Acts 1:9–11 that he was only glorified at his ascension: his resurrection body needed no further transformation. The outpouring of the promised Holy Spirit further confirmed his exalted status (Acts 2:33), and the angelic messengers in Acts 1:11 predicted that he would 'come back in the same way you have seen him go into heaven'.

52–3. As Tannehill observes, 'The sense of closure here is supported by reminders of the birth stories with which the gospel began, for a return to initial themes is a way of rounding off a story.'[58] In those early chapters, people blessed or praised God (1:64, 68; 2:20, 28), sometimes in the context of the Temple, and 'great joy' was promised 'for all the people' (2:10). However, only at the end of his Gospel does Luke tell us that the disciples 'worshipped' Jesus (see Matthew 14:33; 28:9, 17). The verb *proskyneō* means 'to express in attitude or gesture one's complete dependence on or submission to a high authority figure' (BDAG). In 4:7–8, the devil challenges Jesus to worship him and Jesus responds by citing Deuteronomy 6:13 ('Worship the Lord your God and serve him only'). Peter comes close to worshipping Jesus after the miraculous catch of fishes (5:8, 'he fell at Jesus' knees and said, "Go away from me, Lord; I am a sinful man!"'). Likewise, the leper who returned to praise God for healing him 'threw himself at Jesus' feet and thanked him' (17:15–16).[59] When the disciples

---

[57] Harris, *From Grave to Glory*, 183, concludes that the resurrection of Jesus involved his invisible ascent to the Father's right hand, while 'the Ascension was his visible ascent into heaven at the end of forty days'. Metzger, *Textual Commentary*, 162–3, defends the longer reading that includes the words 'and was taken up into heaven'.

[58] Tannehill, *Narrative Unity* 1, 300. 'The joy felt by the devoted Jews who greeted the infant Jesus has been justified by later events, bringing the story to a happy resolution' (301).

[59] In 5:12; 8:28, 41, 47, those seeking help from Jesus fall at his feet. In 5:26; 13:13; 18:43, those who experience his healing power praise God, but they do not strictly 'worship' Jesus.

finally recognised the divinity of their exalted Lord, their gesture of homage could have been linked with praise (as in Genesis 24:26–7; Psalm 95:1–7) or silent adoration (as in Exodus 4:29–31). Either way, this was the logical response to Jesus's resurrection and heavenly ascent (see John 20:28). In obedience to him, the disciples then 'returned to Jerusalem with great joy' and 'stayed continually at the temple, praising God'.[60]

THE SIGNIFICANCE OF JESUS'S ASCENT INTO HEAVEN

This event marked the end of a series of bodily appearances to Jesus's disciples, which revealed to them his divine character and glorified status. As Richard Gaffin observes, 'Ascension and heavenly session are exponential of resurrection.'[61] There were not two stages in Jesus's glorification: his *resurrection* involved 'the final and definitive investiture of his person with glory'.[62] Nevertheless, the ascension began a new era in which his disciples would relate to him as the Lord enthroned in heaven and be empowered and guided by the Holy Spirit to do his will on earth.

When Luke indicates that they worshipped him, he affirms what the entirety of his Gospel has revealed, that Jesus is Lord. The ascension of Jesus should therefore shape our view of reality. God should be at the apex of our 'cosmic hierarchy', as David Bryan puts it, but Luke also wants us to know 'that Jesus of Nazareth dwells in heaven as the resurrected Lord and king who has authority over all'.[63] Moreover, as Matthew Sleeman observes, the ascension in Acts 1:9–11 is not merely a departure, but also 'a heavenly arrival – signalled by the obscuring cloud, which triggers connections with Daniel 7:13–14 – that promises a future earthly return'.[64] The Son of Man is 'seated at the right hand of the mighty God' (Luke 22:69), guaranteeing his promise that in due course he will come 'in a cloud with power and great glory' (21:27).

---

[60] The Temple continued to be a place of prayer, praise and teaching for these first disciples, until they were rejected from its precincts and forced to gather elsewhere (Acts 2:46; 3:1; 4:1–4; 5:42). See Peterson, *Engaging with God*, 136–44, 159–60.

[61] Richard Gaffin, *Resurrection and Redemption: A Study in Paul's Soteriology* (2nd edition; Phillipsburg: Presbyterian and Reformed Publishing Service, 1987), 92.

[62] Gaffin, *Resurrection*, 126. Accordingly, 'what Christ is by virtue of his resurrection, believers will become at their resurrection'. See Philippians 3:20–21.

[63] David K. Bryan, 'A Revised Cosmic Hierarchy Revealed: Apocalyptic Literature and Jesus's Ascent in Luke's Gospel', in Bryan and Pao, *Ascent into Heaven*, 82.

[64] Matthew Sleeman, 'The Ascension and Spatial Theory' in Bryan and Pao, *Ascent into Heaven*, 163. See also my Introduction, pages 25–6.